D1797383

Jane's
SURVEY VESSELS

Edited by Clifford Funnell and Bob Barton

Second Edition
2001-2002

| Total number of entries | 1,007 | New and updated entries | 742 |
| Total number of images | 462 | New images | 240 |

ISBN 0 7106 2331 3
"Jane's" is a registered trade mark

Contents

Front cover: Prince Madog, *the new ocean research vessel operated by a joint venture between Vosper Thornycroft and the University of Wales* **2001**/0121429

How to use *Jane's Survey Vessels*

Jane's Survey Vessels is a one-volume open source reference to the world's governmental and commercial survey and research vessels. Each entry endeavours to give information with regard to the following:

- Operator
- Owner
- Former names
- Current operational status
- Port of registry/flag
- Official number
- Classification
- Call sign
- Place and date of build
- Place and date of rebuild
- Dimensions
- Propulsion
- Speed
- Endurance
- Fuel capacity
- Fuel consumption
- Electrical power
- Fresh water capacity
- Navigation aids
- Communications
- Lifeboats
- Workboat/chase boats
- Lifesaving equipment
- Deck machinery
- Cranes
- Moonpool(s)
- Accommodation
- Scientific deck space
- Scientific Laboratories
- Survey systems
- Vehicles
- Seismic systems

The book is divided into five main sections:

Oceanographic Research (including environmental survey, fisheries and arctic research) Vessels

Almost exclusively operated by government-run scientific establishments with the aim of advancing scientific knowledge of the oceans' physical, chemical and biological properties by means of extensive data-gathering cruises. Often, these are international efforts involving ships of a number of nations – the World Ocean Circulation Experiment and the Global Ocean Observing System (GOOS) are examples.

These vessels are extensively equipped with remote and direct sampling methods. Typically, an oceanographic research ship simultaneously gathers temporal and spatial data on winds, waves, tides, surface and subsurface currents, seabed and sub-seabed sediments, conductivity, temperature, depth, flora and fauna (from plankton to large mammals), turbidity, pH and sound velocity (this is a random list).

Large oceanographic vessels have a sophisticated armoury of systems with which to gather this data. Data is collected using acoustic techniques (for depth measurement, seabed mapping and underwater positioning), and direct sampling by nets, by vertical profiling, by towed vehicles and by gathering telemetered data from networks of fixed or drifting buoys.

Government Hydrographic Vessels

These are almost without exception operated by navies, government departments or government agencies. Their primary activity is to map the seabed in order to produce and sell charts for safe navigation. For many this is their exclusive activity; others may be armed and used in a broader defence role or for specialist work such as fisheries protection; some are involved in limited delineation of resources within a nation's Exclusive Economic Zone (EEZ).

Seismic Exploration Vessels

These are commercial vessels whose sole purpose is to explore for subsea hydrocarbon reservoirs. Although single-purpose, these are vessels of extreme sophistication – a typical ship will tow up to 12 data-gathering "streamers" each up to 6,000 m long. Data from subsea strata are recorded and processed on board with the aid of massive computer power – a typical onboard system has four CPUs, each with three Gbytes of RAM and 200 Gbytes of disk space.

Site and Route Survey Vessels;

This is the "general-purpose" end of the market with a fleet that varies from small launches (of which more below) to 60 m long vessels whose sophistication approaches that of the vessels in the seismic sector. Site survey vessels support the offshore oil industry, the cable-laying industry and nearshore civil engineering activity.

Offshore oil industry. Before a well can be drilled a site survey is undertaken. The site survey vessel uses seismic techniques (although usually with only one streamer) to probe the first few hundred metres of sediments for entrapped gas deposits that, if hit by the drill bit, can cause catastrophic fires on board the drilling rig. If the rig is seabed mounted (a jack-up) the site survey vessel uses acoustic-based sub-bottom profiling and direct sampling techniques to ensure the stability of the seabed on which the rig is placed; if the drilling is to be from an anchored vessel – typically a semi-submersible – the site survey vessel will investigate soil properties at anchoring points. If oil is discovered, the site survey vessel conducts similar seabed mapping and sub-bottom profiling operations before subsea equipment is installed. It will also map the proposed routes of pipelines both within the field development and from the field to shore. The vessel maps the pipeline as it is laid and undertakes annual sonar inspection surveys.

Cable-laying. The massive growth in telecommunications, mostly spawned by the Internet, has led to a corresponding demand for the means to transport those communications and some 90 per cent of this is by subsea fibre optic cables. In the deep ocean where the cable is merely laid on the bottom, the ocean floor is surveyed by multibeam echo-sounder techniques alone. Where the cable has to be buried to protect it from fishing gear – on the continental slope, continental shelf and up to the shoreline – more comprehensive techniques are required, involving the full range of side scan sonar, sub-bottom profiling and direct sampling techniques.

Nearshore civil engineering. Complex underwater surveys are required to support nearshore civil engineering projects. These include the construction of ports and harbours, capital and maintenance dredging, the siting of shore facilities such as refineries, LNG plant and so on. These frequently involve detailed environmental studies to ensure that nearshore flora and fauna are not disturbed by dredging and construction activities. The metocean work involved includes gathering data on winds, waves, tides, currents and chemical properties, as well as the usual seabed mapping and sub-bottom profiling tasks.

Frequently this type of nearshore work is undertaken by small boats – perhaps only 10 m or so long. Users of other Jane's maritime products may be surprised to see such small craft featuring in a guide of this type. However, we felt it important to include a representative selection because these vessels are often just as lavishly equipped with sophisticated survey systems as their ocean-going counterparts. Of course, any boat fitted with a survey echo-sounder and towing a side scan sonar can be termed a "survey vessel" and so we have included only those that have dedicated suites of equipment.

Vessel Operators

Full contact details, including postal, telephone, fax, e-mail and website addresses are provided where possible.

Where possible each entry also includes a photograph and relevant ships' drawings.

To help users of this title evaluate the published data, Jane's Information Group has divided entries into three categories. A full list of all entries indicating their current status is provided in the index.

● **VERIFIED** The editor has made a detailed examination of the entry's content and checked it's relevancy and accuracy for publication in the new edition to the best of his ability.

● **UPDATED** During the verification process, significant changes to content have been made to reflect the latest position known to Jane's at the time of publication.

● **NEW ENTRY** Information on new equipment and/or appearing for the first time in the title.

All new pictures are dated with the year of publication. New pictures this year are dated 2001. Some are followed by a seven digit number for ease of identification by our image library.

Total number of entries	1,007	New and updated entries	742
Total number of images	462	New images	240

Copyright enquiries
Contact: Keith Faulkner, Tel/Fax: +44 (0) 1342 305032, e-mail: keith.faulkner@janes.co.uk

British Library Cataloguing-in-Publication Data.
A catalogue record for this book is available from the British Library.

Printed and bound in Great Britain by Hobbs the Printers, Totton, Hampshire

EDITORIAL AND ADMINISTRATION

Publishing Director: Alan Condron, e-mail: Alan.Condron@janes.co.uk

Managing Editor: Sara Waddington, e-mail: Sara Waddington@janes.co.uk

Content Production Manager: Anita Slade, e-mail: Anita.Slade@janes.co.uk

Content Editing Manager: Jo Fenwick, e-mail: Jo.Fenwick@janes.co.uk

Pre-Press Manager: Christopher Morris, e-mail: Christopher.Morris@janes.co.uk

Team Leaders: Sharon Marshall, e-mail: Sharon.Marshall@janes.co.uk
Neil Grace, e-mail: Neil.Grace@janes.co.uk

Database Editor: Nicola Stuart, e-mail: Nicola.Stuart@janes.co.uk

Content Update: Jacqui Beard, Information Collection Assistant
Tel: (+44 20) 87 00 38 08 Fax: (+44 20) 87 00 39 59
e-mail: yearbook@janes.co.uk

Jane's Information Group Limited, Sentinel House, 163 Brighton Road, Coulsdon,
Surrey CR5 2YH, UK
Tel: (+44 20) 87 00 37 00 Fax: (+44 20) 87 00 37 88
e-mail: jsv@janes.co.uk

SALES OFFICE

Send EMEA enquiries to: *Group Sales Manager*
Jane's Information Group Limited, Sentinel House, 163 Brighton Road, Coulsdon,
Surrey CR5 2YH, UK
Tel: (+44 20) 87 00 37 00 Fax: (+44 20) 87 63 10 06
e-mail: info@janes.co.uk

Send USA enquiries to: *Robert Loughman – Vice-President Product Sales*
Jane's Information Group Inc, 1340 Braddock Place, Suite 300, Alexandria, Virginia
22314-1651, USA
Tel: (+1 703) 683 37 00 Fax: (+1 703) 836 02 97 Telex: 6819193
Tel: (+1 800) 824 07 68 Fax: (+1 800) 836 02 971
e-mail: info@janes.com

Send Asia enquiries to: *David Fisher – Group Sales Manager*
Jane's Information Group Asia, 60 Albert Street, #15-01 Albert Complex, Singapore
189969
Tel: (+65) 331 62 80 Fax: (+65) 336 99 21
e-mail: info@janes.com.sg

Send Australia/New Zealand enquiries to: *David Moden – Business Manager*
Jane's Information Group, PO Box 3502, Rozelle Delivery Centre, New South Wales
2039, Australia
Tel: (+61 2) 85 87 79 00 Fax: (+61 2) 85 87 79 01
e-mail: info@janes.thomson.com.au

ADVERTISEMENT SALES OFFICES

(Head Office)
Jane's Information Group
Sentinel House, 163 Brighton Road,
Coulsdon, Surrey CR5 2YH, UK
Tel: (+44 20) 87 00 37 00
Fax: (+44 20) 87 00 38 59/37 44
e-mail: defadsales@janes.co.uk

Richard West, Senior Key Accounts Manager
Tel: (+44 1892) 72 55 80 Fax: (+44 1892) 72 55 81
e-mail: richard.west@janes.co.uk

Kate Hamlin, Advertising Sales Manager
Tel: (+44 20) 87 00 38 53 Fax: (+44 20) 87 00 38 59/37 44
e-mail: kate.hamlin@janes.co.uk

Joni Beeden, Advertising Sales Executive
Tel: (+44 20) 87 00 39 63 Fax: (+44 20) 87 00 38 59/37 44
e-mail: joni.beeden@janes.co.uk

Steve Soffe, Advertising Sales Executive
Tel: (+44 20) 87 00 39 43 Fax: (+44 20) 87 00 38 59/37 44
e-mail: steven.soffe@janes.co.uk

USA/Canada
Jane's Information Group
1340 Braddock Place, Suite 300,
Alexandria, Virginia 22314-1651, USA
Tel: (+1 703) 683 37 00
Fax: (+1 703) 836 55 37
e-mail: defadsales@janes.com

USA and Canada
Katie Taplett, US Advertising Sales Director
Tel: (+1 703) 683 37 00 Fax: (+1 703) 836 55 37
e-mail: katie.taplett@janes.com

Northern USA and Eastern Canada
Harry Carter, Northeast Region Advertising Sales Manager
Tel: (+1 703) 683 37 00 Fax: (+1 703) 836 55 37
e-mail: harry.carter@janes.com

South Eastern USA
Kristin D Schulze, Advertising Sales Manager
PO Box 270190, Tampa, Florida 33688-0190
Tel: (+1 813) 961 81 32 Fax: (+1 813) 961 96 42
e-mail: kristin@intnet.net

Western USA and West Canada
Richard L Ayer
127 Avenida Del Mar, Suite 2A, San Clemente, California 92672
Tel: (+1 949) 366 84 55 Fax: (+1 949) 366 92 89
e-mail: ayercomm@earthlink.com

Australia: *Richard West* (see UK Head Office)

Benelux: *Steve Soffe* (see UK Head Office)

Brazil: Katie Taplett, (see USA address)

Eastern Europe: *MCW Media & Consulting Wehrstedt*
Dr. Uwe H. Wehrstedt
Hagenbreite 9, D-06463 Ermsleben, Germany
Tel: (+49) 0700/WEHRSTEDT / (+49) 03 47 43/620 90
Fax: (+49) 03 47 43/620 91
e-mail: info@Wehrstedt.org

France: *Patrice Février*
BP 418, 35 avenue MacMahon,
F-75824 Paris Cedex 17, France
Tel: (+33 1) 45 72 33 11 Fax: (+33 1) 45 72 17 95
e-mail: patrice.fevrier@wandadoo.fr

Germany and Austria: *MCW Media & Consulting Wehrstedt* (see Eastern Europe)

Greece: *Steve Soffe* (see UK Head Office)

Hong Kong: *Joni Beeden* (see UK Head Office)

India: *Joni Beeden* (see UK Head Office)

Israel: Oreet – International Media
15 Kinneret Street, IL-51201 Bene Berak, Israel
Tel: (+972 3) 570 65 27 Fax: (+972 3) 570 65 27
e-mail: admin@oreet-marcom.com
Defence: Liat Shaham
e-mail: liat_s@oreet-marcom.com

Italy and Switzerland: Ediconsult Internazionale Srl
Tel: (+39 010) 58 36 59 Fax: (+39 010) 56 65 78
e-mail: genova@ediconsult.com

Japan: Skynet Media, Inc
748, 1-7 Akasaka 9-chome, Minato-ku, Tokyo 107-0052, Japan
Contact: Mr Osamu Yoneda
Tel: (+81 3) 54 74 78 35
Fax: (+81 3) 54 74 78 37
e-mail: skynetme@wonder.ocn.ne.jp

Middle East: *Steve Soffe* (see UK Head Office)

Pakistan: *Joni Beeden* (see UK Head Office)

Russian Federation: *Simon Kay*
33 St John's Street, Crowthorne, Berkshire RG45 7NQ, UK
Tel: (+44 1344) 77 71 23 Mobile: (+44 7702) 54 96 84
Fax: (+44 1344) 77 58 85
e-mail: crowkay@msn.com/crowkay@yahoo.com

Scandinavia: *The Falsten Partnership*
PO Box 21175, London N16 6ZG, UK
Tel: (+44 20) 88 06 23 01 Fax: (+ 44 20) 88 06 81 37
e-mail: sales@falsten.com

Singapore: *Richard West/Joni Beeden* (see UK Head Office)

South Africa: *Richard West* (see UK Head Office)

South Korea: *JES Media Inc*
2nd Floor, ANA Building, 257-1 Myungil-Dong, Kandong-Gu, Seoul 134-070, Korea
Contact: Mr Young-Seoh Chinn, President
Tel: (+82 2) 481 34 11/34 13
Fax: (+82 2) 481 34 14
e-mail: jesmedia@unitel.co.kr

Spain: *Via Exclusivas SL*
Contact: Julio de Andres
Viriato 69SC, E-28010 Madrid, Spain
Tel: (+34 91) 448 76 22 Fax: (+34 91) 446 02 14
e-mail: j.a.deandres@viaexclusivas.com

Turkey: *Richard West* (see UK Head Office)

ADVERTISING COPY
Sue Tucker (Jane's UK Head Office)
Tel: (+44 20) 87 00 37 42 Fax: (+44 20) 87 00 38 59/37 44
e-mail: sue.tucker@janes.co.uk

For North America, South America and Caribbean only:
Shanee Johnson (Jane's USA address)
Alexandria, Virginia 22314-1651, USA
Tel: (+1 703) 683 37 00 Fax: (+1 703) 836 55 37
e-mail: shanee.johnson@janes.com

Alphabetical list of advertisers

R

Rodman
PO Box 501, E-36200 Vigo, Spain .... *Inside front cover*

Foreword

This second edition of *Jane's Survey Vessels* is divided into four sections:

(1) Hydrographic
(2) Oceanographic
(3) Seismic exploration
(4) Site and route survey.

Hydrographic survey vessels

Hydrographic vessels are usually operated by navies, government departments or other public sector agencies. In addition, their role may fall into either supporting civil activities, for example, delineation of Exclusive Economic Zones (EEZs), or in support of military or naval operations, for example charting the seabed in relation to anti-submarine warfare.

Although many of these vessels form part of the armed forces in most countries, they are not always part of the fleet that engages in traditional military operations. Consequently, some countries have taken the opportunity to be more innovative in looking for cost savings relating to both construction and operational costs. An example is the UK government's contract to Vosper Thornycroft to manage and support two new multirole hydrographic and oceanographic survey vessels throughout their 25-year life. The vessels, HMS *Echo* and HMS *Enterprise*, are building at Appledore Shipbuilders and will enter service with the RN's survey squadron in 2002 and 2003.

Oceanographic vessels

As with hydrographic vessels, this sector is primarily owned and operated by national governments, research institutes and universities for marine science, fisheries research and environmental monitoring activities. As a consequence there have been major efforts to encourage co-operation between the larger operators of the research fleets to reduce costs, including the exchange of ship time between countries. Much of this effort is undertaken through the auspices of the International Research Ship Operators' Meeting (ISOM). ISOM is an informal annual meeting (September/October) of managers of ocean research ship fleets for the purpose of discussing subjects and solving problems of mutual interest. Part of this work has included the funding of the OCEANIC research ships database at the University of Delaware, which holds information on research ship cruise schedules. Another discussion area involves the sharing of major research equipment, such as manned and unmanned submersibles.

Within the US academic sector this activity has been undertaken by the University-National Oceanographic Laboratory System (UNOLS), a consortium of 57 academic institutions with significant marine science programmes that either operate or use the US academic research fleet. UNOLS was set up over 25 years ago in an attempt to manage the use of research vessels. The UNOLS Council is charged with planning for future facility requirements for ocean science research to ensure that the Fleet maintains its effectiveness. This includes planning for replacement of ships as they age. Within Europe, the European Commission, through the Fifth Framework Environment and Sustainable Development sub-programme, has attempted to encourage more effective use of Europe's research vessels through its "Support for Research Infrastructures" initiative, which supports the enhancement of research vessels, and through funding multi-partner marine research activities, including research vessels.

Another continuing issue is the use of commercial research vessels to reduce costs and/or the use of commercial ship managers to operate government-owned research vessels, rather than public sector bodies.

Seismic exploration vessels

In the Foreword to the first edition of *Jane's Survey Vessels* we pointed out the difficulties in obtaining as up-to-date a picture of the marine seismic industry as we would have wished. This, we said, was due to the fluctuating state of the market and we promised a more comprehensive set of data in the second edition.

The fluctuations in the market have continued and only as this edition goes to press does the marine seismic industry show signs of recovery. There were a number of reasons for the downturn. Chief of these was the aftermath of the oil price slump in 1999 where, as Andrew McBarnet, seismic guru and editor of *First Break* magazine points out," oil and gas companies simply closed the books on the seismic business. "This left contractors with the unpalatable option, says McBarnet, of laying up vessels or undertaking multi-client survey work.

Another reason for fluctuating fortunes was, ironically enough, that the industry was hoist on the petard of its own technological success. With the introduction of its Ramform vessels, for example, PGS vastly increased productivity and forced its competitors to upgrade their technology. The result has been that the cost per square kilometre of 3-D marine seismic data is now about a tenth of what it was ten years ago.

There were inevitable losses (Horizon Exploration went bankrupt, Aker Geo sold its vessels) and mergers: the giant Western Geophysical, for example, grew still larger by its merger with Geco-Prakla to become WesternGeco and is now estimated to command 60 per cent of the 3-D marine seismic market.

Site & route survey vessels

The mixed fortunes of the seismic exploration business fortunately were not reflected in those of the site and route survey market. A definition is perhaps needed here: seismic exploration vessels have one function only – to prospect for oil and gas reserves. Site and route survey vessels, while often using some of the technology (albeit diluted) of the seismic industry, perform a wide range of offshore engineering tasks. That those tasks are not exclusively oil-related accounts for the better fortunes of this sector over the past year or so: certainly the number of new buildings listed in *Jane's Survey Vessels* reflects this.

Even so, the oil industry still accounts for some 60 per cent of the work undertaken by the worldwide site and route survey fleet, undertaking pre-drilling surveys of the seabed and underlying sediments; mapping proposed pipeline routes; surveying the pipeline as it is laid and undertaking surveys with sonar, sub-bottom profilers and remotely operated vehicles.

Of survey activities for other industries, we reported last year on the boom in subsea cable laying to support the growth in telecommunications spawned by Internet use. Massive projects were planned, all of which required across-ocean surveys with multibeam swath sounding and, nearer shore, a full range of sidescan sonar, sub-bottom profiling and direct sampling techniques. There were prize pickings for the offshore survey market with some contractors operating up to five ships at a time on 2 to 3 year projects.

Roebuck is currently part of the UK Royal Navy's hydrographic fleet (van Ginderen Collection)   *2000*/0075820

Survey craft come in highly contrasting shapes and sizes. Here's Elf, built by Porta-Bote in the United States for British Waterways. Just 3.2m long and car-transportable it nevertheless carries a sophisticated suite of survey equipment, including differential GPS, multibeam and single beam sounders. Contrast this with PGS Exploration's Ramform Explorer – 82m long and one of a series of craft with a unique shape that has revolutionised the seismic exploration industry
2002/0110528/0088243

How things change! The vast and rapid decline in dot.com business has seen a consequent slackening in demand for cable capacity and a corresponding fall-off in offshore surveys. And the increasing capacity of cables – with transmission capacity of a single cable moving from 40 gigabits per second to 1,000 gigabits per second – means that fewer cables will be required to meet demand – and hence less surveys.

So the site and route market has sought to consolidate in existing areas while looking for new activities.

Several have opened up.

First, the Law of the Sea Conventions have "given" many coastal states vast areas of new territory, rich in living and mineral resources. Sometimes these territories have an area far greater with more potential riches than that of the nation's above-surface area.

But to exploit these riches requires an accurate delineation by the nation involved of its ocean environment, the ocean floor and its sediments. Fortunately, the very vessels that have been undertaking oceanwide surveys of potential cable routes are ideally equipped to survey these Exclusive Economic Zones (EEZs).

Large scale EEZ surveys of this type usually begin with desk studies to look at topics such as geology, seabed physiography, bathymetry and coastal morphology; meteorology and oceanography; marine industries such as hydrocarbon exploitation and fishing; and leisure activities.

Then the at-sea survey work begins, typically using swath bathymetry to map the ocean floor to its full depth; to undertake "quick-look" seismic surveys for underlying hydrocarbon deposits; and to sample sediments. This is backed up by meteorological and oceanographic studies where *in-situ* arrays of instruments are often moored in water depths to 3,000 metres for a year or so at a time,
gathering data on currents, temperature, salinity and other indications of the ocean's health.

Secondly, there has been continuing growth in the market for nearshore environmental and geophysical studies to support a wide range of activities – building ports and harbours, siting coastal power plants, installing long sea effluent outfalls. This is where smaller craft are involved and many of these are listed in this edition. Their inclusion is amply justified: these craft usually carry just as much sophisticated survey equipment as their oceangoing counterparts – just look at the specification for the 3 m-long Land-Rover-transportable foldaway "Elf" boat run by British Waterways and you will see that it is capable of producing just as much data as one of the ocean-going vessels. The only difference is one of having a platform which is capable of withstanding prevailing conditions – at the end of the day it is quality of data that counts.

Many of the smaller craft detailed in this edition will increasingly be deployed in one of the relatively new offshore markets – renewable energy. Throughout Europe there are vast schemes to tap the power of offshore winds, waves and currents. Even the UK is now installing offshore wind and wave facilities. But the installation of offshore wind and wave energy facilities requires equally meticulous site surveys – metocean, geophysical and ground engineering – as any offshore oil project. They will however be closer to shore and require smaller boats. It is a vast new market.

Finally, there's the search for deposits of sand and gravel close to shore for aggregates to support onshore building activity – sidescan, sub-bottom profiling and coring required here; and marina building; as well as beach replenishment. The market for site and route surveys is assured.

Users' Charter

This publication is brought to you by Jane's Information Group, a global company with more than 100 years of innovation and an unrivalled reputation for impartiality, accuracy and authority.

Our collection and output of information and images is not dictated by any political or commercial affiliation. Our reportage is undertaken without fear of, or favour from, any government, alliance, state or corporation.

We publish information that is collected overtly from unclassified sources, although much could be regarded as extremely sensitive or not publicly accessible.

Our validation and analysis aims to eradicate misinformation or disinformation as well as factual errors; our objective is always to produce the most accurate and authoritative data.

In the event of any significant inaccuracies, we undertake to draw these to the readers' attention to preserve the highly valued relationship of trust and credibility with our customers worldwide.

If you believe that these policies have been breached by this title, you are invited to contact the editor.

A copy of Jane's Information Group's Code of Conduct for its editorial teams is available from the publisher.

INVESTOR IN PEOPLE

GOVERNMENT HYDROGRAPHIC VESSELS

ALGERIA

Algerian Navy

El Idrissi

GENERAL		ACCOMMODATION	
Former names	A 673	**Crew**	6 officers; 22 crew
Official number	BH 204		
Built (yard and date)	Matsukara, Japan; 1980		*VERIFIED*
Displacement	548.6 t		

El Idrissi

AUSTRALIA

Royal Australian Navy

Leeuwin Class

GENERAL		Propulsion	
Comments	Leeuwin Class hydrographic vessels include HMAS Leeuwin and Melville	**Main engine(s)**	4 × 810 kW GEC Alsthom 660 V AC diesel generators connected to 1,000 kVA alternator; 2 × 970 kW Alsthom variable speed drive electric propulsion motors
Official number	HMAS Leeuwin: A 245 HMAS Melville: A 246		
Call sign	HMAS Leeuwin: VLSE HMAS Melville: VLSF	**Thrusters**	bow: 1 × 400 kW Schottel variable speed drive flush mounted pump jet
Built (yard and date)	North Queensland Engineering, Cairns; 1998 – 2000 (commissioned 27 May 2000)	**Propellers**	2 × 5-bladed fixed pitch counter rotating propeller
Length overall	71.2 m		
Breadth moulded	15.2 m	**Speed (max)**	14 kt
Working deck width		**Speed (cruising)**	12 kt
Max draught		**Endurance**	8,000 n miles at 12 kt
Operational draught	5.3 m	**Fuel capacity**	373 cz diesel distillate; 34 cz AVCAT
Displacement	2,170 t		

Leeuwin Class   **2000**/0017563

Fuel consumption	7 cz/day (four diesels running)	receiver; SSB T2130 transmitter;
Electrical power	240 V/415 V/660 V AC; 24 V DC	DDRF 5050 direction-finding
Fresh water capacity	44 cz (reverse osmosis water	receiver; Navtex Nav 5 receiver
	making facilities)	Raven & Schwartz XT 452 U8

VHF — Raven & Schwartz XT 452 U8 transceiver; Raven & Schwartz XD 432 U8 transceiver; 2 × Sailor RT 2047 D transceivers; SP 3911; 3 Kyodo KG 209 ICOM AE 22

BRIDGE NAVIGATION AIDS

Satellite	Kelvin Hughes 1020 GPS
Radar	STN Atlas 9600 ARPA; I band
Gyrocompass	2 NAVIGAT X Mod 10
	2 NAVITWIN II
Speed log	E/M log; doppler Velocity Log,
	171.3 kHz, in a Janus
	configuration

Cellular — NEC S1 Optus Satellite telephone

SAFETY

Workboat/chase boat — 3 × 10.7 m, 8 t survey motor boats; 2 × 5 m, 280 kg light utility boats, 27 hp; 4.8 m Zodiac inflatable, 27 hp

COMMUNICATIONS

Inmarsat (type)	Inmarsat C H2095 B, 1.5/1.6 GHz
MF/HF	2 Sunair R9200 receivers; R501
	watch receiver; R2120 duplex

Lifesaving equipment — 6 liferafts: 25 person; 2 EPIRBs

Helideck — 20 × 9.5 m capable of operating intermediate sized utility helicopter

HMAS Leeuwin and HMAS Melville   **2000**/0110205

DECK MACHINERY

Cranes	2 Palfinger Marine, 2 t at 8 m radius
A-frame(s)	boat davit; 1 t at 3.6 m radius; starboard: 1 t at 2 m extension; transom: 500 kg at 1.5 m extension
Winches	starboard: 2 winches adjacent to A-Frame for seabed sampling grab and towed CTD; quarterdeck: hydraulic winch for towed sidescan sonar
Transducer well	multibeam echo-sounder situated at frame 13; forward looking sonar situated at frame 26

ACCOMMODATION

Crew	51 (including 10 officers)
Scientists/surveyors	14

SCIENTIFIC SPACES

Total scientific deck space	150 m²
Oceanographic wet lab	21 m²

SURVEY SYSTEMS

Positioning	NR 230 Mk II DFGPS; NR 103 DGPS; Leica MX 412 DGPS; Racal MicroFix
Sensors	CMAS forward looking sonar 36/39 kHz; Dynabase motion sensor
Echo-sounder (single beam)	Atlas DESO 25 12/33/210 kHz; Atlas DESO 15 33/210 kHz fitted to each Survey Motor Boat
Multibeam/swath system	Atlas Fansweep 20, 100kHz; Atlas Fansweep 20, 200 kHz fitted to each Survey Motor Boat
Sidescan sonar	Klein 2000 dual frequency
Grab(s)	Shipek grab on 200 m wire
Oceanographic sensors (CTDs/XBTs and so on)	hull-mounted CTD; towed CTD; InterOcean S4 tide guage; InterOcean S4 current meter; bottom mounted ADCP; expendable Bathythermographs

UPDATED

Royal Australian Navy

Paluma Class

GENERAL

	Paluma Class hydrographic vessels include HMAS Paluma, Mermaid, Shepparton and Benalla		HMAS Mermaid: AGSC02 HMAS Shepparton: AGSC03 HMAS Benalla: AGSC04
Owner	Royal Australian Navy	**Call sign**	HMAS Paluma: VLRY
Port of reg/flag	AGSC		HMAS Mermaid: VLRX
Official number	HMAS Paluma: AGSC01		HMAS Shepparton: VLRZ HMAS Benalla: VLRW

Shepparton (Ian Edwards)   *2000*

Built (yard and date)	Eglo Engineering, Adelaide; February 1989 – March 1990
Length overall	36.55 m
Breadth moulded	14 m
Max draught	2.65 m
Operational draught	2.2 m
Tonnage (grt)	468

PROPULSION

Main engine(s)	2 × Detroit 12 V-92TA diesels; 1,100 hp: 2 shafts
Propellers	2 × 4 blades fixed pitch: outward turning
Speed (max)	11 kt
Speed (cruising)	11 kt
Endurance	3,500 n miles at 11 kt
Fuel capacity	76,400 litres
Fuel consumption	200 litres/h at 11 kt
Electrical power	2 × 130 kW diesel generators
Fresh water capacity	12,000 litres

BRIDGE NAVIGATION AIDS

Satellite	GPS KH 1020
Radar	KH1007 CTD
Echo-sounder	Skipper S113

COMMUNICATIONS

Inmarsat (type)	Mini – M
MF/HF	Codan HF-4000
VHF	IC-M120
Cellular	Analog
Facsimile	Toshiba

SAFETY

Workboat/chase boat	2 × 4.5 m aluminium utility boats
Lifesaving equipment	3 Liferafts: 10 persons

DECK MACHINERY

Cranes	1 Palfinger 730 kg at total extension

HMAS Paluma

2001/0110206

ACCOMMODATION

Crew	3 officers; 11 crew
Hospital	2 berth

SCIENTIFIC SPACES

Total scientific deck space	23.2 m²

SURVEY SYSTEMS

Positioning	Leica DGPS MX 412
	Sercel DGPS NR 103 UHF & HF
	Racal MicroFix
	KH 1020 GPS

Sensors	Skipper S113 Searchlight Sonar
Echo-sounder(single beam)	2 ELAC LAZ 4700 Dual Frequency
Sidescan sonar	1 ELAC LAZ 72 (hull mounted)
Grab(s)	1 Peterson hand-held; 1 Shipek Grab
Sound velocity profiler	Odom 1100 Digibar

UPDATED

HMAS Shepparton   **2001**/0110204

BELGIUM

Waterways and Maritime Affairs Division

Ter Streep

GENERAL BACKGROUND

Coastal hydrographic vessel

Call sign	ORDJ
Built (yard and date)	NV Scheepswerven van Langerbrugge, Gent, Belgium; October 1985
Length overall	49.55 m
Breadth moulded	9.6 m
Max draught	3.25 m
Tonnage (grt)	643
Propulsion	
Main engine(s)	Twin 4-stroke Anglo Belgian Corp (ABC) diesel engines, 596 kW (810 hp) – 750 rpm
Thrusters	Bow: JASTRAM 250 kW (204 hp) – 1,800 rpm
Propellers	Single 4-bladed variable pitch LIPS, 2.2 m diameter
Speed (max)	13 kt
Speed (cruising)	9 – 10 kt
Fuel capacity	49 m³
Electrical power	2 Scania diesels, 178 kW – 1,500 rpm, 190 kVA, 3 × 380 V, 50 Hz
Fresh water capacity	42 m³

BRIDGE NAVIGATION AIDS

Radar	Racal Decca RM 1290
	Racal Decca 970 BT

Gyrocompass	Anschutz Standard 12
Speed log	JRC JLN 203 Doppler log
Echo-sounder	JRC JFE-570 S
Other ship navigation	Decca Navigator Mk 21

COMMUNICATIONS

MF/HF	Skanti TRP/6000/ER 4800 transmitter
	Skanti WR/6000/R 6020 receiver
VHF	2 Sailor RT 144 C

SAFETY

Workboat/chase boat	2 SPURT 25, SAAB diesels, 18 kW (24 hp)

DECK MACHINERY

Cranes	Aft: HATLAPA, 30 kN
	2 HLC 3500 Davits, 40 kN
A-frame(s)	Stern: 50 kN with 2 REXROTH hydraulic cylinders, combined with 2 BRUSSELLE winches
Winches	9: 2 – port, 7 – starboard; 5 kN at 15, 30 and 60 m/min
Transducer well	Centre well of 1 × 1 m for Sectascan sonar

ACCOMMODATION

Crew	18 (total)

SCIENTIFIC SPACES

SURVEY SYSTEMS
Sensors	Datawell Hippy 120
Echo-sounder(single beam)	3 × Atlas DESO 20; Elas Lac 400; Ultra 3000; Polytechnic Marine SECTASCAN sonar; 2 Decca AUTOCARTA II sounding systems

Multibeam/swath system	Simrad EM 950
Oceanographic sensors (CTDs/XBTs and so on)	3 OTT current meters; 5 Seatracks current meters; 5 Aanderaa WLR-5; 7 Datawell wave rider buoys; 1 Datawell Wavec buoy

UPDATED

BRAZIL

Brazilian Navy

Argus Class

GENERAL

Argus H 31 Orion H 32

Official number	Argus H 31
	Orion H 32
Built (yard and date)	Argus: Arsenal de Marinha, Rio de Janeiro; launched 6 Dec 1957, commissioned 29 Jan 1959
	Orion: Arsenal de Marinha, Rio de Janeiro; launched 5 Feb 1958, commissioned 11 June 1959
Rebuilt (yard and date)	Re-engined in 1974
Length overall	44.7 m
Breadth moulded	6.50 m
Operational draught	2.80 m

PROPULSION
Main engine(s)	2 Caterpillar D 379 diesels; 1,098 hp (818 kW) sustained

Propellers	2
Speed (cruising)	15.0 kt
Endurance	3,000 n miles at 15 kt

BRIDGE NAVIGATION AIDS
Satellite	Yes
Radar	2 Racal Decca 1226C; I-band
Gyrocompass	Yes
Speed log	Yes
Echo-sounder	Yes

ACCOMMODATION
Crew	42

SURVEY SYSTEMS
Echo-sounder (single beam)	Yes

VERIFIED

Argus   **2000**/0017628

Brazilian Navy

Sirius

GENERAL
Official number	H 21
Built (yard and date)	Ishikawajima Co Ltd, Tokyo; launched 30th July 1957
Length overall	78.00 m
Breadth moulded	12.1 m
Operational draught	3.70 m

PROPULSION
Main engine(s)	2 Sulzer 7T6-36 diesels; 2,700 hp(m) (1.98 MW)

Propellers	2 CP propellers
Speed (max)	15.7 kt
Speed (cruising)	11.0 kt
Endurance	12,000 n miles at 11 kt

BRIDGE NAVIGATION AIDS
Satellite	Yes
Radar	Racal Decca TM 1226C; I-band.
Gyrocompass	Yes
Speed log	Yes
Echo-sounder	Yes

HELIDECK

Size, aircraft capacity	1 Bell JetRanger.

ACCOMMODATION

Crew	116
Scientists/surveyors	14

SURVEY SYSTEMS

Echo-sounder (single beam)	Yes

VERIFIED

Sirius   *2000*/0056615

BULGARIA

Navy Hydrographic Service

Admiral Branimir Ormanov

GENERAL

	MOMA (TYPE 861) CLASS (AGS)
	Based at Varna
Built (yard and date)	Northern Shipyard, Gdansk,
	Poland: 1977.
Rebuilt (yard and date)	Bulgaria; 1995-96
Length overall	73.3 m
Breadth moulded	11.2 m
Operational draught	3.90 m

PROPULSION

Main engine(s)	2 Zgoda-Sulzer 6TD48 diesels;
	3,300 hp(m) (2.43 MW) sustained
Propellers	2 CP

Speed (cruising)	17.0 kt
Endurance	9,000 n miles at 15 kt

BRIDGE NAVIGATION AIDS

Satellite	Yes
Radar	2 Don-2; I-band
Gyrocompass	Yes
Speed log	Yes
Echo-sounder	Yes

ACCOMMODATION

Crew	37

UPDATED

Admiral Branimir Ormanov   *2000*/0093765

CANADA

Canadian Coast Guard

F.C.G Smith

GENERAL

	Multihulled survey vessel; home port: Québec
Port of reg/flag	Ottawa
Official number	806310
Classification	Home Trade II
Call sign	CG3006
Built (yard and date)	Georgetown Shipyard, Prince Edward Island; 1985
Length overall	34.8 m
Breadth moulded	14.0 m
Max draught	2.1 m
Tonnage (grt)	438.5

PROPULSION

Main engine(s)	2 Beaudoin diesel, each 596 kW
Propellers	2 CP propeller
Speed (cruising)	10.0 kt
Endurance	1,500 n miles/7 days
Fuel capacity	38 m³
Fuel consumption	0.7 m³/day
Electrical power	2 generators, each 135 kW
Fresh water capacity	12 m³

BRIDGE NAVIGATION AIDS

Satellite	Magnavox MX-200
Radar	2 Bridgemaster II C252 ARPA – X Band
Gyrocompass	Anschutz STD 20
Speed log	Sperry SRD-331
Echo-sounder	ELAC LAZ 72
Other ship navigation	Loran: Northstar 800X

COMMUNICATIONS

Inmarsat (type)	no
MF/HF	Daniels DE1400
VHF	Collins 251; Sailor C403; Sailor RT146
Facsimile	Taiyo TF-733

SAFETY

Workboat/chase boat	Two: Avon Rider 5.4 m

DECK MACHINERY

Cranes	Aft-starboard: HIAB CMU: 1.2 tons
	Aft-port: HIAB

ACCOMMODATION

Crew	7

SURVEY SYSTEMS

Echo-sounder (single beam)	sweep boom with Navitronics multichannel sounder (210 kHz)

UPDATED

F.C.G Smith

2001/0017673

Canadian Coast Guard

Frederick G Creed

GENERAL

Multihulled survey vessel; home port: Rimouski, Québec

Port of reg/flag	Ottawa
Official number	813676
Classification	Coastal I
Call sign	CG3198
Built (yard and date)	Swath Ocean Systems Inc, San Diego; 1988
Length overall	20.4 m
Breadth moulded	9.75 m
Max draught	2.6 m
Tonnage (grt)	151.4

PROPULSION

Main engine(s)	Two Detroit diesel V12 TA, 1,609 kW
Propellers	Two fixed-pitch propellers
Speed (max)	21.0 kt
Speed (cruising)	16.0 kt
Endurance	1,500 n miles/3 days
Fuel capacity	15.8 m^3
Fuel consumption	5 m^3/day
Electrical power	Two John Deere generators, each 33 kW
Fresh water capacity	3 m^3

BRIDGE NAVIGATION AIDS

Satellite	Furuno GP 1500 Trimble NT200 D
Radar	Furuno FR 2110 + ARP 23 Furuno FR 8050 D
Gyrocompass	Anschutz Kiel 110
Speed log	Dataline Robertson
Echo-sounder	Furuno FC 561
Other ship navigation	Loran: Furuno FC 561

COMMUNICATIONS

Inmarsat (type)	Westinghouse 1,000 MSat
MF/HF	Skanti TRP8253 SR
VHF	Two Standard 6 × 2400S
Facsimile	Navtex AE-900; Marine Fax TR1 V

SAFETY

Workboat/chase boat	Zodiac 3.7 m

DECK MACHINERY

Cranes	SWL: 0.3 t

ACCOMMODATION

Crew	4

SCIENTIFIC SPACES

Multipurpose dry lab	13.5 m^2

SURVEY SYSTEMS

Multibeam/swath system	Simrad EM 1000

UPDATED

Frederick G Creed

2001/0102243

Canadian Coast Guard

GC-03

GENERAL	
	Multihulled survey vessel; home port: Sorel, Québec
Port of reg/flag	Ottawa
Official number	344981
Classification	Home Trade II
Call sign	CG2600
Built (yard and date)	Ste Catherine d'Alexandrie, Québec; 1973
Length overall	18.5 m
Breadth moulded	6.4 m
Max draught	1.8 m
Tonnage (grt)	56.64
PROPULSION	
Main engine(s)	Two Caterpillar 3306 BTA, 435 kW
Propellers	Two fixed-pitch propellers
Speed (max)	10.5 kt
Speed (cruising)	9.0 kt
Endurance	400 n miles/5 days
Fuel capacity	1.4 m³
BRIDGE NAVIGATION AIDS	
Satellite	Trimble 4000

Radar	Sperry MIL 1040
Gyrocompass	Sperry Mk 37
Speed log	Sperry
Echo-sounder	Seateck; Nauitronic
Other ship navigation	
COMMUNICATIONS	
VHF	Sailor 146
SAFETY	
Workboat/chase boat	Zodiac RHI
DECK MACHINERY	
Cranes	boat crane
ACCOMMODATION	
Crew	4
SCIENTIFIC SPACES	
Multipurpose dry lab	12 m²
SURVEY SYSTEMS	
Sensors	*UPDATED*

GC-03

2001/0102245

CHILE

Hydrographic & Oceanographic Service (SHOA)

Contralmirante Oscar Viel Toro

GENERAL BACKGROUND

Type 1200 Class (AGS). Antarctic patrol and survey ship. Acquired from the Canadian coastguard on 16 February 1995. The vessel was formally based on the west coast at Victoria, British Columbia, and was laid up in 1993.

Former names	R/V *Norman McLeod Rogers*
Owner	Chilean Navy
Official number	AP 46
Built (yard and date)	Canadian Vickers, Montreal: commissioned October 1960

Length overall	89.90 m
Breadth moulded	19.10 m
Operational draught	6.10 m
Tonnage (grt)	4245

PROPULSION

Main engine(s)	4 Fairbanks-Morse 38D8-1/8-12 diesels; 8,496 hp (6.34 MW) sustained
Propellers	2 shafts
Speed (max)	15.0 kt
Speed (cruising)	12.0 kt
Endurance	12,000 n miles at 12 kt
Electrical power	4 GE generators; 4.8 MW; 2 Ruston RK3CZ diesels; 7,250 hp (5.6 MW) sustained; 2 GE generators; 2.76 MW; 2 GE motors; 12,000 hp (8.95 MW)

BRIDGE NAVIGATION AIDS

Radar	I-band

HELIDECK

Size, aircraft capacity	1 BO 105C

ACCOMMODATION

Crew	33

UPDATED

Contralmirante Oscar Viel Toro

2000/0056728

CHINA

Hydrographic Office of Marine Department

Hydro 1

GENERAL

Owner	Government of the Hong Kong Special Administrative Region
Port of reg/flag	Hong Kong
Built (yard and date)	May 1995
Length overall	12.4 m
Breadth moulded	3.3 m
Max draught	2.1 m
Tonnage (grt)	13

PROPULSION

Main engine(s)	Volvo Penta AD 41
Speed (max)	10 kt
Speed (cruising)	8 kt
Fuel capacity	1,800 litres
Electrical power	220 VAC and 12, 24 V DC
Fresh water capacity	300 litres

BRIDGE NAVIGATION AIDS
Radar   JMA – 2254 Rasterscan
Gyrocompass   Anschutz Standard 20

COMMUNICATIONS
VHF   Apelco VXE75
Cellular   GSM

SURVEY SYSTEMS
Positioning   GPS – Trimble 400 DS
Sensors   TSS POS/MV 320 Mk III

Echo-sounder (single beam) Odom EchoTrac DF – 3200 Mk II
Multibeam/swath system   Reson SeaBat 8101
Sound velocity profiler   Odom Digibar
Oceanographic sensors   CTD – Valeport 600 Mk II; ADCP
  (CTDs/XBTs and so on)   – RDI broadband

UPDATED

Hydro 1

2001/0101474

Hydrographic Office of Marine Department

Hydro 2

GENERAL
Owner   Government of the Hong Kong
                    Special Administrative Region
Port of reg/flag   Hong Kong
Built (yard and date)   January 1998
Length overall   18.4 m
Breadth moulded   8 m
Max draught   2.4 m
Tonnage (grt)   33.9

PROPULSION
Main engine(s)   Caterpillar
Speed (max)   11 kt
Speed (cruising)   8 kt
Fuel capacity   8,000 litres

Electrical power   220 VAC and 12, 24 V DC
Fresh water capacity 1,280 litres

BRIDGE NAVIGATION AIDS
Satellite   Furuno GPS Navigator Model
                    GP80
Radar   Furuno Model 1941 II
Gyrocompass   Furuno GY-700

COMMUNICATIONS
VHF   Furuno FM2610

DECK MACHINERY
Cranes   Sea
Winches   Superwinches

SURVEY SYSTEMS

Positioning	DGPS-Trimble 4000 D	**Sidescan sonar**	EdgeTech LC 100
Sensors	TSS DMS 02 – 05	**Grab(s)**	Valeport Hunter Seabed SK 180
Echo-sounder (single beam)	Simrad EA 502	**Sound velocity profiler**	Odom Digibar Po
Multibeam/swath system	Simrad EM3000		

UPDATED

Hydro 2   ***2001***/0101475

Hydrographic Office of Marine Department

Hydro 3

GENERAL

Owner	Government of the Hong Kong Special Administrative Region
Port of reg/flag	Hong Kong
Built (yard and date)	March 1996
Length overall	7.5 m
Breadth moulded	2.4 m
Max draught	0.8 m
Tonnage (grt)	1.9

PROPULSION

Main engine(s)	Evinrude (E 115 LEDA)
Speed (max)	32 kt
Speed (cruising)	5 kt
Fuel capacity	1,800 litres
Electrical power	220 V AC and 12, 24 V DC
Fresh water capacity	300 litres

COMMUNICATIONS

VHF	Apelco VXE75
Cellular	GSM

Hydro 3   ***2001***/0101476

SURVEY SYSTEMS

Positioning	DGPS – Trimble 4000 D
Sensors	TSS HS 5O motion sensor
Echo-sounder (single beam)	Odom Hydrotrac

UPDATED

COLOMBIA

Colombian Navy

Gorgona

GENERAL		PROPULSION	
Comments	Paid off in 1982 but after a complete overhaul at Cartagena naval base was back in service in late 1992.	Main engine(s)	2 Wartsila Nohab diesels; 910 hp (m) (669 kW)
		Propellers	2 shafts
Former names	ex-BO 154, ex-BO 161, ex-FB 161	Speed (max)	13 kt
Built (yard and date)	Lidingoverken, Sweden; commissioned 28 May 1954	ACCOMMODATION	
		Crew	45
Length overall	41.2 m		
Breadth moulded	9.0 m		*NEW ENTRY*
Max draught	2.8 m		

Gorgona (Colombian Navy)   **2001**/0056835

ESTONIA

Estonian National Marine Board

EVA – 315

GENERAL BACKGROUND		Fuel capacity	38 t
Inshore survey launch		Electrical power	710 kW
Port of reg/flag	Tallinn, Estonia	Fresh water capacity	30 t
Official number	38 AR		
Built (yard and date)	1987 YU	BRIDGE NAVIGATION AIDS	
Length overall	36.06 m	Satellite	DGPS
Breadth moulded	8.99 m	Radar	Furuno
Working deck width	8.5 m	Gyrocompass	KURS – 4
Max draught	2.7 m	Speed log	Debeg 4675
Operational draught	2.7 m	Echo-sounder	Atlas 9205
Tonnage (grt)	371		
		COMMUNICATIONS	
PROPULSION		Inmarsat (type)	RT 4801
Main engine(s)	892 kW	VHF	Tron VHF
Speed (max)	12 kt		
Speed (cruising)	12 kt		*UPDATED*

Estonian National Marine Board

EVA – 319

GENERAL

Port of reg/flag	Tallinn, Estonia
Official number	98 RD O1
Built (yard and date)	Työvene Oy, Finland; 1998
Length overall	12.8 m
Breadth moulded	3.9 m
Working deck width	1.85 m
Max draught	1.3 m
Operational draught	1.3 m
Tonnage (grt)	17

PROPULSION

Main engine(s)	Valmet 620 DSM, 218 hp, 2,200 rpm
Propellers	1
Speed (max)	17 kt
Speed (cruising)	12 kt
Fuel capacity	1 t
Electrical power	5 kVA, 220 Hz
Fresh water capacity	200 kg

BRIDGE NAVIGATION AIDS

Satellite	Magellan DGPS
Radar	Furuno FAP 300
Gyrocompass	Anschutz Standard-20 Compact
Speed log	Interphase Probe

COMMUNICATIONS

Inmarsat (type)	RT 4801
VHF	Tron VHF

SAFETY

Lifesaving equipment	Liferaft, 6 persons

DECK MACHINERY

Transducer well	Yes

ACCOMMODATION

Crew	2
Scientists/surveyors	1/2

SURVEY SYSTEMS

Positioning	RTK DGPS; Ashtech Surveyor
Sensors	MRU-5 heave compensation
Echo-sounder(single beam)	AS Ahero (Estonia) 6CH X A1–PO-PC1

VERIFIED

Estonian National Marine Board

EVA – 320

GENERAL

Port of reg/flag	Tallinn, Estonia
Official number	98 RF O3
Built (yard and date)	Työvene Oy, Finland; 1998
Length overall	18 m
Breadth moulded	6.7 m
Working deck width	1.8 m
Max draught	0.9 m
Operational draught	0.9 m
Tonnage (grt)	57

PROPULSION

Main engine(s)	2 Scania DSI – 11
Thrusters	2 KaMeWa Jets, FF-375
Speed (max)	20 kt
Speed (cruising)	15 kt
Endurance	25 n miles from port; wave height 2.0 m
Fuel capacity	4,000 kg
Fuel consumption	180 litres/h
Electrical power	Vetus CHS 30T1, 30 kVA
Fresh water capacity	0.8 t

BRIDGE NAVIGATION AIDS

Satellite	Northstar DGPS 941 XD
Radar	Furuno FR – 1510 Mk 2
Gyrocompass	Anschutz Standard-20 Compact
Echo-sounder	Furuno FCV-611

COMMUNICATIONS

Inmarsat (type)	RT 4801
VHF	Tron VHF

SAFETY

Lifesaving equipment	Liferaft, 6 persons

DECK MACHINERY

Cranes	Hydraulic, 1 t
Transducer well	Yes

ACCOMMODATION

Crew	2
Scientists/surveyors	1/3

SURVEY SYSTEMS

Positioning	RTK DGPS; Ashtech Surveyor
Sensors	MRU-5 heave compensation
Echo-sounder(single beam)	AS Ahero (Estonia) 6CH X A1–PO-PC1
Sidescan sonar	C – Max C800
Sound velocity profiler	A/S Timan (Estonia) HMS-01
Oceanographic sensors (CTDs/XBTs and so on)	SeaBird Seacat SBE 19-03

VERIFIED

FRANCE

French Navy

Lapérouse Class

GENERAL BACKGROUND

BH2 (Batiments Hydrographiques de 2e classe) vessels.
Four vessels: *Laperouse*; *Borda*; *Laplace*; *Arago*. All vessels are based at Brest, except the *Arago*, based at Papeete

Official number	*Laperouse*: A 791; *Borda*: A 792; *Laplace*: A 793; *Arago*: A 794
Built (yard and date)	*Laperouse*: Lorient Naval Dockyard, launched 20 April 1988; *Borda*: Lorient Naval Dockyard, launched 18 June 1988; *Laplace*: Lorient Naval Dockyard, launched 5 Oct 1989; *Arago*: Lorient Naval Dockyard, launched 9 July 1991
Length overall	59.0 m
Breadth moulded	10.9 m
Operational draught	3.63 m

PROPULSION

Main engine(s)	2 SACM-Wärtsilä UD 30 V12 M6D diesels; 2,500 hp(m) (1.84 MW)
Thrusters	Bow thruster
Propellers	2 CP propellers
Speed (cruising)	15.0 kt

Endurance	6,000 n miles at 12 kt
Electrical power	2 × 250 kW generators; 1 × 120 kW generator

BRIDGE NAVIGATION AIDS

Radar	Decca 1226; I-band

SAFETY

Workboat/chase boat	*Laperouse*: 2 VH8 survey launches

ACCOMMODATION

Crew	31

SCIENTISTS/SURVEYORS

11 hydrographers

SURVEY SYSTEMS

Multibeam/swath system	*Laperouse*: Thomson Sintra DUBM 21C; Simrad EM 1002S; *Borda*; *Laplace*; *Arago*: TSM 5260 Lennermor; Simrad EM 1002S

UPDATED

Lapérouse (J Y Robert)

2000/0069943

French Navy

L'esperance

GENERAL BACKGROUND

Former trawler adapted as a survey ship.

Former names	*Jacques Coeur*
Official number	A 756
Built (yard and date)	Gdynia, Poland: commissioned 25 June 1969
Length overall	63.8 m

Breadth moulded	9.80 m
Operational draught	5.90 m

Propulsion

Main engine(s)	2 MAN diesels; 1,850 hp(m) (1.36 MW)
Thrusters	Bow thruster

Propellers	1 propeller
Speed (cruising)	13.0 kt
Endurance	7,000 n miles at 13 kt

ACCOMMODATION

Crew	32
Scientists/surveyors	14

SURVEY SYSTEMS

Multibeam/swath system	Simrad EM 12D multipath echo-sounder

VERIFIED

L'esperance (van Ginderen Collection)

2000

GERMANY

Bundesamt für Seeschifffahrt und Hydrographie (BSH)

Atair

GENERAL

	Vessel for hydrographic survey and wreck search
Current operational status	Operates in the North Sea and Baltic Sea
Port of reg/flag	Hamburg
Call sign	DBBI
Built (yard and date)	Kröger-Werft, Rendsberg; 1986/87
Length overall	51.5 m
Breadth moulded	11.4 m
Max draught	3.45 m
Operational draught	3.15 m
Tonnage (grt)	915 (Oslo); 950 (London)

PROPULSION

Main engine(s)	Electric propeller motor: 660 kW, driven by 2 × diesel electric motors with 463 kW each
Thrusters	1 × Schottel pump jet; 400 kW
Radar	1 × X-Band; 1 × S-Band

Speed log	1 × Doppler log; 1 × EM log
Other ship navigation	Radio navigation systems: 1 × MNS 2000; 1 × RS 4000; 1 × RS 2000

SAFETY

Workboat/chase boat	2 × 7.4 m long boats with survey systems (1 equipped for diving operations)
Lifesaving equipment	1 × 3-man decompression chamber

DECK MACHINERY

Cranes	Electro-hydraulic; Capacity: 48 kN; 12.5 m outreach Hydraulic heavy-duty beam lifter; Capacity: 42 kN Slewing davit: Capacity: 30 kN 2 × towing davits: Capacity: 30 kN

Winches	Wire rope winch; Capacity: 30 kN; 250 m, 16 mm Stern anchor wire rope winch; Capacity: 50 kN; 250 m, 24 mm Hydraulic single wire and repeat winch; Capacity: 8.5 kN; 600 m, 8.2 mm and 200 m, 6 mm	**SCIENTIFIC SPACES**	
		Oceanographic wet lab	14.6 m²
		Multipurpose dry lab	9.8 m²
		Survey Room	25.5 m²
		SURVEY SYSTEMS	
		Echo-sounder (single beam)	1
		Sidescan sonar	1

ACCOMMODATION

Crew	16
Scientists/surveyors	7

UPDATED

Bundesamt für Seeschiffahrt und Hydrographie (BSH)

Deneb

GENERAL

	Sister ship of Atair and Wega
Built (yard and date)	Peene-Werft, Wolgast; 1993/94
Length overall	52.05 m
Breadth moulded	11.40 m
Tonnage (grt)	969

PROPULSION

Main engine(s)	Diesel-electric; 2 diesel engines
Thrusters	Stem thruster, 58 kW each 640 kW
Propellers	Schotte 1 PumpJet, 530 kW
Speed (max)	11.3 kt

BRIDGE NAVIGATION AIDS

Satellite	MNS 2000; Triumbe DGPS
Radar	2 radars: X- S-Band
Speed log	2 doppler logs, 1 E/M log

SAFETY

Workboat/chase boat	2 aluminium launchers, 7.8 m; jet propulsion

DECK MACHINERY

Cranes	1 electrohydraulic; 48 kW; 24 kW at 12.5 m outreach
Winches	hydraulic: 8.5 kW, 600 m single conductor armoured cable, 8.2 mm
Moonpool(s) – size(s)/ function(s)	0.8 × 0.8 m

ACCOMMODATION

Crew	16
Scientists/surveyors	7

SCIENTIFIC SPACES

Oceanographic wet lab	17.3 m²
Multipurpose dry lab	30.0 m²

SURVEY SYSTEMS

Sensors	OSS-112 object search sonar
Echo-sounder (single beam)	Hydrosearch
Multibeam/swath system	Hydrosweep MD
Sidescan sonar	One

VERIFIED

Deneb

2000/0093788

Bundesamt für Seeschiffahrt und Hydrographie (BSH)

Komet

GENERAL

	Vessel for hydrographic survey and research
Current operational status	Operates in the North Sea and Baltic Sea
Port of reg/flag	Hamburg
Call sign	DBBG
Built (yard and date)	Jadewerft, Wilhelmshaven; 1968/69
Length overall	67.6 m
Breadth moulded	11.5 m
Max draught	4.4 m
Tonnage (grt)	1,252
Displacement	1,590 t

PROPULSION

Main engine(s)	2 × MTU diesel motors: each 1,400 kW, driven by 2 × diesel electric motors with 463 kW each
Thrusters	Bow
Propellers	4-blade variable-pitch propeller
Speed (max)	15 kt

BRIDGE NAVIGATION AIDS

Radar	1 × X-Band; 1 × S-Band
Speed log	1 × EM log
Other ship navigation	Decca Navigator Mk 53

COMMUNICATIONS

Lifeboats	2
Workboat/chase boat	6 × 6.7 m survey motor boats with survey systems (max speed: 18 kt)

DECK MACHINERY

Cranes	2 × derricks; foredeck; capacity: each 2 kN
	1 × work; boat deck; capacity: 3 kN
Winches	1 × single core

ACCOMMODATION

Crew	32
Scientists/surveyors	6

SURVEY SYSTEMS

Positioning	Syledis
Echo-sounder (single beam)	2 × STN ATLAS DESO 10 (30/210 kHz); 1 × Elac 20 kHz
Multibeam/swath system	2 × ATLAS Fansweep 20; ATLAS Fansweep 15 on survey launch
Sidescan sonar	1

UPDATED

Bundesamt für Seeschiffahrt und Hydrographie (BSH)

Wega

GENERAL

	Hydrographic survey and research vessel
Current operational status	Operates in the North Sea and Baltic Sea
Port of reg/flag	Hamburg
Call sign	DBBC
Built (yard and date)	Krager Werft, Rendsberg; 1989/90
Length overall	52.05 m
Breadth moulded	11.4 m
Max draught	3.45 m
Operational draught	3.15 m
Tonnage (grt)	908.72 (Oslo); 969 (London)

PROPULSION

Main engine(s)	Electric DC motor: 760 kW, driven by 2 × diesel electric motors with 545 kW and 288 kW
Thrusters	1 × Schottel pump jet, 530 kW; stern, 48 kW with 8 kN thrust
Speed (max)	11.6 kt

BRIDGE NAVIGATION AIDS

Radar	1 × X-Band; 1 × S-Band
Speed log	1 × Doppler; 1 × EM
Other ship navigation	Radio navigation systems: 1 × MNS 2000; 1 × RS 4000; 1 × Syledis SR3; 1 × GPS AX 4000

SAFETY

Workboat/chase boat	2 × 7.8 m long boats with survey systems (1 equipped for diving operations)
Lifesaving equipment	1 × 3-man decompression chamber

DECK MACHINERY

Cranes	Electrohydraulic; capacity: 48 kN; 12.5 m outreach; slewing davit: capacity: 30 kN; hydraulic heavy-duty beam lifter: capacity: 42 kN; 2 × towing davits: capacity: 30 kN
Winches	Wire rope; capacity: 50 kN; 600 m, 16 mm; stern anchor wire rope; capacity: 50 kN; 250 m, 24 mm hydraulic single wire and repeat; capacity: 8.5 kN; 600 m, 8.2 mm

ACCOMMODATION

Crew	16
Scientists/surveyors	7

SCIENTIFIC SPACES

Oceanographic wet lab	17.3 m²

SURVEY SYSTEMS

Sensors	Heave compensator
Echo-sounder (single beam)	
Multibeam/swath system	Atlas Hydrosweep MD
Sidescan sonar	1
Oceanographic sensors (CTDs/XBTs and so on)	Automatic weather station

UPDATED

GREECE

Hydrographic Service – Hellenic Navy

Naftilos

GENERAL

	Hydrographic and oceanographic survey vessel
Owner	Hellenic Navy
Port of reg/flag	Piraeus, Greece
Official number	A478
Classification	100 A1
Call sign	SZBB
Built (yard and date)	D.C. Anastasiades Shipbuilding Company; 19 November 1975
Rebuilt (yard and date)	5 May 1999
Length overall	63.2 m
Breadth moulded	11.6 m
Working deck width	8.25 m
Max draught	4.5 m
Operational draught	4 m
Tonnage (grt)	1,427

PROPULSION

Main engine(s)	Burmeister: 2 × 1,350 bhp at 775 rpm; 2 × 1,200 bhp at 750 rpm
Thrusters	1
Propellers	1
Speed (max)	12.5 kt
Speed (cruising)	11 kt
Endurance	6,600 n miles

Fuel capacity	215,000 litres
Fuel consumption	280 litres/h
Electrical power	380 V AC, 3-phase
Fresh water capacity	94,500 litres

BRIDGE NAVIGATION AIDS

Satellite	Magellan GPS
Radar	2 Racal Decca
Gyrocompass	1
Speed log	1
Echo-sounder	1
Other ship navigation	Navtex

COMMUNICATIONS

MF/HF	2 RF-301
VHF	2 RF-301, 2 Midland

SAFETY

Lifeboats	2
Workboat/chase boat	6
Lifesaving equipment	6 liferafts

DECK MACHINERY

Cranes	1 × 5 t
Winches	1 general use; CTD; 1 oceanographic

Naftilos (van Ginderen Collection)

2000/0079497

ACCOMMODATION
Crew	45 (up to 49)
Scientists/surveyors	12
Hospital	Yes

SCIENTIFIC SPACES
Total scientific deck space	35 m²
Oceanographic wet lab	24 m²

SURVEY SYSTEMS
Positioning	Trisponder; MicroFix, DGPS, Artemis

Echo-sounder (single beam)	Atlas DESO 20; Atlas DESO 25; Raytheon DE-719
Sidescan sonar	Klein
Sub-bottom profiler	Klein
Corer(s)	Klein, Benthos, Couleburg
Grab(s)	5 (including Van Veen, Dietz la Fond)
Other sampling	2 nets
Oceanographic sensors (CTDs/XBTs and so on)	CTDs – 2 × SBE 19; SBE 911 XBT

UPDATED

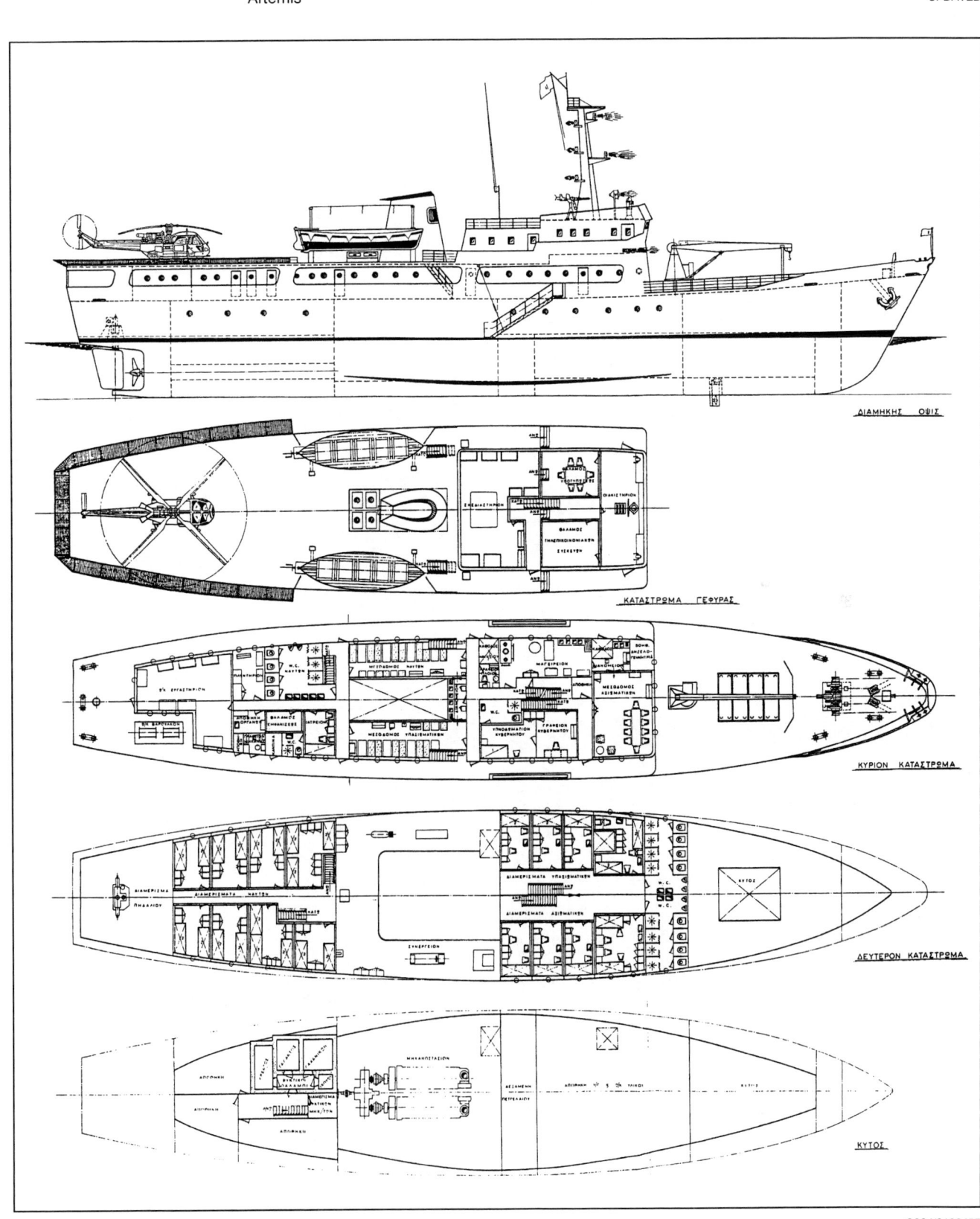

Naftilos

2001/0106453

Hydrographic Service – Hellenic Navy

Pytheas

GENERAL

	Hydrographic and oceanographic survey vessel	Length overall	50.17 m
Owner	Hellenic Navy	Breadth moulded	9.6 m
Port of reg/flag	Piraeus, Greece	Working deck width	8.5 m
Official number	A474	Max draught	3.5 m
Classification	+ A1(E)AMS	Operational draught	3 m
Call sign	SZFF	Tonnage (grt)	568.79
Built (yard and date)	D.C. Anastasiades and A.CH Tsortanides Shipbuilding; 20 September 1983		

PROPULSION

Main engine(s)   General Motors V12-567 ATL, 2 × 900 bhp at 744 rpm

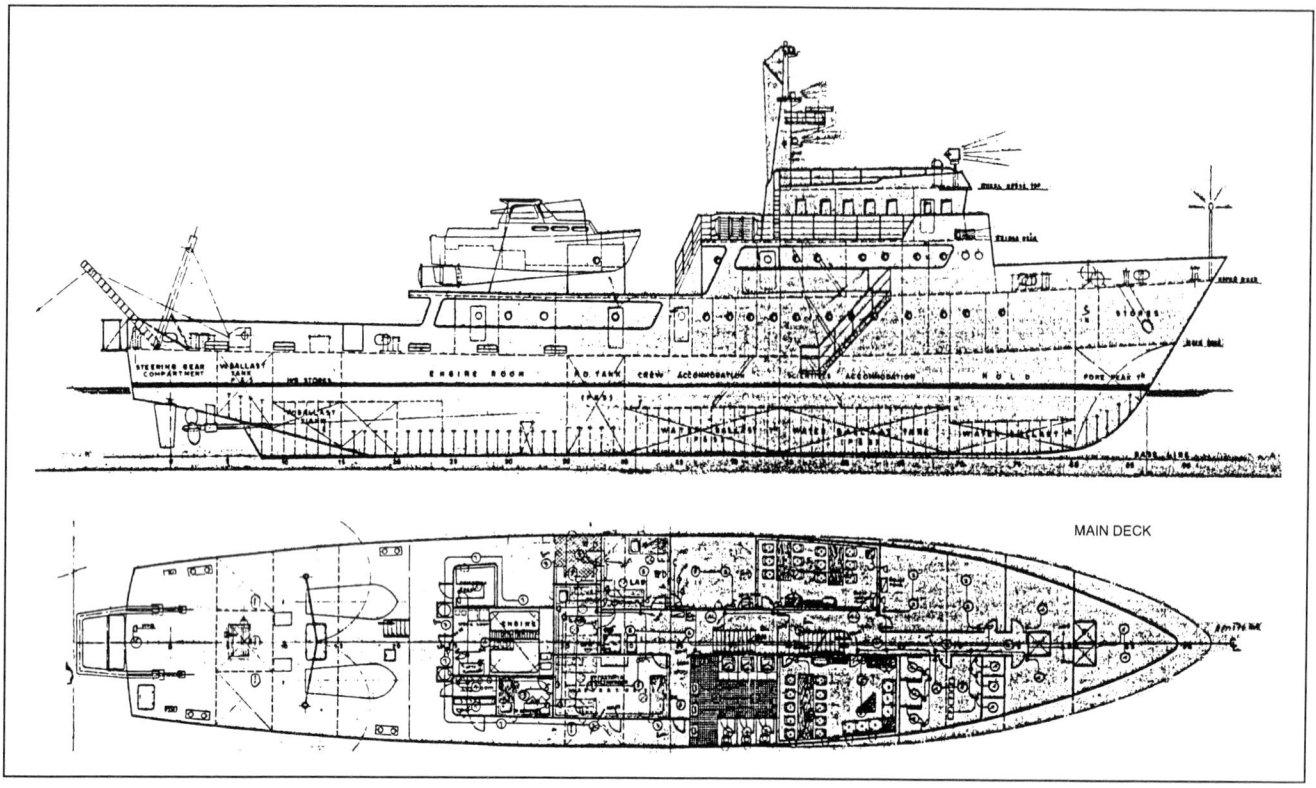

Pytheas (M Verschaeve)

2001/0106452

Pytheas (M Verschaeve)

2000/0052301

Propellers	2
Speed (max)	14 kt
Speed (cruising)	10.6 kt
Endurance	5,300 n miles
Fuel capacity	70,800 litres
Fuel consumption	130 litres/h
Electrical power	2 × 380 V AC, 3-phase
	1 × 380 V AC, 3-phase
	(emergency)
Fresh water capacity	60,000 litres

BRIDGE NAVIGATION AIDS

Satellite	Furuno GPS; 2 Magellan GPS
Radar	1 Racal Decca
Speed log	1
Echo-sounder	1
Other ship navigation	Navtex

COMMUNICATIONS

MF/HF	2 Sunair GSB 900, 100 W; UHF
	GRC 171
VHF	2 Tad M8; 2 Mid 70 442B; RF 440

SAFETY

Lifeboats	1
Workboat/chase boat	1
Lifesaving equipment	3 liferafts; 10 life rings; 70
	lifejackets; 2 × man overboard

DECK MACHINERY

Cranes	2 × 400 kg

A-frame(s)	stern: SWL 3,000 kg
	port: CTD SWL 1,000 kg
Winches	1 general use
	1 CTD
	1 sidescan sonar

ACCOMMODATION

Crew	36
Scientists/surveyors	13
Hospital	Yes

SCIENTIFIC SPACES

Total scientific deck space	14.7 m²
Oceanographic wet lab	12 m²

SURVEY SYSTEMS

Positioning	Trisponder; MicroFix, DGPS,
	Artemis
Echo-sounder (single beam)	Elac LAZ 721
Sidescan sonar	Klein
Sub-bottom profiler	Klein
Corer(s)	Klein, Benthos, Couleburg
Grab(s)	5, including Van Veen, Dietz la
	Fond
Other sampling	2 nets
Oceanographic sensors	CTDs – 2 SBE 19, SBE 911
(CTDs/XBTs and so on)	XBT

UPDATED

Hydrographic Service – Hellenic Navy

Strabon

GENERAL

	Hydrographic survey vessel
Owner	Hellenic Navy
Port of reg/flag	Piraeus, Greece
Official number	A476
Call sign	SZFC
Built (yard and date)	NAFS Ltd; 1988
Length overall	32.72 m
Breadth moulded	6.1 m
Working deck width	4.8 m
Max draught	3.5 m
Operational draught	2.4 m
Tonnage (grt)	252

PROPULSION

Main engine(s)	2 MAN D2842 LE V12, 660 bhp
Propellers	2
Speed (max)	11 kt
Speed (cruising)	9 kt
Endurance	8,000 n miles
Fuel capacity	39,000 litres
Fuel consumption	45 litres/h
Electrical power	1 × 380 V AC, 3-phase
	2 × 220 V AC, 3 phase
	1 × 380 V AC, 3-phase
	(emergency)
Fresh water capacity	8,000 litres

Strabon (van Ginderen Collection)

2000/0079499

BRIDGE NAVIGATION AIDS

Satellite	Furuno GPS; Navstar GPS
Radar	1 Racal Decca
Gyrocompass	1
Speed log	1
Echo-sounder	1
Other ship navigation	Navtex

COMMUNICATIONS

MF/HF	RF-301
VHF	Midland

SAFETY

Workboat/chase boat	1
Lifesaving equipment	2 liferafts; 30 + 40 lifejackets

DECK MACHINERY

Cranes	1 × 400 kg

ACCOMMODATION

Crew	21
Scientists/surveyors	3

SCIENTIFIC SPACES

Total scientific deck space	12.2 m²

SURVEY SYSTEMS

Positioning	Trisponder; MicroFix, DGPS
Echo-sounder (single beam)	Elac LAZ 721

UPDATED

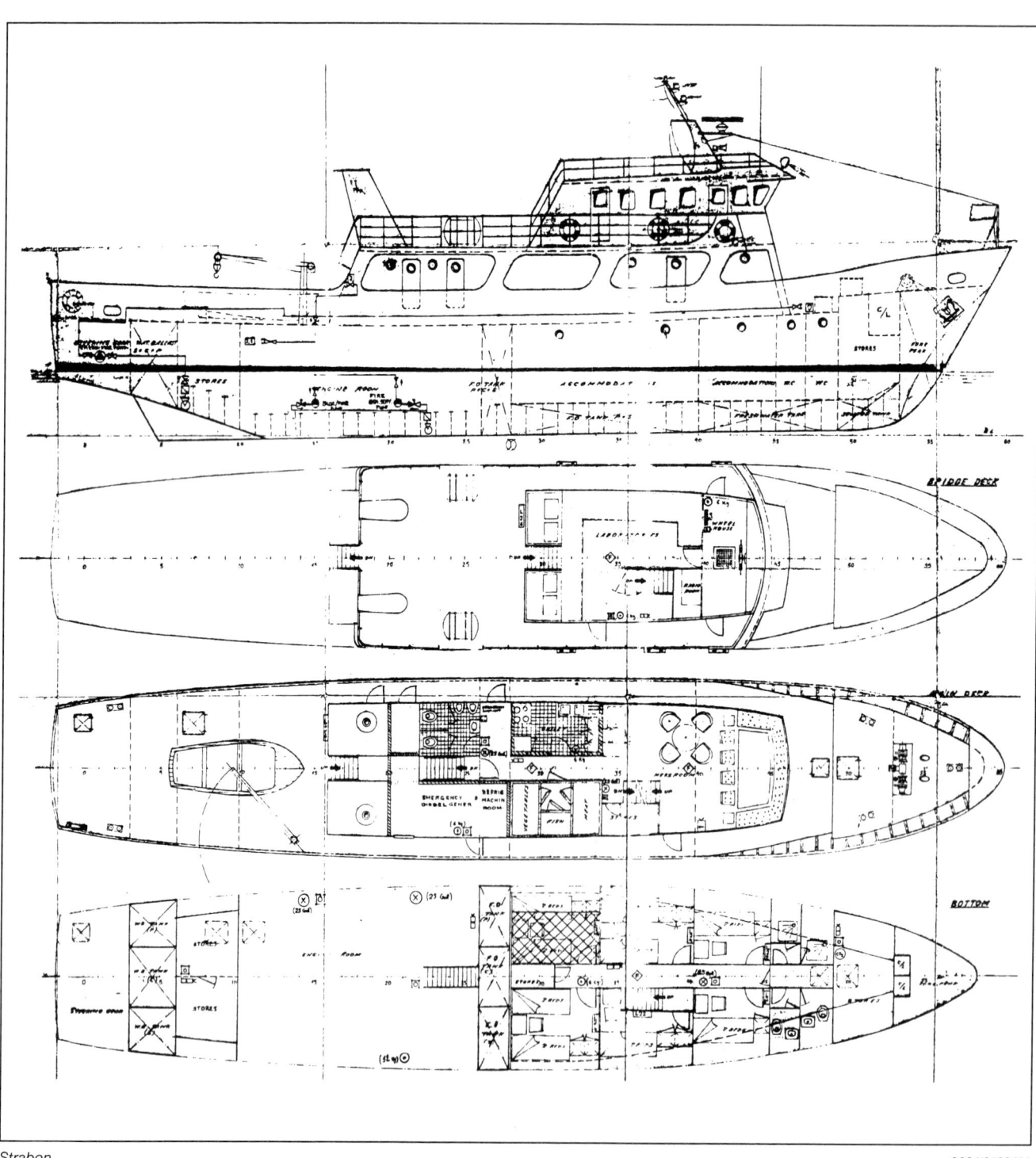

Strabon

2001/0106451

ICELAND

Iceland Hydrographic Service

Baldur

GENERAL

Owner	Icelandic Coast Guard
Port of reg/flag	Reykjavik, Iceland
Official number	2074
Classification	Lloyds Register, + 100 A1
Call sign	TFDA
Built (yard and date)	Velsmiðja Seydisfjardar, May 1991
Length overall	20.06 m
Breadth moulded	5.2 m
Working deck width	5.22 m
Max draught	1.7 m
Operational draught	1.6 m
Tonnage (grt)	64

PROPULSION

Main engine(s)	Caterpillar 3406, 2 × 240 kW/ 326 hp
Propellers	2 fixed
Speed (max)	12 kt
Speed (cruising)	10 kt
Endurance	120 h
Fuel capacity	8 t
Fuel consumption	70 litres/h (max speed)
Electrical power	1 Caterpillar 50 kW, 1 Hatch 22 kW, 380 V AC, 50 Hz
Fresh water capacity	5.5 t

BRIDGE NAVIGATION AIDS

Satellite	Trimble 200 D
Radar	Furuno
Gyrocompass	Anschutz
Echo-sounder	Furuno
Other ship navigation	Forward-looking sonar – Wesmar

COMMUNICATIONS

Inmarsat (type)	Yes (installed April 2000)
MF/HF	Skanti TRP 6000
VHF	Sailor
Cellular	Motorola/Nokia
Facsimile	Richon Lo Kata Navtex 1

SAFETY

Lifeboats	2 Viking, 6- and 10-person
Workboat/chase boat	1 × 12 ft Avon rigid hull inflatable
Lifesaving equipment	VHF Skanti GMDSS
Helideck	Emergency beacon Tron 30 S 406 MHz

DECK MACHINERY

Cranes	MGK Hoes 1.5 t
Winches	1 sidescan sonar cable

ACCOMMODATION

Crew	5 (berths for 8)
Scientists/surveyors	included in crew berths

SCIENTIFIC SPACES

Positioning	Trimble
Sensors	Console heave sensor
Echo-sounder (single beam)	Odom Mk II
Sidescan sonar	EG&G
Grab(s)	Shipek sampler
Sound velocity profiler	SeaBird Electronics

UPDATED

Baldur   *2000*/0064705

INDIA

Indian Navy

'Makar' Class

GENERAL BACKGROUND
4 survey ships (AGS). 2 vessels based at Kochi and 2 based at Chennai

Official number	*Makar*: J 33; *Mithun*: J 34; *Meen*: J 35; *Mesh*: J 36
Built (yard and date)	Goa: 1981-82
Length overall	37.5 m
Breadth moulded	7.50 m
Operational draught	1.90 m

PROPULSION

Main engine(s)	2 diesels; 1,124 hp(m) (826 kW)
Propellers	2 shafts

Speed (cruising)	12.0 kt
Endurance	1,500 n miles at 12.0 kt

BRIDGE NAVIGATION AIDS

Radar	Racal Decca 1629; I-band

ACCOMMODATION

Crew	36

VERIFIED

Makar   **2000**/0064723

Indian Navy

'Sandhayak' Class

GENERAL BACKGROUND
8 survey ships (AGS)

Official number	*Sandhayak*: J 18; *Nirdeshak*: J 19; *Nirupak*: J 14; *Investigator*: J 15; *Jamuna*: J 16; *Sutlej*: J 17; *Darshak*: J 21; *Sarveskhak*: J 22
Built (yard and date)	*Sandhayak*: Garden Reach, Calcutta; launched 6 April 1977; *Nirdeshak*: Garden Reach, Calcutta; launched 16 November 1978; *Nirupak*: Garden Reach, Calcutta; launched 10 July 1981; *Investigator*: Garden Reach, Calcutta; launched 8 August 1987; *Jamuna*: Garden Reach, Calcutta; launched 4 September 1989; *Sutlej*: Garden Reach, Calcutta; launched 1 December 1991; *Darshak*: Goa Shipyard; launched 3 March 1999; *Sarveskhak*: Goa Shipyard; launched 24 November 1999

Length overall	87.8 m
Breadth moulded	12.80 m
Operational draught	3.40 m

PROPULSION

Main engine(s)	2 GRSE/MAN 66V 30/45 ATL diesels; 7,720 hp(m) (5.67 MW) sustained
Propellers	2 shafts with active rudders
Speed (max)	16.0 kt
Endurance	6,000 n miles at 14 kt; 14,000 n miles at 10 kt

BRIDGE NAVIGATION AIDS

Radar	Racal Decca 1629; I-band

SAFETY

Workboat/chase boat	4 GRP survey launches on davits amidships

HELIDECK

Size, aircraft capacity	1 HAL Chetak

ACCOMMODATION

Crew   178
Scientists/surveyors   30

SURVEY SYSTEMS
Echo-sounder (single beam)   3

Multibeam/swath system   Sea Beam 2112 (12 kHz) installed
                                                        on *Darshak*; to be installed on
                                                        Sarveskhak at a later date
Sidescan sonar   1

VERIFIED

Sandhayak

INDONESIA

Hydro-Oceanographic Service (DISHIDROS)

Dewa Kembar

GENERAL BACKGROUND

'Hecla' Class survey ship (AGS). Transferred from UK on 18 April 1986
for refit. Commissioned in Indonesian Navy 10 September 1986

Former names	*Hydra*
Official number	932
Built (yard and date)	Yarrow and Co, Blythswood; commissioned 5 May 1966
Length overall	79.30 m
Breadth moulded	15.00 m
Operational draught	4.70 m

PROPULSION

Main engine(s)	Diesel-electric; 3 Paxman 12YJCZ diesels; 3,780 hp (2.82 MW); 3 generators; 1 motor; 2,000 hp(m) (1.49 MW)
Thrusters	Bow thruster
Propellers	1 shaft
Speed (max)	14.0 kt
Speed (cruising)	11.0 kt
Endurance	12,000 n miles at 11.0 kt

BRIDGE NAVIGATION AIDS
Radar   Kelvin Hughes Type 1006; I-band

ACCOMMODATION
Crew   123

UPDATED

SAFETY
Workboat/chase boat   2 survey launches

HELIDECK
Size, aircraft capacity 1 Westland Wasp

Dewa Kembar (van Ginderen/C Sattler)

2000/0012542

Hydro-Oceanographic Service (DISHIDROS)

'Baruna Jaya' Class

GENERAL BACKGROUND

Baruna Jaya 1 is employed on hydrography, the second on oceanography and the third combines both tasks. *Baruna Jaya IV* is operated by the agency responsible for developing new technology. All are part of the Naval Auxiliary Service

Official number	*Baruna Jaya I:* KAL-IV-02; *Baruna Jaya II:* KAL-IV-03; *Baruna Jaya III:* KAL-IV-04; *Baruna Jaya IV:* KAL-IV-05
Built (yard and date)	*Baruna Jaya I:* CMN, Cherbourg; commissioned 10 August 1989; *Baruna Jaya II:* CMN, Cherbourg; commissioned 25 September 1989; *Baruna Jaya III:* CMN, Cherbourg; commissioned 3 January; *Baruna Jaya IV:* CMN, Cherbourg; commissioned 2 November 1995

Length overall	60.40 m
Breadth moulded	12.10 m
Operational draught	4.20 m
Propulsion	
Main engine(s)	2 Niigata/SEMT-Pielstick 5 PA5 L 255 diesels; 2,990 hp(m) (2.2 MW) sustained
Thrusters	Bow
Propellers	1 cp
Speed (max)	14.0 kt
Speed (cruising)	12.0 kt
Endurance	7,500 n miles at 12.0 kt
SAFETY	
Workboat/chase boat	Survey launch

ACCOMMODATION

Crew	37
Scientists/surveyors	26

SURVEY SYSTEMS

Multibeam/swath system	*Baruna Jaya I & II*; Simrad EM1000; Simrad EM950 (on survey launch); *Baruna Jaya III*: Simrad EM12D

VERIFIED

Baruna Jaya II (John Mortimer)   ***2000**/0052362*

ITALY

Hydrographic Institute of the Navy

Aretusa

GENERAL BACKGROUND

GRP Catamaran design. Hydrographic and oceanographic survey vessel. Sister vessel to *Galatea*

Port of reg/flag	La Spezia, Italy
Official number	A5304
Classification	Hydrographic vessel
Call sign	IABA
Built (yard and date)	Intermarine (Sarzanza-Sp), Italy; launched 8 May 2000
Length overall	39.21 m
Breadth moulded	12.6 m
Working deck width	12 m
Max draught	2.7 m
Operational draught	2.7 m
Tonnage (grt)	390

PROPULSION

Main engine(s)	2 Isotta Fraschini V1708T2 ME
Thrusters	2 Schottel STT 060LK
Propellers	2 Schottel STP 330
Speed (max)	13 kt
Speed (cruising)	11 kt
Electrical power	2 Iveco AIFO GE 8210M22

BRIDGE NAVIGATION AIDS

Radar	ARPA: Gem Elettronica MM/SPN 753 B(V)1; Navigation: Gem Elettronica MM/SPN 753 B(V)2
Gyrocompass	Simrad Robertson RGC 11
Speed log	Atlas Dolog 23
Echo-sounder	Simrad EA 500
Other ship navigation	Dynamic positioning – Simrad SDP 11

COMMUNICATIONS

MF/HF	Skanti TRP 9500
VHF	Skanti 3000 IT and Command Unit CU 300 IT
Facsimile	Skanti R 8003, Aerial Type Fax 5

SAFETY

Lifeboats	4
Workboat/chase boat	1

DECK MACHINERY

Cranes	Gantry for workboat; jib for hydrographic instruments; gantry for towed bodies
Winches	4
Transducer well	Yes

ACCOMMODATION

Crew	27
Scientists/surveyors	4
Hospital	No

SCIENTIFIC SPACES

Total scientific deck space	60 m²
Multipurpose dry lab	9 m²
Chemistry lab	9 m²

SURVEY SYSTEMS

Positioning	Trimble 4000 DGPS; GPS (Code 'P'); Syledis; MicroFix
Echo-sounder (single beam)	Simrad EA 500

Multibeam/swath system	Simrad EM 300
Sidescan sonar	Simrad MS 992
Grab(s)	Yes
Vehicle(s) (ROVs/AUVs and so on)	ROV
Oceanographic sensors (CTDs/XBTs and so on)	ADCP – RDI Ocean Surveyor; CTD – Idronaut Ocean Seven 316

UPDATED

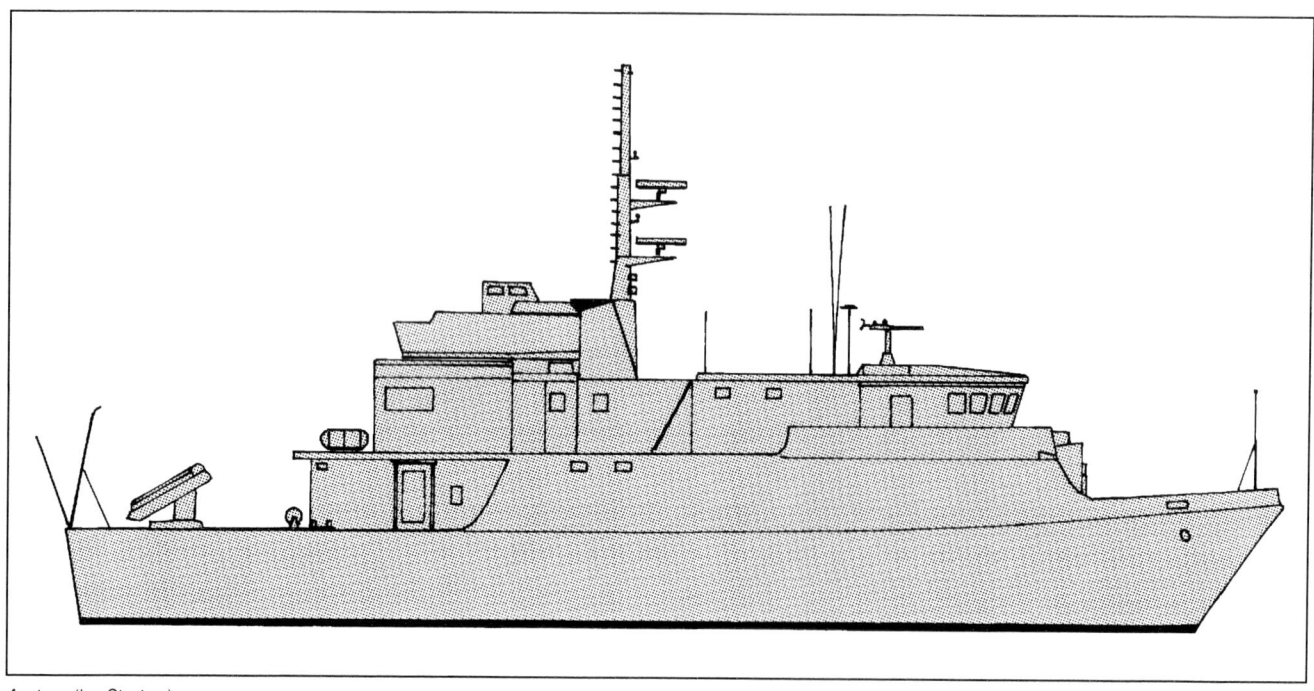

Aretusa (Ian Sturton)

2000/0012606

Hydrographic Institute of the Navy

Galatea

GENERAL BACKGROUND

GRP Catamaran design. Hydrographic and oceanographic survey vessel. Sister vessel to *Aretusa*

Port of reg/flag	La Spezia, Italy
Official number	A5305
Classification	Hydrographic vessel
Call sign	IABC
Built (yard and date)	Intermarine (Sarzanza-Sp), Italy; launched 7 June 2000
Length overall	39.21 m
Breadth moulded	12.6 m
Working deck width	12 m
Max draught	2.7 m
Operational draught	2.7 m
Tonnage (grt)	390

PROPULSION

Main engine(s)	2 Isotta Fraschini V1708T2 ME
Thrusters	2 Schottel STT 060LK
Propellers	2 Schottel STP 330
Speed (max)	13 kt
Speed (cruising)	11 kt
Endurance	1,700 n miles at 13 kt
Electrical power	2 Iveco AIFO GE 8210M22

BRIDGE NAVIGATION AIDS

Radar	ARPA: Gem Elettronica MM/SPN 753 B(V)1; navigation: Gem Elettronica MM/SPN 753 B(V)2
Gyrocompass	Simrad Robertson RGC 11
Speed log	Atlas Dolog 23

Echo-sounder	Simrad EA 500
Other ship navigation	Dynamic positioning – Simrad SDP 11

COMMUNICATIONS

MF/HF	Skanti TRP 9500
VHF	Skanti 3000 IT and Command Unit CU 300 IT
Facsimile	Skanti R 8003, Aerial Type Fax 5

SAFETY

Lifeboats	4
Workboat/chase boat	1

DECK MACHINERY

Cranes	Gantry for workboat; jib for hydrographic instruments; gantry for towed bodies
Winches	4
Transducer well	Yes

ACCOMMODATION

Crew	27
Scientists/surveyors	4
Hospital	No

SCIENTIFIC SPACES

Total scientif deck space ic	60 m²
Multipurpose dry lab	9 m²
Chemistry lab	9 m²

SURVEY SYSTEMS		**Vehicle(s) (ROVs/AUVs and**	ROV
Positioning	Trimble 4000 DGPS; GPS (Code	so on)	
	'P'); Syledis; MicroFix	**Oceanographic sensors**	ADCP – RDI Ocean Surveyor;
Echo-sounder (single beam)	Simrad EA 500	(CTDs/XBTs and so on)	CTD – Idronaut Ocean Seven 316
Multibeam/swath system	Simrad EM 300		
Sidescan sonar	Simrad MS 992		*UPDATED*
Grab(s)	Yes		

Hydrographic Institute of the Navy

Ammiraglio Magnaghi

GENERAL		**Gyrocompass**	2 Microtecnica Torino
Port of reg/flag	La Spezia, Italy	**Speed log**	22 Atlas Dolog; Sagem E/M
Official number	A5303	**Echo-sounder**	Atlas Deso 20
Classification	Hydro-Oceanographic vessel	**Other ship navigation**	ECDIS – C-Map Dkart 'Navigation'
	(AGOR)		
Call sign	IGMA	**COMMUNICATIONS**	
Built (yard and date)	Cantieri Navali del Tirreno e	**MF/HF**	1 ST 1004 HF Elmer; 1 SRT 1000
	Riuniti, Riva Trigoso, 2 May 1975		HF Elmer; 3 RX HF Elmer
Rebuilt (yard and date)	Arsenale M.M. La Spezia – 1990-	**VHF**	3 RTV Elman 1085 A – Cimat
	1991 mid-life works; Arsenale MM		Autolink RT
	La Spezia – 1997-1999 refitting	**Cellular**	GSM (900 – 1,800 MHz)
	works and structural	**Facsimile**	Furuno 108 L Mufax
	improvements		
Length overall	82.65 m	**SAFETY**	
Breadth moulded	13.7 m	**Lifeboats**	1
Working deck width	13.7 m	**Workboat/chase boat**	3 rubber dinghies; 3 launches
Max draught	3.8 m		with data acquisition systems; 1
Operational draught	3.6 m		small launch type 'marino' fitted
Tonnage (grt)	1,744		with keel sounder
		Lifesaving equipment	18 liferaft
PROPULSION			
Main engine(s)	2 GMT B 306 SS (diesel engine),	**DECK MACHINERY**	
	each 1,280 hp; 1 AF 43/25 – 686	**Cranes**	1 type SO.GE.IN, 3 t (max)
	DP, 240 hp	**A-frame(s)**	1 big portal crane with 3 snatch
Thrusters	Variable pitch propeller, 2.3 t		block, 1 t (max) each for CTD /
	(max) of thrust		sampler net and corer
Propellers	Variable pitch propeller	**Winches**	Vidali, 0.75 t (max), 1,000 m,
Speed (max)	12 kt		10 mm of armed cable for towed
Speed (cruising)	9 – 10 kt		fish side scan sonar; Pellegrini
Endurance	8,000 n miles		AS-100H, 1 t (max), 1,500 m,
Fuel capacity	211 m³		5 mm of steel cable for deep
Fuel consumption	0.3 m³/h		corer; Pellegrini AS-70H, 0.75 t
Electrical power	4 diesel engines GMT A 234 ESS,		(max), 2,500 m, 6.41 mm of
	430 kW each; 1 emergency diesel		armed cable for deep CTD or
	engine Isotta Fraschini D 30 SS		sampler; Pellegrini CAB 1000 OR,
	6L, 160 kW		1 t (max) fitted with a free cable or
Fresh water capacity	68 m³		hoist drum; windlass with portal
			crane, Vidali, 4 t (max), 3,000 m,
BRIDGE NAVIGATION AIDS			12 mm of steel cable for deep
Satellite	GPS: Marconi NAVM-06 (P code)		corer type sphincter
Radar	Gem Elettronica MM/SPN 748;		
	Gem Elettronica SC 1510 N		

Ammiraglio Magnaghi (Giorgio Ghiglione)   *2000*/0080094

ACCOMMODATION

Crew	120
Scientists/surveyors	10
Hospital	2

SCIENTIFIC SPACES

Total scientific deck space	125 m²
Oceanographic wet lab	Hydrographic lab 15 m²
Multipurpose dry lab	Main hydrographic room 50 m²; post-process area 60 m²

SURVEY SYSTEMS

Positioning	GPS Marconi type NAVM-06 (P code); 2 DGPS Trimble type 4000 DL/RL – 4000 DL/SI; 1 Sercel Syledis system; 1 Microfix system; 1 Motorola Mini Ranger III system; 1 total station Geotronics AGA 540; 1 Wild T1 with Geotronics geodimeter AGA 210; 1 Wild T2 with Geotronics geodimeter AGA 220
Echo-sounder (single beam)	2 (plus 5 portable for survey boats) Atlas Krupp Deso 20 with 2 transducers each (33-210 kHz) for shallow waters; 1 Elac Laz 4700 with 1 transducer Enif (30 kHz) for deep waters; 1 Elac Laz 4700 with 1 transducer NBS (12 kHz) for deep waters
Multibeam/swath system	Elac Bottom Chart Compact Mk II; Sea Beam 1050 Mk II
Sidescan sonar	Elac SL 72 keel mounted; Mesotech Simrad MS 992 towed
Corer(s)	1 deep corer type sphincter, 8 m; 3 corer type Van Veen
Other sampling	General Oceanics Inc type rosette with Niskin bottle
Oceanographic sensors (CTDs/XBTs and so on)	CTD – Idromar ME OTS 1500; XBT – Plessey Sippican MK 9/12; portable digital tide gauge – Korr-Tech Orpheus; current meters: 2 Aanderaa RCM 4; current meters: 4 Aanderaa RCM 7; current meters: 4 release type Datasonic; current meters: 1 release type Endeco Inc; current meters: 4 buoy type Resinex; automatic Observation station type Sindel CMV2

SEISMIC SYSTEMS

UPDATED

JAPAN

Hydrographic Department of Japan (JHD)

Kaiyo

GENERAL

	Sister vessel to Meiyo
Owner	Marine Safety Agency
Official number	HL 05
Built (yard and date)	Mitsubishi, Shimonoseki; commissioned 7 Oct 1993

Length overall	60.00 m
Breadth moulded	10.50 m
Max draught	3.40 m
Tonnage (grt)	605

Kaiyo (Hachiro Nakai)

2000/0093764

PROPULSION

Main engine(s)	2 Daihatsu 6 DLM-24 diesels; 3,000 hp(m) (2.2 MW)
Thrusters	Bow thruster
Propellers	2 cp propellers
Speed (max)	15 kt
Speed (cruising)	14 kt
Endurance	Cruising range: 5,000 n miles at 14 kt

SAFETY

Workboat/chase boat	Survey launch

ACCOMMODATION

Crew	25
Scientists/surveyors	6

SURVEY SYSTEMS

Positioning	Hybrid positioning system
Sensors	
Echo-sounder (single beam)	Shallow to medium depth
Multibeam/swath system	Seabeam 2000
Oceanographic sensors (CTDs/XBTs and so on)	XBT; Acoustic Doppler current profiler

UPDATED

Hydrographic Department of Japan (JHD)

Meiyo

GENERAL

	Sister vessel to Kaiyo
Owner	Marine Safety Agency
Official number	HL 03
Built (yard and date)	Kawasaki, Kobe; commissioned 24 Oct 1990
Length overall	60.00 m
Breadth moulded	10.50 m
Max draught	3.10 m
Tonnage (grt)	621

PROPULSION

Main engine(s)	2 Daihatsu 6 DLM-24 diesels; 3,000 hp(m) (2.2 MW)
Thrusters	Bow thruster
Propellers	2 cp propellers
Speed (max)	15 kt
Speed (cruising)	14 kt
Endurance	Cruising range: 5,000 n miles at 14 kt

SAFETY

Workboat/chase boat	Survey launch

DECK MACHINERY

Winches	Bottom sampling

ACCOMMODATION

Crew	24
Scientists/surveyors	14

SURVEY SYSTEMS

Positioning	Hybrid positioning system
Echo-sounder (single beam)	Shallow deep sea echo-sounder
Multibeam/swath system	Seabeam 2000
Magnetometer	Proton magnetometer
Gravimeter	Shipborne gravimeter
Oceanographic sensors (CTDs/XBTs and so on)	XBT; Acoustic Doppler current profiler

UPDATED

Meiyo

2000/0093763

Hydrographic Department of Japan (JHD)

Shoyo

GENERAL

Owner	Marine Safety Agency
Official number	HL 01
Built (yard and date)	Mitsui, Tamano; completed 1998
Length overall	98.0 m
Breadth moulded	15.20 m
Max draught	5.30 m
Tonnage (grt)	3,000

PROPULSION

Main engine(s)	Diesel-electric; two diesels; 8,100 hp(m) (5.95 MW); 2 motors; 5,712 hp(m) (4.2 MW)
Thrusters	Bow thruster
Propellers	2 cp propellers
Speed (max)	20.0 kt
Speed (cruising)	17.0 kt
Endurance	Cruise range: 12,000 n miles at 17 kt

SAFETY

Workboat/chase boat	"Mambou II"

ACCOMMODATION

Crew	36
Scientists/surveyors	34

SURVEY SYSTEMS

Positioning	Hybrid positioning system
Multibeam/swath system	SeaBeam 2112; Sys09 ("ANKOU"); SeaBat 9001S on survey launch
Sidescan sonar	Klein 2000
Sub-bottom profiler	Bathy 2000P
Magnetometer	Proton Magnetometer
Gravimeter	Marine gravity meter
Oceanographic sensors (CTDs/XBTs and so on)	MW-A2: Wave meter; AUTOSAL 8400B: Auto Salinometer; HDDR-1: Ocean bottom seismograph

UPDATED

Shoyo

Hydrographic Department of Japan (JHD)

Takuyo

GENERAL

Owner	Marine Safety Agency
Official number	HL 02
Built (yard and date)	Nippon Kokan, Tsurumi; commissioned 31 Aug 1983
Length overall	96.00 m
Breadth moulded	14.20 m
Max draught	4.60 m
Tonnage (grt)	2,600

PROPULSION

Main engine(s)	2 Fuji 6S40B diesels; 6,090 hp(m) (4.47 MW)

Propellers	2 cp propellers
Speed (max)	17 kt
Speed (cruising)	16 kt
Endurance	Cruise range: 12,000 n miles at 16 kt

SAFETY

Workboat/chase boat	2 survey launches

ACCOMMODATION

Crew	60

SURVEY SYSTEMS

Positioning	Hybrid positioning system
Multibeam/swath system	Seabeam 2100
Magnetometer	Proton magnetometer
Gravimeter	Shipborne gravimeter
Vehicle(s) (ROVs/AUVs and so on)	Towed surface CTD

Oceanographic sensors (CTDs/XBTs and so on)	Ship-drift current meter; Shipborne wave analyser; XBT; Acoustic Doppler current profiler; CTD

UPDATED

Takuyo

2000/0093761

Hydrographic Department of Japan (JHD)

Tenyo

GENERAL

Owner	Marine Safety Agency
Official number	HL 04

Built (yard and date)	Sumitomo, Oppama; commissioned 27 Nov 1986
Length overall	56.00 m

Tenyo

2000/0093760

Breadth moulded	9.80 m	**ACCOMMODATION**	
Max draught	2.90 m	**Crew**	24
Tonnage (grt)	430	**Scientists/surveyors**	14

PROPULSION		**SURVEY SYSTEMS**	
Main engine(s)	2 Akasaka diesels; 1,300 hp(m) (955 kW)	**Positioning**	Hybrid positioning system
		Echo-sounder (single beam)	Hydrochart
Propellers	2 shafts	**Multibeam/swath system**	Seabeam 1180
Speed (max)	13 kt	**Oceanographic sensors (CTDs/XBTs and so on)**	XBT; Acoustic Doppler current profiler
Speed (cruising)	12 kt		
Endurance	Cruising range: 5,400 n miles at 12 kt		

UPDATED

BRIDGE NAVIGATION AIDS
Radar   2: JMA 1596; I-band

Maritime Self Defence Force

'Futami' Class

GENERAL		**Thrusters**	Bow thruster
Official number	*Futami:* AGS 5102	**Propellers**	Twin cp propellers
	Wakasa: AGS 5104	**Speed (cruising)**	16 kt
Built (yard and date)	*Futami:* Mitsubishi, Shimonoseki, launched 9 Aug 1978		
	Wakasa: Hitachi, Maizuru; launched 21 May 1985	**BRIDGE NAVIGATION AIDS**	
		Radar	JRC OPS-18-3; G-band
Length overall	97.0 m		
Breadth moulded	15.0 m	**ACCOMMODATION**	
Operational draught	4.20 m	**Crew**	105
		SURVEY SYSTEMS	
PROPULSION		**Vehicle(s) (ROVs/AUVs and so on)**	RCV-225
Main engine(s)	*Futami:* 2 Kawasaki-MAN V8V22/ 30ATL diesels; 4,000 hp(m) (2.94 MW)		
	Wakasa: 2 Fuji 8L27.5XF diesels; 3,250 hp(m) (2.39 MW)		

VERIFIED

Futami (Hachiro Nakai)   ***2000**/0075869*

Maritime Self Defence Force

Suma

GENERAL		**Length overall**	72.0 m
Official number	AGS 5103	**Breadth moulded**	12.8 m
Built (yard and date)	Hitachi, Maizuru; launched 1 September 1981	**Operational draught**	3.40 m

PROPULSION		**SAFETY**	
Main engine(s)	2 Fuji 6L27.5XF diesels; 3,250 hp (m) (2.39 MW)	**Workboat/chase boat**	Survey launch, 11.0 m
Thrusters	Bow thruster	**ACCOMMODATION**	
Propellers	Twin cp propellers	**Crew**	65
Speed (cruising)	15 kt		*VERIFIED*

Suma (Hachiro Nakai)   **2000**/0080180

MALAYSIA

Hydrographic Directorate

Mutiara

GENERAL		**Max draught**	4 m
Owner	Royal Malaysian Navy	**Tonnage (grt)**	1,949
Official number	152		
Built (yard and date)	Hong Leong-Larsen, Butterworth; commissioned 12 January 1978	**PROPULSION**	
		Main engine(s)	2 Deutz SBA 12M528 diesels, 4,000 hp
Length overall	73.6 m		
Breadth moulded	13 m	**Propellers**	2 × 2.55 m diameter, 300 rpm

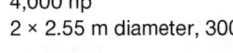

Mutiara (John Mortimer)   **2000**/0012758

Speed (max)	16 kt	Winches	3 × steel wire 4,000 m, SWL 1 t;
Speed (cruising)	13 kt		bottom sampling 6,000 m, SWL
Endurance	4,500 n miles at 16 kt		1 t
Electrical power	440 V AC, 313 kVA, 3 phase,		
	60 Hz	**ACCOMMODATION**	
Fresh water capacity	311 m³	Crew	155

BRIDGE NAVIGATION AIDS

Satellite	Yes	**SCIENTIFIC SPACES**	
Radar	2 Racal Decca 1226/1229; I-Band	Total scientific deck space	250 m²
Gyrocompass	Yes	Oceanographic wet lab	168 m²
Speed log	Doppler log	Multipurpose dry lab	10 m²

SAFETY

Workboat/chase boat	6 survey launches	**SURVEY SYSTEMS**	
		Echo-sounder (single beam)	33/210 kHz

UPDATED

DECK MACHINERY

Cranes	Midships – clearance height 5 m, outboard extension 4 m, SWL 3 t

MEXICO

Mexican Navy

Onjuku

GENERAL BACKGROUND
Survey ship (AGS)

Official number	H 04	Propellers	1 shaft
Built (yard and date)	Uchida shipyard; commissioned 10 January 1980	Speed (max)	12.0 kt
		Speed (cruising)	10.5 kt
		Endurance	5,645 n miles at 10.5 kt
Length overall	36.9 m		
Breadth moulded	8.0 m	**ACCOMMODATION**	
Operational draught	3.50 m	Crew	20

PROPULSION

		Sensors	
Main engine(s)	Yanmar 6UA-UT diesel; 700 hp(m) (515 kW)		Hull-mounted; high-frequency fish-finding sonar

VERIFIED

Onjuku (van Ginderen Collection)

2000/0081256

MOZAMBIQUE

Instituto Nacional de Hydrografia e Navigação (INAHINA)

Bazaruto

GENERAL

Owner	Ministry of Transport and Communications
Port of reg/flag	Maputo
Official number	8801319
Classification	100A1
Call sign	C9130
Built (yard and date)	Svendborgvaerft A/S, 1988
Length overall	51.47 m
Breadth moulded	11.4 m
Max draught	3.51 m
Operational draught	3.4 m
Tonnage (grt)	837

PROPULSION

Main engine(s)	2 Alpha – MAN B&W
Thrusters	1 Brunvoll
Propellers	2
Speed (max)	12 kt
Speed (cruising)	10 kt
Fuel capacity	161 m³
Fuel consumption	4.8 m³/day
Electrical power	220 V
Fresh water capacity	137 t

BRIDGE NAVIGATION AIDS

Satellite	GPS – Sercel
Radar	Furuno RDP – 055 No 320 – 0148; Furuno RDP – 059 No 343 – 0168
Gyrocompass	Sperry No 8190

Speed log	DS 70 No 295 – 0349
Echo-sounder	Furuno FE 680; Furuno FV 0552
Other ship navigation	Steering – two Helmsman

COMMUNICATIONS

Inmarsat (type)	Type C
MF/HF	GMDSS Station – Sailor
VHF	2 Sailor
Facsimile	Furuno

SAFETY

Lifeboats	1
Workboat/chase boat	1
Lifesaving equipment	EPIRB – Skanti 406 MHz 2 SARTS

DECK MACHINERY

Cranes	1 × 2 t; 1 × 15 t
Winches	4

ACCOMMODATION

Charterers	4 cabins
Crew	18
Scientists/surveyors	2 hydrographers

SURVEY SYSTEMS

Positioning	Sercel GPS
Echo-sounder (single beam)	Atlas Deso 17 DS – 33 kHz/210 kHz

UPDATED

MYANMAR (BURMA)

Myanmar Navy

801

GENERAL

Built (yard and date)	Brodogradiliste Tito, Belgrade, Yugoslavia: commissioned 1965

Length overall	62.2 m
Breadth moulded	11.0 m
Operational draught	3.60 m

801   **2001**

PROPULSION	
Main engine(s)	2 MTU 12V 493 TY7 diesels; 2,120 hp(m) (1.62 MW) sustained
Propellers	2 propellers
Speed (cruising)	15.0 kt
BRIDGE NAVIGATION AIDS	
Satellite	Yes
Radar	Racal Decca; I-band.
Gyrocompass	Yes

Speed log	Yes
Echo-sounder	Yes
SAFETY	
Workboat/chase boat	2
ACCOMMODATION	
Crew	99

UPDATED

NETHERLANDS

Hydrographic Service of the Royal Netherlands Navy (RNLN)

Buyskes

GENERAL	
	Hydrographic survey vessel with limited oceanographic and meteorological capability
Current operational status	Hydrographic survey vessels in the North Sea
Port of reg/flag	Den Helder
Official number	A904
Classification	Continental shelf hydrographic survey vessel
Call sign	PAHB
Built (yard and date)	Boeles Shipyards, Bolnes, Netherlands; commissioned 9 March 1973
Rebuilt (yard and date)	Major refit in 1990
Length overall	59.5 m
Breadth moulded	11.2 m
Working deck width	8.00 m
Operational draught	3.7 m
Tonnage (grt)	1,033
PROPULSION	
Main engine(s)	Diesel Electric, 1,400 bhp
Propellers	2.50 m diameter, 250 rpm
Speed (max)	13.5 kt
Speed (cruising)	12.0 kt
Endurance	14 days/3,000 n miles
Fuel capacity	56 m³
Fresh water capacity	74 m³
BRIDGE NAVIGATION AIDS	
Satellite	Sercel NR 103 DGPS
Radar	Racal Decca: 3 and 10 cm
Gyrocompass	Arma Brown/SG Brown
Speed log	Plath EM Log
Echo-sounder	Atlas Deso 25 (33 and 210 kHz)
COMMUNICATIONS	
Inmarsat (type)	Yes

MF/HF	Yes
VHF	Yes
Cellular	Yes
Facsimile	Furuno Dfax
SAFETY	
Lifeboats	4 × liferafts
Workboat/chase boat	1 SMB, type RHIB
Lifesaving equipment	lifejackets, survival suits, oxygen masks
DECK MACHINERY	
Cranes	Stern, 4 t SWL
Winches	Sidescan sonar
ACCOMMODATION	
Crew	7 × 1, 2 × 3, 6 × 4, 1 × 6 berth
Scientists/surveyors	2 × 2 berth
Hospital	2 berths
SCIENTIFIC SPACES	
Oceanographic wet lab	6 m²
SURVEY SYSTEMS	
Positioning	Sercel NR 103 DGPS
Sensors	Wreck sonar: Furuno CH-32, 40/60 kHz
Echo-sounder (single beam)	Atlas Deso 25, 33/210 kHz Atlas Deso 25, 210 kHz (launch)
Multibeam/swath system	Bathyscan 300
Sidescan sonar	Ultra widescan model 3050, 100/325 kHz; Ultra widescan model 3050, 100/325 kHz (launch)
Corer(s)	1 piston (North Sea corer)
Other sampling	Van Veen grips
Sound velocity profiler	Odom Digibar

UPDATED

···

Hydrographic Service of the Royal Netherlands Navy (RNLN)

Tydeman

GENERAL	
	Hydrographic and Oceanographic survey vessel
Current operational status	From January 2000 has been operated solely for hydrographic survey in the North Sea

Port of reg/flag	Den Helder
Official number	A906
Classification	LRS 100A1
Call sign	PAUA
Built (yard and date)	Merwede Shipyards, Hardinxveld-Giesendam, Netherlands; commissioned 10 November 1976

Rebuilt (yard and date)	Major refit in 1992	
Length overall	90.13 m	
Breadth moulded	14.43 m	
Working deck width	3.50 m	
Operational draught	4.80 m	
Tonnage (grt)	2,977	

PROPULSION

Main engine(s)	diesel electric, 2,375 bhp (1,750 kW)
Thrusters	Bow
	Stern: active rudder
Propellers	single
Speed (max)	15 kt
Speed (cruising)	12.5 kt
Endurance	11,000 n miles
Fuel capacity	431 m³
Fresh water capacity	48 m³, water generator 10 m³/day

BRIDGE NAVIGATION AIDS

Satellite	Sercel NR 103 DGPS
Radar	Decca Super 50
Gyrocompass	Arma Brown
Speed log	Plath EM Log
Echo-sounder	Atlas Deso 25 (23 and 210 kHz)
Other ship navigation	Racal Hyperfix receiver type 90569

COMMUNICATIONS

Inmarsat (type)	JUE 45a
MF/HF	Yes
VHF	Yes
Cellular	Yes
Facsimile	Furuno Dfax

SAFETY

Lifeboats	6 × liferafts
Workboat/chase boat	2 Mulder & Rijke, length – 10.2 m, draft – 1.0 m, 13 kt
Lifesaving equipment	Lifejackets, survival suits, oxygen masks

HELIDECK

Size, aircraft capacity	Helideck fitted

DECK MACHINERY

Cranes	1 × 20 kN; 2 × 40 kN; 1 × 3 m boom
A-frame(s)	1 × 170 kN max SWL; 1 × 26 kN max SWL
Winches	1 oceanographic; 2 hydrographic; 1 general purpose; 1 cable (8 slipring); 2 towing; 1 hydrophone
Moonpool(s) – size(s)/ function(s)	1

ACCOMMODATION

Crew	13 × 1; 3 × 2; 11 × 4-berth
Scientists/surveyors	3 × 1; 7 × 2; 1 × 4-berth
Hospital	2 berths

SCIENTIFIC SPACES

Total scientific deck space	Foredeck 90 m²; midships 12 m²; aft 140 m²
Oceanographic wet lab	60 m² wet hall, lab 26 m²
Chemistry lab	Dark room/photolab: 44 m² lab: 30 m² central computer room: 45 m²

SURVEY SYSTEMS

Positioning	Sercel NR 103 DGPS
Sensors	Wreck Sonar: Furuno CH-32, 40/ 60 kHz
Echo-sounder(single beam)	Atlas Deso 25, 33/210 kHz Atlas Deso 25, 210 kHz (launch)
Sidescan sonar	Ultra widescan model 3050, 100/ 325 kHz Ultra widescan model 3050, 100/ 325 kHz (launch)
Sub-bottom profiler	EDO Western 515, 3.5/7 kHz
Magnetometer	Geometrics G-801/3 proton
Corer(s)	3 piston-core sets with 100 core-pipes, length 10 ft, diameter 3.5 in
Sound velocity profiler	Odom Digibar

UPDATED

Tydeman (Michael Mitz)
2000/0081303

NEW ZEALAND

Royal New Zealand Navy

Resolution

GENERAL BACKGROUND
'Stalwart' Class survey ship (AGS).
Laid up by USN in 1995 and acquired in September 1996. Reactivated in October 1996 and commissioned into RNZN 13 February 1997. Converted, mid-1997, for hydrography with secondary role of acoustic research for about three months per year.
A new survey boat with multibeam echo-sounder is to be embarked in 2001.

Former names	*Tenacious* (T-AGOS 17)
Official number	A 14
Built (yard and date)	Halter Marine, Moss Point; commissioned 29 September 1989
Rebuilt (yard and date)	Conversion mid-1997
Length overall	68.0 m
Breadth moulded	13.0 m
Operational draught	4.0 m

PROPULSION

Main engine(s)	Diesel-electric; four Caterpillar D 398B diesel generators; 3,200 hp (2.39 MW); two motors; 1,600 hp (1.2 MW)

Thrusters	Bow thruster, 550 hp
Propellers	2 shafts
Speed (cruising)	11.0 kt
Endurance	4,000 n miles at 11.0 kt

BRIDGE NAVIGATION AIDS

Radar	2 Raytheon; I-band

ACCOMMODATION

Crew	22
Scientists/surveyors	19

SURVEY SYSTEMS

Positioning	DGPS
Multibeam/swath system	STN Atlas Hydrosweep MD 2/30

UPDATED

Resolution   **2000**/0038011

NIGERIA

Nigerian Navy

Lana

GENERAL BACKGROUND
Hydrographic survey vessel (AGS). Similar to UK *'Bulldog class'*

Official number	A 498
Built (yard and date)	Brooke Marine, Lowestoft; launched 4 March 1976
Length overall	57.80 m

Breadth moulded	1.40 m
Operational draught	3.70 m

PROPULSION

Main engine(s)	2 Lister Blackstone diesels; 2,640 hp (1.97 MW)

Thrusters	Bow thruster	**ACCOMMODATION**	
Propellers	2 shafts	**Crew**	52 *UPDATED*
Speed (cruising)	16.0 kt		
Endurance	4,500 n miles at 12.0 kt		

BRIDGE NAVIGATION AIDS
Radar   Racal Decca; I-band

Lana   **2001**/0081334

NORWAY

Norwegian Hydrographic Service

Hydrograf

GENERAL

Former names	M/V *Skomvær*
Current operational status	Operational within Norwegian waters
Owner	Statens Kartverk Sjøkartverket
Port of reg/flag	Stavanger, Norway
Official number	IMO 8416841
Classification	DNV ICE 1B
Call sign	LNOW
Built (yard and date)	February 1985
Length overall	43.80 m
Breadth moulded	10 m
Working deck width	10 m
Max draught	4.05 m
Operational draught	3.30
Tonnage (grt)	629

PROPULSION

Main engine(s)	Bergen diesel, Type KRM-6 995 kW

Thrusters	2 × 136 kW and 67 kW
Propellers	1 × 4-blade reversible
Speed (max)	13.5 kt
Speed (cruising)	11.5 kt
Endurance	40 days
Fuel capacity	220 m³
Fuel consumption	5 m³/day at 11.5 kt
Electrical power	160 kW, 220 V, 50 Hz
Fresh water capacity	35 m³

BRIDGE NAVIGATION AIDS

Satellite	Furuno GP – GP50 Mk II
Radar	JRC JMA 630
	JRC JMA 310
Gyrocompass	Robertson RPG-90
Speed log	Ben Amphrite 210
Echo-sounder	Simrad EA 500
Other ship navigation	Autopilot

COMMUNICATIONS
Inmarsat (type)	Sailor SP 4400, 'B'
MF/HF	Sailor RM 2150-2151
VHF	6 × Sailor RT 2047
Cellular	Yes
Facsimile	Richol

SAFETY
Workboat/chase boat	2 × 9.60 m survey launches
Helideck	

DECK MACHINERY
Cranes	2; 24 t at 4.80 m; 48 t at 8.25 m
Winches	2

ACCOMMODATION
Crew	7
Scientists/surveyors	3
Hospital	Yes

SCIENTIFIC SPACES
Total scientific deck space	10 × 15 m

SURVEY SYSTEMS
Positioning	Seatex Seapos DGPS
Sensors	Seatex Seapos 200 motion reference
Echo-sounder (single beam)	Simrad EA 300 Simrade EA 500
Multibeam/swath system	Simrad EM 3000 (on Survey launches)
Sound velocity profiler	AML SV Plus
Oceanographic sensors (CTDs/XBTs and so on)	

UPDATED

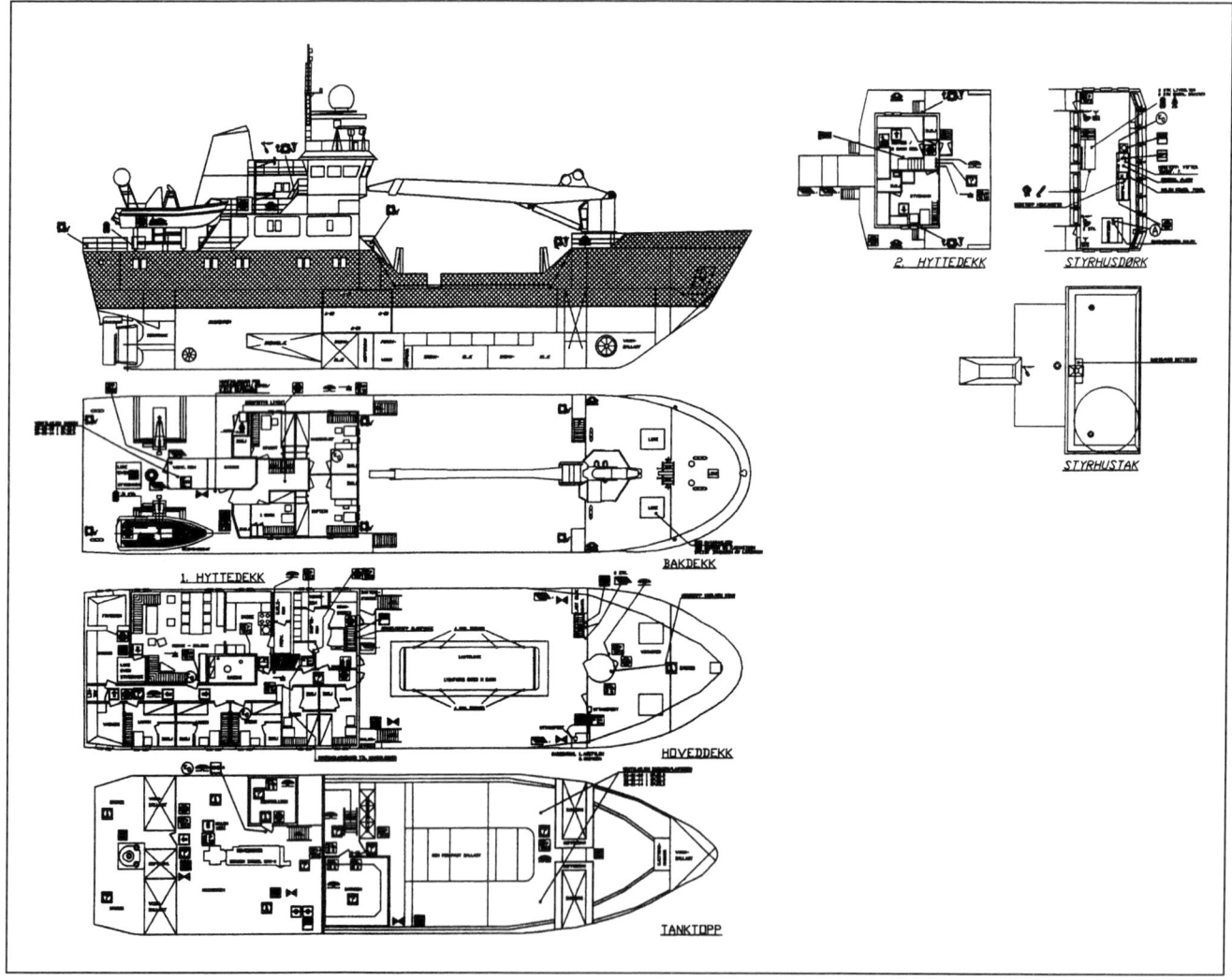

Hydrograf

2001/0106454

Norwegian Hydrographic Service

Sjømåleren

GENERAL
Former names	R/V *Geofjord*; M/S *Ambassador Bay*
Port of reg/flag	Stavanger, Norway
Official number	IMO 8423909
Classification	DNV + 1 A1 EO ICE –C
Call sign	LWXY

Built (yard and date)	1958
Rebuilt (yard and date)	1986, 1996, 1999
Length overall	32.64 m
Breadth moulded	7.02 m
Working deck width	7 × 8 m
Operational draught	4.30 m
Tonnage (grt)	299

PROPULSION

Main engine(s)	Grenaa diesel, Type 6 FR24T/214
Propellers	1
Speed (max)	12 kt
Speed (cruising)	11 kt
Endurance	35 days
Fuel capacity	85 m³
Fuel consumption	2.2 m³/day at 11 kt
Electrical power	200 kW, 220 V, 50 Hz
Fresh water capacity	15 m³; able to produce 1 m³/day

BRIDGE NAVIGATION AIDS

Satellite	Furuno GP – 50 Mk II
Radar	Raytheon ST3410 ARPA; Racal Bridgemaster
Gyrocompass	Robertson SKR 82
Speed log	Skipper EML 224
Echo-sounder	Simrad EA 500
Other ship navigation	Autopilot

COMMUNICATIONS

Inmarsat (type)	Sailor SP 4400
MF/HF	Yes
VHF	Yes
Cellular	Yes
Facsimile	Yes

SAFETY

Lifeboats	1
Workboat/chase boat	1

DECK MACHINERY

Cranes	1
Transducer well	Yes

ACCOMMODATION

Charterers	4
Crew	6
Scientists/surveyors	2

SURVEY SYSTEMS

Positioning	Seatex Seapos
Echo-sounder (single beam)	Simrad EA 300; Simrad EA 500
Multibeam/swath system	Simrad EM 1002
Sound velocity profiler	AML SV Plus
Oceanographic sensors (CTDs/XBTs and so on)	Sensordata SD 204; AML Smart Sensor

VERIFIED

PERU

Directorate of Hydrography & Navigation (HIDRONAV)

Carrillo

GENERAL BACKGROUND
acquired 23 February 1985 for conversion with new engine and survey equipment

Former names	Van Hamel
Port of reg/flag	Callao
Official number	AH 175
Call sign	OBMR
Built (yard and date)	De Vries, Amsterdam; 28 May 1960
Rebuilt (yard and date)	26 June 1985
Length overall	33.08 m
Working deck width	6.87 m
Max draught	2.20 m
Operational draught	1.88 m
Tonnage (grt)	169

PROPULSION

Main engine(s)	2 Wesspor Mk RUB-1612
Propellers	2 shafts
Speed (max)	10 kt
Speed (cruising)	6.0 – 7.0 kt
Endurance	7 days

Fuel capacity	5,500 gallons
Fuel consumption	650 gallons per day
Fresh water capacity	1,000 gallons

BRIDGE NAVIGATION AIDS

Satellite	GPS Magellan
Radar	JRC-JMA 525-6
Gyrocompass	Plath
Echo-sounder	Raytheon

COMMUNICATIONS

MF/HF	PACTOR
VHF	MR 201

SAFETY

Lifeboats	15 person
Workboat/chase boat	Zodiac

SURVEY SYSTEMS

Positioning	DGPS
Echo-sounder (single beam)	Echotrac DF-3200

UPDATED

Directorate of Hydrography & Navigation (HIDRONAV)

Macha

GENERAL

Port of reg/flag	Callao
Official number	AH 174
Call sign	OBMP
Built (yard and date)	SIMA, Chimbote; commissioned April 1982
Length overall	19.60 m
Breadth moulded	5.10 m
Max draught	1.20 m

PROPULSION

Main engine(s)	2 Caterpillar diesels
Propellers	2 shafts
Speed (max)	10.0 kt
Fresh water capacity	950 gallons

ACCOMMODATION

Crew	30

SURVEY SYSTEMS

Sidescan sonar	Yes

UPDATED

Directorate of Hydrography & Navigation (HIDRONAV)

Melo

GENERAL BACKGROUND

Acquired 23 February 1985 for conversion with new engines and survey equipment

Former names	Van der Wel
Port of reg/flag	Callao
Official number	AH 176
Call sign	OBOMS
Built (yard and date)	De Vries, Amsterdam; commissioned 6 October 1961
Length overall	33.08 m
Working deck width	6.87 m
Max draught	2.19 m
Operational draught	1.88 m
Tonnage (grt)	169

PROPULSION

Main engine(s)	2 Wesspor Mk RUB-1612
Propellers	2 shafts
Speed (max)	11 kt
Speed (cruising)	6.0 kt

Endurance	7 days
Fuel capacity	4,800 gallons
Fuel consumption	650 gallons per day

BRIDGE NAVIGATION AIDS

Satellite	Navstar DGPS
Radar	JRC-JMA 525-6

COMMUNICATIONS

Inmarsat (type)	HF-Yaesu Model FT-900
VHF	MR 201

SAFETY

Lifeboats	2 boats
Workboat/chase boat	1 launch

SURVEY SYSTEMS

Positioning	DGPS
Echo-sounder (single beam)	Echotrac DF-3200

UPDATED

Melo

2001/0105212

Directorate of Hydrography & Navigation (HIDRONAV)

Stiglich

GENERAL

Port of reg/flag	Callao
Official number	AH 172
Call sign	OBMP
Built (yard and date)	McLaren, Niteroi; 19 November 1980

Length overall	30.00 m
Breadth moulded	8.00 m
Max draught	1.20 m
Operational draught	0.90 m
Tonnage (grt)	350

PROPULSION

Main engine(s)	2 Caterpillar 33045B, 125 hp
Propellers	2 shafts
Speed (max)	9.5 kt
Endurance	60 days
Fuel capacity	18,680 gallons
Fuel consumption	15 gallons per day

BRIDGE NAVIGATION AIDS

Satellite	NAV-5000 Magellan; 2 GPS Navstar XR5 – M
Radar	Furuno FR-7010D; JRC JMA-6252-6
Gyrocompass	Sperry SR-130 Plath
Echo-sounder	Raytheon 719B-CSS

COMMUNICATIONS

MF/HF	Yaesu FT-900; Kachina KC-103; Kenwood 430-B
VHF	Yaesu VXM-100; Kenwood TKB-720; Motorola

SAFETY

Workboat/chase boat	1 launch

ACCOMMODATION

Crew	30

UPDATED

Stiglich

2001/0081533

Directorate of Hydrography & Navigation (HIDRONAV)

Carrasco

GENERAL BACKGROUND

'Dokkum' Class hydrographic survey vessel

Former names	Abcoude (M 810)
Official number	AH 171
Call sign	OBMQ
Built (yard and date)	Smulders, Schiedam; commissioned 18 May 1956
Rebuilt (yard and date)	1994
Length overall	46.62 m
Breadth moulded	8.75 m
Working deck width	8.75 m
Max draught	3.00 m
Operational draught	2.28 m
Tonnage (grt)	373

PROPULSION

Main engine(s)	2 Fijenoord MAN V64 diesels; 2,500 hp(m) (1.84 MW)
Propellers	2 CP propellers
Speed (max)	15.0 kt
Speed (cruising)	12.0 kt

Endurance	4,363 n miles/13 days
Fuel capacity	16,856 gallons
Fuel consumption	1,200 gallons/day
Electrical power	220 V
Fresh water capacity	3,430 gallons

BRIDGE NAVIGATION AIDS

Satellite	DGPS
Radar	Racal Decca 1226; JRC-JMA 3210
Gyrocompass	Plath
Speed log	Furuno
Echo-sounder	Simrad EQ-30

COMMUNICATIONS

Inmarsat (type)	HF-Yaesu Model FT-900
VHF	MR 201

SAFETY

Lifeboats	3 boats
Workboat/chase boat	FRP launch; Zodiac

ACCOMMODATION		SURVEY SYSTEMS	
Crew	27 to 36	Echo-sounder (single beam)	Simrad EA 500
		Sidescan sonar	Furuno CH-34

UPDATED

Carrasco

2000/0081532

PHILIPPINES

National Mapping and Resource Information Authority (NAMRIA)

Arinya

GENERAL		Electrical power	General Motors Diesel Model 371,
Call sign	DUAK		30 kW, 220 V DC, 3 cylinders,
Length overall	28.4 m		1,200 rpm
Breadth moulded	6.7 m	Fresh water capacity	24.602 t
Max draught	1.98 m (forward), 2.85 m (aft)		
Displacement	250 t	SAFETY	
		Workboat/chase boat	2
PROPULSION			
Main engine(s)	Diesel – General Motors Model	DECK MACHINERY	
	671, 2 cycles, 6 cylinder, 168 hp		
	at 1,800 rpm;	ACCOMMODATION	
Propellers	Twin screw	Crew	6 officers; 25 crew
Speed (cruising)	9 kt		*VERIFIED*

National Mapping and Resource Information Authority (NAMRIA)

Arlunya

GENERAL		Breadth moulded	6.7 m
Call sign	DUAF	Max draught	1.93 m (forward), 2.85 m (aft)
Length overall	28.4 m	Displacement	250 t

PROPULSION

Main engine(s)	Diesel – General Motors Model 671, 2 cycles, 1,800 rpm;		
Propellers	Twin screw		
Speed (cruising)	9 kt		
Electrical power	General Motors Diesel Model 371, 30 kW, 1,200 rpm		
Fresh water capacity	24.602 t		

ACCOMMODATION

Crew	6 officers; 25 crew	*VERIFIED*

National Mapping and Resource Information Authority (NAMRIA)

Atyimba

GENERAL

Call sign	DUAO
Length overall	49.1 m
Breadth moulded	10.1 m
Max draught	2.74 m (forward), 2.77 m (aft)
Displacement	680 t

PROPULSION

Main engine(s)	Diesel – Lister Blackstone Motors Model ES6MGR, 4 cycles, 6 cylinder, 800 hp at 900 rpm
Propellers	Twin screw

Speed (cruising)	9.5 kt
Electrical power	General Motors Diesel, 75 kW, 440 V DC, 4 cylinders, 1,800 rpm, 3-phase
Fresh water capacity	113.55 t

SAFETY

Workboat/chase boat	2

ACCOMMODATION

Crew	8 officers; 46 crew

VERIFIED

National Mapping and Resource Information Authority (NAMRIA)

Hydrographer Presbitero

GENERAL

Call sign	DUXS
Length overall	53.5 m
Breadth moulded	12 m
Max draught	3.8 m
Tonnage (grt)	1,179

PROPULSION

Main engine(s)	Diesel – Caterpillar Models 3512 D1-TA and 3508 D1-TA, 4 cycles, and 8 cylinder, 1,046 hp at 1,200 rpm and 697.32 hp at 1,200 rpm 12 cycles
Propellers	single screw
Speed (cruising)	13 kt

Electrical power	PTO shaft – 448 kW; auxiliary diesel engines – 2 Caterpillar model 3408 (350 kW); emergency diesel engine – Caterpillar 3306 (170 kW)
Fresh water capacity	80 t

SAFETY

Workboat/chase boat	1

ACCOMMODATION

Crew	12 officers; 36 crew

SURVEY SYSTEMS

Multibeam/swath system	Sea Beam 2112

UPDATED

National Mapping and Resource Information Authority (NAMRIA)

Hydrographer Ventura

GENERAL

Call sign	DUXS
Length overall	53.5 m
Breadth moulded	12 m
Max draught	3.8 m
Tonnage (grt)	1,179
Propulsion	
Main engine(s)	Diesel – Caterpillar Models 3512 D1-TA and 3508 D1-TA, 4 cycles, and 12 and 8 cylinder, 1,046 hp at 1,200 rpm and 697.32 hp at 1,200 rpm 12
Propellers	Single screw
Speed (cruising)	13 kt

Electrical power	PTO Shaft – 448 kW; auxilliary diesel engines – 2 Caterpillar model 3408 (350 kW); emergency diesel engine – Caterpillar 3306 (170 kW)
Fresh water capacity	80 t

SAFETY

Workboat/chase boat	1

ACCOMMODATION

Crew	12 officers; 36 crew

SURVEY SYSTEMS

Multibeam/swath system	Sea Beam 2112

UPDATED

POLAND

Polish Navy

Kopernik

GENERAL BACKGROUND
'Moma' Class survey vessel (AGS).

Official number	261
Built (yard and date)	Northern Shipyard, Gdansk; commissioned 20 February 1971
Length overall	73.30 m
Breadth moulded	11.20 m
Operational draught	3.90 m

PROPULSION

Main engine(s)	2 Zgoda-Sulzer 6TD48 diesels; 3,300 hp(m) (2.43 MW) sustained
Propellers	2 shafts

Speed (max)	17.0 kt
Speed (cruising)	12.0 kt
Endurance	9,000 n miles at 12.0 kt

BRIDGE NAVIGATION AIDS

Satellite	SRN 7453 Nogat; SRN 743X; I-band

ACCOMMODATION

Crew	41
Scientists/surveyors	40

UPDATED

Kopernik (J Cislak)   **2000**/0081578

Kopernik (J Cislak)   **2001**/0105247

Polish Navy

Modified 'Finikz' class

GENERAL BACKGROUND
Modified 'Finik 2' Class (Type 874) (AGS) survey vessels (AGS): *Heweliusz* and *Arctowski*.
2 sister ships, *Zodiak* and *Planeta* are civilian operated

Official number
Heweliusz: 265
Arctowski: 266

Built (yard and date)
Northern Shipyard, Gdansk; *Heweliusz* launched 11 September 1981; *Arctowski* launched 20 November 1981; both commissioned 27 November 1982

Heweliusz (J Cislak)

2000/0081577

Heweliusz (J Cislak)

2001/0105245

Length overall	61.60 m	
Breadth moulded	11.20 m	
Operational draught	3.30 m	

PROPULSION
Main engine(s)   2 Cegielski-Sulzer 6AL25/30 diesels; 1,920 hp(m) (1.4 MW); 2 auxiliary motors; 204 hp(m) (150 kW)
Thrusters   Bow thruster
Propellers   2 CP propellers
Speed (max)   13.0 kt
Speed (cruising)   11.0 kt
Endurance   5,900 n miles at 11.0 kt

BRIDGE NAVIGATION AIDS
Radar   SRN 7453 Nogar; SRN 743X; I-band
Speed log   Atlas Dolog

ACCOMMODATION
Crew   49

SURVEY SYSTEMS
Echo-sounder (single beam)   Atlas Deso

UPDATED

Arctowski (Bram Risseeuw)   **2001**/0105246

PORTUGAL

Hydrographic Institute

'Andromeda' Class

GENERAL
Comments   Two Andromeda Class hydrographic launches (AGS). Designed to operate in extreme and coastal areas
Owner   Portuguese Navy

Official number   *Andromeda*: A 5203
Auriga: A 5205
Built (yard and date)   *Andromeda:* Arsenal do Alfeite; commissioned   1 May 1987
Auriga: Arsenal do Alfeite; commissioned   1 March 1988

Auriga   **2001**/0097515

Length overall	31.50 m	**ACCOMMODATION**	
Breadth moulded	7.74 m	**Crew**	13
Operational draught	2.63 m	**Scientists/surveyors**	6

PROPULSION

Main engine(s)	MTU 12V 396 TC62 diesel; 1,100 hp(m) (760 kW) sustained; 60 hp electric motor for low speeds
Propellers	VPP
Speed (max)	12.5 kt
Speed (cruising)	10.0 kt
Endurance	1,980 n miles at 10.0 kt
Electrical power	60 kW main generator; 380 V, 3-phase

SCIENTIFIC SPACES

Total scientific deck space	30 m². Can also receive a 6 m container for scientific purposes

SURVEY SYSTEMS

Echo-sounder (single beam)	2 × Atlas DESO 25
Multibeam/swath system	Andromeda: Fine stabilised-beam transducer (Deep Sea Unit)
Sidescan sonar	Yes
Sub-bottom profiler	Light continuous-reflection seismic equipment
Corer(s)	Shipek, Van Veen
Vehicle(s) (ROVs/AUVs and so on)	Phantom S2

BRIDGE NAVIGATION AIDS

Satellite	DGPS
Radar	Decca RM 914C; I-band.
Gyrocompass	Yes
Speed log	Yes

UPDATED

DECK MACHINERY

Cranes	900 – 3,400 kg hydraulic crane with telescopic jib; 2 t gantry
Winches	Oceanographic CTD

Andromeda (van Ginderen Collection)   **2000**/0012932

Hydrographic Institute

'D Carlos I' Class

GENERAL

Comments	Ex-Stalwart Class hydrographic survey vessels (AGS). D Carlos I integrate into Portuguese Navy in February 1997; Almirante Gago Coutinho, December 1999
Former names	*D Carlos 1:* ex-*Audacious*, ex-*Dauntless* (T-AGOS 11) *Almirante Gago Coutinho:* ex-*Assurance* (T-AGOS 5)
Owner	Portuguese Navy

Official number	D Carlos 1: A 522 *Almirante Gago Coutinho:* A 523
Built (yard and date)	*D Carlos 1:* Tacoma Boat; commissioned 18 June 1989 *Almirante Gago Coutinho:* Tacoma Boat; commissioned 1 May 1985
Length overall	68.20 m
Breadth moulded	13.10 m
Operational draught	5.10 m

PROPULSION		**Speed (max)**	11.0 kt
Main engine(s)	Diesel-electric; four Caterpillar D 398B diesel generators; 3,200 hp (2.39 MW); two GE motors; 1,600 hp (1.2 MW)	**Speed (cruising)**	11.0 kt
		Endurance	4,000 n miles at 11.0 kt
			6,450 n miles at 3.0 kt
Thrusters	Bow thruster: 550 hp	**BRIDGE NAVIGATION AIDS**	
Propellers	2 shafts	**Radar**	2 Raytheon; I-band.

D Carlos 1   *2001*/0097516

D Carlos 1   *2000*/0012931

Almirante Gago Coutinho   *2001*/0097513

ACCOMMODATION

Crew	34
Scientists/surveyors	12

SURVEY SYSTEMS

Multibeam/swath system	Yes
Oceanographic sensors (CTDs/XBTs and so on)	ADCP

UPDATED

RUSSIAN FEDERATION

Department of Navigation and Oceanography

'Sibiriayakov' Class

GENERAL

	Two Sibiriayakov Class hydrographic survey vessels (AGS): *Sibiriayakov* and *Romzuald Muklevitch*
Built (yard and date)	Northern Shipyard, Gdansk; *Sibiryakov:* 1990, *Romzuald Huklevich:* 1992
Length overall	85.60 m
Breadth moulded	15.00 m
Max draught	4.90 m
Operational draught	5.00 m

PROPULSION

Main engine(s)	1 × 3,263 hp
Thrusters	Bow and stern thruster
Propellers	1
Speed (max)	14.6 kt
Speed (cruising)	11.3 kt
Endurance	12,000 n miles
Fuel capacity	530 t
Fuel consumption	7 t per day
Fresh water capacity	74 t

BRIDGE NAVIGATION AIDS

Satellite	Yes
Radar	Two Nayada; I-band
Gyrocompass	Yes
Speed log	Yes
Echo-sounder	Yes

SAFETY

Lifeboats	2: each 37 persons
Lifesaving equipment	4 × liferafts; each 10 persons

HELIDECK

Size, aircraft capacity	No

DECK MACHINERY

Cranes	2: SWL 3.2 t
Winches	6

ACCOMMODATION

Crew	60
Scientists/surveyors	16
Hospital	2 persons

SCIENTIFIC SPACES

Multipurpose dry lab	Total: 111 m²

SURVEY SYSTEMS

Echo-sounder (single beam)	Yes
Magnetometer	Yes
Gravimeter	Yes
Corer(s)	Yes

UPDATED

Sibiriayakov (J Cislak)
2000/0081697

Department of Navigation and Oceanography

'Taiga' class

GENERAL

	Fourteen Taiga (Type 862) Class hydrographic survey vessels (AGS):
	V Adm Vorontsov; Strelets; Taiga; Hydrolog; Stvor; Pegas; Horizont; Gals; Marshal Gelovani; Vizir; Senezh; Donuzlav; Persey; Nikolay Matusevich
Former names	*V Adm Vorontsov: Briz*
Current operational status	4 based in Pacific; 2 in the Black Sea; 4 in the North and 2 in the Baltic Sea
Owner	Russian Navy
Built (yard and date)	Northern Shipyard, Gdansk; 1977-83
Length overall	82.50 m
Breadth moulded	13.50 m
Max draught	3.90 m
Operational draught	4.00 m

PROPULSION

Main engine(s)	2 × Zgoda-Sulzer Type 6TD48 diesels; 2,200 hp(m) sustained; 2 auxiliary motors; 272 hp(m) (200 kW)
Thrusters	Bow thruster
Propellers	2 CP propellers
Speed (max)	16.0 kt
Speed (cruising)	13.0 kt
Endurance	11,300 n miles at 12.0 kt
Fuel capacity	400 t
Fuel consumption	6.5 t per day
Fresh water capacity	85 t

BRIDGE NAVIGATION AIDS

Satellite	Yes
Radar	Palm Frond or Nayada; I-band
Gyrocompass	Yes
Speed log	Yes
Echo-sounder	Yes

Strelets

2000/0019052

Gidrolog

2000/0050052

SAFETY		SCIENTIFIC SPACES	
Lifeboats	1: 50 persons	Multipurpose dry lab	Total: 172.4 m²
Workboat/chase boat	2, each 13 persons		
Lifesaving equipment	3 × liferafts, each 20 persons	SURVEY SYSTEMS	
		Echo-sounder (single beam)	Yes
DECK MACHINERY		Magnetometer	Yes
A-frame(s)	Stern; 5 t	Gravimeter	Yes
Winches	7	Corer(s)	Yes *UPDATED*
ACCOMMODATION			
Crew	66		
Scientists/surveyors	8		
Hospital	2 persons		

Department of Navigation and Oceanography

'Vinograd' Class

GENERAL

Two Vinograd Class hydrographic survey vessels: GS 525; GS 526

Owner	Russian Navy
Built (yard and date)	Rauma-Repola, Finland; 1985
Length overall	32.90 m
Breadth moulded	10.40 m
Max draught	2.70 m

PROPULSION

Main engine(s)	Diesel-electric; 2 diesels; 2 motors
Propellers	2 trainable propellers
Speed (max)	8.5 kt
Speed (cruising)	6.0 kt
Endurance	1,000 n miles at 6.0 kt
Fuel capacity	22 t
Fuel consumption	16 t per day
Fresh water capacity	6.0 t

BRIDGE NAVIGATION AIDS

Satellite	Yes
Gyrocompass	Yes
Speed log	Yes
Echo-sounder	Yes

SAFETY

Lifesaving equipment	4 × liferafts, each 10 persons

DECK MACHINERY

Cranes	2; each 0.9 t SWL
Winches	3

ACCOMMODATION

Crew	12
Scientists/surveyors	7

SURVEY SYSTEMS

Echo-sounder (single beam)	Yes
Multibeam/swath system	GS525: Atlas Fansweep 20
Sidescan sonar	Yes
Corer(s)	Yes

UPDATED

Vinograd (Hartmut Ehlers)   *2000*/0050054

Russian Navy

'Kamenka' Class

GENERAL		**Speed (max)**	14.0 kt
	Eight Kamenka Class hydrographic survey vessels (AGS).	**Speed (cruising)**	10.0 kt
		Endurance	4,000 n miles at 10.0 kt
Built (yard and date)	Northern Shipyard, Gdansk; 1968-69	**BRIDGE NAVIGATION AIDS**	
Length overall	53.50 m	**Radar**	Don 2; I-band.
Breadth moulded	9.10 m		
Operational draught	2.60 m	**DECK MACHINERY**	
		Cranes	Forward: 5 ton
PROPULSION		**ACCOMMODATION**	
Main engine(s)	2 × Sulzer diesels; 1,800 hp(m) (1.32 MW)	**Crew**	25
Propellers	2 × CP propellers		

VERIFIED

Kamenka   2000

Russian Navy

'Nikolay Zubov' Class

GENERAL

Comments — Four Nikolay Zubov (Type 850) Class hydrographic survey vessels (AGS): *Andrey Vilkitsky*; *Boris Davidov*; *Semen Dezhnev*; *Faddey Bellingsgauzen*

Current operational status — Three based in the Northern Fleet

Built (yard and date) — Szczecin Shipyard, Poland; 1964-68

Boris Davidov   2000/0081698

Length overall	89.70 m		
Breadth moulded	13.00 m	**BRIDGE NAVIGATION AIDS**	
Operational draught	4.60 m	Radar	Palm Frond or Don 2; I-band
		SAFETY	
PROPULSION		Workboat/chase boat	2 to 4 survey launches
Main engine(s)	2 × Zgoda-Sulzer 8TD48 diesels;		
	4,400 hp(m) (3.23 MW) sustained	**ACCOMMODATION**	
Propellers	2 shafts	Crew	58
Speed (max)	16.5 kt	Scientists/surveyors	12
Speed (cruising)	14.0 kt		*UPDATED*
Endurance	11,000 n miles at 14.0 kt		

Russian Navy

'Samara' Class

GENERAL		**Propellers**	2 × CP propellers
	Eight Samara Class hydrographic	**Speed (max)**	15.0 kt
	survey vessels (AGS): *Deviator;*	**Speed (cruising)**	10.0 kt
	Gigrometr; Glubomyr; Vostok;	**Endurance**	6,200 n miles at 10.0 kt
	Vaygach; Azimut; Zenit; Tropik		
Current operational status	Only *Deviator; Gigrometr;*	**BRIDGE NAVIGATION AIDS**	
	Glubomyr and *Vostok* active	Radar	Don 2; I-band
Built (yard and date)	Northern Shipyard, Gdansk;		
	1962-65	**SAFETY**	
Length overall	59.00 m	Workboat/chase boat	1 × survey launch
Breadth moulded	10.50 m		
Operational draught	3.80 m	**DECK MACHINERY**	
		A-frame(s)	5 tons
PROPULSION			
Main engine(s)	2 × Zgoda-Sulzer Type 6TD48	**ACCOMMODATION**	
	diesels; 3,300 hp(m) (2.43 MW)	Crew	45
	sustained		*UPDATED*

Samara (van Ginderen Collection)

2000

SOUTH AFRICA

South African Navy

Protea

GENERAL		Classification	Auxiliary Hydrographic Survey
	'Hecla' Class hydrographic survey	Call sign	ZTRX
	vessel (AGS). Hull strengthened	Built (yard and date)	Yarrow (Shipbuilders) Ltd;
	for navigation in ice and fitted		commissioned 23 May 1972
	with a passive roll stabilisation	Rebuilt (yard and date)	Simon's Town Naval Dockyard:
	system.		new main engines and refit in
Official number	A 321		1995-96

Length overall	79.30 m	**COMMUNICATIONS**	
Breadth moulded	15.00 m	Inmarsat (type)	'C'
Max draught	4.70 m	MF/HF	Yes
Operational draught	4.20 m	VHF	Yes
Tonnage (grt)	2,750		

PROPULSION

SAFETY

Main engine(s)	Diesel-electric; 4 MTU diesels; 3,840 hp (2.68 MW) sustained; 3 generators; 1 motor; 2,000 hp (1.49 MW)	Lifeboats	8 × 20-man liferaft
		Workboat/chase boat	2 survey launches; 1 × 3 in 1 Wheter; 1 rigid hull inflatable
Thrusters	Bow		
Propellers	1 CP	**HELIDECK**	
Speed (max)	17.0 kt	Size, aircraft capacity	1 Alouette III
Speed (cruising)	12.0 kt		
Endurance	60 days/12,000 n miles at 12.0 kt	**DECK MACHINERY**	
Fuel capacity	610 t	Cranes	Forecastle: 1 × 2 t SWL
Fuel consumption	10 t/day, at 12 kt	Winches	1 × sweep
Electrical power	440 V, 220 V, 115 V, 24 V: 50/60 Hz		1 × sidescan sonar
		Transducer well	1 × single beam
Fresh water capacity	110 t, 2 Vapomet fresh water generators		1 × multibeam

ACCOMMODATION

		Crew	138 berths
BRIDGE NAVIGATION AIDS			113 crew
Satellite	Trimble GPS	Hospital	4 berth
Radar	Racal Decca Bridgemaster		
Gyrocompass	Sperry 1006; Arma Brown	**SCIENTIFIC SPACES**	
Speed log	Atlas Dolog 22	Oceanographic wet lab	12 m²
Echo-sounder	Atlas Deso 25	Multipurpose dry lab	12 m²

Protea (Robert Pabst)

2000/0019118

Protea (Robert Pabst)

2000/0099194

SURVEY SYSTEMS

Positioning	Racal Landstar; Del Norte transponder; Trimble NT 3000; Racal Hyperfix
Echo-sounder (single beam)	1 × Elac Deepwater
	2 × Atlas Deso 25
Multibeam/swath system	Atlas Hydrosweep MD
Sidescan sonar	EdgeTech Model 260
Grab(s)	1 × Shippek

Oceanographic sensors (CTDs/XBTs and so on)	SBE 19
	SBE 25
SEISMIC SYSTEMS	
Acquisition system	Hinaps Polaris

UPDATED

SPAIN

Spanish Navy

'Castor' Class

GENERAL

	Four 'Castor' Class hydrographic survey vessels (AGS).
Port of reg/flag	Cadiz
Official number	*Castor:* A 21 (ex-H 4)
	Pollux: A 22 (ex-H 5)
	Antares: A 23
	Rigel: A 24
Call sign	*Castor:* EBHC
	Pollux: EBHD
	Antares: EBJY
	Rigel: EBTZ
Built (yard and date)	*Castor:* Bazan, La Carraca; commissioned 10 November 1966
	Pollux: Bazan, La Carraca; commissioned 6 December 1966
	Antares: Bazan, La Carraca; commissioned 21 November 1974
	Rigel: Bazan, La Carraca; commissioned 21 November 1974
Length overall	38.30 m
Breadth moulded	7.60 m

Max draught	3.49 m
Operational draught	2.80 m
PROPULSION	
Main engine(s)	Sulzer 4TD36 diesel; 720 hp(m) (530 kW)
Propellers	1 shaft
Speed (max)	11.0 kt
Speed (cruising)	10.0 kt
Endurance	7 days/3,620 n miles at 8.0 kt
Fuel capacity	55,000 litres
Fuel consumption	100 litres/h
Electrical power	3 × diesel generators
Fresh water capacity	36,000 litres
BRIDGE NAVIGATION AIDS	
Satellite	Omnistar
Radar	Kelvin Hughes HR 3061
Gyrocompass	Sperry SR-120
Speed log	Sagem
Echo-sounder	Atlas Deso 20
COMMUNICATIONS	
MF/HF	Yes
VHF	ITT Marine STR 12 M

Antares (Diego Quevedo)

2000/0019161

SAFETY

Lifeboats	2
Workboat/chase boat	2

DECK MACHINERY

Winches	2

ACCOMMODATION

Crew	37, including surveyors

SURVEY SYSTEMS

Positioning	Trimble 4000RS DGPS; trisponder
Echo-sounder (single beam)	Atlas DESO 20

UPDATED

Spanish Navy

'Malaspina' Class

GENERAL

Two 'Malaspina' Class hydrographic survey vessels (AGS). Developed from British 'Bulldog' class survey vessels

Official number	*Malaspina:* A 31
	Tofiño: A 32
Call sign	*Malaspina:* EBHL
	Tofiño: EBDK
Built (yard and date)	*Malaspina:* Bazan, La Carraca; commissioned 21 February 1975
	Tofiño: Bazan, La Carraca; commissioned 23 April 1975
Length overall	57.60 m
Breadth moulded	11.70 m
Max draught	3.51 m
Operational draught	3.40 m
Tonnage (grt)	1,169.99

PROPULSION

Main engine(s)	2 San Carlos MWM TbRHS-345-61 diesels; 2,700 hp
Thrusters	150 hp
Propellers	2 shafts; acbLIPS cp props
Speed (max)	15.0 kt
Speed (cruising)	14.25 kt

Endurance	3,140 n miles
Fuel capacity	176,483 litres
Electrical power	C/A – 750 kW/30 kW
Fresh water capacity	146,000 litres

BRIDGE NAVIGATION AIDS

Satellite	GPS
Radar	Decca RM 1216 A
	Kelvin Hughes 1006
Gyrocompass	Anschutz

ACCOMMODATION

Crew	63

SCIENTIFIC SPACES

Total scientific deck space	600 m²
Multipurpose dry lab	10 m²
Chemistry lab	22 m²

SURVEY SYSTEMS

fitted with echo-sounders, Egg Mark B sidescan sonar,

Echo-sounder (single beam)	2 Atlas DESO 20
	Retractable Burnett 538-2 sonar for deep sounding

UPDATED

Tofiño (Paul Jackson)

2000/0080632

TAIWAN

Taiwanese Navy

Ta Kuan

GENERAL BACKGROUND
'Alliance' (NATO) Class hydrographic survey vessel (AGS). Designed for oceanography and hydrographic research.

Official number	1601
Built (yard and date)	Fincantieri, Muggiano; launched 17 December 1994
Length overall	93.00 m
Breadth moulded	15.20 m
Operational draught	5.10 m

PROPULSION

Main engine(s)	Diesel-electric; 3 MTU/AEG diesel generators; 5,712 hp(m) (4.2 MW); 2 AEG motors; 5,100 hp(m) (3.75 MW)
Thrusters	Bow; stern trainable and retractable
Propellers	2 shafts

Speed (max)	15.0 kt
Speed (cruising)	12.0 kt
Endurance	12,000 n miles at 12.0 kt

BRIDGE NAVIGATION AIDS

Satellite	Navsat
Radar	H/I-band

ACCOMMODATION

Crew	82

SURVEY SYSTEMS

Echo-sounder (single beam)	Deep and shallow echo-sounders
Multibeam/swath system	Simrad EM 1200
Vehicle(s) (ROVs/AUVs and so on)	ROV

VERIFIED

Ta Kuan (C Chung)

2000/0019239

THAILAND

Thai Navy

Chanthara

GENERAL

Former names	AGS II
Official number	811

Built (yard and date)	Lürssen Werft; commissioned 30 May 1961
Length overall	69.90 m

Breadth moulded	10.50 m	Speed (cruising)	10.0 kt
Operational draught	3.00 m	Endurance	10,000 n miles at 10.0 kt

PROPULSION

ACCOMMODATION

Main engine(s)	Two KHD diesels; 1,090 hp(m) (801 kW)	Crew	68
Propellers	2 shafts		*UPDATED*
Speed (max)	13.25 kt		

Chanthara (Maritime Photographic)   2000/0019280

TUNISIA

Tunisian Navy

Khaireddine

GENERAL BACKGROUND
'Wilkes' Class survey vessel (AGS). Decommissioned on 29 August 1995 and transferred by grant aid on 29 September 1995.

Former names   *Wilkes* (T-AGS 33)

Official number	A 700
Built (yard and date)	Defoe SB Co, Bay City, Michigan; launched 31 July 1969
Length overall	87.00 m

Khaireddine   2000/0080854

Breadth moulded	14.60 m	**Speed (cruising)**	13.0 kt
Operational draught	4.60 m	**Endurance**	8,000 n miles at 13.0 kt

PROPULSION

Main engine(s)   Diesel-electric; 2 Alco diesel generators; Westinghouse/GE motor; 3,600 hp (2.69 MW)

Thrusters   Bow: 350 hp (261 kW)
Propellers   1 shaft
Speed (max)   15.00 kt

BRIDGE NAVIGATION AIDS
Radar   RM 1650/9X; I-band

ACCOMMODATION
Crew   37

UPDATED

TURKEY

Department of Navigation, Hydrography and Oceanography

Cesme

GENERAL

Silas Bent Class survey vessel (AGS). Transferred from US on 28 October 1999

Former names   *Silas Bent* (T-AGS 26)
Owner   Turkish Navy
Official number   A 591
Built (yard and date)   American SB Co, Lorain; commissioned 23 July 1965
Length overall   87.00 m
Breadth moulded   14.60 m
Operational draught   4.60 m

PROPULSION
Main engine(s)   Diesel-electric; two Alco diesel generators; Westinghouse/GE motor; 3,600 hp (2.69 MW)

Thrusters   Bow thruster, 350 hp
Propellers   One shaft
Speed (max)   15.00 kt
Speed (cruising)   14.0 kt
Endurance   12,000 n miles at 14.0 kt

BRIDGE NAVIGATION AIDS
Radar   RM 1650/9X; I-band

ACCOMMODATION
Crew   31

UPDATED

Cesme   *2000*/0093757

Department of Navigation, Hydrography and Oceanography

Cubuklu

GENERAL				
Former names	Y 1251		Gyrocompass	Yes
Owner	Turkish Navy		Speed log	Yes
Built (yard and date)	Golcuk; launched 17 November		Echo-sounder	Yes
	1983			
Length overall	40.50 m		**DECK MACHINERY**	
Breadth moulded	9.60 m		Cranes	Stern, clearance above deck 7 m,
Max draught	3.20 m			outboard extension 4 m, SWL 1
Tonnage (grt)	650			ton
			Winches	4 × oceanographic, steel wire
PROPULSION				1,000 m
Main engine(s)	MWM diesel; 820 hp(m) (603 kW)			CTD winch
Propellers	1 CP propeller			
Speed (max)	10.0 kt		**ACCOMMODATION**	
Speed (cruising)	9.0 kt		Crew	16
Endurance	5,500 n miles/30 days		Scientists/surveyors	8
Fuel capacity	75 m³			
Electrical power	380 V AC, total 110 kVA, 3-phase,		**SCIENTIFIC SPACES**	
	50 Hz		Total scientific deck space	50 m²
Fresh water capacity	35 m³		Oceanographic wet lab	6 m²
			Multipurpose dry lab	30 m²
BRIDGE NAVIGATION AIDS				
Satellite	Yes		**SURVEY SYSTEMS**	
Radar	Racal Decca; I-band.		Multibeam/swath system	SeaBeam 1050D

UPDATED

Cubuklu

2000/0093759

UKRAINE

Ukraine Navy

'Biya' Class

GENERAL BACKGROUND

2 'Biya' Class survey ships (AGS); U 601; U 602. Transferred from Russia in 1997.

Former names	U 601: *GS 273*; U 602: *GS 212*		Length overall	55.00 m
Built (yard and date)	Northern Shipyard, Gdansk;		Breadth moulded	9.80 m
	1972-76		Max draught	2.60 m
			PROPULSION	
			Main engine(s)	2 diesels; 1,200 hp(m) (882 kW)

Propellers	2 CP
Speed (max)	13.0 kt
Speed (cruising)	11.0 kt
Endurance	4,700 n miles at 11.0 kt

DECK MACHINERY

| Cranes | 5 t |

ACCOMMODATION

| Crew | 25 |

BRIDGE NAVIGATION AIDS

| Radar | Don 2; I-band |

VERIFIED

SAFETY

| Workboat/chase boat | Survey launch |

U 601 (W Globke)

2000/0019356

Ukraine Navy

'Finik' Class

GENERAL BACKGROUND

3 'Finik' Class survey ships (AGS); *Pereyaslav; Alchevsk; Skvyra.* Transferred from Russia in 1997.

| Former names | *Pereyaslav*: GS 401; *Alchevsk*: GS 402; *Skvyra*: OS 265 |
| Built (yard and date) | Northern Shipyard, Gdansk; 1978-83 |

Pereyaslav (van Ginderen Collection)

2000/0019355

Length overall	61.30 m		**BRIDGE NAVIGATION AIDS**	
Breadth moulded	10.80 m		Radar	Kivach B; I-band
Max draught	3.30 m			

PROPULSION

DECK MACHINERY

Main engine(s)	2 Cegielski-Sulzer 6AL25/30		Cranes	7 t
	diesels; 1,920 hp(m) (1.4 MW);			
	auxiliary propulsion; 2 motors;		**ACCOMMODATION**	
	204 hp(m) (150 kW)		Crew	26
Thrusters	Bow		Scientists/surveyors	9
Propellers	2 CP			
Speed (cruising)	13.0 kt			*VERIFIED*
Endurance	3,000 n miles at 13.0 kt			

Ukraine Navy

Simferopol

GENERAL BACKGROUND

'Moma' Class (Type 861M) survey ship (AGS). Transferred from Russia in February 1996

Former names	*Jupiter*
Official number	U 511
Length overall	73.30 m
Breadth moulded	11.20 m
Max draught	3.90 m

PROPULSION

| Main engine(s) | 2 Zgoda-Sulzer diesels; 3,300 hp (m) (2.43 MW) sustained |

Propellers	2 CP
Speed (max)	17.0 kt
Speed (cruising)	11.0 kt
Endurance	9,000 n miles at 11 kt

BRIDGE NAVIGATION AIDS

| Radar | Don 2; I-band. |

ACCOMMODATION

| Crew | 56 |

UPDATED

Simferopol   *2000*/0019347

UNITED KINGDOM

Royal Navy

Beagle

GENERAL

Comments   Normally employed in home waters. Due to pay off in 2002. The sister vessel *Bulldog* paid off in August 2001

Official number   H319

Built (yard and date)   Brooke Marine, Lowestoft; launched 7 September 1967

Length overall   57.8 m

Breadth moulded   11.4 m

Operational draught   3.70 m

PROPULSION

Main engine(s)   4 Lister-Blackstone ERS8M diesels; 2,640 hp (1.97 MW)

Propellers   2 CPPs

Speed (max)   13 kt

Speed (cruising)   12 kt

Endurance   4,500 n miles at 12 kt

BRIDGE NAVIGATION AIDS

Radar   Kelvin Hughes type 1007, I-band

SAFETY

Workboat/chase boat   9 m survey motor boat; 7 m RIB

DECK MACHINERY

Winches   Lebus sidescan

ACCOMMODATION

Crew   46

Hospital   2

SURVEY SYSTEMS

Sensors

Echo-sounder(single beam)   Atlas Deso 25; Kelvin Hughes 778

Sidescan sonar   GeoAcoustics 2094

Magnetometer   Proton

Grab(s)   Shipek; Mudsnapper

Sound velocity profiler   Hand-held SV probe

Oceanographic sensors (CTDs/XBTs and so on)   XBTs; CTDs

UPDATED

Beagle (H M Steele)   **2000**/0075819

Royal Navy

Confidante

GENERAL

Comments   Survey vessel contracted to the Royal Navy and operated by Naval Party NP 1016. Works mainly in the Dover Strait and southern North Sea conducting routine re-surveys in onshore and coastal waters.

Owner   Reid Marine

Port of reg/flag   Kirkwall, UK

Official number   901825

Classification   Specialist Survey Vessel

Call sign   ZQZI 5

Built (yard and date)   Halter Marine Inc, Louisiana, USA; 1989

Rebuilt (yard and date)   Reid Marine, Ramsgate; 1999

Length overall   32.684 m

Breadth moulded   7.315 m

Operational draught   2.0 m

Tonnage (grt)   208.12

PROPULSION

Main engine(s)	2 × 380 hp Detroit Diesels
Thrusters	Bow: 60 hp
Propellers	Twin
Speed (max)	15 kt
Speed (cruising)	12 kt
Endurance	24 h at 12 kt
Fuel capacity	400 gallons

BRIDGE NAVIGATION AIDS

Satellite	Koden GPS
Radar	Simrad; Furuno
Gyrocompass	Sperry
Speed log	Simrad
Echo sounder	Simrad Colour
Other ship navigation	Simrad CA250 Chart Plotter System
	Simrad & Brooks & Gatehouse Auto Pilots

COMMUNICATIONS

Inmarsat (type)	Inmarsat-C
VHF	2 Simrad DSC/GMDSS

SAFETY

Workboat/chase boat	6-man 90 hp RIB

DECK MACHINERY

A-frame(s)	Twin
Winches	3: fwd; midships; aft

ACCOMMODATION

Charterers	12
Crew	6

SURVEY SYSTEMS

Positioning	MN8
Echo sounder (single beam)	Atlas Deso 25 210kHz/33 kHz
Sidescan sonar	GeoAcoustics 2094
Magnetometer	Proton
Grab(s)	Shipek; Mudsnapper
Sound velocity profiler	Handheld SV probe

NEW ENTRY

Royal Navy

"Echo" Class

GENERAL

Comments	Multi-role hydrographic and oceanographic survey vessels. Two vessels, HMS *Echo* and HMS *Enterprise*, presently under construction. The prime contract with Vosper Thornycroft Ltd was placed in June 2000. It is worth around £130 million and includes support of the ships throughout their 25-year life.
Classification	Lloyds +100A1, Survey Vessel, Ice Class IC +LMC, PSMR*, UMS, ES(2)
Built (yard and date)	Appledore Shipbuilders, Devon; *Echo* due to be floated out early in 2002, commissioned date due to be November 2002; *Enterprise* due to be commissioned in May 2003

Length overall	90.0 m
Breadth moulded	16.8 m
Max draught	5.5 m

PROPULSION

Main engine(s)	Diesel electric: Ruston 6RK270; power: 1,600 kW at 900 rpm, nominal power: 1882 kVA
Propellers	Azimuthing thrusters
Speed (max)	> 15 kt
Endurance	> 9,000 n miles at 12 kt
Electrical power	3 main generators: ABB Automation AMG 660 L 8 L, 690 V, 60 Hz
	Harbour generator: ABB Automation AMG 400 S 4, Engine: Cummins VTA28G5M, 550 kW at 1,800 rpm, nominal power: 688 kVA, 690 V, 60 Hz
	Emergency generator: Newage;

Echo class (artist's impression) (Vosper Thornycroft)

2001/0106722

Engine: Cummins KTA19D2M, 350 kW at 1,800 rpm, nominal power: 438 kVA, 450 V, 60 Hz	**SURVEY SYSTEMS**
	Multibeam/swath system Simrad EM 1002; Simrad EM 3000 on survey motor boat
SAFETY	**Sidescan sonar** Towed
	Vehicle(s) (ROVs/AUVs and Towed undulating environmental
Workboat/chase boat Survey motor launch	**so on)** sensors

NEW ENTRY

ACCOMMODATION
Crew   46 (accommodation for 81)

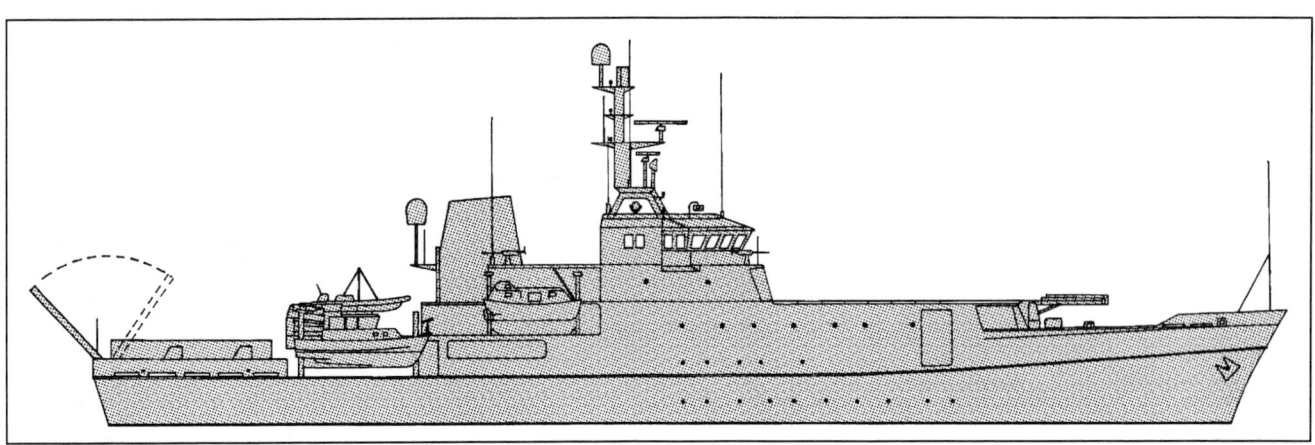

Echo (Ian Sturton)   *2001*/0084423

Royal Navy

Endurance

GENERAL

Comments	Antarctic Patrol Ship (AGOB) that assists in scientific research programmes in co-operation with the British Antarctic Survey. Leased in 1991 as the *Polar Circle* and bought outright in 1992. Ice-strengthened hull capable of breaking 1 m thick ice at 3 kt.	**Max draught**	8.5 m
		Tonnage (grt)	2,198
		PROPULSION	
		Main engine(s)	2 Bergen BRM8 diesels, 8,160 hp (m) (6 MW) sustained
Former names	*Polar Circle; A 176*	**Thrusters**	Bow and stern
Official number	A171	**Propellers**	Single CP Propellers
Built (yard and date)	Ulstein Hatlo, Norway; commissioned 21 Nov 1991	**Speed (max)**	15 kt
		Speed (cruising)	12 kt
		Endurance	6,500 n miles at 12 kt
Length overall	91.0 m	**BRIDGE NAVIGATION AIDS**	
Breadth moulded	17.9 m	**Radar**	Kelvin Hughes Type 1007; I-band.

Endurance (J Brodie)   *2001*/0106717

SAFETY		**SURVEY SYSTEMS**	
Workboat/chase boat	2 survey boats; 7 m RIB	Positioning	MN8
Lifesaving equipment	GMDSS	Echo sounder (single beam)	Simrad EA500
		Sidescan sonar	GeoAcoustics 2094
HELIDECK		Magnetometer	Proton
Size, aircraft capacity	2 Westland Lynx HAS 3	Grab(s)	Shipek; Mudsnapper
		Sound velocity profiler	Handheld SV probe
ACCOMMODATION		Oceanographic sensors	CTDs and XBTs
Crew	130	(CTDs/XBTs and so on)	

NEW ENTRY

Royal Navy

Marine Explorer

GENERAL		**SAFETY**	
Comments	Survey vessel contracted to the Royal Navy and operated by Naval Party NP 1008. Works in coastal and offshore waters conducting routine re-surveys in onshore and coastal waters.	Workboat/chase boat	6-man 90 hp RIB
		DECK MACHINERY	
		A-frame(s)	1
		Winches	MPD sidescan
Owner	Eidesvik Shipping (UK)Ltd	**SURVEY SYSTEMS**	
Port of reg/flag	Plymouth, UK	Positioning	MN8
Official number	359119	Echo sounder (single beam)	Atlas Deso 25 210kHz/33 kHz
Classification	Survey Vessel	Sidescan sonar	GeoAcoustics 2094
Call sign	GUIY	Magnetometer	Proton
Length overall	82.7 m	Grab(s)	Shipek; Mudsnapper
Working deck width	13.6 m	Sound velocity profiler	Handheld SV probe
Tonnage (grt)	2,198		

NEW ENTRY

Marine Explorer (NP 1008)   **2001**/0084422

Royal Navy

Roebuck

GENERAL		**PROPULSION**	
Comments	Coastal survey vessel designed to conduct surveys on UK Continental Shelf	Main engine(s)	4 Mirlees-Blackstone ESL8 Mk 1 diesels; 2.27 MW (3,040 hp)
Official number	H 130	Propellers	2 CPPs
Built (yard and date)	Brooke Marine, Lowestoft; launched 14 November 1985	Speed (max)	14 kt
		Speed (cruising)	12 kt
Length overall	63.9 m	Endurance	4,000 n miles at 12 kt
Breadth moulded	13 m		
Operational draught	4 m	**BRIDGE NAVIGATION AIDS**	
		Radar	Nautilus 6000C ARPA

SAFETY
Workboat/chase boat   7 m RIB; survey launch

DECK MACHINERY
A-frame(s)   1
Winches   Lebus sidescan; Aquashuttle

ACCOMMODATION
Crew   54

SURVEY SYSTEMS
Positioning   MN8

Echo-sounder (single beam)	Atlas Deso 25; Kelvin Hughes 778
Sidescan sonar	GeoAcoustics 2094
Magnetometer	Proton
Grab(s)	Shipek; Mudsnapper
Vehicle(s) (ROVs/AUVs and so on)	AquaShuttle
Sound velocity profiler	Hand-held SV probe
Oceanographic sensors (CTDs/XBTs and so on)	CTDs; XBTs
SEISMIC SYSTEMS	

UPDATED

Roebuck (van Ginderen Collection)   **2000**/0075820

UNITED STATES OF AMERICA

Military Sealift Command

Pathfinder

GENERAL BACKGROUND INFORMATION

Designed and constructed to provide multiple capabilities, including physical, chemical and biological oceanography; multidiscipline environmental investigations; ocean engineering and marine acoustics; marine geology and geophysics and bathymetric, gravimetric and magnetometric surveying.

Pathfinder   **2001**/0016561

The surveys are conducted for the Naval Meteorology and Oceanography Command, Stennis Space Center, by personnel of the Naval Oceanographic Office

Owner	Oceanographer of the Navy
Official number	TAGS 60
Classification	American Bureau of Shipping, US Coast Guard
Built (yard and date)	Halter Marine Shipyard, Moss Point, Mississippi; 1994
Length overall	98.70 m (329 ft)
Breadth moulded	17.40 m (58 ft)
Max draught	5.70 m (19 ft)
Operational draught	5.40 m (18 ft)

PROPULSION

Main engine(s)	4 EMB/Baylor diesel generators; 11,425 hp) (8.52 MW); 2 GE CDF 1944 motors; 8,000 hp (5.97 MW) sustained; 6,000 hp (4.48 MW);
Thrusters	bow thruster; 1,500 (1.19 MW)
Propellers	2 acbLIPS Z drives;
Speed (cruising)	16.0 kt
Endurance	12,000 n miles

SAFETY

Workboat/chase boat	2 × 10 m (34 ft) Hydrographic Survey Launches (HSLs)

DECK MACHINERY

Cranes	3 multipurpose
Winches	5

ACCOMMODATION

Crew	25
Scientists/surveyors	30

SCIENTIFIC SPACES

Total scientific deck space	3,500 sq ft
Multipurpose dry lab	4,000 sq ft

SURVEY SYSTEMS

Positioning	Dynamic Position Systems
Multibeam/swath system	Simrad EM 121A/EM 1000
Sidescan sonar	towed digital sidescan sonars
Vehicle(s) (ROVs/AUVs and so on)	May be carried

NEW ENTRY

NOAA Office of Marine and Aviation Operations

Rainier

GENERAL

	Designed for conducting hydrographic surveys in support of nautical charting. The ship operates off the US Pacific coast, and in Alaskan coastal waters. Home Port: Seattle, Washington
Official number	S 221
Classification	American Bureau of Shipping
Call sign	WTEF
Built (yard and date)	Aerojet-General Shipyards, Jacksonville, Florida; delivered: April 1968
Length overall	70.4 m (231 ft)
Breadth moulded	12.8 m (42 ft)
Max draught	4.4m (14.3 ft)
Tonnage (grt)	1,591

PROPULSION

Main engine(s)	2 General Motors EMD geared diesel; rated power (each): 1,200 hp
Thrusters	Detroit Diesel/Bird Johnson through hull bow; rated power: 200 hp
Propellers	2 controllable pitch; diameter: 8.5 ft; blades: 3
Speed (cruising)	12 kt
Endurance	5,898 n miles/22 days
Fuel capacity	107,000 gallons

Rainier

2000/0093758

Fuel consumption	120 gallons/h
Electrical power	2 Detroit Diesel/GE generators; output voltage: 450 V AC, 60 Hz, 3-phase; power rating: 300 kW Detroit Diesel/GE emergency generator; output voltage: 450 V AC, 60 Hz, 3-phase; power rating: 75 kW Electrical service: 450/120 V AC, 3-phase; 120 V AC, 1-phase
Fresh water capacity	16,000 gallons

BRIDGE NAVIGATION AIDS

Satellite	Differential Global Positioning System (DGPS) receivers
Radar	X-band radar with an ARPA display
Gyrocompass	Yes

COMMUNICATIONS

Inmarsat (type)	Standard A radio transceiver; Standard C radio transceiver
MF/HF	HF Marine band transceivers; HF Alarm Watch radio receiver (2,182 kHz)
VHF	VHF-FM Marine band transceivers; portable VHF-FM transceivers
Cellular	Telephone
Facsimile	NAVTEX receiver; weather receiver

SAFETY

Workboat/chase boat	5 aluminium survey launches; manufacturer: The Boatyard (Jensen); length: 29 ft; propulsion: diesel Aluminium survey launch; manufacturer: American Eagle (Munson); length: 29 ft; propulsion: diesel/Hamilton Jet Drive AmonArk aluminium open boat; length: 17 ft; propulsion: gasoline outboard American Eagle aluminium SAFE boat; length: 19 ft; propulsion: gasoline outboard Zodiac inflatable open boat; length: 13 ft; propulsion: gasoline outboard

DECK MACHINERY

Cranes	2 Skagit telescoping boom; location: foredeck, port and starboard; boom length: 25 ft; lifting capacity: 2,500 lb (boom extended) Skagit fixed-length; location: aft mast; boom length: 40 ft; lifting capacity: 5,000 lb
A-frame(s)	Movable, electrohydraulic; location: main deck, starboard quarter; clearance over side: 3 ft
Winches	Northern Line electrohydraulic oceanographic winch; location: main deck, starboard quarter; line speed: 0 to 400 ft/min; maximum pull: 1,000 lb; drum capacity: 30,000 ft of ³/₁₆ in wire rope

ACCOMMODATION

Crew	49
Scientists/surveyors	4

SCIENTIFIC SPACES

Multipurpose dry lab	Dry oceanographic lab: 20.9 m² (240 sq ft)

SURVEY SYSTEMS

Echo-sounder (single beam)	Deep water; shallow water hydrographic
Multibeam/swath system	SeaBeam HydroChart II Multibeam Swath System; 2 SeaBeam 1180 multibeam systems for use on survey launches; 2 Reson SeaBat 8101 EG&G
Sidescan sonar	
Oceanographic sensors (CTDs/XBTs and so on)	Sea-Bird Electronics Inc SBE 19, SEACAT CTD profilers; Shipboard Environmental *Data* Acquisition System (SEAS); air and seawater temperature sensors

UPDATED

Office of Coast Survey, NOAA

Bay Hydrographer

GENERAL BACKGROUND INFORMATION
Survey operations in Chesapeake Bay; multibeam sonar, sidescan sonar, diver investigation of submerged wrecks and obstructions to navigation for update of nautical charts; testing and development platform for NOAA's Nautical Charting Laboratory in Silver Spring, Maryland; home port: Norfolk, Virginia

Length overall	16.80 m
Breadth moulded	5.10 m
Max draught	1.50 m

PROPULSION

Speed (cruising)	10 kt
Endurance	3 days/700 n miles

BRIDGE NAVIGATION AIDS

Satellite	DGPS

ACCOMMODATION

Crew	2
Scientists/surveyors	7

SURVEY SYSTEMS

Multibeam/swath system	Klein 5000; Reson SeaBat 9001
Sidescan sonar	EdgeTech 260

NEW ENTRY

URUGUAY

Uruguay Navy

'Oyarvide' Class

GENERAL

"Helgoland" Class Survey Ship (AGS). Former German ocean-going tug. Recommissioned in 1998. Ice-strengthened hull.

Former names	*Helgoland* (A 1457)
Official number	22
Built (yard and date)	Unterweser, Bremerhaven; commissioned 8 March 1966
Length overall	68.00 m
Breadth moulded	12.70 m
Max draught	4.80 m

PROPULSION

Main engine(s)	Diesel-electric; 4 MW 12-cylinder diesel generators; 2 motors; 2.43 MW (3,000 hp(m))
Propellers	2 shafts
Speed (max)	17.0 kt
Speed (cruising)	16.0 kt
Endurance	6,400 n miles at 16.0 kt

BRIDGE NAVIGATION AIDS

Radar	Raytheon; I-band

ACCOMMODATION

Crew	34

SURVEY SYSTEMS

Positioning	DGPS
Sensors	Hull-mounted sonar for wreck search
Echo-sounder (single beam)	Dual-frequency 200/12 kHz
Multibeam/swath system	Seabeam 1180
Oceanographic sensors (CTDs/XBTs and so on)	Multiparameter profiling probe

UPDATED

Oyarvide 3 / 2000 (A E Galarce)

VENEZUELA

OCHINA (Hydrographic Department)

Miguel Rodriguez

GENERAL BACKGROUND

'Cherokee' Class survey ship (AGS). Acquired from USA on 1 September 1978

Former names	*Salinan* ATF 161 (R 23)
Built (yard and date)	Charleston SB and DD Co; commissioned 9 November 1945

Length overall	62.50 m	**Speed (cruising)**	15.0 kt
Breadth moulded	11.70 m	**Endurance**	7,000 n miles at 15.0 kt
Max draught	5.20 m		
		BRIDGE NAVIGATION AIDS	
PROPULSION		**Radar**	Sperry SPS-53; I/J-band
Main engine(s)	Diesel-electric; 4 GM 16-278A		
	diesels; 4,400 hp (3.28 MW); 4	**ACCOMMODATION**	
	generators; motor; 3,000 hp (2.24	**Crew**	85
	MW)		
Propellers	1 shafts		*VERIFIED*

Miguel Rodriguez   *2000*/0050735

VIETNAM

Vietnam Navy

Kamenka

GENERAL		**PROPULSION**	
	Transferred from USSR in	**Main engine(s)**	2 Sulzer diesels; 1,800 hp(m)
	December 1979		(1.32 MW)
Built (yard and date)	Northern Shipyard, Gdansk;	**Propellers**	2 cp propellers
	1968-69	**Speed (max)**	14 kt
Length overall	53.50 m	**Speed (cruising)**	10 kt
Breadth moulded	9.10 m	**Endurance**	4,000 n miles at 10 kt
Max draught	2.60 m		

BRIDGE NAVIGATION AIDS
Radar   Don 2; I-band

ACCOMMODATION
Crew   25

DECK MACHINERY
Cranes   Forward: 5 t

UPDATED

Kamenka   **2000**

OCEANOGRAPHIC RESEARCH VESSELS

ARGENTINA

Armarda Argentina

Puerto Deseado

GENERAL

Current operational status	Operates in the southwest Atlantic Ocean
Owner	Consejo Nacional de Investigaciones Cientificas y Tecnicas (CONICET)
Port of reg/flag	Argentina
Official number	Q 20
Classification	ABS
Call sign	LOPD
Built (yard and date)	Astarsa, San Fernando; 26 April 1978
Length overall	76.8 m
Breadth moulded	13.2 m
Working deck width	13.00 m
Max draught	5.00 m
Tonnage (grt)	2,400

PROPULSION

Main engine(s)	2 × MAN diesels, 900 kW each, Model 9L 2027
Thrusters	Bow: Schottel, S-150-L
Propellers	2
Speed (max)	14 kt
Speed (cruising)	12 kt
Endurance	40 days
Fuel capacity	700 m³
Fuel consumption	10 m³/day
Electrical power	4 × Stanford 380 W; 1 × EGA 400 W, 50 Hz
Fresh water capacity	105 m³

BRIDGE NAVIGATION AIDS

Satellite	Magnavox MX200 Leica MX400
Radar	Kelvin Hughes Nucleus 2 5000T Decca RM 1229 Raytheon 1660/125B
Gyrocompass	Anschutz Standard III
Echo-sounder	Kelvin Hughes MS 32
Other ship navigation	Omega

COMMUNICATIONS

MF/HF	1 × RF 130 TX, 1 TX Redifon, 1 TX/RX YAAAESSU FT 840 1 × EGA HAAGENUK MS 90N
VHF	Motorola; 1 com; 1 CM 127

SAFETY

Lifeboats	6 inflatable liferafts (20 persons each)
Workboat/chase boat	1 Harding, Model MOB 20
Lifesaving equipment	110 lifejackets

DECK MACHINERY

Cranes	Stern, 9 m clearance
A-frame(s)	1 × coring; 1 × streamer; 2 × CTD
Winches	7

ACCOMMODATION

Crew	75
Scientists/surveyors	19
Hospital	2 berths

Puerto Deseado (Luis Oscar Zunino)

SCIENTIFIC SPACES

Total scientific deck space	200 m²
Oceanographic wet lab	50 m²
Multipurpose dry lab	50 m³
Chemistry lab	35 m³

SURVEY SYSTEMS

Echo-sounder (single beam)	Edo Western NBBS 16/25/34 kHz Raytheon
Sub-bottom profiler	Raytheon 3.5 kHz
Magnetometer	Varian Mod V-75
Gravimeter	Askania Mod 6553
Corer(s)	1
Oceanographic sensors (CTDs/XBTs and so on)	Sippican XBT Mk II; Neil Brown CTD Mk III; Sparton XBT Mod 101

SEISMIC SYSTEMS

Energy source (type and manufacturer)	Airguns
Number of airguns	4
Size of airguns	10/20/40 CINC
Compressor numbers and types	Bauer Mod 1K-21-50E
Total capacity	1,500 m³, 1,750 hp, 200 bar
Streamer type	Single channel
Streamer numbers and lengths per number	2 × 50 m
Acquisition system	EG & G
Recording system	EG & G for 255/UGR – Raytheon

UPDATED

Consejo Nacional de Investigaciones Cientificas y Tecnicas (CONICET)

El Austral

GENERAL

Current operational status	Operates in the southwest Atlantic Ocean
Classification	Lloyds Register
Built (yard and date)	1930
Length overall	44.3 m
Breadth moulded	8.2 m
Operational draught	5.3 m
Tonnage (grt)	490

PROPULSION

Main engine(s)	1 diesel engine, 400 hp at 350 rpm; Auxiliary engine, 180 hp
Propellers	1.6 m diameter, 350 rpm
Speed (cruising)	8 kt
Endurance	4,000 n miles
Fuel capacity	30 m³
Electrical power	200/110 V AC, 70 kVA, 50 Hz; 110/50 V DC
Fresh water capacity	20 m³

BRIDGE NAVIGATION AIDS

Satellite	Yes
Radar	Yes
Gyrocompass	Yes
Speed log	Doppler

DECK MACHINERY

Winches	2 oceanographic, 3,600 m, 1 t; Trawl, 1,400 m, 17 t

ACCOMMODATION

Crew	14
Scientists/surveyors	11

SCIENTIFIC SPACES

Total scientific deck space	80 m²
Oceanographic wet lab	20 m²
Multipurpose dry lab	24 m²

SURVEY SYSTEMS

Echo-sounder (single beam)	12 kHz
Magnetometer	Yes
Gravimeter	Yes

VERIFIED

National Institute for Fishery Research & Development (INIDEP)

Capitan Oca Balda

GENERAL

Current operational status	Operates in the southwest Atlantic Ocean
Classification	Germanischer Lloyd
Built (yard and date)	Germany; 1982
Length overall	65 m
Breadth moulded	11.4 m
Operational draught	4.2 m
Tonnage (grt)	1,179

PROPULSION

Main engine(s)	1 diesel engine, 2,600 hp at 650 rpm
Propellers	2.75 m diameter, 270 rpm
Speed (max)	14 kt
Speed (cruising)	12 kt
Endurance	6,000 n miles/23 days
Electrical power	380 V AC, 995 kVA, 3 phase, 50 Hz; 690 V AC, 475 kVA, 50 Hz
Fresh water capacity	121 m³

BRIDGE NAVIGATION AIDS

Satellite	Yes
Radar	Yes
Gyrocompass	Yes
Speed log	Doppler

COMMUNICATIONS

Facsimile	Fax

DECK MACHINERY

Winches	2 oceanographic, steel wire, 3,000 m; conducting cable, 1,500 m

ACCOMMODATION

Crew	24
Scientists/surveyors	14

SURVEY SYSTEMS

Echo-sounder (single beam)	Fisheries, 38/120 kHz

UPDATED

National Institute for Fishery Research & Development (INIDEP)

Dr Eduardo Holmberg

GENERAL		BRIDGE NAVIGATION AIDS	
Current operational status	Operates in the southwest Atlantic Ocean	Satellite	Yes
		Radar	Yes
Built (yard and date)	Japan; 1980	Gyrocompass	Yes
Length overall	62.0 m	Speed log	Doppler
Breadth moulded	11 m		
Operational draught	4.2 m	COMMUNICATIONS	
Tonnage (grt)	950	Facsimile	Fax
PROPULSION		DECK MACHINERY	
Main engine(s)	1 diesel engine, 2,100 hp at 680 rpm	Cranes	Midships, 1 t
		A-frame(s)	Stern
Propellers	2.75 m diameter, 650 rpm	Winches	2 oceanographic
Speed (max)	14 kt		
Speed (cruising)	13.5 kt	ACCOMMODATION	
Endurance	3,200 n miles/24 days	Crew	24
Fuel capacity	245 m^3	Scientists/surveyors	13
Electrical power	385 V AC, 350 kVA, 3 phase, 50 Hz		
		SURVEY SYSTEMS	
Fresh water capacity	125 m^3	Echo-sounder (single beam)	Fisheries, 120 kHz

UPDATED

AUSTRALIA

Australian Institute of Marine Science (AIMS)

Harry Messel

GENERAL		SAFETY	
	Decommissioned December 2000	Workboat/chase boat	2 dinghies
Built (yard and date)	Stannard Bros, Sydney; 1973	DECK MACHINERY	
Length overall	20.7 m	Winches	Hydrographic winch; Benthos/plankton winch
Breadth moulded	7 m		
Operational draught	2 m	Transducer well	
PROPULSION		ACCOMMODATION	
Main engine(s)	6-71GM engines; 290 kW	Crew	4
Propellers	Twin screw	Scientists/surveyors	6
Speed (cruising)	9 kt		
Endurance	1,000 n miles	SCIENTIFIC SPACES	
Fuel capacity	18,500 litres	Total scientific deck space	26 m^2 (aft)
		Multipurpose dry lab	13.2 m^2
BRIDGE NAVIGATION AIDS			
Satellite	Yes	SURVEY SYSTEMS	
Gyrocompass	Yes	Echo-sounder (single beam)	Yes

UPDATED

Australian Institute of Marine Science (AIMS)

Lady Basten

GENERAL		BRIDGE NAVIGATION AIDS	
Built (yard and date)	Ocean Shipyards, Fremantle; 1978	Satellite	Yes
		Gyrocompass	Yes
Length overall	27.4 m		
Breadth moulded	8 m	SAFETY	
Operational draught	2.5 m	Workboat/chase boat	3 dinghies
PROPULSION		DECK MACHINERY	
Main engine(s)	8V-71 GM engines; 360 kW	A-frame(s)	3 t
Speed (cruising)	10 kt	Winches	Hydrographic; Bertros/Plankton
Endurance	2,500 n miles		
Fuel capacity	27,000 litres		

ACCOMMODATION

Crew	7
Scientists/surveyors	7

SCIENTIFIC SPACES

Total scientific deck space	32.0 m² (aft)
Oceanographic wet lab	5.7 m²
Multipurpose dry lab	18.7 m²

SURVEY SYSTEMS

Sensors	Scanning sonar
Echo-sounder (single beam)	Yes

VERIFIED

Australian Maritime College

Wyuna

GENERAL

Current operational status	Operates in the Pacific Ocean and Tasman Sea
Classification	Lloyds Register
Built (yard and date)	1953
Length overall	63.5 m
Breadth moulded	11.89 m
Operational draught	4.59 m
Tonnage (grt)	1,313

PROPULSION

Main engine(s)	3 diesel-electric engines, each 1,941 hp at 700 rpm; Auxiliary diesel, 615 hp
Propellers	3.66 m diameter, 150 rpm
Speed (max)	13.5 kt
Speed (cruising)	12 kt
Endurance	6,000 n miles
Fuel capacity	297 m³
Electrical power	415/240 V AC, 100/70 kVA, 3 phase, 50 Hz
Fresh water capacity	169 m³

BRIDGE NAVIGATION AIDS

Satellite	Yes
Radar	Yes
Gyrocompass	Yes
Speed log	E/M Log; Doppler Log

DECK MACHINERY

Cranes	Stern, 1 t

ACCOMMODATION

Crew	9
Scientists/surveyors	37

SCIENTIFIC SPACES

Total scientific deck space	100 m²
Multipurpose dry lab	43 m²

SURVEY SYSTEMS

Echo-sounder (single beam)	35/210 kHz

VERIFIED

CSIRO Division of Fisheries

Southern Surveyor

GENERAL

	Fisheries research vessel
Former names	MT *Ranger Callisto* (1972-73); MT *Kurd* (1973-1982)
Classification	Lloyds 100A1 Ice Class 3 DP(AM) (temporarily suspended)
Built (yard and date)	Brooke Marine, Lowestoft, UK; 1972
Rebuilt (yard and date)	August 1990; re-engined 1994
Length overall	66.1 m
Breadth moulded	12.3 m
Max draught	5.3 m
Tonnage (grt)	1,594

PROPULSION

Main engine(s)	Wartsila Vasa 6R32, 2,460 kW driving a Leroy-Somer alternator-type LSA 54 M8, 1,875 kVA
Thrusters	Bow: 2 × 540 hp (403 kW) Brunvoll SPX-VP units; stern: 2 × 540 hp (403 kW) Brunvoll SPX-VP units; azimuth thruster, 740 hp (552 kW), retractable
Propellers	Kort nozzle, controllable pitch, 552 kW
Speed (max)	14 kt
Speed (cruising)	12 kt
Endurance	26 days at 12 kt
Fuel capacity	260 t

Electrical power	3 Deutz diesel engines driving a Stamford Generator, 3,500 kVA 415/240 V AC, 50 Hz
Fresh water capacity	72 t

BRIDGE NAVIGATION AIDS

Satellite	Ashtech 12 channel DGPS Trimble Nav Trac XL
Radar	Furuno FR2010; Furuno FR1011
Gyrocompass	2 Sperry Mk 37
Echo-sounder	Furuno TE 881, 50 Hz; Furuno FCV 140, 28/200 kHz colour sounder

COMMUNICATIONS

Inmarsat (type)	Inmarsat C; Inmarsat A with fax and telex; Optus mobilesat; Magnavox MX2400
MF/HF	2 Sailor HF 1300
VHF	3 Sailor VHF RT 144

DECK MACHINERY

Winches	Fishing: 30 t; Net Drum, Hydrographic, Towed Body and Scientific
Moonpool(s) – size(s)/ function(s)	1.2 m × 1.0 m with a vertical instrument carriage

ACCOMMODATION

Scientists/surveyors 12

SURVEY SYSTEMS

Sensors Furuno FNR 700 – net recorder; Scanmar net monitor; Bottom classification: RoxAnn; Simrad SD570; Deep water viseo system

Echo-sounder (single beam) Simrad EK 500, 12/38/120 kHz – hull mounted; Simrad EK 400, 12/38/120 kHz – towed body

Other sampling Demersal and Pelagic trawls to 2,000 m; Benthic sleds; Instrumented Bongo; Net Hyball ROV; CI AquaShuttle

Vehicle(s) (ROVs/AUVs and so on)

Oceanographic sensors (CTDs/XBTs and so on) XBT system; Salinometer; Fluorometer; Sea-surface temperature; RDI 150 kHz broadband ADCP; Neil Brown WOCE CTD; General Oceanics rosette sampling system

VERIFIED

Southern Surveyor

2000/0099236

CSIRO Division of Oceanography

Franklin

GENERAL

Oceanographic research vessel

Classification Lloyds 100A + LMC, UMS

Built (yard and date) North Queensland Engineers & Agents, Cairns, North Queensland, 1985

Length overall 55.2 m

Breadth moulded 11.8 m

Max draught 3.8 m

PROPULSION

Main engine(s) Wartsila-Vasa 12 V 22 developing 1,590 kW

Thrusters Bow: Schottel S302 LSVCP

Propellers Controllable pitch, four blades, 2.55 m diameter

Speed (cruising) 13 kt

Endurance 7,500 n miles

Electrical power 1 × 800 kVA diesel generator, 415 V, 3 phase, 50 Hz; 240 V, 1 phase, 50 Hz; 24 V DC

Satellite GPS: Ashtech OEM; NCS Mk 2

Radar JRC JMA-630 (10 cm); JRC JMA-626 (3 cm)

Gyrocompass SG Brown Mk 10

Speed log Doppler Log: JRC JCN-203

Echo-sounder JRC JFU-216, 28/200 kHz

COMMUNICATIONS

MF/HF Sailor 1000; Codan 6801 Mk 2

VHF Dancom RT 408

DECK MACHINERY

Cranes Hiab 180 Sea, 100 kN at 1.7 m; 1.56 kN at 10.3 m

A-frame(s) Starboard: maximum 90 kN

Winches Oceanographic: 10,000 m, 6 mm; Oceanographic: 6,000 m CTD cable, 6.45 mm

ACCOMMODATION

Crew 13

Scientists/surveyors 12

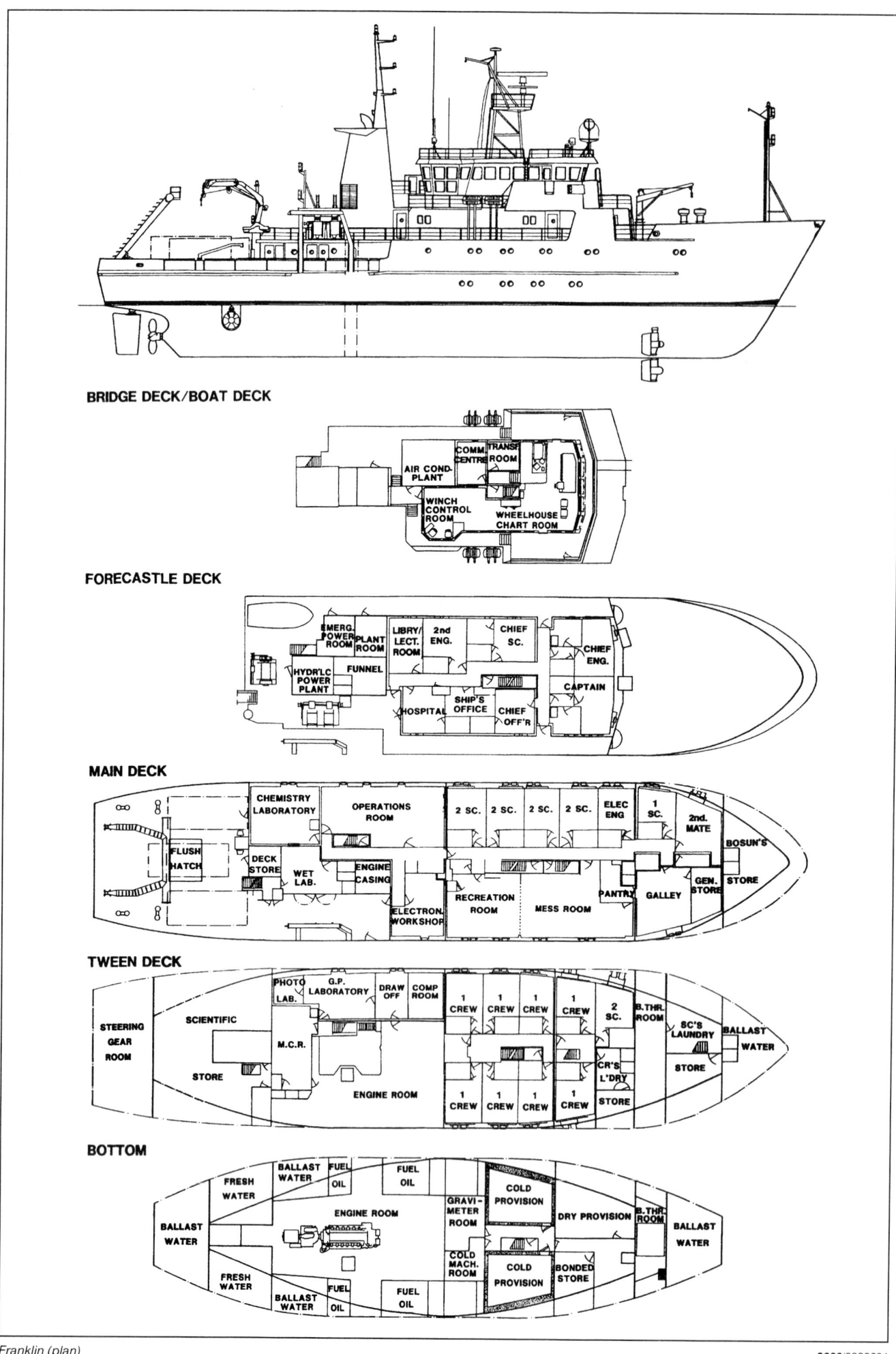

Franklin (plan)

SURVEY SYSTEMS		**Oceanographic sensors**	ADCP – RDI 150 kHz; CTD – Neil
Positioning	Deep Sea Pinger – Benthos 2216	**(CTDs/XBTs and so on)**	Brown WOCE standard;
Echo-sounder (single beam)	Simrad EA500, 12/120 kHz		thermosalinograph – Ocean Data
Other sampling	General Oceanics 12 and		TSG-103; XBT – Sippican
	24 bottle rosette system		meteorology station

Franklin   *2000*/0099203

James Cook University

James Kirby

GENERAL		**MF/HF**	Codan
Comments	Steel-hulled fisheries research	**VHF**	GME
	vessel based on a commercial		
	prawn trawler hull	**DECK MACHINERY**	
Built (yard and date)	Horn Engineering, Brisbane; 1972	**A-frame(s)**	Stern, SWL of 1 t, 3 m high, 1.9 m
Length overall	19.5 m		wide
Breadth moulded	5.2 m	**Winches**	2 × side: used for trawling; Jaden
Max draught	2.15 m		No 6, 500 m, 10 mm cable.
			Centre: used for dredging, grab
PROPULSION			sampling, sledging; Jaden No 6,
Main engine(s)	Cummins NT855 diesel, 300 bhp		1,000 m, 8 mm wire
	at 1,800 rpm		Hydrographic: used mainly for
Propellers	Hundestad variable pitch		water sampling, 200 m, 4 mm
Speed (max)	> 10 kt		wire
Electrical power	Cummins generator, 34 kVA;		Electromagnetic: used for side
	Yanmar generator, 20 kVA;		scan sonar equipment, holds
	415 VAC, 50 Hz		300 m of electrical conductor
			core cable
BRIDGE NAVIGATION AIDS			
Satellite	DGPS	**ACCOMMODATION**	
Radar	Yes	**Crew**	2
Gyrocompass	Yes	**Scientists/surveyors**	6 (14 for day trips)
Echo sounder	Colour		
		SURVEY SYSTEMS	
COMMUNICATIONS		**Multibeam/swath system**	Reson SeaBat 8101
Inmarsat (type)	Yes	**Sidescan sonar**	Benthos Chirp II 6600

NEW ENTRY

P & O Polar Australia Pty Ltd

Aurora Australis

GENERAL

COMMENTS
Antarctic supply/research ship

Owner	Australian government
Classification	Lloyds Register Ice Class 1A Super Icebreaker
Built (yard and date)	Newcastle, Australia; 1989
Length overall	94.91 m

Aurora Australis (van Ginderen Collection)   ***2001****/0056515*

BRIDGE NAVIGATION AIDS
Satellite	Ashtech 3DF GPS; Koden GPS

SAFETY
Workboat/chase boat	2 inflatable boats, 4.9 m; 1 inflatable boat, 5.5 m

DECK MACHINERY
A-frame(s)	
Winches	2
Crew	24
Scientists/surveyors	116

SURVEY SYSTEMS
Sensors	Camera: Benthos
Echo-sounder (single beam)	Simrad EK 500 12/38/120/200 kHz
Other sampling Oceanographic sensors (CTDs/XBTs and so on)	General Oceanics rosette sampler CTD Ned Brown MK 3B; fluorometer: Sea-Tech; SBE 21 thermosalinograph; fluorometer: Turner Designs TD 10

SEISMIC SYSTEMS
Energy source (type and manufacturer)	RDI ADCP 150 kHz; XBT: Sippican Mk 12

UPDATED

BELGIUM

Management Unit of the North Sea Mathematical Models (MUMM)

Belgica

GENERAL BACKGROUND
A multipurpose oceanographic vessel

Owner	The Belgian Federal Ministry of Science
Port of reg/flag	Belgian Navy
Official number	A962
Classification	Germanischer Lloyds +100 A4+MC AUT 16/24 Research Vessel
Call sign	ORGQ
Built (yard and date)	Boelwerf, Temse; commissioned 5 July 1984

Length overall	51.12 m
Breadth moulded	10 m
Working deck width	10 m
Max draught	4.6 m
Operational draught	4 m
Tonnage (grt)	965

PROPULSION
Main engine(s)	1 × 6 cylinder, 4-stroke, turbocharged ABC6 DZ medium-speed diesel (1,030 rpm) 1,150 kW (1,570 hp)

Belgica   ***2000****/0099205*

Thrusters	2 transverse (bow and stern) JASTRAM hydraulically driven: 2 × 150 kW	**Lifesaving equipment**	1 EPIRB ; 2 SART; 8 portable VHF Motorola GP300 PL
Propellers	KaMeWa-type skewed bac, rotational speed of 360 rpm, 1.95 m diameter	**DECK MACHINERY** **Cranes**	1 folding/telescopic hydraulic – HIAB FOCO 36: 2 t at 11 m; 8 t at 2 m
Speed (max)	13.5 kt	**A-frame(s)**	1 stern gantry: 8 t
Speed (cruising)	12 kt	**Winches**	2 combined trawling/fishing:
Fuel capacity	165 m³		6.4 t; 1 fishing net drum: 7 m³/5 t;
Fuel consumption	4 t/day – full ahead (pitch 100 per cent – 850 rpm)		2 hydraulic winches
Electrical power	2 diesel-driven alternators: Caterpillar 275 kW; Van Kaick 325 kW, 440 V, 60 Hz 1 static converter/regulator (220 V ± 1% and 50 Hz ± 0.5%) 20 kVA	**Transducer well**	transducer installed in a hull unit which allows the transducer to be retracted into the hull
Fresh water capacity	100 m³	**ACCOMMODATION** **Crew**	15
		Scientists/surveyors	15
BRIDGE NAVIGATION AIDS			
Satellite	DGPS Sercel NR 103; Magnavox MX 200; Leica MX51R DGPS Beacon receiver	**SCIENTIFIC SPACES** **Total scientific deck space**	115 m²
Radar	2 Decca Bridgemaster, MA 180/04 and CD252/6 connected with a colour video track plotter Racal Decca Fishmaster 2	**Oceanographic wet lab**	20 m²: Frigo: deep freezer; filtration system Milli-RO, Milli-Q (Millipore)
Gyrocompass	Anschutz STD 20	**Multipurpose dry lab**	12 m²: Lab 1 – biology; Cardan table; Labo centrifuge; fume
Speed log	Dual-axis Doppler log – Raytheon DSN 450		extractor 12 m²: Lab 2 – microbiology: Cardan table; laminar flow
Echo-sounder	Atlas Echograph 481 digigraph		cabinet; incubators; autoclave;
Other ship navigation	Autopilot – Anschutz 102-834		oven 20 m²: fish lab: fish tank; fish 'throw away tube'; Cardan table.
COMMUNICATIONS			14 m²: computer room: data
Inmarsat (type)	Saturn B Marine Bm Class 1 W/PC 9000 Nera Worldphone Marine		acquisition and processing system 4 m²: ship's office; multibeam
MF/HF	HF Transmitter – Debeg D7313; MF/HF Transmitter – Debeg E7313; MF/HF Transmitter – Debeg 7204 SSB		transceiver unit 13 m²: container lab (20 ft container)
VHF	D72A; JHS32A	**Chemistry lab**	10 m²: Cardan table; laminar flow cabinet; nutrient auto-analyser
Cellular	GSM Siemens S4r		
Facsimile	1 Okifax 460	**SURVEY SYSTEMS**	
SAFETY		**Positioning**	DGPS Sercel NR 103; Magnavox MX 200; Leica MX51R DGPS Beacon receiver
Lifeboats	1 rescue boat; 4 automatic inflatable liferaft (20 persons)	**Sensors**	Meteo station – TH Friedrichs;
Workboat/chase boat	RIB – 5 m hull, 40 pK outboard motor		heave compensator – TSS 320B;

Belgica

2000/0099206

Echo-sounder (single beam)	bottom classification – Roxann; solarimeter – Kipp & Zonen CM 5 Atlas Deso 20 – 33/200 kHz; Furuno FE 824 – 50/200 kHz; Furuno FCV 381 – 28/88 kHz	Oceanographic sensors (CTDs/XBTs and so on)	SBE 19; SBE 911 connected with SBE 32 Carousel equipped with 12; Niskin bottles or 10 litre or 5 litre GO-FLO bottles; 3 Niskin sampling bottles of 30 litres and Niskin sampling bottles of 5 litres;
Multibeam/swath system	Kongsberg Simrad EM 1002S		thermosalinograph – SBE 21;
Magnetometer	Marine data		fluorimeter – Turner Designs 10-
Corer(s)	Spade – USNEL; multicorer – Bowers & Connelly		AU-005; current meter – NBA DNC 3
Grab(s)	modified Van Veen; Shipec Grabs		
Other sampling	High-speed encased gulfstream plankton sampler Benthic sledge		
Sound velocity profiler	Applied Microsystems SV Plus		

UPDATED

BERMUDA

Bermuda Biological Station for Research (BBSR)

Weatherbird II

GENERAL		Speed log	Yes
Classification	American Bureau of Shipping	Echo-sounder	Yes
Call sign	WAH 4677		
Built (yard and date)	1982	**DECK MACHINERY**	
Length overall	35.05 m	Cranes	Hiab Sea stern, clearance above deck 13 m, SWL 2 t
Breadth moulded	8.53 m		
Max draught	2.59 m	A-frame(s)	Stern, midships SWL 9 tons
Tonnage (grt)	194	Winches	CTD: Markey DUSH, TSE winch: Model SPD-70, 12,000 m
PROPULSION			
Main engine(s)	2 Detroit 16V71 diesel engines, each 500 bhp at 1,800 rpm	**ACCOMMODATION**	
Thrusters	Bow: Schottel	Crew	8
Propellers	2	Scientists/surveyors	12
Speed (max)	10 kt		
Speed (cruising)	9.5 kt	**SCIENTIFIC SPACES**	
Endurance	4,500 n miles/14 days	Total scientific deck space	46 m²
Fuel capacity	132 m³	Multipurpose dry lab	Radiation lab; electronics lab
Electrical power	AC voltage: 110 V/208 VAC, 3-phase, 60 Hz	Chemistry lab	Yes
		SURVEY SYSTEMS	
BRIDGE NAVIGATION AIDS		Oceanographic sensors (CTDs/XBTs and so on)	SeaBird CTD
Radar	Yes		
Gyrocompass	Yes		

UPDATED

BRAZIL

Brazilian Navy

Almirante Câmara

GENERAL		Breadth moulded	12.2 m
	'Robert D Conrad' Class (Oceanographic Ship) (AGOR), equipped for gravimetric, magnetic and geological research	Operational draught	4.70 m
		PROPULSION	
Former names	Sands T-AGOR 6; transferred from USA 1 July 1974	Main engine(s)	Diesel-electric; 2 Caterpillar diesel generators; 1 motor; 1,000 hp (746 kW)
Official number	H 41	Thrusters	Bow
Built (yard and date)	Marietta Co, Point Pleasant; commissioned 8 February 1965	Speed (max)	13.5 kt
		Speed (cruising)	12.0 kt
Length overall	63.70 m	Endurance	12,000 n miles at 12 kt

BRIDGE NAVIGATION AIDS		**ACCOMMODATION**	
Satellite	Yes	Crew	36
Radar	RCA CRM-NIA-75; I/J-band		
Gyrocompass	Yes	**SURVEY SYSTEMS**	
Speed log	Yes	Magnetometer	Yes
Echo-sounder	Yes	Gravimeter	Yes

VERIFIED

DECK MACHINERY
Cranes   10 t

Almirante Câmara (Hartmut Ehlers)   *2000*/0012953

Brazilian Navy

Ary Rongel

GENERAL

	Polar Research Ship (AGOB)	**Built (yard and date)**	Eides, Norway; commissioned 22
Former names	*Polar Queen*. Acquired by sale 19		January 1981
	April 1994. Ice-strengthened hull	**Length overall**	75.300 m
	fitted.	**Breadth moulded**	13.0 m
Official number	H 44	**Operational draught**	5.30 m

Ary Rongel   *2000*/0056613

PROPULSION

Main engine(s)	2 MAK 6M-453 diesels; 4,500 hp(m) (3.3 MW)
Thrusters	2 bow thrusters; 1 stern thruster
Propellers	CP propeller
Speed (cruising)	14.50 kt
Endurance	19,500 n miles at 14 kt

BRIDGE NAVIGATION AIDS

Satellite	Yes
Radar	Yes
Gyrocompass	Yes
Speed log	Yes
Echo-sounder	Yes

HELIDECK

Size, aircraft capacity	Platform for Ecureuil 2

ACCOMMODATION

Crew	51

SURVEY SYSTEMS

Positioning	Simrad Albatross dynamic positioning system

VERIFIED

Brazilian Navy

Bãrao De Teffé

GENERAL

	Polar Research Ship (AGOB) recommissioned as a lighthouse tender but operates in reserve to *Ary Rongel*
Former names	*Thala Dan*
Official number	H 42
Built (yard and date)	Aalborg Vaerft, Denmark; commissioned 8 May 1957
Length overall	75.2 m
Breadth moulded	14.2 m
Operational draught	6.30 m
Tonnage (grt)	2,183

PROPULSION

Main engine(s)	Burmeister & Wain diesel; 1,970 hp(m) (1.45 MW)

Propellers	CP propeller
Speed (cruising)	12.00 kt

BRIDGE NAVIGATION AIDS

Satellite	Yes
Radar	Yes
Gyrocompass	Yes
Speed log	Yes
Echo-sounder	Yes

HELIDECK

Size, aircraft capacity	2 Aerospatiale UH-13 Ecureuil 2

ACCOMMODATION

Crew	76

UPDATED

Bãrao De Teffé (Hartmut Ehlers)   **2000**/0017626

Brazilian Navy

Suboficial Oliveira

GENERAL

	Commissioned at Fortaleza for Naval Research Institute. Decommissioned in 1991 but retained in service as an AvPqOc (ocean survey craft).

Former names	DHN 02
	U 15
Official number	Camr 02
Built (yard and date)	Inace; commissioned 22 May 1981
Length overall	35.5 m

Breadth moulded	6.70 m		**Gyrocompass**	Yes
Operational draught	4.80 m		**Speed log**	Yes
			Echo-sounder	Yes

PROPULSION
Main engine(s)	2 diesels; 740 hp(m) (544 kW)
Propellers	2 shafts
Speed (cruising)	8.0 kt
Endurance	1,400 n miles at 8 kt

ACCOMMODATION
Crew	10

SURVEY SYSTEMS
Magnetometer	Yes
Gravimeter	Yes

BRIDGE NAVIGATION AIDS
Satellite	Yes
Radar	Racal Decca 110; I-band

VERIFIED

Suboficial Oliveira

2000/0056618

Directorate of Hydrography and Navigation

Taurus

GENERAL

Background information   Transferred from Royal Navy on 31 January 1995; ex "River Class" Buoy Tender fitted with second crane amidships for oceanographic research. Reclassified as a Naval Hydroceanographic vessel (NHo) on 7 May 1996.

Former names   *HMS Helmsdale (M 2010)*

Owner	Brazilian Navy	**Speed (cruising)**	10 kt
Official number	H 36	**Endurance**	4,500 n miles at 10 kt
Built (yard and date)	Richards (Shipbuilders) Ltd, Lowesoft, UK; commissioned 1 March 1986	**BRIDGE NAVIGATION AIDS**	
Length overall	47.5 m	**Radar**	2 × Racal Decca TM 1226C; I band
Breadth moulded	10.5 m		
Max draught	2.9 m	**ACCOMMODATION**	
		Crew	33
PROPULSION			
Main engine(s)	2 × Ruston 6RKC diesels; 3,100 hp (2.3 MW) sustained	**SURVEY SYSTEMS**	
		Multibeam/swath system	Simrad EM 1000
Propellers	twin shafts		
Speed (max)	14 kt		*NEW ENTRY*

Taurus   **2001**/0012954

Oceanographic Institute, São Paulo University

Prof W Besnard

GENERAL		**Gyrocompass**	Yes
Current operational status	Operates in the Atlantic Ocean	**Speed log**	Doppler log
Classification	DNV		
Built (yard and date)	1967	**DECK MACHINERY**	
Length overall	49.35 m	**A-frame(s)**	Stern
Breadth moulded	9.3 m	**Winches**	Oceanographic, 4,000 m, 1 t; trawl, 500 m, 2 t
Operational draught	4.3 m		
Tonnage (grt)	577		
		ACCOMMODATION	
PROPULSION		**Crew**	22
Main engine(s)	1 diesel engine, 960 hp at 310 rpm; auxiliary diesel, 290 hp	**Scientists/surveyors**	15
Propellers	2.26 m diameter, 310 rpm	**SCIENTIFIC SPACES**	
Speed (max)	12.5 kt	**Total scientific deck space**	60 m²
Speed (cruising)	10.5 kt	**Oceanographic wet lab**	7 m²
Endurance	5,000 n miles	**Multipurpose dry lab**	30 m²
Fuel capacity	103 m³		
Electrical power	110/220 V AC, 210 kVA, 3 phase, 60 Hz	**SURVEY SYSTEMS**	
		Echo-sounder (single beam)	38/120 kHz
Fresh water capacity	57 m³		
			UPDATED
BRIDGE NAVIGATION AIDS			
Satellite	Yes		
Radar	Yes		

BULGARIA

Institute of Oceanology

Akademik

GENERAL

Classification	KM*13-SRS
Built (yard and date)	1979
Length overall	56 m
Breadth moulded	10 m
Max draught	4.80
Tonnage (grt)	905
Displacement	1,225 t

PROPULSION

Main engine(s)	diesel, 1,000 hp at 375 rpm
Speed (cruising)	11.5 kt
Endurance	7,500 n miles/35 days
Fuel capacity	180 m³
Electrical power	400/230 V AC, 500 kVA, 3-phase, 50 Hz

BRIDGE NAVIGATION AIDS

Satellite	Yes
Radar	Yes
Gyrocompass	Yes
Speed log	Doppler log

DECK MACHINERY

Cranes	Stern, clearance above deck 11 m, outboard extension 10 m
A-frame(s)	Stern
Winches	3

ACCOMMODATION

Crew	26
Scientists/surveyors	16

SCIENTIFIC SPACES

Total scientific deck space	140 m²
Survey systems	
Sidescan sonar	Klein model 530T
Magnetometer	MPMP 01
Corer(s)	Gantry and vibro corers
Other sampling	SBE 32 carousel
Vehicle(s) (ROVs/AUVs and so on)	Manned submersible: PC-8B
Oceanographic sensors (CTDs/XBTs and so on)	SBE 911 plus CTD; Aarderaa current meter

SEISMIC SYSTEMS

Energy source (type and manufacturer)	SAK-3 sparker up to 10 kJ; GID boomer

VERIFIED

CANADA

Canadian Coast Guard

Alfred Needler

GENERAL

Comments	Home port: Dartmouth, Nova Scotia
Owner	Department of Fisheries and Oceans
Port of reg/flag	Ottawa
Official number	800746
Classification	Home Trade I; 1 ce Class 2
Call sign	CG2683
Built (yard and date)	Ferguson Industries Ltd, Pictou, Nova Scotia; 1982
Length overall	50.30 m
Breadth moulded	11.00 m
Max draught	4.90 m
Tonnage (grt)	958.9

PROPULSION

Main engine(s)	One Caterpillar 6 cyl diesel, 2,600 kW
Propellers	1 CPP
Speed (max)	14.0 kt
Speed (cruising)	12.00 kt
Endurance	3,000 n miles/30 days
Fuel capacity	209.5 m³
Fuel consumption	4.5 m³/day
Electrical power	1 × 250 kW generator; 2 × 200 kW generator; 1 × 125 kW emergency generator
Fresh water capacity	45 m³

BRIDGE NAVIGATION AIDS

Satellite	Magnavox MX-51R; Northstar 8000
Radar	Racal RM-1690 – S-Band; Racal 2490 X-Band; Racal RM-1690 X-Band
Gyrocompass	Sperry Mk 37
Speed log	Ben/Galatec Mk 3
Echo-sounder	Elac Laz 4400
Other ship navigation	Loran: Northstar 800X

COMMUNICATIONS

Inmarsat (type)	Magnavox MX2400
MF/HF	Harris RF3200; Skanti 8000; Skanti TRP8255S
VHF	King KY92; Sailor RT 146; Sailor RT 2048
Facsimile	Taiyo TF-733

SAFETY

Workboat/chase boat	Zodiac; RHI-5.48 m

DECK MACHINERY

Cranes	Atlas Polar – SWL 7 tons; HIAB hydrographic; plankton; net sounder
Winches	

ACCOMMODATION

Crew	29

SCIENTIFIC SPACES

Total scientific deck space	90 m²
Oceanographic wet lab	60 m²
Multipurpose dry lab	12 m²

SURVEY SYSTEMS

Sensors	
Echo-sounder (single beam)	ELAC LAZ 4400; Simrad EK38

UPDATED

Canadian Coast Guard

Calanus II

GENERAL

Background information	Inshore Fisheries research vessel; home port: Ste Flavie, Quebec
Port of reg/flag	Ottawa
Official number	814685
Classification	Home Trade II
Call sign	CG3187
Built (yard and date)	Chantier Naval Matane, Matane-sur-Mer, Québec; 1991
Length overall	19.92 m
Breadth moulded	6.9 m
Max draught	3.2 m
Tonnage (grt)	160

PROPULSION

Main engine(s)	geared diesel, 412 kW
Thrusters	yes
Propellers	1 × VPP
Speed (cruising)	9.5 kt
Endurance	30 days / 2,000 n miles
Fuel capacity	31 m³
Electrical power	1 × 50 kW generator; 1 × 40 kW generator
Fresh water capacity	5 m³

BRIDGE NAVIGATION AIDS

Satellite	2 × Northstar 941X; Motarola Port
Radar	2 × Racal Bridgemaster

Gyrocompass	Anschutz
Echo-sounder	YRC JFU216; Skipper GDS61
Other ship navigation	Loran: Raytheon 780

COMMUNICATIONS

Inmarsat (type)	Westinghouse
MF/HF	Skanti
VHF	Icom L; 2 × Motorola, Icom
Facsimile	Furuno Fax 207

SAFETY

Workboat/chase boat	Zodiac

DECK MACHINERY

Cranes	HIAB; telescopic swing arm aft
A-frame(s)	
Winches	Scientific: 2 at 250 kg; 1 at 150 kg; 2 at 1.8 t (one on 'A' frame)

ACCOMMODATION

Crew	5

SCIENTIFIC SPACES

Oceanographic wet lab	11 m²
Multipurpose dry lab	18.36 m²

NEW ENTRY

Canadian Coast Guard

Caligus

GENERAL

Background information	Inshore Fisheries research vessel; home port: Patricia Bay, British Columbia
Current operational status	operates in Pacific Ocean
Port of reg/flag	Ottawa
Official number	328127
Classification	Home Trade I
Call sign	CG2338
Built (yard and date)	John Manly Ltd, New Westminster, British Columbia; 1967
Length overall	16.8 m
Breadth moulded	4.5 m
Max draught	2.0 m
Tonnage (grt)	41.36

PROPULSION

Main engine(s)	GM 8V-71 geared diesel, 171 kW
Propellers	1 × FPP
Speed (cruising)	9 kt
Endurance	10 days / 1,000 n miles
Fuel capacity	4.5 m³
Electrical power	1 × 10 kW generator 1 × 7.5 kW generator

BRIDGE NAVIGATION AIDS

Satellite	Northstar 941X
Radar	Anritsu Simrad RA-722VA
Echo-sounder	FCW-1000
Other ship navigation	Loran: Furuno LP 1000

COMMUNICATIONS

MF/HF	Daniels DE1200
VHF	2 × Raytheon RAY-55

SAFETY

Workboat/chase boat	Zodiac

DECK MACHINERY

Cranes	boom on main mast: SWL 1.5 t
Winches	trawl; trawl drum; crab and prawn trap puller

ACCOMMODATION

Crew	5

NEW ENTRY

Canadian Coast Guard

J L Hart

GENERAL

Background information	Inshore Fisheries research vessel; home port: St Andrews, New Brunswick
Current operational status	operates in Canadian Maritimes
Port of reg/flag	Ottawa
Official number	347504
Classification	Home Trade II
Call sign	CG2661
Built (yard and date)	Industrie Marine de Caraquet, New Brunswick; 1974
Length overall	19.8 m
Breadth moulded	5.9 m
Max draught	3.2 m
Tonnage (grt)	89

PROPULSION

Main engine(s)	Caterpillar 6 cylinder, 317 kW
Propellers	1 × CPP
Speed (cruising)	9 kt
Endurance	14 days / 3,000 n miles
Fuel capacity	17 m³
Fuel consumption	1.2 m³/day
Electrical power	Detroit Diesel 3 cylinder, 550 kW
Fresh water capacity	1.5 m³

BRIDGE NAVIGATION AIDS

Satellite	Magnavox MX-200

Radar	Racal Bridgemaster ARPA; Furuno ARPA
Gyrocompass	Sperry Mk 37
Speed log	Sperry Doppler SRD-301
Echo-sounder	Elac LAZ 440; Elac LAZ 2110
Other ship navigation	Loran: Raytheon 398

COMMUNICATIONS

Inmarsat (type)	Westinghouse 1000 MSat
MF/HF	Daniels 24; Icom IC-M710
VHF	3 × Sailor RT144

SAFETY

Workboat/chase boat	Zodiac Hurricane

DECK MACHINERY

Cranes	HIAB seacrane: SWL 3.4 t
A-frame(s)	aft
Winches	yes

ACCOMMODATION

Crew	5

SCIENTIFIC SPACES

Oceanographic wet lab	78.48 m²

NEW ENTRY

J L Hart   *2001*/0102435

Canadian Coast Guard

Hudson

GENERAL

Comments	Home port: Dartmouth, Nova Scotia
Owner	Department of Fisheries and Oceans
Port of reg/flag	Ottawa
Official number	320936
Classification	Lloyds Register 100A
Call sign	CGDG
Built (yard and date)	Saint John SB & DD Ltd, New Brunswick; 1963
Rebuilt (yard and date)	Saint John Drydock; 1990
Length overall	90.39 m
Breadth moulded	15.40 m
Max draught	6.80 m
Tonnage (grt)	3,740

PROPULSION

Main engine(s)	16 cylinder 4 × Alco diesel-electric, 6,469 kW; auxiliary diesels, 1,640 hp
Thrusters	Bow
Propellers	2 fixed pitch
Speed (max)	17.0 kt
Speed (cruising)	10.5 kt
Endurance	23,100 n miles/105 days
Fuel capacity	1,268 m³
Fuel consumption	7.6 m³/day
Electrical power	2 Caterpillar D358D each 611 kW
Fresh water capacity	105 m³

BRIDGE NAVIGATION AIDS

Satellite	Magnavox MX-380
Radar	Racal Bridgemaster II – X-Band Racal Bridgemaster – S-Band
Gyrocompass	Sperry Mk 37
Speed log	Sperry Doppler SRD-301
Echo-sounder	Yes
Other ship navigation	Loran: Trimble 10X

COMMUNICATIONS

MF/HF	Harris RF-3200E; 2 Skanti HF-55B
VHF	2 Sailor C-403A
Facsimile	Taiyo Fax TF-733

SAFETY

Lifeboats	1
Workboat/chase boat	Avon RHI; workboat; launch

HELIDECK

Size, aircraft capacity	Flight deck: 1,380 m² Hangar: 280 m²

DECK MACHINERY

Cranes	Arva Telescopic; Hampton; SWL 4.3 t; grove crane
A-frame(s)	stern, clearance above deck 4 m, outboard extension 2 m, SWL 5 t
Winches	Pengo 150; Swan 29

ACCOMMODATION

Crew	37
Scientists/surveyors	37

SCIENTIFIC SPACES

Oceanographic wet lab	20 m²
Multipurpose dry lab	hydrographic: 112 m²; general purpose: 18 m²
Chemistry lab	Geo-chem: 40 m²

SURVEY SYSTEMS

Echo-sounder (single beam)	Elac Laz 440

UPDATED

Hudson

2001/0101387

Canadian Coast Guard

John P Tully

GENERAL

Comments	Offshore research and survey vessel; home port: Patricia Bay, British Columbia
Owner	Department of Fisheries and Oceans
Port of reg/flag	Ottawa
Official number	804457
Classification	Lloyds Register A1
Call sign	CG2958
Built (yard and date)	Bel-Air Shipyard Ltd, Vancouver; 1985
Length overall	68.9 m
Breadth moulded	14.5 m
Max draught	4.50 m
Tonnage (grt)	2,021

PROPULSION

Main engine(s)	Two Deutz 8-cylinder geared diesels, 2,757 kW
Thrusters	Bow: 800 hp; Stern: 350 hp
Propellers	One CP propeller
Speed (max)	13.5 kt
Speed (cruising)	10.0 kt
Endurance	12,000 n miles/50 days
Fuel capacity	483 m^3
Fuel consumption	2.1 m^3/day
Electrical power	Three generators, one emergency generator: each 470 kW
Fresh water capacity	31 m^3

BRIDGE NAVIGATION AIDS

Satellite	Trimble XL-GPS
Radar	Sperry 3400M; Sperry 2500M
Gyrocompass	Sperry Mk 227; Anschutz 20
Speed log	Furuno CI-30
Echo-sounder	JRC Jev-216; Furuno FE-881
Other ship navigation	Loran: JRC JNA-760

COMMUNICATIONS

Inmarsat (type)	1560602/TULL
MF/HF	Shanti TRP-8253-S
VHF	Sailor C-403
	Collins
Facsimile	Furuno 207 R 214

SAFETY

Workboat/chase boat	Four sounding launchers

HELIDECK

Size, aircraft capacity	190 m^2 flight deck

DECK MACHINERY

Cranes	Hampton Crane SWL: 5 tons; HIAB stores crane – forward
A-frame(s)	4.3 m
Winches	Yes

ACCOMMODATION

Crew	20
Scientists/surveyors	20

SCIENTIFIC SPACES

Oceanographic wet lab	6 m^2
Multipurpose dry lab	50 m^2

SURVEY SYSTEMS

Sensors	
Echo-sounder (single beam)	Simrad EA-500

UPDATED

John P Tully

2001/0101389

Canadian Coast Guard

Limnos

GENERAL

Background information	Coastal research and survey vessel
Current operational status	operates in Central and Arctic region
Port of reg/flag	Ottawa
Official number	328088
Classification	Inland Waters I; 900 A1 Ice Class 1
Call sign	CG2350
Built (yard and date)	Port Weller Dry Docks Ltd, St Catherines, Ontario; 1968
Rebuilt (yard and date)	New engines; 1981
Length overall	44.81 m
Breadth moulded	9.75 m
Max draught	2.6 m
Tonnage (grt)	459.95

PROPULSION

Main engine(s)	2 × Caterpillar 3412, 750 kW
Propellers	2
Speed (max)	10 kt
Speed (cruising)	10 kt
Endurance	14 days / 3,500 n miles at 10 kt
Fuel capacity	80 m³
Fuel consumption	3.5 m³/day
Electrical power	2 × 150 kW generators 1 × 100 kW emergency generator
Fresh water capacity	60 m³

BRIDGE NAVIGATION AIDS

Satellite	2 × Trimble NT 200D
Radar	2 × Racal Decca Bridgemaster
Gyrocompass	Arma Brown Mk 10
Echo-sounder	Lowrange; Elac

COMMUNICATIONS

VHF	3 × Sailor Compact VHF-RT 2047
Facsimile	Alden AE 900

SAFETY

Workboat/chase boat	Boston Whaler, 5m Crane; Ambar 550, Crane

DECK MACHINERY

Cranes	Galion crane SWL: 15 t; 2 × Hiabs
A-frame(s)	yes
Winches	6 × Limnological

ACCOMMODATION

Crew	14 (16 berths available)

SCIENTIFIC SPACES

Oceanographic wet lab	6 m²
Multipurpose dry lab	10 m²

SURVEY SYSTEMS

Echo-sounder (single beam)	Atlas DESO 10

NEW ENTRY

Canadian Coast Guard

Louis M Lauzier

GENERAL

Background information	Coastal research and survey vessel; under charter to Memorial University of Newfoundland; home port: Burlington, Ontario
Current operational status	Operates in Central and Arctic region
Port of reg/flag	Ottawa
Official number	370575
Classification	Home Trade II
Call sign	CG3159
Built (yard and date)	Breton Industries Ltd, Port Hawkesbury, Nova Scotia; 1976
Rebuilt (yard and date)	New engines; 1986
Length overall	37.1 m
Breadth moulded	8.2 m
Max draught	2.13 m
Tonnage (grt)	322.25

PROPULSION

Main engine(s)	2 × Cummins K2300, 1,200 kW
Thrusters	bow
Propellers	2 × FPP
Speed (cruising)	12.5 kt
Endurance	1,800 n miles
Fuel capacity	53 m³
Electrical power	2 × 140 kW generators

BRIDGE NAVIGATION AIDS

Satellite	Trimble Navtrac XL
Radar	JRC JMA-627-6 – X band; Decca Racal 6520/CAD- X band
Gyrocompass	Sperry Mk 37
Echo-sounder	Elac LAZ 72; Lowrange X-16
Other ship navigation	Loran: Furuno LC 90

COMMUNICATIONS

VHF	Motorola PT 400; Sailor RT 2047

NEW ENTRY

Canadian Coast Guard

Matthew

GENERAL

Owner	Department of Fisheries and Oceans
Port of reg/flag	Ottawa
Official number	813730
Classification	Lloyds Register
Call sign	VOSR
Built (yard and date)	Versatile Pacific Shipyards Inc, North Vancouver, BC; 1990
Length overall	50.30 m

Breadth moulded	10.50 m	**MF/HF**	2 Skanti TRP82535; Unident Grant
Max draught	4.3 m	**VHF**	3 Sailor C403
Tonnage (grt)	857	**Facsimile**	Taiyo TF-733

PROPULSION

Main engine(s)	2 Caterpillar 3508 – 8 cylinder diesels	**SAFETY**	
		Workboat/chase boat	Zodiac 520; 2 Sheppard Dunlop; 2 hydrographic launchers
Thrusters	Bow		
Propellers	2 cpp		
Speed (max)	12 kt	**HELIDECK**	
Speed (cruising)	12 kt	**Size, aircraft capacity**	Flight Deck: 90 m²
Endurance	4,000 n miles/20 days		
Fuel capacity	120 m³	**DECK MACHINERY**	
Fuel consumption	6 m³/day	**Cranes**	Hiab 60 Sea SWL: 3.4 t; Hiab 200 Sea
Electrical power	3 Caterpillar generators; each 250 kW		
Fresh water capacity	7 m³	**ACCOMMODATION**	
		Crew	13

BRIDGE NAVIGATION AIDS

Satellite	Magnavox MX-300	**SURVEY SYSTEMS**	
Radar	Racal Bridgemaster; Racal BT502	**Echo-sounder (single beam)**	Elac LAZ 4400
Gyrocompass	Anschutz Kiel Mk 4	**Multibeam/swath system**	Simrad BM 100
Speed log	Yes		
Echo-sounder	Yes		*UPDATED*

COMMUNICATIONS

Inmarsat (type)	Magnavox Mk 2400

Canadian Coast Guard

Navicula

GENERAL

Background information	Inshore Fisheries research vessel; home port: Dartmouth, Nova Scotia	**Length overall**	19.8 m
		Breadth moulded	5.8 m
		Max draught	3.2 m
Current operational status	operates in Canadian Maritimes	**Tonnage (grt)**	80.2
Port of reg/flag	Ottawa		
Official number	328673	**PROPULSION**	
Classification	Fishing/Home Trade II	**Main engine(s)**	Detroit diesel 12 cylinder, 272 kW
Call sign	CG2364	**Propellers**	1 × FPP
Built (yard and date)	Atlantic Shipbuilding, Lunenburg, Nova Scotia; 1968	**Speed (max)**	10 kt
		Speed (cruising)	9 kt
		Endurance	5 days / 1,000 n miles

Navicula   *2001*/0102436

Fuel capacity	8.8 m³	**SAFETY**	
Fuel consumption	1.6 m³/day	**Workboat/chase boat**	Zodiac
Electrical power	General Motors, 10 kW		
Fresh water capacity	4.5 m³	**DECK MACHINERY**	
		Cranes	cargo boom
BRIDGE NAVIGATION AIDS		**A-frame(s)**	aft
Satellite	Magnavox MX-200	**Winches**	trawl
Radar	2 × Racal Bridgemaster		
Gyrocompass	Sperry Mk 37	**ACCOMMODATION**	
Speed log	Sperry Doppler SRD-301	**Crew**	3
Echo-sounder	Elac LAZ 72; Elac LAZ 2220		
Other ship navigation	Loran: Northstar 800	**SCIENTIFIC SPACES**	
		Oceanographic wet lab	26 m²
COMMUNICATIONS		**Multipurpose dry lab**	20 m²
Inmarsat (type)	H9		
MF/HF	2 × Daniels 1200	**SURVEY SYSTEMS**	
VHF	Sailor Compact RT 2048	**Other sampling**	flounder trawl

NEW ENTRY

Canadian Coast Guard

Opilio

GENERAL		**Gyrocompass**	Anschutz
Background information	Inshore Fisheries research vessel; home port: Shippegan, New Brunswick	**Echo-sounder**	Furuno UIO; Sitex 1500EX
		Other ship navigation	Loran: Raytheon 570
Current operational status	operates in Canadian Maritimes	**COMMUNICATIONS**	
Port of reg/flag	Ottawa	**Inmarsat (type)**	Westinghouse 1000 M-Sat
Official number	811804	**MF/HF**	Motorola IC-M700
Classification	Home Trade II	**VHF**	Raytheon 53; King 7200
Call sign	CFD2576	**Facsimile**	Furuno NX-500
Built (yard and date)	Sea Boats Ltd, Cocagne, New Brunswick; 1989	**SAFETY**	
		Workboat/chase boat	Zodiac, 16 ft
Length overall	18.2 m		
Breadth moulded	6.2 m	**DECK MACHINERY**	
Max draught	3.0 m	**Cranes**	HIAB: SWL 1 t; cargo derrick
Tonnage (grt)	73.98	**Winches**	2 × drag winches 3.9 t at 240 rpm; sampling; gantry
PROPULSION			
Main engine(s)	Beaudoin geared diesel, 285 kW	**ACCOMMODATION**	
Thrusters	bow	**Crew**	3
Propellers	1 × VPP		
Speed (cruising)	9 kt	**SCIENTIFIC SPACES**	
Endurance	4 days / 800 n miles	**Total scientific deck space**	wet trawl deck: 12 m²
Fuel capacity	8.2 m³		
Fuel consumption	1.1 m³/day	**SURVEY SYSTEMS**	
Electrical power	2 × 40 kW generators	**Other sampling**	flounder trawl
Fresh water capacity	3.6 m³		
BRIDGE NAVIGATION AIDS			
Satellite	Northstar 941X		
Radar	Racal Bridgemaster; Furuno		

NEW ENTRY

Canadian Coast Guard

Pandallus III

GENERAL		**Breadth moulded**	4.5 m
Background information	Inshore Fisheries research vessel; home port: St Andrews, New Brunswick	**Max draught**	1.8 m
		Tonnage (grt)	28.1
Current operational status	operates in Canadian Maritimes	**PROPULSION**	
Port of reg/flag	Ottawa	**Main engine(s)**	Detroit 6 cylinder geared diesel, 692 kW
Official number	195320		
Classification	Home Trade II	**Propellers**	1 × FPP
Call sign	CF4703	**Speed (cruising)**	9 kt
Built (yard and date)	Navy Island Marine, Dartmouth, Nova Scotia; 1986	**Endurance**	216 n miles
		Fuel capacity	2.3 m³
Length overall	12.8 m	**Electrical power**	Kobota 4 cylinders, 15 kW

BRIDGE NAVIGATION AIDS

Satellite	Raytheon Raystar 390
Radar	Furuno FR-1830 – X band
Echo-sounder	Simrad Skipper 603

COMMUNICATIONS

VHF	Sailor R/T 144

DECK MACHINERY

Cranes	HIAB 60 SWL: 1.1 t

ACCOMMODATION

Crew	2

NEW ENTRY

Canadian Coast Guard

Parizeau

GENERAL

Comments	Home port: Dartmouth, Nova Scotia
Owner	Department of Fisheries and Oceans
Port of reg/flag	Ottawa
Official number	328076
Classification	Home Trade II
Call sign	CGBS
Built (yard and date)	Burrard Dry Dock Co Ltd, North Vancouver; 1967
Length overall	64.5 m
Breadth moulded	12.2 m
Max draught	4.60 m
Tonnage (grt)	1,314

PROPULSION

Main engine(s)	2 Deutz 8 cylinder diesel, 1,967 kW
Thrusters	bow
Propellers	2 CPP
Speed (max)	14.0 kt
Speed (cruising)	10.0 kt
Endurance	17,250 n miles/60 days
Fuel capacity	416.5 m³
Fuel consumption	6.9 m³/day
Electrical power	3 Caterpillar 3,400 each 312 kW
Fresh water capacity	120 m³

BRIDGE NAVIGATION AIDS

Satellite	Magnavox MX-300
Radar	2 Racal Bridgemasters
Gyrocompass	Sperry Mk 37

Echo-sounder	Elac LAZ 4400
Other ship navigation	Loran: Northstar 800

COMMUNICATIONS

Inmarsat (type)	1561504/PARI Magnavox UX 2400
MF/HF	Skanti TRP 82535
VHF	Sailor CH03; RT 2048
Facsimile	Taiyo TF-733

SAFETY

Lifeboats	1
Workboat/chase boat	Zodiac Hurricane

DECK MACHINERY

Cranes	Jacobs Crane SWL 119 t HIAB 180
A-frame(s)	Stern, clearance above deck 4 m, outboard extension 1 m
Winches	CTD

ACCOMMODATION

Crew	20

SCIENTIFIC SPACES

Total scientific deck space	200 m²
Multipurpose dry lab	Upper Hydrographic: 70 m² Lower Hydrographic: 40 m² Dry: 15 m²

SURVEY SYSTEMS

Echo-sounder (single beam)	Elac Laz 4400

UPDATED

Canadian Coast Guard

W E Ricker

GENERAL

Background information	Offshore Fisheries research vessel; home port: Patricia Bay, British Columbia
Former names	*Callistratus*
Current operational status	operates in Pacific Ocean
Port of reg/flag	Ottawa
Official number	372369
Classification	Ice Class: 100A1; Home Trade II
Call sign	CG2965
Built (yard and date)	Narasaki Senpakukogyo Ltd, Muroran Hokkaido, Japan; 1978
Length overall	58.0 m
Breadth moulded	9.5 m
Max draught	4.5 m
Tonnage (grt)	1104.5

PROPULSION

Main engine(s)	Akasaka AH 40 6-cylinder geared diesel, 1,863 kW

Thrusters	bow
Propellers	1 × CPP
Speed (max)	11.5 kt
Speed (cruising)	10 kt
Endurance	50 days / 6,000 n miles
Fuel capacity	290 m³
Fuel consumption	5 m³/day
Electrical power	3 × 150 kW generators
Fresh water capacity	31 m³

BRIDGE NAVIGATION AIDS

Satellite	2 × Northstar 941
Radar	JRC JMA-830 – S band; Raytheon M34 – X band
Gyrocompass	Sperry Mk 37
Speed log	JRC JLN-202
Echo-sounder	Simrad ITI; Simrad EQ55; Skipper SRP690
Other ship navigation	Loran: Raytheon Raynav 780

COMMUNICATIONS

Inmarsat (type)	JRC JUE-45A
MF/HF	Kenwood R-2000
VHF	Collins VHF 251; Sailor RT146; Vertex 99
Facsimile	Furuno Fax 108

SAFETY

Workboat/chase boat	2 × RHI Zodiac

DECK MACHINERY

Winches	Swan CTD

ACCOMMODATION

Crew	19

SCIENTIFIC SPACES

Oceanographic wet lab	51 m²
Multipurpose dry lab	13 m2; Hydrographic: 11 m²

SURVEY SYSTEMS

Echo-sounder (single beam)	Simrad ED 500
Sidescan sonar	Wesmar

NEW ENTRY

Canadian Coast Guard

Shamook

GENERAL

Background information	Inshore Fisheries research vessel; home port: St John's, Newfoundland
Current operational status	operates off of Newfoundland
Port of reg/flag	Ottawa
Official number	347507
Classification	Home Trade II
Call sign	CG2676
Built (yard and date)	Georgetown Shipyard, Georgetown, Prince Edward Island; 1975
Length overall	24.9 m
Breadth moulded	6.7 m
Max draught	3.5 m
Tonnage (grt)	117

PROPULSION

Main engine(s)	Caterpillar D3795SCAC 8 cylinders, 416 kW
Propellers	1 × CPP
Speed (max)	10 kt
Speed (cruising)	8 kt
Endurance	5 days / 2,500 n miles
Fuel capacity	23 m³
Fuel consumption	1.6 m³/day
Electrical power	1 × 40 kW generator; 1 × 15 kW generator
Fresh water capacity	2.3 m³

BRIDGE NAVIGATION AIDS

Satellite	2 × Northstar

Radar	Racal BM 914 – X band; Raython R41 – X band
Gyrocompass	Sperry Mk 37
Speed log	Sperry SRD-301
Echo-sounder	3 × Simrad EQ100; Simrad EQ50; Suzuri Sonar

COMMUNICATIONS

Inmarsat (type)	M-Sat
MF/HF	Harris RF-3200
VHF	Raython 580; Triton M100

SAFETY

Workboat/chase boat	Zodiac

DECK MACHINERY

Cranes	TICO: SWL: 8 t
A-frame(s)	2 × Gallows Frames
Winches	2 × trawl, aft

ACCOMMODATION

Crew	6

SCIENTIFIC SPACES

Total scientific deck space	wet aft deck: 13 m²
Multipurpose dry lab	10 m²

SURVEY SYSTEMS

Sidescan sonar	yes

NEW ENTRY

Canadian Coast Guard

Shark

GENERAL

Background information	Inshore Fisheries research vessel; home port: Burlington, Ontario
Current operational status	operates in central Canada and Arctic regions
Port of reg/flag	Ottawa
Official number	314694
Classification	Inland Waters II
Call sign	VX5809
Built (yard and date)	Hike Metal Products Ltd, Wheatley, Ontario; 1971
Rebuilt (yard and date)	New engines; 1997/98
Length overall	16.0 m
Breadth moulded	4.5 m
Max draught	1.2 m
Tonnage (grt)	29.82

PROPULSION

Main engine(s)	2 × Caterpillar 3126 6 cylinders, 630 kW
Propellers	2 × FPP
Speed (max)	14 kt
Speed (cruising)	12 kt
Endurance	1.5 days / 200 n miles
Fuel capacity	1.8 m³
Fuel consumption	0.5 m³/day
Electrical power	Onan, 15 kW
Fresh water capacity	0.5 m³

BRIDGE NAVIGATION AIDS

Satellite	Trimble Nautrac XL
Radar	Racal Bridgemaster; Racal Decca 130

Gyrocompass	Arma Brown	A-frame(s)	yes
Echo-sounder	Lowrange X-16	Winches	Hawbolt HSF 1216 AS Trawl
Other ship navigation	Loran: Micrologic ML 8000 II		

COMMUNICATIONS

VHF	2 × Sailor 2000

ACCOMMODATION

Crew	2

SAFETY

Workboat/chase boat	Zodiac

SCIENTIFIC SPACES

Multipurpose dry lab	7.5 m²

DECK MACHINERY

SURVEY SYSTEMS

Echo-sounder (single beam)	SI-TEX-CUS III
Sidescan sonar	yes

Cranes	HIAB: SWL: 0.5 t

NEW ENTRY

Shark   *2001*/0102252

Canadian Coast Guard

Teleost

GENERAL

	Offshore fisheries research vessel home port: St John's, Newfoundland
Port of reg/flag	Ottawa
Official number	808657
Classification	LR Ice Class 1A; Home Trade II
Call sign	CGCB
Built (yard and date)	Langston Ship – Batbyggeri AS, Tomrefjord, Norway; 1988
Rebuilt (yard and date)	Marystown Shipyard; 1994
Length overall	63.0 m
Breadth moulded	14.2 m
Max draught	7.2 m
Tonnage (grt)	2,405

PROPULSION

Main engine(s)	Caterpillar 3606TA, 2982 kW
Thrusters	Bow
Propellers	1 CPP
Speed (max)	13.5 kt
Speed (cruising)	12.0 kt

Endurance	12,000 n miles
Fuel capacity	400 m³
Electrical power	2 generators: 1,456 kW, 1,070 kW

BRIDGE NAVIGATION AIDS

Satellite	Furuno GP-300; Furuno GP-500
Radar	Furuno 2830S X band; Furuno 8030S S band
	Furuno FR-8030D X band
Gyrocompass	2 Sperry Mk 37
Speed log	Sperry SRD-331
Echo-sounder	2 Simrad ES-500
Other ship navigation	Loran: Furuno LC 90

COMMUNICATIONS

MF/HF	Skanti TRP 7000; ICOM IC-R71A
VHF	Skanti RT 2047; Skanti VHF 3000
Facsimile	Furuno FAX-208

SAFETY

Workboat/chase boat	Seabearer FRC, 7 m

DECK MACHINERY

Winches   6 hydraulic; 4 oceanographic

ACCOMMODATION

Scientists/surveyors   20

SURVEY SYSTEMS

Echo-sounder (single beam)   Simrad EA500; Simrad EK500

Sidescan sonar   Simrad 240 SR

UPDATED

Teleost   *2001*/0056713

Canadian Coast Guard

Vector

GENERAL

Background information   Coastal research and survey vessel; home port: Patricia Bay, British Columbia

Current operational status   operates in Pacific Ocean

Port of reg/flag   Ottawa

Official number   328079

Classification   Home Trade II

Vector   *2001*/0101392

Call sign	CGBW	**Gyrocompass**	Sperry Mk 37
Built (yard and date)	Yarrows Ltd, Esquimault, British Columbia; 1967	**Echo-sounder**	Furuno FCV-251 JRC RD-5000
Rebuilt (yard and date)	main engine modernisation; 1995	**Other ship navigation**	Loran: Furuno LC 80
Length overall	39.74 m		
Breadth moulded	9.46 m		
Max draught	3.5 m	**COMMUNICATIONS**	
Tonnage (grt)	515	**MF/HF**	2 × Scanti TRP 8253 S
		VHF	Sailor RM2042; ICOM IC-M80
PROPULSION		**Facsimile**	Furuno Fax 208 Mk2
Main engine(s)	Caterpillar 3208 geared diesel, 597 kW	**SAFETY**	
Thrusters	bow	**Workboat/chase boat**	Boston Whaler, 4.9m
Propellers	1 × CPP		
Speed (max)	12 kt	**DECK MACHINERY**	
Speed (cruising)	10 kt	**Cranes**	ARVA crane SWL: 4 t
Endurance	20 days / 3,500 n miles	**A-frame(s)**	aft deck: 2
Fuel capacity	74 m³	**Winches**	various
Fuel consumption	1.8 m³/day		
Electrical power	Caterpillar 3306, 370 kW Caterpillar 3406, 370 kW	**SCIENTIFIC SPACES**	
		Multipurpose dry lab	65 m²
Fresh water capacity	46 m³		
		SURVEY SYSTEMS	
BRIDGE NAVIGATION AIDS		**Echo-sounder (single beam)**	Simrad EA 500
Radar	Decca Racal 2090 BT; Raytheon M25		

NEW ENTRY

Canadian Coast Guard

Wilfred Templeman

GENERAL		**Built (yard and date)**	Ferguson Industries Ltd, Pictou, Nova Scotia; 1981
Background information	Offshore Fisheries research vessel; home port: St John's, Newfoundland	**Length overall**	50.3 m
		Breadth moulded	11.0 m
Current operational status	operates off Newfoundland	**Max draught**	4.3 m
Port of reg/flag	Ottawa	**Tonnage (grt)**	925
Official number	800741		
Classification	Ice Class: 100A1 Class 2; Home Trade I	**PROPULSION**	
		Main engine(s)	Alco 12 cylinder Geared Diesel, 1,471 kW
Call sign	CGDV		

Wilfred Templeman

Propellers	1 × CPP
Speed (max)	11 kt
Speed (cruising)	9 kt
Endurance	25 days / 6,000 n miles
Fuel capacity	228.5 m³
Fuel consumption	6.8 m³/day
Electrical power	350 kW DC generator for trawl winch; 2 × 196 kW generators; 125 kW Emergency Generator
Fresh water capacity	45 m³

BRIDGE NAVIGATION AIDS

Satellite	Trimble NT200D
Radar	Raytheon M34 – S band; Raytheon M34 – X band
Gyrocompass	Sperry Mk 37
Speed log	JRC JLN-612
Echo-sounder	Furuno CN100; Simrad 11000; Furuno CN110
Other ship navigation	Loran: Furuno LC 90; Seimac 8000

COMMUNICATIONS

Inmarsat (type)	Magnavox MX2400
MF/HF	Marconi SM100; Skanti TRP8253S
VHF	Telex TEL66T; SRA ME61
Facsimile	Furuno Fax 208

SAFETY

Workboat/chase boat	FRC Hurricane 470

DECK MACHINERY

Cranes	HIAB: SWL 1.25 t; HIAB: port
Winches	trawl; plankton

ACCOMMODATION

Crew	19

SCIENTIFIC SPACES

Oceanographic wet lab	60 m²
Multipurpose dry lab	10 m²; Hydrographic: 10 m²

SURVEY SYSTEMS

Echo-sounder (single beam)	Simrad EK 500; Simrad EK 38

NEW ENTRY

Canadian Coast Guard

R B Young

GENERAL

Background information	Inshore research and survey vessel; home port: Patricia Bay, British Columbia
Current operational status	operates in Pacific Ocean
Port of reg/flag	Ottawa
Official number	811822
Classification	Home Trade II
Call sign	CG3253
Built (yard and date)	Allied Shipbuilders Ltd, North Vancouver, British Columbia; 1990
Length overall	32.3 m
Breadth moulded	8.0 m
Max draught	2.3 m
Tonnage (grt)	299.96

PROPULSION

Main engine(s)	2 × Caterpillar 6 cylinders, 480 kW
Thrusters	bow
Propellers	2 × CPP
Speed (max)	11.6 kt
Speed (cruising)	10 kt
Endurance	20 days / 5,000 n miles
Fuel capacity	51 m³
Fuel consumption	2 m³/day
Electrical power	2 × 95 kW Generators
Fresh water capacity	11.1 m³

BRIDGE NAVIGATION AIDS

Satellite	Northstar 941X
Radar	2 × Ratheon R81
Gyrocompass	Sperry Mk 37
Speed log	DRC 203 Dopplet
Echo-sounder	Furuno FE880
Other ship navigation	Loran: Raynav 780

COMMUNICATIONS

Inmarsat (type)	Autotel
MF/HF	Skanti
VHF	ICOM M120; MCX 1000 / Skanti
Facsimile	Navtex / Furuno

SAFETY

Workboat/chase boat	RHI Zodiac; 2 × hydrographic launches

DECK MACHINERY

Cranes	Hiab
A-frame(s)	yes

SCIENTIFIC SPACES

Oceanographic wet lab	17 m²

SURVEY SYSTEMS

Multibeam/swath system	Simrad EM1002

NEW ENTRY

Naval Research Establishment

Quest

GENERAL

Built for the Naval Research Establishment of the Defence Research Board for acoustic, hydrographic and general oceanographic work.

Capable of operating in heavy ice in the company of an icebreaker. Based at Halifax and does line array acoustic research in the straits of the northern archipelago.

Planned to conduct TIAPS trials (towed integrated active/passive sonar) in 2000.

Official number   AGOR 172
Built (yard and date)   Burrard, Vancouver; launched 9 July 1968, commissioned 21 August 1969
Rebuilt (yard and date)   Mid-life update in 1997-99 included new communications and navigation equipment and improved noise insulation
Length overall   71.6 m
Breadth moulded   12.8 m
Operational draught   4.60 m

PROPULSION
Main engine(s)   Diesel-electric; four Fairbanks-Morse 38D8-1/8-9 diesel generators; 4.36 MW; 2 GE motors
Propellers   2 cp propellers
Speed (max)   16 kt
Speed (cruising)   12 kt
Endurance   10,000 n miles at 12 kt

ACCOMMODATION
Crew   55

VERIFIED

Quest (van Ginderen Collection)   *2000*/0056684

CHILE

Hydrographic and Oceanographic Service, (SHOA)

Vidal Gormaz

GENERAL BACKGROUND
'Robert D Conrad' Class (AGOR)
Transferred from USA on 28 September 1992. This is the first class of ships designed and built by the US Navy for oceanographic research. Fitted with instrumentation and laboratories to measure gravity and magnetism, water temperature, sound transmission in water, and the profile of the ocean floor. Special features include 10 t capacity boom and winches for handling over-the-side equipment

Former names   *Thomas Washington*
Owner   Chilean Navy
Official number   AGOR 60
Built (yard and date)   Marinette Marine, USA; Commissioned 27 Sep 1965
Length overall   63.60 m
Breadth moulded   12.0 m
Operational draught   4.65 m
Tonnage (grt)   1,490

PROPULSION
Main engine(s)   2 Cummins diesel generators; 1,000 hp (746 kW)
Thrusters   Bow: Western Gear
Propellers   1 × 2.41 m diameter

Speed (max)   12.5 kt
Speed (cruising)   10 kt
Endurance   12,000 n miles at 12 kt
Fuel capacity   306 m³
Electrical power   450 V AC, 250/750 kVA, 3 phase, 60 Hz
Fresh water capacity   27 m³

BRIDGE NAVIGATION AIDS
Satellite   Yes
Radar   2 × Furuno FR 1662S
Gyrocompass   Sperry Mk 37
Speed log   Ametek Straza MRK 4015A
Echo-sounder   3 × Furuno FE-600

DECK MACHINERY
Cranes   Stern
A-frame(s)   Yes
Winches   2 × oceanographic, 5,000 m; Western Gear HWH 30A, 70 mm conducting cable; Interocean Western Gear geological, 7,000 m

Accommodation	
Crew	32
Scientists/surveyors	13

SCIENTIFIC SPACES

Total scientific deck space	102 m²
Oceanographic wet lab	19 m²
Multipurpose dry lab	130 m²

SURVEY SYSTEMS

Sensors	Sector scan sonar, 3/12 kHz
Echo-sounder (single beam)	Edo western 3.5/12 kHz
Multibeam/swath system	Sea Beam
Magnetometer	Yes
Corer(s)	Piston, 3 m
Grab(s)	Yes
Other sampling	24 bottle rosette, 3 litre Niskin bottles
Oceanographic sensors (CTDs/XBTs and so on)	XBT; CTD: SBE 19; SBE 25

Vidal Gormaz (van Ginderen Collection)   **2000**/0056729

UPDATED

Instituto de Fomento Pesquero (IFOP)

Abate Molina

GENERAL

Current operational status	Operates in the Pacific Ocean
Classification	NKK
Built (yard and date)	1990
Length overall	43.6 m
Breadth moulded	8.3 m
Operational draught	3.1 m
Tonnage (grt)	426

PROPULSION

Main engine(s)	1 diesel engine, 1,400 hp at 800 rpm; Auxiliary diesel, 440 hp
Propellers	2.3 m diameter, 289 rpm
Speed (cruising)	12 kt
Endurance	8,000 n miles
Fuel capacity	150 m³
Electrical power	225/460 V AC, 180 kVA, 3 phase, 60 Hz
Fresh water capacity	50 m³

BRIDGE NAVIGATION AIDS

Satellite	JRC JLR-4200
Radar	2 × JRC JMA 527
Gyrocompass	Tokimec
Speed log	JRC NEU-51

COMMUNICATIONS

Inmarsat (type)	Furuno S-18
MF/HF	Taiyo Musen. TD-C338 Mk II
Facsimile	JRC JAX-39; Navtex: NCR-300A

DECK MACHINERY

Cranes	Hydraulic, midships, 10.9 m, SWL 500 kg
Winches	1 × hydraulic; 2 × oceanographic; 1 × electric

ACCOMMODATION

Crew	13
Scientists/surveyors	13

SCIENTIFIC SPACES

Oceanographic wet lab	10 m²
Multipurpose dry lab	9 m²

SURVEY SYSTEMS

Sensors	Net sounder: Furuno FNR-80
Echo-sounder (single beam)	Simrad EK-500
Corer(s)	Piston: TSK 1101-C
Oceanographic sensors (CTDs/XBTs and so on)	EG&G CTDO Mk III; TSK/ Sippican XBT; TSK Mod 1103-A; Furuno: ADCP

UPDATED

CHINA, PEOPLE'S REPUBLIC

Dalian Fisheries College

Fisheries College No. 2

GENERAL			Length overall	43.5 m
Classification	ZC		Breadth moulded	7.60 m
Built (yard and date)	1988		Operational draught	2.80 m

PROPULSION		ACCOMMODATION	
Main engine(s)	Diesel; 600 bhp at 450 rpm	Crew	18
Speed (max)	12.5 kt	Scientists/surveyors	20
Speed (cruising)	12.0 kt		
Endurance	22 days		*VERIFIED*
Fuel capacity	54 m³		
Fresh water capacity	40 m³		

East China Sea Branch S.O.A

Xiang Yang Hong 10

GENERAL

Owner	State Oceanic Administration (SOA)	Gyrocompass	Yes
		Speed log	Yes
Built (yard and date)	1979		
Length overall	156.09 m	**COMMUNICATIONS**	
Breadth moulded	20.60 m	Inmarsat (type)	Yes
Operational draught	8.19 m		
Tonnage (grt)	9,999	**DECK MACHINERY**	
		Cranes	Midships: clearance above deck 9 m, outboard extension 1 m, SWL 28 tons

PROPULSION

Main engine(s)	2 diesels; 18,000 bhp at 165 rpm	Winches	9 oceanographic: steel wire 10,000 m, SWL 1 ton; conducting cable 2,500 m, SWL 2 tons
Speed (max)	20.0 kt		
Speed (cruising)	18.0 kt		
Endurance	18,000 n miles/120 days		
Fuel capacity	3,660 m³	**ACCOMMODATION**	
Electrical power	400/220 V AC, 3-phase, 50 Hz	Crew	80
Fresh water capacity	924 m³	Scientists/surveyors	20

BRIDGE NAVIGATION AIDS

		SCIENTIFIC SPACES	
Satellite	Yes	Multipurpose dry lab	99 m²
Radar	Yes		*VERIFIED*

Institute of Oceanology

Science 1

GENERAL

Length overall	104.0 m	**ACCOMMODATION**	
Breadth moulded	13.7 m	Crew	50
Max draught	4.9 m	Scientists/surveyors	50
Tonnage (grt)	2,250		
			VERIFIED

PROPULSION

Main engine(s)	11,600 bhp

North China Sea Branch S.O.A

Ji Di

GENERAL

Owner	State Oceanic Administration	**BRIDGE NAVIGATION AIDS**	
Built (yard and date)	1971	Satellite	Yes
Length overall	152.4 m	Radar	Yes
Breadth moulded	20.0 m	Gyrocompass	Yes
		Speed log	Yes

PROPULSION

Main engine(s)	Diesel; 8,300 bhp	**COMMUNICATIONS**	
Speed (max)	15.1 kt	Inmarsat (type)	Yes
Speed (cruising)	14.0 kt		
Endurance	20,000 n miles/100 days		*UPDATED*
Fuel capacity	2,116 m³		
Fresh water capacity	731 m³		

North China Sea Branch S.O.A

Xiang Yang Hong 07

GENERAL

Comments	Also *Xiang Yang 08*
Owner	State Oceanic Administration (SOA)
Built (yard and date)	1972
Length overall	74.0 m
Breadth moulded	10.0 m
Operational draught	3.33 m

PROPULSION

Main engine(s)	2 diesels; 3,700 bhp
Speed (max)	17.5 kt
Endurance	4,000 n miles/40 days

VERIFIED

North China Sea Branch S.O.A

Xiang Yang Hong 09

GENERAL

Owner	State Oceanic Administration (SOA)
Built (yard and date)	1977
Length overall	112.01 m
Breadth moulded	15.20 m
Operational draught	5.50 m

PROPULSION

Main engine(s)	2 diesels; 9,000 bhp at 200 rpm
Speed (max)	18.2 kt
Speed (cruising)	17.0 kt
Endurance	10,000 n miles/60 days
Fuel capacity	1,096 m³

Electrical power	380/220 V AC, 3-phase, 50 Hz
Fresh water capacity	340 m³

BRIDGE NAVIGATION AIDS

Satellite	Yes
Radar	Yes
Gyrocompass	Yes

DECK MACHINERY

Winches	6 oceanographic
Sensors	

VERIFIED

Ocean University of QuingDao

Dong Fang Hong 2

GENERAL

Comments	
Built (yard and date)	1995
Length overall	96.0 m
Breadth moulded	15.0 m
Max draught	8.0 m
Tonnage (grt)	3,235

PROPULSION

Speed (max)	18 kt
Speed (cruising)	16 kt

ACCOMMODATION

Scientists/surveyors	196

NEW ENTRY

South China Sea Branch S.O.A

Xiang Yang Hong 05

GENERAL

Owner	State Oceanic Administration (SOA)
Built (yard and date)	1967
Length overall	152.6 m
Breadth moulded	19.4 m
Operational draught	7.20 m

PROPULSION

Main engine(s)	Diesel; 7,200 bhp
Speed (max)	16.4 kt
Speed (cruising)	15.2 kt
Endurance	120 days
Fuel capacity	1,804 m³
Electrical power	380/220 V AC
Fresh water capacity	1,000 m³

BRIDGE NAVIGATION AIDS

Satellite	Yes
Radar	Yes

Gyrocompass	Yes
Speed log	Yes

COMMUNICATIONS

Inmarsat (type)	Yes

DECK MACHINERY

Cranes	Stern, midships
Winches	8 oceanographic

ACCOMMODATION

Crew	40
Scientists/surveyors	70

SCIENTIFIC SPACES

Multipurpose dry lab	40 m²

VERIFIED

South China Sea Branch S.O.A

Xiang Yang Hong 14

GENERAL			
Owner	State Oceanic Administration (SOA)	Gyrocompass	Yes
		Speed log	Yes
Built (yard and date)	1981		
Length overall	110.59 m	**COMMUNICATIONS**	
Breadth moulded	15.20 m	Inmarsat (type)	Yes
Operational draught	5.50 m		
Tonnage (grt)	2,985	**DECK MACHINERY**	
		Cranes	Midships: clearance above deck 9 m, outboard extension 1 m, SWL 28 tons
PROPULSION			
Main engine(s)	2 diesels; 9,000 bhp at 200 rpm	Winches	6 oceanographic: steel wire 10,000 m, SWL 1 ton; conducting cable 1,000 m, SWL 1 ton
Speed (max)	18.6 kt		
Speed (cruising)	17.0 kt		
Endurance	10,000 n miles/60 days		
Fuel capacity	1,055 m³	**ACCOMMODATION**	
Electrical power	380/220 V AC, 3-phase, 50 Hz	Crew	40
Fresh water capacity	413 m³	Scientists/surveyors	70
BRIDGE NAVIGATION AIDS		**SCIENTIFIC SPACES**	
Satellite	Yes	Multipurpose dry lab	99 m²
Radar	Yes		*VERIFIED*

South China Sea Institute of Oceanography

Shiyan 2

GENERAL			
Classification	China Bureau (ZC)	**SCIENTIFIC SPACES**	
Built (yard and date)	1981	Total scientific deck space	60 m²
Length overall	68.45 m	Multipurpose dry lab	80 m²
Breadth moulded	10.0 m		
Operational draught	3.50 m	**SURVEY SYSTEMS**	
Tonnage (grt)	655	Echo-sounder (single beam)	Knudsen 320M
		Multibeam/swath system	Reson SeaBat 8111
PROPULSION		Sidescan sonar	GeoAcoustics SS941; Klein 531
Main engine(s)	2 diesels; each 2,200 bhp at 600 rpm	Sub-bottom profiler	GeoAcoustics GeoPulse; GeoChirp
Speed (max)	13.5 kt	Magnetometer	MAPM-92; DSM-1
Speed (cruising)	12.5 kt	Gravimeter	KSS-30
Endurance	5,500 n miles/45 days	Sound velocity profiler	Falmouth SVP3
Fuel capacity	180 m³	Oceanographic sensors (CTDs/XBTs and so on)	RDI Workhorse ADCP; S4ADW wave, current and tide meter; Wave Track-1156 wave buoy Aanderaa: RCM-7/8; WLR7; TR7 Falmouth Micro-CTD
Electrical power	380/220 V AC, total 960 kVA, 3-phase, 50 Hz		
Fresh water capacity	140 m³		
BRIDGE NAVIGATION AIDS		**SEISMIC SYSTEMS**	
Satellite	Yes	Energy source (type and manufacturer)	DFS-V 48-channel seismic system
Radar	Yes		
Gyrocompass	Yes		*UPDATED*
Speed log	Yes		
ACCOMMODATION			
Crew	30		
Scientists/surveyors	24		

South China Sea Institute of Oceanography

Shiyan 3

GENERAL			
Comments	Undertaking oceanographic expeditions. Fourteen laboratories	Breadth moulded	13.74 m
		Operational draught	5.00 m
		Tonnage (grt)	2,609
Classification	China Bureau (ZC)	**PROPULSION**	
Built (yard and date)	1981	Main engine(s)	2 diesels; each 10,600 bhp at 220 rpm
Length overall	102.0 m		

Speed (max)	20.2 kt	**SCIENTIFIC SPACES**	
Speed (cruising)	16.7 kt	**Total scientific deck space**	304 m²
Endurance	9,000 n miles/40 days	**Oceanographic wet lab**	40 m²
Fuel capacity	600 m³	**Multipurpose dry lab**	20 m²
Electrical power	380/220V AC, total 129 kVA, 3-phase, 50 Hz		
		SURVEY SYSTEMS	
Fresh water capacity	600 m³	**Echo-sounder (single beam)**	Knudsen 320M
		Multibeam/swath system	Reson SeaBat 8111
BRIDGE NAVIGATION AIDS		**Sidescan sonar**	GeoAcoustics SS941; Klein 531
Satellite	Yes	**Sub-bottom profiler**	GeoAcoustics GeoPulse; GeoChirp
Radar	Yes		
Gyrocompass	Yes	**Magnetometer**	MAPM-92; DSM-1
Speed log	Yes	**Gravimeter**	KSS-30
		Sound velocity profiler	Falmouth SVP3
DECK MACHINERY		**Oceanographic sensors**	RDI Workhorse ADCP; S4ADW
Cranes	Stern: clearance above deck 7 m, outboard extension 2 m	**(CTDs/XBTs and so on)**	wave, current and tide meter; Wave Track-1156 wave buoy
Winches	6 oceanographic, wire length 6,000 m		Aanderra: RCM-7/8; WLR7; TR7 Falmouth Micro-CTD
		SEISMIC SYSTEMS	
ACCOMMODATION		**Energy source (type and**	DFS-V 48-channel seismic system
Crew	38	**manufacturer)**	
Scientists/surveyors	50		

UPDATED

State Oceanic Administration

Shijian

GENERAL		**Fuel capacity**	486 m³
Built (yard and date)	1969	**Electrical power**	380/220 V AC, total 50 kVA/560 kVA, 3-phase, 50 Hz
Length overall	94.73 m		
Breadth moulded	14.0 m	**Fresh water capacity**	330 m³
Operational draught	5.00 m		
Tonnage (grt)	2,955	**ACCOMMODATION**	
		Crew	52
PROPULSION		**Scientists/surveyors**	65
Main engine(s)	2 diesels; each 4,000 bhp at 200 rpm		
		SCIENTIFIC SPACES	
Speed (max)	16.0 kt	**Multipurpose dry lab**	99 m²
Speed (cruising)	14.5 kt		
Endurance	7,500 n miles/45 days		*VERIFIED*

Yellow Sea Fisheries Research Institute

Beidou Hao

GENERAL		**COMMUNICATIONS**	
Classification	DNV, class A1A	**Inmarsat (type)**	Yes
Built (yard and date)	1984		
Length overall	56.2 m	**DECK MACHINERY**	
Breadth moulded	12.5 m	**Cranes**	Stern, midships: clearance above deck 9 m, outboard extension 4 m, SWL 3 tons
Operational draught	6.50 m		
Tonnage (grt)	1,147	**A-frame(s)**	Midships: clearance above deck 7 m, outboard extension 6 m, SWL 3 tons
PROPULSION			
Main engine(s)	Diesel; 2,250 bhp at 825 rpm	**Winches**	Oceanographic, steel wire 3,500 m, SWL 1 ton
Speed (max)	13.7 kt		
Speed (cruising)	12.0 kt		
Endurance	9,000 n miles/30 days	**ACCOMMODATION**	
Fuel capacity	300 m³	**Crew**	22
Electrical power	220 V AC, total 1,140 kVA/560 kVA, 3-phase, 50 Hz	**Scientists/surveyors**	8
Fresh water capacity	60 m³	**SCIENTIFIC SPACES**	
		Total scientific deck space	60 m²
BRIDGE NAVIGATION AIDS		**Oceanographic wet lab**	25 m²
Satellite	Yes	**Multipurpose dry lab**	25 m²
Radar	Yes		
Gyrocompass	Yes		
Speed log	Yes		*UPDATED*

COLOMBIA

Communidad Cientifico Nacional Colombia

Providencia

GENERAL

Comments	Sister vessel of *Malpelo*. Geophysical research vessel
Current operational status	Operates in the Caribbean Sea and Pacific Ocean
Owner	Colombian Navy
Official number	BO 155
Classification	Germanischer Lloyd
Built (yard and date)	Martin Jansen SY, Leer; commissioned 24 July 1981
Length overall	50.3 m
Breadth moulded	10 m
Max draught	4 m
Tonnage (grt)	780

PROPULSION

Main engine(s)	2 MAN-Augsberg diesels, 1,570 hp (1.15 MW); auxiliary diesel, 550 hp
Thrusters	Bow
Propellers	1 Kort nozzle
Speed (max)	13 kt
Speed (cruising)	10 kt
Endurance	15,000 n miles at 12 kt
Fuel capacity	210 m^3
Electrical power	440/220 V AC, 315 kVA, 3-phase, 60 Hz
Fresh water capacity	88 m^3

BRIDGE NAVIGATION AIDS

Satellite	Yes
Radar	Raytheon
Gyrocompass	Yes
Speed log	E/M; Doppler

DECK MACHINERY

Cranes	Midships, 5 t
A-frame(s)	Stern
Winches	2 oceanographic, steel wire, 120 cable, 2,200 m, 1 t; bottom sampling, 500 m, 2 t

ACCOMMODATION

Crew	48
Scientists/surveyors	6

SCIENTIFIC SPACES

Total scientific deck space	60 m^2
Oceanographic wet lab	35 m^2
Multipurpose dry lab	18 m^2

SURVEY SYSTEMS

Sensors	12 kHz

UPDATED

Direccion General Maritima y Portuaria (DIMAR)

Malpelo

GENERAL

Comments	Sister vessel of *Providencia*. Fisheries research vessel

Current operational status	Operates in the Caribbean Sea and Pacific Ocean
Owner	Colombian Navy

Malpelo 2000 (Colombian Navy)

2001/0103704

Official number	BO 156		
Classification	Germanischer Lloyd		
Built (yard and date)	Martin Jansen SY, Leer 1981		
Length overall	50.3 m		
Breadth moulded	10 m		
Max draught	4 m		
Tonnage (grt)	780		

PROPULSION

Main engine(s)	2 MAN-Augsberg diesels, 1.15 MW (1,570 hp); auxiliary diesel, 550 hp
Thrusters	Bow
Propellers	1 Kort nozzle
Speed (max)	13 kt
Speed (cruising)	12 kt
Endurance	15,000 n miles at 12 kt
Fuel capacity	198 m³
Electrical power	440/220 V AC, 315 kVA, 3-phase, 60 Hz
Fresh water capacity	89 m³

BRIDGE NAVIGATION AIDS

Satellite	Yes
Radar	Raytheon
Gyrocompass	Yes
Speed log	E/M

COMMUNICATIONS

Inmarsat (type)	Yes

DECK MACHINERY

Cranes	Stern, 5 t
A-frame(s)	Midships
Winches	1 oceanographic, 3,000 m, 4 t; bottom sampling, 3,000 m, 2 t; Bt

ACCOMMODATION

Crew	48
Scientists/surveyors	6

SCIENTIFIC SPACES

Total scientific deck space	60 m²
Oceanographic wet lab	35 m²
Multipurpose dry lab	18 m²

SURVEY SYSTEMS

Sensors	Fisheries sonar

UPDATED

DENMARK

Danish Institute for Fisheries Research (DIFRES)

Dana

GENERAL

Current operational status	Operates in the Atlantic Ocean, North Sea and Baltic Sea
Classification	Norske Ventas + 1A1, Ice 1A
Call sign	OHXB
Built (yard and date)	Dannebrog Shipyard 1981
Length overall	78.43 m
Breadth moulded	14.7 m
Max draught	5.93 m
Operational draught	5.7 m
Tonnage (grt)	2,483

PROPULSION

Main engine(s)	2 B & W Alpha diesels, 16V23LU at 800 rpm
Thrusters	Bow and stern
Propellers	3.8 m diameter, 160 rpm
Speed (max)	15.5 kt
Speed (cruising)	12.5 kt
Endurance	14,000 n miles/50 days
Fuel capacity	557 m³
Electrical power	380/220 V AC, 2,200 kVA, 3-phase, 50 Hz
Fresh water capacity	93 m³

Dana (van Ginderen Collection)

2000

BRIDGE NAVIGATION AIDS

Satellite	Yes
Radar	Yes
Gyrocompass	Yes
Speed log	E/M; Doppler
Other ship navigation	Loran; Decca

DECK MACHINERY

Cranes	Stern, 5 t
Winches	Oceanographic, steel wire, 1,800 m, 8.2 mm
	Oceanographic, conducting cable, 800 m
	Trawl, 1,000 m, 2 t
	Plankton, 3,000 m
	Sampling hose, 150 m

ACCOMMODATION

Crew	27
Scientists/surveyors	12

SCIENTIFIC SPACES

Total scientific deck space	60 m²
Oceanographic wet lab	35 m²
Multipurpose dry lab	18 m²

SURVEY SYSTEMS

Sensors	Fisheries sector scan sonar, 38/120 kHz

NEW ENTRY

National Environment Research Institute

Gunnar Thorson

GENERAL

Current operational status	Operates in the North Sea and Baltic Sea
Classification	Lloyds Register
Call sign	OWPB
Built (yard and date)	Ørskov Christensens Stålskibsvaerft a/s, 1981
Length overall	56 m
Breadth moulded	12.3 m
Max draught	4.6 m
Tonnage (grt)	868

PROPULSION

Main engine(s)	2 diesel, each 2,360 hp at 825 rpm; auxiliary diesel, 825 hp
Propellers	2.1 m diameter, 300 rpm
Speed (cruising)	11 kt
Endurance	9,600 n miles/40 days
Fuel capacity	310 m³
Electrical power	380 V AC, 184/524 kVA, 3 phase, 50 Hz
Fresh water capacity	82 m³

BRIDGE NAVIGATION AIDS

Satellite	DGPS Northstar 951X
Radar	Yes
Gyrocompass	Furuno Marine
Speed log	Doppler Log
Other ship navigation	Decca

COMMUNICATIONS

VHF	Sailor VHF RT 2048

DECK MACHINERY

Cranes	Midships, 1 t
Winches	2 oceanographic, steel wire, 1,000 m

ACCOMMODATION

Crew	16
Scientists/surveyors	18

SCIENTIFIC SPACES

Oceanographic wet lab	4 m²
Multipurpose dry lab	40 m²

SURVEY SYSTEMS

Echo-sounder (single beam)	Elac Laz 5000
Other sampling	General Oceanic; OTE; KC Denmark
Oceanographic sensors (CTDs/XBTs and so on)	SBE 25; fluorometer: Dr Hardt; ADCP: RDI Instruments; Biospherical QSP-200PD

UPDATED

Gunnar Thorson (M Declerck)   **2000**/0017790

ECUADOR

Instituto Oceanografico de la Armada (INOCAR)

Orion

GENERAL

Comments	Research vessel for oceanographic, hydrographic and meteorological work
Former names	*Dometer*, HI91, HI92
Owner	Armada del Ecuador
Official number	HI-91
Classification	ABS – AAIE – AMS – ACCU
Call sign	HCOR
Built (yard and date)	Ishikawajima, Tokyo; commissioned 10 November 1982
Length overall	70.21 m
Breadth moulded	10.7 m
Working deck width	10.6 m
Max draught	3.6 m
Operational draught	3.4 m
Tonnage (grt)	1,418

PROPULSION

Main engine(s)	Diesel-electric; 3 Detroit 16V-92TA diesel generators; 1.54 MW (2,070 hp) sustained; 2 motors; 1.42 MW (1,900 hp)
Propellers	1
Speed (max)	12.25 kt
Speed (cruising)	10 kt
Endurance	6,000 n miles at 12 kt/30 days
Fuel capacity	237 m³ (62,400 gallons)
Fuel consumption	80 gallons/h
Electrical power	440 V AC, 600 kVA, 3 phase, 60 Hz; 115 V AC, 20 kVA, 60 Hz
Fresh water capacity	155 m³ (40,800 gallons)

BRIDGE NAVIGATION AIDS

Satellite	Trimble Navtrac XL; Trimble NT200D
Radar	Decca ARPA 340; Decca 250
Gyrocompass	Tokyo Keiki
Speed log	Furuno E/M
Echo-sounder	Furuno FCV-561

COMMUNICATIONS

Inmarsat (type)	Telex – Fax – Phone
MF/HF	Telex Arq
VHF	Furuno
Facsimile	Yaesu FT 900

SAFETY

Lifeboats	2
Workboat/chase boat	2

DECK MACHINERY

Cranes	Stern, 5 t
A-frame(s)	Stern
Winches	Oceanographic, steel wire, 6,000 m; conducting cable, 1,500 m

ACCOMMODATION

Crew	42
Scientists/surveyors	20
Hospital	2

SCIENTIFIC SPACES

Total scientific deck space	135 m²
Oceanographic wet lab	105 m²

Orion (T J Gander)

2000

Multipurpose dry lab	20 m²	Oceanographic sensors	CTD, XBT; InterOcean
Chemistry lab	10 m²	(CTDs/XBTs and so on)	thermosalinograph; Hydro Bios
			bathythermograph
SURVEY SYSTEMS			
Positioning	DGPS; Decca Trisponder	**SEISMIC SYSTEMS**	
Echo-sounder (single beam)	Echotrack DF-3200; Raytheon	Energy source (type and	Electrical, EG&G
Sub-bottom profiler	SMS, EG&G	manufacturer)	
Corer(s)	Piston	Recording system	Javelin; Philips
Other sampling	General oceanic multisample		
	Rosette; Niskin		

UPDATED

ESTONIA

Estonian Marine Institute

Livonia

GENERAL		Gyrocompass	Yes
Former names	*Arnold Veimar*	Speed log	EM; Doppler
Built (yard and date)	1984		
Length overall	71.6 m	**COMMUNICATIONS**	
Breadth moulded	12.8 m	Inmarsat (type)	Yes
Max draught	4.5 m	Facsimile	Yes
Tonnage (grt)	1,832		
		DECK MACHINERY	
PROPULSION		Cranes	Stern; midships, height 8 m,
Main engine(s)	2 diesel, each 3,000 bhp at		outboard extension 6 m, 5 t SWL
	485 rpm	Winches	5 oceanographic, 5 t SWL
Propellers	2.45 m diameter, 275 rpm		
Speed (max)	13 kt	**ACCOMMODATION**	
Speed (cruising)	12 kt	Crew	13
Endurance	12,000 n miles/45 days	Scientists/surveyors	36
Fuel capacity	400 m³		
Electrical power	0/380 V AC, 600 kVA, 3 phase,	**SCIENTIFIC SPACES**	
	50 Hz	Total scientific deck space	100 m²
Fresh water capacity	240 m³	Oceanographic wet lab	80 m²
		Multipurpose dry lab	170 m²
BRIDGE NAVIGATION AIDS			
Satellite	Yes	**SURVEY SYSTEMS**	
Radar	Yes	Echo-sounder(single beam)	33/210 kHz

UPDATED

FINLAND

Finnish Institute of Marine Research

Aranda

Port of reg/flag	Helsinki, Finland	Speed (max)	13.5 kt
Classification	Research vessel	Speed (cruising)	10.5 kt
Call sign	OIRY	Endurance	60 days
Built (yard and date)	Wärtsilä Shipyards, Helsinki; 1989	Fuel capacity	441 m³
Length overall	59.2 m	Fuel consumption	230 litres/h
Breadth moulded	13.8 m	Electrical power	Strømberg 2 × 1,570 kVA, 1 × 350
Working deck width	10 m (132 m²)		kVA;
Max draught	5 m		400/660 V AC, 3 phase, 50 Hz;
Operational draught	4.6 m		400/230 V AC, 3 phase, 50 Hz
Tonnage (grt)	1,734	Fresh water capacity	68 m³
PROPULSION		**BRIDGE NAVIGATION AIDS**	
Main engine(s)	Wärtsilä Vasa 8 R 22 MD 1,000	Satellite	DGPS: Northstar 951 X; DGPS:
	rpm – 1,300 kW		Magnavox MX 200; Trimble/
	Wärtsilä Vasa 12 V 22 MD 1,000		Fugro via Inmarsat A
	rpm – 1,700 kW	Radar	2 Selesmar X/S band
Thrusters	Bow: Bakker, azimuth, 400 kW	Gyrocompass	2 Robertson RGC 11
	Stern: Bakker, Pd160-900, 150 kW	Speed log	Atlas Dolog 20

Echo-sounder	Atlas echograph 481/100 kHz
Other ship navigation	Autopilot: Robertson AP9 Mk 2

COMMUNICATIONS

Inmarsat (type)	A – JRC-JUE 35B; C – Thrane & Thrane
MF/HF	Skanti
VHF	Skanti; Sailor RT 2048; Sailor RT 4822

SAFETY

Lifeboats	1 × 6 person MOB boat
Workboat/chase boat	Water-jet: 6.25 m
Lifesaving equipment	6 × 20-person liferafts

HELIDECK

Size, aircraft capacity	Helicopter hangar facility to carry 2 helicopters

DECK MACHINERY

Cranes	Forward, Effer 1 t/15 m; aft, Hägglunds 3 t/12.5 m
A-frame(s)	2 aft 1.5 t/10 t
Winches	2 electric, 4 mm, 1,000 m, 200 kg; 1 hydraulic, 6 mm, 3,000 m, 800 kg; 1 hydraulic CTD, 8 mm, 4,000 m, 800 kg

ACCOMMODATION

Crew	12 – 13
Scientists/surveyors	27

SCIENTIFIC SPACES

Total scientific deck space	110 m²
Oceanographic wet lab	9 m²
Multipurpose dry lab	Various 210 m²; computer lab 25 m²
Chemistry lab	40 m²

SURVEY SYSTEMS

Positioning	Dynamic: Simrad/Robertson SDP 600
Echo-sounder (single beam)	Atlas DESO 25, 15/210 kHz; Atlas DESO 25, 12/33 kHz; JRC JFV 200R 50/28 kHz; Meridata MD DSS 15 kHz
Corer(s)	2 Benthos; Gemini; Aquarius, Niemistö, 2 Selena
Grab(s)	Van Veen
Other sampling	Technicap PPS; Hydro Bios water sampler
Vehicle(s) (ROVs/AUVs and so on)	Benthos ROV; W S Oceans U-Tow
Oceanographic sensors (CTDs/XBTs and so on)	RDI 150 kHz ADCP; SBE 911CD; General Oceanics 1015 rosette; SIS Plus 500 CTD

UPDATED

Aranda

2001/0114491

Regional Environment Centre of South Savo and University of Joensuu, Saimaa Research

Muikku

GENERAL

Background information	Home port: Savonlinna, Finland
Former names	*Särkkä* (until 1989)
Official number	OHMMM 230298000
Classification	Reasearch vessel
Call sign	OHMMM
Built (yard and date)	Rauma, Hollming Shipyards; 1989
Rebuilt (yard and date)	Savonlinna shipyards; 1989
Length overall	27.70 m
Breadth moulded	6.90 m
Working deck width	6.00 m
Max draught	2.20 m
Operational draught	2.00 m
Tonnage (grt)	129

PROPULSION

Main engine(s)	Machinery output 2 × 279 kW
Thrusters	bow thruster 50 kW
Speed (max)	12.0 kt
Speed (cruising)	10.0 kt
Endurance	10 days
Fuel capacity	17 t
Fuel consumption	80 litres/h
Electrical power	main generator: 45 kW; Auxiliary generator: 22 kW; 62 kW
Fresh water capacity	12 t

BRIDGE NAVIGATION AIDS

Satellite	Northstar 921XD DGPS
Radar	Selescan 1024/20 ARPA, 25 kW
	Furuno 841/4 kW
Gyrocompass	Sperry 2205R
Speed log	Furuno DS-70
Echo-sounder	Autohelm
	SALL Log

COMMUNICATIONS

VHF	Navall EF-2465+DSC
Cellular	Nokia Premicell 09l, Nokia 6080/3110
Facsimile	Cannon FAX-120

SAFETY

Lifeboats	2 liferafts
Workboat/chase boat	Watercat/Alamarin 105 hp Volvo diesel and Sun-Buster (Yamaha; 30 hp)
Lifesaving equipment	52 lifejackets, 5 life suits

DECK MACHINERY

Cranes	Fore (Hiab 031 ALTW; 30 tm, 5.8 m); CTD (Hiab 011 B; 1.1 tm, 3.2 m); rear (Ferrari 087-2; 7.0 tm, 10.8 m)
Winches	Research 1 (4.5 kN, 110 m, forecrane); Research 2 (3.0 kN, 110 m, CTD-crane); Research 3 (4.5 kN, 250 m rear crane); split net drum and capstan (13 kN); split (2) (10 kN, 300 m); ball (2) (7 kN, 300 m); net sound (3 kN, 300 m)

ACCOMMODATION

Crew	3-4
Scientists/surveyors	8-10

SCIENTIFIC SPACES

Total scientific deck space	30 m²
Oceanographic wet lab	12 m²
Multipurpose dry lab	11 m²

SURVEY SYSTEMS

Positioning	DGPS satellite navigator (Northstar 921 XD)
Sensors	Furuno FE-606, Simrad EK-500
Echo-sounder (single beam)	Atlas Deso 10; Atlas echograph 420; MD DSS (digital echo-sounder)
Corer(s)	Limnos, Ekman, bottom dredge, modified Livingstone
Other sampling	Hydrobios, Limnos, plankton pump (Grundfos JP 5 VA)
Oceanographic sensors (CTDs/XBTs and so on)	CTD-system (2) (SBE 19-03, 335 m acoustic Doppler current profiler (RDI, 600 kHz); ultrasonic current meter (Sensotec UCM-50); fluorometer (Turner Designs 10-AU)

NEW ENTRY

FRANCE

French Navy

D'entrecasteaux

GENERAL BACKGROUND

Oceanographic survey vessel, batiment oceanographique (BO). Designed for oceanographic surveys to depths of 6,000 m.

Official number	A 757
Built (yard and date)	Brest Naval Dockyard; commissioned 8 October 1971
Length overall	95.65 m
Breadth moulded	13.00 m
Operational draught	4.20 m

PROPULSION

Main engine(s)	Diesel-electric; 2 diesel SACM-Wärtsila; 2,720 hp(m) (2 MW); 2 motors
Propellers	2 shafts; acbLIPS cp; auxiliary propulsion; 2 Schottel trainable and retractable propellers
Speed (max)	15.0 kt
Speed (cruising)	12.0 kt
Endurance	12,000 n miles at 12 kt

BRIDGE NAVIGATION AIDS		ACCOMMODATION	
Radar	2 Racal Decca 1226; I-band	Crew	77
		Scientists/surveyors	38 hydrographers
COMMUNICATIONS			
Inmarsat (type)	"A"	**SURVEY SYSTEMS**	
		Vehicle(s) (ROVs/AUVs and so on)	Chelsea Instruments SeaSoar
SAFETY			
Workboat/chase boat	3 survey launches	Oceanographic sensors (CTDs/XBTs and so on)	ADCP
HELIDECK			
Size, aircraft capacity	SA 319B Alouette III		

UPDATED

D'entrecasteaux (H M Steele)   *2000*/0069942

Institut de Recherche pour le Developpement (IRD)

Alis

GENERAL			
Comments	Fisheries research vessel	**Fuel consumption**	2,400 litres/day
Port of reg/flag	Concarneau, France	**Electrical power**	1 × 85 kVA; 1 × 125 kVA (380/220 V, 50 Hz)
Official number	CC 683 407 J		
Classification	Bureau Veritas No 13/3E	**Fresh water capacity**	20 m³
Call sign	FHQB		
Built (yard and date)	Chantiers Piriou, Concarneau, 1987	**BRIDGE NAVIGATION AIDS**	
		Satellite	Litton MLX 400; Magnavox MX 200; Furuno
Length overall	28.6 m	**Radar**	Racal Decca Bridgemaster; Furuno
Breadth moulded	8.4 m		
Max draught	3.85 m	**Gyrocompass**	Sperry SR-50
Tonnage (grt)	198.8 (269 UMS)	**Speed log**	Ben
Displacement	330 t	**Echo-sounder**	Skipper 810; EDO; Furuno
PROPULSION		**COMMUNICATIONS**	
Main engine(s)	1 diesel engine – Deutz SBA 16 M 816; 649 kW	**Inmarsat (type)**	C/Standard M
		MF/HF	Blu – Skanti TRP, 8750-S 750 W
Thrusters	50 kW	**VHF**	Navicom RT 175
Propellers	1 cp		
Speed (max)	12 kt	**SAFETY**	
Speed (cruising)	10 kt	**Workboat/chase boat**	2 Yamaha 45CV
Fuel capacity	40 m³	**Lifesaving equipment**	Rigolet

DECK MACHINERY

Cranes	1 Hiab: 3.4 t at 1.7 m, 0.9 t at 6.2 m
A-frame(s)	Portico
Winches	2 fishing: 1,500 m, 18 mm diameter; CTD: 2,000 m, 5.5 mm diameter; hydrology: 2,000 m, 5.5 mm diameter; dredging: 4,000 m, 12.7 mm; winding trawl: 2 m³

ACCOMMODATION

Crew	12
Scientists/surveyors	8

SCIENTIFIC SPACES

Total scientific deck space	100 m²
Oceanographic wet lab	10 m²
Multipurpose dry lab	15 m²

SURVEY SYSTEMS

Sensors	Net Sounder – Skipper 815 50 kHz
Echo-sounder (single beam)	EDO 323C 12 kHz
Multibeam/swath system	Simrad SR 240 24 Hz
Magnetometer	Yes
Oceanographic sensors (CTDs/XBTs and so on)	Met Station – POMAR MO 4-3412A-3.00 SeaBird SME 19

SEISMIC SYSTEMS

Energy source (type and manufacturer)	Yes
Number of airguns	1
Compressor numbers and types	1
Acquisition system	Yes
Recording system	Yes

VERIFIED

Alis
2000/0099235

Institut de Recherche pour le Developpement (IRD)

Antéa

GENERAL COMMENTS
Fisheries research vessel

Port of reg/flag	Pavillon, France
Official number	CC 854 508
Classification	Bureau Veritas No 39 Y 352
Call sign	FNUR
Built (yard and date)	Chantiers Ocean, les Sables d'Olonne, December 1995
Length overall	34.95 m
Breadth moulded	11.7 m

Max draught	3.4 m
Tonnage (grt)	4,214 (571 UMS)
Displacement	405 t

PROPULSION

Main engine(s)	2 diesel – Deutz TBD 604
Propellers	2 cp
Speed (max)	12 kt
Speed (cruising)	11.5 kt
Fuel capacity	68 m³

Fuel consumption	5,200 litres/day
Electrical power	2 × 180 kVA (380/220 V, 50 Hz)
Fresh water capacity	32 m³

BRIDGE NAVIGATION AIDS

Satellite	Trimble NT 100; Trimble NT 200 D
Radar	Furuno 25 kW; Furuno 10 kW
Gyrocompass	Robertson RGC-50
Speed log	Ben Galatée Mk 3; Sagem
Echo-sounder	Furuno FCV 1000

COMMUNICATIONS

Inmarsat (type)	C/Standard M
VHF	Sailor

SAFETY

Lifeboats	Piel; Sidep
Workboat/chase boat	Bombard

DECK MACHINERY

Cranes	Aft – 3 t at 11 m; forward – 0.9 t at 6 m
A-frame(s)	1 Portico
Winches	2 fishing: 1,900 m, 19 mm diameter; CTD: 6,000 m, 10.8 mm diameter; hydrology: 2,000 m, 6.5 mm diameter; 2 winding trawls: 3 m³

ACCOMMODATION

Crew	13
Scientists/surveyors	10

SCIENTIFIC SPACES

Total scientific deck space	40 m²
Oceanographic wet lab	16 m²
Multipurpose dry lab	18 m²

SURVEY SYSTEMS

Positioning	DGPS – Sercel NR 230 Mk II; Simrad ITI
Sensors	Ossian 38-120 kHz
Echo-sounder (single beam)	Simrad EK-500
Multibeam/swath system	Simrad SR 240 24 Hz
Oceanographic sensors (CTDs/XBTs and so on)	SBE-19; SBE-31; SBE-911 including Seabird Rosette and 12 bottles; RDI broadband ADCP 150 kHz

VERIFIED

Antéa   **2000**/0099232

Institut Français de Recherche pour l'exploitation de la Mer (IFREMER)

Gwen Drez

GENERAL COMMENTS

Atlantic coastal fisheries research vessel

Port of reg/flag	Brest
Official number	BR 278970 D
Classification	Bureau Veritas
Call sign	FZYB
Built (yard and date)	CMN, Cherbourg; 1976
Length overall	24.5 m
Breadth moulded	7.4 m

Operational draught	3.5 m
Tonnage (grt)	106.31

PROPULSION

Main engine(s)	Baudoin DVX 12, 440 kW
Fuel capacity	32 m³
Electrical power	56 kVA, 380 V; Perkins 70 kVA, 220 V
Fresh water capacity	12 m³

BRIDGE NAVIGATION AIDS		Winches	2 BOPP fishing, 1,500 m, 18 mm;
Satellite	Sercel NR 53 DGPS; MLR CM015 DGPS		2 BOPP winching trawls; netsonde; hydrology 2,000 m, 6.45 mm
Radar	Furuno FR 8100, FR 810		
Gyrocompass	Anschutz, type 110-106		
Speed log	Ben Galatée 400 E/M	**ACCOMMODATION**	
Echo-sounder	Skipper 815; Koden CVS 8805 KH	**Crew**	7
		Scientists/surveyors	5
COMMUNICATIONS		**SCIENTIFIC SPACES**	
Inmarsat (type)	Mini M Nera ABB	**Oceanographic wet lab**	15 m²
VHF	TRP 2500	**Multipurpose dry lab**	3.6 m²
DECK MACHINERY		**SURVEY SYSTEMS**	
Cranes	Hiab 60 CMU 6 t/m	**Echo-sounder(single beam)**	Micrel Ossian 1500, 38 kHz, Furuno fishing sounder
A-frame(s)	Stern CMU 5 t (fishing); rotating, CMU 1 t		

VERIFIED

Institut Français de Recherche pour l'exploitation de la Mer (IFREMER)

L'Atalante

GENERAL		**Speed (max)**	15.3 kt
Comments	Capable of operating the manned submersible Nautile and ROV Victor 6000	**Speed (cruising)**	11 kt
		Fuel capacity	580 m³
		Electrical power	3 Duvant-Crepel diesel engines/ alternators (3 × 1,100 kW)
Port of reg/flag	Brest		
Official number	BR 732996 K	**Fresh water capacity**	261 m³
Classification	Bureau Veritas 13/3E, open sea, Ice II, oceanographic research vessel		
		BRIDGE NAVIGATION AIDS	
Call sign	FNCM	**Radar**	Sercel DGPS 103/203
Built (yard and date)	Ateliers et Chantiers du Havre; 1989	**Gyrocompass**	2 SGB 1000
		Speed log	Alma CL1 60 E/M; Thomson TSM 5750
Length overall	84.6 m		
Breadth moulded	15.85 m		
Operational draught	5.05 m	**COMMUNICATIONS**	
Tonnage (grt)	3,559	**Inmarsat (type)**	Sailor; 2 ABB Nera Inmarsat B
		Facsimile	JRC NRC 300 A
PROPULSION		**DECK MACHINERY**	
Main engine(s)	2 Jeumont-Schneider CCP 138-53-8 main engines (2 × 1,000 kW)	**Cranes**	Travelling, SWL 4 t; telescoping: SWL 10 t at 10 m
Thrusters	Schottel bow	**A-frame(s)**	Rotating stern, SWL 22 t; lateral, SWL 10 t; lateral SWL 2.6-5.2 t

L'Atalante

2000/0099223

L'Atalante (stern view)

Winches	4 oceanographic: deep water: 8,000 m, 19 mm, SWL 15 t; dredging: 8,000 m, 19 mm; hydrology: 8,000 m, 10.8 mm, SWL 5 t; CTD: 8,000 m, 10.8 mm, SWL 5 t	**Survey systems** **Positioning**	 TMS Posidonia 2 Applanix Hippy 120 HDMS
		Echo-sounder (single beam)	Furuno 200 Hz
		Multibeam/swath system	Simrad EM12 (dual); EM 950
		Sub-bottom profiler	3.5 kHz (chirp mode)
Moonpool(s) – size(s)/ function(s)	3 Travocean type, diameter 300 mm	**Magnetometer**	Barringer M244
		Gravimeter	Lockheed Martin BGM5
		Vehicle(s) (ROVs/AUVs and so on)	Nautile; Victor 6000
ACCOMMODATION			
Crew	17-30	**Oceanographic sensors (CTDs/XBTs and so on)**	RDI ADCP 300 kHz and 75 kHz; SIS CTD 1000
Scientists/surveyors	30-33		thermosalinometer; Sippican Mk 12 XBT launcher
SCIENTIFIC SPACES			
Total scientific deck space	Wet lab 17 m², lab 11 m²		*UPDATED*
Oceanographic wet lab	30 m²		
Multipurpose dry lab	23 m², cold lab: 16 m², clean lab: 11 m², photo lab: 7 m², clean lab 15 m²		

Institut Français de Recherche pour l'exploitation de la Mer(IFREMER)

L'Europe

GENERAL		**Electrical power**	2 connectable generating sets – 380 V; port – 150 kVA, starboard – 80 kVA
Comments	Catamaran. Mediterranean coastal research vessel		
Port of reg/flag	Sète	**Fresh water capacity**	18 m³
Official number	ST 819589 H		
Classification	Bureau Veritas	**BRIDGE NAVIGATION AIDS**	
Call sign	FKJB	**Satellite**	Sercel NR 103 DGPS
Built (yard and date)	Ocean Shipyards, les Sables d'Olonne	**Radar**	2 Racal Bridgemaster C
		Gyrocompass	SGB 1000
Length overall	29.6 m	**VHF**	2 TRP 3000 Skanti
Breadth moulded	10.6 m		
Operational draught	3.45 m	**DECK MACHINERY**	
Tonnage (grt)	335	**Cranes**	Hydrology (quarterdeck) CMU 5.3 t at 2 m, 0.6 t at 12.5 m; hydrology (forward deck) CMU 3.4 t at 1.8 m, 0.58 t at 9.10 m
PROPULSION			
Main engine(s)	2 SACM diesels (2 × 345 kW)	**A-frame(s)**	Rotating stern, CMU 5 t
Propellers	2 Renou Dardel CCPs		
Fuel capacity	32 m³		

Winches	Hydrology, 3,200 m, 6.45 mm; CTD, 3,200 m, 6.45 mm; 2 fishing, 2,700 m, 6.45 mm; Oceano, 5,000 m, 10.8 mm; Netsonde 1,500 m, 10 mm	**SCIENTIFIC SPACES**	
		Oceanographic wet lab	50 m²
Moonpool(s) – size(s)/ function(s)	1.3 m × 1.3 m	**SURVEY SYSTEMS**	
		Sensors	Scanner trawl, 42 kHz; Simrad SR 240 omnidirectional sonar 24 kHz
ACCOMMODATION		**Echo-sounder(single beam)**	Micrel Ossian 1500, 35/200 kHz; Simrad EK 500, 38 kHz; Ossian 500, 12/49 kHz; Ossian 200
Crew	8	**Oceanographic sensors (CTDs/XBTs and so on)**	SeaBird SBE21, CTD
Scientists/surveyors	8		

UPDATED

L'Europe

2000/0099225

Institut Français de Recherche pour l'exploitation de la Mer (IFREMER)

Le Suroît

GENERAL		**BRIDGE NAVIGATION AIDS**	
Comments	Multipurpose research vessel	**Satellite**	2 Dassault Sercel NR203 DGPS
Port of reg/flag	Brest	**Radar**	Atlas 9600 (X and S)
Official number	BR 267206S	**Gyrocompass**	2 SG Brown 1000S
Classification	Bureau Veritas 13/3E, *, special service, oceanographic research, open sea, Ice III	**Speed log**	Ben Galatée Mk 3 E/M
		Echo-sounder	Skipper ED 161
Call sign	FZVN		
Built (yard and date)	Ateliers et Chantiers de la Manche, Dieppe; 1975	**COMMUNICATIONS**	
		Inmarsat (type)	2 NGRA Saturn Bm Standard B
Rebuilt (yard and date)	Modernised 1999	**VHF**	Sailor RT 4800 E/R
Length overall	56.34 m	**Facsimile**	JMC FX-220 Meteofax
Breadth moulded	11 m		
Operational draught	4.1 m	**Deck machinery**	
Tonnage (grt)	946 UMS	**Cranes**	CMU 7.3 t at 5.60 m
		A-frame(s)	Stern CMU 10 t; side, CMU 8 t; side, hydrological, CMU 1 t
PROPULSION		**Winches**	KLEY France: 6,000 m, 17.7 mm; FARMO bathysonde, 6,000 m, 6.45 mm
Main engine(s)	2 BSHR MGO V12 (2 × 600 kW)		
Thrusters	Pleuger bow, 150 kW		
Speed (cruising)	10 kt		
Fuel capacity	130 m²		
Electrical power	2 alternators (2 × 625 kVA); Geoentry set 180 kVA	**ACCOMMODATION**	
		Crew	16-23
Fresh water capacity	59 m²	**Scientists/surveyors**	14-17

SCIENTIFIC SPACES

Oceanographic wet lab	16 m²
Multipurpose dry lab	16 m²

SURVEY SYSTEMS

Positioning	TMS Posidonia, USBL
Echo-sounder (single beam)	Simrad EA 500, 12 kHz, Furuno 200 kHz

Multibeam/swath system	Simrad EM 300, Simrad EM 1000
Sub-bottom profiler	ELICS
Oceanographic sensors (CTDs/XBTs and so on)	Sippican Mk 12 bathythermograph; SBE 19; RDI ADCP 150 kHz; SBE 21

UPDATED

Le Suroît   2000/0099221

Institut Français de Recherche pour l'exploitation de la Mer (IFREMER)

Nadir

GENERAL

Comments	Support vessel for the Nautile manned submersible

Port of reg/flag	Brest
Official number	BR 282844P
Classification	Bureau Veritas

Nadir   2000/0099222

Call sign	FZOP	
Built (yard and date)	Auroux Shipyards, Arcachon; 1974	

Length overall	55.74 m
Breadth moulded	11.91 m
Operational draught	4.68 m
Tonnage (grt)	1,142

PROPULSION

Main engine(s)	2 × 2 Baudoin DVX12
Thrusters	Gil jet auxiliary
Propellers	2 DNP12SRM multidirectional, 440 kW
Fuel capacity	310 m³
Electrical power	2 AT315 LB 7/4 alternators (300 kVA)
Fresh water capacity	109 m³

BRIDGE NAVIGATION AIDS

Satellite	Sercel NR 51 DGPS; Sercel NR109 DGPS
Gyrocompass	2 S G Brown 1000
Speed log	Ben Galatée Mk 6 E/M

COMMUNICATIONS

Inmarsat (type)	ABB Nera M/B

DECK MACHINERY

Cranes	SWL 3 t at 15 m, 15 t at 3 m
A-frame(s)	Rotating stern, SWL 22 t
Winches	Hauling CMU 3 t

ACCOMMODATION

Crew	15
Scientists/surveyors	25

SCIENTIFIC SPACES

Oceanographic wet lab	2

SURVEY SYSTEMS

Positioning	TMS – Posidonia
Echo-sounder(single beam)	Simrad EA 500 (12 kHz)
Vehicle(s) (ROVs/AUVs and so on)	Nautile

UPDATED

Institut Français de Recherche pour l'exploitation de la Mer (IFREMER)

Thalassa

GENERAL COMMENTS
Fisheries research vessel and support for Victor 6000 ROV

Official number	868095G
Classification	Bureau Veritas: 13/3E, *, fishing, open sea, Ice II, AUT-Port
Call sign	FNFP
Built (yard and date)	1996
Length overall	73.65 m

Breadth moulded	14.9 m
Max draught	6.10 m
Tonnage (grt)	2,803 UMS
Displacement	2,300 – 2,900 t

PROPULSION

Main engine(s)	4 MWM Deutz TBD 604 BV 1,128 kW, 1,500 rpm; electric motor, 2,200 kW, 150 rpm

Thalassa

2000/0099231

Thrusters	Brunvoll: bow, 440 kW (electrical); Brunvoll: stern, 264 kW (hydraulic)
Propellers	Six blades – fixed
Speed (max)	14.7 kt
Speed (cruising)	11 kt
Endurance	45 days
Fuel capacity	460 m³
Fresh water capacity	190 m³

BRIDGE NAVIGATION AIDS

Satellite	2 Dassault Sercel NR103 DGPS
Radar	2 Racal Decca ARPA 340
Gyrocompass	2 S G Brown 1000S
Speed log	Ben Galatée Mk 3
Echo-sounder	Skipper GDS 101

COMMUNICATIONS

Inmarsat (type)	2 ABB Nera Standard B
VHF	Sailor RT 4800 E/R

DECK MACHINERY

Cranes	Stern, 10 t at 10 m; 4 t at 18.5 m; forward, 6 t at 1.91 m; 1.25 t at 8.6 m
Winches	Trawl warps, 2 × 4,500 m, 26 mm; net drums: 16 m³ and 12 m³

ACCOMMODATION

Crew	16 – 25
Scientists/surveyors	25

SCIENTIFIC SPACES

Oceanographic wet lab	Biology: 27 m²
Multipurpose dry lab	Hydrology: 24 m²; physics: 18 m²
Chemistry lab	15 m²

SURVEY SYSTEMS

Positioning	Cegelec DPS 901; Scanmar Trawl-eye and trawl sensors 42/75 kHz
Sensors	Scanmar fishing gear parameter system; TMS PACHA 2000
Echo-sounder (single beam)	Micrel Ossian 1500, 38/200; Simrad EK500, 38/120 kHz; Ossian 500, 12/49 kHz; Ossian 2500, 37.5 kHz
Multibeam/swath system	Simrad SR 240 omnidirectional sonar
Oceanographic sensors (CTDs/XBTs and so on)	ADCP: RDI 75/300 kHz; CTD: SeaBird 21; bathythermograph: Sippican Mk 12

UPDATED

Institut Français de Recherche pour l'exploitation de la Mer (IFREMER)

Thalia

GENERAL

Comments	Atlantic coastal research vessel
Port of reg/flag	Brest
Official number	BR 385795N
Classification	Bureau Veritas
Call sign	FPCS
Built (yard and date)	CMN, Cherbourg; 1978
Length overall	24.5 m
Breadth moulded	7.4 m
Operational draught	3.6 m
Tonnage (grt)	135.4

PROPULSION

Main engine(s)	2 Poyand A 12150M engines (2 × 265 kW)
Thrusters	Sauer bow 37 kW
Fuel capacity	25 m³
Electrical power	Alternator: 180 kVA
Fresh water capacity	15.5 m³

BRIDGE NAVIGATION AIDS

Satellite	MLR CM 015 DGPS
Radar	Furuno FR 1931; FR 8100

Gyrocompass	SGB 1000
Speed log	12e ANTEA E/M
Echo-sounder	Furuno FCV 582

DECK MACHINERY

Cranes	Hiab ALTW 1165, CMU 6 t/m
A-frame(s)	Rotating stern, CMU 3 t
Winches	SERN hydrology, 2,000 m, 6.45 mm; 2 BOPP 2500 1B, 14 mm

SURVEY SYSTEMS

Echo-sounder (single beam)	Furuno FE 881, 200 kHz
Oceanographic sensors (CTDs/XBTs and so on)	SBE 21 CTD; TPP seawater thermometer

UPDATED

Institut Français pour la Recherche et la Technologie Polaires (IFRTP)

La Curieuse

GENERAL

Comments	Coastal logistics and oceanographic vessel
Owner	IFRTP
Length overall	25 m

Breadth moulded	7.6 m
Max draught	3.8 m
Tonnage (grt)	162 (UMS)
Displacement	310 t

PROPULSION
Main engine(s)   2 × 414 kW

ACCOMMODATION
Crew   6
Scientists/surveyors
                                  12

UPDATED

La Curieuse   *2000*/0099217

Institut Français pour la Recherche et la Technologie Polaires (IFRTP)

L'Astrolabe

GENERAL
Comments   Logistics and oceanographic vessel
Owner   Ferronia International Shipping
Classification   Class A-Super; Polar ship with ice capacity
Length overall   65 m
Breadth moulded   12.8 m
Max draught   4.8 m

Tonnage (grt)   1,837 (UMS)
Displacement   2,000 t

PROPULSION
Main engine(s)   2 × 2,270 kW

ACCOMMODATION
Scientists/surveyors   48 (13 cabins)

NEW ENTRY

L'Astrolabe   *2000*/0099220

Institut Français pour la Recherche et la Technologie Polaires (IFRTP)

Marion Dufresne

GENERAL

Comments	Oceanographic research vessel
Owner	Compagnie Générale Maritime
Classification	Bureau Veritas
Built (yard and date)	Ateliers et Chantiers du Havre; 1995
Length overall	120.5 m
Breadth moulded	20.6 m
Operational draught	6.95 m
Tonnage (grt)	9,403

PROPULSION

Main engine(s)	3 × diesel-generating sets, total 8,250 kW; 2 × AC synchronous electric propulsion motors (2 × 3,000 kW)
Thrusters	Bow; 750 kW
Propellers	2 × propeller shafts; 2 × flap rudders
Speed (max)	17 kt
Speed (cruising)	15.7 kt
Fuel capacity	Diesel oil; 1,170 m³

Communications

Inmarsat (type)	3 × satellite terminals (Navstar B, C and M standards)
VHF	SSb, VHF

SAFETY

Workboat/chase boat	2 × general purpose/ oceanographic craft; 2 × container barges

HELIDECK

Size, aircraft capacity	2 × helicopters

DECK MACHINERY

Cranes	2 × high-speed, 25 t SWL; logistic/oceanographic, 18 t SWL; service, 3 t SWL

ACCOMMODATION

Scientists/surveyors	110 passengers (59 cabins)

SCIENTIFIC SPACES

Total	650 m²

SURVEY SYSTEMS

Multibeam/swath system	Simrad EM 1000; EM 300
Corer(s)	Astern Integrated Heavy Sampling Equipment (SIAMOIS), 1 × 30 t winch, 3 × storing drums, 7,500 m, 30 mm; 2 × 10/30 t A-frames (aft and lateral); 3 × manoeuvrable winches, 18 t and 3 t cranes Calypso high length corer (10 t, 60 m); ILOT system for lightweight sampling; 2 × 4 t winches; 3 × storage drums; 1 × A-frame
Other sampling	Double seawater pumping system for analysis purposes
Oceanographic sensors (CTDs/XBTs and so on)	2 × large-volume CTD Rosettes

SEISMIC SYSTEMS

Compressor numbers and types	2 × air compressors

UPDATED

Marion Dufresne

2000/0099218

GERMANY

Alfred Wegener Institute/Martini GmbH

Polarstern

GENERAL

Comments	*Polarstern* is a double-hulled icebreaker used for polar research and as a supply vessel
Owner	Federal Ministry of Science, Education, Research and Technology (BMBF)

Classification	Germanischer Lloyd, 100 A 4 Arc 3, MC Arc 3 Aut 16/24	**DECK MACHINERY**	
Built (yard and date)	Howaldtswerke/Deutsche Werft, Kiel and Werft Nobiskrug, Rendsberg; 1982	**Cranes**	15 t, working radius of 4-24 m; 25 t, bow
		Winches	8 for the deployment of scientific gear
Length overall	118 m		
Breadth moulded	25.0 m	**ACCOMMODATION**	
Max draught	11.2 m	**Crew**	41-44
Displacement	17,300 t	**Scientists/surveyors**	50

PROPULSION

SCIENTIFIC SPACES

Main engine(s) — 4 × diesel; 2 × variable pitch propellers; 14,000 kW (20,000 hp) — 9 scientific labs

Speed (max) — 16 kt

Speed (cruising) — 10-12 kt

SURVEY SYSTEMS

BRIDGE NAVIGATION AIDS

Echo-sounder (single beam) — Yes

Satellite — GPS

Multibeam/swath system — Atlas Hydrosweep DS-2

Sub-bottom profiler — Parasound

Oceanographic sensors (CTDs/XBTs and so on) — Meteorological station

SAFETY

Workboat/chase boat — 12 m research launch; inflatable craft

UPDATED

HELIDECK

Size, aircraft capacity — 2 × helicopters

Bundesamt fur Seeschiffahrt und Hydrographie (BSH)

Gauss

GENERAL		**Built (yard and date)**	Schlichting-Werft, Travemunde; 1979/80
	Marine research vessel for environmental protection and fisheries support	**Length overall**	68.68 m
Current operational status	Operates in the North Sea and Baltic Sea	**Breadth moulded**	13.09 m
		Max draught	4.60 m
		Operational draught	4.30 m
Port of reg/flag	Hamburg	**Tonnage (grt)**	1,684
Call sign	DBBX	**Displacement**	1,964 t

Gauss

2000/0099237

PROPULSION

Main engine(s)	Diesel-electric, 3 × MaK diesel motors, each 589 kW at 750/min
Thrusters	Gill's bow; passive secondary propeller – Grim's guide wheel
Propellers	1 × double-rotor AEG propeller motor, maximum 2 × 560 kW
Speed (max)	13.3 kt
Speed (cruising)	11.0 kt
Electrical power	3 × AEG generators, each 910 kVA, 660 V, 50 Hz

BRIDGE NAVIGATION AIDS

Satellite	Yes

DECK MACHINERY

Cranes	Main deck, starboard; capacity: 30 kN; 14 m swing range; heavy-duty beam lifter; capacity: 80 kN at 10° slope

Winches	Heavy-duty: 1,200 m, 16 mm; single wire: 6,000 m, 11 mm; repeat: 6,000 m, 6 mm; wire rope: 1,000 m, 16 mm

ACCOMMODATION

Crew	19
Scientists/surveyors	12

SCIENTIFIC SPACES

Oceanographic wet lab	29.7 m²
Dry Lab	17.0 m²
Multipurpose dry lab	19.4 m²

SURVEY SYSTEMS

Sub-bottom profiler	Parasound

UPDATED

Centre for Marine and Climate Research (ZMK) University of Hamburg

Meteor

GENERAL

Owner	Federal Ministry for Research and Technology; Managing Owner: RF Reedereigemeinschaft Forschungsschiffahrt GmbH
Port of reg/flag	Germany
Classification	GL + 100 A4 E2 + MC Aut

Call sign	DBBH
Built (yard and date)	Schlichting Werft, Travemunde; 1985/86
Length overall	97.50 m
Breadth moulded	16.50 m
Max draught	5.60 m
Displacement	4,780 t

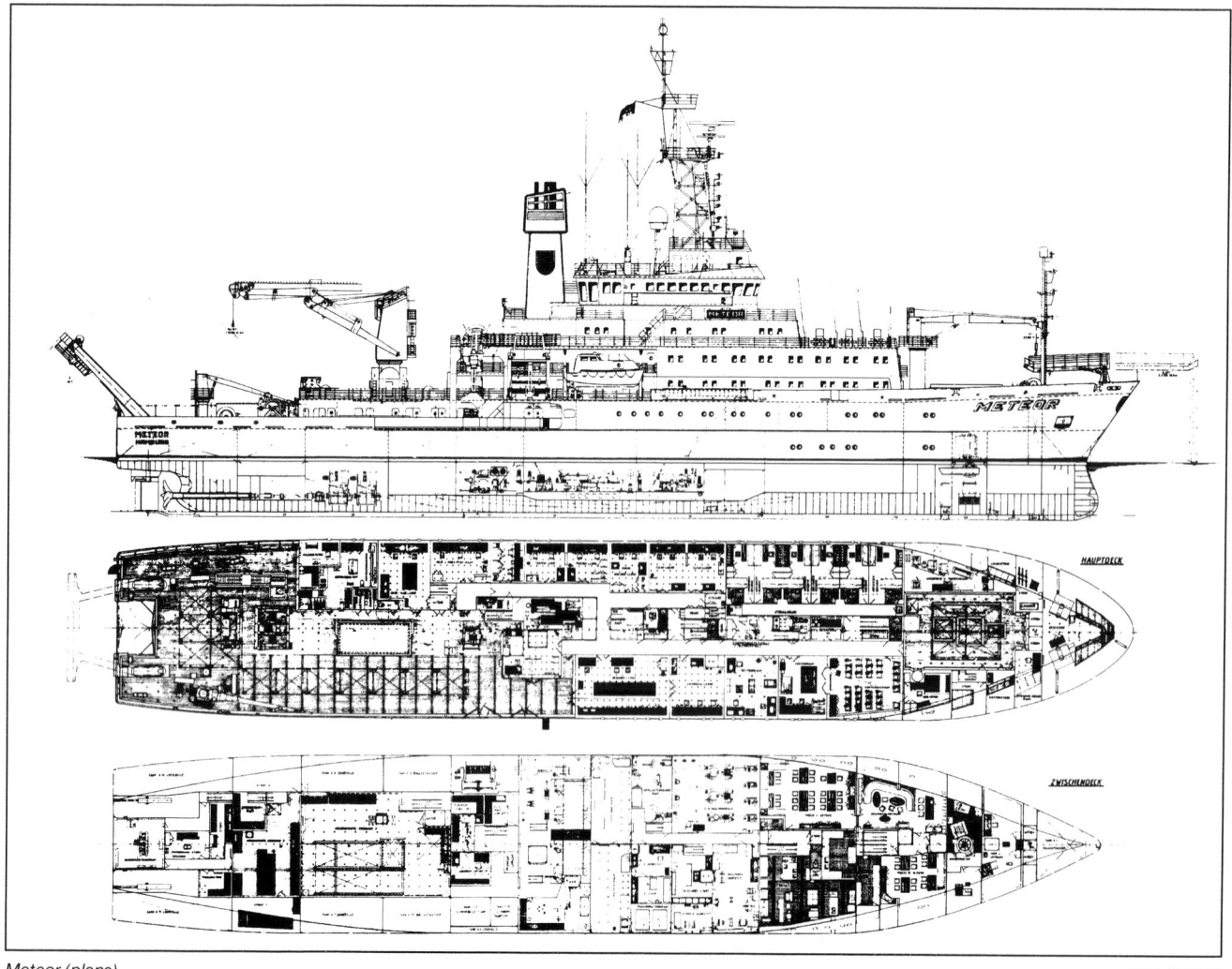

Meteor (plans)

2000/0099229

PROPULSION

Main engine(s)	4 MaK 6 M 332, 1,000 kW at 750 rpm
Thrusters	Bow: omnithruster, 919 kW, 10 t thrust athwartships; 8 t thrust fore and aft; Becker rudder, type FKSR
Speed (cruising)	12 kt
Endurance	60 days
Fuel capacity	655 t IFO 80; 60 t MDO
Fuel consumption	12 t IFO/day at 12 kt
Electrical power	4 AEG generators, each 1,350 kVA, 660 V, 50 Hz; 1 AEG harbour generator, 510 kVA, 380/220 V, 50 Hz
Fresh water capacity	130 t

BRIDGE NAVIGATION AIDS

Satellite	Yes
Radar	X and S band
Gyrocompass	Yes
Speed log	Doppler EM
Echo-sounder	2
Other ship navigation	Loran C; Omega; radio direction-finder

SAFETY

Lifeboats	Yes
Workboat/chase boat	Yes

DECK MACHINERY

Cranes	Main (15 t), two auxiliary, jib-boom (20 t), corer, handling device, side gallow
A-frame(s)	Stern: 20.0 t
Winches	17, equipped with up to 11,000 m of wires and cables for geological sampling, underwater video, oceanographic data collection and fisheries research.

ACCOMMODATION

Crew	32
Scientists/surveyors	28 plus 2 German Weather Service

SCIENTIFIC SPACES

Total scientific deck space	400 m², 20 laboratories on the main deck.
Oceanographic wet lab	Yes
Multipurpose dry lab	Yes
Chemistry lab	Yes

SURVEY SYSTEMS

Multibeam/swath system	Atlas Hydrosweep DS

UPDATED

Meteor   **2000**/0099230

Federal Agency for Agriculture and Food (BLE)

Clupea

GENERAL

Comments	Side trawler type. Home port: Rostock – Marienehe
Built (yard and date)	Bodden shipyard, Damgarten; 1949

Rebuilt (yard and date)	Modernised 1987
Length overall	17.6 m
Breadth moulded	5.12 m
Max draught	2.42 m
Tonnage (grt)	46

PROPULSION		ACCOMMODATION	
Speed (cruising)	8.5 kt	Crew	4
		Scientists/surveyors	3-4

NEW ENTRY

Federal Agency for Agriculture and Food (BLE)

Solea

GENERAL		Speed (cruising)	12 kt
Comments	Stern trawler type. Home port: Hamburg	Electrical power	170 kVA
Classification	GL + 100 A 5KE + MC AUT 10	**BRIDGE NAVIGATION AIDS**	
Call sign	DBFI	Radar	2
Built (yard and date)	Commissioned 29 May 1974		
Length overall	35.4 m	**DECK MACHINERY**	
Breadth moulded	9.0 m	Winches	2 fishing, 1,500 m, 9 t
Max draught	3.6 m		
Tonnage (grt)	338	**ACCOMMODATION**	
		Crew	11
PROPULSION		Scientists/surveyors	5
Main engine(s)	Diesel, 640 kW		

UPDATED

Federal Agency for Agriculture and Food (BLE)

Walther Herwig III

GENERAL		BRIDGE NAVIGATION AIDS	
Comments	Stern trawler type vessel. Home port: Bremerhaven	Satellite	MNS 2000
		Radar	X-band; S-band + ARPA
Owner	Federal Ministry for Consumer Protection, Food and Agriculture	Gyrocompass	Yes
		Speed log	Doppler; EM
Classification	GL + 100 A 5E2, + MCE 2 AUT		
Call sign	DBFR	**DECK MACHINERY**	
Built (yard and date)	Berne and Wolgast; 1992/93	Winches	2 trawl, 3,000 m, 165 kN; 2, 6,000 m, 30 kN
Length overall	64.5 m		
Breadth moulded	14.8 m		
Max draught	5.96 m	**ACCOMMODATION**	
Tonnage (grt)	2,131	Crew	21
		Scientists/surveyors	12
PROPULSION			
Main engine(s)	Diesel/diesel-electric, 2,900 kW in total; main diesel engine 1,800 kW; MaK 453C	**SURVEY SYSTEMS**	
		Echo-sounder (single beam)	2 × Simrad EK500
Propellers	cp, fixed Kort nozzle		
Speed (cruising)	13.5 kt		

UPDATED

Forschungsansalt der Bundeswehr fur Wasserschall und Geophysik

Planet

GENERAL	
Official number	A 1450
Built (yard and date)	Norderwerft, Hamburg; 1967
Length overall	80.4 m
Breadth moulded	12.6 m
Operational draught	4 m

PROPULSION	
Main engine(s)	Diesel-electric, 4 MWM diesel
Thrusters	Bow generators; 1 motor; 1.02 MW (1,390 hp)
Speed (cruising)	13 kt
Endurance	9,400 n miles at 13 kt

BRIDGE NAVIGATION AIDS	
Radar	2 Raytheon; I-band

Planet (Harald Carstens)   ***2001***/0104541

HELIDECK

Size, aircraft capacity	1 Bell 206B or MBB BO 105 CB

ACCOMMODATION

Crew	39
Scientists/surveyors	22

SURVEY SYSTEMS

Sensors	Hull-mounted search sonar

UPDATED

Institute for Baltic Sea Research Warnemünde/Baltic Marine Service GmbH

Alexander von Humboldt

GENERAL

Comments	Constructed as a modified fishing vessel. Converted in 1970 to a research vessel.
Former names	*Georgius Agricola*, renamed in 1970
Owner	Land Mecklenburg-Vorpommern
Classification	GL 100 A4 E1
Call sign	Y3CW
Built	Penewerft Wolgast: 1967
Rebuilt (yard and date)	Fully reconstructed in 1977/78 as an oceanographic research vessel
Length overall	64.23 m
Breadth moulded	10.50 m
Max draught	5.20 m
Tonnage (grt)	1,249 grt

PROPULSION

Main engine(s)	Type 6 NZD 72; 1,286 kW
Thrusters	Bow: 70 kW; active rudder: 70 kW
Propellers	VPP
Speed (max)	12 kt
Speed (cruising)	10 kt
Endurance	50 days
Fuel capacity	330 m³
Fuel consumption	4.5 t per day
Electrical power	3 × diesel generators; 330/150/75 kVA, shaft generator 400 kVA; 380/220V, 50 Hz
Fresh water capacity	50 m³ fresh water, 55 m³ drinking water, production 8 m³/day

BRIDGE NAVIGATION AIDS

Satellite	2 × DGPS
Radar	2

Gyrocompass	1
Speed log	Doppler
Echo-sounder	3

DECK MACHINERY

Cranes	Slewing boom, 4 t
A-frame(s)	Stern, SWL 50 kN
Winches	2 drum, 3,000 m, 7 mm and 6,000 m, 4 mm Lerok 12 kN, 10,000 m, 5 mm Lerok 5 kN, 4,000 m, 4 mm Geological 20 kN, 5,000 m, 8 mm

ACCOMMODATION

Crew	16
Scientists/surveyors	12/15

SCIENTIFIC SPACES

Total scientific deck space	130 m²
Oceanographic wet lab	Biological lab: 22.5 m²
Multipurpose dry lab	17 m²
	Physics lab: 11 m²
	C14 lab: 4.5 m²
	Photolab: 4 m²
	Weather lab: 2.7 m²
Chemistry lab	20 m²

SURVEY SYSTEMS

Echo-sounder (single beam)	Atlas Deso 25
Oceanographic sensors (CTDs/XBTs and so on)	Surface water themosalinograph CTD

UPDATED

Alexander von Humboldt   2001/0079770

Institute for Baltic Sea Research Warnemünde/Baltic Marine Services GmbH

Professor Albrecht Penck

GENERAL

Owner	Land Mecklenburg-Vorpommern
Classification	GL 100 A4 G1
Call sign	Y3CH
Built (yard and date)	Roßlau and Peene-yard, Wolgast: 1951
Rebuilt (yard and date)	Extensive improvement of scientific equipment: 1993
Length overall	38.58 m
Breadth moulded	7.28 m
Max draught	3.5 m
Tonnage (grt)	307

PROPULSION

Main engine(s)	Type 8 NVD 36, 220 kW
Speed (max)	9 kt
Speed (cruising)	8 kt
Endurance	20 days
Fuel capacity	40 m³
Fuel consumption	1.5 t per day at service speed
Electrical power	2 diesel generators, 2 × 67 kW; 380/220V, 50 Hz
Fresh water capacity	36 m³ (drinking water)

BRIDGE NAVIGATION AIDS

Satellite	2 × DGPS
Radar	2
Gyrocompass	Yes
Echo-sounder	2

COMMUNICATIONS

VHF	Yes
Cellular	Yes
Facsimile	Yes

DECK MACHINERY

Cranes	Hydraulic cantilever, 3 t at 7 m (3 m outboard)
Winches	CTD, 1,500 m coaxial tross cable 8.2 mm
	hydraulic drum 2 t, 600 m coaxial tross cable 8.2 mm, 1,000 m steel rope 6 mm

ACCOMMODATION

Crew	10
Scientists/surveyors	11/12

SCIENTIFIC SPACES

Oceanographic wet lab	Biological lab: 6 m²
	Computer lab: 6 m²
	Hydro lab: 9 m²
	Evaluation room: 4 m²
Chemistry lab	13 m²

SURVEY SYSTEMS

Echo-sounder (single beam)	Yes
Oceanographic sensors (CTDs/XBTs and so on)	Surface water thermosadnograph ADCP CTD

UPDATED

Institute for Coastal Research, GKSS

Ludwig Prandtl

GENERAL

Classification	Germanischer Lloyd 100A 4K
Length overall	24.5 m
Breadth moulded	6.3 m

PROPULSION

Main engine(s)	2 × 184 kW
Propellers	2 Schottel jets
Speed (cruising)	10 kt
Electrical power	2 generators, 24 V, 220 V, 380 V

BRIDGE NAVIGATION AIDS

Satellite	GPS

SAFETY

Workboat/chase boat	Dinghy

DECK MACHINERY

Cranes	Yes
A-frame(s)	Yes
Winches	2 hydraulic

SURVEY SYSTEMS

Echo-sounder (single beam)	2

UPDATED

Institut fur Meereskunde, University of Kiel

Polarfuchs

GENERAL

Comments	Planned as an auxiliary craft for the Research Vessel *Polarstern*. Modernised, refitted and integrated into the research vessel fleet on 28 November 1997
Built (yard and date)	Fassmer shipyard, Motzen; 1982
Length overall	12.7 m
Breadth moulded	4.4 m
Max draught	1.35 m

PROPULSION

Speed (max)	7.5 kt
Endurance	60 n miles range

DECK MACHINERY

A-frame(s)	Stern
Winches	2: 250 m/6 mm wire, 350 kg
	1: 80 m/6 mm, 100 kg

ACCOMMODATION

Crew	2
Scientists/surveyors	6

NEW ENTRY

Institut fur Meersekunde, University of Kiel

Littorina

GENERAL

Comments	Research cutter
Built (yard and date)	Julius Dietrich Shipyard, Oldersum; 1975
Length overall	29.8 m
Breadth moulded	7.42 m
Operational draught	3.0 m
Tonnage (grt)	168

PROPULSION

Speed (cruising)	10 kt
Endurance	2,000 n miles range

BRIDGE NAVIGATION AIDS

Satellite	GPS

ACCOMMODATION

Crew	5
Scientists/surveyors	6 (12 on 1-day voyages)

SCIENTIFIC SPACES

Multipurpose dry lab	12 m^2

SURVEY SYSTEMS

Echo-sounder (single beam)	30 kHz/200 kHz

VERIFIED

K & K Nordseeforschungsschiff – Bereederung GmbH

Senckenberg

GENERAL

Current operational status	Certified for operation in the North Sea, Baltic Sea, English Channel, Celtic Sea and Irish Sea
Owner	Senckenberg Natural History Society, Frankfurt
Port of reg/flag	Wilhelmshaven, Germany
Classification	GL + 100 A 4 ME + MC AUT
Call sign	DDAW
Built (yard and date)	Schiffswerft Diedrich, Oldersum, Germany: 1976
Length overall	29.71 m
Breadth moulded	7.42 m
Working deck width	6.8 m
Max draught	2.74 m
Operational draught	2.74 m
Tonnage (grt)	164.99

PROPULSION

Main engine(s)	1 KHD SBF 12M 716, 346 kW at 1,500 rpm; 2 MWM D 226-4, 32 kW at 1,500 rpm
Thrusters	Becker high-performance rudder
Propellers	Variable pitch
Speed (max)	12 kt
Speed (cruising)	9 kt
Endurance	14 days (2,000 n miles)
Fuel capacity	23 t
Fuel consumption	1.15 t per 100 n miles (at cruising speed)
Electrical power	2 Piller NKT 50-4, 35 kVA, 1,500 rpm, 380 V, 50 Hz
Fresh water capacity	15 t

BRIDGE NAVIGATION AIDS

Satellite	Raytheon Raystar 920 GPS, Shipmate RS 5400 DGPS
Radar	Koden MD 2000 (daylight)
Gyrocompass	Plath
Speed log	Shipmate RS 2800 power plotter/recorder
Echo-sounder	Elac LAZ 51 ATR 303, 30 kHz

COMMUNICATIONS

MF/HF	Sailor SSB RE 2100
VHF	Sailor Compact RT 2048
Cellular	D-net
Facsimile	D-Net

SAFETY

Lifeboats	1 dinghy, solid body, 4 m
Workboat/chase boat	Viking rubber dinghy, 14.72 kW
Lifesaving equipment	2 liferafts, 12 survival suits

DECK MACHINERY

Cranes	Main deck, 1 hydraulic, foldable, 2.5 t (max); aft deck, hydraulic pocket, 1 t
Winches	Main deck, trawling

ACCOMMODATION

Crew	5
Scientists/surveyors	5

SCIENTIFIC SPACES

Total scientific deck space	70 m^2
Multipurpose dry lab	12 m^2 (wet/dry)

SURVEY SYSTEMS

Positioning	Shipmate RS 5400 DGPS/RS 2800 power plotter
Echo-sounder (single beam)	Furuno FZ 1000, 50/200 kHz with QTC seabed classification
Sidescan sonar	Klein Hydroscan 520, 100/500 kHz
Sub-bottom profiler	Geo-Pulse boomer
Corer(s)	Reineck box corer (0.2 × 0.3 × 0.4 m) Vibrocorer (0.1 × 0.1 × 3 m)
Grab(s)	Shipek, Van Heen (0.1 m^2 and larger)
Vehicle(s) (ROVs/AUVs and so on)	Hyball ROV (300 m depth rating)
Oceanographic sensors (CTDs/XBTs and so on)	CTD – ME multiprobe CTD – Aanderaa CMR 9 multiprobe ADCP – RDI 1,200 kHz

UPDATED

RF Reedereigemeinschaft Forschungsschiffahrt GmbH

Alkor

GENERAL

Sister ship of RV *Heincke*

Owner	Institut fur Meersekunde, University of Kiel
Port of reg/flag	Germany
Classification	GL + 100 A4 E2 "Special ship" MC E2 AUT
Call sign	DBND
Built (yard and date)	Schiffs- und Maschinenfabrik Cassens GmbH, Emden; 1990
Length overall	55.2 m
Breadth moulded	12.5 m
Operational draught	4.16 m
Tonnage (grt)	1,322
Displacement	1,463 t

PROPULSION

Main engine(s)	3 KHD-MWM TBD-604 L 6, 525 kW each
Thrusters	Schottel pump-jet 620 kW; Becker rudder
Speed (cruising)	12.5 kt
Fuel capacity	144.06 t
Electrical power	3 generators: 800 kVA, 380 V, 50 Hz 228 kVA, 380 V, 50 Hz 40 kVA, 380 V, 50 Hz
Fresh water capacity	21.92 t, 3 t/day production

BRIDGE NAVIGATION AIDS

Satellite	NMS 2000, Mk 53B, Trimble 10X
Radar	2
Gyrocompass	1
Speed log	Dolog 22D; Naviknot II
Echo-sounder	2
Other ship navigation	Radio direction-finder

COMMUNICATIONS

Inmarsat (type)	Satcom Standard A
MF/HF	HF-SSB R/T
VHF	Yes
Facsimile	Weather receiver

DECK MACHINERY

Cranes	Main, 6.0 t; auxiliary, 0.99 t; gallow, 3.0 t
A-frame(s)	3 t
Winches	Deep sea anchor, 1,000 m, 16 mm; fishery, 2 × 1,200 m, 20 mm; net winder, 4.0 t Winch for net monitoring system, 1,200 m

ACCOMMODATION

Crew	10
Scientists/surveyors	12

SCIENTIFIC SPACES

Oceanographic wet lab	28 m²
Multipurpose dry lab	Multipurpose: 22 m² Dry lab: 42 m² Freezing lab: 9 m²
Chemistry lab	15 m²

SURVEY SYSTEMS

Sensors	Net monitoring systems
Echo-sounder (single beam)	2 fishery; sediment

UPDATED

Alkor

2000/0099233

RF Reedereigemeinschaft Forschungsschiffahrt GmbH

Heincke

GENERAL

	Sister ship of RV *Alkor*
Owner	Biologische Ansalt Helgoland, Hamburg
Port of reg/flag	Germany
Classification	GL + 100 A4 E2 "Special ship" MC E2 AUT
Call sign	DBCK
Built (yard and date)	Detlef Hegemann Roland-Werft GmbH & Co, KG, Berne; 1990
Length overall	55.2 m
Breadth moulded	12.5 m
Operational draught	4.16 m
Tonnage (grt)	1,322
Displacement	1,463 t

PROPULSION

Main engine(s)	3 KHD-MWM TBD-604 L 6, 525 kW each
Thrusters	Schottel pump-jet 620 kW, Becker rudder
Speed (cruising)	12.5 kt
Fuel capacity	144.06 t
Electrical power	3 generators: 800 kVA, 380 V, 50 Hz 228 kVA, 380 V, 50 Hz 40 kVA, 380 V, 50 Hz
Fresh water capacity	21.92 t, 3 t/day production

BRIDGE NAVIGATION AIDS

Satellite	NMS 2000, Mk 53B, Trimble 10X
Radar	2
Gyrocompass	1
Speed log	Dolog 22D; Naviknot II
Echo-sounder	2
Other ship navigation	Radio direction-finder

COMMUNICATIONS

Inmarsat (type)	Satcom Standard A
MF/HF	HF-SSB R/T
VHF	Yes
Facsimile	Weather receiver

DECK MACHINERY

Cranes	Main, 6 t; auxiliary, 0.99 t; gallow, 3 t
A-frame(s)	3 t
Winches	Deep sea anchor, 1,000 m, 16 mm; fishery, 2 × 1, 200 m, 20 mm; net winder, 4 t Winch for net monitoring system, 1,200 m

ACCOMMODATION

Crew	10
Scientists/surveyors	12

SCIENTIFIC SPACES

Oceanographic wet lab	28 m²
Multipurpose dry lab	Multipurpose: 22 m² Dry lab: 42 m² Freezing lab: 9 m²
Chemistry lab	15 m²

SURVEY SYSTEMS

Sensors	Net monitoring systems
Echo-sounder (single beam)	2 fishery

UPDATED

RF Reedereigemeinschaft Forschungsschiffahrt GmbH

Poseidon

GENERAL

Owner	State of Schleswig Holstein	Port of reg/flag	Germany
		Classification	GL + 100 A4 EM + MC Aut 16/24

Poseidon

2000/0099228

Call sign	DBKV
Built (yard and date)	Schichau Unterweser AG, Bremerhaven; 1976
Length overall	60.8 m
Breadth moulded	11.4 m
Operational draught	4.365 m
Tonnage (grt)	1,105
Displacement	1,509 t

PROPULSION

Main engine(s)	3 MWM TD-602 V 16; each 550 kW
Thrusters	Bow: Gill-Jet, 290 kW, thrust 4 t Becker rudder
Speed (cruising)	12.5 kt
Fuel capacity	130 t
Fuel consumption	4.8 t/day at 12.5 kt
Electrical power	3 AEG generators, type DKBH 408/04, each 810 kVA, 660 V, 50 Hz 1 AEG, type DKBH 282/04, 100 kVA, 385 V, 50 Hz
Fresh water capacity	60 t, 2 t/day production

BRIDGE NAVIGATION AIDS

Satellite	Yes
Radar	3
Gyrocompass	Yes
Speed log	Yes
Echo-sounder	2
Other ship navigation	Radio direction-finder

COMMUNICATIONS

MF/HF	SSB/AM/IW/FM transmitter 1.4 kW, 10 kHz – 30 MHz
VHF	Yes
Facsimile	Weatherfax receiver

DECK MACHINERY

Cranes	Main, 6 t; jib boom, 10 t; travelling hoist in front store, 2.5 t; travelling hoist in Wet lab, 1.1 t
A-frame(s)	Stern: 5.0 t
Winches	Fishery, 2 × 1,500 m, 16 mm, each 5 t and 2 auxiliary drums, 140 m, 16 mm Single core towing, 2,000 m, 10 mm, 2 t Multiconductor and serial, 250 m, 15 mm; 1,500 m, 6 mm; vertical, 2,000 m, 16 mm, 8/4 t; single core, 1,500 m, 10 mm, 0.5 t

ACCOMMODATION

Crew	18
Scientists/surveyors	12

SCIENTIFIC SPACES

Total scientific deck space	135 m²
Oceanographic wet lab	Yes
Multipurpose dry lab	Yes
Chemistry lab	Yes

SURVEY SYSTEMS

Positioning	Pinger registration system, 12 kHz
Sensors	Net Sounder
Echo-sounder (single beam)	30 kHz; fisheries; sediment, 18 kHz
Multibeam/swath system	150 kHz

UPDATED

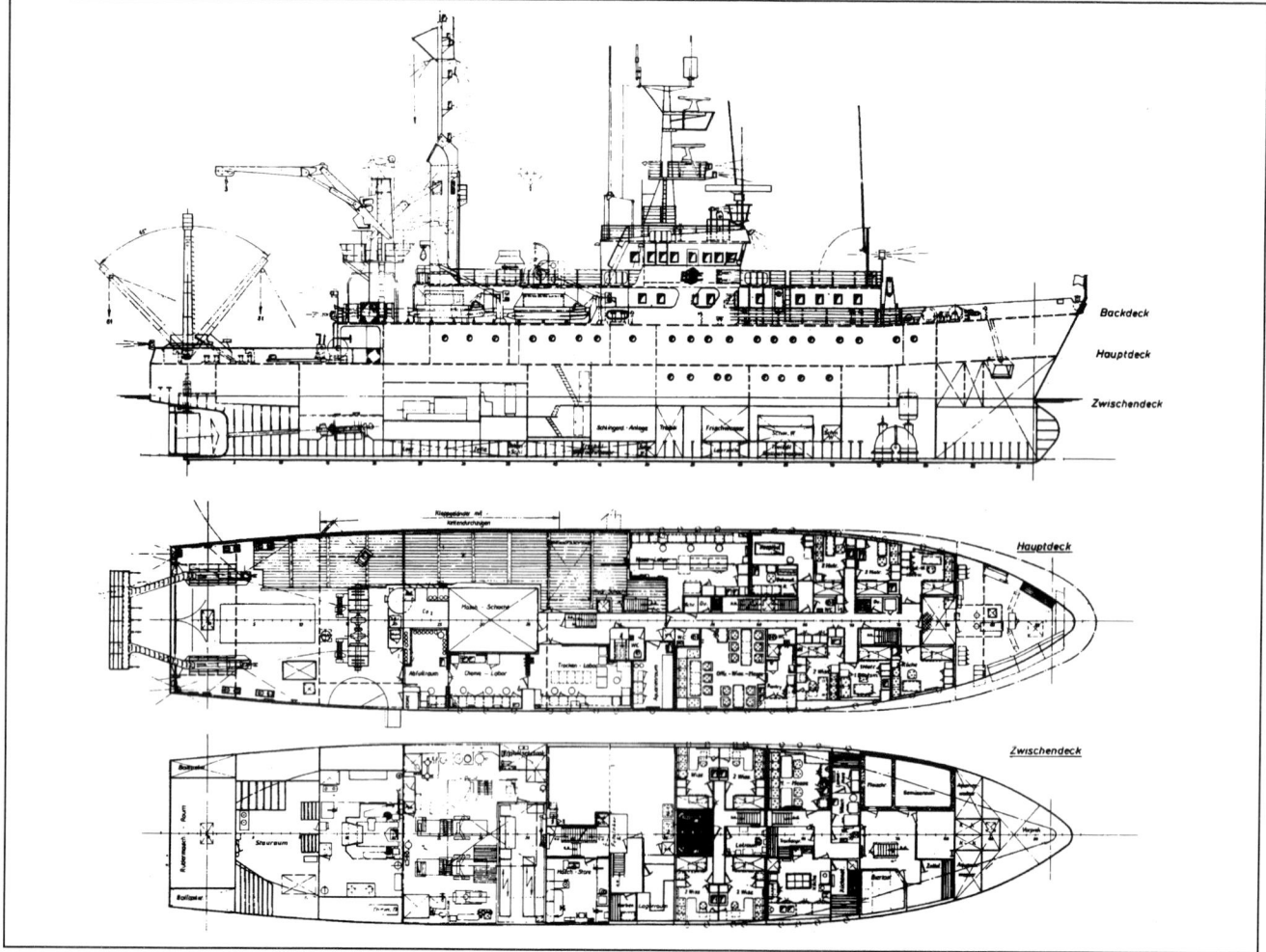

Poseidon (plans)   **2000**/0099227

RF Reedereigemeinschaft Forschungsschiffahrt GmbH

Sonne

GENERAL

Comments	Originally built as a stern-fishing trawler
Owner	Partenreederei MS Sonne
Port of reg/flag	Bremen, Germany
Classification	GL + 100 A4 EF + MC
Call sign	DFCG
Built (yard and date)	Rickmers-Werft, Bremerhaven; 1969
Rebuilt (yard and date)	1977 – Schichau Unterweser AG, Bremerhaven
	1978 – Rickmers-Werft, Bremerhaven
	1991 – Schichau Unterweser AG, Bremerhaven
Length overall	97.61 m
Breadth moulded	14.2 m
Max draught	6.8 m
Displacement	4,734 t

PROPULSION

Main engine(s)	3 MaK 8 M 282, 1,500 kW at 1,000 rpm; port diesel, MaK 8 M 281, 735 kW at 7,500 rpm

Thrusters	Bow: azimuth, 1,115 kW; Becker rudder
Speed (cruising)	12.5 kt
Endurance	50 days
Fuel capacity	657 t
Electrical power	3 DMT generators, each 2,000 kVA, 660 V, 50 Hz
	1 AEG, harbour generator, 510 kVA, 380/220 V, 50 Hz
Fresh water capacity	43 t

BRIDGE NAVIGATION AIDS

Satellite	Skyfix DGPS
Radar	1 ARPA; 1 AC
Gyrocompass	2
Speed log	Doppler EM
Echo-sounder	2
Other ship navigation	Loran C; radio direction-finder

SAFETY

Lifeboats	Yes
Workboat/chase boat	Yes

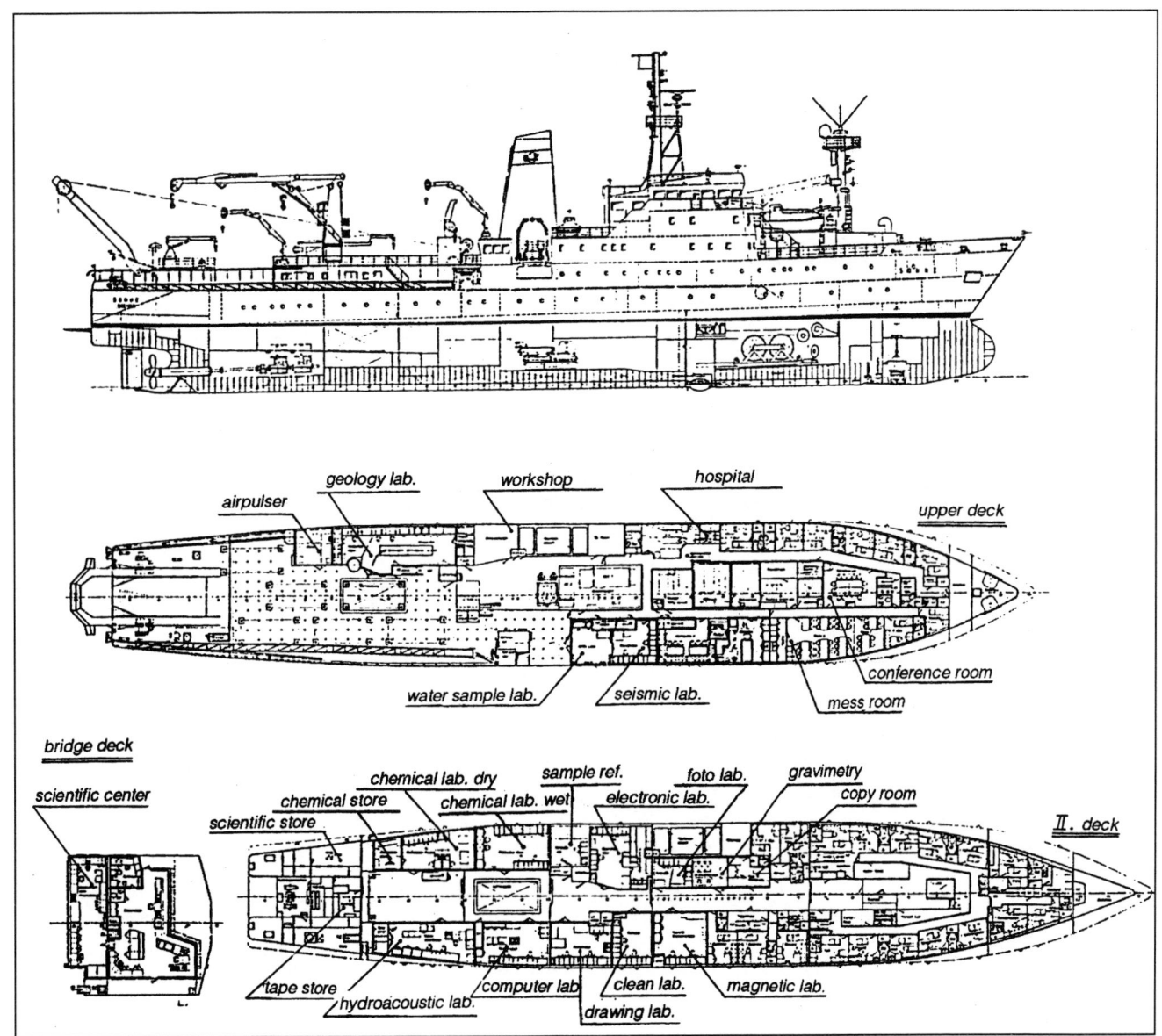

Sonne (plans)

Sonne   **2000**/0099219

DECK MACHINERY

Cranes	2 assistant, 20 kN; assistant, 17 kN; central, 53/177 kN, 17/7 m range; derrick, 50 kN; jib-boom, 100 kN, 3 m (max); corer frame, 24 m; magnetometer, 9 kN; side gallow, 30 kN; main (15 t), two auxiliary, jib-boom (20 t), corer, handling device, side gallow
A-frame(s)	Stern: 120.0 kN, 125° slewable
Winches	Deeptow with two storage, 8,000 m, 18 mm, 2 m/s; geological, 8,000 m, 18 mm, 2 m/s; Hatlapa hydrographic, 7,000 m, 11 mm; 10 auxiliary for scientific instruments

ACCOMMODATION

Crew	30
Scientists/surveyors	25

SCIENTIFIC SPACES

Total scientific deck space	Main deck: 260 m² plus 5 container spaces II deck: 116 m²
Oceanographic wet lab	Main deck: 15 m²
Multipurpose dry lab	Main deck: Geology lab 51 m²; Seismic lab 11 m²; Sample preparation lab 5 m² II deck: Electronics lab 24 m²; gravimeter lab 11 m²; photo lab 12 m²; hydroacoustic lab 32 m²; gravimetry/magnetic lab 28 m²

Chemistry lab	II deck: dry chemistry lab 28 m² ; wet chemistry lab 28 m²

SURVEY SYSTEMS

Positioning	Ashtech ADU-II GPS attitude sensor; USBL and LBL acoustic positioning systems
Echo-sounder (single beam)	Atlas DESO 25, 12 kHz Elac 30 kHz
Multibeam/swath system	Atlas Hydrosweep DS
Sub-bottom profiler	Atlas Parasound
Grab(s)	2 deep sea TV
Other sampling	Ocean floor observation system (Video, stereo photo, CTD)
Oceanographic sensors (CTDs/XBTs and so on)	Multiprobe; rosette water sampler; X-ray fluoroscopy; X-ray defractometry; thermosalinograph

SEISMIC SYSTEMS

Number of airguns	2 × 21 connectors, 2 airgun arrays, 2 trigger relays
Compressor numbers and types	4 for reflexion seismic
Total capacity	2 × 25 m³/min; 2 × 2 m³/min, working pressure 150 bar

UPDATED

RF Reedereigemeinschaft Forschungsschiffart GmbH

Victor Hensen

GENERAL

Comments	Multipurpose research vessel
Owner	RF Reedereigemeinschaft Forschungsschiffahrt GmbH
Port of reg/flag	Bremerhaven

Classification	GL + 100 A4 E + MC E Aut 16/24
Call sign	DBAW
Built (yard and date)	Schichau Unterweser AG, Bremerhaven; 1974/75
Length overall	39.22 m

Breadth moulded	9.4 m
Operational draught	3.53 m

PROPULSION

Main engine(s)	2 MTU 6 R 362 TB 61
	(2 × 353 kW)
	Schottel bow thruster 129 kW
Propellers	Escher-Wyss CPP
Speed (cruising)	12.3 kt
Fuel consumption	3.2 t/day
Electrical power	MAN-diesel 135 kVA, shaft
	generator 375 kVA

BRIDGE NAVIGATION AIDS

Echo-sounder	30 kHz

DECK MACHINERY

Cranes	AK 6000 2 (5) t; AK 3006 0.5
	(1.5) t
Winches	Fishing, 2 drums, SWL 5 t,
	1,500 m, 14 mm

ACCOMMODATION

Crew	11
Scientists/surveyors	12

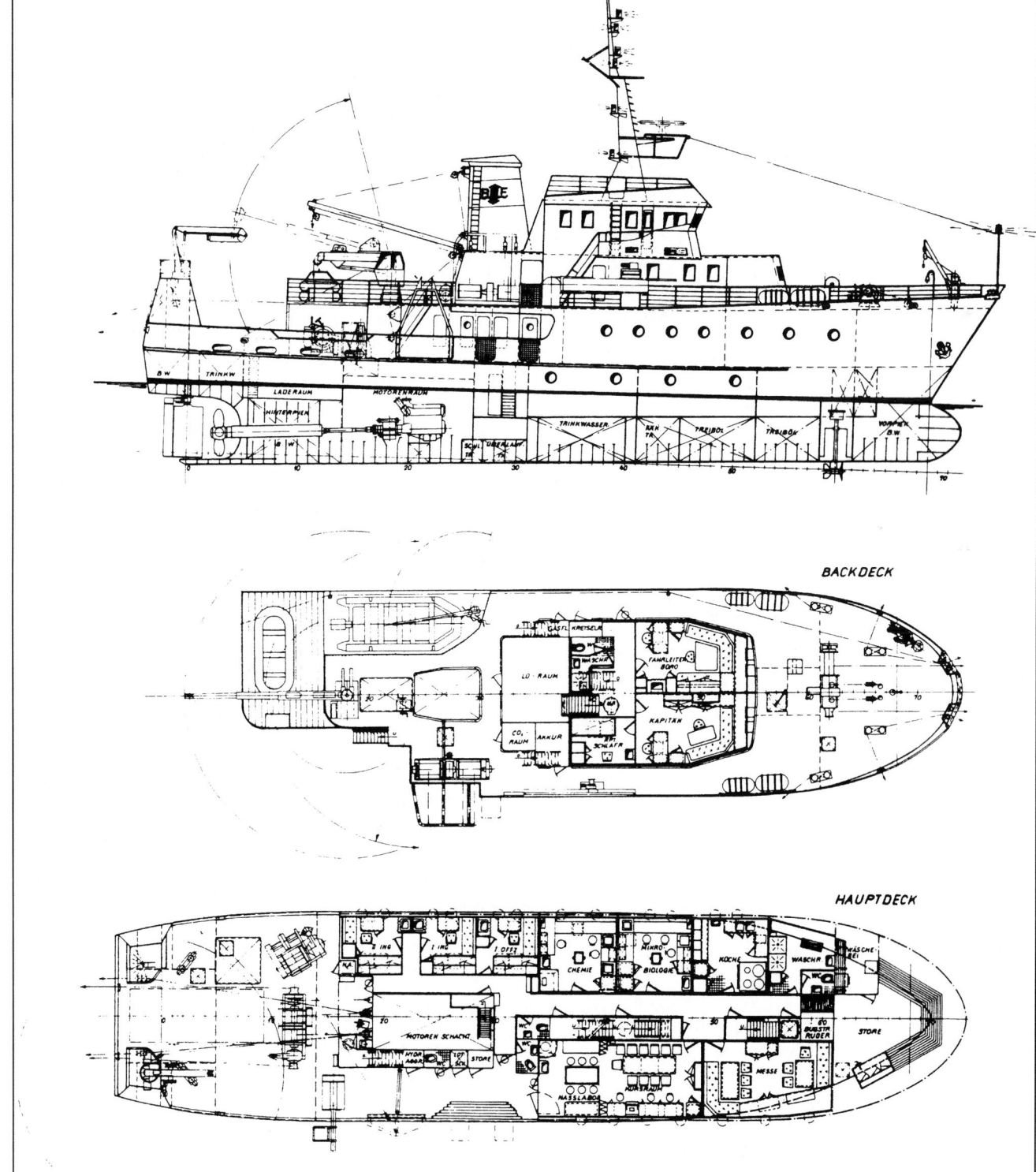

Victor Hensen (plans)

2000/0099216

SCIENTIFIC SPACES		SURVEY SYSTEMS	
Oceanographic wet lab	10 m²	Echo-sounder (single beam)	18 kHz
Multipurpose dry lab	16 m²		
Chemistry lab	12 m²		

UPDATED

Victor Hensen

2000/0099215

GREECE

Institute of Marine Biology of Crete

Philia

GENERAL

Port of reg/flag	Iraklion, Greece
Official number	12
Classification	+H100 A1 R(F, HMC)
Call sign	SW 2204
Built (yard and date)	Piraeus, 1986
Length overall	26.1 m
Breadth moulded	7.25 m
Working deck width	6.5 m
Max draught	3.2 m
Operational draught	2.55 m
Tonnage (grt)	142.72

PROPULSION

Main engine(s)	Twin Mann diesel: each 350 shp
Thrusters	Bow: 25 hp
Propellers	vp
Speed (max)	10 kt
Speed (cruising)	9 kt
Fuel capacity	22 t
Fuel consumption	Approx 1,600 litres/day
Electrical power	2 Mann 85 kW generators
Fresh water capacity	6 t

BRIDGE NAVIGATION AIDS

Satellite	Fugro DGPS
Radar	2 Furuno
Gyrocompass	Anschutz
Speed log	Simrad
Echo-sounder	Furuno 15/28/50/200 kHz

COMMUNICATIONS

Inmarsat (type)	GMDSS A2
MF/HF	Yes
VHF	3

SAFETY

Workboat/chase boat	1 × 4.6 m, 40 hp
Lifesaving equipment	2 × 25 person liferafts

DECK MACHINERY

Cranes	Hiab, 2 t with extending arm
Winches	2 net drums; 2 fishing winches, 12 mm, 1,200 m; 1 hydrographic, 4 mm × 2,000 m; 6 mm × 1,300 m
Transducer well	Yes

ACCOMMODATION

Crew	7
Scientists/surveyors	6

SCIENTIFIC SPACES

Total scientific deck space	35 m^2
Oceanographic wet lab	9 m^2
Multipurpose dry lab	9 m^2 (additional 12.5 m^2 electronics lab)

SURVEY SYSTEMS

Positioning	Fugro DGPS
Sensors	Seabed classification: RoxAnn
	Furuno colour net recorder
Echo-sounder (single beam)	Simrad EK 500, 38/120 kHz
	Simrad EK 400, 120 kHz
Multibeam/swath system	Biosonics dual-beam 120 kHz V-Fin

Sidescan sonar	Yes
Corer(s)	Box
Grab(s)	Various
Other sampling	Benthic & Pelagic trawls; plankton samplers; Simrad cameras and sledge
Vehicle(s) (ROVs/AUVs and so on)	ROV: MiniRover Mk II
Sound velocity profiler	Yes
Oceanographic sensors (CTDs/XBTs and so on)	CTD – SeaBird Electronics Current meters (7) – Aanderaa RC7 Weather station – Aanderaa Meteostar 2000 irradiance, oxygen, fluorimeter

UPDATED

Philia   **2000**/0099214

National Centre for Marine Research

Aegaeo

GENERAL

Port of reg/flag	Chalkis, Greece
Classification	+H 100 A1
Call sign	SXYY
Built (yard and date)	Chalkis Shipyards, 1985

Rebuilt (yard and date)	Length extended by 10 m: completed 1997
Length overall	61.51 m
Breadth moulded	9.6 m
Operational draught	2.9 m (summer)
Tonnage (grt)	778

PROPULSION

Main engine(s)	2 × 950 bhp MAN ZL 20/27VO
Thrusters	Bow – Schottel ski-87 unit of 1 mph
Propellers	2
Speed (max)	13.5 kt
Speed (cruising)	12 kt
Endurance	20 days
Fuel capacity	80 t
Fuel consumption	6 t/day at12 kt
Electrical power	3 phase: 380 V AC, 50 Hz 1 phase: 220 V AC/110 V AC/24 V DC (50 Hz)

BRIDGE NAVIGATION AIDS

Satellite	Trimble Navigation 4000 AX North Star 941X
Radar	Furuno with Plotter FCR-1421 Mk II, 96 miles Racal Decca 250 with Geographics, 96 miles
Gyrocompass	Sperry SR 120
Speed log	Doppler – Simrad NL
Echo-sounder	Furuno FE824ET
Other ship navigation	Autopilot – A/P Neco 728

COMMUNICATIONS

Inmarsat (type)	VHF/DSC
VHF	Sailor Compact RT2047 Navico
Facsimile	Furuno FAX 108 Navtex NMR 100

DECK MACHINERY

Cranes	3.5 t
A-frame(s)	Stern – 10 t SWL, 7.3 m height; port – 1 t
Winches	2 main – 2 drums, 2,500 m, 16 mm; oceanographic – 1 drum, 2,500 m for CDT; 1 drum, 6,000 m, 4 mm; oceanographic – 1 drum, 6,000 m for CDT

ACCOMMODATION

Crew	22
Scientists/surveyors	21 (8 × 2-berth, 1 × 1 berth, 1 × 4-berth cabins)

SCIENTIFIC SPACES

Oceanographic wet lab	10 m^2
Multipurpose dry lab	29 m^2: general lab – chemistry/biology; 6 m^2: primary productivity lab; 32 m^2: geological acoustics survey room; 6 m^2: computers lab; 12 m^2: Clean room – dissolved trace elements analysis (container)

SURVEY SYSTEMS

Echo-sounder (single beam)	ODEC Bathy 1000
Multibeam/swath system	SeaBeam 2120 (20 kHz)
Sub-bottom profiler	2 × 3.5 kHz towed systems (4-16 transducers
Magnetometer	1
Corer(s)	3 × gravity core samplers (3-6 m long); 1 × box corer
Other sampling	Rosette, 12 Nisken Bottles
Oceanographic sensors (CTDs/XBTs and so on)	CTD; ADCP

SEISMIC SYSTEMS

Energy source (type and manufacturer)	1 × 19 kg Sparker system
Size of airguns	40 in^3 with 2 hydrophone arrays

UPDATED

ICELAND

Marine Research Institute

Árni Friöriksson

GENERAL

	Fisheries and oceanographic research vessel
Owner	Government of Iceland
Port of reg/flag	Iceland
Official number	Sk No 2350
Classification	Lloyds Register LRS + 11 A1 Research Vessel + LMC Ice Class 1C
Call sign	TFNA
Built (yard and date)	Asmar, Chile, 2000
Length overall	69.9 m
Breadth moulded	14 m
Working deck width	14 m
Max draught	6.8 m
Operational draught	6.5 m
Tonnage (grt)	2,200

PROPULSION

Main engine(s)	Alstom diesel-electric, 3,300 kW at 150 rpm; 4 Caterpillar 3512 B, 1,080 kW at 1,200 rpm
Thrusters	Schottel pump-jet 82RD bow and stern 400 kW
Propellers	1 KaMeWa FPP
Speed (max)	16 kt
Speed (cruising)	13 kt
Endurance	30 days
Fuel capacity	Approx 430,000 litres
Fuel consumption	Max 12.3 litres/h
Electrical power	AVK DSG 86 M1-6 generators, 1,200 kVA
Fresh water capacity	60,000 litres

BRIDGE NAVIGATION AIDS

Satellite	Trimble NT200D DGPS
Radar	Furuno FAR-28355 S-band; Furuno FR2115 X-band
Gyrocompass	Anschutz std 20
Speed log	Yes
Echo-sounder	Yes

COMMUNICATIONS

Inmarsat (type)	Type B and Type C

MF/HF	Sailor 250 W radio station	**SCIENTIFIC SPACES**	
VHF	Yes	**Total scientific deck space**	180 m²
Cellular	Yes	**Oceanographic wet lab**	47 m²
Facsimile	Yes	**Multipurpose dry lab**	45 m²
		Chemistry lab	16 m²

SAFETY
Lifeboats	Yes
Workboat/chase boat	Yes
Lifesaving equipment	Yes

SURVEY SYSTEMS
Sensors	Kaijo KCS-2882, KCH-1828 search sonars
Echo-sounder (single beam)	2 Simrad EK 500, 18, 38 and 120 kHz
Multibeam/swath system	Simrad EM-300
Other sampling	Bottom and pelagic trawls
Oceanographic sensors (CTDs/XBTs and so on)	RDI ADCP

DECK MACHINERY
Cranes	70 t/m, max length 19 m; 36 t/m, max length 16 m
Winches	3 trawl, 32 t; 2 net: various auxiliary CTD; hydrographic 200 plankton 2 × electrical cable

UPDATED

ACCOMMODATION
Crew	14
Scientists/surveyors	18
Hospital	2

Marine Research Institute

Bjarni Saemundsson

GENERAL
	Fisheries and oceanographic research vessel
Owner	Government of Iceland
Port of reg/flag	Reykjavik, Iceland
Official number	Sk No 1131
Classification	Germanischer Lloyd
Call sign	TFEA
Built (yard and date)	Bremerhaven, Germany, 1970
Length overall	55.88 m
Breadth moulded	10.6 m
Working deck width	10 m
Max draught	7 m
Operational draught	5.2 m
Tonnage (grt)	822

PROPULSION
Main engine(s)	3 × 410 kW diesel-electric
Thrusters	Bow: Schottel 175 hp
Propellers	1 fixed
Speed (max)	12 kt
Speed (cruising)	10-11.5 kt
Endurance	24 days
Fuel capacity	180 t
Fuel consumption	1.9-2.5 t/day
Electrical power	3 × 410 kW
Fresh water capacity	71 tons

BRIDGE NAVIGATION AIDS
Satellite	3 DGPS
Radar	Kelvin Hughes 96 n miles 10 cm Furuno FR 2120 96 n miles 3 cm
Gyrocompass	Anschutz 130-507
Speed log	Sagem

COMMUNICATIONS
Inmarsat (type)	Standard C
MF/HF	GMDSS (A1, A2, A3)
VHF	GMDSS IMO
Cellular	3 NMT Mobile Telephones
Facsimile	Yes

SAFETY
Workboat/chase boat	5 m fixed-hull Zodiac
Lifesaving equipment	5 liferafts, 12 persons

DECK MACHINERY
Cranes	Palfinger 12 m boom 36 t/m and 1 × 6 m 1 t/m
Winches	2 × 6.5 t trawl, 2,650 m, 28 mm diameter; 6 auxiliary; 3 scientific

ACCOMMODATION
Crew	13
Scientists/surveyors	13

Bjarni Saemundsson

2000/0099213

SCIENTIFIC SPACES

Total scientific deck space	200 m²
Oceanographic wet lab	Oceanographic: 7 m²
	Fish lab: 56 m²
	Phytoplankton: 6 m²
Multipurpose dry lab	40 m²

SURVEY SYSTEMS

Sensors	Kayjo Denki net sonar
	Maq fishing sonar
	Simrad FS 3300 trawl surveillance
	sonar

Sidescan sonar	Simrad EK 500
Other sampling	Bottom and pelagic trawls
Oceanographic sensors	SBE 911 plus CTD with 12 bottle
(CTDs/XBTs and so on)	rosette (3,000 m depth); SBE 16;
	two Scanmar temperature and
	depth sensors

UPDATED

Marine Research Institute

Dröfn

GENERAL

	Fisheries and oceanographic
	research vessel
Owner	Government of Iceland
Port of reg/flag	Iceland

BRIDGE NAVIGATION AIDS

Satellite	Yes
Radar	Yes
Gyrocompass	Yes
Speed log	Yes
Echo-sounder	Yes

COMMUNICATIONS

MF/HF	Yes
VHF	Yes
Cellular	Yes
Facsimile	Yes

SAFETY

Lifeboats	Yes

Workboat/chase boat	Zodiac
Lifesaving equipment	4 liferafts, 12 person

DECK MACHINERY

Cranes	Yes

SCIENTIFIC SPACES

Total scientific deck space	80 m²
Oceanographic wet lab	Fish lab: 5 m²; phytoplankton:
	50 m²

SURVEY SYSTEMS

Positioning	2 DGPS
Sensors	Furuno net sonar; Atlas
	Fishfinder-701
Echo-sounder (single beam)	Elac Laz 4400
Oceanographic sensors	2 Scanmar depth and
(CTDs/XBTs and so on)	temperature sensors

VERIFIED

Dröfn

2000/0077282

INDIA

Department of Ocean Development

Gaveshani

GENERAL	
Classification	Indian Register of Shipping
Built	1975
Length overall	68.33 m
Breadth moulded	12.19 m
Operational draught	3.44 m
Tonnage (grt)	1,634

PROPULSION	
Main engine(s)	2 diesel, each 3,200 bhp at 1,360 rpm
Propellers	2.1 m diameter, 230 rpm
Speed (cruising)	10 kt
Endurance	6,000 n miles/26 days
Fuel capacity	200 m³
Electrical power	440/220 V AC, 70 kVA, 3 phase, 50 Hz

BRIDGE NAVIGATION AIDS	
Satellite	Yes
Radar	Yes
Gyrocompass	Yes
Speed log	EM

DECK MACHINERY	
Winches	4 oceanographic: 4,000 m, SWL 2 t; hydrographic: 4,000 m, SWL 2 t; trawl: 4,000 m, 2 t

ACCOMMODATION	
Crew	38
Scientists/surveyors	19

SCIENTIFIC SPACES	
Oceanographic wet lab	22 m²
Multipurpose dry lab	99 m²

SURVEY SYSTEMS	
Sensors	Fisheries sector-scan sonar
Echo-sounder (single beam)	Yes

UPDATED

Department of Ocean Development

Sagar Kanya

GENERAL	
Comments	Ocean research vessel
Classification	Lloyds Register of Shipping
Built	1983
Length overall	100.34 m
Breadth moulded	16.39 m
Operational draught	5.6 m
Tonnage (grt)	4,209

PROPULSION	
Main engine(s)	5 diesel-electric, each 4,825 bhp at 750 rpm
Propellers	2.75 m diameter, 220 rpm
Speed (max)	14.2 kt
Speed (cruising)	12 kt
Endurance	9,999 n miles/45 days
Fuel capacity	200 m³
Electrical power	660/400 V AC, 630 kVA, 3 phase, 50 Hz

BRIDGE NAVIGATION AIDS	
Satellite	Yes
Radar	Yes
Gyrocompass	Yes
Speed log	EM; Doppler

COMMUNICATIONS	
Inmarsat (type)	Yes
VHF	Yes

DECK MACHINERY	
Cranes	Stern, midships: 12 m height, 9 m outboard extension, SWL 1 t
A-frame(s)	Stern, midships: 9 m height, 3 m outboard extension, SWL 22 t
Winches	Steel wire: 9,999 m, SWL 2 t Conducting cable: 6,000 m, SWL 2 t Trawl: 4,000 m, 2 t

ACCOMMODATION	
Crew	60
Scientists/surveyors	31

SCIENTIFIC SPACES	
Total scientific deck space	470 m²
Oceanographic wet lab	80 m²
Multipurpose dry lab	290 m²

SURVEY SYSTEMS	
Echo-sounder (single beam)	12 kHz/30 kHz
Multibeam/swath system	Atlas Hydrosweep DS

UPDATED

Department of Ocean Development

Sagar Purvi and Sagar Paschmi

GENERAL	
Comments	Coastal research vessels
Classification	Indian Register of Shipping
Built	*Sagar Purvi* — December 1996; *Sagar Paschmi* — November 1996
Length overall	30.15 m

Breadth moulded	6.5 m	
Operational draught	1.8 m	
Tonnage (grt)	187	

PROPULSION

Main engine(s)	2 × 105 kW
Thrusters	2 × Detroit diesels
Propellers	2
Speed (cruising)	8 kt
Endurance	10 days
Fuel capacity	17,000 litres

BRIDGE NAVIGATION AIDS

Satellite	GPS
Radar	Yes
Gyrocompass	Yes
Speed log	Yes
Echo-sounder	Yes

COMMUNICATIONS

Inmarsat (type)	Yes
MF/HF	Yes
VHF	Yes
Facsimile	Yes

SAFETY

Workboat/chase boat	Inflatable boat

DECK MACHINERY

A-frame(s)	Aft
Winches	3 SEAMAC: stainless steel wire – 4 mm; PVC coated wire – 9 mm; steel wire rope – 8 mm; Norlan RV-125 electrohydraulic trawl, twin drum

ACCOMMODATION

Crew	7
Scientists/surveyors	11

SCIENTIFIC SPACES

Oceanographic wet lab	12 m²
Multipurpose dry lab	15 m²

SURVEY SYSTEMS

Multibeam/swath system	*Sagar Purvi* — yes
Corer(s)	Gravity
Grab(s)	SS Van Veen
Other sampling	Niskin water samplers; plankton net; trawl net
Oceanographic sensors (CTDs/XBTs and so on)	SBE 25

UPDATED

Department of Ocean Development

Sagar Sampada

GENERAL

Comments	Fisheries and ocean research vessel
Owner	Department of Ocean Development
Classification	DNV; Indian Register of Shipping
Built	1984
Length overall	71.5 m
Breadth moulded	16.4 m
Operational draught	5.6 m
Tonnage (grt)	2,661

PROPULSION

Main engine(s)	1 diesel, 2,285 bhp at 725 rpm
Speed (max)	13 kt
Speed (cruising)	12 kt
Endurance	13,000 n miles/15 days
Fuel capacity	425 m³
Electrical power	415/230 V AC, 3 phase, 50 Hz
Fresh water capacity	204 m³

BRIDGE NAVIGATION AIDS

Satellite	Yes

Radar	Yes
Gyrocompass	Yes
Speed log	Doppler

DECK MACHINERY

Winches	3, steel wire 9,999 m, conducting cable 4,000 m; Rosette, 6,000 m; plankton, 10,000 m

ACCOMMODATION

Crew	34
Scientists/surveyors	22

SURVEY SYSTEMS

Sensors	Fisheries sonar
Echo-sounder (single beam)	38/120 kHz
Seismic systems	

UPDATED

Fishery Survey of India

Matsya Nireekshani

GENERAL

Built	1978
Length overall	40.55 m
Breadth moulded	8 m
Operational draught	4.25 m
Tonnage (grt)	329

PROPULSION

Main engine(s)	1 diesel, 2,030 bhp
Speed (max)	13 kt

Speed (cruising)	10 kt
Endurance	22 days
Fuel capacity	180 m³
Electrical power	440 V AC, 205 kVA, 3 phase, 50 Hz
Fresh water capacity	120 m³

BRIDGE NAVIGATION AIDS

Satellite	Yes
Radar	Yes

Gyrocompass	Yes	**SURVEY SYSTEMS**	
Speed log	EM	**Sensors**	Fisheries sector-scan sonar

VERIFIED

ACCOMMODATION
Crew 24
Scientists/surveyors 1

INDONESIA

Indonesian Navy

Burujulasad

GENERAL
Comments Research ship (AGOR)
Official number 931
Built (yard and date) Schlichting, Lubeck-Travemunde; launched August 1965, commissioned 1967

Length overall 82.20 m
Breadth moulded 11.40 m
Operational draught 3.50 m

PROPULSION
Main engine(s) 4 × 4 MAN V6V 22/30 diesels; 6,850 hp(m) (5.03 MW)
Propellers 2 shafts
Speed (max) 19.1 kt
Speed (cruising) 15.0 kt
Endurance 14,500 n miles at 15 kt

BRIDGE NAVIGATION AIDS
Radar Decca TM 262; I-band

SAFETY
Workboat/chase boat 3 survey boats

HELIDECK
Size, aircraft capacity Bell 47J

ACCOMMODATION
Crew 108
Scientists/surveyors 28

UPDATED

Burujulasad **2000**/0052361

Indonesian Navy

Jalanidhi

GENERAL

Oceanographic research ship (AGOR)
Official number 933

Built (yard and date) Sasebo Heavy Industries; commissioned 12 January 1963
Length overall 53.90 m
Breadth moulded 9.50 m
Operational draught 4.30 m

PROPULSION

Main engine(s)	MAN G6V 30/42 diesel; 1,000 hp (m) (735 kW)
Propellers	1 shaft
Speed (max)	11.5 kt
Speed (cruising)	15.0 kt
Endurance	7,200 n miles at 10 kt

BRIDGE NAVIGATION AIDS

Radar	Nikkon Denko; I-band. Furuno; I-band

ACCOMMODATION

Crew	87
Scientists/surveyors	26

VERIFIED

Jalanidhi (van Ginderen Collection)   *2000*/0080024

INTERNATIONAL

NATO Sacant Undersea Research Centre

Alliance

GENERAL

NATO research vessel with German, British and Italian crew. Based at La Spezia.

Port of reg/flag	Germany
Official number	A1456
Built (yard and date)	Fincantieri – Cantieri Navali Italiani, Muggiani Shipyard; La Spezia; 1988

Length overall	93.0 m
Breadth moulded	15.20 m
Max draught	5.20 m
Tonnage (grt)	3,180

PROPULSION

Main engine(s)	2 Fincantieri GMT, 12 cylinder Type B230-12, 1,890 kW at 1,200 rpm

Alliance (Giorgio Ghiglione)   *2001*/0081284

Thrusters	Bow	**DECK MACHINERY**	
Propellers	2	**Cranes**	4 electrohydraulic
Speed (max)	16.30 kt	**A-frame(s)**	3 m wide, max load 32,000 kg
Speed (cruising)	12.0 kt	**Winches**	2 towing; 3 oceanographic/
Endurance	7,500 n miles at 12 kt		hydrographic; 1 chain
Fuel capacity	315 m³		
Fuel consumption	8 t/day at 11.5 kt IF, 6 cylinder	**ACCOMMODATION**	
	Type ID36 SS 6V, 480 kW at	**Crew**	24
	1,800 rpm	**Scientists/surveyors**	23
Fresh water capacity	100 t		

		SCIENTIFIC SPACES	
BRIDGE NAVIGATION AIDS		**Total scientific deck space**	400 m²
Satellite	Magnavox MX 200; 2 Fugro MN8		
	DGPS	**SURVEY SYSTEMS**	
Radar	2 Kelvin Hughes Nucleus 6000 A	**Sensors**	TVDS towed active VDS 200 Hz –
Gyrocompass	2 Anschutz Standard 4		4 kHz; medium and low frequency
Speed log	Magnavox MX610D Doppler;		passive towed line arrays.
	Sagem E/M	**Echo-sounder (single beam)**	2 Atlas Deso 20
Echo-sounder	Atlas 481	**Multibeam/swath system**	Atlas Hydrosweep MD 20; Simrad
			3000
COMMUNICATIONS		**Oceanographic sensors**	C.Sonde SVP 10 – Sound velocity
Inmarsat (type)	Magnavox MX 2400 – A EB –	**(CTDs/XBTs and so on)**	probe
	Nera HSD – B		RDI – ADCP
	Skanti/Nera Saturn C – C		Sea Bird – CTD
MF/HF	Skanti/Nera DSC		

UPDATED

SAFETY	
Workboat/chase boat	2 watercraft R6 RIB

NATO Saclant Undersea Research Centre

Leonardo

GENERAL		**DECK MACHINERY**	
Comments	Coastal Research Vessel under	**Cranes**	Effer
	construction. Delivery scheduled	**A-frame(s)**	Effer
	for delivery on 30 April 2002. Will	**Winches**	Marine Project Development
	operate as an Italian Public		
	Vessel.	**ACCOMMODATION**	
Classification	ABS	**Crew**	10
Built (yard and date)	McTay Marine Ltd, UK; 2002		
Length overall	28 m	**SURVEY SYSTEMS**	
		Positioning	Dynamic Positioning
PROPULSION			
Main engine(s)	Cummins. Twin Schottel		*NEW ENTRY*
	azimuthing thrusters		
Thrusters	Bow: Schottel azimuthing		

IRELAND

Marine Institute

Celtic Explorer

		Port of reg/flag	Ireland
GENERAL		**Built (yard and date)**	Damen Shipyards, Netherlands;
Comments	Newbuild oceanographic		due Autumn 2002
	research vessel to be delivered in	**Length overall**	65.5 m
	Autumn 2002.	**Breadth moulded**	14.8 m
	The vessel has been developed	**Max draught**	5.7 m
	for a key role in Ireland's National	**Tonnage (grt)**	2,300
	Seabed Survey and will undertake		
	oceanographic work, fisheries	**PROPULSION**	
	research, water and	**Speed (max)**	14 kt
	environmental and geological	**Endurance**	45 days
	sampling, acoustic research		
	operations, and instrumentation	**ACCOMMODATION**	
	deployment and recovery (e.g.	**Crew**	12
	data buoys).	**Scientists/surveyors**	19

SCIENTIFIC SPACES	
Oceanographic wet lab	1 fish/wet lab, 1 water lab
Multipurpose dry lab	1 dry/IT lab
Chemistry lab	1

SURVEY SYSTEMS	
Sensors	Scanning Sonar
Echo sounder (single beam)	Scientific Echo Sounder (18-38-120 kHz)
Multibeam/swath system	Yes

Sub-bottom profiler	Yes
Oceanographic sensors (CTDs/XBTs and so on)	CTD Rosette water sampling system
	Meteorological instruments
	Data Acquisition System
	Acoustic Doppler Current Profiler (ADCP)
	Thermosalinograph

NEW ENTRY

Marine Institute

Celtic Voyager

GENERAL	
Comments	Replaced the RV *Lough Beltra*
Classification	Lloyds 100A1 Research Vessel, LMC
Built (yard and date)	Scheepswerf Visser bv, Den Helder; delivered July 1997
Length overall	31.40 m
Breadth moulded	8.50 m
Max draught	3.80 m

PROPULSION	
Main engine(s)	Wartsila UD25M5 (626 kW); ZF Marine gearbox + Berg propeller
Thrusters	Bow: Berg 104 kW
Propellers	Van der Giessen wing nozzle
Speed (cruising)	10.00 kt
Endurance	17 days
Electrical power	1 × 100 kW – 380 V – 3-phase – 50 Hz water-cooled generator; 1 × 60 kW – 380 V – 3-phase – 50 Hz air-cooled generator; 380/220 V 50 Hz supply net; 220 V 50 Hz special domestic use net; 220 V 50 Hz clean net for scientific instrumentation 24V DC net (emergency and start-up)

BRIDGE NAVIGATION AIDS	
Satellite	Trimble NT differential GPS Scorpio MBX-2 DGPS receiver
Radar	Decca Bridgemaster ARPA C251/6
Gyrocompass	Anschutz STD 20m
Speed log	Yes
Echo-sounder	Furuno FCV 281

COMMUNICATIONS	
MF/HF	Skanti TRP 8401S SSB radio Skanti DSC9001 MFDSC receiver
VHF	Furuno FM 8000 ICOM 120
Cellular	Motorola GSM 2500
Facsimile	Navtex Receiver Furuno NX500

DECK MACHINERY	
Cranes	Side derrick forward, hydraulically operated with one luffing ram and 1 extension ram controlled as 2 separate functions; length extended 3 m; length retracted 2 m; maximum static load at full extension 1,000 kg.
A-frame(s)	Stern-mounted, clear opening 2.5 m wide × 4 m high; SWL at the centre of the crossbeam – 10,000 kg; hydraulically operated;

Winches	3 eye plates on the crossbeam each with a SWL of 10,000 kg. 2 general purpose, wire capacity 1,000 m of 16 mm wire; pull on bare drum 10,000 kg; bare drum diameter 260 mm minimum; diamond screw spooling gear with variable ratio to accommodate various wire diameters from 8 to 24 mm Oceanographic, wire capacity 1,000 m of 4 mm wire; pull on bare drum 1,000 kg; bare drum diameter 200 mm; provision for mounting slip rings; free fall facility; variable speed control (forward and reverse); automatic spooling via diamond screw to be adjustable within fine limits + or – 0.2 mm to allow for various wire sizes from 4 to 12 mm Portable single net drum, 1 net drum (approximate dimensions of drum – 1.6 m diameter × 2 m wide) mounted on a common shaft; mounted between the vertical legs of the A-frame; maximum speed 20 rpm, control variable both forward and reverse; pull on bare drum 4,000 kg

Celtic Voyager   *2001*/0059326

ACCOMMODATION

Crew	7
Scientists/surveyors	9

SCIENTIFIC SPACES

Oceanographic wet lab	1
Chemistry lab	1

Sensors	Scanmar net sensors
Echo-sounder (single beam)	Furuno depth sounder dual-frequency sounder operating at 28/200 kHz RoxAnn sounder (28/200 kHz)
Multibeam/swath system	Simrad EM 950/EM 1002S
Corer(s)	Multi – can take up to 4 simultaneous cores with a diameter of 59 and 150 mm sediment length and 150 mm supernatant length. Reineck; Shipek; Gravity; Benthic Day and van Veen; anchor dredge
Grab(s)	
Other sampling	6 × 1.7 litre NIO bottles are available in the wet lab. In addition, 4 × 2.5 litre and 2 × 5 litre GO-FLOW bottles
Vehicle(s) (ROVs/AUVs and so on)	Aquashuttle Compact ROV, 360° vision, auto heading and depth, trim, compass, rate gyro, high-resolution colour video camera, stills camera, 300 m cable capable of operating in depths of up to 300 m, >2.5 kt speed, manipulator arm

Celtic Voyager at sea   **2001**/0102810

Oceanographic sensors (CTDs/XBTs and so on)	Sea-Bird SBE 19 CTD; Seacat thermosalinograph; Model 10-AU-005 field fluorometer turbidimeter model 850l; reversing thermometers (RTM 4002); broadband acoustic Doppler current profiler (150 kHz); Recording Current Meters (RCM 7)

UPDATED

ISRAEL

Red Sea Surveyor Ltd

Sea Surveyor

GENERAL

Comments	Oceanographic and hydrographic research vessel in Red Sea and Indian Ocean
Port of reg/flag	Panama
Classification	DNV +1A1 Ice-C
Call sign	HP 7358
Built (yard and date)	Martin Jensen Shipwerft; 1974
Length overall	33.5 m
Breadth moulded	7.2 m
Max draught	3.2 m
Tonnage (grt)	246

PROPULSION

Main engine(s)	B & W Alpha diesel, 550 hp
Propellers	cp
Speed (cruising)	8 kt
Endurance	11,000 n miles/30 days
Fuel capacity	38 t
Electrical power	2 Perkins generators 140 kVA each
Fresh water capacity	60 m^3

BRIDGE NAVIGATION AIDS

Satellite	Nav Add 700
Radar	Koden, 48 miles
Gyrocompass	Microtechnica
Echo-sounder	Koden 4,000 m

COMMUNICATIONS

Inmarsat (type)	SATCOM M Sailor
MF/HF	SSB Icom 700; SSB Sailor RT 64
VHF	Sailor

SAFETY

Workboat/chase boat	2 Tornado RIB, 5.1 m with marine outboards

DECK MACHINERY

Cranes	Hiab 550, aft, 1 t at 4.50 m; Hiab 360, midships, 0.5 t at 3.0 m
A-frame(s)	Midships, starboard side, 2 t
Winches	Sea Mac hydrographic, 2 t, 4,000 m cable

ACCOMMODATION

Crew	9
Scientists/surveyors	18

SCIENTIFIC SPACES

Oceanographic wet lab	5 m × 4 m; 4 m × 3 m
Multipurpose dry lab	4 m × 3 m

UPDATED

ITALY

Institute of Marine Biology

Umberto D'Ancona

GENERAL

Owner	National Council of Research
Port of reg/flag	Venice, Italy
Built (yard and date)	Cantiere Riva Trigoso; 1967
Rebuilt (yard and date)	1970
Length overall	24.2 m
Breadth moulded	5.0 m
Max draught	1.60 m
Tonnage (grt)	82

PROPULSION

Main engine(s)	2 diesel DAF DK 1160, each 145 kW
Propellers	2
Speed (cruising)	10 kt
Electrical power	2 diesel DAF DA 475, each 62 kW coupled to one 25 kW generator, 220 V, 3 phase, 50 Hz

BRIDGE NAVIGATION AIDS

Satellite	GPS
Radar	Furuno 1510; Furuno FRS 48
Gyrocompass	Sperry SR 120
Other ship navigation	Track display Koden TD 050, GPS-linked electronic chart NAV-ADD

COMMUNICATIONS

MF/HF	Yes
VHF	Yes

DECK MACHINERY

Cranes	2
A-frame(s)	1 – port side
Winches	2: 1 oceanographic

ACCOMMODATION

Crew	5
Scientists/surveyors	6

SCIENTIFIC SPACES

Oceanographic wet lab	14 m^2
Multipurpose dry lab	2 m^2

SURVEY SYSTEMS

Positioning	GPS Trimble Acutis
Echo-sounder (single beam)	Elac; Furuno
Grab(s)	Van Veen
Oceanographic sensors (CTDs/XBTs and so on)	CTD – Idronaut; EG&G Mark V; SBE SeaCat; Biospherical PNF; Quantaspectrometer; Micros Automatic Station

VERIFIED

Istituto Nazionale di Oceanografia Geofisico Sperimentale

OGS Explora

GENERAL

	Seismic research vessel
Port of reg/flag	Trieste
Official number	764/Trieste
Classification	RINA 100 A1, 1-Nav IL
Call sign	IXWQ ST 1AQ-1 Ice 1B
Built (yard and date)	Elmsfleth, Germany; 1973
Length overall	72.63 m
Breadth moulded	11.8 m
Max draught	4.18 m
Operational draught	4.15 m
Tonnage (grt)	1,408

PROPULSION

Main engine(s)	2 Deutz Diesel engines, 2 × 1,294-5 kW (1,760 hp)
Thrusters	Electric, 260 kW
Propellers	1 VPP
Speed (max)	13.5 kt
Speed (cruising)	12 kt
Endurance	approx 40 days
Fuel capacity	approx 320 t
Fuel consumption	approx 8 t/day
Electrical power	860 kVA, 3 phase, 230/400 V, 50 Hz

BRIDGE NAVIGATION AIDS

Satellite	DGPS

Radar	Selesmar Mod 1645 9X Sperry Rascar 3,400 m Racal Bridge Master
Gyrocompass	Anschutz std
Speed log	EM Plath Naviknot Atlas DOLOG 12A

COMMUNICATIONS

Inmarsat (type)	Inmarsat B Saturn Nera 3S EB Skanti complete station

DECK MACHINERY

Cranes	Stern – height 6 m, outboard extension 5 m, SWL 1 t Bow derrick – SWL 10 t
A-frame(s)	Midships – height 4 m, outboard extension 1 m, SWL 8 t
Winches	1 – conducting cable 600 m; steel wire 2,300 m

ACCOMMODATION

Crew	17
Scientists/surveyors	25
Hospital	2

SCIENTIFIC SPACES

Total scientific deck space	200 m^2
Oceanographic wet lab	116 m^2
Multipurpose dry lab	12 m^2

SURVEY SYSTEMS		Streamer manufacturer	ITI (Syntron)
Echo-sounder (single beam)	Simrad EA 500	Streamer type	Stealth array solid-state streamer
Gravimeter	Bodenseewerk KSS 31	Streamer numbers and	1 single streamer, 1,200 m long,
Corer(s)	8 m, 10 cm diameter, gravity	lengths per number	96 channels; 1 hydrophone array
Grab(s)	Van Veen light		for single channel acquisition
		Recording system	OYO DAS-1, 96 channels
SEISMIC SYSTEMS			
Energy source (type and manufacturer)	2-4 Sodera GI guns; 3.5 litres each		*VERIFIED*
Compressor numbers and types	3 LMF for a total net output of 200 litres/min at 140 bar		

So. Pro. Mar.

Minerva

GENERAL		Gyrocompass	Yes
Owner	National Research Council (CNR)	Speed log	Yes
Classification	RINA	Echo-sounder	Yes
Built (yard and date)	1956		
Length overall	60.07 m	DECK MACHINERY	
Breadth moulded	8.90 m	A-frame(s)	Midships – outboard extension 5.0 m
Max draught	3.40 m	Winches	2 – conducting cable 2,000 m;
Tonnage (grt)	635		steel wire 6,000 m, SWL 7 tons
		Moonpool(s) -	
PROPULSION			
Main engine(s)	2 diesel, each 1,710 bhp at 1,600 rpm	Accommodation	
Propellers	1.72 m at 316 rpm	Crew	13
Speed (max)	16.0 kt	Scientists/surveyors	16
Speed (cruising)	12.0 kt		
Endurance	4,600 n miles/16 days	SCIENTIFIC SPACES	
Fuel capacity	91 m³	Total scientific deck space	265 m²
Electrical power	220/380 V AC, 500 kVA, 3-phase, 50 Hz	Oceanographic wet lab	10 m²
		Multipurpose dry lab	90 m²
Fresh water capacity	46 m³		
		SURVEY SYSTEMS	
BRIDGE NAVIGATION AIDS		Echo-sounder (single beam)	30/50 kHz
Satellite	Yes		
Radar	Yes		*UPDATED*

So. Pro. Mar.

Urania

		DECK MACHINERY	
		Cranes	Stern, midships – clearance 5 m, clearance 10 m, outboard extension 2 m, SWL 1 ton
GENERAL			
Owner	National Research Council (CNR)		
Classification	RINA	A-frame(s)	Midships – clearance 5 m, SWL 4 tons
Built	1992		
Length overall	61.3 m	Winches	4 – conducting cable 5,000 m,
Breadth moulded	11.1 m		SWL 1 t; steel wire 7,000 m, SWL
Max draught	3.6 m		7 t
Tonnage (grt)	1,000		CTD, 450 m
			Magnetometer, 150 m
PROPULSION			
Main engine(s)	2 diesel, each 2,640 bhp at 750 rpm	ACCOMMODATION	
		Crew	13
Propellers	1.72 m at 316 rpm	Scientists/surveyors	16
Speed (max)	14.5 kt		
Speed (cruising)	12 kt	SCIENTIFIC SPACES	
Endurance	11,000 n miles/45 days	Total scientific deck space	208 m²
Electrical power	220/380 V AC, 394 kVA, 3 phase, 50 Hz	Oceanographic wet lab	55 m²
		Multipurpose dry lab	81 m²
BRIDGE NAVIGATION AIDS		SURVEY SYSTEMS	
Satellite	Yes	Echo-sounder (single beam)	30/50 kHz
Radar	Yes	Magnetometer	Yes
Gyrocompass	Yes	Oceanographic sensors (CTDs/XBTs and so on)	CTD
Speed log	Yes		
Echo-sounder	Yes		*UPDATED*

JAPAN

Fisheries Agency of Japan

Shoyo Maru

GENERAL

	Fisheries Research Vessel
Official number	135883
Call sign	JLOJ
Built (yard and date)	NKK Corporation, Tsurumi Shipyard, Japan; completed 12 May 1998
Length overall	87.60 m
Breadth moulded	14.00 m
Max draught	5.30 m
Tonnage (grt)	2,494

PROPULSION

Main engine(s)	2 Yanmar 6N330-EN2, each 2,206.5 kW at 620 rpm; 1 Tayo electric motor for propulsion, 350 kW; 3 Yanmar generators, each 350 kW
Thrusters	Bow
Propellers	Kamome CP
Speed (max)	18.75 kt
Speed (cruising)	16.0 kt
Endurance	13,900 n miles cruising range
Fuel capacity	650.3 m³
Electrical power	3 Taiyo FEK45AS-8 generators, each 750 kVA
Fresh water capacity	200.1 m³

BRIDGE NAVIGATION AIDS

Satellite	Furuno DGPS

Radar	Tokimec ARPA X-band; Tokimec ARPA S-band
Gyrocompass	Tokimec
Echo-sounder	Furuno

COMMUNICATIONS

Inmarsat (type)	JRC "B"; JRC "C"; JRC GMDSS console
MF/HF	JRC
VHF	JRC
Facsimile	JRC

SAFETY

Workboat/chase boat	IHI craft: unmanned in-water observation system

DECK MACHINERY

Cranes	Dynacon CTD Octopus winch and heave motion; Palfinger folding knuckle; Nippon Ican telescopic; Mansei Kogyo electrical hoist
A-frame(s)	Tateno, 5 tonnes
Winches	Dynacon CTD; Tsurumi-Seiki Mocness; Tsurumi-Seiki towing CTD; Tsurumi-Seiki 8,000 m; Tsurumi-Seiki 3,000 m; Tsurumi-Seiki towing biomass evaluator fish finder

ACCOMMODATION

Crew	37
Scientists/surveyors	12

Shoyo Maru

2000/0093752

SCIENTIFIC SPACES

Oceanographic wet lab	Yes
Multipurpose dry lab	Yes

SURVEY SYSTEMS

Sensors	Vemco net sonde; Furuno scanning sonar; Kaijo biomass evaluation fish finder
Echo-sounder (single beam)	NEC 12 kHz; Furuno
Multibeam/swath system	Furuno
Sub-bottom profiler	Raytheon 3.5 kHz
Magnetometer	Gauss

Other sampling	Sea Bird/Bess Mocness net; Nippon Kaiyo IKMT net; Ocean Instruments Bongo net; Challenger Oceanic Congo net
Vehicle(s) (ROVs/AUVs and so on)	MES ROV; Chelsea Instruments SeaSoar; Endeco V-Fin towed vehicle
Oceanographic sensors (CTDs/XBTs and so on)	Sea Bird CTD; Tsurumi-Seiki XBT/XCTD; RDI ADCP; Guildline Autosal; biospherical profiling natural fluorometer

UPDATED

Japanese Marine Science & Technology Centre (JAMSTEC)

Kairei

GENERAL

Comments	*Kairei* operates the 10,000 m ROV *Kaiko* and performs deep sea floor surveys
Built (yard and date)	1997
Length overall	104.9 m
Breadth moulded	16 m
Max draught	4.5 m
Tonnage (grt)	4,628

PROPULSION

Main engine(s)	2 diesel, each 3,000 hp
Propellers	2 controllable pitch
Speed (cruising)	16 kt
Endurance	9,600 n miles

BRIDGE NAVIGATION AIDS

Radar	Yes
Gyrocompass	Yes
Speed log	Yes
Echo-sounder	Yes

DECK MACHINERY

Winches	Survey

ACCOMMODATION

Crew	29
Scientists/surveyors	31

SCIENTIFIC SPACES

Oceanographic wet lab	Yes
Multipurpose dry lab	Yes

SURVEY SYSTEMS

Multibeam/swath system	Sea Beam 2112
Sub-bottom profiler	Yes
Magnetometer	Proton; shipboard
Gravimeter	Shipboard
Corer(s)	Piston
Other sampling	Bottom sampler
Vehicle(s) (ROVs/AUVs and so on)	*Kaiko* ROV
Oceanographic sensors (CTDs/XBTs and so on)	XBT (expendable bathythermograph)

UPDATED

Kairei

2000/0093786

Japanese Marine Science & Technology Centre (JAMSTEC)

Kaiyo

GENERAL

Comments	SWATH vessel designed to perform oceanographic surveys	**BRIDGE NAVIGATION AIDS**	
		Radar	Yes
		Gyrocompass	Yes
Built (yard and date)	1985	Speed log	Yes
Length overall	61.6 m	Echo-sounder	Yes
Breadth moulded	28.0 m		
Max draught	6.3 m	**ACCOMMODATION**	
Tonnage (grt)	2,893	Crew	29
		Scientists/surveyors	40
PROPULSION			
Main engine(s)	4 diesel, each 1,250 hp	**SURVEY SYSTEMS**	
Thrusters	4 forward, each 6.8 t thrust; 4 aft, each 4 t thrust	Multibeam/swath system	Sea Beam
Propellers	2 controllable pitch		*UPDATED*
Speed (cruising)	13 kt		
Endurance	5,100 n miles		

Japanese Marine Science & Technology Centre (JAMSTEC)

Mirai

GENERAL

Built (yard and date)	1997	**ACCOMMODATION**	
Length overall	130 m	Crew	34
Breadth moulded	19 m	Scientists/surveyors	46 (observation staff 18, and researchers 28)
Max draught	6.9 m		
PROPULSION		**SURVEY SYSTEMS**	
Main engine(s)	4 diesel, each 2,500 hp	Multibeam/swath system	Sea Beam 2112
Propellers	2 controllable pitch	Sub-bottom profiler	Yes
Speed (cruising)	16 kt	Magnetometer	Proton; shipboard
Endurance	12,000 n miles	Gravimeter	Shipboard
		Corer(s)	20 ml piston (for 10,000 m depth)
BRIDGE NAVIGATION AIDS		Other sampling	Rosette water sampling instrument 200 litre water sampler
Radar	Yes	Oceanographic sensors (CTDs/XBTs and so on)	Acoustic current meter; Ocean Lidar System; XBT (expendable bathythermograph); XCP (expendable current profiler); XCTD (expendable conductivity temperature depth profiler)
Gyrocompass	Yes		
Speed log	Yes		
Echo-sounder	Yes		
DECK MACHINERY			
Cranes	Articulated deck SWL 3 t; jib deck SWL 10 t; gallows SWL 11 t		
A-frame(s)	SWL 22 t		*UPDATED*
Winches	7 survey; 3 traction		

Mirai   *2000*/0093785

Japanese Marine Science & Technology Centre (JAMSTEC)

Natsushima

GENERAL

Comments	*Natsushima* operates the Shinkai 2000 manned submersible and the ROV Dolphin 3K in addition to undertaking oceanographic surveys
Built (yard and date)	1981
Length overall	67.4 m
Breadth moulded	13.0 m
Max draught	3.6 m
Tonnage (grt)	1,553

PROPULSION

Main engine(s)	2 diesel, each 850 hp
Propellers	2 controllable pitch
Speed (cruising)	12 kt
Endurance	10,800 n miles

BRIDGE NAVIGATION AIDS

Radar	Yes
Gyrocompass	Yes
Speed log	Yes
Echo-sounder	Yes

ACCOMMODATION

Crew	49
Scientists/surveyors	6

SURVEY SYSTEMS

Vehicle(s) (ROVs/AUVs and so on)	Shinkai 2000; Dolphin 3K

UPDATED

Natsushima

2001/0114487

Japanese Marine Science & Technology Centre (JAMSTEC)

Yokosuka

GENERAL

Comments	*Yokosuka* operates the manned submersible Shinkai 6500 and performs oceanographic surveys
Built (yard and date)	1990
Length overall	105 m
Breadth moulded	16 m
Max draught	4.5 m

PROPULSION

Main engine(s)	2 diesel, each 3,000 hp
Propellers	2 controllable pitch
Speed (cruising)	16 kt
Endurance	9,500 n miles

BRIDGE NAVIGATION AIDS

Radar	Yes
Gyrocompass	Yes
Speed log	Yes
Echo-sounder	Yes

ACCOMMODATION		**Gravimeter**	Shipboard
Crew	45	**Vehicle(s) (ROVs/AUVs and**	Shinkai 6500
Scientists/surveyors	15	**so on)**	*UPDATED*

SURVEY SYSTEMS
Magnetometer   Towed Proton; shipboard

Yokosuka   ***2001**/0114488*

Tokai University

Bosei Maru

GENERAL

	Research and Training Vessel
Classification	NK: NS*MNS*Ice Class 1D
Built (yard and date)	Miho Shipyard Co, Japan; 1993
Length overall	87.98 m
Breadth moulded	12.80 m
Max draught	4.80 m
Tonnage (grt)	2,174

PROPULSION

Main engine(s)	2 Yanmar diesel, each 1,838 kW at 720 rpm; 2 Yanmar generator sets, each 530 kW
Thrusters	Bow: Kamome 308 kW, 50 kN thrust
Propellers	1 Kamome cp
Speed (max)	19.1 kt
Speed (cruising)	17.0 kt
Fuel capacity	401 m³
Electrical power	2 Shinko generators, each 445 V AC, 600 kVA, 60 Hz; 1 Deutz emergency generator, 100 kW, 100 kVA
Fresh water capacity	185 m³

BRIDGE NAVIGATION AIDS

Satellite	JRC
Radar	JRC 50 kW, X-band; JRC 60 kW, S-band
Gyrocompass	2: Tokimec
Speed log	JRC Doppler
Echo-sounder	JRC

COMMUNICATIONS

Inmarsat (type)	Anritsu "A" (telephone and fax); Anritsu "C" (telex)
MF/HF	Anritsu 800 kW
VHF	2: Anritsu
Facsimile	Anritsu Navtex; Anritsu weather

SAFETY

Lifeboats	2: Shigi partially enclosed, 89 person; 2: Toyo rescue boats, 6 person; 4: Mitsubishi inflatable liferafts, 25 person

DECK MACHINERY

Cranes	Hiab Foco hinged, 9 kN; Hiab Foco, 9 kN

A-frame(s)	3: Sekiryo 60, 20 and 10 kN	**Magnetometer**	Gauss
Winches	4 Mitsubishi oceanographic; 1 Mitsubishi CTD, 6,000 m, 7.4 mm	**Oceanographic sensors (CTDs/XBTs and so on)**	EMS ADCP; EMS CTDOV; EMS thermosalinograph; Kaijo salinometer; Okura CO_2 analyser
ACCOMMODATION			
Crew	190 (including students)	**SEISMIC SYSTEMS**	
		Energy source (type and manufacturer)	Toyo Tech air gun system
SCIENTIFIC SPACES			
Oceanographic wet lab	Yes		*VERIFIED*
Multipurpose dry lab	Yes		
SURVEY SYSTEMS			
Echo-sounder (single beam)	NEC 12 kHz; Furuno		
Sub-bottom profiler	Raytheon 3.5 kHz		

Bosei Maru   **2000**/0093751

KOREA, SOUTH

Korea Ocean Research & Development Institute (KORDI)

Eardo

GENERAL		**Call sign**	D8GQ
Port of reg/flag	Masan, Korea	**Built (yard and date)**	KTMA; 1992
Official number	7	**Length overall**	48.95 m
Classification	KR	**Breadth moulded**	8.60 m

Max draught	2.80 m	
Operational draught	2.60 m	
Tonnage (grt)	357	

PROPULSION

Main engine(s)	2: 5L 20/27, each 612 hp at 900 rpm;
	Motors: 3: N-855G, 195 hp at 1,800 rpm
Thrusters	Bow: 90 TV Ulstein
Speed (max)	12.0 kt
Speed (cruising)	9.5 kt
Endurance	10 days/5,000 n miles
Fuel capacity	119.92 m³
Fuel consumption	2 t/day
Electrical power	3 generators: 162.5 kVA, 130 kW
Fresh water capacity	62.98 m³

Eardo   **2001**/0101674

BRIDGE NAVIGATION AIDS

Satellite	Trimble Procon; Magnavox MX-200
Radar	Krupp Atlas 7600AC/RM; Krupp Atlas 7600 ARPA
Gyrocompass	C-Plath VAVIPAGAT
Speed log	Chernikeef Mk 4
Other ship navigation	Loran C: Micrologic ML-8000

COMMUNICATIONS

Inmarsat (type)	JRC JUE 45E MII "A"; SC-2051 "C"
MF/HF	2: RC-2095; Skanti Sait T900
VHF	Haeyang HSD-3100
Facsimile	Chokwang Electronics CF-3300 Weather

SAFETY

Workboat/chase boat	FRP: 40 hp

DECK MACHINERY

Cranes	M1AB 120
A-frame(s)	10 t; J-frame
Winches	Deepsea; CTD; hydrographic

ACCOMMODATION

Crew	15
Scientists/surveyors	17

SCIENTIFIC SPACES

Oceanographic wet lab	13.81 m²
Multipurpose dry lab	13.30 m²

SURVEY SYSTEMS

Positioning	Oceano SBL Acoustic Positioning System
Sensors	Scientific Fish Finder: Furuno FCV-32
Echo-sounder (single beam)	STN ATLAS DESO-20
Multibeam/swath system	Simrad EM1002
Sidescan sonar	EdgeTech Model-260
Sub-bottom profiler	Ferranti ORE; ORE-140
Oceanographic sensors (CTDs/XBTs and so on)	XBT: Sippican, MK-9; CTD: EG&G Mk V; ADCP: RDI RDVM-0150

SEISMIC SYSTEMS

Sparker Array System: EG&G 16000J

UPDATED

Korea Ocean Research & Development Institute (KORDI)

Onnuri

GENERAL

Official number	8
Classification	+KRS1 – special purpose ship, research, +KRM1 – UMA
Call sign	D9XJ
Built (yard and date)	M.K; 1992
Length overall	63.80 m
Breadth moulded	12.0 m
Max draught	6.0 m
Operational draught	5.60 m
Tonnage (grt)	1,422

PROPULSION

Main engine(s)	2 Wärtsilä 8R22/26 4-cycle diesel, 1,160 kW at 900 rpm
Thrusters	Bow: cp, 230 kW, 3,500 kg; stern: cp, 190 kW, 3,000 kg
Propellers	1 cp
Speed (max)	15.50 kt
Speed (cruising)	13.5 kt
Endurance	35 days
Fuel capacity	358 m³
Fuel consumption	5.5 t/day

Electrical power	2 generators: 550 kVA at 1,800 rpm; emergency generator: 80 kVA at 1,800 rpm
Fresh water capacity	108 m³

BRIDGE NAVIGATION AIDS

Satellite	Trimble DSM Magnavox MX-4200, 4810
Radar	JRC/Raytheon ARPA 3430/1200, TM 3425/7-X4
Speed log	Krupp Atlas Dolog

COMMUNICATIONS

Inmarsat (type)	JRC JUE 45E "A"; SC-2051 "C"
MF/HF	2: RC-2095
VHF	2: RH-2050
Facsimile	Furuno 214 weather

SAFETY

Lifeboats	43 person
Workboat/chase boat	Yes

DECK MACHINERY

Cranes	Hiab 200 sea
A-frame(s)	Mjellern & Karlsen
Winches	1 hydraulic: Rapp Hyderna; 1 deep sea: Rapp Hyderna

ACCOMMODATION

Crew	16
Scientists/surveyors	25
Hospital	Yes

SCIENTIFIC SPACES

Oceanographic wet lab	32.5 m²
Multipurpose dry lab	60.5 m²

SURVEY SYSTEMS

Positioning	Dynamic Positioning System: Simrad Albatross ADP 700
Sensors	Scanning sonar: Simrad SR-240; Scientific Fish Finder: Simrad EK-500
Echo-sounder (single beam)	Simrad EA 500
Multibeam/swath system	SeaBeam 2000
Sidescan sonar	Benthos: SIS 3000; KORDI assembled system

Onnuri 2001/0101673

Sub-bottom profiler	Bathy 2000P
Gravimeter	Lacoste & Romberg SL type
Corer(s)	Benthos 2450 Piston
Oceanographic sensors (CTDs/XBTs and so on)	Wave Meter: WS Oceans Mk-3; CTD: SBE 911; ADCP: RDI VM0150

SEISMIC SYSTEMS

Compressor numbers and types	CGG LMF

UPDATED

Onnuri 2000/0093753

LIBYA

Marine Biological Research Center

Nour

GENERAL

Classification	Bureau Veritas
Built	1970
Length overall	48.7 m
Breadth moulded	10 m
Max draught	4.55 m
Tonnage (grt)	598

PROPULSION

Main engine(s)	2 diesel, each 1,380 bhp at 430 rpm
Speed (max)	12 kt
Speed (cruising)	10 kt
Endurance	5,000 n miles/26 days
Fuel capacity	154 m³

Electrical power	380 V AC, 330 kVA, 3 phase, 50 Hz
Fresh water capacity	60 m³

BRIDGE NAVIGATION AIDS

Satellite	Yes
Radar	Yes
Gyrocompass	Yes
Speed log	Yes
Echo-sounder	Yes

DECK MACHINERY

Cranes	Midships, clearance above deck 12 m, outboard extension 8 m, SWL 1 ton

A-frame(s)	Stern
Winches	1 – 4,000 m

ACCOMMODATION

Crew	23
Scientists/surveyors	12

SCIENTIFIC SPACES

Oceanographic wet lab	65 m²
Multipurpose dry lab	23 m²

SURVEY SYSTEMS

Echo-sounder (single beam)	38/120 kHz
Magnetometer	Yes
Oceanographic sensors (CTDs/XBTs and so on)	CTD

UPDATED

LITHUANIA

Center of Marine Research

Véjas

GENERAL

Owner	State of the Environment Lithuania
Built	1980
Length overall	55.63 m
Breadth moulded	9.32 m
Max draught	4.3 m
Tonnage (grt)	697

PROPULSION

Main engine(s)	1 diesel, 1,000 bhp at 428 rpm
Propellers	1.65 m diameter
Speed (max)	11 kt
Speed (cruising)	8 kt
Endurance	8,000 n miles/32 days
Fuel capacity	178 m³
Electrical power	220 V AC, 450 kVA, 3 phase, 50 Hz
Fresh water capacity	45 m³

BRIDGE NAVIGATION AIDS

Satellite	Yes
Radar	Yes
Gyrocompass	Yes

Speed log	EM
Echo-sounder	Yes

DECK MACHINERY

A-frame(s)	Stern – clearance height 8 m, outboard extension 5 m, SWL 1 ton
Winches	4 – conducting cable 1,000 m, SWL 1 t; steel wire 1,200 m, SWL 4 t; bottom sampling 1,200 m

ACCOMMODATION

Crew	21
Scientists/surveyors	20 – 25

SCIENTIFIC SPACES

Total scientific deck space	90 m²
Oceanographic wet lab	10 m²
Multipurpose dry lab	50 m²

SURVEY SYSTEMS

Echo-sounder (single beam)	25 kHz

UPDATED

Lithuanian Navy

Vetra

GENERAL

Comments	"Valerian Uryvavev" Class (AGOR/AX). Built at Khabarovsk in early 1980s. Transferred from the Russian Navy in 1992 where she was used as a civilian oceanographic research vessel. Now used as the Flag ship for the Baltic States MCMV unit which includes *Olev* and *Kalev* (from Estonia) and *Viesturs* and *Imanta* (from Latvia). A second of class, *Véjas*, works for the Ministry of Environment.
Former names	*Rudolf Samoylovich*
Official number	A 41
Length overall	54.9 m
Breadth moulded	9.5 m
Max draught	4.0 m

PROPULSION

Main engine(s)	Deutz diesel; 850 hp(m) (625 kW)
Propellers	one
Speed (max)	12 kt

BRIDGE NAVIGATION AIDS

Radar	Racal Decca RM 1290; I-band

ACCOMMODATION

Crew	34

Vetra (Michael Nitz)   ***2001**/0097760*

NEW ENTRY

MALAYSIA

University College Terengganu

Unipertama V

GENERAL

Built (yard and date)	1978
Length overall	50.5 m
Breadth moulded	8.7 m
Tonnage (grt)	477

PROPULSION

Main engine(s)	1 diesel, 1,400 bhp at 750 rpm
Speed (cruising)	11.3 kt
Endurance	14,000 n miles/60 days
Fuel capacity	252 m³
Electrical power	445 V AC, 350 kVA
Fresh water capacity	43 m³

BRIDGE NAVIGATION AIDS

Satellite	Yes

Radar	Yes
Gyrocompass	Yes
Speed log	Yes
Echo-sounder	Yes

DECK MACHINERY

A-frame(s)	Stern
Winches	1 – steel wire 200 m

ACCOMMODATION

Crew	23
Scientists/surveyors	34

UPDATED

MEXICO

Dirección General de Oceanografía Naval

Altair

GENERAL

	"Robert D Conrad" class (AGOR)
Former names	*James M Gilliss* (until 1983), AGOR 4
Owner	Secretaría de Marina-Armada de México
Official number	H-05
Classification	ABS
Built (yard and date)	Christy Corp, WI; commissioned 5 November 1962
Rebuilt (yard and date)	Mexico, refitted and modernised. Recommissioned 14 June 1983
Length overall	63.7 m
Breadth moulded	12.2 m
Max draught	4.7 m
Tonnage (grt)	975

PROPULSION

Main engine(s)	2 Caterpillar diesel-electric generators, 1,200 hp (895 kW); 2 motors; 1,000 hp (746 kW)
Thrusters	Bow
Propellers	1
Speed (max)	13.5 kt
Speed (cruising)	10 kt
Endurance	10,500 n miles at 10 kt
Fuel capacity	160 m³
Electrical power	110/440 V AC, 375 kVA, 3 phase, 60 Hz
Fresh water capacity	65 m³

BRIDGE NAVIGATION AIDS

Satellite	Yes

Altair   **2000**/0081257

Radar	Raytheon 1025; Raytheon R4iY
Gyrocompass	Yes
Speed log	Yes
Echo-sounder	Yes

DECK MACHINERY

Winches	2 – steel wire 1,500 m; conducting cable 3,000 m, SWL 1 t

ACCOMMODATION

Crew	41
Scientists/surveyors	15

SCIENTIFIC SPACES

Total scientific deck space	130 m²
Oceanographic wet lab	19 m²
Multipurpose dry lab	44 m²

UPDATED

Dirección General de Oceanografía Naval

Antares

GENERAL

	"Robert D Conrad" class (AGOR)
Former names	S P Lee (until 1992), AG192
Owner	Secretaría de Marina-Armada de México
Official number	H 06
Classification	ABS
Built (yard and date)	Defoe, Bay City; commissioned 2 December 1962
Length overall	63.7 m
Breadth moulded	12.2 m
Max draught	4.7 m
Tonnage (grt)	975

PROPULSION

Main engine(s)	2 Caterpillar diesel-electric generators, 1,200 hp (895 kW); 2 motors; 1,000 hp (746 kW)
Thrusters	Bow
Propellers	1
Speed (max)	13.5 kt
Speed (cruising)	10 kt
Endurance	10,500 n miles at 10 kt
Fuel capacity	160 m³

Electrical power	110/440 V AC, 375 kVA, 3 phase, 60 Hz
Fresh water capacity	65 m³

BRIDGE NAVIGATION AIDS

Satellite	Yes
Radar	Raytheon 1025; Raytheon R4iY
Gyrocompass	Yes
Speed log	Yes
Echo-sounder	Yes

DECK MACHINERY

Winches	1 – steel wire 9,999 m, SWL 6 t

ACCOMMODATION

Crew	41
Scientists/surveyors	15

SCIENTIFIC SPACES

Total scientific deck space	130 m²
Oceanographic wet lab	19 m²
Multipurpose dry lab	44 m²

UPDATED

Instituto de Ciencías del Mar y Limnología

El Puma

GENERAL

Owner	Universidad Nacional Autonoma de México-Unam
Classification	DNV
Built (yard and date)	1980
Length overall	49.99 m
Breadth moulded	10.30 m
Max draught	4.70 m
Tonnage (grt)	638

PROPULSION

Main engine(s)	1 diesel, 1,680 hp at 770 rpm
Propellers	2.55 m diameter
Speed (max)	12.5 kt
Speed (cruising)	12 kt
Endurance	9,000 n miles/30 days
Fuel capacity	200 m³
Electrical power	440 V AC, 225 kVA, 3-phase, 60 Hz
Fresh water capacity	44 m³

BRIDGE NAVIGATION AIDS

Satellite	Yes
Radar	Yes

Gyrocompass	Yes
Speed log	Yes
Echo-sounder	Yes

DECK MACHINERY

Cranes	Stern, SWL 3 t
A-frame(s)	Stern, midships: clearance above deck 7 m, outboard extension 3 m, SWL 3 t
Winches	3 oceanographic, steel wire 1,800 m; conducting cable 7,000 m; synthetic cable 5,000 m, SWL 12 t; bottom sampling, steel wire 5,000 m, SWL 13 t

ACCOMMODATION

Crew	15
Scientists/surveyors	20
Scientific spaces	

VERIFIED

Instituto de Ciencías del Mar y Limnología

Justo Sierra

GENERAL

Owner	Universidad Nacional Autonoma de México-Unam
Classification	Lloyds Register
Built (yard and date)	1982
Length overall	49.99 m
Breadth moulded	10.30 m
Max draught	4.70 m
Tonnage (grt)	780

PROPULSION

Main engine(s)	1 diesel, 1,680 hp at 800 rpm
Propellers	2.60 m diameter
Speed (max)	12.5 kt
Speed (cruising)	12 kt
Endurance	10,000 n miles/30 days
Fuel capacity	200 m³
Electrical power	440 V AC, 225 kVA, 3-phase, 60 Hz
Fresh water capacity	42 m³

BRIDGE NAVIGATION AIDS

Satellite	Yes
Radar	Yes
Gyrocompass	Yes
Speed log	Yes
Echo-sounder	Yes

DECK MACHINERY

Cranes	Stern, clearance above deck 8 m, outboard extension 8 m
A-frame(s)	Stern, midships: SWL 8 t
Winches	3 oceanographic, steel wire 2,000 m; conducting cable 5,000 m; synthetic cable 5,000 m, SWL 12 t; bottom sampling, steel wire 5,000 m, SWL 8 t

ACCOMMODATION

Crew	15
Scientists/surveyors	21
Scientific spaces	

VERIFIED

MOROCCO

Moroccan Navy

Abu El Barakat Al Barbari

GENERAL

	"Robert D Conrad" class research ship (AGOR). Leased from the USA on 26 July 1993
Former names	*Bartlett* (T-AGOR 13)
Official number	702
Built (yard and date)	Northwest Marine Iron Works, Portland, Oregon; commissioned 31 March 1969
Length overall	63.70 m
Breadth moulded	12.20 m
Operational draught	4.70 m

PROPULSION

Main engine(s)	Diesel-electric; 2 Caterpillar D 378 diesel generators; one motor; 1,000 hp (746 kW)
Thrusters	Bow
Propellers	1 shaft
Speed (max)	13.5 kt

Abu El Barakat Al Barbari   *2000*/0081278

Speed (cruising)	12.0 kt		**ACCOMMODATION**	
Endurance	12,000 n miles at 12 kt		**Crew**	26
			Scientists/surveyors	15
BRIDGE NAVIGATION AIDS				
Radar	TM 1660/12S; I-band		**SURVEY SYSTEMS**	
			Magnetometer	Yes
DECK MACHINERY			Gravimeter	Yes
Cranes	Boom, 10 t		Sound velocity profiler	Yes
Winches	Yes			

UPDATED

MYANMAR (BURMA)

Myanmar Navy

802

GENERAL			**PROPULSION**	
	A fishery research ship of		**Main engine(s)**	Niigata diesel
	Singapore origin, arrested on 8		**Propellers**	1 shaft
	April 1974 and taken into service		**Speed (cruising)**	13.0 kt
	as a survey vessel in about 1981.			
	Stern trawler type.		**BRIDGE NAVIGATION AIDS**	
Former names	R/V *Changi*		**Radar**	I-band
Built (yard and date)	Miho Shipyard, Shimizu:			
	commissioned 20 June 1973		**ACCOMMODATION**	
Length overall	47.0 m		**Crew**	45
Breadth moulded	8.70 m			
Operational draught	3.60 m			

VERIFIED

802   *2000*/0056657

NETHERLANDS

The Netherlands Institute for Fisheries Research (RIVO)

Tridens

GENERAL			**Breadth moulded**	13.86 m
Classification	Lloyds Register		**Max draught**	4.60 m
Built (yard and date)	1990		**Tonnage (grt)**	659
Length overall	73.54 m			

PROPULSION

Main engine(s)	2 diesel, each 4,352 bhp at 1,000 rpm
Speed (max)	17.0 kt
Speed (cruising)	14.0 kt
Fuel capacity	361 m³
Electrical power	380 V AC, 2,120 kVA, 3-phase, 50 Hz; 220 V AC, 259 kVA, 3-phase, 50 Hz
Fresh water capacity	80 m³

DECK MACHINERY

Cranes	Stern, clearance above deck 8 m, outboard extension 5 m; hydrographic
A-frame(s)	Stern

ACCOMMODATION

Crew	21
Scientists/surveyors	12

SCIENTIFIC SPACES

Total scientific deck space	200 m²
Oceanographic wet lab	20 m²
Multipurpose dry lab	15 m²

UPDATED

Netherlands Institute for Sea Research (NIOZ)

Pelagia

GENERAL COMMENT

Comments	*Pelagia* is designed for multidisciplinary research, cruises in coastal seas and continental shelves. NIOZ also operates *Navicula* and *Griend* in the shallow Wadden Sea
Port of reg/flag	Texel
Official number	18179 ZR 1991; IMO nr: 9001461
Classification	Bureau Veritas 1 3/3 E Deep Sea, Ice 111. AUT. MS
Call sign	PGRQ
Built (yard and date)	Verolme Shipyard Heusden, Heusden; 1991
Length overall	66.045 m
Breadth moulded	12.80 m
Max draught	4.00 m (Summer)
Tonnage (grt)	1,615

PROPULSION

Main engine(s)	Diesel: port: 673 kW, 673 kVA; starboard: 1,020 kW, 1,030 kVA
Thrusters	Bow: omnidirectional, 450 kW, thrust 4,200 kg
Propellers	1 fixed pitch
Speed (max)	12.5 kt
Endurance	30 days
Fuel capacity	200 m³
Fuel consumption	7.5 m³/day
Electrical power	Main generators: 2 main diesel driven; 275 kVA
Fresh water capacity	100 m³

BRIDGE NAVIGATION AIDS

Satellite	DGPS: Sercel NR 53
Radar	KH-HR 3000 A/2/6 X-band
Speed log	Ben Galatee Mk3
Echo-sounder	Furuno FCV140 – 50/200 kHz; Radio Holland EL- 4242 C; Furuno FE-606 registrating

COMMUNICATIONS

Facsimile	Navtex receiver: Lokata NL-2; weather receiver: Furuno FAX-214

SAFETY

Lifesaving equipment	4 25-person dinghies plus 17 survival suits; 1 × 6-person man-overboard boat

Deck machinery

Cranes	C-deck starboard: SWL: 10 / 7.5 t
A-frame(s)	C-deck starboard: SWL 10 t; reach outboard/inboard: 3 m/3 m; height above deck: 8 m; frame-width: 3 m; stern: SWL 10 t; reach-out/inboard: 3 m/5.5 m; height above deck: 8 m working height; frame width: 6.5 m/8 m, total width 12 m
Winches	CTD: C – deck starboard; max pull: 5 t; Rochester wire/type: 1-H-285A; wire size: 0.288 in (7.32 mm); wire length: 8,800 m; workload: 18.5 kN (4,150 lb/ft); breaking strength (min): 46.3 kN (10,400 lb/ft); side: C – deck starboard; max pull: 10 t; wire: steel 3 × 36; 14 mm; 3,000 m; 131 kN; auxiliary: max pull: 5 t; wire: steel; 12 mm; 250 m; hydrographic: D-deck midship starboard; max pull: 200 kg; wire: stainless steel; 6 mm; 500 m; towing: C – deck aft; max pull: 5 t; Rochester type: 90463 I 3 cond + 3 coax; wire size: 0.463 in (11.76 mm); 900 m; stern: C – deck aft; max pull: 10 t; wire: steel 6 × 36 ws+st c; 18 mm; 2,000 m

ACCOMMODATION

Crew	10
Scientists/surveyors	15

SCIENTIFIC SPACES

Total scientific deck space	135 m²
Oceanographic wet lab	Wet chem. lab: 15 m² on D-deck; salt water lab: 12 m² on E-deck; general wet lab: 30 m² on D-deck
Multipurpose dry lab	Computer room: 8 m² on C-deck; measuring room: 20 m² on C-deck; dry laboratory: 15 m² on D-deck

SURVEY SYSTEMS

Echo-sounder (single beam)	Simrad EK 500
Sub-bottom profiler	Datasonic Chirp CAP – 6000; Oretech 3010, 10 kW, 3.5 kHz

Corer(s)	Pistoncore: up to 24 m at 8,000 m depth; Vibrocore: up to 6 m at 100 m depth
Grab(s)	Various
Oceanographic sensors (CTDs/XBTs and so on)	CTD/rosette sampler: Seabird/ Technicap Towed ADCP

Aqua flow system: Chelsea Instruments, connected via: ABC-system

UPDATED

Netherlands Institute of Ecology, Centre for Estuarine and Coastal Ecology

Luctor

GENERAL

	Marine Research Vessel
Owner	KNAW, NIOO – CEMO
Port of reg/flag	Yerseke, Netherlands
Official number	IMO No 8510697
Call sign	PFQN
Built (yard and date)	Gebr. Kooiman bv, 17 April 1985
Length overall	34.0 m
Breadth moulded	7.0 m
Working deck width	7.27 m
Max draught	2.4 m
Operational draught	1.5 m
Tonnage (grt)	176

PROPULSION

Main engine(s)	Cummins Diesel Model KTA-1150-M, 500 hp (375 kW)
Thrusters	1 bow thruster; 1 stern thruster
Propellers	Lips cunial bronze propeller

Speed (max)	9 kt
Speed (cruising)	9 kt
Fuel consumption	400 litres/50 n miles; 70 litres/h

SAFETY

Lifesaving equipment	2 × 8-person Viking inflatable liferafts

DECK MACHINERY

Cranes	Hydraulic crane: "v.d. Sluys & Kampers"

SCIENTIFIC SPACES

Total scientific deck space	70 m²
Oceanographic wet lab	15 m²
Multipurpose dry lab	14 m²

VERIFIED

Luctor

2000/0099211

North Sea Directorate

Arca

GENERAL

Oil recovery and research vessel

Owner
Netherlands Ministry of Transport, Public Works and Water Management

Port of reg/flag
Netherlands

Classification
Bureau Veritas 3V+1 3/3/-E special service/research vessel/ oil recovery ship + Mach/+ AUT-MS/+ ALS DP

Call sign
PDHT

Built (yard and date)
Damen Shipyards, Gorinchem, Netherlands; August 1998

Length overall
83.02 m

Breadth moulded
12.8 m

Tonnage (grt)
2,388

PROPULSION

Main engine(s)
2 Caterpillar 3508B DI-TA SCAC; 2 Caterpillar 3512B DI-TA SCAC; output: max 2 × 1,230 kW/1,000 rpm

Thrusters
600 kW (FPP) electrical driven

Propellers
2 azimuth thrusters

Fuel capacity
200 m³

Electrical power
2 Van Kaik generators, 1,056 kW/1,500 rpm 690 V; 2 Van Kaik generators, 858 kW/1,500 rpm 690 V; auxiliary set: 312.5 kVA 400 V; total power: 3,600 kW + 175 kW, 690/400/230 V, 50 Hz

Fresh water capacity
175 m³

COMMUNICATIONS

Inmarsat (type)
Satcom B/C

MF/HF
GMDSS

SAFETY

Life boats
2 × 25 persons

Workboat/chase boat
9.6 m, 1 t bollard pull, 12 kt

DECK MACHINERY

Cranes
Knuckle Type: 1 t at 8.5 m; Knuckle Type: 10 t at 11 m; Knuckle Type: 10/20 t at 11/8 m; 2 davits: 1 t at 2 m

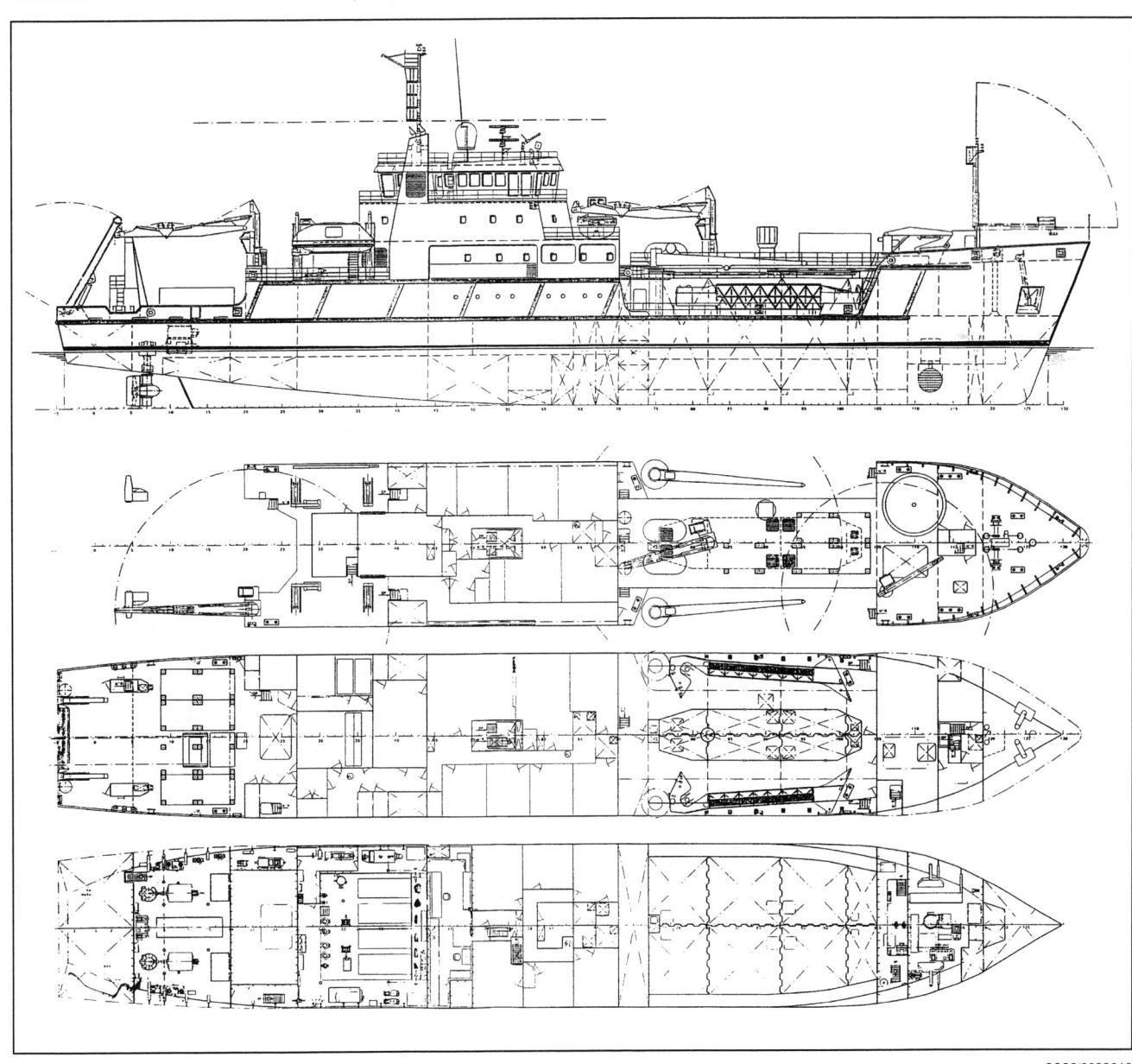

2000/0099210

A-frame(s)	Stern: 6 t at 6 m	**Sensors**	Furuno CH-34 – obstacle avoidance sonar; Datawell Hippy-120 C motion sensor; TSS DMS 205
Winches	2: 10 t, 400 m; hydrographic: 5 t, 400 m		
ACCOMMODATION			
Crew	20 total	**Echo-sounder (single beam)**	Atlas DESO 25
		Multibeam/swath system	Simrad EM 3000 dual
		Sidescan sonar	Ultra Minescan
SURVEY SYSTEMS		**Sound velocity profiler**	Plessey 4031; Applied Microsystems SVP 16
Positioning	Sercel 203 DGPS; Simrad SDP – Dynamic Positioning		

UPDATED

NEW ZEALAND

NIWA Vessel Management Ltd

Kaharoa

GENERAL

Port of reg/flag	Wellington
Classification	Class 10
Call sign	ZM 7552
Built (yard and date)	1981
Length overall	28.00 m
Breadth moulded	8.20 m
Max draught	3.20 m

PROPULSION

Main engine(s)	Lister Blackstone 511 kW at 750 rpm
Propellers	Liaanen cp
Speed (cruising)	10.5 kt
Endurance	30 days
Fuel capacity	48.8 m³
Electrical power	Main generators: 2 Lister JWA 6MA – 140 bhp at 1,500 rpm
Fresh water capacity	21.3 m³

BRIDGE NAVIGATION AIDS

Satellite	2 Furuno GP 50
Gyrocompass	Tokyo Keiki
Speed log	Doppler: Ametek
Echo-sounder	Koden CV 8814 colour sounder; Furuno FE 881 dry paper sounder

COMMUNICATIONS

MF/HF	Skanti 400 W SSB radio telephone ; Coden 120 W SSB marine transceiver
VHF	ICOM; Sailor R 501
Facsimile	Furuno Dfax

SAFETY

Lifeboats	Lancer Inflatable SOLAS B

DECK MACHINERY

Cranes	Hiab Seacrane
A-frame(s)	Heavy-duty, stern-mounted gantry. Operates through an arc of 75°
Winches	2 main trawl: Norwinch 1,500 m 14 mm 6 × wire rope per winch; 2 Gilson: Norwinch ; 1 net drum: Norwinch ; acoustic: holds approx 1,000 m ; 12.5 mm faired cable, slipring fitted; hydrology: holds 3,000 m 6 mm wire; CTD: holds 2,000 m 6 mm cable, slipring fitted; camera: holds 1,500 m camera cable, slipring fitted.

ACCOMMODATION

Scientists/surveyors	8 (max)

SURVEY SYSTEMS

Positioning	Trimble DGPS systems
Sensors	Net monitors: Scanmar system; Furuno CN22; heave compensator: TSS
Echo-sounder (single beam)	Odom Echotrac
Sidescan sonar	Klein 595 dual-frequency, sidescan sonar
Corer(s)	Various
Grab(s)	Various
Vehicle(s) (ROVs/AUVs and so on)	Chelsea Instruments Nu Shuttle
Oceanographic sensors (CTDs/XBTs and so on)	Seismic Eel Uniboom, 450 m cable

UPDATED

NIWA Vessel Management Ltd

Tangaroa

GENERAL

Port of reg/flag	Wellington
Classification	DNV + 1A1 Ice
Call sign	ZMFR
Built (yard and date)	1991
Length overall	70.00 m
Breadth moulded	13.80 m
Max draught	7.20 m
Tonnage (grt)	2,282

PROPULSION

Main engine(s)	Wärtsilä Vasa 8R 32D, 4,023 bhp
Thrusters	Bow: Brunvoll 368 kW
Propellers	Wärtsilä Wichman PR 90/4
Speed (cruising)	12.0 kt
Endurance	22,000 n miles/45 days
Fuel capacity	681 m³
Electrical power	Main generator: Leroy Sommer 1,800 kVA; auxiliary generator:

	Cummins KTA 38 GI / Leroy Sommer 900 kVA; harbour generator: Cummins 400 kVA		CTD: 3,000 m 6 mm cable; slipring fitted; camera: 3,000 m 15.1 mm cable; slipring fitted; 6,000 m 8 mm CTD cable.
Fresh water capacity	82 m³		

BRIDGE NAVIGATION AIDS		**ACCOMMODATION**	
Satellite	Magnavox 4200; Furuno GP 500; Ashtech.3DF ADU	Crew	19
		Scientists/surveyors	17
Radar	Furuno 2830 S; Furuno 1530 D		
Gyrocompass	Sperry RPG 90	**SCIENTIFIC SPACES**	
Speed log	Atlas Naviknot 11/NF; Doppler: CI 30	Oceanographic wet lab	Hydrology; Plankton
		Multipurpose dry lab	Chemical Lab equipped with fume cabinet; temperature-controlled lab equipped with filtered water supply; hydrology dry lab; photographic lab; electronics lab
Echo-sounder	Kaijo Denki KMC 2000		
COMMUNICATIONS			
Inmarsat (type)	Furuno Falcom 5B		
MF/HF	Sailor 1000B		
VHF	Sailor RT2047		
Facsimile	Furuno 208A Panasonic	**SURVEY SYSTEMS**	
		Positioning	Trimble DGPS systems
SAFETY		Sensors	Net monitors: Scanmar system; Furuno CN22; Kaijo Denki; heave compensator TSS
Lifeboats	Rigid bottom inflatable		
Workboat/chase boat	Dive tender: 6 m rigid bottom Zodiac	Echo-sounder (single beam)	Simrad EK 500; Odom Echotrac
		Sidescan sonar	Klein 595 dual-frequency, sidescan sonar
DECK MACHINERY		Corer(s)	Coring wire 5,500 m of 16 mm 3 × 19 held on main winch; corer recovery device athwartship mounted track and car system to handle up to 6 m barrels
Cranes	3 Seacranes: lifting capacity 2 t		
A-frame(s)	Starboard mounted, lifting capacity 5 t; deck clearance 6 m		
Winches	2 Main Trawl: 4,000 m 28 mm 6 × 19 wire rope each self-tensioning; 2 Gilson; 4 Sweepline; 1 Outhaul; 1 Cod End; 1 Windlass; 2 Net drum; 2 acoustic – each holds 1,200 m; 12.5 mm faired cable or 2,000 m 12.5 mm unfaired sliprings fitted; hydrology: 3,000 m 6 mm wire;	Grab(s)	Various
		Vehicle(s) (ROVs/AUVs and so on)	Chelsea Instruments Nu Shuttle
		Oceanographic sensors (CTDs/XBTs and so on)	ADCP: RDI broadband acoustic profiler, 150 kHz; seismic Eel Uniboom, 450 m cable.

UPDATED

NORWAY

Department of Fisheries and Marine Biology

Hans Brattström

GENERAL		**BRIDGE NAVIGATION AIDS**	
Owner	University of Bergen	Satellite	Magnavox MX 200 with DGPS
Classification	Den Norske Skipskontrollen	Radar	Furuno 7040
Call sign	LERS	Gyrocompass	Robertson RGC 10
Built (yard and date)	Batutrustning A/S, Rubbestadneset;1992	Other ship navigation	Autopilot – Robertson AP 9 Mk II
Length overall	24.3 m	**COMMUNICATIONS**	
Breadth moulded	6.5 m	VHF	Sailor RT2047
Max draught	6.5 m		
Tonnage (grt)	97		
Displacement	50 t	**SAFETY**	
		Workboat/chase boat	Rubber dinghy, 15 hp outboard
PROPULSION			
Main engine(s)	2 GM 12v-71ta; 2-stroke, 2,100 rpm, 650 bhp each	**DECK MACHINERY**	
		Cranes	1 × 6.1 t/m; 1 × 2.4 t/m
Propellers	Servogear, controllable pitch	Winches	2 hydraulic 2,500 m, 10 mm; hydraulic 1,500 m, 6.8 mm diameter
Speed (max)	22 kt		
Speed (cruising)	20 kt		
Fuel capacity	6,000 litres		
Electrical power	GM 6-71n: 165 bhp, 63 kW, 220 V, 50 Hz; Volvo 17.4 bhp, 10 kW, 220 V, 50 Hz (110 V/60 Hz available)	**ACCOMMODATION**	
		Crew	2
		Scientists/surveyors	4
Fresh water capacity	3,000 litres	**SCIENTIFIC SPACES**	
		Oceanographic wet lab	1
		Multipurpose dry lab	1

SURVEY SYSTEMS

Sensors	Trawl sensors – Scanmar; Kaijo Denki KCH 1827
Echo-sounder (single beam)	Simrad EQ50 38 kHz

Oceanographic sensors (CTDs/XBTs and so on)	CTD and water sampling rosette

VERIFIED

Hans Brattström

2000/0099212

Institute of Marine Research

Dr Fridtjof Nansen

GENERAL

Owner	Norwegian Agency for Development Co-operation
Port of reg/flag	Bergen, Norway
Official number	IMO-9062934
Classification	DNV + 1A1 ICE 1C MV, E0
Call sign	LGWS
Built (yard and date)	Flekkefjord Slipp og Maskinfabrikk, Norway; 1993
Length overall	56.75 m
Breadth moulded	12.5 m
Max draught	5.4 m
Tonnage (grt)	1,444

PROPULSION

Main engine(s)	3,264 hp
Thrusters	Bow: 408 hp
Propellers	1
Speed (max)	15 kt
Speed (cruising)	13.5 kt
Endurance	10,000 n miles/40 days
Fuel capacity	316 m³
Electrical power	220/440 V AC, 1,170 kW, 50-60 Hz
Fresh water capacity	108 m³

BRIDGE NAVIGATION AIDS

Satellite	2 Furuno GP-500 Mk-2 GPS
Radar	Furuno FAR-2830S S-band; Furuno FAR-2822S X-band
Gyrocompass	Robertson RGC 11
Speed log	BEN 48 mm Flat Surface Sensor
Echo-sounder	Simrad EK 500
Other ship navigation	MaxSea chart plotter

COMMUNICATIONS

Inmarsat (type)	Nera Saturn B, Sailor C Std C
MF/HF	Sailor Compact GMDSS Station
VHF	Sailor Compact RT2048
Cellular	GSM
Facsimile	Yes

SAFETY

Lifeboats	1 × 33 person
Workboat/chase boat	1 × 6 person
Lifesaving equipment	3 liferafts, total 56 persons

DECK MACHINERY

Cranes	2 × 2.0 t/10.0 m; 1 × 5.0 t/12.5 m
Winches	2 × 30.5 t, 2,470 m, 24 mm

ACCOMMODATION

Crew	33
Scientists/surveyors	20

SCIENTIFIC SPACES

Oceanographic wet lab	40 m²
Multipurpose dry lab	35 m²

SURVEY SYSTEMS

Positioning	Seatex Seapath II
Echo-sounder(single beam)	Simrad EK 500, 18/38/120 kHz split beam
Multibeam/swath system	Simrad EM 950, 95 kHz
Vehicle(s) (ROVs/AUVs and so on)	Macartney Focus ROTV
Oceanographic sensors (CTDs/XBTs and so on)	CTD – SBE 911 plus and water sample carousel

UPDATED

Institute of Marine Research

GM Dannevig

GENERAL

Port of reg/flag	Arendal, Norway
Official number	IMO-8899665
Classification	DNV + 1A1* R90 E0
Call sign	LINW
Built (yard and date)	Kystvagen Verft, Norway; 1979
Rebuilt (yard and date)	Bentsen & Son, Norway; 1987
Length overall	27.85 m
Breadth moulded	6.75 m
Max draught	2.66 m
Tonnage (grt)	171

PROPULSION

Main engine(s)	2 Volvo Penta TMD 121C, 350 hp
Thrusters	Bow: 100 hp
Propellers	1
Speed (max)	9 kt
Speed (cruising)	8.5 kt
Endurance	1,150 n miles/6 days
Fuel capacity	16.5 m³
Electrical power	220 V AC, 80 kW, 50 Hz
Fresh water capacity	9 m³

BRIDGE NAVIGATION AIDS

Satellite	GPS
Radar	Yes
Gyrocompass	Yes
Echo-sounder	Yes

COMMUNICATIONS

MF/HF	Yes
VHF	Yes
Cellular	Yes
Facsimile	Yes

SAFETY

Workboat/chase boat	1 × 4.0 m, 25 hp
Lifesaving equipment	2 liferafts, total 31 persons

DECK MACHINERY

Cranes	1 × 0.8 t/9.0 m, 1.2 – 2 t
Winches	2 trawl, 2 drums, 13.0 t

ACCOMMODATION

Crew	3
Scientists/surveyors	12

SCIENTIFIC SPACES

Total scientific deck space	43 m²
Oceanographic wet lab	7 m²
Multipurpose dry lab	2: total 40 m²

NEW ENTRY

Institute of Marine Research

G. O. Sars

GENERAL

Classification	DNV
Built (yard and date)	1970
Length overall	70.00 m
Breadth moulded	13.03 m
Max draught	7.30 m
Tonnage (grt)	1,447

PROPULSION

Main engine(s)	1 diesel engine, 2,250 bhp at 750 rpm
Speed (max)	14.0 kt
Speed (cruising)	11.0 kt
Endurance	7,000 n miles/30 days
Fuel capacity	359 m³
Electrical power	AC voltage: 380 V, total 1,000 kVA, 3-phase, 50Hz; AC voltage: 380 V, total 650 kVA, 3-phase, 50Hz
Fresh water capacity	97 m³

BRIDGE NAVIGATION AIDS

Radar	Yes

Gyrocompass	Yes
Speed log	Yes
Echo-sounder	Yes

DECK MACHINERY

Cranes	Stern, midships: clearance above deck 6 m, SWL 24 t
Winches	3 oceanographic, steel wire, 4,000 m, SWL 2 t; CTD: 4,000 m; hydrographic

ACCOMMODATION

Crew	17
Scientists/surveyors	15

SCIENTIFIC SPACES

Total scientific deck space	50 m²
Oceanographic wet lab	35 m²
Multipurpose dry lab	40 m²

UPDATED

Institute of Marine Research

Håkon Mosby

GENERAL

Owner	University of Bergen
Port of reg/flag	Bergen, Norway
Official number	IMO-7922233
Classification	1A1 Stern Trawler E0

Call sign	LJIT
Built (yard and date)	Mjellum & Karlsen, Norway; 1980
Length overall	47.24 m
Breadth moulded	10.32 m
Max draught	5.0 m
Tonnage (grt)	701

PROPULSION

Main engine(s)	1,500 hp
Thrusters	Bow: 200 hp; stern: 200 hp
Propellers	1
Speed (max)	14 kt
Speed (cruising)	12 kt
Endurance	6,500 n miles/21 days
Fuel capacity	160 m³
Fuel consumption	3.5 m³/day (economical); 5.0 m³/day (full speed)
Electrical power	220/400 V, 50 Hz
Fresh water capacity	44 m³

BRIDGE NAVIGATION AIDS

Satellite	GPS & DGPS
Radar	S-band and X-band
Gyrocompass	Yes
Speed log	Yes
Echo-sounder	Yes
Other ship navigation	Loran C

COMMUNICATIONS

Inmarsat (type)	Standard A
MF/HF	Yes
VHF	Yes
Cellular	Yes
Facsimile	Yes

SAFETY

Lifeboats	1 × 25 person
Workboat/chase boat	Rubber dinghy, 25 hp
Lifesaving equipment	5 liferafts

DECK MACHINERY

Cranes	1 × 3 tonnes/9.0 m; 2 × 1 tonne/3.5 m; 1 × 1 tonne/4.0 m
A-frame(s)	Starboard
Winches	Double drum, 5,000 m, 12 mm; 2 trawl, 1,600 m, 20 mm; hydrographic, 5,000 m, 4 mm; CTD, 6,000 m, 6.4 mm; magnetometer; trawl eye, 2,500 m

ACCOMMODATION

Crew	9
Scientists/surveyors	16
Scientific spaces	
Total scientific deck space	100 m²
Oceanographic wet lab	20 m²
Multipurpose dry lab	30 m²

SURVEY SYSTEMS

Echo-sounder (single beam)	Yes
Multibeam/swath system	Yes
Magnetometer	Yes
Gravimeter	Yes
Oceanographic sensors (CTDs/XBTs and so on)	CTD

SEISMIC SYSTEMS

Energy source (type and manufacturer)	LMF 10.4 m³/min – 200 bar (VHGD 55 22 W 70)

UPDATED

Institute of Marine Research

Johan Hjort

GENERAL

Port of reg/flag	Bergen, Norway
Official number	IMO-8915768
Classification	+ 1A1 ICE 1B E0
Call sign	LDGJ
Built (yard and date)	Flekkefjord Slipp og Maskinfabrikk, Norway; 1990
Length overall	64.4 m
Breadth moulded	13.0 m
Max draught	6.4 m
Tonnage (grt)	1,828

PROPULSION

Main engine(s)	3,264 hp
Thrusters	360° water jet
Propellers	1
Speed (max)	14.25 kt
Speed (cruising)	11 kt
Endurance	10,000 n miles/40 days
Fuel capacity	280 m³
Fuel consumption	5.0 m³/day (economical); 10.0 m³/day (full speed)
Fresh water capacity	80 m³

BRIDGE NAVIGATION AIDS

Satellite	Trimble NT200D DGPS; Racal Mk 90 GPS
Radar	Racal Decca 2690 BT Series S-band; Racal Decca BT 502 X-band
Gyrocompass	2 Anschutz Std 20
Speed log	Bergen Nautik
Echo-sounder	Simrad EQ 100, 50 kHz
Other ship navigation	MaxSea chart plotter

COMMUNICATIONS

Inmarsat (type)	Nera Saturn 3S Std. A; Sailor H2095B Std C
MF/HF	Skandi TRP 8400D
VHF	Sailor Compact RT2048
Cellular	NMT and GSM
Facsimile	Yes

SAFETY

Lifeboats	2 × 48 person
Lifesaving equipment	4 liferafts

DECK MACHINERY

Cranes	3 1.44 t/11.4 m; 1 × 5.0 t/4.0 m

ACCOMMODATION

Crew	13
Scientists/surveyors	19

SCIENTIFIC SPACES

Total scientific deck space	316 m²
Oceanographic wet lab	50 m²
Multipurpose dry lab	75 m²
Chemistry lab	50 m²

SURVEY SYSTEMS

Sensors	Simrad SR240 omnisonar, 24 kHz
Echo-sounder (single beam)	Simrad EK 500, 18/38/120 kHz split beam; Simrad EK 500, 200 kHz
Oceanographic sensors (CTDs/XBTs and so on)	CTD – SBE 911 plus and water sample carousel

VERIFIED

Institute of Marine Research

Michael Sar

GENERAL	
Classification	DNV
Built (yard and date)	1979
Length overall	49.00 m
Breadth moulded	10.0 m
Max draught	6.00 m
Tonnage (grt)	493

PROPULSION	
Main engine(s)	1 diesel engine, 1,500 bhp at 825 rpm
Speed (max)	13.5 kt
Speed (cruising)	11.5 kt
Endurance	5,000 n miles/20 days
Fuel capacity	180 m³
Electrical power	AC voltage: 380/220 V, total 158 kVA, 3-phase, 50 Hz
Fresh water capacity	90 m³

BRIDGE NAVIGATION AIDS	
Radar	Yes
Gyrocompass	Yes
Speed log	Yes
Echo-sounder	Yes

DECK MACHINERY	
Cranes	Stern, midships: clearance above deck 6 m, SWL 2 t
Winches	2 oceanographic, steel wire, 1,500 m, SWL 10 t; hydrographic: 4,000 m

ACCOMMODATION	
Crew	12
Scientists/surveyors	6

SCIENTIFIC SPACES	
Total scientific deck space	70 m²
Oceanographic wet lab	25 m²
Multipurpose dry lab	25 m²

NEW ENTRY

University of Tromso

Jan Mayen

GENERAL	
Comments	Stern trawler type, chartered by University of Tromso until 2002. Designed for fishery and marine biological, geological and oceanographic surveys in open and ice-covered waters. Other vessels operated include *Johann Ruud* and *Hyas*.
Classification	DnV Ice 1A
Built (yard and date)	Danyard a/s, Norway; 1988
Rebuilt (yard and date)	Båtbygg a/s; 1992 redesigned and refurbished as a research vessel
Length overall	63.80 m
Breadth moulded	13.0 m
Max draught	7.00 m
Tonnage (grt)	1,118

PROPULSION	
Main engine(s)	1 diesel, 4,080 bhp at 750 rpm
Speed (max)	16 kt
Speed (cruising)	12 kt
Endurance	20,000 n miles/70 days
Fuel capacity	574 m³
Electrical power	AC voltage: 440 V, total 2,180 kVA, 3-phase, 60 Hz
Fresh water capacity	60 m³

BRIDGE NAVIGATION AIDS	
Radar	Yes
Gyrocompass	Yes
Speed log	Yes
Echo-sounder	Yes

COMMUNICATIONS	
Inmarsat (type)	Thrane and Thrane C; Mini-M satellite telephone

DECK MACHINERY	
Cranes	Stern, outboard extension 13 m, SWL 4 t
A-frame(s)	Stern
Winches	CTDO: 4,000 m cable; hydrography: 3,000 m cable; dredge: 3 t, 3.500 m/12 mm; trawl eye: 2,400 m/11.4 mm; net drum: 25 t
Transducer well	3.5 m × 1.0 m section can be lowered 3.5 m below normal keel level

ACCOMMODATION	
Crew	12
Scientists/surveyors	23

SCIENTIFIC SPACES	
Total scientific deck space	50 m²
Oceanographic wet lab	4 labs: 30 m², 30 m², 19 m², 24 m²
Multipurpose dry lab	Hydrography lab 13 m²; isotope room 5.5 m²; data processing centre 55 m²

SURVEY SYSTEMS	
Sensors	Furuno CSH.70 fish-finding sonar
Echo-sounder (single beam)	Simrad EK-500 (38/120 kHz)
Sub-bottom profiler	GeoPulse 5430A; GeoPulse 5210A
Corer(s)	Various
Grab(s)	Various
Other sampling	Double 50 m trawlways for bottom trawling
Oceanographic sensors (CTDs/XBTs and so on)	RDI ADCP-150; Seabird SBE 911 Plus with compact rosette fluorometer

UPDATED

PAKISTAN

Ministry of Communications, Hydrographic Department

Beh Paima

GENERAL

Owner	Ministry of Communications, Government of Islamic Republic of Pakistan
Port of reg/flag	Karachi
Classification	LRS +100A1 +1mc
Call sign	AQPD
Built (yard and date)	Ishikawajima Harima Heavy Industries Co Ltd, Japan; 1982
Length overall	61 m
Breadth moulded	11.8 m
Working deck width	11.7 m
Max draught	6 m
Operational draught	3.7 m
Tonnage (grt)	1,183.52

PROPULSION

Main engine(s)	2 diesel engines – 1,000 PS
Thrusters	1 bow: Model TCN-175
Propellers	2 CPP 3-bladed
Speed (max)	13.99 kt
Speed (cruising)	9 kt
Endurance	5,400 n miles
Fuel capacity	265,000 litres
Fuel consumption	220 litres/h
Electrical power	563 A, 320 kW, 410 V AC, 50 Hz, 3-phase
Fresh water capacity	110 t

BRIDGE NAVIGATION AIDS

Satellite	GPS, DGPS, DDMU-586
Radar	JMA 650.7; 9,345-9,435 MHz, range 120 n miles
Gyrocompass	Sperry Mk 307 MOD-D
Speed log	Type EML-12
Echo-sounder	NJA 193S

COMMUNICATIONS

Inmarsat (type)	'C' TT-3020B Cap Sat
MF/HF	NSD-53; 405 – 535 kHz
	JSB-400; 1.6 – 25 MHz
VHF	JHV 212 TX/RX 88 channels; 156 – 163 MHz

SAFETY

Lifeboats	2
Workboat/chase boat	6 Zulu (rubber) boats with 25 hp outboard engine
Lifesaving equipment	Liferaft capacity – 215 persons

DECK MACHINERY

Cranes	1 × 1 t SWL
A-frame(s)	2 at quarterdeck
Winches	6

ACCOMMODATION

Crew	84
Scientists/surveyors	15
Hospital	Sick bay with 1 bed

SCIENTIFIC SPACES

Total scientific deck space	77.02 m²
Oceanographic wet lab	20.46 m²
Multipurpose dry lab	40.68 m²
Chemistry lab	14.88 m²

SURVEY SYSTEMS

Positioning	Trimble 4000 SST, 4000 DS DMU-586, Trisponders 218E
Echo-sounder (single beam)	DESO 20, 21, 22; 33/210 kHz
Sidescan sonar	EG&G Mk 1B
Sub-bottom profiler	Uniboom & Spark Array
Magnetometer	EG&G Gradiometer Model G-801G
Gravimeter	Lacoste & Romberg
Grab(s)	2
Other sampling	Nansen bottles 1.3 litres Zooplankton net NORPAC Plankton net
Oceanographic sensors (CTDs/XBTs and so on)	Current, wave and tide gauges STD Model 3 TS-MICOM B.T. – 2,000 m

UPDATED

PERU

Instituto del Mar del Perú (IMARPE)

Humboldt

GENERAL

Classification	Germanischer Lloyd
Built (yard and date)	1978
Length overall	76.2 m
Breadth moulded	12.6 m
Tonnage (grt)	1,731.06

PROPULSION

Main engine(s)	2 B & W Alpha diesels, each 1,118.55 hp
Speed (max)	14.0 kt
Speed (cruising)	12.0 kt

Endurance	10,000 n miles/37 days
Fuel capacity	409 m³
Electrical power	2 Deutz, each 388 kW, 1 Deutz, 188 kW
Fresh water capacity	125 m³

BRIDGE NAVIGATION AIDS

Satellite	Yes
Radar	Yes
Gyrocompass	Yes
Speed log	Yes
Echo-sounder	Yes

DECK MACHINERY		SCIENTIFIC SPACES	
Winches	1 oceanographic, steel wire, 2,000 m ; bottom sampling, 4,000 m	Oceanographic wet lab	8 m²
		Multipurpose dry lab	80 m²

UPDATED

ACCOMMODATION	
Crew	100

Instituto del Mar del Perú (IMARPE)

"IMARPE" Class

GENERAL		PROPULSION	
Comments	Three coastal research vessels, IV, V and VI	Main engine(s)	Caterpillar 190 hp
		Fuel capacity	1,000 gallons
Built (yard and date)	1995	Fresh water capacity	800 gallons
Length overall	16.5 m		
Breadth moulded	5.3 m		
Tonnage (grt)	46.03		

Instituto del Mar del Perú (IMARPE)

José Olaya Balandra

GENERAL		ACCOMMODATION	
Comments		Crew	30
Built (yard and date)	Mitubishi Heavy Industries, Shimonoseki, Japan; 1998		
		SURVEY SYSTEMS	
Length overall	40.50 m	Sensors	Net Sounder
Breadth moulded	8.30 m	Echo sounder (single beam)	Simrad
Max draught	3.0 m	Corer(s)	Piston
Tonnage (grt)	370	Grab(s)	Van Veen
		Other sampling	Rosette of Niskin bottles
PROPULSION		Oceanographic sensors	ADCP
Speed (cruising)	10.5 kt	(CTDs/XBTs and so on)	XBT
Endurance	7,200 n miles		Fluorometer
Fuel capacity	135 m³		
Fresh water capacity	45 m³		

PHILIPPINES

Bureau of Fisheries and Aquatic Resources (BFAR)

Researcher

GENERAL		DECK MACHINERY	
Built (yard and date)	1966	Cranes	Midships, outboard extension 1 m
Length overall	44.50 m	A-frame(s)	Midships
Breadth moulded	8.20 m	Winches	Oceanographic, steel wire, 1,000 m
Max draught	3.30 m		
Tonnage (grt)	419		
		ACCOMMODATION	
PROPULSION		Crew	27
Main engine(s)	1 diesel, 850 bhp at 365 rpm	Scientists/surveyors	18
Speed (max)	9.0 kt		
Speed (cruising)	8.3 kt	SCIENTIFIC SPACES	
Endurance	6,000 n miles/32 days	Total scientific deck space	9 m²
Fuel capacity	63 m³	Oceanographic wet lab	6 m²
Fresh water capacity	82 m³	Multipurpose dry lab	19 m²

VERIFIED

BRIDGE NAVIGATION AIDS	
Radar	Yes
Gyrocompass	Yes
Speed log	Yes
Echo-sounder	Yes

Mines and Geosciences Bureau

Explorer

GENERAL	
Classification	American Bureau of Shipping
Built (yard and date)	1984
Length overall	55.00 m
Breadth moulded	9.40 m
Max draught	3.80 m
Tonnage (grt)	500

PROPULSION	
Main engine(s)	2 diesel, each 1,200 bhp at 1,200 rpm
Speed (max)	12.0 kt
Speed (cruising)	11.0 kt
Endurance	4,200 n miles/30 days
Fuel capacity	101 m³
Electrical power	AC voltage: total 187 kVA, 3-phase, 60 Hz
Fresh water capacity	150 m³

BRIDGE NAVIGATION AIDS	
Radar	Yes
Gyrocompass	Yes
Speed log	Yes
Echo-sounder	Yes

DECK MACHINERY	
Cranes	Stern, clearance above deck 7 m, outboard extension 2 m, SWL 3 tons
Winches	Oceanographic, steel wire, 8,000 m, SWL 2 t; bottom sampling, 8,000 m, SWL 2 t

ACCOMMODATION	
Crew	21
Scientists/surveyors	10

SCIENTIFIC SPACES	
Oceanographic wet lab	18 m²

UPDATED

University of Philippines in the Visayas

Sardinella

GENERAL	
Classification	NKK
Built (yard and date)	1980
Length overall	40.22 m
Breadth moulded	8.80 m
Max draught	2.20 m
Tonnage (grt)	411

PROPULSION	
Main engine(s)	1 diesel, 1,200 bhp at 390 rpm
Speed (max)	11.0 kt
Speed (cruising)	9.0 kt
Endurance	15 days

Fuel capacity	128 m³
Fresh water capacity	50 m³

BRIDGE NAVIGATION AIDS	
Radar	Yes
Gyrocompass	Yes
Speed log	Yes
Echo-sounder	Yes

ACCOMMODATION	
Crew	22
Scientists/surveyors	30

VERIFIED

POLAND

Institute of Oceanology

Oceania

GENERAL	
Background information	Wind-powered survey vessel
Owner	Polish Academy of Sciences
Built (yard and date)	1985
Length overall	48.93 m
Breadth moulded	8.99 m
Max draught	3.49 m

PROPULSION	
Main engine(s)	Sails: 700 m², hydraulically raised and driven; auxiliary diesel, 310 hp
Thrusters	Bow: 70 hp
Propellers	cp
Speed (max)	Sails: 15 kt; Engine: 9 kt
Endurance	60 days
Fuel capacity	47 t
Electrical power	3 × generators: 135 kVA (50, 50 and 35 kVA), 400/220 VAC, 3-phase, 50 Hz

Fresh water capacity	40 t, 2 t/day from desalination unit

BRIDGE NAVIGATION AIDS	
Satellite	GPS 8800 Honeywell-Elac; Magnavox 4102
Radar	Furuno FR 1505 DA; Furuno 1830
Speed log	Electromagnetic: 4601 Radmor
Echo-sounder	Radmor

COMMUNICATIONS	
Facsimile	Furuno 108L

SAFETY	
Lifeboats	Inflatable, DSB 420 JRB, Yamaha engine
Workboat/chase boat	Kormoran, crew: 6, Yamaha outboard

DECK MACHINERY		SURVEY SYSTEMS	
A-frame(s)	6 t	Echo-sounder (single beam)	Atlas Deso 20 (33, 210 kHz); LAZ 4700 (30, 50, 210 kHz)
Winches	2 × deep-trawl, pull 1 t, drum capacity 2,000 m, (cable wire); 4 × cable wire for shallow water uses, pull 150 kg, drum capacity 350 m	Corer(s)	Yes
		Other sampling	Rosette: 12 × 3 litres; Nansen-type bottles, 1 and 2 litres; set of plankton nets
ACCOMMODATION		Oceanographic sensors (CTDs/XBTs and so on)	CTD probe: operational depth to 300 m, time constant of the temperature sensor 1.5 s; fluorometer, operational depth 100 m
Crew	15		
Scientists/surveyors	18		

NEW ENTRY

Polareks S.A.

Polarex

GENERAL		Speed log	Yes
Classification	Polish Register of Shipping	Echo-sounder	Yes
Built (yard and date)	1992		
Length overall	46.80 m	DECK MACHINERY	
Breadth moulded	11.40 m	Cranes	Stern, clearance above deck 5 m, outboard extension 6 m
Max draught	4.80 m		
Tonnage (grt)	624	A-frame(s)	Stern, clearance above deck 3 m, outboard extension 6 m, SWL 20 tons
PROPULSION			
Main engine(s)	1 diesel, 1,224 bhp at 720 rpm	Winches	2 oceanographic: steel wire 6,000 m, SWL 1 t; conducting cable 2,000 m, SWL 1 t
Speed (max)	12.0 kt		
Speed (cruising)	10.8 kt		
Endurance	30 days		
Fuel capacity	196 m³	ACCOMMODATION	
Electrical power	AC voltage: 380 V, 140 kVA, 3-phase, 50 Hz	Crew	10
		Scientists/surveyors	36
Fresh water capacity	58 m³		
		SCIENTIFIC SPACES	
BRIDGE NAVIGATION AIDS		Total scientific deck space	122 m²
Radar	Yes	Multipurpose dry lab	25 m²
Gyrocompass	Yes		

VERIFIED

Sea Fisheries Institute

Baltica

GENERAL		BRIDGE NAVIGATION AIDS	
Comments	Oceanographic, biological and fisheries research vessel. Operates in the Baltic Sea.	Radar	Yes
		Gyrocompass	Yes
		Speed log	Yes
Classification	Polish Register of Shipping	Echo-sounder	Yes
Built (yard and date)	1993		
Length overall	41.00 m	DECK MACHINERY	
Breadth moulded	9.00 m	Cranes	
Max draught	4.45 m	A-frame(s)	Stern, rotating; 3 t
Tonnage (grt)	614	Winches	Various
PROPULSION		ACCOMMODATION	
Main engine(s)	Cegielski 8S20D diesel; 140 kW at 900 rpm	Crew	11
		Scientists/surveyors	11
Thrusters	Bow		
Speed (max)	11.5 kt	SCIENTIFIC SPACES	
Speed (cruising)	8.0 kt	Total scientific deck space	150 m²
Endurance	30 days	Oceanographic wet lab	Biology: 25 m²; Ichthyology: 18 m²
Fuel capacity	174 m³	Multipurpose dry lab	Physics: 12 m²
Electrical power	AC voltage: 380 V, 472 kVA, 3-phase, 50 Hz; 220 V, 60 kVA, 3-phase, 50 Hz	Chemistry lab	20 m²
		SURVEY SYSTEMS	
		Oceanographic sensors (CTDs/XBTs and so on)	ADCP
Fresh water capacity	55 m³		

UPDATED

PORTUGAL

Hydrographic Institute

Almeida Carvalho

GENERAL

	AGS Class vessel.
Owner	Portugese Navy
Built (yard and date)	Commissioned: July 1966
Length overall	63.60 m
Breadth moulded	12.0 m
Operational draught	4.60 m

PROPULSION

Main engine(s)	Diesel-electric; 1,000 hp
	(840 kW), 200 rpm

PROPELLERS

	1
Speed (max)	11.0 kt
Endurance	60 days / 12,000 n miles
Fuel capacity	300 t
Electrical power	3 x 200 kW generators, 440 V, 60 Hz
	1 x 100 kW generator, 440 V, 60 Hz
Fresh water capacity	19 t

BRIDGE NAVIGATION AIDS

Satellite	DGPS
Radar	Kelvin Hughes 1007 F
	JRC JMA 3525
Gyrocompass	Yes
Speed log	Yes
Echo sounder	Elac Castor

COMMUNICATIONS

MF/HF	Yes
VHF	Yes

SAFETY

Workboat/chase boat	Betran 7.9 m, 8 kt

DECK MACHINERY

Cranes	10 t
Winches	1 x Dredging
	2 x Oceanographic
	1 x CTD

ACCOMMODATION

Crew	52

SURVEY SYSTEMS

Sensors	TSS Heave Compensator
Echo sounder (single beam)	2 x Atlas Deso 20
	1 x Atlas Deso 25
Oceanographic sensors (CTDs/XBTs and so on)	CTD

NEW ENTRY

Almeida Carvalho   *2001*/0097517

Instituto Português de Investigação Pesqueria (IPIMAR)

Capricornio

GENERAL

Comments	
Built (yard and date)	1969
Length overall	46.55 m

PROPULSION

Main engine(s)	1,200 hp
Speed (max)	12 kt
Endurance	30 days / 7,000 n miles

NEW ENTRY

Instituto Português de Investigação Pesqueria (IPIMAR)

Donax

GENERAL		PROPULSION	
Comments		Main engine(s)	173 hp
Built (yard and date)	1977	Speed (max)	9 kt
Length overall	15.45 m		

NEW ENTRY

Instituto Português de Investigação Pesqueria (IPIMAR)

Mestre Costeiro

GENERAL		PROPULSION	
Comments		Main engine(s)	463 hp
Built (yard and date)	1960	Speed (max)	10 kt
Length overall	27.02 m	Endurance	8 days / 1,920 n miles

NEW ENTRY

Instituto Português de Investigação Pesqueria (IPIMAR)

Noruega

GENERAL			
Classification	Bureau Veritas	Gyrocompass	Yes
Built (yard and date)	1978	Speed log	Yes
Length overall	47.50 m	Echo-sounder	Yes
Breadth moulded	10.30 m		
Max draught	5.90 m	**DECK MACHINERY**	
Tonnage (grt)	495	Winches	Oceanographic, steel wire
			5,000 m
PROPULSION			
Main engine(s)	1 diesel, 1,500 bhp at 825 rpm	**ACCOMMODATION**	
Speed (max)	13.0 kt	Crew	18
Speed (cruising)	11.0 kt	Scientists/surveyors	12
Endurance	9,500 n miles		
Fuel capacity	174 m³	**SCIENTIFIC SPACES**	
Electrical power	AC Voltage: 220 V, 380 kVA, 3-phase, 50 Hz	Oceanographic wet lab	20 m²
		Multipurpose dry lab	6 m²
Fresh water capacity	80 m³		

UPDATED

BRIDGE NAVIGATION AIDS
Radar   Yes

ROMANIA

National Institute for Marine Research and Development "Grigore Antipa"

Steaua de Mare I

GENERAL			
Current operational status	Marine research	Thrusters	570 hp
Port of reg/flag	Constanta, Romania	Propellers	1
Classification	Trawler	Speed (max)	10 kt
Call sign	YQLA	Speed (cruising)	9 kt
Built (yard and date)	Poland; 1981	Endurance	14 days
Length overall	25.8 m	Fuel capacity	30 t
Breadth moulded	7.2 m	Fuel consumption	85 kg/h
Working deck width	3.15 m	Electrical power	37 kVA
Max draught	2.1 m	Fresh water capacity	6 m³
Tonnage (grt)	109		
Displacement	60 t	**BRIDGE NAVIGATION AIDS**	
		Satellite	1
PROPULSION		Echo-sounder	1
Main engine(s)	6AL 20/24		

COMMUNICATIONS			**Transducer well**	1
VHF	1		Gate valve	2
SAFETY			**ACCOMMODATION**	
Lifeboats	2		Crew	7
			Scientists/surveyors	5
DECK MACHINERY				
Cranes	1		**SURVEY SYSTEMS**	
A-frame(s)	2		Sensors	1
Winches	3			

VERIFIED

Grigore Antipa (Diego Quevedo)

RUSSIAN FEDERATION

Department of Navigation and Oceanography

'Abxaziy' Class

GENERAL		**Thrusters**	Yes
Comments	Two vessels: *Cronchtadt* and	Propellers	2
	Nevelscoy	Speed (max)	17.5 kt
Owner	Russian Navy	Speed (cruising)	14.70 kt
Built (yard and date)	Germany; 1972-1973	Endurance	19,800 n miles
Length overall	124.0 m	Fuel capacity	1,380 t
Breadth moulded	17.0 m	Fuel consumption	15 t per day
Max draught	6.50 m	Fresh water capacity	230 t
PROPULSION		**BRIDGE NAVIGATION AIDS**	
Main engine(s)	2 x 4,000 hp	Satellite	Yes

Radar	Yes
Gyrocompass	Yes
Speed log	Yes
Echo sounder	Yes

SAFETY

Lifeboats	2, each 85 persons
Workboat/chase boat	2, each 15 persons
Lifesaving equipment	7 × life rafts, each 10 persons

HELIDECK

Size, aircraft capacity	Yes

DECK MACHINERY

A-frame(s)	4, each 4 t SWL
Winches	18

ACCOMMODATION

Crew	130
Scientists/surveyors	25
Hospital	4 persons
Scientific spaces	
Multipurpose dry lab	Total: 640 m²

SURVEY SYSTEMS

Echo sounder (single beam)	Yes
Magnetometer	Yes
Gravimeter	Yes
Corer(s)	Yes

NEW ENTRY

Department of Navigation and Oceanography

'Akademik Krylov' class

GENERAL

Comments	Three Akademik Krylov Class hydrographic survey vessels: Akademik Krylov; Admiral Vladimirskiy
Owner	Russian Navy
Built (yard and date)	Szczecin; 1974-79
Length overall	146.00 m
Breadth moulded	18.60 m
Max draught	6.39 m

PROPULSION

Main engine(s)	2 × 8,000 hp
Thrusters	Bow and stern thrusters
Propellers	2 shafts
Speed (max)	20.4 kt
Speed (cruising)	15.3 kt
Endurance	23,800 n miles
Fuel capacity	2,432 t
Fuel consumption	20 t per day
Fresh water capacity	166.5 t

BRIDGE NAVIGATION AIDS

Satellite	Yes
Radar	Nayada, Palm Frond and Don 2; I-band
Gyrocompass	Yes
Speed log	Yes
Echo-sounder	Yes

SAFETY

Lifeboats	2: each 70 persons
Workboat/chase boat	Two survey launches: each 22 persons
Lifesaving equipment	22 liferafts: each 10 persons

HELIDECK

Size, aircraft capacity	One Hormone

DECK MACHINERY

Cranes	1 × SWL 7t
A-frame(s)	2 × SWL 9t
Winches	11

ACCOMMODATION

Crew	125
Scientists/surveyors	36
Hospital	6 persons

SCIENTIFIC SPACES

Total scientific deck space	1,575 m²
Multipurpose dry lab	26 laboratories: 712.5 m²

SURVEY SYSTEMS

Echo-sounder (single beam)	Yes
Sidescan sonar	Yes
Magnetometer	Yes
Gravimeter	Yes
Corer(s)	Yes

UPDATED

Leonid Demin

2000/0081696

Navigation and Oceanography Department

'GS-439' Class

GENERAL	
Comments	Two GS-439 Class vessels: GS-439 and GS-440
Owner	Russian Navy
Built (yard and date)	Russia; 1993-1994
Length overall	39.60 m
Breadth moulded	9.80 m
Max draught	2.30 m

PROPULSION	
Main engine(s)	2 x 450 hp
PROPELLERS	2
Speed (max)	10.8 kt
Speed (cruising)	7.8 kt
Endurance	1,450 n miles
Fuel capacity	26 t
Fuel consumption	1.9 t per day
Fresh water capacity	24 t

BRIDGE NAVIGATION AIDS	
Satellite	Yes
Radar	Yes

Gyrocompass	Yes
Speed log	Yes
Echo sounder	Yes

SAFETY	
Lifesaving equipment	4 liferafts, each 10 persons

DECK MACHINERY	
Cranes	1: 2.5 t SWL
Winches	3

ACCOMMODATION	
Crew	20
Scientists/surveyors	3
Scientific spaces	

SURVEY SYSTEMS	
Echo sounder (single beam)	Yes
Corer(s)	Yes

NEW ENTRY

Polar Marine Geosurvey Expedition (PMGE)

Academik A. Karpinsky

GENERAL	
Comments	
Owner	Ministry of Mineral Resources
Port of reg/flag	St. Petersburg; Russia
Official number	IMO 8227238, Registration number: M-37040
Classification	USSR Register Class KM L2 F A2 research
Call sign	UIZO
Built (yard and date)	Black Sea Shipbuilding Plant, Ukraine; 1984
Length overall	103.0 m
Breadth moulded	16.0 m
Working deck width	8.0 m
Max draught	6.6 m
Operational draught	5.8 m
Tonnage (grt)	4430

PROPULSION	
Main engine(s)	2 × 6ЧH40/46-OM4, engine power 2 × 3,500 hp
Propellers	1 variable pitch
Speed (max)	15 kt
Speed (cruising)	10 kt (single engine)
Endurance	100 days
Fuel capacity	1,350 t
Fuel consumption	19.4 t at 15 kt; 11.5 t at 10 kt; stand-by – 3t
Electrical power	Two shaft generator , each 1,600 kW; 3 MSS, each 200 kW
Fresh water capacity	104 t, makes 50 t/day

BRIDGE NAVIGATION AIDS	
Satellite	GPS – Magnavox MX-4400; GLONASS – GP-80; Briz-K
Radar	Okean-C Furuno
Gyrocompass	Kurs-4; Vega
Speed log	IEL-2M
Echo sounder	Gel-3

COMMUNICATIONS	
Inmarsat (type)	Inmarsat-A: "Volna-C"; Inmarsat-B: Mini-M
MF/HF	"Musson"; "Korvet", "Brig"
VHF	"Reid-1"; "Sirena-1A"; radio station "Prizyv", "Prichal"
Facsimile	Yes

SAFETY	
Lifeboats	2 × 55 person; 2 × 20 person liferafts
Workboat/chase boat	7 m

DECK MACHINERY	
A-frame(s)	Stern: 10 t
Winches	Two wire sampling: 18 t Sampling: 2.5 t Seismic streamer: 1.2 t, 2,000 m/77 mm 2 magnetometer 0.5 t 2 airgun: 1 t

ACCOMMODATION	
Charterers	32
Crew	39
Scientists/surveyors	21

SCIENTIFIC SPACES	
Total scientific deck space	120 m^2 free deck, 40 m^2 work deck
Oceanographic wet lab	80 m^2
Multipurpose dry lab	270 m^2
Chemistry lab	50 m^2

SURVEY SYSTEMS	
Positioning	Asud-4 DP system
Echo sounder (single beam)	GEL-3
Magnetometer	VOSTOK (DMV), sensitivity: 0.02 nT; Range: 20,000 – 84,000 nT

Gravimeter	MGK "CHETA-AGG" (Marine Gravimetry Complex); Accuracy for the reduced gravity: 0.6-0.8 mgal; Drift: 4 – 6 mgal/month; Sampling interval: 0.16 sec; Measuring range: up to 14,000 mgal	Compressor numbers and types	6 electrocompressors EK-7.5, working pressure 140 bar
		Total capacity	18-24 litres/min
		Streamer manufacturer	Geko Prakla
		Streamer type	120/240 channels, (Nominal configuration: 78 channels); Group interval: 25 m; Shot interval: 50 m
Grab(s)	Photo – grab sampler		
SEISMIC SYSTEMS		Streamer numbers and lengths per number	1; 3,000 m
Energy source (type and manufacturer)	Airguns: 6 PI 20, Russia;	Acquisition system	Promax-2D on base of IBM RISC-SYSTEM-6000
Number of airguns	2 (total volume up to 80 litres, nominal pressure -130-150 kg/cm²)	Recording system	Seismic recording system: GAK-120 – IBM PC Pentium111 – Epson 1170 – EXABYTE
Size of airguns	Each airguns: Length 0.7 m, diameter 0.2 m, weight 30 kg		*NEW ENTRY*

Polar Marine Geosurvey Expedition (PMGE)

Professor Logachev

GENERAL		Working deck width	8.0 m
Owner	Ministry of Mineral Resources	Max draught	6.6 m
Port of reg/flag	St Petersburg; Russia	Operational draught	5.8 m
Official number	IMO 8834691, Registration No: M-42153	Tonnage (grt)	4,504
		Displacement	5,620 t
Classification	KM*L2 1 A2; Ice Class 30% floating ice		
		PROPULSION	
Call sign	UIJT	Main engine(s)	2 × Pielstick 3,500 bhp;
Built (yard and date)	Black Sea Shipbuilding Plant, Ukraine; 1991		2 × 1,600 kW shaft generators; 3 × 200 kW diesel generators
Rebuilt (yard and date)	Croatia; 1995	Thrusters	2 × 680 hp
Length overall	104 m	Propellers	1 × controllable pitch
Breadth moulded	16.0 m	Speed (max)	13.5 kt

Professor Logachev   ***2001**/0102834*

Speed (cruising)	12.0 kt
Endurance	90 days
Fuel capacity	1,117 t
Fuel consumption	20 t/day at 13.5 kt; 10.4 t at 9 kt (single engine)
Electrical power	2 shaft generators, each 1,600 kW; 3 MSS, each 200 kW
Fresh water capacity	104 t, makes 50 t/day

BRIDGE NAVIGATION AIDS

Satellite	GPS – Magnovox-4400; GLONASS-GG24
Radar	OKEAN-C
Gyrocompass	Kurs-4; Vega
Speed log	Aqua-2 L
Echo-sounder	Gel-4

COMMUNICATIONS

Inmarsat (type)	A: Volna-C; B: Mini-M
MF/HF	Musson; Koruet; Brig
VHF	Reid-1; Sirena-1A; radio station Prizyu; Prichel
Facsimile	Yes

SAFETY

Lifeboats	2 × 55 person: 2 × 20 person (liferafts)
Workboat/chase boat	7 m

DECK MACHINERY

Cranes	Bow: 3 t; stern: 5 t
A-frame(s)	Stern: 15 t; port: 16 t; starboard derrick: 10 t
Winches	Deepsea towing: 16 t, 10,000 m/17 mm; video: 10 t, 5,000 m/26 mm; 2 long-range sonar: 0.5 t, 500 m/12 mm and 300 mm/17 mm; wire: 18 t; electric: 2.5 kN; seismic streamer: 1.2 t, 2,000 m/50 mm; magnetometer: 0.5 t; CTD: 2.5 t
Transducer well	4

ACCOMMODATION

Charterers	30
Crew	40
Scientists/surveyors	22
Hospital	Yes

SCIENTIFIC SPACES

Total scientific deck space	150 m² free deck, 70 m² workdeck
Oceanographic wet lab	40 m²
Multipurpose dry lab	200 m²
Chemistry lab	55 m²

SURVEY SYSTEMS

Positioning	ASUD-6 DP system; "SIGMA" underwater navigation system
Sensors	"ABYSSAL" photographic and geoacoustic survey systems
Echo-sounder(single beam)	GEL-4
Multibeam/swath system	
Sidescan sonar	MAK-1M, 30 kHz/100 kHz/profiler 5 kHz; OCEAN, 9kHz
Sub-bottom profiler	"ORETEX-M", 3.5-10 kHz
Corer(s)	Various
Grab(s)	Preussag with TV camera
Other sampling	SBE 32 Carousel

Professor Logachev

2001/0102832

Vehicle(s) (ROVs/AUVs and so on)	ORETECH-M colour video systems	Compressor numbers and types	2 EK-7.5 electrocompressors
Oceanographic sensors (CTDs/XBTs and so on)	SBE 911 plus	Total capacity	18-24 litres/min
		Streamer manufacturer	Russia
		Streamer type	6 channel streamer
SEISMIC SYSTEMS		Streamer numbers and lengths per number	1, length 0.5 km
Energy source (type and manufacturer)	Puls-3 (31 litre airguns)	Recording system	HD PC Pentium III
Number of airguns	4		*UPDATED*
Size of airguns	Length 0.7 m, diameter 0.2 m, 30 kg		

Sea Technology Institute

'Akademik Kurchatov' Class

GENERAL		**PROPULSION**	
Comments	Two vessels: *Akademik Kurchatov* and *Dmitry Mendeleev*	Main engine(s)	2 × diesels, each 4,000 hp
		Speed (max)	13.8 kt
Owner	Shirshov Institute, Russian Academy of Sciences	Fuel capacity	1,000 t
		Electrical power	6 × 560 hp diesel alternators
Official number	*Akademik Kurchatov:* Lloyds Register 6806896		
	Dmitry Mendeleev: Lloyds Register 6610924	**DECK MACHINERY**	
		A-frame(s)	1
Built (yard and date)	Math as Thesen Werft, Wismar; *Dmitry Mendeleev* commissioned August 1968	Winches	5
	Akademik Kurchatov commissioned December 1968	**ACCOMMODATION**	
		Crew	76
		Scientists/surveyors	77
Length overall	124.0 m	Scientific spaces	
Breadth moulded	17.00 m	Multipurpose dry lab	10
			NEW ENTRY

Sea Technology Institute

Akademik Loffe

GENERAL		****	
Comments		Fuel capacity	1,220 t
Owner	Shirshov Institute, Russian Academy of Sciences	Electrical power	2 × 1,200 hp
		HELIDECK	
Official number	Lloyds Register 8507729	Deck machinery	
Built (yard and date)	Hollming Oy, Finland; launched December 1986, commissioned February 1988	Cranes	2
		A-frame(s)	1
		Winches	11
Length overall	117.0 m		
Breadth moulded	18.20 m	**ACCOMMODATION**	
		Crew	76
		Scientists/surveyors	52
PROPULSION		Scientific spaces	
Main engine(s)	2 × diesels, 3,500 hp	Multipurpose dry lab	18 laboratories
Speed (max)	13.0 kt		*NEW ENTRY*
Speed (cruising)	10.5 kt		

Sea Technology Institute

Akademik Matislav Keldysh

GENERAL		**PROPULSION**	
Owner	Shirshov Institute, Russian Academy of Sciences	Main engine(s)	4 × diesels, each 1,460 hp
		Speed (max)	12.5 kt
Official number	Lloyds Register 7711018	Speed (cruising)	10.5 kt
Built (yard and date)	Holming Oy, Finland; commissioned January 1981	Fuel capacity	1,150 t
		Electrical power	2 × 1,100 hp diesel alternators
Rebuilt (yard and date)	Converted to submersible carrier in 1987	**DECK MACHINERY**	
Length overall	122.2 m	Cranes	4
Breadth moulded	17.80 m	A-frame(s)	1
		Winches	15

Crew	53	Scientific spaces	
Scientists/surveyors	47 plus 25 technicians	Multipurpose dry lab	17

NEW ENTRY

Sea Technology Institute

'Akademik Sergei Vavliov' Class

GENERAL		Speed (cruising)	10.5 kt
Comments	Two vessels; *Akademik Sergei Vavliov* and *Akademik Lotte*	Fuel capacity	1,220 t
		Electrical power	2 x 1,200 hp
Owner	Shirshov Institute, Russian Academy of Sciences		
Official number	*Akademik Sergei Vavliov:* Lloyds Register 8507729	**DECK MACHINERY**	
		Cranes	2
		A-frame(s)	1
	Akademik Lotte: Lloyds Register 8507731	Winches	11
Built (yard and date)	Hollming Oy, Finland;	**ACCOMMODATION**	
	Akademik Sergei Vavliov: launched December 1986, commissioned February 1988	Crew	76
		Scientists/surveyors	52
		Scientific spaces	
	Akademik Lotte: launched August 1987, commissioned February 1989	Multipurpose dry lab	18 laboratories
		Survey systems	
Length overall	117.0 m	Multibeam/swath system	Hollming Ekhoss II
Breadth moulded	18.20 m		
PROPULSION			
Main engine(s)	2 × diesels, 3,500 hp		
Speed (max)	13.0 kt		

NEW ENTRY

Sea Technology Institute

Akvenavl

GENERAL		**DECK MACHINERY**	
Comments		A-frame(s)	1
Owner	Shirshov Institute, Russian Academy of Sciences	Winches	2
Built (yard and date)	USSR; commissioned August 1976	**ACCOMMODATION**	
		Crew	13
Length overall	34.0 m	Scientists/surveyors	7
Breadth moulded	7.10 m		
		SCIENTIFIC SPACES	
PROPULSION		Multipurpose dry lab	1
Main engine(s)	1 x diesel, 305 hp		
Speed (max)	8.5 kt		
Fuel capacity	15 t		
Electrical power	3 x 115 hp; 3 x 80 hp; 3 x 35 hp diesel alternators		

NEW ENTRY

Sea Technology Institute

Professor Shtockman

GENERAL		Fuel capacity	260 t
Owner	Shirshov Institute, Russian Academy of Sciences	Electrical power	3 x 225 hp diesel alternators
Official number	Lloyds Register 7703927	**DECK MACHINERY**	
Built (yard and date)	Laivaieollissuus, Finland; commissioned January 1979	Cranes	2
		A-frame(s)	1
Length overall	68.9 m	Winches	5
Breadth moulded	12.40 m		
		ACCOMMODATION	
PROPULSION		Crew	34
Main engine(s)	1 x diesel, 2,000 hp	Scientists/surveyors	25
Speed (max)	12.0 kt	Scientific spaces	
		Multipurpose dry lab	6

NEW ENTRY

Sea Technology Institute

Rift

GENERAL

Owner	Shirshov Institute, Russian Academy of Sciences
Official number	Lloyds Register 7826295
Built (yard and date)	USSR
Length overall	53.7 m
Breadth moulded	10.50 m

PROPULSION

Main engine(s)	1 x diesels, 1,320 hp
Speed (max)	10.0 kt

Fuel capacity	150 t
Electrical power	3 x 225 hp diesel alternators
Winches	2
Crew	27
Scientists/surveyors	11
Scientific spaces	
Multipurpose dry lab	3

NEW ENTRY

Sea Technology Institute

Shelf

GENERAL

Owner	Shirshov Institute, Russian Academy of Sciences
Built (yard and date)	USSR; commissioned August 1977
Length overall	34.0 m
Breadth moulded	7.10 m

PROPULSION

Main engine(s)	1 x diesel, 305 hp
Speed (max)	8.5 kt
Fuel capacity	22 t
Electrical power	3 x 115 hp; 3 x 80 hp; 3 x 35 hp diesel alternators

DECK MACHINERY

Cranes	4
A-frame(s)	1
Winches	15
Crew	13
Scientists/surveyors	7
Scientific spaces	
Multipurpose dry lab	17 laboratories

NEW ENTRY

Sea Technology Institute

Vityaz II

GENERAL

Owner	Shirshov Institute, Russian Academy of Sciences
Official number	Lloyds Register 7826295
Built (yard and date)	Poland; commissioned December 1981
Length overall	110.9 m
Breadth moulded	16.60 m

PROPULSION

Main engine(s)	2 x diesels, each 3,200 hp
Speed (max)	15.0 kt

Fuel capacity	1,150 t
Electrical power	3 x 930 hp diesel alternators
A-frame(s)	1
Crew	62
Scientists/surveyors	59
Scientific spaces	
Multipurpose dry lab	15

NEW ENTRY

YUZHMORGEOLOGIYA Federal Marine Scientific Centre

17 Syezd Profsoyuzov

GENERAL

Owner	YUZHMORGEOLOGIYA Federal Marine Scientific Centre
Built (yard and date)	1982
Length overall	103 m
Breadth moulded	16 m
Max draught	6.1 m

PROPULSION

Endurance	60 days (food and fuel); 20,000 n miles at 17 kt

ACCOMMODATION

Crew	52
Scientists/surveyors	42

SURVEY SYSTEMS

Gravimeter	Several Russian-developed systems, plus Lacoste & Romberg S-113

VERIFIED

YUZHMORGEOLOGIYA Federal Marine Scientific Centre

Akademik Sidorenko

GENERAL	
Owner	YUZHMORGEOLOGIYA Federal Marine Scientific Centre
Classification	KM*L2 1 A2; Ice Class 30% floating ice
Built (yard and date)	1988/89
Length overall	104.5 m
Breadth moulded	16.6 m
Max draught	7.2 m
Operational draught	5.8 m
Tonnage (grt)	4,430
Displacement	5,715 t

PROPULSION	
Main engine(s)	2 × Pielstick 3,500 bhp; 2 × 1,600 kW shaft generators; 3 × 200 kW diesel generators
Thrusters	1 × 500 hp
Propellers	1 × controllable pitch
Speed (max)	16.3 kt
Endurance	90 days (fuel); 58 days (food); cruising range: 21,000 n miles
Fuel capacity	1,220 t

BRIDGE NAVIGATION AIDS	
Satellite	GPS – MX-4400; SNS transit system
Radar	Furuno
Gyrocompass	2
Speed log	Doppler

DECK MACHINERY	
Cranes	Port stern, hydraulic J-frame: 1.2 t; 4 × cargo booms: 3.6 t (each)
A-frame(s)	Stern: 16 t
Winches	Traction: 16 t

ACCOMMODATION	
Crew	52
Scientists/surveyors	42

VERIFIED

YUZHMORGEOLOGIYA Federal Marine Scientific Centre

Gelendzhik

GENERAL	
Owner	YUZHMORGEOLOGIYA Federal Marine Scientific Centre
Port of reg/flag	Russian Federation
Official number	885858
Classification	KM*L2 1 A2; Ice Class 30% floating ice
Call sign	UFII
Built (yard and date)	Nikolaev; 1989
Rebuilt (yard and date)	Croatia; 1995
Length overall	104.5 m
Breadth moulded	16.0 m
Max draught	5.88 m
Tonnage (grt)	4,504
Displacement	5,700 t

PROPULSION	
Main engine(s)	2 × Pielstick 3,500 bhp;
Thrusters	2 × 680 hp
Propellers	1 × controllable pitch
Speed (max)	14 kt
Speed (cruising)	10 kt
Endurance	90 days (fuel); 70 days (food); cruising range: 21,000 n miles
Fuel capacity	1,220 t
Fuel consumption	22.5 t/day in transit; 8 t/day in operation; 3 t/day on standby
Electrical power	2 × 1,600 kW shaft generators; 3 × 200 kW diesel generators
Fresh water capacity	104.2 t

BRIDGE NAVIGATION AIDS	
Satellite	GPS – Furuno
Radar	Furuno
Gyrocompass	Yes
Speed log	Doppler: IEL-2M
Echo-sounder	NEL-M1

COMMUNICATIONS	
Inmarsat (type)	Mini-M; GMDSS Sailor (Area A3)
Facsimile	Navtex receiver

SAFETY	
Lifeboats	2 × 55 persons
Lifesaving equipment	4 × 10 persons

DECK MACHINERY	
Cranes	Lifting system: 3 t; hydraulic J-frame: 5 t derrick: 16 t
A-frame(s)	Stern: 16 t
Winches	Deepsea towing: 160 kN; oceanographic: 8 kN; oceanographic: 12 kN; lifting: 18 kN; electric: 2.5 kN; seismic streamer: 12 kN; geophysical: 5 kN; geophysical: 25 kN

ACCOMMODATION	
Crew	42
Scientists/surveyors	46

SCIENTIFIC SPACES	
Total scientific deck space	120 m²
Oceanographic wet lab	646 m² (incl Dry lab)

SURVEY SYSTEMS	
Positioning	GPS: Trimble 4000 DL-II; SBL positioning – SIGMA-M
Sensors	Seatex MRU
Multibeam/swath system	Simrad EM12S-120
Sidescan sonar	Mak-1M, 30/100 kHz
Corer(s)	Kadr-1, 5.5 m length; gravity, 4 m length; box – Ocean-025
Grab(s)	Grab sampler
Other sampling	Cone penetrometer
Vehicle(s) (ROVs/AUVs and so on)	Raduga deep towed vehicle
Sound velocity profiler	ME OTS; AML SVP-16; SV Plus

VERIFIED

YUZHMORGEOLOGIYA Federal Marine Scientific Centre

Impuls

GENERAL		PROPULSION	
	Research vessel	Speed (max)	12.3 kt
Length overall	41 m	Endurance	1,870 n miles cruising range
Breadth moulded	8 m		
Max draught	2 m	ACCOMMODATION	
Displacement	306 t	Crew	22 (including scientists)

VERIFIED

YUZHMORGEOLOGIYA Federal Marine Scientific Centre

Issledovatel

GENERAL		PROPULSION	
	"Valerian Uryvayev" class research vessel	Speed (max)	11.8 kt
		Endurance	10,000 n miles cruising range
Built (yard and date)	1977		
Length overall	58 m	ACCOMMODATION	
Breadth moulded	9.3 m	Crew	23
Max draught	3.2 m	Scientists/surveyors	17
Displacement	1,128 t		

VERIFIED

YUZHMORGEOLOGIYA Federal Marine Scientific Centre

Yantar

GENERAL		PROPULSION	
	Research vessel	Speed (max)	9 kt
Built (yard and date)	1975	Endurance	1,400 n miles cruising range
Length overall	34 m		
Breadth moulded	7 m	ACCOMMODATION	
Max draught	2.6 m	Crew	22 (including scientists)
Displacement	266 t		

VERIFIED

YUZHMORGEOLOGIYA Federal Marine Scientific Centre

Yuzhmorgeologiya

GENERAL		
Owner	YUZHMORGEOLOGIYA Federal Marine Scientific Centre	
Port of reg/flag	Russian Federation	
Official number	841099	
Classification	KM*L2 1 A2; Ice Class 30% floating ice	
Call sign	UBSZ	
Built (yard and date)	Nikolaev, 1985	
Length overall	104.5 m	
Breadth moulded	16.6 m	
Max draught	7.2 m	
Operational draught	5.8 m	
Tonnage (grt)	4,430	
Displacement	5,660 t	

PROPULSION	
Main engine(s)	2 × Pielstick 3,500 bhp;
Thrusters	1 × 500 hp
Propellers	1 × controllable pitch
Speed (max)	14.5 kt
Endurance	90 days (fuel); 70 days (food); cruising range: 21,000 n miles
Fuel capacity	1,220 t
Fuel consumption	19.6 t/day in transit; 10 t/day in operation; 3 t/day on standby

Electrical power	2 × 1,600 kW shaft generators; 2 × 200 kW diesel generators

BRIDGE NAVIGATION AIDS	
Satellite	GPS – MX-4400; SNS transit system
Radar	Furuno FR-2110
Gyrocompass	2
Speed log	Doppler – IEL-2M
Echo sounder	NEL-10

COMMUNICATIONS	
Inmarsat (type)	Furuno GMDSS (Area A3); Saturn-B

SAFETY	
Lifeboats	2 × 55 persons
Workboat/chase boat	Zodiac
Lifesaving equipment	3 liferafts: 10 persons

DECK MACHINERY	
Cranes	Port stern, hydraulic J-frame: 1.2 tonnes; 4 × cargo booms: 3.6 t (each)
A-frame(s)	Stern: 16 t
Winches	Traction: 16 t

ACCOMMODATION

Crew	52
Scientists/surveyors	42

SURVEY SYSTEMS

Sensors	M-140 profiler; AWS 2700
Sidescan sonar	MAK-1M
Corer(s)	Gravity

Grab(s)	Grab sampler
Other sampling	Dredge
Vehicle(s) (ROVs/AUVs and so on)	Neptune deep-towed TV-photo system
Oceanographic sensors (CTDs/XBTs and so on)	CTD – SeaCat with General Oceanics rosette

VERIFIED

SOUTH AFRICA

Marine and Coastal Management, Department of Environmental Affairs and Tourism

Africana

GENERAL

FRS *Africana* is the flagship of the Marine and Coastal Management fleet of oceanographic research ships. Her main role is as a platform for research and monitoring undertaken to guide the management of South Africa's offshore fisheries

Classification	Lloyds Register 100 A1 + Ice Class II
Call sign	ZAUB
Built (yard and date)	Dorbyl Marine, Durban; keel laid: 1979 (Commissioned in March 1982)
Length overall	77.85 m
Breadth moulded	15.25 m
Max draught	5.70 m
Tonnage (grt)	2,471.11

PROPULSION

Main engine(s)	Single screw, diesel electric: 3 APE Allen diesel each developing 1,044 kW at 600 rpm; 3 Siemens 750 kW DC generators supplying Siemens motor of 1,790 kW at 174 rpm
Thrusters	Omnidirectional bow
Propellers	Fixed pitch

Speed (max)	14.5 kt
Speed (cruising)	12.0 kt
Endurance	20,000 n miles/45 days
Fuel capacity	532 t
Electrical power	Generated at 380 V, 3-phase, 50 Hz by 2 Siemens 550 kW alternators driven by 2 of the main engines. Auxiliary power by 437 kW Deutz diesel engine driving 350 kW Siemens alternator. 220 V AC 50 Hz domestic supply. 220 V AC 50 Hz stabilised supply from 10 or 5 kVA units
Fresh water capacity	90 m³

BRIDGE NAVIGATION AIDS

Satellite	GPS
Radar	Yes
Gyrocompass	2
Speed log	Yes

SAFETY

Helideck	
Size, aircraft capacity	Medium-sized helicopter

DECK MACHINERY

Cranes	2 Pesci P1700 Pesci P555

Africana

2000/0093792

Winches	Main trawl: Clarke Chapman; 2 × 25 t finger capstans, 2 storage drums each with 4,000 m × 32 mm warp; net drum: Petrel, 7,5 m – 6,2 t; fishing/ mooring: Petrel, 2 × 10 t; auxiliary trawl: Petrel, 2 × 10 t; net sonde: Elac; 2,500 mm cable, constant tension; hydrographic: Clarke Chapman, single finger capstan, storage drum; 5,000 m × 9.5 mm conductor cable, 1 storage drum 6,000 m × 6 mm SWR; large towing: Lebus, one drum 2,500 m × 12.5 mm conductor cable, 1 drum 2,500 m × 12.5 mm conductor cable SWR; vertical plankton: Lebus, 1 drum 1,000 m × 7.2 mm conductor cable; small towing: Lebus, 1 drum 1,000 m × 9.5 mm conductor cable

SURVEY SYSTEMS

Sensors	Simrad SU sonar ; Simrad FR 500 net sonde system
Echo-sounder (single beam)	Simrad EK500 scientific with 38 and 120 kHz split-beam transducers with 18 kHz single-beam option; Simrad ES500 commercial with 18 and 50 kHz single-beam frequencies
Oceanographic sensors (CTDs/XBTs and so on)	Neil Brown CTD; General Oceanics 12 × 5 litre rosette; Seacat thermosalinograph; Turner Designs flow through fluorometer; RDI ADCP; expendable bathythermograph; retractable calibration monitor for echo-sounders retractable underway water sampling probe; SFRI universal underwater unit; SFRI electronic fish measuring boards

VERIFIED

ACCOMMODATION

Crew	52
Scientists/surveyors	19

Marine and Coastal Management, Department of Environmental Affairs and Tourism

Agulhas

Classification	Lloyds Register Ice Class 1
Call sign	ZSAF

Built (yard and date)	Mitsubishi Heavy Industries, Shimonoseki, Japan; keel laid: 1977
Length overall	111.95 m

Agulhas

2000/0093791

Breadth moulded	18.05 m	**DECK MACHINERY**	
Max draught	6.045 m	**Cranes**	Julius Wolff and Co 5 t travelling
Tonnage (grt)	6,122.96		deck servicing all three hatches;
			O & K 25 t at 17 m luffing/slewing
PROPULSION			situated on focsle head; 2 t
Main engine(s)	2 unidirectional Mirrlees KmR6		telescopic stores
	Major turbo-charged and	**Winches**	Mitsubishi electric windlass with
	intercooled 6-cylinder 4-stroke;		2 × 5 t warping drums; deep
	total power MCR 4,476 kW,		hydrographic with capacity of
	service power 3,804 kW		7,000 m of 9.5 mm diameter
Thrusters	750 hp Samuel White Gill		4-core conductor cable; vertical
	omnidirectional bow, 500 hp		plankton with capacity of 1,000 m
	Pleuger tunnel stern		of 7 mm diameter 4-core
Propellers	Single, controllable pitch		conductor cable; Lebus
Speed (max)	14.0 kt		deepwater coring with capacity of
Speed (cruising)	12.5 kt		10,000 m of 12 mm diameter
Endurance	15,000 n miles/90 days		steel cable; towing/mooring
Fuel capacity	1,099 t		comprising 2 warping drums and
Electrical power	Generated at 380 V, 3-phase,		2 clutched towing drums, the port
	50 Hz by 3 Mitsubishi alternators		drum with a capacity of 2,500 m
	driven by Daihatsu 6-DS-22		of 12 mm diameter 10-core
	engines each developing 768 kW.		conductor cable, and the
	Alternator output each 700 kW.		starboard drum with a capacity of
	Mitsubishi emergency generator		2,500 m of 12.5 mm diameter
	driven by 145 kW Deutz BF-121-		steel wire rope.
	714 engine. 220 V AC, 50 Hz		
	domestic supply. 220 V AC, 50 Hz	**ACCOMMODATION**	
	stabilised supply from 10 or 5	**Crew**	40
	kVA units.	**Scientists/surveyors**	98
Fresh water capacity	213 m³		
		SCIENTIFIC SPACES	
BRIDGE NAVIGATION AIDS		**Total scientific deck space**	130 m²
Satellite	GPS		
Radar	Yes	**SURVEY SYSTEMS**	
Gyrocompass	Yes	**Echo-sounder (single beam)**	Nippon Electric Co. MS 74 deep
Speed log	Yes		sea, 12 kHz; tank-mounted
			Simrad EK 500 120 kHz
SAFETY			transducer; Simrad EK 38 kHz;
Workboat/chase boat	2 workboats of 50 hp drive; 4		Furuno FCV 262 multifunction
	large 10 m inflatable rafts with a		colour sounder with flush-
	working capacity of 15 t per		mounted 28/50 kHz transducer.
	paired rafts; One 2 × 40 hp 10	**Sub-bottom profiler**	Nippon Electric Co. NE 515, 3.5
	man SOLAS rescue boat; One 30		and 7 kHz
	hp 6 man inflatable SOLAS	**Oceanographic sensors**	Neil Brown CTD General
	rescue boat; One 25 hp 4 man	**(CTDs/XBTs and so on)**	Oceanics 12 × 8 litre rosette;
	inflatable for inshore scientific		Seacat thermosalinograph;
	work.		expendable bathythermograph
HELIDECK			*UPDATED*
Size, aircraft capacity	Enclosed hangar facilities for 2		
	Aerospatiale Puma SA 330 J		
	helicopters		

Marine and Coastal Management, Department of Environmental Affairs and Tourism

Algoa

GENERAL		**Max draught**	3.75 m
	Used mainly for pelagic,	**Tonnage (grt)**	759.38
	mesopelagic and inshore		
	demersal surveys	**PROPULSION**	
Classification	Bureau Veritas	**Main engine(s)**	Single Crepelle SN, turbocharged
Call sign	ZR 4311		and intercooled 12-cylinder
Built (yard and date)	Ateliers et Chantiers, France;		4-stroke diesel driving an Eyscher
	1975		Weiss
Rebuilt (yard and date)	Converted at Dorbyl Marine, Cape	**Thrusters**	Bow: Schottel SRP 170 LSV,
	Town; 1993		280 kW retractable/
Length overall	52.55 m		omnidirectional
Breadth moulded	10.80 m	**Propellers**	Single, controllable pitch

Speed (max)	12.5 kt
Speed (cruising)	11.0 kt
Endurance	6,000 n miles/15 days
Fuel capacity	138 t
Electrical power	2 MAN diesel gensets, each 280 kVA, 380/220 V, 3-phase, 50 Hz at 0.8 PF; shaft generator; stabilised supply

BRIDGE NAVIGATION AIDS

Satellite	GPS
Radar	Yes
Gyrocompass	Yes
Speed log	Yes

DECK MACHINERY

Winches — Main trawl: Brissoneau and Lotz, electric, warp capacity 3,500 m × 26 mm, 4 auxiliary drums; net drum: gear driven from main trawl; mooring: 1 port, 1 starboard, electric; net sonde: Atlas, electric; hydrographic: LEBUS, medium pressure, hydraulic, drum capacity 2,000 m × 9.5 mm, 4 core conductor cable, via accumulator system to hydraulic A-frame, midships; vertical plankton: LEBUS, medium pressure, hydraulic, drum capacity 1,500 × 9.5 mm, 4 core conductor cable via accumulator to hydraulic A-frame, midships;

towing 1: PETREL, medium pressure, hydraulic, drum capacity 500 m × 11, 76 mm, 10 core conductor cable, fair lead direct to main gantry aft; towing 2: PETREL, medium pressure, hydraulic, drum capacity 1,000 m × 9.5 mm, 4 core conductor cable, cable lead to hydraulically slewed davit and accumulator on starboard aft gantry platform.

ACCOMMODATION

Crew	22
Scientists/surveyors	14

SCIENTIFIC SPACES
Survey systems

Sensors	Simrad EQ 50 kHz net sounder (paper recorder)
Echo-sounder (single beam)	Simrad EQ 50 kHz colour sounder; Simrad EK500 scientific, 38 and 120 kHz split beam operating frequencies.
Oceanographic sensors (CTDs/XBTs and so on)	Neil Brown CTD; General Oceanics 12 × 5 litre rosette; Seacat thermosalinograph; expendable bathythermograph; RDI; ADCP; SFRI universal underwater unit; SFRI electronic fish measuring boards

VERIFIED

Algoa   *2000*/0093790

Marine and Coastal Management, Department of Environmental Affairs and Tourism

Sardinops

GENERAL

	Used mainly for experimental and exploratory trap and line fishing, and current meter deployment/retrieval
Classification	Lloyds Register
Call sign	ZSNG
Built (yard and date)	Globe Engineering Works, Cape Town; 1958
Length overall	36.58
Breadth moulded	7.62 m
Max draught	3.68 m
Tonnage (grt)	255.2

PROPULSION

Main engine(s)	1 B & W 5-cylinder 2-stroke diesel, single setting type VD, developing 600 hp at 310 rpm
Propellers	Single, three-bladed variable-pitch manganese bronze
Speed (max)	10.5 kt
Speed (cruising)	10.0 kt
Endurance	3,600 n miles/15 days
Fuel capacity	36 t
Electrical power	2 Detroit Diesel gensets, 135 kVA, 380/220 V, 3-phase, 50 Hz; Ford 25 kVA, 380/220 V, 3-phase, 50 Hz, at 0.8 PF, auxiliary harbour set.
Fresh water capacity	24.4 t

BRIDGE NAVIGATION AIDS

Satellite	GPS
Radar	Yes
Gyrocompass	Yes
Speed log	Yes

DECK MACHINERY

A-frame(s)	Aft
Winches	Hydraulics A/S type B4 Special Windlass with 165 m of 25.4 mm stud link chain with 0.32 t anchor, 1 spare 0.32 t bower anchor and one kedge 0.13 t stock anchor; hydraulics A/S type G16 hydrological with 1,500 m of 4.76 mm wire; hydraulics A/S type 34 hydrological with 1,500 m of 4 mm wire; line hauler is IZVI A/S Type CL fitted with a line coiler head.

ACCOMMODATION

Crew	16
Scientists/surveyors	4

VERIFIED

Sardinops   **2000**/0093789

SPAIN

Comisión Interministerial de Ciencia y Tecnología (CICYT)

Hespérides

Former names	*Mar Antártico*	Built (yard and date)	Bazan, Cartagena; commissioned 16 May 1991
Official number	A33		
Classification	Lloyd's Register of Shipping 100 A1 Ice Class 1B	Length overall	82.50 m
		Breadth moulded	14.30 m
		Max draught	4.35 m

PROPULSION

Main engine(s)	4 MAN – Bazan 14 V 20/27 diesels, 6,680 hp (5 MW); 2 × DC electric motors assembled in tandem. Each motor is able to supply 1,400 kW between 184 and 220 rpm.
Thrusters	Transverse bow
Propellers	Fixed pitch
Speed (max)	14.7 kt
Speed (cruising)	13.0 kt
Endurance	12,000 n miles at 12 kt
Electrical power	2 diesel generators BAZAN-MAN 14 V 20/27: 1,300 kW, 675 V, 50 Hz; 2 diesel generators BAZAN-MAN 7L 20/27: 650 kW, 675 V, 50 Hz
Fresh water capacity	90 m³

BRIDGE NAVIGATION AIDS

Satellite	2 GPS receivers with DGPS capability; Ashtech 3DF GPS receiver

Radar	S-band and X-band with ARPA console
Gyrocompass	2
Speed log	Dual-axis Doppler
Echo-sounder	Navigation

HELIDECK

Size, aircraft capacity	Medium-size helicopter

ACCOMMODATION

Crew	56
Scientists/surveyors	30

SURVEY SYSTEMS

Sensors	Simbad Ice Sonar

VERIFIED

Hespérides (Diego Quevedo)

2000/0080631

Consejo Superior de Investigaciones Cientificas (CSIC)

García del Cid

GENERAL

Call sign	EHUU
Built (yard and date)	1977
Length overall	37.2 m
Breadth moulded	8.40 m
Max draught	4.20 m
Tonnage (grt)	285.5

PROPULSION

Main engine(s)	1 Deutz diesel, 1,160 hp
Thrusters	1 bow, 150 hp
Propellers	VPP
Speed (max)	10 kt

Speed (cruising)	5,700 nm/12 days
Fuel consumption	400 kVA, 220 , 40 Hz, 3-phase

BRIDGE NAVIGATION AIDS

Satellite	Magnavox MX-1107
Radar	Anritsu C AR-12A; Anntsu B/N RA-720-VA
Gyrocompass	Sperry UK 37E

COMMUNICATIONS

MF/HF	25 karti
VHF	SRA ME-60

SAFETY	
Workboat/chase boat	Zodiac Mk II, 25 hp
DECK MACHINERY	
Cranes	500 kg at 10 m; 4,000 kg at 1 m extension
A-frame(s)	Stern; 15 t m (max)
ACCOMMODATION	
Crew	14
Scientists/surveyors	12

SCIENTIFIC SPACES	
Oceanographic wet lab	25 m²
Multipurpose dry lab	16 m²
SURVEY SYSTEMS	
Sensors	Simrad
Echo sounder (single beam)	EA 500 (18 kHz)
Oceanographic sensors (CTDs/XBTs and so on)	ADCP CTD Thermosaluometer

VERIFIED

Instituto Canarias de Ciencias Marinas

Taliarte

GENERAL	
	Oceanographic and fisheries research vessel
Call sign	EEXL
Length overall	39.6 m
Breadth moulded	7.24 m
Operational draught	3.95 m
Tonnage (grt)	267
PROPULSION	
Main engine(s)	Mack 1070 CV
Propellers	Variable pitch
Speed (max)	11 kt
Speed (cruising)	9 kt
Endurance	18 days/3,880 n miles
Fuel capacity	77 m³
Fresh water capacity	48 m³
BRIDGE NAVIGATION AIDS	
Satellite	Magnavox MX-1142; Furuno GP-70 Mk II

Radar	Sperry MK-12A; Koden MD-3711
Gyrocompass	Tokyo Keiki
Speed log	Simrad NL Doppler
Echo-sounder	JMC Colour V-122
COMMUNICATIONS	
MF/HF	Skanti TRP 5000
VHF	Skanti TRP 2000
Facsimile	Rayfax 1200
DECK MACHINERY	
Winches	Oceanographic: Tecco marine, 4,000 m, 6 m; 2 fisheries: 2,000 m, 22 m
ACCOMMODATION	
Crew	12
Scientists/surveyors	9

UPDATED

Taliarte   **2001**/0101672

Instituto Español de Oceanografia

Cornide de Saavedra

GENERAL	
Call sign	EDSV
Built (yard and date)	1993
Length overall	66.7 m
Breadth moulded	11.25 m
Max draught	4.65 m
Tonnage (grt)	1,113.13

PROPULSION	
Main engine(s)	2 × 290 kW
Speed (max)	13 kt
Endurance	120 days
Fuel capacity	264,000 litres
Electrical power	380/220/24/12 V; 2 × 290 kW generators
Fresh water capacity	4/6 t/24 h

BRIDGE NAVIGATION AIDS
Echo sounder   Skipper ET-127

DECK MACHINERY
Cranes   2 hydraulic 7,500/3,500 kg
Winches   2 oceanographic, 6,000 m, 6 mm

ACCOMMODATION
Crew   27
Scientists/surveyors   31

SURVEY SYSTEMS
Sensors   Simrad F R-500
Echo sounder (single beam)   2 Elac 600; Simrad EK 500; Simrad EK 400

UPDATED

Instituto Español de Oceanografia

Francisco de Paula Navarro

GENERAL

Call sign	EGES
Built (yard and date)	1991
Length overall	30.46 m
Breadth moulded	7.40 m
Max draught	4.26 m
Tonnage (grt)	178

PROPULSION

Main engine(s)	2 × 50 kW
Speed (max)	11 kt
Endurance	10 days
Fuel capacity	32,000 litres
Electrical power	380/220/24/12 V; 2 × 50 kW generators
Fresh water capacity	9,400 litres

BRIDGE NAVIGATION AIDS

Satellite	GPS
Radar	1 Kioritsu; 1 Kelvin Hughes
Gyrocompass	Decca – Microtechnica
Echo-sounder	3 Furuno; Skipper ET-127

COMMUNICATIONS

MF/HF	1
VHF	2
Facsimile	Furuno FX-240

SAFETY

Lifeboats	Zodiac

DECK MACHINERY

Cranes	Hydraulic 1,100 kg
A-frame(s)	2 winches, 2,000 m

ACCOMMODATION

Crew	10
Scientists/surveyors	7

SCIENTIFIC SPACES

Multipurpose dry lab	15 m²

UPDATED

Instituto Español de Oceanografia

Odón de Buen

GENERAL

	Oceanographic and fisheries research vessel
Call sign	EA 7637
Built (yard and date)	1991
Length overall	22.50 m
Breadth moulded	6.0 m
Max draught	2.70 m
Tonnage (grt)	63.55

PROPULSION

Speed (max)	11 kt
Endurance	14 days
Fuel capacity	9,250 litres
Electrical power	20 kW; 220/24/12/380 V
Fresh water capacity	2,800 litres

BRIDGE NAVIGATION AIDS

Satellite	GPS
Radar	2 Koden
Gyrocompass	Okushin
Echo-sounder	2 Skipper 802; Simrad EQ 100
Other ship navigation	Loran

COMMUNICATIONS

MF/HF	1
VHF	2
Facsimile	Alden MarineFax

DECK MACHINERY

Cranes	Hydraulic
Winches	Oceanographic, 2,000 m, 6 mm; CTD, 4,000 m, 6 mm

ACCOMMODATION

Crew	6
Scientists/surveyors	6

SURVEY SYSTEMS

Sensors	Simrad FS 3,300

UPDATED

SWEDEN

Kristineberg Marine Research Station

Arne Tiselius

GENERAL

Owner	Royal Swedish Academy of Sciences
Port of reg/flag	Fiskebäcksil
Official number	IMO No 7517624
Call sign	SDBF
Built (yard and date)	Th. Hellesöy Skibsbyggeri A/S; 1976
Rebuilt (yard and date)	Pvarvet; 1996
Length overall	31.0 m
Breadth moulded	7.0 m
Working deck width	7.0 m
Max draught	3.66 m
Operational draught	3.47 m
Tonnage (grt)	237

PROPULSION

Main engine(s)	B&W Alpha; 500 kW
Thrusters	2 × Brunvoll SPH – 105
Propellers	1
Speed (max)	12 kt
Speed (cruising)	10 kt
Fuel capacity	15 m³
Fuel consumption	70 litres/h
Electrical power	2 Stamford generators, 60 kVA each
Fresh water capacity	10 m³

BRIDGE NAVIGATION AIDS

Satellite	Shipmate DGPS
Radar	Furuno FR – 1505 D
Echo-sounder	Skipper CS 1421

COMMUNICATIONS

VHF	Sailor

SAFETY

Lifesaving equipment	4 liferafts, 50 persons total

DECK MACHINERY

Cranes	Hiab Foco HKB 60 sea
A-frame(s)	3.5 m height, 2.7 m width
Winches	1 – 3 drums, 8/12 mm wire, 5,000 kp; 1 – 4 mm, 250 kp

ACCOMMODATION

Crew	4 or 2 (daytime)
Scientists/surveyors	10

SCIENTIFIC SPACES

Total scientific deck space	40 m²
Oceanographic wet lab	20 m²
Multipurpose dry lab	14 m²
Chemistry lab	10 m²

SURVEY SYSTEMS

Positioning	Transas Navi Fisher
Echo-sounder single (beam)	Simrad EK 600
Corer(s)	Yes
Grab(s)	Yes
Vehicle(s) (ROVs/AUVs and so on)	ROV with depth of 350 m
Oceanographic sensors (CTDs/XBTs and so on)	General Oceanics Mk 3c

VERIFIED

Kristineberg Marine Research Station

Oscar von Sydow

GENERAL

Owner	Royal Swedish Academy of Sciences
Port of reg/flag	Fiskebäcksil
Call sign	SFC – 4766
Built (yard and date)	A S Fjellstrand; 1976
Length overall	12.19 m
Breadth moulded	3.7 m
Working deck width	3.5 m
Max draught	1.78 m
Operational draught	1.5 m

PROPULSION

Main engine(s)	Volvo Penta, 130 kW
Thrusters	1 bow
Propellers	1
Speed (max)	9 kt
Speed (cruising)	8 kt
Fuel capacity	1,000 litres
Fuel consumption	20 litres/h
Electrical power	7.5 kW
Fresh water capacity	175 litres

BRIDGE NAVIGATION AIDS

Satellite	Shipmate DGPS
Radar	Raytheon R 40
Echo-sounder	Fuso 803

COMMUNICATIONS

VHF	Sailor

SAFETY

Lifesaving equipment	Liferaft, 28 persons

DECK MACHINERY

Winches	1 – 8 mm wire, 2,050 kp; 1 – 4 mm, 1,075 kp

SCIENTIFIC SPACES

Total scientific deck space	16 m²

SURVEY SYSTEMS

Positioning	Transas Navi Fisher
Corer(s)	Yes
Grab(s)	Yes
Vehicle(s) (ROVs/AUVs and so on)	ROV with depth of 350 m

VERIFIED

National Board of Fisheries

Ancylus

GENERAL	
Comments	
Built (yard and date)	Marinteknik AB, Östhammar, Sweden; 1971
Length overall	24.0 m
Breadth moulded	6.0 m
Max draught	2.7 m
Tonnage (grt)	108

PROPULSION	
Main engine(s)	2 Scania 500 hp
Thrusters	bow
Propellers	1
Speed (max)	9 kt
Fuel capacity	11 t
Electrical power	45 kW, 380/220 VAC, 24/12/6 V
Fresh water capacity	4 t

BRIDGE NAVIGATION AIDS	
Satellite	DGPS
Radar	2
Gyrocompass	Yes
Echo sounder	Yes

DECK MACHINERY	
Cranes	Hydraulic: 1 t Davit: 150 kg
Winches	Trawling: 3.3 t Hydrographic: 5 mm wire

SCIENTIFIC SPACES	
Oceanographic wet lab	54 m²
Multipurpose dry lab	38 m²

NEW ENTRY

National Board of Fisheries

Argos

GENERAL	
Classification	DNV
Built (yard and date)	1974
Length overall	61.25 m
Breadth moulded	11.70 m
Max draught	4.90 m
Tonnage (grt)	1,261

PROPULSION	
Main engine(s)	2 Alpha diesel, each 900 bhp at 400 rpm
Speed (max)	14 kt
Speed (cruising)	11.0 kt
Endurance	1,000 n miles/50 days
Fuel capacity	284 m³
Electrical power	380/220 V AC, total 1,300 kVA, 3-phase, 50 Hz; 220 V AC, total 250 kVA, 3-phase, 50 Hz
Fresh water capacity	78 m³

BRIDGE NAVIGATION AIDS	
Satellite	Yes
Radar	Yes
Gyrocompass	Yes
Speed log	Yes
Echo-sounder	Yes

DECK MACHINERY	
Cranes	Stern midships, outboard extension 12 m, SWL 1 ton
A-frame(s)	Midships, clearance above deck 5 m, outboard extension 2 m, SWL 3 tons
Winches	3 oceanographic, steel wire 7,000 m, SWL 1 ton; conducting cable 1,500 m, SWL 1 ton; bottom sampling 2,000 m, SWL 1 ton

ACCOMMODATION	
Crew	19
Scientists/surveyors	12

SCIENTIFIC SPACES	
Total scientific deck space	90 m²
Oceanographic wet lab	80 m²
Multipurpose dry lab	72 m²

UPDATED

Swedish Navy

Ale

GENERAL	
Background information	Combined icebreaker and survey vessel
Owner	Swedish Maritime Administration
Built (yard and date)	Wärtillä, Helsinki; June 1973
Length overall	47.00 m
Breadth moulded	13.00 m
Operational draught	5.00 m

PROPULSION	
Main engine(s)	2 diesels; 4,750 hp(m) (3.49 MW)
Propellers	2 shafts
Speed (cruising)	14.0 kt

ACCOMMODATION		SURVEY SYSTEMS	
Crew	32	**Multibeam/swath system**	Elac bottomchart compact 180 kHz MK II; SeaBeam 1180

NEW ENTRY

Ale   *2001*/0050197

Swedish Navy

Jacob Hagg

GENERAL

Owner	Swedish Maritime Administration
Built (yard and date)	Djupviks Shipyard; launched 12 March 1983
Length overall	36.5 m
Breadth moulded	7.50 m
Operational draught	1.70

PROPULSION

Main engine(s)	4 Saab Scania DSI 14 diesels; 1,592 hp(m) (1.17 MW) sustained
Speed (max)	16.0 kt

ACCOMMODATION

Crew	13

SURVEY SYSTEMS

Multibeam/swath system	Elac Bottomchart Compact 180 kHz MK II; SeaBeam 1180

UPDATED

Jacob Hagg (J Cislak)   *2000*/0050199

Swedish Navy

Nils Strömcrona

GENERAL		**PROPULSION**	
Background information	Catamaran aluminium construction	Main engine(s)	4 Saab Scania DSI 14 diesels; 1,592 hp(m) (1.17 MW)
Owner	Swedish Maritime Administration	Thrusters	bow and stern
Built (yard and date)	1985		
Length overall	30.00 m	**ACCOMMODATION**	
Breadth moulded	10.00 m	Crew	14
Operational draught	1.80 m		

NEW ENTRY

Nils Strömcrona

2001/0080747

THAILAND

Department of Fisheries

Chulabhorn

GENERAL		Gyrocompass	Yes
Classification	NKK	Speed log	Yes
Built (yard and date)	1986	Echo-sounder	Yes
Length overall	67.25 m		
Breadth moulded	12.00 m	**DECK MACHINERY**	
Max draught	4.40 m	Cranes	Stern, SWL 2 tons
Tonnage (grt)	1,424	Winches	Oceanographic, steel wire 6,000 m, SWL 1 t
PROPULSION			
Main engine(s)	1 diesel, 2,800 bhp at 240 rpm	**ACCOMMODATION**	
Speed (max)	14.5 kt	Crew	40
Speed (cruising)	13.0 kt	Scientists/surveyors	30
Endurance	12,000 n miles/30 days		
Fuel capacity	450 m^3	**SCIENTIFIC SPACES**	
Electrical power	385 V AC, total 350 kVA, 3-phase, 50 Hz	Oceanographic wet lab	6 m^2
		Multipurpose dry lab	6 m^2
Fresh water capacity	140 m^3		

UPDATED

BRIDGE NAVIGATION AIDS
Satellite   Yes
Radar   Yes

Department of Fisheries

Samruat Pramong 4

GENERAL			
Classification	NKK	Radar	Yes
Built (yard and date)	1964	Gyrocompass	Yes
Length overall	48.00 m	Speed log	Yes
Breadth moulded	12.00 m	Echo-sounder	Yes
Max draught	4.50 m		
Tonnage (grt)	518	**DECK MACHINERY**	
		Winches	Oceanographic, steel wire 2,000 m, SWL 3 t
PROPULSION			
Main engine(s)	1 diesel, 1,000 bhp	**ACCOMMODATION**	
Speed (max)	11.0 kt	Crew	37
Speed (cruising)	10.0 kt	Scientists/surveyors	46
Endurance	6,000 n miles/30 days		
Fuel capacity	120 m³	**SCIENTIFIC SPACES**	
Fresh water capacity	100 m³	Total scientific deck space	60 m²
		Multipurpose dry lab	12 m²
BRIDGE NAVIGATION AIDS			
Satellite	Yes		

VERIFIED

Hydrographic Department

Suk

GENERAL			
Owner	Royal Thai Navy	Radar	Racal Decca 1226; I-band.
Official number	812	Gyrocompass	Yes
Built (yard and date)	Bangkok Dock Co Ltd; commissioned 3 March 1982	Speed log	Yes
		Echo-sounder	Yes
Length overall	62.90 m	**DECK MACHINERY**	
Breadth moulded	11.00 m	Cranes	Stern
Max draught	4.10 m	A-frame(s)	Stern
Tonnage (grt)	1,526	Winches	2 oceanographic, steel wire 6,000 m; conducting cable length 6,000 m
PROPULSION			
Main engine(s)	2 MTU diesels; 2,400 hp(m) (1.76 MW)		
Speed (max)	15.0 kt	**ACCOMMODATION**	
Speed (cruising)	12.0 kt	Crew	60
Endurance	5,000 n miles/15 days	Scientists/surveyors	20
Fuel capacity	144 m³		
Electrical power	440 V AC, total 240 kVA, 3-phase, 60 Hz	**SCIENTIFIC SPACES**	
		Oceanographic wet lab	50 m²
Fresh water capacity	156 m³	Multipurpose dry lab	10 m²
BRIDGE NAVIGATION AIDS			
Satellite	Yes		

VERIFIED

Suk (van Ginderen Collection)

2000/0080828

SEAFDEC/TD

Seafdec

GENERAL		Electrical power	225/385 V AC, total 600 kVA, 3-phase, 50 Hz
Comments	Steel purse seiner, built under a grant from the Japanese government	Fresh water capacity	138 m³
Port of reg/flag	Bangkok, Thailand	**BRIDGE NAVIGATION AIDS**	
Official number	35 09 0085 5	Satellite	Yes
Classification	NK, NS*, MNS*, Fisheries training and research vessel	Radar	Yes
		Gyrocompass	Yes
Call sign	HSHE	Speed log	Yes
Built (yard and date)	Miho Shipyard Co Ltd; 1992	Echo-sounder	Yes
Length overall	65.02 m		
Breadth moulded	12.00 m	**DECK MACHINERY**	
Max draught	4.66 m	Winches	2 oceanographic, steel wire 2,200 m
Operational draught	4.5 m		
Tonnage (grt)	1,178		
		ACCOMMODATION	
PROPULSION		Crew	33
Main engine(s)	1 diesel, 2,800 bhp at 620 rpm	Scientists/surveyors	30
Speed (max)	16.64 kt		
Speed (cruising)	14.3 kt	**SCIENTIFIC SPACES**	
Endurance	12,000 n miles/36 days	Oceanographic wet lab	15 m²
Fuel capacity	429 m³		

UPDATED

TURKEY

General Directorate of Mineral Research & Exploration (MTA)

Mta Sismik-1

GENERAL		BRIDGE NAVIGATION AIDS	
Classification	Lloyd's Register	Satellite	Yes
Built (yard and date)	1976	Radar	Yes
Length overall	56.45 m	Gyrocompass	Yes
Breadth moulded	8.80 m	Speed log	Yes
Max draught	3.90 m	Echo-sounder	Yes
Tonnage (grt)	720		
		DECK MACHINERY	
PROPULSION		Winches	1, steel wire 2,500 m, SWL 3 t
Main engine(s)	1 diesel, 1,050 bhp at 335 rpm		
Speed (max)	12.0 kt	**ACCOMMODATION**	
Speed (cruising)	11.0 kt	Crew	23
Endurance	2,400 n miles/25 days	Scientists/surveyors	12
Fuel capacity	100 m³		
Electrical power	220/380 V AC, total 180 kVA, 3-phase, 50 Hz; 220 V AC, total 113 kVA, 3-phase, 50 Hz	**SCIENTIFIC SPACES**	
		Total scientific deck space	140 m²
		Oceanographic wet lab	40 m²
Fresh water capacity	100 m³		

UPDATED

Institute of Marine Science

Bilim

GENERAL		Propellers	Single variable pitch
Owner	Middle East Technical University	Speed (max)	11.5 kt
Classification	ABS	Speed (cruising)	9.5 kt
Built (yard and date)	1983	Endurance	6,500 n miles/45 days
Length overall	40.36 m	Fuel capacity	120 m³
Breadth moulded	9.47 m	Electrical power	2 MWM generators, each 200 hp, 380/220 V AC; 1 MWM 12 kW emergency generator
Max draught	3.80 m		
Tonnage (grt)	433		
		Fresh water capacity	120 m³
PROPULSION			
Main engine(s)	MWM diesel, 820 bhp at 700 rpm		

BRIDGE NAVIGATION AIDS

Satellite	Magnavox MX 100 GPS
Radar	Racel Decca RM1226
Gyrocompass	Arma Brown Mk 10
Speed log	Raytheon DSL-200
Echo-sounder	1

COMMUNICATIONS

MF/HF	SAIT-6
VHF	Skanti; Shipmate RS8000; ICOM IC-M2
Facsimile	SAIT Electronic XH 5121 Navtex

DECK MACHINERY

Cranes	Electrohydraulic articulated boom crane: 3 t SWL
A-frame(s)	Double multipurpose: 500 kg and 8 t
Winches	Lebus oceanographic: 2,000 m, 8 mm wire; Norlan hydraulic trawl: 7.5 t, 2 × 1,500 m, 18 mm steel wire; Norlan hydraulic net: 6 t, 6 m³ nets; telescopic: 250 kg at 10 m, 600 m boom length

ACCOMMODATION

Crew	12
Scientists/surveyors	14

SCIENTIFIC SPACES

Total scientific deck space	72 m²
Oceanographic wet lab	15 m²
Multipurpose dry lab	40 m²

SURVEY SYSTEMS

Sensors	BioSonics towed system
Echo-sounder (single beam)	Atlas EDIG10/DESO 10
Sidescan sonar	Yes
Corer(s)	Various
Other sampling	General Oceanics rosette (12 × 5 litre)
Vehicle(s) (ROVs/AUVs and so on)	Mini Rover Mk II Rov
Oceanographic sensors (CTDs/XBTs and so on)	SBE 9 CTD; RDI ADCP

SEISMIC SYSTEMS

Energy source (type and manufacturer)	EG & G Uniboom shallow seismic system

UPDATED

Institute of Marine Sciences & Management

Arar

GENERAL

Owner	University of Istanbul
Port of reg/flag	Turkey
Built (yard and date)	Germany 1951
Length overall	31.27 m
Breadth moulded	6.50 m
Max draught	2.76 m
Tonnage (grt)	178

PROPULSION

Main engine(s)	MAN 1951-CGV42, 375 bhp at 380 rpm
Speed (max)	11.0 kt
Speed (cruising)	10.0 kt
Endurance	15 days
Fuel capacity	30 m³
Electrical power	Perkins 55 kW generator, 380/220 V AC; Perkins 110 kW generator
Fresh water capacity	7 m³

Arar   0102836

BRIDGE NAVIGATION AIDS

Satellite	Furuno GPS; Seiwa Plorad 730 DT NT GPS
Radar	Furuno FR-7040; Koden MD-300
Gyrocompass	Sperry SR-50
Speed log	Yes
Echo-sounder	Simrad

COMMUNICATIONS

MF/HF	GBS-900 SSB
VHF	Sailor RT 2047/D; Dancom RT-408
Facsimile	Furuno Navtex Nx500

DECK MACHINERY

Cranes	Midships
Winches	1 oceanographic, steel wire 500 m

ACCOMMODATION

Crew	13
Scientists/surveyors	15

SCIENTIFIC SPACES

Total scientific deck space	55 m²
Oceanographic wet lab	8 m²
Multipurpose dry lab	10 m²

SURVEY SYSTEMS

Echo-sounder (single beam)	Furuno FE-6200
Corer(s)	Gravity core sampler
Grab(s)	Grab and snapper sediment sampler
Other sampling	Rosette (12 × 5 litre bottles)
Oceanographic sensors (CTDs/XBTs and so on)	SBE 911 CTD system; SBE Sealogger SBE25; fluorometer; DO sensor; Aanderaa RCM4 current meter; RDI ADCP

UKRAINE

Marine Hydrophysical Institute

Akademik Vernadsky

GENERAL		**Gyrocompass**	Yes
Owner	Ukrainian Academy of Sciences	**Speed log**	Yes
Built (yard and date)	1968	**Echo-sounder**	Yes
Length overall	124.20 m		
Breadth moulded	17.00 m	**DECK MACHINERY**	
Max draught	6.10 m	**Cranes**	Stern: clearance above deck 9 m,
Tonnage (grt)	5,560		outboard extension 4 m, SWL
			5 tons
PROPULSION		**A-frame(s)**	Midships: clearance above deck
Main engine(s)	2 diesel-electric, 8,000 hp at		3 m, outboard extension 2 m,
	225 rpm		SWL 4 tons
Speed (max)	18.0 kt	**Winches**	8: oceanographic: steel wire
Speed (cruising)	16.0 kt		8,500 m; conducting cable
Endurance	20,000 n miles/52 days		5,000 m, SWL 5 tons
Fuel capacity	1,596 m³		
Fresh water capacity	125 m³	**ACCOMMODATION**	
		Crew	81
BRIDGE NAVIGATION AIDS		**Scientists/surveyors**	76
Satellite	Yes		
Radar	Yes		*VERIFIED*

Marine Hydrophysical Institute

Mikhail Lomonsov

Owner	Ukrainian Academy of Sciences	**Radar**	Yes
Built (yard and date)	1957	**Gyrocompass**	Yes
Length overall	102.40 m	**Speed log**	Yes
Breadth moulded	14.40 m	**Echo-sounder**	Yes
Max draught	6.31 m		
Tonnage (grt)	3,897	**DECK MACHINERY**	
		Winches	9: oceanographic: steel wire
PROPULSION			10,000 m, SWL 6 tons
Main engine(s)	1 diesel, 2,450 hp at 90 rpm		
Speed (max)	12.0 kt	**ACCOMMODATION**	
Speed (cruising)	10.0 kt	**Crew**	73
Endurance	11,000 n miles/35 days	**Scientists/surveyors**	60
Fuel capacity	1,380 m³		
Fresh water capacity	115 m³		*VERIFIED*
BRIDGE NAVIGATION AIDS			
Satellite	Yes		

Marine Hydrophysical Institute

Professor Kolesnikov

Owner	Ukrainian Academy of Sciences	**BRIDGE NAVIGATION AIDS**	
Built (yard and date)	1962	**Satellite**	Yes
Length overall	63.80 m	**Radar**	Yes
Breadth moulded	93.40 m	**Gyrocompass**	Yes
Max draught	3.50 m	**Speed log**	Yes
Tonnage (grt)	997	**Echo-sounder**	Yes
PROPULSION		**ACCOMMODATION**	
Main engine(s)	1 diesel, 1,000 hp at 375 rpm	**Crew**	35
Speed (max)	12.5 kt	**Scientists/surveyors**	24
Speed (cruising)	10.0 kt		
Endurance	4,300 n miles/15 days		*VERIFIED*
Fuel capacity	74 m³		
Fresh water capacity	55 m³		

Marine Hydrophysical Institute

Trepang

Owner	Ukrainian Academy of Sciences	Gyrocompass	Yes
Built (yard and date)	1984	Speed log	Yes
Length overall	29.80 m	Echo-sounder	Yes
Breadth moulded	8.00 m		
Max draught	3.60 m	**DECK MACHINERY**	
Tonnage (grt)	249	Cranes	Stern, midships: clearance above deck 1 m, outboard extension 2 m, SWL 1 ton
PROPULSION			
Main engine(s)	1 diesel, 750 hp at 900 rpm	A-frame(s)	Stern: outboard extension 3 m
Speed (max)	10.0 kt	Winches	3: oceanographic: steel wire 5,000 m, SWL 3 tons
Speed (cruising)	9.0 kt		
Endurance	4,800 n miles/12 days		
Fuel capacity	65 m^3	**ACCOMMODATION**	
Fresh water capacity	12 m^3	Crew	14
		Scientists/surveyors	6
BRIDGE NAVIGATION AIDS			
Satellite	Yes		*VERIFIED*
Radar	Yes		

Underwater Scientific Research Centre

Gidronavt

GENERAL		**BRIDGE NAVIGATION AIDS**	
Built (yard and date)	1978	Radar	Yes
Length overall	53.74 m	Gyrocompass	Yes
Breadth moulded	10.52 m	Speed log	Yes
Max draught	4.47 m	Echo-sounder	Yes
Tonnage (grt)	788		
		DECK MACHINERY	
PROPULSION		A-frame(s)	Stern
Main engine(s)	1 diesel, 1,320 hp at 428 rpm	Winches	2: oceanographic
Speed (max)	9.0 kt		
Endurance	6,000 n miles/24 days	**ACCOMMODATION**	
Fuel capacity	130 m^3	Crew	32
Fresh water capacity	70 m^3	Scientists/surveyors	6
			VERIFIED

Underwater Scientific Research Centre

Gydrobiolog

GENERAL		**BRIDGE NAVIGATION AIDS**	
Built (yard and date)	1978	Radar	Yes
Length overall	53.74 m	Gyrocompass	Yes
Breadth moulded	10.52 m	Speed log	Yes
Max draught	4.47 m	Echo-sounder	Yes
Tonnage (grt)	788		
		DECK MACHINERY	
PROPULSION		A-frame(s)	Stern
Main engine(s)	1 diesel, 1,320 hp at 428 rpm	Winches	2: oceanographic
Speed (max)	9.0 kt		
Endurance	6,000 n miles/24 days	**ACCOMMODATION**	
Fuel capacity	130 m^3	Crew	32
Fresh water capacity	70 m^3	Scientists/surveyors	6
			VERIFIED

Underwater Scientific Research Centre

Ikhtiandr

GENERAL		Breadth moulded	14.02 m
Built (yard and date)	1973	Max draught	5.80 m
Length overall	84.50 m	Tonnage (grt)	2,270

PROPULSION		Speed log	Yes
Main engine(s)	1 diesel, 2,000 hp at 560 rpm	Echo-sounder	Yes
Speed (max)	12.5 kt		
Speed (cruising)	10.0 kt	**DECK MACHINERY**	
Endurance	11,000 n miles/50 days	A-frame(s)	Stern
Fuel capacity	420 m³	Winches	3: oceanographic
Fresh water capacity	220 m³		
		ACCOMMODATION	
BRIDGE NAVIGATION AIDS		Crew	70
Satellite	Yes	Scientists/surveyors	19
Radar	Yes		
Gyrocompass	Yes		*VERIFIED*

Underwater Scientific Research Centre

Khronometr

GENERAL		BRIDGE NAVIGATION AIDS	
Built (yard and date)	1973	Satellite	Yes
Length overall	82.20 m	Radar	Yes
Breadth moulded	13.02 m	Gyrocompass	Yes
Max draught	5.10 m	Speed log	Yes
Tonnage (grt)	2,150	Echo-sounder	Yes
PROPULSION		**DECK MACHINERY**	
Main engine(s)	2 diesel, 2,320 hp at 375 rpm	A-frame(s)	Stern
Speed (max)	14.5 kt	Winches	2: oceanographic
Speed (cruising)	13.0 kt		
Endurance	12,000 n miles/60 days	**ACCOMMODATION**	
Fuel capacity	480 m³	Crew	63
Fresh water capacity	160 m³	Scientists/surveyors	16
			VERIFIED

Underwater Scientific Research Centre

Oddissej

GENERAL		BRIDGE NAVIGATION AIDS	
Built (yard and date)	1973	Satellite	Yes
Length overall	84.50 m	Radar	Yes
Breadth moulded	14.02 m	Gyrocompass	Yes
Max draught	5.80 m	Speed log	Yes
Tonnage (grt)	2,270	Echo-sounder	Yes
PROPULSION		**DECK MACHINERY**	
Main engine(s)	1 diesel, 2,000 hp at 560 rpm	A-frame(s)	Stern
Speed (max)	12.5 kt	Winches	3: oceanographic
Speed (cruising)	10.0 kt		
Endurance	11,000 n miles/50 days	**ACCOMMODATION**	
Fuel capacity	420 m³	Crew	70
Fresh water capacity	220 m³	Scientists/surveyors	19
			VERIFIED

UNITED KINGDOM

British Antarctic Survey

Ernest Shackleton

GENERAL			
		Former names	*MV Polar Queen*
		Port of reg/flag	Falkland Islands
Comments	Built for the Norwegian company	Classification	DnV*A1 Icebreaker ICE 05
	Rieber Shipping of Bergen in	Built (yard and date)	Kverner Klevin Leirvik A/S,
	1995. The British Antarctic Survey		Norway; 1995
	acquired the ship in August 1999,		
	renamed RRS *Ernest Shackleton*	Length overall	80.0 m
	and re-registered in the Falkland	Breadth moulded	17.0 m
	Islands.	Operational draught	7.35 m (6.35 m icebreaking)
		Tonnage (grt)	4,028

PROPULSION

Main engine(s)	2 × Bergen diesel BRM 6 each 2,550 kW at 720 rpm
Thrusters	Bow: Brunvoll Transverse Thrusters 600 kW, Brunvoll Transverse Thrusters 800 kW, Brunvoll Retractable Azimuth Thruster 800 kW
	Stern: 2 × Brunvoll Transverse Thrusters each 600 kW
Propellers	Single screw C.P. propeller in nozzle from twin output/single output gearbox
Endurance	130 days/40,000 n miles
Electrical power	2 × 2,200 kW shaft generators
	2 × 600 kW auxilliary generators
	1 × 150 kW emergency generator

Bridge navigation aids	
Satellite	Trimble Navtrac XL 6 ch.
Radar	X- and S-Band
Gyrocompass	2 x Anschutz STD 20
Speed log	Yes
Echo sounder	Skipper GDS 101
	Furuno CH36
	Furuno C160
Other ship navigation	Loran C

HELIDECK

Size, aircraft capacity	Designed for a Super Puma, diameter of deck 18 m

DECK MACHINERY

Cranes	Norlift Telescopic Crane: 10 t at 5 m
	Norlift GP Crane: 2 t at 7 m
	Norlift Folded Jib ROV Crane: 5 t at 10 m
	Norlift Offshore Crane: 50 t at 10 m

ACCOMMODATION

Crew	21
Scientists/surveyors	59
Hospital	1

SCIENTIFIC SPACES

Oceanographic wet lab	45 m²
Multipurpose dry lab	45 m²
Survey systems	
Positioning	Simrad Albatross ADP 702 Mk 3
Sensors	Seatex Seapath 200
Echo sounder (single beam)	Simrad EA 500

NEW ENTRY

British Antarctic Survey

James Clark Ross

GENERAL

Current operational status	Operates principally in polar seas
Owner	Natural Environment Research Council
Port of reg/flag	Stanley, Falkland Islands
Classification	Lloyds +100A1 Ice 1AS + LMS UMS (DP-AM)
Call sign	ZDLP
Built (yard and date)	Swan Hunter, Wallsend; 1991
Length overall	99.04 m
Breadth moulded	18.85 m
Max draught	6.40 m
Freeboard to Working Deck	3.308 m
Tonnage (grt)	5,732

PROPULSION

Main engine(s)	Diesel electric: 2 Wärtsilä Vasa 6R32; 2 Wärtsilä Vasa 8R22: 8,200 kW
Thrusters	Bow: White Gill 360° controllable, 10 t thrust
	Stern: White Gill 360° controllable, 4 t thrust
Propellers	1: fixed pitch
Speed (max)	15.7 kt
Speed (cruising)	12 kt
Endurance	57 days at sea

James Clark Ross

2000/0099207

BRIDGE NAVIGATION AIDS

Radar	Sperry Rasterscan 3400 – 25 kW X-band; Sperry Rasterscan 3400 – 30 kW S-band
Gyrocompass	Mk 37 Mod E dual
Speed log	Sperry SRD 421S dual-axis Doppler log; Chernikeef Aquaprobe Mk V E/M
Echo-sounder	Marconi Maritime Seachart 3 Navigation Sounder; Seachart 3 Manoeuvring Sounder
Other ship navigation	Sperry Marine integrated bridge system; Model ADG autopilot; Decca Navigator; Loran 'C' Omega

COMMUNICATIONS

MF/HF	GMDSS – SAIT

DECK MACHINERY

Cranes	Main cargo: forward: capacity: 20 t at 20 m; stores: forward: capacity: 4 t at 10 m; science: forward: capacity: 2 t at 4 m; cargo/science: aft: capacity: 10 t at 17 m; science: port aft: capacity: 2.5 t at 13 m; science: starboard aft: capacity: 2.5 t at 10 m;
A-frame(s)	Aft: capacity: 20 t at 9 m; midships: capacity: 30 t at 8 m
Winches	Superaramid warp: 8,000 m, 29 mm; coring warp: 7,000 m, 16.8 mm; trawl warp: 15,000 m; tapered CTD/hydrographic; hydrographic wire: 9,000 m, 6 mm; conducting cable: 8,000 m, 10 mm; biological: 3,000 m, 14 mm; 2 × trawling: 5,000 m, 25 mm 2 × trawling; 2 × Gilson: 500 m, 20 mm

ACCOMMODATION

Crew	12 officers; 16 crew; 1 doctor
Scientists/surveyors	31

SCIENTIFIC SPACES

Total scientific deck space	650 m²
Oceanographic wet lab	23.5 m²
Multipurpose dry lab	44.2 m²
Chemistry lab	18.1 m²

SURVEY SYSTEMS

Positioning	Leica MX 400 DGPS Ashtech G12 DGPS
Echo-sounder (single beam)	2 × Simrad EA 500; 1 × Simrad EK 500 (38, 200 and 120 kHz)
Multibeam/swath system	Furuno CSH50 directional sonar; Simrad EM 120; Simrad EM 102
Sub-bottom profiler	Simrad EK 500 (3.5 kHz); Simrad TOPAS
Oceanographic sensors (CTDs/XBTs and so on)	ADCP – RDI VDM150

SEISMIC SYSTEMS

Energy source (type and manufacturer)	Air: 4 × Hamworthy 4TH 565 W 100

UPDATED

Centre for Environment, Fisheries and Aquaculture Science (CEFAS)

Cirolana

GENERAL

Comments	Fisheries and environmental research vessel
Current operational status	Operating in North Atlantic and North Sea
Owner	Ministry of Agriculture, Fisheries and Food (MAFF)
Port of reg/flag	Grimsby; UK
Official number	338774
Classification	DTp X Fishing Vessel; Lloyds Register + 100A1 + LMC CCS ICE 1B
Call sign	GNAM
Built (yard and date)	Ferguson Brothers, Port Glasgow; 1970
Length overall	72.54 m
Breadth moulded	14.02 m
Max draught	5.05 m
Tonnage (grt)	1,919
Displacement	2,400 t

PROPULSION

Main engine(s)	3 W H Allen 6S37E, each 1,100 bhp at 500 rpm
Thrusters	Bow: Stone Vickers, 260 kW; 3 × Laurence Scott + Electromotors DG generators, each 700 kW DC; 2 × 500 kW 415 V 50 Hz
Propellers	1 vp
Speed (max)	15 kt
Speed (cruising)	14 kt
Endurance	>35 days, 60 days (food)/10,000 n miles at 14 kt
Fuel capacity	344 t
Fuel consumption	8.5 t/day (full power), 4 t/day (routine)
Electrical power	Auxiliary generator: Paxman 8 RPHCZ driving an LSE alternator giving 375 kW, 415 V, 50 Hz at 1,500 rpm
Fresh water capacity	147 t

BRIDGE NAVIGATION AIDS

Satellite	DGPS
Radar	Kelvin Hughes Anticol and 340
Gyrocompass	Arma Brown Mk 10; SG Brown 1000
Speed log	KAE DOLOG 22; Colnbrook E/M
Echo-sounder	Kelvin Hughes MS44
Other ship navigation	Autopilot: SG Brown

DECK MACHINERY

Cranes	Hiab 1808, main deck (stbd): capacity: 18 t at 1 m; Hiab 110, forecastle: capacity: 11 t at 1 m
A-frame(s)	Forecastle: capacity: 1 t at 3.5 m
Winches	Trawl: capacity: 2,300 m, 18 mm diameter; hydro: various; CTD: various; cable: various; coring: various; net drum: various; Gilson: various; headline

ACCOMMODATION		Echo-sounder (single beam)	2 × Simrad EK400; Simrad
Crew	36 (incl scientists)		ES400; Simrad SM600; Kelvin
Scientists/surveyors			Hughes MS44; Kelvin Hughes
			MS29
SCIENTIFIC SPACES		Corer(s)	Yes
Total scientific deck space	280 m²	Grab(s)	Yes
Oceanographic wet lab	Biological: 15 m²	Vehicle(s) (ROVs/AUVs and	Towed vehicle
Multipurpose dry lab	42 m²; clean biological lab; 8 m²	so on)	
Chemistry lab	25 m²	Oceanographic sensors	Air and sea surface temperature,
		(CTDs/XBTs and so on)	humidity, windspeed and
SURVEY SYSTEMS			direction, and barometric
Sensors	RoxAnn		pressure

UPDATED

Centre for Environment, Fisheries and Aquaculture Science (CEFAS)

Corystes

GENERAL		Radar	Litton ARPA 340 & 280
Comment	Fisheries and environmental	Gyrocompass	SG Brown 1000
	research vessel	Speed log	KAE DOLOG 22; Colnbrook E/M
Current operational status	Operating in North Atlantic and	Echo-sounder	Simrad ED161
	North Sea	Other ship navigation	Autopilot: Decca Arkas
Owner	Ministry of Agriculture, Fisheries		
	and Food (MAFF)	DECK MACHINERY	
Port of reg/flag	Lowestoft; UK	Cranes	Hiab 180: main deck: capacity:
Official number	706142		18 t at 1 m; Hiab 180: aft:
Classification	DTp X Fishing Vessel, Lloyds		capacity: 18 t at 1 m; Hiab 180:
	Register + 100A1 + LMC CCS		forecastle: capacity: 18 t at 1 m
	UMS	A-frame(s)	Stern: capacity: 12 t at 7 m; side:
Call sign	GHRU		capacity: 5 t at 8 m
Built (yard and date)	Ferguson Ailsa, Troon; 1987	Winches	Trawl: 1,000 m, 26 mm; coring:
Length overall	53.25 m		1,000 m, 12 mm; hydro: 1,000 m,
Breadth moulded	12.8 m		4/6 mm; CTD: 1,000 m, 12 mm;
Max draught	4.30 m		Gilson: various; headline: various;
Tonnage (grt)	1,280		net drum
Displacement	1,550 t		
		ACCOMMODATION	
PROPULSION		Crew	27 (incl scientists)
Main engine(s)	2 × W H Allen 8S12F, each 1,400		
	bhp at 750 rpm; 2 × Laurence	SCIENTIFIC SPACES	
	Scott + Electromotors brushless	Total scientific deck space	230 m²
	AC alternators, each 962.5 kW,	Oceanographic wet lab	Biological: 24 m²
	660 V 50 Hz	Multipurpose dry lab	27 m²; acoustic lab: 13 m²
Thrusters	Bow: White Gill 40VST Unit		
Speed (max)	13.25 kt	SURVEY SYSTEMS	
Speed (cruising)	12.5 kt	Sensors	RoxAnn
Endurance	>50 days/8,500 n miles at	Echo-sounder (single beam)	Simrad EK400; Simrad ES400;
	13.25 kt		Simrad SM600; ET 105
Fuel capacity	185 t	Corer(s)	Yes
Fuel consumption	6.8 t/day (full power), 3 t/day	Grab(s)	Yes
	(routine)	Vehicle(s) (ROVs/AUVs and	Towed vehicle
Electrical power	Auxiliary generator: Caterpillar	so on)	
	3408B driving Marker Alternator,	Oceanographic sensors	ADCP; air and sea surface
	269 kW, 415 V at 1,500 rpm	(CTDs/XBTs and so on)	temperature, humidity,
Fresh water capacity	82 t		windspeed and direction, and
			barometric pressure
BRIDGE NAVIGATION AIDS			
Satellite	DGPS		

UPDATED

Defence & Evaluation Research Agency (DERA)

Colonel Templer

GENERAL		Port of reg/flag	UK
	Underwater research vessel.	Classification	DTp VII; Lloyds 100A1+LMC
	Converted deep water stern	Call sign	GTTA
	trawler	Built (yard and date)	Hall Russell, Aberdeen; 1966
Owner	Defence & Evaluation Research	Rebuilt (yard and date)	1992
	Agency (DERA)	Length overall	56.55 m

Breadth moulded	10.97 m
Max draught	5.6 m
Freeboard to Working Deck	1.12 m
Tonnage (grt)	1,005
Displacement	1,332.3 t

PROPULSION

Main engine(s)	2 × Cummings KTA38G4(M) 940 kW generator sets driving an Aquamaster US 2001 fixed-pitch semi-skewed contrarotating azimuthing thruster. Drive to thruster achieved by a 1,324 kW infinitely variable DC motor.
Thrusters	Bow: 300 bhp Brunvol C.P.
Propellers	Liam C.P in Kort nozzle
Speed (max)	14 kt (2 engines)
Speed (cruising)	11.6 kt (1 engine)
Endurance	16 days at sea
Fuel capacity	145 t
Fuel consumption	4.2 t/day at MCR (1 engine)
Electrical power	450 kVA transformer off main bars; 2 × 180 kW Volvo Penta alternators
Fresh water capacity	10 t potable, 34 t domestic

BRIDGE NAVIGATION AIDS

Satellite	MNS 2000G; Racal Skyfix DGPS
Radar	Racal Decca 'S' band 2690 BT ARPA inter-switched to BT 502
Gyrocompass	Plath NAVIGAT XII mod 07
Speed log	Chernikeef Mk V Aquaprobe dual-axis E/M log
Echo-sounder	Raytheon JFV 200
Other ship navigation	Racal Decca MIRANS 3000; autopilot: Plat NAVPILOT V/GM Loran; NNSS OMEGA

COMMUNICATIONS

Inmarsat (type)	Saturn 3S90 Inmarsat 'A'; Skant; TRP 8753; Sailor 2047 duplex; Sailor 2048 simplex
MF/HF	
VHF	
Facsimile	Navtex

SAFETY

Workboat/chase boat	Quest Q26, Castoldi Jet, David Still Rigid inflatable, Avon Sea Rider

DECK MACHINERY

Cranes	Hiab 1165/A articulated, Boat deck port: capacity 1 t at 8 m; Tico 270HT articulated, main deck, starboard: capacity 2.3 t at 10 m
A-frame(s)	Main deck, stern: capacity: 5 t at 8 m
Winches	Trials, drum diameter: 1.5 m, duty 6.25 t on top layer, brake holding 10 t; deck 5.0 t (fixed); deck 2.5 t (fixed); deck 5.0 t (portable); deck 2.5 t (portable)
Moonpool(s) – size(s)/ function(s)	28 in moonpool

ACCOMMODATION

Crew	6 officers; 8 crew
Scientists/surveyors	12

SCIENTIFIC SPACES

Total scientific deck space	143 m²
Multipurpose dry lab	51 m² (main), 28 m² (secondary)

SURVEY SYSTEMS

Oceanographic sensors (CTDs/XBTs and so on)	ADCP; air and sea surface temperature, humidity, windspeed and direction, solar radiation and barometric pressure

SEISMIC SYSTEMS

Energy source (type and manufacturer)	5 × Gearing and Watson SS300X; 2 × Gearing and Watson SS350X; 3 × Argo Technology Inc Type 219
Compressor numbers and types	2 × Hamworthy 25F4 – air

UPDATED

Colonel Templer (Maritime Photographic)

2000/0075840

Department of Agriculture and Rural Development for Northern Ireland (DANI)

Lough Foyle

GENERAL

	Oceanographic and Fisheries Research vessel
Current operational status	Operating in the Irish Sea and Celtic Sea.
Port of reg/flag	UK
Official number	GYAR
Classification	DTp VII, BV 13/3/E
Built (yard and date)	S.I.C.C.Na., St. Malo 1974
Rebuilt (yard and date)	1982
Length overall	43.5 m
Breadth moulded	9.4 m
Max draught	4.6 m
Freeboard to Working Deck	2.0 m
Tonnage (grt)	546 grt
Displacement	768 t

PROPULSION

Main engine(s)	MAK; 895 kW
Thrusters	Bow: White Gill azimuthing unit
Speed (max)	14 kt
Speed (cruising)	11 kt
Endurance	14 days

BRIDGE NAVIGATION AIDS

Radar	Furuno Racal Decca Bridgemaster II 250 ARP A
Gyrocompass	Arma Brown Mk 10
Speed log	Walker E4, JRC JNL203 Doppler
Echo-sounder	Atlas Echograph 600, Koden CVS 820C 50
Other ship navigation	Autopilot: Decca 450M and 450G

DECK MACHINERY

Cranes	Tico crane: aft: Capacity: 2 t at 12 m
A-frame(s)	Stern: Capacity: 10 t at 6 m Port: Capacity: 2 t at 4 m
Winches	2 × Trawl (port & starboard): 2,300 m, 18 mm Dredge: 7,000 m Hydro: 7,000 m, 6 mm Conducting wire: 3,000 m, 6 mm Net drum Oceanographic towing: 800 m, 12 mm coaxial

ACCOMMODATION

Crew	9 officers; 11 crew
Scientists/surveyors	8

SCIENTIFIC SPACES

Total scientific deck space	70.7 m²
Oceanographic wet lab	6.5 m²; Biological wet lab: 23.5 m²
Chemistry lab	6.7 m²

SURVEY SYSTEMS

Echo-sounder (single beam)	2 × Simrad EY200 and Furuno CSH50 sonar display
Oceanographic sensors (CTDs/XBTs and so on)	Air and sea surface temperature, humidity, windspeed and direction, and barometric pressure

UPDATED

Dove Marine Laboratory

Bernicia

GENERAL

Current operational status	North Sea and local estuaries for research and teaching.
Owner	University of Newcastle-upon-Tyne
Port of reg/flag	UK
Classification	DTp VIIIA; Lloyds 100A1
Call sign	MLER
Built (yard and date)	Ryton Marine, Wallsend; 1973
Length overall	16.2 m
Breadth moulded	4.3 m
Max draught	2.4 m
Freeboard to Working Deck	0.8 m
Tonnage (grt)	46.25
Displacement	58.24 t

PROPULSION

Main engine(s)	Gardner 6 LX; 110 hp at 1,300 rpm
Speed (max)	9.0 kt
Speed (cruising)	8.0 kt
Endurance	3 days/5,000 n miles at 9 kt

BRIDGE NAVIGATION AIDS

Satellite	DGPS
Radar	Racal Decca Bridgemaster
Echo-sounder	JMC CVS; Kelvin Hughes MS45
MF/HF	Yes
VHF	Yes

DECK MACHINERY

Cranes	Main deck; capacity: 0.5 t at 3 m
A-frame(s)	Stern: capacity: 1.5 t; max height: 2 m
Winches	Spencer Carter trawl winch, 2 drums: 2 × 200 m, 12 mm
Crew	4
Scientists/surveyors	12 (day basis)

SCIENTIFIC SPACES

Total scientific deck space	20 m²
Oceanographic wet lab	4 m²
Multipurpose dry lab	7 m²
Survey systems	
Corer(s)	Yes

UPDATED

Dunstaffnage Marine Laboratory

Calanus

GENERAL

	Oceanographic and fisheries research vessel
Current operational status	Operates Scottish west coast
Owner	Natural Environment Research Council, Dunstaffnage Marine Laboratory
Port of reg/flag	UK
Classification	DTp Fishing Vessel
Call sign	GBJK
Built (yard and date)	Hinks Ltd, Appledore; 1980
Length overall	18.59 m
Breadth moulded	6.71 m
Max draught	3.2 m
Freeboard to Working Deck	1.3 m
Tonnage (grt)	59
Displacement	116.8 t

PROPULSION

Main engine(s)	Kelvin Model TA8; 280 shp at 1,200 rpm
Propellers	VPP
Speed (max)	8.9 kt
Speed (cruising)	8.7 kt
Endurance	8 days at sea
Electrical power	John Deere generator, 240 V, 50 Hz, 1-phone, 45 kVA

BRIDGE NAVIGATION AIDS

Satellite	Sercel DGPS
Radar	Decca Bridgemaster 180/4
Speed log	Ben Log
Echo-sounder	Simrad EL, 38 kHz; RMC, 50 kHz and 200 kHz
Other ship navigation	Autopilot: Decca Pilot 350

COMMUNICATIONS

MF/HF	Sailor, Rx type R104, Tx type T128
VHF	RT 144B
Facsimile	Furuno FAX-108

SAFETY

Workboat/chase boat	4 m Zodiac with 15 hp outboard motor

DECK MACHINERY

Cranes	Atlas: Stern: Capacity: 1 t at 5 m
A-frame(s)	Stern, Capacity: 3 t at 4 m
Winches	Trawl 2 × 500 m, 13 mm
	Lebus Hydrographic, 300 m, 5 mm (hydrographic cable)
	300 m, 8 mm (conducting CTD cable)

ACCOMMODATION

Crew	3 officers; 2 crew;
Scientists/surveyors	6

SCIENTIFIC SPACES

Total scientific deck space	40 m²
Oceanographic wet lab	3.8 m²
Multipurpose dry lab	19.5 m²

SURVEY SYSTEMS

Oceanographic sensors (CTDs/XBTs and so on)	Barometric pressure

UPDATED

Dunstaffnage Marine Laboratory

Seol Mara

GENERAL

Background information	
Current operational status	operates in sea lochs and shallow inshore waters
Owner	Scottish Association for Marine Science (SAMS)
Port of reg/flag	UK
Built (yard and date)	Tyler Boat Co, Tonbridge; 1972
Length overall	10.5 m
Breadth moulded	4.1 m
Operational draught	1.8 m

PROPULSION

Main engine(s)	Lister 6 cylinder diesel, 88.5 bhp
Propellers	single
Speed (max)	6 kt
Electrical power	dieselite generator, 240 V AC, 50 Hz, single phase, 3 kW

BRIDGE NAVIGATION AIDS

Satellite	Furuno GP-50 Mark 2; Racal Decca Navstar 2000
Radar	Furuno 2400 Mk 3
Echo-sounder	JMC colour video echo sounder; Simrad EL

COMMUNICATIONS

MF/HF	Sailor MF Communications Rx Type 104 Tx Type 121
VHF	ICOM VHF Type M120

SAFETY

Lifeboats	for 10 persons

DECK MACHINERY

A-frame(s)	SWL 0.5 t
Winches	Spencer Carter triple barrel trawl: 325 m, 5 mm (hydro wire), 8 mm (trawl wire)

ACCOMMODATION

Crew	2
Scientists/surveyors	4 (day cruises only)

SCIENTIFIC SPACES

Total scientific deck space	6 × 4 m

NEW ENTRY

Environment Agency National Marine Service

Coastal Guardian

GENERAL

Current operational status	UK home waters, west coast
Owner	Environment Agency
Port of reg/flag	UK
Classification	DTp VIII Lloyds
Call sign	MQJT3
Built (yard and date)	David Abels, Bristol; 1992
Length overall	16.45 m
Breadth moulded	5.5 m
Max draught	1.8 m
Freeboard to Working Deck	0.6 m
Tonnage (grt)	46.6
Displacement	55 t

PROPULSION

Main engine(s)	2 × Ford Sabre 180c turbocharged: each 132 kW
Speed (max)	10 kt
Speed (cruising)	8 kt
Endurance	2 days at sea

BRIDGE NAVIGATION AIDS

Satellite	DGPS
Radar	Raytheon R70
Gyrocompass	Tokimec ES 140
Speed log	Sagem LH 92 E/M
Echo-sounder	JMC V122 colour, dual frequency
Other ship navigation	Autopilot: Robertson AP45

DECK MACHINERY

Cranes	Hiab Type 31: port quarter: Capacity: 2.5 t at 1.1 m, 0.6 t at 4.8 m
A-frame(s)	Aft: Capacity: 1 t at 2 m
Winches	Trawl; 2 drums: 200 m, 12 mm Tow fish cable; 50 m Hydro; 100 m, 2.5 mm

ACCOMMODATION

Crew	2
Scientists/surveyors	6

SCIENTIFIC SPACES

Total scientific deck space	25 m²
Multipurpose dry lab	12 m²

SURVEY SYSTEMS

Positioning	Qubit Trac V
Echo-sounder (single beam)	Simrad EA 300
Oceanographic sensors (CTDs/XBTs and so on)	ADCP; sea surface temperature; windspeed and direction

UPDATED

Environment Agency National Marine Service

Sea Vigil

GENERAL

Owner	Environment Agency
Port of reg/flag	UK, home waters
Classification	DTp VIII Lloyds
Call sign	MNRH9
Built (yard and date)	David Abels, Bristol; 1991
Length overall	16.4 m
Breadth moulded	5.5 m
Max draught	1.7 m
Freeboard to Working Deck	0.6 m
Tonnage (grt)	49.79
Displacement	55 t

PROPULSION

Main engine(s)	2 × Sabre Perkins M215c turbocharged: each 156 kW
Speed (max)	9.9 kt
Speed (cruising)	8.5 kt
Endurance	2 days at sea

BRIDGE NAVIGATION AIDS

Satellite	DGPS
Radar	Racal BT 360/4
Gyrocompass	Robertson RGC50
Speed log	JMC DL-100
Echo-sounder	JMC V-7 Colour
Other ship navigation	Autopilot: Robertson AP45

DECK MACHINERY

Cranes	Hiab Type 31: starboard rear Deck: Capacity: 0.6 t at 6.5 m
A-frame(s)	Aft: Capacity: 0.75 t at 2.5 m
Winches	Trawl: 150 m, 12 mm

ACCOMMODATION

Crew	2
Scientists/surveyors	6

SCIENTIFIC SPACES

Total scientific deck space	19 m²
Multipurpose dry lab	19 m²; scientific hold: 7 m²

SURVEY SYSTEMS

Positioning	Qubit Trac C
Echo-sounder (single beam)	Atlas Deso 15

UPDATED

Environment Agency National Marine Service

Vigilance

GENERAL

Owner	Environment Agency
Port of reg/flag	UK; home waters, mid-Wales to Lands End
Classification	DTp VIII Lloyds
Call sign	MLCA5
Built (yard and date)	David Abels, Bristol; 1990
Length overall	15.77 m
Breadth moulded	5.5 m
Max draught	1.6 m
Freeboard to Working Deck	0.6 m
Tonnage (grt)	40.12

PROPULSION

Main engine(s)	2 × Ford Sabre 180 c turbocharged: each 132 kW
Speed (max)	10 kt
Speed (cruising)	9 kt
Endurance	2 days

BRIDGE NAVIGATION AIDS

Satellite	DGPS
Radar	Raytheon R41 raster scan
Gyrocompass	Robertson RGC50
Speed log	Dana 200
Echo-sounder	Raytheon V720 + V700 Rayplot
Other ship navigation	Autopilot: Cetrec

DECK MACHINERY

Cranes	Effer: fore deck, port: Capacity: 2.5 t at 1 m; 0.6 t at 6.5 m

A-frame(s)	Stern: Capacity: 1 t at 2m
Winches	Trawl, two drums: 300 m, 12 mm

ACCOMMODATION

Crew	2
Scientists/surveyors	10

SCIENTIFIC SPACES

Total scientific deck space	27 m²
Multipurpose dry lab	10 m²

SURVEY SYSTEMS

Positioning	Qubit Trac C
Echo-sounder (single beam)	Simrad EA 300
Sidescan sonar	C-Max CM800
Oceanographic sensors (CTDs/XBTs and so on)	Sea surface temperature; wind-speed and direction

UPDATED

Environment Agency National Marine Service

Water Guardian

GENERAL

Owner	Environment Agency
Port of reg/flag	UK home waters, east coast
Classification	DTp VIII Lloyds
Call sign	MPUJ4
Built (yard and date)	David Abels, Bristol; 1992
Length overall	16.45 m
Breadth moulded	5.5 m
Max draught	1.8 m
Freeboard to Working Deck	1.0 m
Tonnage (grt)	51.31

PROPULSION

Main engine(s)	2 × Ford Sabre 180 c turbocharged: each 132 kW
Speed (max)	10 kt
Speed (cruising)	9 kt
Endurance	3/4 days at sea

BRIDGE NAVIGATION AIDS

Satellite	DGPS
Radar	Racal Bridgemaster with Geographics
Gyrocompass	Robertson RGC50

Speed log	Doppler
Echo-sounder	JMC Fishfinder
Other ship navigation	Autopilot: Robertson AP45

DECK MACHINERY

Cranes	Hiab: port quarter: Capacity: 2.5 t at 1.1 m; 0.6 t at 5 m
A-frame(s)	Stern: Capacity: 1 t at 2 m
Winches	Trawl: 300 m, 12 mm Trawl: 100 m, 12 mm

ACCOMMODATION

Crew	2
Scientists/surveyors	6

SCIENTIFIC SPACES

Total scientific deck space	27 m²
Multipurpose dry lab	13 m²; scientific hold: 25 m²

SURVEY SYSTEMS

Positioning	Qubit Trac C
Oceanographic sensors (CTDs/XBTs and so on)	Sea surface temperature

UPDATED

Marr Vessel Management Ltd

Clupea

GENERAL

Comment	Fisheries research vessel
Current operational status	operates in North Sea and off the west coast of Scotland
Owner	Scottish Office, Agriculture and Fisheries Department, Marine Laboratory
Port of reg/flag	Leith
Official number	335167
Classification	DTp VIII
Call sign	GYWG
Built (yard and date)	Hall Russell, Aberdeen; 1968
Rebuilt (yard and date)	1988
Length overall	28.9 m
Breadth moulded	7.92 m
Max draught	3.51 m
Freeboard to Working Deck	0.77 m

Tonnage (grt)	231
Displacement	381.66 t

PROPULSION

Main engine(s)	Lister ES8M geared diesel; 660 shp
Thrusters	Brunvoll, athwartships
Propellers	Slack & Parr CP propeller
Speed (max)	11.0 kt
Speed (cruising)	9 kt
Endurance	2,300 n miles/12 days
Fuel capacity	30 t
Electrical power	port and starboard Gardner Type 6L3B with 106 kVA alternators; 2 × Lawrence Scott 106 kVA alternators, 230 V l-phase AC
Fresh water capacity	15 t

BRIDGE NAVIGATION AIDS

Satellite	2 × NR51 DGPS
Radar	2 × Racal Decca Bnd generator
Gyrocompass	Sperry SR 120
Speed log	Decca; Walker
Echo-sounder	2 × Skipper echo sounder; Simrad EQ

COMMUNICATIONS

Inmarsat (type)	Iridium Sat Phone
MF/HF	Sailor RE 2 100
VHF	DSC
Facsimile	Furuno Weatherfax D-fax

DECK MACHINERY

Cranes	Tico Marine 150T: Trawl deck: Capacity 6.4 t at 2 m
A-frame(s)	Aft: Capacity: 1.5 t at 4 m
Winches	2 × trawl: 750 m, 20 mm Hydro: 1,000 m, 8 mm TV slip ring, 500 m Net drum Netsonde winch

ACCOMMODATION

Crew	4 officers; 6 crew
Scientists/surveyors	8

SCIENTIFIC SPACES

Total scientific deck space	150 m²
Oceanographic wet lab	10 m²
Multipurpose dry lab	5 m²

SURVEY SYSTEMS

Echo-sounder (single beam)	Simrad EK500 120 kHz; Simrad EK500 120 kHz and 38 kHz
Other sampling	Simrad FS3300 Net Monitor; Netsonde
Oceanographic sensors (CTDs/XBTs and so on)	Air and sea surface temperature, humidity, wind speed and direction, and barometric pressure

UPDATED

Marr Vessel Management Ltd

Scotia

GENERAL

	Fisheries Research Vessel
Current operational status	Operates in the North Sea and Northeast Atlantic
Owner	Scottish Office, Agriculture and Fisheries Department, Marine Laboratory
Port of reg/flag	Leith
Classification	LR +100A1 + LMC Ice Class 1D UMS SCM
Call sign	MXHR6
Built (yard and date)	Ferguson Shipbuilders, Port Glasgow; 1998
Length overall	68.6 m
Breadth moulded	15.0 m
Max draught	5.65 m
Freeboard to Working Deck	2.6 m
Tonnage (grt)	2,619
Displacement	2,850 t

PROPULSION

Main engine(s)	3 × Wartsila type 9620 diesels; total 4,455 kW
Thrusters	bow: 'Elliot' White Gill; 720 kW, 750 V DC; stem: Brunvoll tunnel; 980 kW, 660 V AC
Speed (max)	15 kt
Speed (cruising)	12 kt
Endurance	11,000 n miles/30 days
Fuel capacity	340 t
Electrical power	3 × 1,400 kW generators, 1,000 rpm, 8 pole 660 V, 3-phase; harbour: Cummins 240 kW, 415 V, 3-phase; emergency: Cummins 81 kW, 415 V, 3-phase
Fresh water capacity	

BRIDGE NAVIGATION AIDS

Satellite	2 × DGPS
Radar	2 × Decca 'S' + 'X' band
Speed log	doppler
Echo-sounder	yes
Other ship navigation	Loran

COMMUNICATIONS

Inmarsat (type)	GMDSS area 3

DECK MACHINERY

Cranes	articulated telescopic cod-end handly crane, hydrographic; plankton: 10 t; container: 10 t; gamma: 6 t
Winches	2 × trawl: 3,500 m, 25 mm
Transducer well	2 × gilson: 200 m, 28 mm; 8 × hydrographic
Gate valve	3 × split-net; 1 × auto trawl system

ACCOMMODATION

Crew	17
Scientists/surveyors	12

SCIENTIFIC SPACES

Total scientific deck space	100 m²
Oceanographic wet lab	40 m²
Multipurpose dry lab	30 m²
Survey systems	
Sensors	Scanmar
Echo-sounder (single beam)	Simrad EK500: 200 kHz, 120 kHz, 38 kHz; Fishing sonar: 50 kHz, 120 kHz
Multibeam/swath system	15-25 kHz hull mounted
Other sampling	Simrad FS3300 Net Monitor; Netsonde
Oceanographic sensors (CTDs/XBTs and so on)	ADCP; air temperature, humidity, windspeed and direction, short-wave radiation, and barometric pressure

UPDATED

Natural Environment Research Council, Research Vessel Services

Charles Darwin

GENERAL

Owner	Natural Environment Research Council, Research Vessel Services
Port of reg/flag	London, UK
Official number	705613
Classification	DTp VII, Lloyds 100A1 LMP UMS 16 h
Call sign	GDLS
Built (yard and date)	Appledore Shipbuilders, Appledore; 1982
Length overall	69.4 m
Breadth moulded	14.4 m
Max draught	4.80 m
Freeboard to Working Deck	2.6 m
Tonnage (grt)	1,936
Displacement	2,556 t

PROPULSION

Main engine(s)	Mirlees Blackstone MB275; 1,900 kW
Thrusters	Bow: White Gill azimuthing unit
Speed (max)	12.5 kt
Speed (cruising)	10.5 kt
Endurance	Max: 45 days Operational: 22 days

BRIDGE NAVIGATION AIDS

Satellite	DGPS
Radar	ARPA 1626C; AC1226C
Gyrocompass	2 × Arma Brown Mk 10
Speed log	Magnavox Doppler MX6100; Colnbrook E/M
Echo-sounder	Simrad ED 162
Other ship navigation	Autopilot: RD DP780

DECK MACHINERY

Cranes	Atlas 6002 hydraulic crane, amidships: capacity: 8 t at 2 m
A-frame(s)	Stern, Capacity: 15 t at 6 m Starboard, Capacity: 8 t at 6 m
Winches	Coring winch, 13,000 m, 13.2 mm /Trawl warp, 13,000 m, 13.2 mm Hydro winch, 6,000 m, 6 mm CTD winch, 7,500 m, 8 mm Trawl winch (starboard), 3,400 m, 22 mm Trawl winch (port), 3,400 m, 22 mm

ACCOMMODATION

Crew	9 officers; 12 crew
Scientists/surveyors	18

SCIENTIFIC SPACES

Total scientific deck space	260 m^2
Oceanographic wet lab	16.25 m^2
Multipurpose dry lab	70.25 m^2
Echo-sounder (single beam)	Simrad EA 500, 10.2/12 kHZ
Multibeam/swath system	Simrad EM125/120
Oceanographic sensors (CTDs/XBTs and so on)	ADCP; air and sea surface temperature, humidity, windspeed and direction, and barometric pressure

SEISMIC SYSTEMS

Energy source (type and manufacturer)	Air: 2 × Hamworthy VTH 190

UPDATED

Charles Darwin

2000/0099208

Natural Environment Research Council, Research Vessel Services

Discovery

GENERAL

Owner	Natural Environment Research Council, Research Vessel Services
Port of reg/flag	London, UK
Official number	304401
Classification	DTp VII, Lloyds 100A1 UMS 16 h
Call sign	GLNE
Built (yard and date)	Hall Russell, Aberdeen; 1963
Rebuilt (yard and date)	ENVC Viana do Castello, Portugal, 1992
Length overall	90.25 m
Breadth moulded	14.0 m
Max draught	5.32 m
Freeboard to Working Deck	2.6 m
Tonnage (grt)	3,008
Displacement	4,378 t

PROPULSION

Main engine(s)	Diesel electric: four Mirlees Blackstone ESL6 Mk II: 2 Mirlees Blackstone ESL9 Mk II; 3,716 kW
Thrusters	Bow: White Gill thruster and Becker rudder
Speed (max)	12.5 kt
Speed (cruising)	11 kt
Endurance	Max: 55 days
	Operational: 45 days

BRIDGE NAVIGATION AIDS

Satellite	DGPS
Radar	ARPA 2690: RM5028T
Gyrocompass	2: SG Brown 1000
Speed log	Chernikeef Aquaprobe Mk V E/M
Echo-sounder	Simrad Skipper
Other ship navigation	Autopilot: Decca 42E14 550/650 Series

DECK MACHINERY

Cranes	ACTA hydraulic knuckle crane: forward: Capacity: 30 t at 1 m ACTA hydraulic knuckle crane: midships: Capacity: 120 t at 1 m ACTA hydraulic knuckle crane: mid/aft: Capacity: 75 t at 1 m ACTA hydraulic knuckle crane: aft port: Capacity: 30 t at 1 m ACTA hydraulic knuckle crane: aft starboard: Capacity: 30 t at 1 m
A-frame(s)	Stern: Capacity: 20 t at 6 m Starboard: Capacity: 15 t at 5 m Forward: Capacity: 3 t at 4 m
Winches	Superaramid Warp: 8,000 m, 25 mm Trawl warp: 15,000 m, 13/18 mm Coring wire: 7,000 m, 17 mm Conductor wire: 10,000 m, 17 mm Hydro winch: 9,000 m, 6 mm CTD winch: 8,000 m, 10 mm

ACCOMMODATION

Crew	9 officers; 13 crew
Scientists/surveyors	28

SCIENTIFIC SPACES

Total scientific deck space	460 m²
Oceanographic wet lab	61 m²
Multipurpose dry lab	65 m²
Chemistry lab	21 m²

SURVEY SYSTEMS

Echo-sounder (single beam)	Simrad EA 500, 10.2/12 kHz
Multibeam/swath system	Gloria
Oceanographic sensors (CTDs/XBTs and so on)	ADCP; air and sea surface temperature, humidity, windspeed and direction, and barometric pressure

SEISMIC SYSTEMS

Energy source (type and manufacturer)	Air: 4 x Hamworthy 4TH 565 W 100

UPDATED

Discovery

2000/0099209

Plymouth Marine Laboratory

Sepia

GENERAL		Speed (cruising)	8 kt
	Inshore and Estuarine Research Vessel	Endurance	1 day at sea
Current operational status	Operates in Plymouth sea area	BRIDGE NAVIGATION AIDS	
Owner	Natural Environment Research Council, Plymouth Marine Laboratory	Radar	Decca
		Echo-sounder	Simrad 160; Kelvin Hughes MS 315
Port of reg/flag	UK	Other ship navigation	Autopilot
Classification	DTp fishing vessel		
Call sign	MYUT	DECK MACHINERY	
Built (yard and date)	Halmatic, Southampton; 1967	A-frame(s)	Stern
Length overall	12 m	Winches	Trawl: 250 m, 8 mm
Breadth moulded	3.4 m		
Max draught	1.2 m	ACCOMMODATION	
Freeboard to Working Deck	0.3 m	Crew	2/3
Tonnage (grt)	12		
		SCIENTIFIC SPACES	
PROPULSION		Total scientific deck space	5 m²
Main engine(s)	2 × Perkins V8 510M; 240 kW		
Speed (max)	10 kt		*UPDATED*

Plymouth Marine Laboratory

Squilla

GENERAL		BRIDGE NAVIGATION AIDS	
	Inshore Scientific Support Vessel	Radar	Decca
Current operational status	Operates in Plymouth sea area	Speed log	Decca
Owner	Natural Environment Research Council, Plymouth Marine Laboratory	Echo-sounder	Simrad; Fuso 200
		Other ship navigation	Autopilot: Decca Pilot 350
Port of reg/flag	UK	DECK MACHINERY	
Classification	DTp fishing vessel	Cranes	Hiab: starboard deck: Capacity: 1 t at 4 m
Call sign	GTHM		
Built (yard and date)	Tyler, Tyneside; 1974	A-frame(s)	Stern: Capacity: 3 t at 2.6 m
Length overall	19.5 m	Winches	Trawl: 400 m, 14 mm
Breadth moulded	5.7 m		Hydro: 100 m, 8 mm
Max draught	3.0 m		
Freeboard to Working Deck	0.5 m	ACCOMMODATION	
Tonnage (grt)	73	Crew	4
PROPULSION		SCIENTIFIC SPACES	
Main engine(s)	Kelvin Model TS8; 240 kW	Multipurpose dry lab	31.2 m²
Speed (max)	10 kt		
Speed (cruising)	9 kt		
Endurance	5 days at sea		*UPDATED*

Plymouth Marine Laboratory

Tamaris

GENERAL		Freeboard to Working Deck	0.1 m
	Inshore and Estuarine Research Vessel	Displacement	6 t
Current operational status	Operates in Plymouth sea area	PROPULSION	
Owner	Natural Environment Research Council, Plymouth Marine Laboratory	Main engine(s)	Twin 135 hp Volvo Penta; 200 kW
		Speed (max)	12 kt
		Speed (cruising)	8 kt
Port of reg/flag	UK	Endurance	1 day at sea
Call sign	2SWL		
Built (yard and date)	RTK Marine, Poole; 1974	BRIDGE NAVIGATION AIDS	
Length overall	12.5 m	Radar	Decca
Breadth moulded	3.2 m	Speed log	Euromarine
Max draught	1.2 m	Echo-sounder	Euromarine

HELIDECK
Deck machinery

ACCOMMODATION

Crew	2

SCIENTIFIC SPACES

Total scientific deck space	16 m²
Oceanographic wet lab	4 m²

UPDATED

Port Erin Marine Laboratory

Roagan

GENERAL

Current operational status	Operates in the Irish Sea
Owner	University of Liverpool, Port Erin Marine Laboratory
Port of reg/flag	Isle of Man
Classification	Isle of Man DHPP VII
Call sign	MNCN7
Built (yard and date)	A Hokeman BV, The Netherlands; 1982
Rebuilt (yard and date)	1991
Length overall	23.75 m
Breadth moulded	6.5 m
Max draught	3.2 m
Freeboard to Working Deck	0.4 m
Tonnage (grt)	104
Displacement	227.32 t

PROPULSION

Main engine(s)	2 × Caterpillar 34067
Speed (max)	10 kt
Speed (cruising)	10 kt
Endurance	8 days at sea
Electrical power	240 V AC and 24 V DC

BRIDGE NAVIGATION AIDS

Satellite	DGPS
Radar	Furuno
Echo-sounder	Skipper CS119 (38 kHz); Furuno Colour Sounder (50 kHz and 200 kHz)
Other ship navigation	Autopilot: Wagner

DECK MACHINERY

A-frame(s)	Stern: Capacity: 6 t at 5 m
Harbour side: 1 t at 1 m
Winches	CTD: 200 m, 8 mm
Trawl, 4 drum: 2 × 200 m, 12 mm
Trawl: 200 m, 10 mm

ACCOMMODATION

Crew	4
Scientists/surveyors	4/6

SCIENTIFIC SPACES

Total scientific deck space	35 m²
Oceanographic wet lab	Multipurpose wet/dry: 12.74 m²
Multipurpose dry lab	7.75 m²

SURVEY SYSTEMS

Sensors	RoxAnn; Furuno CN8 colour net recorder trawleye
Echo-sounder (single beam)	Simrad EY200 50 kHz, 120 kHz, 200 kHz; Simrad EY 500 38 kHz
Sidescan sonar	C-Max CM 800
Corer(s)	various
Grab(s)	various
Other sampling	Gulf III plankton sampler
Vehicle(s) (ROVs/AUVs and so on)	Mini Rover Mk I
Oceanographic sensors (CTDs/XBTs and so on)	Sea surface temperature; SBE Seacat Profiler (CTD); SBE rosette with SBE19 CTD and fluorometer; Turner flow-through fluorometer

UPDATED

Port Erin Marine Laboratory

Sula

GENERAL

Current operational status	Operates in Isle of Man coastal waters
Owner	University of Liverpool, Port Erin Marine Laboratory
Port of reg/flag	Isle of Man
Classification	Isle of Man DHPP
Call sign	MDX24
Built (yard and date)	Cygnus, Penryn; 1984
Length overall	8.0 m
Breadth moulded	3.0 m
Max draught	1.0 m
Displacement	6.5 t

PROPULSION

Main engine(s)	Sabre 80; 60 kW
Speed (max)	7 kt
Speed (cruising)	7 kt
Endurance	1 day at sea

BRIDGE NAVIGATION AIDS

Satellite	DGPS
Echo-sounder	Furuno FE450

DECK MACHINERY

Winches	Trawl winch: ost, 100 m, 8 mm
Pot/Trap hauler

ACCOMMODATION

Crew	2
Scientists/surveyors	4

SCIENTIFIC SPACES

Total scientific deck space	9 m²

SURVEY SYSTEMS

Other sampling	various trawls: various water bottles

UPDATED

Royal Navy

Scott

GENERAL

Comments	Designed by BAeSEMA/YARD and ordered 20 January 1995 to replace *Hecla*. Ice-strengthened bow. Foredeck strengthened for helicopter operations.
Official number	H131
Classification	Lloyds: + 100A1 + LMC, Ice Class 1A
Built (yard and date)	Appledore Shipbuilders, Bideford; launched 13 October 1996; commissioned 1997
Length overall	131.13 m
Breadth moulded	21.50 m
Max draught	8.3 m
Tonnage (grt)	9,498

PROPULSION

Main engine(s)	2 Krupp MaK 9M32 9-cyl diesels; 3,960 kW at 600 rpm
Thrusters	Bow: HRP400 series, 7 t thrust
Propellers	1 shaft; acbLIPS cp
Speed (max)	17.5 kt
Speed (cruising)	12 kt
Endurance	25,000 n miles at 12 kt
Fuel capacity	1,728 t
Electrical power	Main: 440 V, 3-phase, 60 Hz; emergency: 230 V, 1-phase, 60 Hz
Fresh water capacity	141.9 t

BRIDGE NAVIGATION AIDS

Satellite	GPS
Radar	Kelvin Hughes ARPA 1626; I-band.
Gyrocompass	Mk 29
Other ship navigation	Loran C

Scott (John Brodie) **2000**/0075817

ACCOMMODATION

Crew	71 berths (42 embarked at any one time)

SURVEY SYSTEMS

Sensors	MINICINS INS
Echo-sounder (single beam)	Atlas Deso 25 210 kHz/33 kHz
Multibeam/swath system	SASS (Sonar Array Sounding System) IV multibeam depth-sounder
Sidescan sonar	GeoAcoustics 2094
Magnetometer	Towed proton
Gravimeter	Yes
Grab(s)	Shipek; Mudsnapper
Sound velocity profiler	Hand-held SV probe
Oceanographic sensors (CTDs/XBTs and so on)	XBTs and CTDs

UPDATED

School of Ocean & Earth Science, Southampton University

Bill Conway

GENERAL

Current operational status	Operates in the English Channel, River Solent and Poole Harbour
Owner	Southampton University
Port of reg/flag	UK
Classification	MCA workboat certificate category 3
Call sign	MNAT6
Built (yard and date)	Lochin Marine, Rye; 1991
Length overall	11.74 m
Breadth moulded	3.96 m
Max draught	1.3 m
Freeboard to Working Deck	1.0 m
Tonnage (grt)	8.4

PROPULSION

Main engine(s)	2 × Mermaid Manta: 260 kW
Propellers	2
Speed (max)	12 kt
Speed (cruising)	10 kt
Endurance	1 day/150 n miles at 10 kt

BRIDGE NAVIGATION AIDS

Satellite	Trimble survey DGPS
Radar	APELCO, 16 n miles
Speed log	Stowe Data Line
Echo-sounder	Stowe
VHF	2

DECK MACHINERY

A-frame(s)	stern, capacity: 750 kg, 3 m
Winches	trawl: 70 m, 8 mm diameter

ACCOMMODATION

Crew	2
Scientists/surveyors	12

SCIENTIFIC SPACES

Total scientific deck space	15 m²
Sensors	
Oceanographic sensors (CTDs/XBTs and so on)	Sea temperature; windspeed and direction

UPDATED

University Marine Biological Station, Millport

Aora

GENERAL

Current operational status	Operates in the North Irish Sea and off the Scottish west coast
Owner	University Marine Biological Station, Millport
Port of reg/flag	UK
Classification	Category 2 workboat, MCA
Call sign	2JMN
Built (yard and date)	Morris & Lorimer Ltd, Argyll; 1975
Length overall	15.0 m
Breadth moulded	5.5 m
Max draught	2.5 m
Freeboard to Working Deck	1.0 m
Tonnage (grt)	48

PROPULSION

Main engine(s)	2 × Daewoo MD136; each 147 hp
Speed (max)	10 kt
Speed (cruising)	9 kt
Endurance	14 days at sea

BRIDGE NAVIGATION AIDS

Satellite	DGPS & GPS
Radar	Racal Decca RM270 Bright Track
Echo-sounder	Skipper CS 119; Simrad EL38
Other ship navigation	Autopilot: Racal Decca DP150

DECK MACHINERY

Cranes	Derrick: midships; capacity: 1 t at 4 m Gilson derrick: midships; capacity: 1.5 t
A-frame(s)	Stern; capacity 1.5 t; max height: 4 m
Winches	Hydro: 600 m: 4 mm diameter Trawl, 2 drums: 2 × 400 m; 12 mm diameter Gilson, 1 t

ACCOMMODATION

Crew	4
Scientists/surveyors	4

SCIENTIFIC SPACES

Total scientific deck space	20 m²
Oceanographic wet lab	yes
Multipurpose dry lab	yes

UPDATED

University Marine Biological Station, Millport

Aplysia

GENERAL

Current operational status	Operates in the Scottish west coast area, inshore waters
Owner	University Marine Biological Station, Millport
Port of reg/flag	UK
Official number	1 × A
Classification	DTp 1XA, MCA
Call sign	2MXC

Built (yard and date)	Aberdour Marine Ltd, Aberdour; 1977
Length overall	11 m
Breadth moulded	4 m
Max draught	1.6 m
Tonnage (grt)	16.11

PROPULSION

Main engine(s)	Ford Model 2715E: 81 kW
Speed (max)	9 kt
Speed (cruising)	7 kt
Endurance	5 days at sea

BRIDGE NAVIGATION AIDS

Satellite	GPS
Radar	Racal Decca RD80
Echo-sounder	JMC colour V105

DECK MACHINERY

A-frame(s)	Gilson derrick: midships (starboard); Capacity: 1.0 t Stern: Capacity: 1 t; Max height: 3 m
Winches	Trawl, 2 drums: 2 × 300 m; 10 mm diameter Pothauler: 150 m; 4 mm diameter Hydrographic

ACCOMMODATION

Crew	2
Scientists/surveyors	1

SCIENTIFIC SPACES

Total scientific deck space	17.5 m²

Aplysia   **2001**/0101263

UPDATED

VT Ocean Sciences

Prince Madog

GENERAL

Comments	VT Ocean Sciences is a joint venture between the University of Wales at Bangor and Vosper Thornycroft (UK) Ltd. Home port: Menai Bridge, North Wales
Port of reg/flag	UK
Classification	Lloyds Register +100 A1 "Research Vessel", LMC
Built (yard and date)	Visser; 2001
Length overall	34.9 m
Breadth moulded	8.5 m
Max draught	3.5 m
Tonnage (grt)	350

PROPULSION

Main engine(s)	1,080 kW Wartsila 6L20C. Gearbox includes PTO/PTI, a combined Shaft Generator and Slow Speed Drive Motor
Thrusters	Bow: 150 kW
Propellers	CP Propeller
Speed (max)	10.5 kt
Endurance	10 days
Fuel capacity	62.7 m³ (at 80%)
Electrical power	415 V / 240 V, 50Hz 240 V, 50Hz clean net for sensitive equipment 24 V DC net
Fresh water capacity	32 m³

BRIDGE NAVIGATION AIDS

Satellite	Furuno DGPS
Radar	Furuno S-Band
Gyrocompass	Plath
Echo sounder	Furuno

COMMUNICATIONS

Inmarsat (type)	Inmarsat-B/C
Cellular	Nokia
Facsimile	Toshiba

DECK MACHINERY

Cranes	Boom starboard. Outreach 2.5 m 1.0 t Aft: Atlas 140.1 marine crane. 14 t/m, 12.1 m boom reach Foredeck: Atlas 3008 marine crane. 8 t/m, 6.5 m boom reach

Prince Madog   0102838

A-frame(s)	Aft: 5 t SWL. Outreach 4 m, Height above deck 6.5 m
Winches	2 Rapp TWS-705/B270 split trawl winches arranged for one person operation on main deck. Remote control in wheelhouse and aft deck. Capacity 1,000 m × 18 mm. Pull on 1st layer 9.5 ton/30 m/min. Pull on top layer 2.8 ton/108 m/min 1 Rapp GW200 CDT winch, slip ring for 4 conductors. Capacity 1,000 m × 8 mm. Pull on 1st layer 0.9 ton/51 m/min. Pull on top layer 0.5 ton/100 m/min 1 Rapp GW200 hydrographic winch. Capacity 1000m x 4mm. Pull on 1st layer 0.35 ton/76 m/min. Pull on top layer 0.2 ton/100 m/min 1 Rapp HW 100-5 middle winch. Capacity 400 m × 14 mm. Pull on top layer 1 ton/100 m/min.

ACCOMMODATION

Crew	8
Scientists/surveyors	9 + 1

SCIENTIFIC SPACES

Total scientific deck space	80 m²
Oceanographic wet lab	29 m²
Multipurpose dry lab	26 m²

SURVEY SYSTEMS

Positioning	Kongsberg Simrad HPR-410P
Sensors	QTC View Acoustic seabed classification system.
Echo sounder (single beam)	Kongsberg Simrad EK-60 120/38 kHz split beam
Sub-bottom profiler	Geoacoustics/ORE 3.5-7 kHz Pinger transducer.
Oceanographic sensors (CTDs/XBTs and so on)	RDI Workhorse Mariner. 300 kHz broadband, hull mounted, remote speed log display W S Ocean Systems meteorological and oceanographic sensor suites. Seabird 911*plus* CTD with SBE-13B dissolved oxygen sensor.

Prince Madog   0102839

NEW ENTRY

UNITED STATES OF AMERICA

California Department of Fish and Game

Mako

Built (yard and date)	Steiner Shipyards; 1991	**DECK MACHINERY**	
Length overall	24.00 m	Cranes	Articulated: Hiab Sea Crane 80, mounted midships on aft boat deck; max lift capacity 2,100 lb at full extension; gallows-mounted net reel: Yaquina NR95-2, 7 ft wide with 6 ft diameter end flanges
Breadth moulded	7.20 m		
Max draught	3.00 m		
Tonnage (grt)	143		
PROPULSION			
Main engine(s)	Caterpillar 3412, 550 hp; auxiliary: Caterpillar 3306 – hydraulics and 14 kW emergency generator		
		Winches	Hydrographic: davit-mounted Markey DYH-3 with 500 m of 3/16 in wire; lift capacity 600 lb, speed 70 m/min at mid-drum; 2 × trawl; Yaquina YB9P-2 with 4,000 ft of 5/16 in wire each
Thrusters	Bow: Wesmar DPC 75		
Propellers	Single in Kort Nozzle		
Speed (cruising)	9 kt		
Endurance	14 days/4,000 n miles		
Fuel capacity	14,000 gallons		
Electrical power	Generator set: Northern Lights 40 kW, 110/208 VAC, 32/12 VDC	**ACCOMMODATION**	
		Crew	3 – 5
Fresh water capacity	7,000 gallons	Scientists/surveyors	7
BRIDGE NAVIGATION AIDS		**SCIENTIFIC SPACES**	
Satellite	GPS	Oceanographic wet lab	Main deck; 2 × live wells 2,700 gallons each with 180 gallons/min pumps
Radar	2		
Echo-sounder	Fathometer		
Other ship navigation	Loran		
		SURVEY SYSTEMS	
COMMUNICATIONS		Sensors	sonar; net sounder
MF/HF	SSB		*NEW ENTRY*
VHF	Transceivers		
Cellular	Phone		
SAFETY			
Workboat/chase boat	12 ft Achilles inflatable with 20 hp outboard; 17 ft Boston Whaler with 60 hp outboard		

Cape Fear Community College

Dan Moore

GENERAL		**COMMUNICATIONS**	
Current operational status	Coastal/estuarine waters in vicinity of Wilmington, North Carolina	MF/HF	SSB
		VHF	Yes
		Cellular	Yes
Built (yard and date)	1967		
Length overall	25.50 m	**DECK MACHINERY**	
Breadth moulded	7.20 m	Cranes	Morgan 143FSC; 4,850 lb capacity at 27 ft extension
Tonnage (grt)	157		
		A-frame(s)	Stern ramp with heavy lift; 5 t SWL
PROPULSION			
Main engine(s)	Cummins KTA 19M2 diesel	Winches	Pullmaster H18 trawl/towing; 3,000 ft 1/2 in wire; Sea Mac 215 oceanographic tow; 15,000 ft 3/16 in wire
Speed (cruising)	9 kt		
Fuel capacity	9,000 gallons		
Fuel consumption	75 gallons/day		
Electrical power	2 × 50 kW diesel-driven generators: 230 VAC three-phase; 220/110 VAC single-phase		
		ACCOMMODATION	
		Crew	7
Fresh water capacity	3,000 gallons	Scientists/surveyors	18
BRIDGE NAVIGATION AIDS		**SCIENTIFIC SPACES**	
Satellite	GPS	Total scientific deck space	Aft: 600 sq ft
Radar	Yes	Oceanographic wet lab	170 sq ft
Gyrocompass	Yes	Multipurpose dry lab	150 sq ft
Echo-sounder	Omnidirectional sonar		
Other ship navigation	Loran C		*NEW ENTRY*

Centre for Great Lakes and Aquatic Sciences

Laurentian

GENERAL COMMENTS
Purchased by the University of Michigan in 1974.
Home port: Grand Haven Michigan

Owner	The University of Michigan
Built (yard and date)	1973
Length overall	24.00 m
Breadth moulded	6.55 m
Max draught	2.67 m
Tonnage (grt)	129

PROPULSION

Main engine(s)	Detroit Diesel 12V-71, 340 bhp at 2,100 rpm
Propellers	1
Speed (max)	9.6 kt
Speed (cruising)	8.5 kt
Endurance	3,000 n miles/10 days
Fuel capacity	36 m³
Electrical power	208/120 V, total 40 kVA, 3-phase, 60 Hz Detroit Diesel 4-71; Onan 20 kW 120/208 VAC 3-phase
Fresh water capacity	17 m³

BRIDGE NAVIGATION AIDS

Satellite	Furuno FSN-80 GPS; Magnavox DGPS
Radar	Sperry Mk-12, 50 kW; Raytheon R-40X
Gyrocompass	Sperry Mk 37
Speed log	Yes
Echo-sounder	Ross 250C
Other ship navigation	Loran C: Trimble 10X

COMMUNICATIONS

MF/HF	1 × SSB transceiver
VHF	2 × Raytheon Ray-55

SAFETY

Workboat/chase boat	Boston Whaler, 13 ft, 15 hp

DECK MACHINERY

Cranes	Dunbar Hiab, 3,600 lb at min
A-frame(s)	Height: 10 ft, width 3 ft, SWL 2,000 lb; extension; 2,460 lb at maximum extension
Winches	BT: 1,700 ft, ½ in cable; Stbd: conducting cable, 2,300 ft, ½ in cable; Stbd: dual: 2,000 ft, ½ in cable; Stern: port side: 2,000 ft, ³⁄₁₆ in cable; crane: stbd: 1,000 ft, ⅛ in cable

ACCOMMODATION

Crew	4-6
Scientists/surveyors	8-10

SCIENTIFIC SPACES

Total scientific deck space	58 m²
Oceanographic wet lab	13 m²
Multipurpose dry lab	36 m²

SURVEY SYSTEMS

Echo-sounder (single beam)	Ross 801C, 100 kHz
Sidescan sonar	Klein 595, 100 kHz
Corer(s)	MK-V Soutar/Van Veen box corer; gravity
Grab(s)	Wildco No. 1725 Ponar grab sampler
Other sampling	Various nets; Niskin bottles
Oceanographic sensors (CTDs/XBTs and so on)	Mechanical bathythermographs

UPDATED

Centre for Marine Science Research, University of North Carolina

Cape Fear

GENERAL

Length overall	21.00 m
Breadth moulded	6.30 m
Operational draught	1.95 m
Tonnage (grt)	77

PROPULSION

Main engine(s)	Twin Caterpillar 3406; 700 hp
Speed (cruising)	16 kt
Fuel capacity	1,800 gallons
Fuel consumption	50 gallons/h @ 16 kt
Electrical power	20 kW Lugger diesel generator, 220/120 VAC, single phase; 16 kW Lugger diesel generator
Fresh water capacity	800 gallons

SURVEY SYSTEMS

Sidescan sonar	EdgeTech DF1000-DCI
Sub-bottom profiler	GeoAcoustics
Oceanographic sensors (CTDs/XBTs and so on)	Richard Brancker Research – conductivity, temperature loggers; RD Instruments – 300 kHz Workhorse; Seabird SBE 19 – CTD

NEW ENTRY

College of Oceanic & Atmospheric Sciences, Oregon State University

Elakha

GENERAL

Background information	Designated oceanographic research vessel by US Coast Guard; home port: Newport, Oregon

Official number	1100178 (USCG)
Classification	Class III Motorboat
Call sign	WCZ 7501
Length overall	16.20 m
Breadth moulded	4.95 m
Max draught	1.50 m

PROPULSION

Main engine(s)	Caterpillar 3176B 6-cyl, 400 hp @ 2,000 rpm; Reduction gear: Twin Disc, Model MG5111A, 2.444:1 ratio
Thrusters	Bow: 12 in Key Power hydraulically driven off main engine
Endurance	400 n miles
Fuel capacity	1,200 gallons
Fuel consumption	19 gallons/h
Electrical power	Northern Lights, 230/117 VAC, 60 Hz, 7.5 kW

BRIDGE NAVIGATION AIDS

Satellite	Furuno GP36; Garman 128
Radar	Furuno 1761
Echo-sounder	Furuno 582L

COMMUNICATIONS

MF/HF	ICOM IC-M700PRO-21
VHF	ICOM IC-M59; 2 Uniden (hand-held)
Cellular	Motorola 2950

SAFETY

Lifeboats	10-person SOLAS A pack inflatable liferaft
Lifesaving equipment	10 × immersion suits

DECK MACHINERY

Cranes	Morgan M/N 14; 13 ft reach, 716 lb capacity at full reach; portable – bolts to deck and connects to vessel hydraulics
A-frame(s)	2,000 lb SWL
Winches	Sound Ocean Systems STW-1012L-7 with 600 m of ¼ in 3 × 19 wire; capable of spooling ¼ in electromechanical cable with hollow shaft for slip ring installation; auxiliary: Marco W0800; capable of 4,200 lb of pull on bare drum at 86 ft/min, can spool 500 ft of ½ in wire; portable – bolts to deck and connects to vessel hydraulics
Transducer well	15 in ID, through hull

NEW ENTRY

Duke University Marine Laboratory

Cape Hatteras

GENERAL COMMENTS
Home port: Beaufort, North Carolina

Current operational status	Operates between Nova Scotia, Caribbean Sea and Bermuda
Owner	National Science Foundation
Official number	NC 3233 AU
Classification	ABS * A1 AMS Research Vessel Uninspected, Undocumented
Call sign	WRZ -934
Built (yard and date)	Atlantic Marine Ship Builders, 1981
Length overall	41.0 m
Breadth moulded	9.7 m
Max draught	2.70 m
Tonnage (grt)	296

PROPULSION

Main engine(s)	Twin diesel Caterpillar, Model 379TA, 1,130 hp, Pay and Brinck clutch;
Propellers	Twin screw, controllable-pitch propellers
Speed (max)	12 kt
Speed (cruising)	10 kt
Endurance	7,000 n miles at 10 kt/25 days
Fuel capacity	28,695 gallons
Electrical power	2 diesel Caterpillar, Model 3406T, 1,800 rpm, 175 kW each; primary power 480 V AC 3-phase, 60 cycle
Fresh water capacity	6,000 gallons

BRIDGE NAVIGATION AIDS

Satellite	Yes
Radar	Yes
Gyrocompass	Yes
Speed log	Yes

COMMUNICATIONS

Facsimile	Yes

SAFETY

Workboat/chase boat	Inflatable work boat: Avon 19 ft – 8 person capacity
Work boat: Boston Whaler 13 ft – 4 person capacity

DECK MACHINERY

Cranes	Alaska Marine, located on main deck aft, 24,000 lb capacity at 10 ft, with a maximum lift of 2,610 lb at 40 ft.
Alaska Marine, forward of deckhouse, starboard side, 2,500 lb capacity at 27 ft.
A-frame(s)	Stern, located on main deck aft, with 15,000 lb capacity
Portable located on main deck, aft starboard quarter with 20,000 lb capacity
Winches	Trawl – Markey hydraulic. Line pull, 17,000 lb; line speed, hoist 6,000 lb payload (water weight), average speed, 65 m/min; diamond level-wind; wire, US Steel, ½ in 3 × 19 torque balanced, 30,000 ft.
Hydrographic – Markey hydraulic (DUSH-4) with slip-ring capabilities, aft; wire, 30,000 ft ¼ in 3 × 19 torque balanced; line speed, 100 m/ min, average CTD – Markey hydraulic (DUSH-5) with slip-ring capabilities located on 01 deck; wire, 30,000 ft EM cable, 0.322 in; line speed, 100 m/min average.

ACCOMMODATION

Crew	11
Scientists/surveyors	11

SURVEY SYSTEMS

Echo-sounder (single beam)	Hull-mounted 3.5 kHz transducers (array of 9 each) Hull-mounted 12 kHz transducers (2 each)
Sub-bottom profiler	ODEC Bathy-2000P CHIRP sub-bottom profiler
Corer(s)	Piston (barrel lengths expandable to 80 ft in 10 ft increments); Box, Ocean Instruments Mark III (50 × 50 cm box); Box, Ocean Instruments Soutar (modified with steel frame); Box, Ocean Instruments Multicorer, MC-800; takes eight 10 cm diameter samples; Gravity; Shipek grab; Cerame-Vivas rock dredge
Oceanographic sensors (CTDs/XBTs and so on)	Sea Bird CTD (6,000 m depth limit); Sea Tech in situ transmissometer (20 cm path length); 6,000 m depth limit; Sea Tech in situ fluorometer (500 m depth limit); Chelsea Instruments in situ fluorometer (6,000 m depth limit); Quantum Sensor – Biospherical Instruments QSP-200L (1,000 m depth limit); altimeter – TRITECH ST-200; 6,800 m depth limit; General Oceanics rosette water sampler with 30-1 Niskin bottles, 5-1 Niskin bottles; Guildline Model 8410 Portasal salinometer (permanently installed in main lab); Turner Designs Model 10 fluorometer; Hitachi Model V-2000 spectrophotometer (1 and 10 cm cells); Sippican MK-12 XBT System (probes available at cost); ADCP, RDI 150 kHz (350 m maximum profiling depth)

UPDATED

Duke University Marine Laboratory

Susan Hudson

GENERAL

Background information	Welded aluminium hull
Current operational status	Estuarine waters and into the Gulf Stream in the vicinity of Beaufort, North Carolina
Length overall	15.00 m
Breadth moulded	4.80 m
Max draught	1.35 m

PROPULSION

Main engine(s)	Twin 350 hp diesel
Speed (max)	18 kt
Speed (cruising)	14 kt
Endurance	400 n miles
Fuel capacity	750 gallons
Electrical power	12 kW diesel generator

BRIDGE NAVIGATION AIDS

Satellite	GPS
Radar	Yes
Echo-sounder	Yes
Other ship navigation	Loran C

COMMUNICATIONS

MF/HF	SSB
VHF	Yes
Cellular	Yes

DECK MACHINERY

Winches	Sea Mac 302HM split-drum; 500 lb capacity, with two-conductor slip rings; Goins double drum trawl

SCIENTIFIC SPACES

Multipurpose dry lab	120 sq ft

SURVEY SYSTEMS

Other sampling	Rock dredge; trawl net(s); water bottles
Oceanographic sensors (CTDs/XBTs and so on)	CTD system with transmissometer, fluorometer, and PAR sensors; fluorometer; scanning spectroradiometer; radiation sensor

NEW ENTRY

Florida Atlantic University

Oceaneer IV

GENERAL

Current operational status	Southeast coast of Florida including the Florida Keys
Built (yard and date)	1978
Length overall	10.20 m
Breadth moulded	3.90 m
Max draught	1.05 m

PROPULSION

Main engine(s)	Caterpillar 3208, 210 hp
Speed (max)	9 kt
Speed (cruising)	8 kt
Endurance	700 n miles
Electrical power	Onan MDKD 8 kW generator, 120/240 VAC

BRIDGE NAVIGATION AIDS

Satellite	Magnavox MX-200 GPS with DGPS
Echo-sounder	Horizon DS-50 digital depth sounder; Raytheon digital fathometer

COMMUNICATIONS

VHF	Standard Eclipse+; Apelco VXL7500
Cellular	Telephone; SLIP/PPP Internet connection

DECK MACHINERY

Winches	Hydraulic Cat-head, mounted on davit, 1,400 lb line pull @ 41 ft/min

ACCOMMODATION

Crew	1-2
Scientists/surveyors	8 (day operations only)

SCIENTIFIC SPACES

Total scientific deck space	Aft deck: 12 × 12 ft

SURVEY SYSTEMS

Positioning	USBL: ORE Trackpoint II and LXT systems

Sensors	Hi-8mm underwater video camera; underwater video system 300 ft cable + SVHS; water jet probe (max water depth 70 ft)
Sidescan sonar	digital (100/500 kHz)
Sub-bottom profiler	Chirp sonar high-resolution (sub-bottom profiler 5 – 40 m)
Grab(s)	Clamshell
Other sampling	Secchi disc and 3 × 1 litre Niskin bottles
Oceanographic sensors (CTDs/XBTs and so on)	FSI CTD; refractometer; digital thermometer; InterOcean S4 current meter

NEW ENTRY

Florida Institute of Oceanography

Bellows

GENERAL

Current operational status	Gulf of Mexico, southeast Atlantic, Bahamas and the northern Caribbean Sea.
Owner	State of Florida
Call sign	WBC 8717
Length overall	21.30 m
Breadth moulded	6.00 m
Operational draught	1.20 m

PROPULSION

Main engine(s)	2 × GM 6-71 diesel through Allison marine gears; 400 hp total
Speed (cruising)	8.5 kt
Endurance	10 days/1,200 n miles
Fuel capacity	3,000 gallons
Electrical power	2 × Detroit 3-71 diesels with 40 kW, 120/208 V AC, 3-phase generators
Fresh water capacity	1,500 gallons

BRIDGE NAVIGATION AIDS

Satellite	Trimble NavTrac XL GPS
Radar	Furuno 1411, 72 n miles colour; Furuno 1941, 48 n miles
Echo-sounder	Raytheon V860 split-screen colour video, 4,800 W
Other ship navigation	M800 Northstar LORAN C

COMMUNICATIONS

MF/HF	M700 ICOM SSB transceiver; Stevens Sea 222 SSB transceiver
VHF	M100 ICOM transceiver; Motorola 440 transceiver; standard HX220S hand-held transceiver
Facsimile	Furuno DFAX weather receiver

SAFETY

Workboat/chase boat	14 ft Boston Whaler, 25 hp outboard

DECK MACHINERY

Cranes	Starboard extending 13 ft for plankton/neuston tows
A-frame(s)	Starboard aft; width 6 ft, height 10 ft, fixed with 2 × 6 ft hero platform; U-frame: stern, width 14 ft, height 16 ft, hydraulic rams, travel distance 3 ft fore, 3 ft aft
Winches	Electromechanical hydraulic CTD with slip rings, with 800 m, 0.303 in two conductor cable with 1,000 lb line pull; hydraulic trawling with 1,800 m, $5/16$ in cable, 6,000 lb line pull; hydro winch on 01 deck with 1,800 m, $3/16$ in cable, 800 lb line pull; auxiliary davit winch on 01 deck for small boat deployment

ACCOMMODATION

Crew	3
Scientists/surveyors	10

SCIENTIFIC SPACES

Total scientific deck space	275 sq ft
Oceanographic wet lab	185 sq ft dry/wet air conditioned

SURVEY SYSTEMS

Echo-sounder (single beam)	Furuno DE 881 depth recorder, 2,000 m
Corer(s)	Piston
Grab(s)	Bottom
Other sampling	Niskin bottles
Oceanographic sensors (CTDs/XBTs and so on)	CTD; XBT; reversing thermometers

NEW ENTRY

Graduate College of Marine Studies, University of Delaware

Cape Henlopen

GENERAL

Current operational status	Operates between Cape Hatteras, North Carolina, the Gulf of Maine and Bermuda
Classification	American Bureau of Shipping

Built (yard and date)	1976
Length overall	36.58 m
Breadth moulded	7.10 m
Max draught	2.83 m
Tonnage (grt)	197

PROPULSION

Main engine(s)	2 diesel engines, 2,500 bhp at 1,800 rpm
Speed (max)	15 kt
Speed (cruising)	12 kt
Endurance	2,400 n miles/10-14 days
Fuel capacity	37 m³
Electrical power	208 VAC, 3-phase
Fresh water capacity	7 m³

BRIDGE NAVIGATION AIDS

Satellite	GPS
Radar	Yes
Gyrocompass	Yes
Speed log	Yes
Echo-sounder	Yes

COMMUNICATIONS

Inmarsat (type)	C
Cellular	Yes
Facsimile	Yes

DECK MACHINERY

Cranes	Heila 19-35 7,000 lb at 15 ft; 2,800 lb at 35 ft
A-frame(s)	Stern, SWL 5 t
Winches	Trawl: Marco 1501 double drum; Hydro: Marco W198; SeaMac portable; DEME portable

ACCOMMODATION

Crew	6
Scientists/surveyors	12

SCIENTIFIC SPACES

Total scientific deck space	15 m²
Oceanographic wet lab	11 m²
Multipurpose dry lab	17 m²

SURVEY SYSTEMS

Echo-sounder (single beam)	Knudsen 320 B/R
Corer(s)	Various
Grab(s)	Various
Other sampling	Rosette: General Oceanic 1015, 10 litre bottles
Vehicle(s) (ROVs/AUVs and so on)	Scanfish towed vehicle
Oceanographic sensors (CTDs/XBTs and so on)	CTD profiler: SBE 911 Plus; ADCP: RDI NBVM 300 kHz; Profiling light meter: Biospherical Instruments XBT system

UPDATED

Great Lakes National Program Office, Environmental Protection Agency

Lake Guardian

GENERAL

Background information	Research and monitoring vessel; former offshore supply vessel; acquired by EPA in December 1988; home port: Bay City, Michigan
Former names	M/V *Marsea Fourteen*
Classification	Ice-strengthened to ABS class 'C'
Built (yard and date)	Halter Marine, Moss Point, Mississippi; 1981
Rebuilt (yard and date)	Converted by Halter Marine, Moss Point, Mississippi;
Length overall	54.00 m
Breadth moulded	12.00 m
Operational draught	3.30 m
Tonnage (grt)	299

PROPULSION

Main engine(s)	2 × Caterpillar D-399 16-cyl diesels each developing 1,200 hp
Thrusters	Bow: Caterpillar 3406 6-cyl diesel engine developing 300 hp and driving a Schottel tunnel thruster
Propellers	84 in diameter 4-blade stainless steel propellers housed in Kort nozzles
Speed (cruising)	11 kt
Endurance	6,000 n miles
Fuel capacity	79,000 gallons
Fuel consumption	75 gallons/h
Electrical power	3 × Caterpillar 3306 6-cyl diesel engines driving KATO generators rated at 135 kW each; any two generators may be linked to achieve a maximum of 270 kW
Fresh water capacity	29,000 gallons

BRIDGE NAVIGATION AIDS

Satellite	Furuno GP 500
Radar	2 × Racal Decca BT 500
Gyrocompass	Sperry SR 130
Speed log	JEC JLN-203
Echo sounder	Furuno FE 881 Mk-11
Other ship navigation	Loran: Northstar 800; Furuno LC 90 GPS

COMMUNICATIONS

MF/HF	Harris RF 3200
VHF	Standard Titan+; Raytheon Ray 88
Facsimile	Weatherfax receiver: Furuno 214

SAFETY

Workboat/chase boat	33 ft workboat – Mudpuppy; 22 ft workboat – Monark (2 × 85 hp Johnson motors, Loran C, 110 VAC generator, depth-sounder, radio); 2 × Zodiacs (one with 50 hp Evinrude motor, the other, used for trace metal sampling, with wooden oars)

DECK MACHINERY

Cranes	Hiab 450 Sea Crane (11,620 lb at 26-3/4 ft, 48,500 lb at 6.5 ft)
A-frame(s)	2 × starboard hydraulic, max capacity 5,000 lb; stern hydraulic, max capacity 30,000 lb
Winches	Rosette: Interocean (220 VAC 3-phase electric, 500 lb line pull); Seabird/Pump: Sea-Mac (220 VAC 3-phase electric/hydraulic, 1,000 lb line pull); coring: Sea-

---

Mac 3540 EH (480 VAC -3-phase electric/hydraulic, 6,600 lb line pull); zooplankton: Hyde (440 VAC, 400 lb line pull); general purpose: Interocean (220 VAC 3-phase, 500 lb line pull)

ACCOMMODATION

Crew	16 cabins – accommodates 42 (inc scientists)

SCIENTIFIC SPACES

Total scientific deck space	2,260 sq ft; full bottom tier of container labs: 1,335 sq ft (ability to embark up to eight 20-ft modular (container) laboratories)

Multipurpose dry lab	300 sq ft
Chemistry lab	208 sq ft

SURVEY SYSTEMS

Sub-bottom profiler	Datasonics 3.5 kHz
Oceanographic sensors (CTDs/XBTs and so on)	SBE 16 Seacat CTD; SBE 19 Seacat CTD; SBE 25-03 Sealogger CTD; SBE 911plus CTD

NEW ENTRY

Great Lakes Water Institute

Neeskay

GENERAL

Official number	512553
Call sign	WY 8293
Built (yard and date)	Higgins Inc, New Orleans, Louisiana; 1953
Rebuilt (yard and date)	1970 Peterson Builders Inc, Sturgeon Bay, Wisconsin; 1970; Hanna Marine, Lamont, Illinois; 1984 (2 m aft extension and gantry system)
Length overall	21.60 m
Breadth moulded	5.40 m
Operational draught	2.40 m
Tonnage (grt)	75

PROPULSION

Main engine(s)	Single 340 hp Detroit Diesel 12-cylinder 71 series engine; twin disc 514-M marine gear with 3:1 reduction with trolling valve control
Propellers	Diameter 42 in, shaft diameter 4 in
Speed (max)	11 kt
Speed (cruising)	9.5 kt
Endurance	3 days/600 n miles
Electrical power	One Northern Lights 20 kW, 83 A 110/220; one 11.7 A uninterruptible power system; one Northern Lights 45 kW, 480 VAC, 3-phase generator

BRIDGE NAVIGATION AIDS

Satellite	Northstar 951XD DGPS
Radar	Furuno 72 mile
Gyrocompass	KVH Azimuth 314 AC fluxgate; Sperry Mk 27
Echo-sounder	Lorance X-16 depth chart recorder interfaced with Loran-C; Lorance 3400 digital depth-sounder; two transducers 8 and 20°
Other ship navigation	2 × Northstar 800 Loran-C receivers

COMMUNICATIONS

VHF	2 × VHF-FM radiotelephones

SAFETY

Lifeboats	2 × 10-person inflatable liferafts
Lifesaving equipment	Category I 406 EPIRB; 17 × survival suits

DECK MACHINERY

Cranes	Forward: Hiab articulated hydraulic
A-frame(s)	Forward: with max load capacity of 2,000 lb; Aft: hydraulic ram gallows frame on stern with 4 m clearance under frame and 1 m swing clearance over stern, max load capacity 2,000 lbs
Winches	Forward: Otis Oceanographic hydraulic with free-fall capability and 460 m (1,500 ft) of ¼ in conducting cable with slip-ring; Aft: Lantec two-speed hydraulic with free-fall capability and 400 m of ¼ in cable; Aft: one Lantec single-speed high-power hydraulic with 400 m of ¼ in cable

ACCOMMODATION

Crew	3

SCIENTIFIC SPACES

Oceanographic wet lab	Yes
Multipurpose dry lab	Yes

SURVEY SYSTEMS

Corer(s)	Box coring and sediment sampling
Other sampling	Vertical and horizontal net tows, trawling, dredging
Vehicle(s) (ROVs/AUVs and so on)	Small ROV
Oceanographic sensors (CTDs/XBTs and so on)	Seabird CTD profiler; rosette sampler; hydrographic casts; current meters

NEW ENTRY

Gulf Coast Research Laboratory

Tommy Munro

GENERAL
Background Information
Official number   634430
Classification   ABS; USCG
Call sign   WRB 2908
Built (yard and date)   Bender Shipyard, Mobile,
                                  Alabama; 1981
Length overall   29.25 m
Breadth moulded   7.50 m
Max draught   2.70 m

PROPULSION
Main engine(s)   Twin GM V12-71 each capable of
                                  300 hp @ 1,800 rpm
Speed (max)   > 10 kt
Endurance   20 days/2,500 n miles
Fuel capacity   10,850 gallons
Fuel consumption   50 gallons/h @ 10 kt
Electrical power   2 × GM-4-71 diesel-powered
                                  generators supplying 50 kW (208/
                                  120 VAC)
Fresh water capacity   10,294 gallons

BRIDGE NAVIGATION AIDS
Satellite   DGPS
Radar   2 × Furuno, 5 and10 kW, 48 n
                                  miles
Gyrocompass   Sperry
Echo-sounder   Atlas Echograph 680 recording
                                  fathometer with graphic scale
                                  expander; Datamarine System
                                  2300B digital depth indicator;
                                  Skipper Model CS115 colour
                                  echo-sounder with 50 kHz
                                  transducer

COMMUNICATIONS
MF/HF   Hull Model 922 SSB WRB 2908
                                  radio
VHF   Ray-53-A WRB 2908

SAFETY
Lifeboats   2 × 12-man Givens Buoy Liferafts
Workboat/chase boat   ZODIAC with outboard

DECK MACHINERY
A-frame(s)   Port and stern
Winches   3 × trawl (all hydraulic) port and
                                  starboard McElroy with level wind,
                                  7,000 ft of ½ in cable;
                                  hydrographic with level wind and
                                  12 conductor slip rings; 13,000 ft
                                  of ¼ in cable or 6,000 ft of ⅜ in;
                                  stern-mounted hydraulically
                                  operated net reel with 4 × 5 ft
                                  spool with line pull capacity of 3
                                  to 4 tons and drum torque at ½
                                  drum @ 90,000 lb

ACCOMMODATION
Crew   5
Scientists/surveyors   12

SCIENTIFIC SPACES
Total scientific deck space   25 × 45 ft

NEW ENTRY

Harbor Branch Oceanographic Institution

Edwin Link

GENERAL
Former names   *Sea Diver*
Port of reg/flag   Fort Pierce, Florida

Classification   American Bureau of Shipping
Built (yard and date) 1959
Rebuilt (yard and date) 1992

Edwin Link   *2000*/0093755

Length overall	33.90 m (113 ft)
Breadth moulded	6.90 m (23 ft)
Operational draught	2.55 m (8.5 ft)
Tonnage (grt)	174.6

PROPULSION

Main engine(s)	2 × 3406-B Cat. diesels; 375 shp each at 1,800 rpm
Thrusters	Bow
Speed (cruising)	10.0 kt
Endurance	5,000 n miles
Fuel capacity	10,500 gallons
Fuel consumption	36 gallons p/h
Electrical power	2 Caterpillar 3,306 diesel generators, 95 kW each, 440/208/110 V AC 3-phase
Fresh water capacity	3,200 gallons

BRIDGE NAVIGATION AIDS

Radar	Simrad/Anritsu Furuno 8050D
Gyrocompass	Sperry Mk 37
Echo-sounder	Autohem Tri-data

COMMUNICATIONS

Inmarsat (type)	JRC 45A Satcom
MF/HF	Furuno/Skanti-TRP 8258S SSB transceiver
VHF	2
	3 ICOM hand-held
Facsimile	Aldin Faxmate II weather recorder; Aldin Navtek receiver AE900

SAFETY

Workboat/chase boat	Avon rigid hull inflatable – 17 ft, 70 hp outboard; Avon rigid hull inflatable – 13 ft, 40 hp outboard

DECK MACHINERY

Cranes	Articulating: 10 t capacity; Cargo: 1 t capacity
A-frame(s)	5 t capacity
Winches	Optional: SEA-MAC Model 3540 EHCLWR – towing, trawling, coring with optional 14 conductor slip-ring, drum capacity up to 1,500 m of wire SMATCO Model HCSR-2-100 hydraulic storage reel/tow, capacity up to 1,600 m of wire

ACCOMMODATION

Crew	7
Scientists/surveyors	12

SURVEY SYSTEMS

Positioning	Trackpoint II
Echo-sounder (single beam)	Simrad EQ50

UPDATED

Harbor Branch Oceanographic Institution

Seward Johnson

GENERAL

	Oceanographic and submersible-support research vessel
Classification	American Bureau of Shipping
Built (yard and date)	1984
Rebuilt (yard and date)	1994
Length overall	61.20 m (204 ft)

Breadth moulded	10.80 m (36 ft)
Operational draught	3.6 m (12 ft)
Tonnage (grt)	285

PROPULSION

Main engine(s)	2 Caterpillar 3512 TI, 850 hp each at 1,200 rpm

Seward Johnson

2000/0093754

Thrusters	Bow and stern: two 360° rotatable, Elliot White-Gill 32 T3, each powered by GE 325 hp DC/SCR-drive motors		
Propellers	2 fixed-pitch		
Speed (max)	13.0 kt		
Speed (cruising)	12.0 kt		
Endurance	6,000 n miles		
Fuel capacity	63,000 gallons		
Fuel consumption	70 gallons/h at 12 kt		
Electrical power	3 CAT 3406 diesel generators, 295 kW each, 1 CAT 3304 emergency diesel generator, 110 kW		
Fresh water capacity	18,000 gallons		

DECK MACHINERY

Cranes	Appleton lifting, 10 t capacity at 38 ft outreach; Appleton lightweight, 3.5 t capacity with 21 ft outreach
A-frame(s)	Stern: for submersible/towed systems launch and recovery, 18 t capacity; side: with forward (1.5 t), centre (10 t) and aft (5 t) lifting points
Winches	Various

ACCOMMODATION

Crew	11
Scientists/surveyors	29

BRIDGE NAVIGATION AIDS

Satellite	2 Magnavox MX300 DGPS 1 Magnavox MX200 DGPS
Radar	Raytheon Pathfinder ST ARPA S-band; Raytheon Pathfinder ST Alphax X-Band
Gyrocompass	2 Sperry Mk 37
Speed log	Sperry SRD 331
Echo-sounder	Data Marine 1000 digital Furuno FE 502

SCIENTIFIC SPACES

Oceanographic wet lab	288 sq ft
Multipurpose dry lab	468 sq ft
	Submersible maintenance lab: 264 sq ft
Chemistry lab	Environmental lab: 85 sq ft

SURVEY SYSTEMS

Positioning	ORE-Trackpoint Model 4410C acoustic system Simrad/Robertson dynamic System
Echo-sounder (single beam)	Simrad EQ50, 38/50 kHz
Sub-bottom profiler	3.5 kHz transducer
Oceanographic sensors (CTDs/XBTs and so on)	RDI 150 kHz ADCP; RDI 600 kHz ADCP; RDI 38 kHz ADCP; real-time continuous flow sampling system; SeaBird 911 CDT/Carousel

UPDATED

COMMUNICATIONS

Inmarsat (type)	NERA Satcom: "A"; "B" voice, fax, data; "C" (data only)
MF/HF	SEA 330 SSB Harris RF 230M SSB
VHF	Simrad Model 1550
Facsimile	NAVTEX receiver Weatherfax

SAFETY

Workboat/chase boat	Willard rigid hull inflatable – 22 ft, 2 × 70 hp outboard Various

---

Harbor Branch Oceanographic Institution

Seward Johnson II

GENERAL

	Offshore supply vessel converted to support marine science research in 1988
Former names	*Edwin Link*
Classification	American Bureau of Shipping
Built (yard and date)	1982
Rebuilt (yard and date)	1998
Length overall	50.40 m (168 ft)
Breadth moulded	11.40 m (38 ft)
Operational draught	3.3 m (11 ft)
Tonnage (grt)	288.19

PROPULSION

Main engine(s)	2 × 16V 149 Detroit diesels; 940 shp each at 1,800 rpm
Thrusters	Bow: 360° rotatable, high volume, axial pump thruster, powered by CAT 3406-T; 465 hp, 10,000 lb thrust
Speed (cruising)	11.0 kt
Endurance	7,000 n miles
Fuel capacity	62,000 gallons
Fuel consumption	85 gallons p/h
Electrical power	3 GM 871 diesel generator, 190 kW (all paralleling) 440/208/110 V AC 3-phase 1 emergency GM 471T, 99 kW

Fresh water capacity	39,000 gallons with reverse osmosis unit (50 gallons/h)

BRIDGE NAVIGATION AIDS

Satellite	2 Magnavox MX200 GPS
Radar	2 Simrad & Enritsu
Gyrocompass	Sperry Mk 37
Speed log	Sperry Doppler
Echo-sounder	Data Marine digital Furuno FE-D 814 AF Furuno FM 220

COMMUNICATIONS

Inmarsat (type)	JRC 45A Satcom
MF/HF	Furuno/Skanti-TRP 8258S SSB transceiver; Harris RF 230M SSB
VHF	1 Drake; 3 ICOM IC-M120 hand-held
Facsimile	Alden Marinefax TR-IV with NAVTEX

SAFETY

Workboat/chase boat	Avon rigid hull inflatable – 17 ft, 50 hp outboard; Willard rigid hull inflatable – 22 ft, 2 × 70 hp outboard

DECK MACHINERY

Cranes	Articulating: 10 t capacity; cargo: 5 t capacity
A-frame(s)	For submersible/towed systems launch and recovery, 18 t capacity; Side J-frame, 3,500 lb capacity
Winches	SEA-MAC 88 electro/hydraulic hydro
	Optional:
	SEA-MAC Model 3540 EHCLWR – towing, trawling, coring with optional 14 conductor slip-ring, drum capacity up to 1,500 m of wire; SMATCO Model HCSR-2-100 hydraulic storage reel/tow winch, capacity up to 1,600 m of wire

ACCOMMODATION

Crew	11
Scientists/surveyors	27

SCIENTIFIC SPACES

Oceanographic wet lab	220 sq ft
Multipurpose dry lab	342 sq ft
	Submersible maintenance lab: 264 sq ft
Chemistry lab	2 environmental labs: 66 sq ft

SURVEY SYSTEMS

Positioning	ORE Trackpoint Model 4410C acoustic system
	Straza Model 9010 passive tracker
Echo-sounder (single beam)	Simrad EQ50, 38/50 kHz
Sub-bottom profiler	Datasonics chirp, 3.5 kHz
Oceanographic sensors (CTDs/XBTs and so on)	RDI 150 and 600 kHz ADCPs

UPDATED

Seward Johnson II (Bob Barton)   *2001*/0059327

Institute of Marine/Coastal Sciences, Rutgers University

Arabella

GENERAL

Background information	Fibre-glass hull (lobster-boat type)
Current operational status	Near-shore (up to 25 n miles) and estuarine research
Length overall	14.40 m
Breadth moulded	5.28 m
Max draught	1.50 m

PROPULSION

Main engine(s)	Detroit 12V71TA diesel; Twin Disc 514 gearing and trolling valve for 1-2 kt operation

Thrusters	Bow
Speed (cruising)	15 kt
Fuel capacity	750 gallons
Electrical power	12.5 kW diesel-driven generator; 208/110 VAC triple-phase

BRIDGE NAVIGATION AIDS

Satellite	DGPS
Radar	Yes
Echo-sounder	2 × digital fathometers; Amber depth-sounder
Other ship navigation	Loran C

COMMUNICATIONS		Winches	Single drum hydraulic with capstan and four-conductor slip ring; 900 ft of ¼ in electromechanical wire
VHF	2		
Cellular	Yes		

DECK MACHINERY		SCIENTIFIC SPACES	
Cranes	Mast and boom with electric winch; 90 ft of ¼ in wire	Total scientific deck space	Aft: 300 sq ft
A-frame(s)	Hydraulic		*NEW ENTRY*

Institute of Marine/Coastal Sciences, Rutgers University

Caleta

GENERAL		Echo-sounder	Recording fathometer
Current operational status	Near-shore (up to 25 n miles) and estuarine research	Other ship navigation	2 Loran C
Length overall	8.85 m	COMMUNICATIONS	
Breadth moulded	3.30 m	VHF	Yes
Max draught	0.83 m	Cellular	Yes

PROPULSION		DECK MACHINERY	
Main engine(s)	ADQ41B diesel	Cranes	Mast and boom with electric winch; 90 ft of ¼ in wire; 2,000 lb capacity
Propellers	DuoProp outdrive		
Speed (cruising)	18 kt		
Fuel capacity	150 gallons	A-frame(s)	Hydraulic; 6,000 lb capacity
Electrical power	2.8 kW inverter (1.5 kW continuous); 110 VAC single-phase	Winches	Hydraulic with capstan; 1,700 ft of ¼ in wire; 1,500 lb capacity

BRIDGE NAVIGATION AIDS		SCIENTIFIC SPACES	
Satellite	2	Total scientific deck space	Aft: 117 sq ft
Radar	Yes		*NEW ENTRY*

Lamont-Doherty Earth Observatory, Columbia University

Maurice Ewing

GENERAL COMMENTS		Breadth moulded	14.10 m
Originally constructed as a seismic vessel. Acquired in 1989		Max draught	5.30 m
Owner	National Science Foundation	Tonnage (grt)	1,976
Classification	American Bureau of Shipping: A-1 Baltic Ice Class IA and Coast Guard inspected	PROPULSION	
		Speed (max)	13.5 kt
Rebuilt (yard and date)	Modified 1989	Speed (cruising)	10 – 11 kt
Length overall	70.20 m	Endurance	15,000 n miles/50 days

Maurice Ewing   ***2001***/0101530

BRIDGE NAVIGATION AIDS
DGPS: Trimble 200D
Satellite	GPS: Ashtech 3DF
Radar	Furuno FR20305
Gyrocompass	2 × Sperry Mk 37
Speed log	Furuno CI-30
Echo-sounder	Furuno FGG80

COMMUNICATIONS
JRC Inmarsat receiver
Inmarsat (type)	C: Thrane & Thrane T13020A

DECK MACHINERY
Cranes	Hiab; SWL 3,000 lb or 44 ft Appleton: SWL 11,900 lb at 20 ft; Slattery stiff boom crane; SWL 4,000 lb at 50 ft
A-frame(s)	Starboard and stern SWL 15 t
Winches	Multipurpose: hydrographic/camera: CTD: all L-DEO-LEBOS design Dynacon Traction.

ACCOMMODATION
Crew	22
Scientists/surveyors	28

SCIENTIFIC SPACES
Oceanographic wet lab	Analytical lab: 225 sq ft; CTD sampling lab: 380 sq ft
Multipurpose dry lab	550 sq ft; Instrument lab: 1,400 sq ft

SURVEY SYSTEMS
Echo-sounder (single beam)	Edo hull-mounted 3.5 and 12 kHz transducers
Multibeam/swath system	STN Atlas Hydrosweep DS
Magnetometer	Geometries 880
Gravimeter	Bell BGM-3
Corer(s)	Various
Grab(s)	Various
Oceanographic sensors (CTDs/XBTs and so on)	ADCP: RDI 150 kHz thermosalinograph

SEISMIC SYSTEMS
Number of airguns	20
Size of airguns	2,000 psi, 8,300 cu in tuned sound source array
Streamer manufacturer	ITI streamer cable
Streamer type	6 km hydrophone streamer cable
Recording system	Syntrak 480-24 seismic recording system

UPDATED

The Large Lakes Observatory

Blue Heron

GENERAL
Background information	Home port: Duluth, Minnesota
Owner	University of Minnesota
Built (yard and date)	1985
Length overall	25.88 m
Breadth moulded	7.00 m
Max draught	3.33 m
Tonnage (grt)	< 200

PROPULSION
Main engine(s)	Caterpillar 3508TA diesel, 775 bhp; reverse reduction gear 4.07:1
Propellers	Kort nozzle; 5.5 SS 4-blade propeller
Speed (max)	10 kt

Blue Heron

2001/0101643

Speed (cruising)	9 kt
Endurance	14 days/3,000 n miles
Fuel capacity	8,000 gallons
Electrical power	One Caterpillar 3304: 65 kW, 480 VAC, 3-phase, 208/110 VAC; one Lister AC: 30 kW, 3-phase, 208/110 VAC
Fresh water capacity	2,400 gallons

BRIDGE NAVIGATION AIDS

Satellite	2 × Northstar 941X DGPS
Radar	Furuno Model 1721; Furuno Model 7112
Other ship navigation	Loran: Northstar 800

COMMUNICATIONS

VHF	King VHF 7000 radio
Cellular	Telephone

DECK MACHINERY

Cranes	Morgan Model 070 (Hiab) capable of lifting 1,200 lb at 30 ft
A-frame(s)	Hydraulic 5 t capacity
Winches	SeaMac 220 trawl with 3,000 ft ½ in wire rope, level wind; SeaMac 310 hydrographic with 1,500 ft ¼ in wire rope, level wind; SeaMac electromechanical winch with 3,000 ft, 0.322 in conducting cable, level wind

ACCOMMODATION

Crew	4
Scientists/surveyors	5

SCIENTIFIC SPACES

Total scientific deck space	800 sq ft

Oceanographic wet lab	240 sq ft
Multipurpose dry lab	575 sq ft

SURVEY SYSTEMS

Positioning	TSS POS-MV 320 motion referencing unit (inertial with twin differential GPS)
Echo-sounder (single beam)	Knudsen Model 320/R with 28 kHz transducer
Multibeam/swath system	Sea Bat Model 8101
Sidescan sonar	ORE Model 168 analogue system
Sub-bottom profiler	Geopulse high-resolution seismic reflection profiling system (1-3 kHz)
Corer(s)	Ocean Instruments multi-corer; piston; Benthos gravity
Other sampling	Seabird 32 Carousel with 12 × 8 litre bottle capacity plankton nets; Niskin bottles: 12 × 8 litre and 6 × 5 litre
Oceanographic sensors (CTDs/XBTs and so on)	RDI acoustic Doppler current profiler, 150 kHz; SeaBird Model 19-01 CTD (internal recording) with fluorometer and transmissometer; SeaBird Model 911 plus CTD (deck unit) with fluorometer, transmissometer, PAR sensor, and altimeter; expendable bathythermographs

SEISMIC SYSTEMS

Size of airguns	Bolt Model 600B airguns with 1, 5, 10 and 40 in chambers

NEW ENTRY

Louisiana Universities Marine Consortium

Acadiana

GENERAL

Background information	Outfitted to support research and educational activities in Louisiana coastal bays and near-shore waters; home port: Defelice Marine Center, Cocodrie, Louisiana
Built (yard and date)	Breaux's Bay Craft , Inc, Loreauville, Louisiana
Length overall	17.40 m
Breadth moulded	5.40 m
Operational draught	1.20 m

PROPULSION

Main engine(s)	Twin Caterpillar 3406, 650 total hp
Speed (max)	10 kt
Endurance	5 days
Fuel capacity	900 gallons
Electrical power	Northern Lights 20 kW 110/220 VAC single phase 60 Hz generator; Northern Lights 14 kW 110/220 VAC single phase 60 Hz generator

BRIDGE NAVIGATION AIDS

Satellite	DGPS
Echo sounder	2
Other ship navigation	2 × Loran C

COMMUNICATIONS

MF/HF	1 SSB
VHF	2
Cellular	Telephone

DECK MACHINERY

Winches	Trawl with 500 ft of ¼ in cable; hydro with 500 ft of 3/16 in cable; electromechanical with 500 ft of 3/16 in single conductor cable

ACCOMMODATION

Crew	2
Scientists/surveyors	4 (25 for day trips)

SCIENTIFIC SPACES

Oceanographic wet lab	144 sq ft

NEW ENTRY

Louisiana Universities Marine Consortium

Pelican

GENERAL
Classification	ABS +A1 and AMS coastal research vessel
Length overall	31.50 m
Breadth moulded	7.80 m
Operational draught	2.85 m

PROPULSION
Endurance	18 days/3,490 n miles
Fuel capacity	15,725 gallons

BRIDGE NAVIGATION AIDS
Satellite	Northstar 800X with an 8000 GPS receiver and an 8401 DGPS; Northstar 9400 GPS and a portable Garmin GPS 45; Cochrane Technologies with Trimble GPS and Micronet receiver station
Gyrocompass	Sperry Marine

COMMUNICATIONS
Inmarsat (type)	INMARSAT A satellite phone; Ku-band satellite comm station (Boatracs); SeaNet satellite communications console
Cellular	Telephone

DECK MACHINERY
Cranes	Nautilus 4 t, 25 ft with 360° radius; typical configuration: 300 ft wire rope for loading at dock and load transfer at sea and limited over-the-side use for instrument towing and deployments
Winches	Trawl: Marco WT 244 with 7 × conductor slip ring assembly; typical configuration: 16,000 ft of ½ in wire rope for trawling and coring; hydro: InterOcean with 3 × conductor slip ring assembly; typical configuration: 10,000 ft of 0.250 in, single conductor cable for hydro casts and back-up for primary CTD; CTD: Dynacon with 3 × conductor slip ring assembly; typical configuration: 10,000 ft of 0.322 in, triple conductor cable for CTD, MocNess, and so on

ACCOMMODATION
Crew	6
Scientists/surveyors	14

SCIENTIFIC SPACES
Total scientific deck space	1,056 sq ft
Oceanographic wet lab	350 sq ft
Multipurpose dry lab	124 sq ft

SURVEY SYSTEMS
Echo-sounder (single beam)	Odom DF3200 MkII
Corer(s)	Benthos Model 2175 piston; variety of box
Grab(s)	Variety
Vehicle(s) (ROVs/AUVs and so on)	Endeco wing-towed vehicle; sled (used for towing 1,200 kHz ADCP)
Oceanographic sensors (CTDs/XBTs and so on)	SBE 911+ CTD (inc Sea Tech transmissometer; Sea Tech fluorometer; dual SBE 13 Beckman type dissolved oxygen sensors; D&A Instruments optical backscatterance sensor; Datasonics altimeter; CI Aquatracka fluorometer); SBE32 12 position carousel; RDI acoustic Doppler current profiler; MIDAS – underway sampling system (incl SBE21; thermosalinograph; WetLabs WetStar; Sea Tech transmissometer); Sippican MK12 XBT

NEW ENTRY

Marine Center, University of Hawaii

Kilomoana

GENERAL
Background information	AGOR 26. SWATH ship being designed and constructed, under a contract supervised by NAVSEA, to replace the R/V *Moana Wave* for the Office of Naval Research (ONR) and will be entering service in 2002. General purpose oceanographic research in coastal and deep ocean areas. Also able to operate ROVs and AUVs.
Current operational status	Under construction
Owner	US Office of Naval Research
Built (yard and date)	Atlantic Marine, Jacksonville, Florida; keel-laying ceremony 5 February 2001
Length overall	55.68 m
Breadth moulded	26.40 m
Max draught	7.50 m

PROPULSION
Speed (cruising)	12 kt survey in Sea State 6
Endurance	10,000 n miles

DECK MACHINERY
Winches	0.680 in traction

ACCOMMODATION
Crew	48
Scientists/surveyors	> 30

SCIENTIFIC SPACES
Total scientific deck space	4,460 sq ft
Oceanographic wet lab	Total lab space: 2,762 sq ft

SURVEY SYSTEMS
Positioning	HPR 418
Echo-sounder (single beam)	EA 500
Multibeam/swath system	EM 120; EM 1002
Oceanographic sensors (CTDs/XBTs and so on)	CTD system; Sontek ADCP 125

NEW ENTRY

Marine Physical Laboratory, Scripps Institute of Oceanography

Flip

GENERAL COMMENTS

The Floating Instrument Platform (FLIP) is a non-propelled research platform owned by the US Navy and operated by the Marine Physical Laboratory, Scripps Institution of Oceanography, as a stable platform for oceanographic research.

FLIP operates from the Scripps Nimitz Marine Facility in San Diego.

Owner	US Navy
Built (yard and date)	Gunderson Brothers Engineering Company, Portland, Oregon; launched June 22, 1962
Length overall	108.0 m
Breadth moulded	7.93 m
Max draught	3.83 m
Tonnage (grt)	700 grt

PROPULSION

Speed (cruising)	7 – 10 kt (under tow)
Electrical power	2 x 150 kW Generators
	1 x 40 kW Generator (aux)

BRIDGE NAVIGATION AIDS

Satellite	Yes
Radar	Yes
Gyrocompass	Yes

COMMUNICATIONS

Inmarsat (type)	Yes
MF/HF	Yes
VHF	Yes
Cellular	Yes

ACCOMMODATION

Crew	5

NEW ENTRY

Flip manoeuvring into position   **2001**/0009322

Flip in position   **2001**/0009323

Marine Science Institute, University of Texas

Longhorn

GENERAL COMMENTS

Coastal oceanographic research vessel

Built (yard and date)	Allied Shipyard, 1971
Rebuilt (yard and date)	Master Marine Shipyard, 1986
Length overall	32.0 m
Breadth moulded	7.38 m
Max draught	2.23 m
Tonnage (grt)	175

PROPULSION

Main engine(s)	2 GM 12V71 diesels, each 360 hp
Propellers	2, fixed pitch
Speed (max)	10 kt
Speed (cruising)	9.5 kt
Endurance	3,000 n miles/14 days
Fuel capacity	11,000 gallons
Electrical power	2 × 75 kW diesel generator sets.

BRIDGE NAVIGATION AIDS

Satellite	Trimble NT200D GPS with differential, Trimble Navtrac XL

Radar	Furuno FCR-1400 Mark 3 colour radar
Gyrocompass	Sperry SR-220

COMMUNICATIONS

Inmarsat (type)	QualComm Omnitracs 200 SatCommunicator, MarineSat
MF/HF	Stephens 222 and Harris RF3200
VHF	Unimetrics Sea Com 55 and Hummingbird (3 units)
Cellular	Southwestern Bell (361-850-3038) and Marine Sat (888-626-5440)
Facsimile	Alden Faxmate

SAFETY

Workboat/chase boat	16 ft Carolina Skiff; 16 ft Zodiac

DECK MACHINERY

Cranes	TICO 150 marine. Lifting capacity 14,109 lb at 6 ft 6 in extension; 5,666 lb at 16 ft 5 in extension (4 ft 5 in over the side); and

A-frame(s)	1,433 lb at 41 ft extension (29 ft over the side). The crane is mounted amidships Hydraulic; 12 ft horizontal clearance; 18 ft 6 in vertical clearance; 8 ft clearance overboard; 9 ft 6 in reach inboard, 20,000 lb rated.
Winches	Main – Dynacon, carries 9,600 ft of ½ in 3 × 19. There is a four-conductor slip-ring and a capability of handling 6,000 ft of 680 conductor cable. 2 hydro, Dynacon Model 8000A, are available for water-bottle sampling, light coring, dredging, plankton net, and CTD (conductivity, temperature, depth) work. One has 10,000 ft of ¼ in 7 × 19 stainless wire rope, the other has 11,666 ft of 0.322 diameter 3 conductor wire

ACCOMMODATION

Crew	6
Scientists/surveyors	13
Scientific spaces	
Oceanographic wet lab	400 sq ft
Multipurpose dry lab	400 sq ft

SURVEY SYSTEMS

Echo-sounder (single beam)	Knudsen 320M
Corer(s)	Box: Ocean Instruments Mark 1, 8 × 12 × 24 in. Piston: Two each, 3 in diameter. Rock dredge: Kahl #215WA400 benthic rock dredge, mouth opening 24 × 15 in.
Other sampling	Trawls: 35 ft and 40 ft shrimp (otter), 60 × 30 in doors; 1 m plankton nets. Smith-McIntyre sediment samplers: 1 stainless steel; 2 steel.
Oceanographic sensors (CTDs/XBTs and so on)	Sea-Bird 911-Plus, SBE-32 Carousel water sampler, water sampling bottles, Sea-Bird SBE-13 dissolved oxygen sensor, Sea Tech TR2025 25 cm transmissometer, Sea Tech FL0500 fluorometer (500 m depth case), Datasonics altimeter. Niskin bottles: Four 30 litre and four 5 litre. Reversing thermometers: Six unprotected deep-sea, two thermometer frames.

UPDATED

Marine Sciences Research Center, State University of New York

Onrust

GENERAL

Background information	Steel-hulled modified offshore lobster boat design.
Current operational status	Long Island Sound, New York Harbor, the Hudson River, and in the Atlantic from the south shore of Long Island to the continental shelf edge (approximately 100 miles offshore)
Owner	State University of New York
Built (yard and date)	Rhode Island Marine Service; 1974
Rebuilt (yard and date)	5 ft section added to stern; February 1990
Length overall	18.00 m
Breadth moulded	4.98 m
Operational draught	1.95 m
Tonnage (grt)	50

PROPULSION

Main engine(s)	Detroit Diesel 12V-71N 400 hp
Propellers	36 in four-bladed propeller
Speed (cruising)	10 kt
Endurance	50 h
Electrical power	Northern Lights 20 kW diesel generator 110 V/220 VAC single phase; Onan 8 kW diesel generator 110 V/220 VAC single phase, 32 VDC 65 A alternator, 12 VDC 80 A alternator
Fresh water capacity	300 gallons

BRIDGE NAVIGATION AIDS

Satellite	Magnavox MX200 GPS; Leica MX51R DGPS
Radar	Furuno FF-7100 72 mile; Raytheon R20 24 mile

COMMUNICATIONS

MF/HF	SEA 222 SSB
VHF	ICOM IC-M125; Intermarine SR30; Apelco Clipper 90AS
Cellular	Motorola

SAFETY

Lifeboats	15-person SOLAS ocean liferaft
Workboat/chase boat	13 ft inflatable with 15 hp outboard
Lifesaving equipment	10 survival suits

DECK MACHINERY

Cranes	Hydrographic davit: light duty electric winch, 300 ft 3/16 in 7 × 19 stainless steel wire
A-frame(s)	Gantry: 2,000 lb capacity U-frame hydraulic, 3 × block positions, min height clearance to deck 10 ft (9 ft with electromechanical block), min opening 8.33 ft
Winches	Main: Hathaway in-line double drum trawl, line pull 2,000 lb @ 40 rpm, with 1,000 ft of 5/16 in 7 × 19 stainless steel wire and 700 ft of 3/8 in seven-conductor electromechanical cable
Moonpool – size/function	20 in diameter

ACCOMMODATION

Crew	2
Scientists/surveyors	6 (20 on day cruises)

SCIENTIFIC SPACES

Total scientific deck space	340 sq ft work area, 16 ft clear deck area
Multipurpose dry lab	168 sq ft

NEW ENTRY

Maryland Department of Natural Resources

Kerhin

GENERAL

Background information	Welded aluminium hull
Current operational status	Chesapeake Bay and its tributaries; Maryland waters of the mid-Atlantic continental shelf
Length overall	15.30 m
Breadth moulded	4.80 m
Max draught	1.20 m

PROPULSION

Main engine(s)	Twin Detroit Diesel 8V-71
Speed (cruising)	18 kt
Endurance	220 n miles
Electrical power	15 kW diesel generator; 220/110 VAC single-phase; 21.5 kW diesel generator; 110 VAC three-phase
Fresh water capacity	100 gallons

BRIDGE NAVIGATION AIDS

Satellite	2 × Leica DGPS
Radar	2
Echo-sounder	Video fathometer
Other ship navigation	Loran C

COMMUNICATIONS

VHF	2
Cellular	Yes

SAFETY

Lifeboats	8-person automatic inflating liferaft; 15-person life float
Lifesaving equipment	Cold water immersion suits

DECK MACHINERY

Cranes	Mast with two adjustable booms: aft: 2,500 lb capacity with 21.5 ft deck clearance; rail: 2,000 lb capacity with 16 ft deck clearance
Winches	Double drum, variable speed, free-spool, trawl-type deck; each drum outfitted with 500 ft of 5/16 in stainless wire
Transducer well	Internal

ACCOMMODATION

Crew	Sleeps 4

SCIENTIFIC SPACES

Total scientific deck space	Forward: 225 sq ft

NEW ENTRY

Military Sealift Command

Bowditch

GENERAL

	'Pathfinder' class T-AGS 60 Class Oceanographic Survey Ship
Owner	Oceanographer of the Navy
Official number	TAGS 62
Classification	USCG certified/ABS classed; ABC Class C Ice strengthening
Built (yard and date)	Halter Marine, Inc, Moss Point; delivered July 1996
Length overall	98.70 m (329 ft)
Breadth moulded	17.40 m (58 ft)
Max draught	5.70 m (19 ft)
Operational draught	5.40 m (18 ft)

PROPULSION

Main engine(s)	4 EMD/Baylor diesel generators; 11,425 hp, (8.52 MW); GE CDF 1944 motors; 8,000 hp, (5.97 MW) sustained; 6000 hp (4.48 MW)
Thrusters	Bow; 1,500 hp (1.19 MW)
Propellers	2 acbLIPS Z drives
Speed (cruising)	16 kt
Endurance	12,000 n miles at 12 kt plus 29 days at 3 kt with 10% fuel reserve
Electrical power	8,520 kW at 600 V AC

BRIDGE NAVIGATION AIDS

Satellite	Rockwell Collins AN/WRN-6(V)1
Radar	Yes
Gyrocompass	Sperry MK39 RLG
Speed log	Yes
Echo-sounder	Yes

SAFETY

Workboat/chase boat	Two

DECK MACHINERY

Cranes	Telescoping boom (Allied Marine TB 80-80); foldable boom (HIAB 180 sea); towing (Appleton Marine KEB 50-35)
A-frame(s)	Davit (Fritz Culver FCAD-4120) Stern U-frame (Fritz Culver FCDB-151Z0) Side U-frame (Fritz Culver FCDB-1096)
Winches	Trawl/coring traction system; (Dynacon TWS 30600-DSW-SSW-HC); (2) CTD/hydro (Dynacon 11040); general purpose (Dynacon 9840LW-RC); magnetometer (Dynacon 1001045); (2) hydrostreamer (Dynacon 20002-ELSS)

ACCOMMODATION

Crew	25
Scientists/surveyors	30

SCIENTIFIC SPACES

Total scientific deck space	3,500 sq ft
Multipurpose dry lab	4,000 sq ft

SURVEY SYSTEMS

Positioning	Bottom transponder navigation system – Benthos Inc. DS-7000-16, a 5 to 50 kHz real-time navigation system for positioning the ship with regard to a fixed, acoustic, deep ocean pinger (Datasonic BFP-312) transponder network Simrad/Robertson DP System

Echo-sounder (single beam)	ODEC BATHY-2000 12/33 kHz	Sound velocity profiler	Sippican XSV
Multibeam/swath system	Simrad EM121A		ME SV-PROBE OTS
Sub-bottom profiler	ODEC BATHY-2000 3.5 kHz	Oceanographic sensors	ADCP – RD Instruments VM-0150
Magnetometer	EG&G G811/813	(CTDs/XBTs and so on)	Sippican XBT
Other sampling	General Oceanic water sampler – operates with the CTD to collect water samples in depths to 7,000 m using a Rosette sampler, Niskin bottles and a (Guideline Portasal 8410) salinometer. Sea surface – OMEGA DP82Y		Falmouth ICTD

UPDATED

Military Sealift Command

Bruce C. Heezen

GENERAL

Background information	'Pathfinder' T-AGS 60 class vessel. Designed and constructed to provide multiple capabilities, including physical, chemical and biological oceanography; multidiscipline environmental investigations; ocean engineering and marine acoustics; marine geology and geophysics; and bathymetric, gravimetric and magnetometric surveying. The surveys are conducted for the Naval Meteorology and Oceanography Command, Stennis Space Centre, by personnel of the Naval Oceanographic Office. Expected to be delivered in late 2001.
Owner	Oceanographer of the Navy
Official number	TAGS 65
Classification	American Bureau of Shipping, US Coast Guard
Built (yard and date)	Halter Marine Shipyard, Moss Point, Mississippi, completed January 2000.
Length overall	98.70 m (329 ft)
Breadth moulded	17.40 m (58 ft)
Operational draught	5.40 m (18 ft)

PROPULSION

Main engine(s)	4 EMD/Baylor diesel generators; 11,425 hp (8.52 MW); 2 GE CDF 1944 motors; 8,000 hp (5.97 MW) sustained; 6,000 hp (4.48 MW)

Thrusters	Bow, 1,500 hp (1.19 MW)
Propellers	2 acbLIPS Z drives;
Speed (cruising)	16.0 kt
Endurance	12,000 n miles

SAFETY

Workboat/chase boat	2 × 34 ft (10 m) Hydrographic Survey Launches (HSLs) equipped with EM3000 multibeam systems operating at 300 kHz

DECK MACHINERY

Cranes	3 multipurpose
Winches	5

ACCOMMODATION

Crew	25
Scientists/surveyors	30

SCIENTIFIC SPACES

Total scientific deck space	3,500 sq ft
Multipurpose dry lab	4,000 sq ft

SURVEY SYSTEMS

Positioning	Dynamic Position Systems
Multibeam/swath system	Kongsberg Simrad EM1002/ EM121A EM 3000 on survey launches
Sidescan sonar	Towed digital
Vehicle(s) (ROVs/AUVs and so on)	May be carried

NEW ENTRY

USNS Bruce C Heezen, the fifth of the UNS's six-strong 'Pathfinder' class fleet (US Naval Hydrographic Office)   ***2001***/0094104

Military Sealift Command

Henson

GENERAL	'Pathfinder' class T-AGS 60 Class Oceanographic Survey Ship	**DECK MACHINERY**	
		Cranes	Telescoping boom (Allied Marine TB 80-80); foldable boom (HIAB 180 Sea crane); towing (Appleton Marine KEB 50-35)
Owner	Oceanographer of the Navy		
Official number	TAGS 63		
Classification	USCG Certified/ABS Classed; ABC Class C Ice Strengthening	**A-frame(s)**	Davit (Fritz Culver FCAD-4120); Stern U-frame (Fritz Culver; FCDB-151Z0); side U-frame (Fritz Culver FCDB-1096)
Built (yard and date)	Halter Marine, Inc, Moss Point; delivered February 1998		
Length overall	98.70 m (329 ft)	**Winches**	Trawl/coring traction system (Dynacon TWS 30600-DSW-SSW-HC); (2) CTD/hydro (Dynacon 11040); general purpose (Dynacon 9840LW-RC); magnetometer (Dynacon 1001045); (2) hydrostreamer (Dynacon 20002-ELSS)
Breadth moulded	17.40 m (58 ft)		
Max draught	5.70 m (19 ft)		
Operational draught	5.40 m (18 ft)		

PROPULSION

Main engine(s) 4 EMD/Baylor diesel generators; 11,425 hp, (8.52MW); 2 GE CDF 1944 motors; 8,000 hp, (5.97 MW) sustained; 6000 hp (4.48 MW)

ACCOMMODATION

Crew 25
Scientists/surveyors 30

Thrusters Bow; 1,500 hp (1.19 MW)
Propellers 2 acbLIPS Z drives
Speed (cruising) 16 kt

SCIENTIFIC SPACES

Total scientific deck space 3,500 sq ft
Multipurpose dry lab 4,000 sq ft

Endurance 12,000 n miles at 12 kt plus 29 days at 3 kt with 10% fuel reserve
Electrical power 8,520 kW at 600 V AC

SURVEY SYSTEMS

Positioning Bottom transponder navigation system – Benthos Inc DS-7000-16, a 5 to 50 kHz real-time navigation system for positioning the ship with regard to a fixed, acoustic, deep ocean pinger (Datasonic BFP-312) transponder network Simrad/Robertson DP system

BRIDGE NAVIGATION AIDS

Satellite Rockwell Collins AN/WRN-6(V)1
Radar Yes
Gyrocompass Sperry MK39 RLG
Speed log Yes
Echo-sounder Yes

SAFETY

Workboat/chase boat 2

Henson (Halter Marine)

2000/0053398

Echo-sounder (single beam)	ODEC BATHY-2000 12/33 kHz	Sound velocity profiler	Sippican XSV
Multibeam/swath system	Simrad EM121A		ME SV-PROBE OTS
Sub-bottom profiler	ODEC BATHY-2000 3.5 kHz	Oceanographic sensors	ADCP – RD Instruments
Magnetometer	EG&G G811/813	(CTDs/XBTs and so on)	VM-0150; Sippican XBT/Falmouth
Other sampling	General Oceanic water sampler –		ICTD
	operates with the CTD to collect		
	water samples in depths to		
	7,000 m using a Rosette sampler,		*UPDATED*
	Niskin bottles and a (Guideline		
	Portasal 8410) salinometer.		
	Sea surface – OMEGA DP82Y		

Military Sealift Command

Mary Sears

GENERAL		**Thrusters**	Bow; 1,500 hp (1.19 MW)
Background information	'Pathfinder' T-AGS 60 class	**Propellers**	2 acbLIPS Z drives;
	vessel. Designed and constructed	**Speed (cruising)**	16.0 kt
	to provide multiple capabilities,	**Endurance**	12,000 n miles
	including physical, chemical and		
	biological oceanography;	**SAFETY**	
	multidiscipline environmental	Workboat/chase boat	2 × 34 ft (10 m) Hydrographic
	investigations; ocean engineering		Survey Launches (HSLs)
	and marine acoustics; marine		equipped with EM3000
	geology and geophysics; and		multibeam systems operating at
	bathymetric, gravimetric and		300 kHz
	magnetometric surveying.		
	The surveys are conducted for	**DECK MACHINERY**	
	the Naval Meteorology and	Cranes	3 multipurpose
	Oceanography Command,	Winches	5
	Stennis Space Centre, by		
	personnel of the Naval	**ACCOMMODATION**	
	Oceanographic Office.	Crew	25
	Expected to be delivered in late	Scientists/surveyors	30
	2001.		
Owner	Oceanographer of the Navy	**SCIENTIFIC SPACES**	
Official number	TAGS 65	Total scientific deck space	3,500 sq ft
Classification	American Bureau of Shipping, US	Multipurpose dry lab	4,000 sq ft
	Coast Guard		
Built (yard and date)	Halter Marine Shipyard, Moss	**SURVEY SYSTEMS**	
	Point, Mississippi, due to be	Positioning	Dynamic Position Systems
	delivered in late 2001	Multibeam/swath system	Kongsberg Simrad EM1002; EM
Length overall	98.70 m (329 ft)		121A; EM 3000 on survey
Breadth moulded	17.40 m (58 ft)		launches; towed digital sidescan
Operational draught	5.40 m (18 ft)		sonars
		Vehicle(s) (ROVs/AUVs and	May be carried
PROPULSION		so on)	
Main engine(s)	4 EMD/Baylor diesel generators;		*NEW ENTRY*
	11,425 hp (8.52 MW); 2 GE CDF		
	1944 motors; 8,000 hp (5.97 MW)		
	sustained; 6,000 hp (4.48 MW)		

Military Sealift Command

Sumner

GENERAL		**PROPULSION**	
	'Pathfinder' Class T-AGS 60 Class	Main engine(s)	4 EMD/Baylor diesel generators;
	Oceanographic Survey Ship		11,425 hp, (8.52 MW); GE CDF
Owner	Oceanographer of the Navy		1944 motors; 8,000 hp, (5.97
Official number	TAGS 61		MW) sustained; 6,000 hp (4.48
Classification	USCG Certified/ABS Classed;		MW)
	ABC Class C Ice Strengthening	**Thrusters**	Bow; 1,500 hp (1.19 MW)
Built (yard and date)	Halter Marine, Inc, Moss Point;	**Propellers**	2 acbLIPS Z drives
	delivered June 1995	**Speed (cruising)**	16 kt
Length overall	98.70 m (329 ft)	**Endurance**	12,000 n miles at 12 kt plus 29
Breadth moulded	17.40 m (58 ft)		days at 3 kt with 10% fuel reserve
Max draught	5.70 m (19 ft)	**Electrical power**	8,520 kW at 600 V AC
Operational draught	5.40 m (18 ft)		

BRIDGE NAVIGATION AIDS

Satellite	Rockwell Collins AN/WRN-6(V)1
Radar	Yes
Gyrocompass	Sperry MK39 RLG
Speed log	Yes
Echo-sounder	Yes

SAFETY

Workboat/chase boat	2

DECK MACHINERY

Cranes	Telescoping boom (Allied Marine TB 80-80); foldable boom (HIAB 180 Sea Crane); towing (Appleton Marine KEB 50-35)
A-frame(s)	Davit (Fritz Culver FCAD-4120); stern U-frame (Fritz Culver FCDB-151Z0); side U-frame (Fritz Culver FCDB-1096)
Winches	Trawl/coring traction system; (Dynacon TWS 30600-DSW-SSW-HC); (2) CTD/hydro (Dynacon 11040); general purpose (Dynacon 9840LW-RC); magnetometer (Dynacon 1001045); (2) hydrostreamer (Dynacon 20002-ELSS)

ACCOMMODATION

Crew	25
Scientists/surveyors	30

SCIENTIFIC SPACES

Total scientific deck space	3,500 sq ft
Multipurpose dry lab	4,000 sq ft

SURVEY SYSTEMS

Positioning	Bottom transponder navigation system – Benthos Inc. DS-7000-16, a 5 to 50 kHz real-time navigation system for positioning the ship with regard to a fixed, acoustic, deep ocean pinger (Datasonic BFP-312) transponder network Simrad/Robertson DP system
Echo-sounder (single beam)	ODEC BATHY-2000 12/33 kHz
Multibeam/swath system	Simrad EM121A/EM 1000
Sub-bottom profiler	ODEC BATHY-2000 3.5 kHz
Magnetometer	EG&G G811/813
Other sampling	General Oceanic water sampler – operates with the CTD to collect water samples in depths to 7,000 m using a Rosette sampler, Niskin bottles and a (Guideline Portasal 8410) salinometer Sea surface – OMEGA DP82Y
Sound velocity profiler	Sippican XSV ME SV-PROBE OTS
Oceanographic sensors (CTDs/XBTs and so on)	ADCP – RD Instruments; VM-0150; Sippican XBT; Falmouth ICTD

UPDATED

Monterey Bay Aquarium Research Institute (MBARI)

Point Lobos

GENERAL

Former names	*Lolita Chanest*
Call sign	WTE 4907
Length overall	33.5 m
Breadth moulded	7.9 m
Operational draught	2.4 m

PROPULSION

Main engine(s)	2 × 16 V 92 Detroit diesels, 1,200 hp
Speed (max)	12 kt
Speed (cruising)	11 kt
Endurance	9,000 n miles at 11 kt
Fuel capacity	20,500 gallons
Electrical power	2 generators, 40 kW 353 Detroit Diesel
Fresh water capacity	2,500 gallons

BRIDGE NAVIGATION AIDS

Satellite	Trimble 4000 DL DGPS
Radar	Furuno FR-1510D

Gyrocompass	Sperry Mk 37
Echo-sounder	Furuno FCV252

COMMUNICATIONS

VHF	3
Cellular	Motorola SCN 2449A

SAFETY

Lifeboats	2 Switlik inflatable 10-man rafts
Workboat/chase boat	1 Avon 6 m RIB, 70 hp

DECK MACHINERY

Cranes	2 Hiab 290 Sea
A-frame(s)	TMS
Winches	1 Markey CTD DYWS-3

SURVEY SYSTEMS

Vehicle(s) (ROVs/AUVs and so on)	Ventana ROV

UPDATED

Monterey Bay Aquarium Research Institute (MBARI)

Western Flyer

GENERAL

	SWATH oceanographic vessel designed for deep sea ROV operations
Owner	Monterey Bay Aquarium Research Institute
Length overall	36.0 m
Breadth moulded	15.9 m

Max draught	3.70 m
Tonnage (grt)	499 (US)

PROPULSION

Main engine(s)	Diesel-electric 2,500 hp; 2 Caterpillar 3512, 850 kW; 2 Caterpillar 3408, 350 kW; 1 Caterpillar 3304, 105 kW; 2

	propulsion motors: GE, 1,250 hp (each)
Thrusters	2 bow thrusters; omni thrusters HCT 600, each 300 hp
Speed (max)	14.5 kt
Endurance	4,000 n miles at 8 kt
Fuel capacity	17,900 gallons
Fresh water capacity	2,400 gallons

BRIDGE NAVIGATION AIDS

Satellite	Trimble 4000 DS
Radar	Furuno, FR2110 and FR1941
Gyrocompass	Anschutz std 20

SAFETY

Lifeboats	1 Willard 540; 2 Viking (25 person)

DECK MACHINERY

Cranes	2 Hiab 290; Effer 62 TXM
A-frame(s)	Stern: SWL 5,900 kg; ROV UH system: Dynacon TV 3615K/SW 3616K
Winches	CTD: Dynacon 12030

ACCOMMODATION

Crew	9
Scientists/surveyors	10 plus 5 ROV pilots

SURVEY SYSTEMS

Positioning	Nautronic ASK 4001
Echo-sounder(single beam)	Odom Echotrac DF 3200 Mk II
Vehicle(s) (ROVs/AUVs and so on)	Tiburon ROV

UPDATED

Moss Landing Marine Laboratories

Point Sur

GENERAL

Comments	Operates off California, Oregon and Washington, with extended cruises to Mexico, Hawaii and Alaska
Owner	National Science Foundation
Classification	American Bureau of Shipping
Built (yard and date)	Atlantic Marine Inc; 1981
Length overall	41.15 m
Breadth moulded	9.75 m
Max draught	2.74 m
Tonnage (grt)	298

PROPULSION

Main engine(s)	2 Caterpillar 379TA , each 565 shp
Propellers	2 cp
Speed (max)	11.5 kt
Speed (cruising)	10 kt
Endurance	21 days/6,800 n miles at 10 kt
Fuel capacity	278 m³
Electrical power	2 generators, each 175 kW
Fresh water capacity	31 m³

BRIDGE NAVIGATION AIDS

Satellite	Magnavox 200 6 channel DGPS; Furuno GP80 DGPS
Radar	2 Furuno digital colour
Gyrocompass	Sperry Mk 37
Speed log	Sperry SRD 301A
Echo-sounder	Furuno colour sounder

COMMUNICATIONS

Inmarsat (type)	Yes

MF/HF	Yes
VHF	Yes
Facsimile	Yes

DECK MACHINERY

Cranes	Stern: Appleton KEB 20-34-27; bow: Alaska Marine MCK-1500
A-frame(s)	Stern: 11,000 lb; gallows frame: stdb: 5,000 lb
Winches	Trawl: Northern line 3352 EHMOW; CTD: Markey DUSH-5; hydro: Northern line 1210D

ACCOMMODATION

Crew	9
Scientists/surveyors	12

SCIENTIFIC SPACES

Total scientific deck space	1,100 sq ft
Oceanographic wet lab	96 sq ft
Multipurpose dry lab	488 sq ft; electronics 120 sq ft

SURVEY SYSTEMS

Sensors	Fisheries sonar
Echo-sounder (single beam)	Knudsen 3.5 kHz/12 kHz; Raytheon PTR
Oceanographic sensors (CTDs/XBTs and so on)	RDI: 150 kHz ADCP (vessel mounted); 2 Seabird SBE 911 plus CTD systems; thermosalinograph; fluorometer

UPDATED

NOAA Office of Marine and Aviation Operations

Albatross IV

GENERAL

Conducts fishery and living marine resource research in support of NOAA's National Marine Fisheries Service (NMFS), Northeast Fisheries Science Center's Woods Hole Laboratory in Woods Hole, Massachusetts. The ship's normal operating area is the Gulf of Maine, Georges Bank, and the continental shelf and slope from southern New England to Cape Hatteras, North Carolina. Typical assessment work includes groundfish assessment surveys and Marine Resources Monitoring, Assessment and Prediction

	(MARMAP) surveys. Home Port: Woods Hole, Massachusetts
Official number	R342
Classification	American Bureau of Shipping
Call sign	WMVF
Built (yard and date)	Southern Shipbuilding, Slidell, Louisiana; delivered November 1962
Length overall	57.0 m (187 ft)
Breadth moulded	10.1 m (33 ft)
Max draught	4.9 m (16.2 ft)
Tonnage (grt)	1,115

PROPULSION

Main engine(s)	2 Caterpillar geared diesels, rated power (each): 565 hp
Thrusters	1 Murrat and Tregurtha through hull tunnel thruster; rated power: 125 hp
Propellers	1 Liaaen controllable pitch/Kort Nozzle; diameter: 8 ft
Speed (cruising)	10 kt
Endurance	3,933 n miles/16 days
Fuel capacity	44,700 gallons
Fuel consumption	50 gallons/h
Electrical power	2 Caterpillar ship service generators; output voltage: 450 V AC, 60 Hz, 3-phase; power rating (each): 215 kW. 1 John Deere emergency generator; output voltage: 450 V AC, 60 Hz, 3-phase; power rating: 45 kW Electrical service: 450 V AC, 60 Hz, 3-phase; 120/220 V AC, 60 Hz, 1-phase; 120/230 V DC
Fresh water capacity	22,324 gallons

BRIDGE NAVIGATION AIDS

Satellite	Differential Global Positioning System (DGPS) receivers
Radar	X- and S-Band with ARPA display
Gyrocompass	Yes
Speed log	Doppler

COMMUNICATIONS

Inmarsat (type)	Standard A radio transceiver; Standard C radio transceiver; Skycell satellite transceiver
MF/HF	HF marine band transceivers; HF Alarm Watch radio receiver (2,182 kHz)
VHF	VHF/FM marine band transceivers
Cellular	Yes
Facsimile	NAVTEX receiver

SAFETY

Workboat/chase boat	1 Willard Marine diesel Utility/Rescue Boat; Length: 18 ft

DECK MACHINERY

Cranes	1 Marine Hydraulics Inc fixed length boom; boom length: 35 ft; location: boat deck, aft; lifting capacity: 10,000 lb
A-frame(s)	1 movable gantry; clearance over the side: 11 ft; location: stern 1 movable hydrographic winch; clearance over the side: 13 ft; location: starboard boat deck, Frame 64 1 movable aft J-frame; clearance over the side: 8 ft; location: starboard main deck, aft
Winches	2 New England Trawler electrohydraulic trawl; line speed: 215 ft/min; maximum pull: 16,000 lb; drum capacity: 6,000 ft of ⅞ in wire rope 1 New England Trawler electrohydraulic dredge; line

Albatross IV

2000/0093806

speed: 185 ft/min; maximum pull:
4,000 lb; drum capacity: 3,900 ft
of ⅝ in wire rope
1 New England Trawler electric
oceanographic; line speed:
200 ft/min; maximum pull: 3,500
lb; drum capacity: 6,000 ft of ⅜ in
wire rope
1 New England Trawler
electrohydraulic hydrographic;
line speed: 250 ft/min; maximum
pull: 3,800 lb; drum capacity:
20,000 ft of ¼ in wire rope

ACCOMMODATION
Crew   20
Scientists/surveyors   14

SCIENTIFIC SPACES

Stern: 1,080 sq ft of open deck
space (accessible by 5 t boom),
and sufficient area to house 2
standard deck lab containers.

Oceanographic wet lab

Multipurpose dry lab

SURVEY SYSTEMS
Echo-sounder (single beam)

**Oceanographic sensors
(CTDs/XBTs and so on)**

Plankton lab: 110 sq ft; Biological
lab: 300 sq ft
Photographic/oceanographic/
chemistry lab: 110 sq ft; scientific
study lab: 100 sq ft; electronics
lab: 180 sq ft

Simrad EK500 high-resolution
scientific sounder with Sun Sparc
processing station; deep water
echo-sounder; shallow water
echo-sounder; vertical fish finder
Acoustic Doppler current profiler.
thermosalinograph; fluorometer;
XBT system; Shipboard
Environmental data Acquisition
System (SEAS); heave and pitch
sensor

UPDATED

NOAA Office of Marine and Aviation Operations

David Starr Jordan

GENERAL

A western rigged stern trawler
designed for mid-water trawling,
but is also capable of conducting
bottom trawls, longline sets,
plankton tows, oceanographic
vertical casts, mud sample
bottom grabs, scuba dives, and
marine mammal and seabird
surveys. The vessel conducts
fisheries, oceanographic and
living marine resource research in
support of the National Marine
Fisheries Service (NMFS),
Southwest Fisheries Science
Center (SWFSC) laboratory in La
Jolla, CA (San Diego). The ship
normally operates off the coast of
California, USA and Baja

California, Mexico in international
waters. The ship has been used
extensively in the Eastern Tropical
Pacific (ETP) for monitoring the
dolphin-tuna associations, and in
California waters to investigate
the habitat and prey of blue
whales and humpback whales.
Home Port: San Diego, CA

Official number	R 444
Classification	American Bureau of Shipping
Call sign	WTDK
Built (yard and date)	Christy Corporation, Sturgeon Bay, Wisconsin; delivered: November 5, 1965
Length overall	52.1 m (171 ft)
Breadth moulded	11.2 m (36.6 ft)
Max draught	3.8 m (12.5 ft)
Tonnage (grt)	873

David Starr Jordan

2000/0093805

PROPULSION

Main engine(s)	2 White-Superior geared diesel engines; rated power (each): 534 hp
Thrusters	1 Hundested tunnel thruster; rated power: 200 hp
Propellers	2 Bird Johnson controllable pitch
Speed (max)	10 kt
Speed (cruising)	12 kt
Endurance	7,500 n miles/30 days
Fuel capacity	50,000 gallons
Fuel consumption	50 gallons/hour
Electrical power	2 General Motors/Delco ship service generators; rated power (each): 200 kW; output voltage: 450 V AC, 60 Hz, 3-phase; 1 General Motors/Delco emergency generator; rated power: 30 kW; output voltage: 450 V AC, 60 Hz, 3-phase; electrical service: 450/220 V AC, 60 Hz, 3-phase; 120 V AC, 60 Hz, 1-phase
Fresh water capacity	8,000 gallons

BRIDGE NAVIGATION AIDS

Satellite	Global Positioning System (GPS) receivers (standard, "P" Code, and differential units)
Radar	X- and S-Band radars, with an ARPA display
Gyrocompass	Sperry Mk 37, Mod D

COMMUNICATIONS

Inmarsat (type)	Standard A radio transceiver; Standard C radio transceiver
MF/HF	HF marine band transceivers
VHF	VHF/FM marine band transceivers; VHF/AM aircraft band transceiver
Cellular	Phone
Facsimile	Weather receiver; NAVTEX receiver
Safety	
Workboat/chase boat	1 Zodiac Rigid Hull Inflatable Boat (RHIB) rescue boat; length: 5.5 m (18.5 ft); 2 × 40 hp Yamaha gasoline outboards; 1 Avon Rigid Hull Inflatable Boat (RHIB) utility boat; length: 5.4 m (18 ft); propulsion: 75 hp Yamaha gasoline outboard; 1 open Boston Whaler Utility Boat; length: 3.7 m (12 ft); 25 hp Johnson gasoline outboard

DECK MACHINERY

Cranes	1 Alaska Marine telescoping boom; lifting capacity: 11,838 lb; lifting capacity (with boom extended): 3,750 lb; boom length: 50 ft; location: 01 level, frame 54, centreline 1 Husky Marine articulated boom; boom length: 18 ft; lifting capacity: 4,650 lb; lifting capacity (with boom extended): 1,800 lb; location: 01 level, frame 10, port
A-frame(s)	1 gantry (A-frame); SWL 11,750 lb; clearance over the side: 3.3 m (11 ft) outboard of the transom; horizontal clearance: 4.1 m (13.5 ft) inside of the gantry; vertical clearance: 6.6 m (21.5 ft) in the vertical position; 5.9 m (19.3 ft) in the full back position; location: main deck, aft, centreline (removable) 1 J-frame; SWL 8,000 lb; clearance over the side: 3 m (10 ft) outboard of deck edge; location: main deck, frame 50, port; 1 port davit; capacity: lightweight towed devices (less than 100 lb); clearance over the side: 3.5 m (11.5 ft) outboard of deck edge; location: 01 level, frame 43, port
Winches	1 Markey Model: DESH-5 CTD; line speed: 100 m/min. (max); 60 m/min (typical); maximum pull: 7,000 lb mid-scope; drum capacity: 6,000 m of 0.322 in EM cable (3 conductor); location: 01 level, frame 44, port 1 Marco Model: W-1920 hydraulic hydrographic winch; line speed: 780 ft/min; maximum pull: 1,600 lb; drum capacity: 5,500 m (18,000 ft) of ¼ in wire rope; location: 01 level, frame 52, starboard 1 Marco Model: W-1816 hydraulic combination winch; 2 trawl drums (1-port & 1-stbd); line speed: 200 ft/min; maximum pull: 12,000 lb; drum capacity: 2,750 m (9,000 ft) of ⅝ in wire rope. 1 centre drum; line speed: 160 ft/min; maximum pull: 6,500 lb; drum capacity: 1,800 m (6,000 ft) of 0.322 in EM cable (3 conductor); location: winch room (1st platform, frame 57, centreline) 1 hydraulic net reel winch; drum width: 2.44 m (96 in) between flanges; drum diameter: 1.25 m (49.5 in) at flange; 0.41 m (16 in) at hub; location: main deck, frame 70, centreline (removable) 1 choker winch; maximum pull: 6,000 lb; drum capacity: 37 m (120 ft) of ½ in wire; location: 01 level, frame 55, centreline

ACCOMMODATION

Crew	18
Scientists/surveyors	15

SCIENTIFIC SPACES

Oceanographic wet lab	Seawater lab: 182 sq ft; wet specimen lab: 146 sq ft
Multipurpose dry lab	Hydro lab: 198 sq ft; dry specimen lab: 72 sq ft
Chemistry lab	340 sq ft

SURVEY SYSTEMS

Sensors	Wesmar 600E 12 kHz scanning sonar system, different line Furuno Netsonde
Echo-sounder (single beam)	Simrad EQ-50, with 38 and 200 kHz transducers Simrad EQ-50, with 38 and 50 kHz transducers
Other sampling	Rosette water sampling system

Oceanographic sensors (CTDs/XBTs and so on)	RD Instruments ADCP CTD System – Sea-Bird Model SBE 911+ (maximum depth capability of 6,800 m) Sea-Bird Model SBE 19 Seacat (maximum depth capability of 1,500 m) XBT system		Shipboard Environmental Data Acquisition System (SEAS); thermosalinograph, Sea-Bird Model SBE 21; autosalinometer, Guildline Model 8400

UPDATED

NOAA Office of Marine and Aviation Operations

Delaware II

GENERAL

Conducts fishery and living marine resource research in support of NOAA's National Marine Fisheries Service (NMFS), Northeast Fisheries Science Center's Woods Hole Laboratory in Woods Hole, MA. The ship's normal operating area is the Gulf of Maine, Georges Bank, and the continental shelf and slope from southern New England to Cape Hatteras, NC. Typical assessment work includes groundfish assessment surveys and Marine Resources Monitoring, Assessment and Prediction (MARMAP) surveys. Research conducted from the *Delaware II* provides an understanding of the physical and biological processes that control year-class strength of key economical fish species

Home Port: Woods Hole, Massachusetts

Official number	R 445
Classification	American Bureau of Shipping
Call sign	KNBD
Built (yard and date)	South Portland Engineering, S Portland, Maine; delivered: October 1968
Length overall	47.2 m (155 ft)
Breadth moulded	9.1 m (30 ft)
Max draught	5.1 m (16.6 ft)
Tonnage (grt)	600

PROPULSION

Main engine(s)	1 General Motors/Electro-Motive Division Model: EMD-567C, V-12 geared diesel engine; Rated power: 1,200 hp
Propellers	1 fixed pitch
Speed (cruising)	10 kt
Endurance	5,318 n miles/24 days
Fuel capacity	24,500 gallons
Fuel consumption	52 gallons/h
Electrical power	2 Detroit Diesel/General Motors 6VT-92 ship service generators; output voltage: 480 V AC, 60 Hz, 3-phase; power rating: 270 kW (each) 1 Perkins, 1000 series, 6 cylinder emergency generator; output voltage: 480 V AC, 60 Hz, 3-phase; power rating: 70 kW Electrical service: 460/220 V AC, 60 Hz, 3-phase; 110 V AC, 60 Hz, 1-phase
Fresh water capacity	7,300 gallons

BRIDGE NAVIGATION AIDS

Satellite	Global Positioning System (GPS) receivers
Radar	X- and S-Band, with an ARPA display
Gyrocompass	Yes
Speed log	Doppler
Echo-sounder	Yes

COMMUNICATIONS

Inmarsat (type)	Standard A radio transceiver, with 56 kb high-speed data modem Standard C radio transceiver
MF/HF	HF Marine Band transceivers with digital selective calling HF Alarm Watch radio receiver (2,182 kHz)
VHF	VHF-FM Marine Band transceivers with digital selective calling
Cellular	Phone
Facsimile	Weather receiver NAVTEX receiver

SAFETY

Workboat/chase boat	1 Rigid Hull Inflatable Boat (RHIB); length: 18 ft; 25 hp

DECK MACHINERY

Cranes	1 Aurora telescoping deck; boom length: 35 ft maximum; location: starboard quarter; lifting capacity: 6,000 lb.
A-frame(s)	1 movable gantry; clearance over the side: 4 ft; work area below: 10 ft wide by 17 ft high; location: stern 1 movable forward; clearance over the side: 8 ft; work area below: 6 ft wide by 13.3 ft high; SWL 5,000 lb; location: stbd side, forward Aft movable; clearance over the side: 8 ft; work area below: 6 ft wide by 16.5 ft high; SWL 7,000 lb; location: stbd side, aft
Winches	2 Marine Hydraulics Inc diesel hydraulic trawl; line speed: 119 ft/min; maximum pull: 20,000 lb; drum capacity: 3,000 m of 1 in wire rope 1 NETEC electrohydraulic oceanographic; drive: line speed: 60 m/min at 10,000 lb; Maximum pull: 20,000 lb at 30 m/min; drum capacity: 4,400 m of 0.625 in. or 600 m of 1.0 in conducting cable (interchangeable drum) 1 NETEC electrohydraulic constant tension; drive: line

speed: 320 ft/min; maximum pull: 3,500 lb tension; drum capacity: 329 m of 0.5 in conducting cable
1 NETEC diesel hydraulic net reel; drive: maximum pull: 20,000 lb; line speed: 100 ft/min
1 Almon Johnson hydraulic forward hydrographic; drive: line speed: 80 m/min; line pull: 5,000 lb; drum capacity: 2,000 m of 0.25 in and 0.322 in conducting wire (2 drum winch)
1 Almon Johnson hydraulic aft hydrographic; drive: line speed: 100 m/min; line pull: 5,000 lb; drum capacity: 6,000 m of 0.25 in or 0.322 in conducting wire (interchangeable drums)

ACCOMMODATION
Crew   16
Scientists/surveyors   14

SCIENTIFIC SPACES
Total scientific deck space	Protected work area: 172 sq ft
Oceanographic wet lab	264 sq ft
Multipurpose dry lab	Dry/chemistry lab: 230 sq ft
	Scientific freezer: forward main deck, walk-in, 201 cu ft

SURVEY SYSTEMS
Echo-sounder (single beam)	Colour video sounder (50 and 200 kHz)
	Simrad EK-500 scientific sounder (12, 38 and 120 kHz), with BI500 software running on a SUN workstation
Oceanographic sensors (CTDs/XBTs and so on)	Acoustic Dopplers current profiler thermosalinograph
	3 hull-mounted sea surface temperature probes; fluorometer; CTD profiler; Shipboard Environmental Acquisition System (SEAS); XBT system; digital fish rulers; digital fish scales

UPDATED

Delaware II   **2000**/0093804

NOAA Office of Marine and Aviation Operations

Ferrel

GENERAL

Equipped specifically for oceanographic studies of coastal and inshore waters along the east and Gulf coasts.
Home Port: Charleston, SC

Official number	S 492
Classification	American Bureau of Shipping
Call sign	WTEZ
Built (yard and date)	Ziegler Shipyards, Inc, Jennings, LA; delivered: May 1968
Length overall	40.5 m (133 ft)
Breadth moulded	9.8 m (32 ft)
Max draught	2.4 m (8.0 ft)
Tonnage (grt)	349

PROPULSION

Main engine(s)	2 geared diesel Caterpillar; rated power (each): 375 hp
Thrusters	General Electric through hull bow thruster; rated power: 100 hp
Propellers	Twin fixed pitch
Speed (cruising)	9.7 kt
Endurance	1,200 n miles/9 days
Fuel capacity	12,800 gallons
Fuel consumption	50 gallons/h
Electrical power	2 Caterpillar generators; output voltage: 450 V AC, 60 Hz, 3-phase; power rating: 100 hp electrical service: 450 V AC, 3-phase 220/110 V AC, 1-phase
Fresh water capacity	9,000 gallons

BRIDGE NAVIGATION AIDS

Satellite Differential Global Positioning
System (DGPS) receiver
Radar X-Band with an ARPA display;
S-Band
Gyrocompass Yes

COMMUNICATIONS

Inmarsat (type) Standard C Radio Transceiver
MF/HF HF Marine Band transceivers
HF Alarm Watch radio receiver
(2,182 kHz)
VHF VHF-FM Marine Band transceivers
portable
VHF-FM transceivers
Cellular Yes

SAFETY

Workboat/chase boat SeaArk aluminium open boat;
length: 23 ft; propulsion: diesel
outdrive; equipment: davit arm
and winch; electronics: DGPS,
VHF radio, cellular phone, digital
depth sounder
SeaArk aluminium open boat;
length: 21 ft; propulsion: gasoline
outboard; equipment: davit arm
and winch; electronics: DGPS,
VHF radio, cellular phone, digital
depth sounder
Nautica inflatable open boat;
length: 13 ft; propulsion: gasoline
outboard
Boston Whaler glass fibre open
boat; length: 14 ft; propulsion:
gasoline outboard

DECK MACHINERY

Cranes Austin Westin telescoping boom;
location: forecastle deck,
amidships; boom length: 35 ft;
lifting capacity: 4,500 lb (boom
extended – 1,050 lb)/
2 Beebe Brothers Inc davit arms;
location: forecastle deck, port
side and stern; arm length: 4 ft;
lifting capacity: 2,000 lb
Appleton articulated boom; boom
length: 40 ft; location: main deck,
port side, aft; lifting capacity:
12,000 lb (boom extended –
2,000 lb)
A-frame(s) Movable, electro-hydraulic;
location: main deck, starboard
midship; clearance over side: 6 ft;
opening: 6 ft wide × 9 ft high
Winches Electrohydraulic skipper
oceanographic; location: main
deck, starboard side; line speed:
0 to 60 ft/min; maximum pull:
6,000 lb; drum capacity: 1,700 ft
of ⅜ in stainless steel wire rope
Sea-Mac electrohydraulic
trawling; location: forecastle
deck, midship; line speed: 0 to
150 ft/min; maximum pull: 4,600
lb; drum capacity: 2,750 ft of ½ in
wire rope
Portable Sea-Mac electric side
scan sonar; line speed: 0 to
150 ft/min; maximum pull: 500 lb;
drum capacity: 300 m of 7
conductor wire rope

ACCOMMODATION

Crew 13
Scientists/surveyors 8

SCIENTIFIC SPACES

Oceanographic wet lab 20.9 m² (225 sq ft)

SURVEY SYSTEMS

Positioning Transponder sonar locator
system

Ferrel

2000/0093803

Echo-sounder (single beam)	Deep water echo-sounder Innerspace 448; shallow water hydrographic echo-sounder; Simrad EQ-50 fish finding echo-sounder	**Oceanographic sensors (CTDs/XBTs and so on)**	Seacat SBE 19-02 and SBE 19-03 CTD profilers; air and seawater temperature sensors; Shipboard Environmental Data Acquisition System (SEAS)
Sidescan sonar	Edgetech Model 260-TH side scan sonar recorder; EG&G Model 272 side scan towfish		

UPDATED

NOAA Office of Marine and Aviation Operations

Gordon Gunter

GENERAL

Conducts fishery and marine resource research supporting NOAA's National Marine Fisheries Service (NMFS), Pascagoula Laboratory in Pascagoula, Mississippi. The ship collects fish and crustacean specimens using trawls and benthic longlines and fish larvae and eggs, and plankton using plankton nets and surface and midwater larval nets. The *Gunter* will normally operate in the Gulf of Mexico and Caribbean Sea.
Home Port: Pascagoula, Mississippi

Former names
Relentless (T-AGOS 18) operated by the Military Sealift Command as an Ocean Surveillance Ship until her transfer to NOAA on 17 March, 1993

Official number R 336
Classification American Bureau of Shipping

Call sign WTEO
Built (yard and date) Halter Marine, Inc, Moss Point, Mississippi; delivered: 12 January, 1990
Rebuilt (yard and date) Brooklyn, New York; commissioned August 28, 1998
Length overall 68.3 m (224 ft)
Breadth moulded 13.1 m (43 ft)
Max draught 4.6 m (15 ft)
Tonnage (grt) 2,014

PROPULSION
Main engine(s) 2 General Electric Model: 42G972; Type: 750 V DC, reversible; rated power (each): 800 hp
Thrusters 1 Schottel tunnel thruster Model: S-300-L; Motor: 750 V DC, reversible; rated power: 550 hp; diameter: 300 mm (51.2 in); blades: 4
Propellers 2 fp
Speed (cruising) 11 kt
Endurance 8,000 n miles/45 days

Gordon Gunter

2000/0093802

Fuel capacity	116,000 gallons	1 Avon W520 inflatable utility boat; length: 17 ft; capacity: 12 people; propulsion: 25 hp OMC gasoline outboard
Fuel consumption	35 gallons/h/generator	
Electrical power	4 Caterpillar diesel Model: D398TA; rated power (each): 600 kW; output voltage: 600 V AC, 60 Hz, 3-phase; 1 emergency generator; Caterpillar 3406TA; rated power: 250 kW; output voltage: 450 V AC, 60 Hz, 3-phase; electrical service: 450 V AC, 60 Hz, 3-phase; 120 V AC, 60 Hz, 1-phase	

DECK MACHINERY

Cranes — 1 Allied Marine Crane Model: TB9-37 aft working deck; boom length: 37 ft (extended); lifting capacity: 4,600 lb at 17 ft radius; 1,100 lb at 37 ft radius; location: 01 level aft, on centreline

Fresh water capacity	4,882 gallons

Winches — 1 Markey Model: Compact CTD/Science, Type COM7X ; drive: electric, 7.5 hp; deck lift capacity: 2,203 lb; drum capacity: 2,000 m; line speed: 15 to 32 m/min; location: aft working deck, port
1 SEAMAC Model: 1015 HLW hydraulic oceanographic; drum capacity: 2,000 m; line speed: 0 to 35 m/min; location: aft working deck, starboard

BRIDGE NAVIGATION AIDS

Satellite	Global Positioning System (GPS) receivers: Magnavox MX-200 differential GPS; Trimble Centurion P-Code GPS; Magnavox MX-50R Beacon receiver
Radar	X- and S-Band, with an ARPA display
Gyrocompass	Sperry Mk 227
Speed log	Sperry SRD-421
Echo-sounder	Yes

ACCOMMODATION

Crew	18
Scientists/surveyors	15

COMMUNICATIONS

Inmarsat (type)	Standard A radio transceiver Standard C radio transceiver Skycell transceiver
MF/HF	HF Marine Band transceivers (2 – Raytheon RAY-152s)
VHF	NOAA Frequency VHF-FM transceiver (Motorola MaxTrax); portable VHF-FM transceivers (8 Motorola Saber R)
Cellular	Yes
Facsimile	Weather receiver; NAVTEX receiver

SCIENTIFIC SPACES

Oceanographic wet lab	207 sq ft
Multipurpose dry lab	576 sq ft; computer lab: 143 sq ft

SURVEY SYSTEMS

Sensors	12 kHz scanning sonar system, Wesmar 600E Furuno Netsonde
Echo-sounder (single beam)	Simrad EQ-50, with 38 and 200 kHz transducers Simrad EQ-50, with 38 and 50 kHz transducers
Other sampling	Rosette water sampling system
Oceanographic sensors (CTDs/XBTs and so on)	CTD system (Sea-Bird SBE 19 SEACAT profiler and SBE 25 Sealogger CTD); uncontaminated sea water sampling system; thermosalinograph (Sea-Bird SBE 21); flourometer (Turner Design Model 10AU); Shipboard Environmental *Data* Acquisition System (SEAS)

SAFETY

Workboat/chase boat	1 Zodiac Hurricane Rigid Hull Inflatable Boat (RHIB) 7500 rescue boat; length: 24 ft; capacity: 20 people; propulsion: Volvo Penta diesel; davit: single-point launching system, with constant tension crane 1 Boston Whaler glass fibre utility boat; length: 22 ft; capacity: 11 people; propulsion: 150 hp OMC gasoline outboard

VERIFIED

NOAA Office of Marine and Aviation Operations

John N Cobb

GENERAL

A wooden research ship. Conducts fishery and living marine resource research in southeast Alaska and in US Pacific coastal waters, supporting the research of the National Marine Fisheries Service (NMFS) Auke Bay Laboratory in Juneau, Alaska
Home Port: Seattle, Washington

Official number	R 552
Classification	American Bureau of Shipping
Call sign	WMVC

Built (yard and date)	Western Boatbuilding Co, Tacoma, WA; delivered: February 1950
Length overall	28.3 m (93 ft)
Breadth moulded	7.9 m (26 ft)
Max draught	3.4 m (11.0 ft)
Tonnage (grt)	185

PROPULSION

Main engine(s)	1 Fairbanks Morse diesel; rated power: 325 hp
Propellers	1 fixed pitch
Speed (cruising)	10 kt
Endurance	2,850 n miles/13 days

Fuel capacity	8,200 gallons	
Fuel consumption	25 gallons/h	
Electrical power	2 GM/Electric Machine diesel generators; rated power (each): 30 kW; output voltage: 240 V AC, 60 Hz, 3-phase	
	Honda emergency generator; rated power: 500 W; output voltage: 110 V AC, 60 Hz, 1-phase; electrical service: 240/ 220 V AC, 60 Hz, 3-phase; 220/ 110 V AC, 60 Hz, 1-phase	
Fresh water capacity	6,000 gallons	

BRIDGE NAVIGATION AIDS

Satellite	GPS receiver
Radar	2 X-Band
Gyrocompass	Yes

COMMUNICATIONS

Inmarsat (type)	Mini-M radio transceiver; Standard C radio transceiver
MF/HF	2
VHF	2
Cellular	Yes

SAFETY

Workboat/chase boat	1 Boston Whaler glass fibre open utility boat; length: 17 ft; propulsion: gasoline outboard, 70 hp

DECK MACHINERY

Cranes	1 fixed-length boom; boom length: 30 ft; lifting capacity: 4,800 lb; location: aft
Winches	1 Rowe hydraulic trawl (double drum); maximum pull: 14,000 lb; drum capacity: 4,800 ft of 9/16 in wire rope, or 7,200 ft of 1/2 in wire rope; 1 hydraulic net reel; 1 oceanographic; drum capacity: 6,000 ft of 3/16 in wire rope; pot hauler; line coiler; automated long line coiler

ACCOMMODATION

Crew	7
Scientists/surveyors	4

SCIENTIFIC SPACES

Multipurpose dry lab	General lab: 150 sq ft

SURVEY SYSTEMS

Sensors	Forward-looking sonar; fish finder; net sonde
Echo-sounder (single beam)	Shallow water; colour sounder

VERIFIED

John N Cobb

2000/0093801

NOAA Office of Marine and Aviation Operations

Ka'imimoana

GENERAL

Fully operational, supporting NOAA's oceanographic and climate research missions in the Pacific. Home Port: Honolulu, Hawaii

Former names	*Titan* (T-AGOS 15) operated by the Military Sealift Command as an Ocean Surveillance Ship until her transfer to NOAA on 31 August 1993.
Official number	R 333

Classification	American Bureau of Shipping	Speed log	Doppler
Call sign	WTEU	Echo-sounder	Navigation depth sounder
Built (yard and date)	Halter Marine, Inc, Moss Point, Mississippi; delivered 1989		

COMMUNICATIONS

Rebuilt (yard and date)	Maritime Contractors, Inc Shipyard, Bellingham, Washington, redelivered to NOAA in April 1996.	Inmarsat (type)	Standard A radio transceiver, with 56 kbyte high-speed data modem; Standard C radio transceiver; GMDSS compliant
Length overall	68.3 m (224 ft)	MF/HF	HF Marine Band transceivers with digital selective calling
Breadth moulded	13.1 m (43 ft)		
Max draught	4.6 m (15 ft)	VHF	VHF-FM Marine Band transceivers with digital selective calling
Tonnage (grt)	2,014	Cellular	Phone

PROPULSION

		Facsimile	Weather receiver; NAVTEX receiver
Main engine(s)	2 General Electric Model: 42G972 diesel electric; 750 V DC, reversible; rated power (each): 800 hp		

SAFETY

Thrusters	1 Schottel Model: S-300-L tunnel thruster; 750 V DC, reversible; rated power: 550 hp; diameter: 300 mm; blades: 4	Workboat/chase boat	1 Zodiac Hurricane Rigid Hull Inflatable Boat (RHIB) rescue boat; length: 22.5 ft; 200 hp Volvo diesel outdrive
Propellers	2 fixed pitch		1 Avon inflatable utility boat; length: 17 ft; propulsion: 25 hp gasoline outboard
Speed (cruising)	10.5 kt		
Endurance	8,000 n miles/30 days		

DECK MACHINERY

Fuel capacity	116,000 gallons	Cranes	2 Hiab Model: 450 aft working deck; lifting capacity: 4,000 lb at 33ft radius, 5,200 lb at 25 ft radius, 8,000 lb at 15 ft radius; location: aft working deck, frame 93, port and starboard
Fuel consumption	35 gallons/h		
Electrical power	4 Caterpillar Model: D398TA ship service/propulsion diesel generators; rated power (each): 600 kW; output voltage: 600 V AC, 60 Hz, 3-phase electrical service: 450/120 V AC, 60 Hz, 3-phase; 120 V AC, 60 Hz, 1-phase		1 Hiab Model 120 midship; lifting capacity: 1,500 lb at 21 ft radius; location: upper deck, frame 65, starboard
Fresh water capacity	7,300 gallons	A-frame(s	1; SWL 20,000 lb; sheave travel: 12 ft forward of the transom to 12 ft aft of the transom; vertical clearance: 28 ft between cross member and deck; horizontal clearance: 15 ft between legs at deck to 12 ft between legs at cross member; location: stern

BRIDGE NAVIGATION AIDS

Satellite	Global Positioning System (GPS) receivers/Ashtech 3DF attitude and position determining GPS receiver		
Radar	X- and S-Band, with an ARPA display		
Gyrocompass	Sperry MK 227		1 J-Frame; SWL 10,000 lb; sheave

Ka'imimoana

2000/0093800

travel: 6 ft inboard of the deck edge to 8 ft outboard of the deck edge; vertical clearance: 13 ft between cross member and deck, at the deck edge; location: forecastle deck, starboard

Winches	2 Markey WETG-60 brailing; drive: electric two-speed/reversing motor, 15 hp; Warping Head: 18 in diameter gypsy, horizontal axis; pull: 10,000 lb at 33 ft/min, 2,500 lb at 132 ft/min; location: aft working deck, port and starboard 1 Market Model DESH-5 CTD; drive: electric AC-SCR/DC motor, 75 hp; maximum pull: 7,000 lb mid-scope; drum capacity: 10,000 m of 0.322 in conductor cable; location: 02 level

ACCOMMODATION

Crew	21
Scientists/surveyors	12

SCIENTIFIC SPACES

Multipurpose dry lab	Lab space: 950 sq ft

SURVEY SYSTEMS

Echo-sounder (single beam)	Deep water system; shallow water system
Oceanographic sensors (CTDs/XBTs and so on)	CTD system XBT system acoustic Doppler current profiler; atmospheric profiler; Vaisala upper air sounding system; uncontaminated sea water sampling system; thermosalinograph; autosalinometer; Shipboard Environmental Data Acquisition System (SEAS)

VERIFIED

NOAA Office of Marine and Aviation Operations

McArthur

GENERAL

	Conducts oceanographic research and assessments, primarily throughout the area of the Exclusive Economic Zone of the Pacific coast of the United States. Home Port: Seattle, Washington
Official number	R 330
Classification	American Bureau of Shipping
Call sign	WTEJ
Built (yard and date)	Norfolk Shipbuilding and Drydock Norfolk, VA; delivered: November 1966
Length overall	53.3 m (175 ft)
Breadth moulded	11.6 m (38 ft)
Max draught	3.7 m (12.1 ft)
Tonnage (grt)	854

PROPULSION

Main engine(s)	2 General Motors geared diesel; rated power (each): 800 hp
Propellers	2 Bird Johnson controllable pitch; diameter: 6.8 ft; blades: 3
Speed (cruising)	10 kt
Endurance	6,600 n miles/30 days
Fuel capacity	63,000 gallons
Fuel consumption	80 gallons/h
Electrical power	2 Detroit Diesel/GE generators; output voltage: 450 V AC, 60 Hz, 3-phase; power rating: 220 kW; Detroit Diesel/Delco emergency generator; output voltage: 450 V AC, 60 Hz, 3-phase; power rating: 60 kW; electrical service: 450 V AC, 3-phase; 120 V AC, 1-phase
Fresh water capacity	6,000 gallons

BRIDGE NAVIGATION AIDS

Satellite	Differential Global Positioning Receivers (DGPS)
Radar	X- and S-Band
Gyrocompass	Sperry MK227
Echo-sounder	Bridge fathometer

COMMUNICATIONS

Inmarsat (type)	Standard A radio transceiver; Standard C radio transceiver
MF/HF	HF Marine Band transceivers HF Alarm Watch radio receiver (2,182 kHz)
VHF	Yes
Cellular	Yes
Facsimile	NAVTEX receiver Weather fax receiver

SAFETY

Workboat/chase boat	Zodiac Rigid Hull Inflatable Boat (RHIB); length: 19 ft; propulsion: Volvo-Penta diesel 2 Zodiac Rigid Hull Inflatable Boats (RHIB); length: 21 ft; propulsion: Yamaha 130 hp gasoline outboards Jensen diesel aluminium work boat; length: 29 ft; equipment: A-Frame (SWL 600 lb) and winch (¼ in wire rope, SWL 600 lb) SAFE boat; length: 17 ft; propulsion: Johnson 115 hp gasoline outboard; gasoline storage capacity aboard ship: 550 gallons

DECK MACHINERY

Cranes	Husky Hydraulics articulated boom; boom length: 22 ft; location: starboard quarter; lifting capacity: 3,600 lb; Baldwin-UMA-Hamilton telescoping boom; boom length: 32 ft; location: foredeck; lifting capacity: boom extended 10 ft: 3,200 lb, boom extended 32 ft: 2,400 lb; Allied Systems Co rescue boat crane; location: E-deck, starboard; SWL: 3,500 lb
A-frame(s)	Movable, location: stern; clearance over side: 10 ft; usable

Winches

width: 10 ft; vertical clearance (deck to padeye): 17 ft 9 in; lifting capacity: 8,000 lb
Movable, location: starboard quarter; clearance over quarter: 6 ft; usable width: 6 ft; vertical clearance (deck to padeye): 14 ft 2 in; lifting capacity: 2,000 lb
Markey electrohydraulic oceanographic; line speed: 50 to 60 m/min; maximum pull, low speed: 12,000 lb; maximum pull, high speed: 8,000 lb; maximum drum capacity: 6,000 m of 0.322 in conducting cable (3 conductor); currently rigged with: 3,500 m of 0.322 in conducting cable; maximum working load: 5,000 lb; recommended working load: 2,500 lb
Braden electrohydraulic oceanographic; line speed: 50 m/min; maximum pull: 16,000 lb; maximum drum capacity: 800 m of ⁵⁄₁₆ in wire rope; currently rigged with: 325 m of ⁷⁄₁₆ in galvanized wire rope; SWL: 5,000 lb

Pullmaster hydraulic A-frame; line speed: 50 to 80 m/min; maximum pull, bare drum: 12,000 lb; maximum pull, full drum: 7,300 lb; maximum drum capacity: 1,600 m of ¼ in wire rope

ACCOMMODATION
Crew   22
Scientists/surveyors   13

SCIENTIFIC SPACES
Oceanographic wet lab   150 sq ft
Multipurpose dry lab   Instrument lab (E Deck): 150 sq ft

SURVEY SYSTEMS
Echo-sounder (single beam)   Bathy 1000 deep water; Simrad EQ-50 depth sounder
Oceanographic sensors (CTDs/XBTs and so on)   RDI acoustic Doppler Current Profiler (ADCP) CTD system; thermosalinograph; autosalinometer; Shipboard Environmental Data Acquisition System (SEAS)

UPDATED

McArthur   **2000**/0093799

NOAA Office of Marine and Aviation Operations

Miller Freeman

GENERAL

Stern trawler capable of operating a variety of biological and oceanographic sampling gear. Its primary mission is to provide a working platform for the study of the ocean's living resources.
Home Port: Seattle, Washington

Official number	R 223
Classification	American Bureau of Shipping
Call sign	WTDM

Built (yard and date)	American Shipbuilding, Toledo, OH; delivered: June 1967
Rebuilt (yard and date)	Recommissioned 1974
Length overall	65.5 m (215 ft)
Breadth moulded	12.8 m (42 ft)
Max draught	6.1 m (20.0 ft)
Tonnage (grt)	1,515

PROPULSION

Main engine(s)	1 General Motors geared diesel; rated power: 2,200 hp

Thrusters	1 Schottel lowerable electric bow thruster; rated power: 400 hp
Propellers	1 controllable pitch; manufacturer: Bird Johnson; diameter: 10.1 ft; blades: 3
Speed (cruising)	12 kt
Endurance	12,582 n miles/31 days
Fuel capacity	8,200 gallons
Fuel consumption	25 gallons/h
Electrical power	2 Caterpillar generators; output voltage: 450 V AC, 60 Hz, 3-phase; power rating: 600 kW Caterpillar/GE emergency generator; output voltage: 450 V AC, 60 Hz, 3-phase; power rating: 100 kW; electrical service: 450 V AC, 3-phase; 120 V AC, 1-phase
Fresh water capacity	7,350 gallons

BRIDGE NAVIGATION AIDS

Satellite	Global Positioning System (GPS) receivers: P-Code GPS receiver; Differential GPS receivers; Ashtech 3DF location and attitude determining receiver
Radar	X-Band and S-Band; one with an ARPA display
Gyrocompass	Sperry MK227
Speed log	Ametek MRQ-4015D Doppler
Echo-sounder	Navigation depth sounder

COMMUNICATIONS

Inmarsat (type)	Standard B radio transceiver with 56 kbyte high-speed data modem; Standard C radio transceiver; Mini-M radio transceiver
MF/HF	HF Marine band transceivers HF Alarm Watch radio receiver (2,182 kHz)
VHF	Portable VHF-FM transceivers
Cellular	Yes
Facsimile	NAVTEX receiver Weather fax receiver

SAFETY

Workboat/chase boat	Munson Launch, a 26 ft HammerHead; aluminium V-hull; 10 ft beam; 3 ft loaded draft; CAT 3208 engine, 185 hp; 115 V AC electrical capability; radar, GPS system, depth sounder, VHF/FM radio; capacity 9 persons; 21 kt. Novurania Launch, a rigid hull inflatable rescue boat, 60 hp outboard motor; 16.5 ft length; maximum speed approx 30 mph; capacity 4 persons. Zodiac inflatable; length 15 ft; 25 hp outboard motor.

DECK MACHINERY

Cranes	Port Rowe; 1,500 lb, 360° range; ⅜ in starboard Rowe; 1,500 lb, 360° range; ⅜ in Bow; 2,750 lb at 27 ft Cargo boom; 14,400 lb
A-frame(s)	Aft Marco trawl gantry; 29 ft height; 14.5 ft width; 4.5 ft aft extension; 6.0 ft forward extension Port Markey Oceanographic; 14.5 ft height; 4.5 ft outboard extension Starboard Markey Oceanographic; 13.5 ft height; 4.5 ft outboard extension
Winches	Starboard Markey; 2-layer, 3 conductor; 0.322 in; 3,100 m; 1,150 lb Port Markey; 2-layer, 3 conductor; 0.322 in; 3,215 m; 1,150 lb Aft Marco; 6 × 19 IWRC; 7⁄16 in; 2,940 m; 3,550 lb Aft Rowe; galvanised 2-layer, single conductor, Oceo wire; ⅜ in; 2,450 m; 3,300 lb 2 Rapp-Hydema trawl; 6 × 19

Miller Freeman

2000/0093798

galvanised, improved plow,
IWRC; 1 in; 2,200 m; 22,000 lb
2 net reels; 18,000 lb – 20,000
lb max pull
Port Lantec; Spectra; 1.25 in;
250 ft; 23,000 lb
Starboard Lantec; 6 × 19 plow
steel 1.125 in; 250 ft; 23,000 lb
Haul-out; Spectra; ½ in; 250 ft;
40,700 lb

ACCOMMODATION
Crew   39
Scientists/surveyors   11

SCIENTIFIC SPACES
Oceanographic wet lab   Fish processing lab: 400 sq ft;
                                Rough lab: 240 sq ft; Wet lab: 340
                                sq ft
Chemistry lab   Ocean chemistry lab: 170 sq ft

SURVEY SYSTEMS
Sensors   Wesmar HD-670 scanning sonar
                                Netsond

Echo-sounder (single beam)   Simrad EQ-50 fish finding (38 and
                                50 kHz)
                                Simrad EK-500 scientific sounder
                                (18, 38 and 120 kHz)
                                Deep water (12 kHz)
Oceanographic sensors   RDI acoustic Doppler current
(CTDs/XBTs and so on)   profiler; scientific computer
                                system, for data acquisition and
                                analysis; Sea-Bird Electronics, Inc
                                SBE 21; thermosalinograph; Sea-
                                Bird Electronics, Inc SBE 9/11
                                Plus CTD profiler; Shipboard
                                Environmental *Data* Acquisition
                                System (SEAS); XBT system; wind
                                speed and direction sensors; air
                                temperature and relative humidity
                                sensors

VERIFIED

NOAA Office of Marine and Aviation Operations

Oregon II

GENERAL

Conducts fishery and living
marine resource research,
supporting the research of the
National Marine Fisheries Service
(NMFS), Pascagoula Laboratory
in Pascagoula, Mississippi.
Home Port: Pascagoula,
Mississippi

Official number   R 332
Classification   American Bureau of Shipping
Call sign   WTDO
Built (yard and date) Ingalls Shipbuilding, Pascagoula,
                       MS; delivered: August 1967
Length overall   51.8 m (170 ft)

Breadth moulded   10.4 m (34 ft)
Max draught   4.3 m (14.0 ft)
Tonnage (grt)   703

PROPULSION
Main engine(s)   2 Caterpillar Model: 3512 DITA;
                       rated power (each): 900 hp
Thrusters   Hundested bowthruster; tunnel
                       diameter: 1 m; rated power: 250
                       hp
Propellers   1 Bird Johnson controllable pitch;
                       diameter: 6 ft; blades: 4
Speed (cruising)   12 kt
Endurance   7,810 n miles/33 days
Fuel capacity   71,500 gallons

Oregon II

2000/0093797

Fuel consumption	78 gallons/h		capacity: 6,000 lb at 26 ft; constant tension rescue boat crane
Electrical power	2 Caterpillar generators; output voltage: 450 V AC, 60 Hz, 3-phase; power rating (each): 246 kW		Allied Systems; location: starboard quarter; lifting capacity: 6,000 lb
	Kato emergency generator; output voltage: 450 V AC, 60 Hz, 3-phase; power rating: 75 kW electrical service: 450 V AC, 60 Hz, 3-phase; 120 V AC, 60 Hz, 1-phase	**A-frame(s)**	Movable, clearance over the side: 10 ft; location: port side, forward; lifting capacity: 3,500 lb
Fresh water capacity	7,640 gallons	**Winches**	Marco hydraulic seine/trawl; line speed: 180 ft/min; maximum pull: 30,000 lb; drum capacity: 1,200 ft of 9/16 in wire rope

BRIDGE NAVIGATION AIDS

Satellite	Differential Global Positioning System (DGPS) receivers
Radar	X- and S-Band
Gyrocompass	Yes
Speed log	Doppler

Marine Hydraulics hydrographic; line speed: 45 m/min; maximum pull: 3,000 lb; drum capacity: 3,700 m of 0.322 in EM cable
Markey electric hydrographic; drum capacity: 4,000 m of 0.322 in EM cable

COMMUNICATIONS

Inmarsat (type)	Standard A radio transceiver; Standard C radio transceiver; Skycell satellite transceiver
MF/HF	HF Marine band transceivers HF Alarm Watch radio receiver (2,182 kHz)
VHF	VHF-FM Marine band transceivers Portable VHF-FM transceivers
Cellular	Yes
Facsimile	NAVTEX receiver

New England Trawler self-contained hydraulic MOCNESS; line speed: 100 ft/min; maximum pull: 3,000 lb; drum capacity: 8,000 ft of 0.68 in wire rope

ACCOMMODATION

Crew	17
Scientists/surveyors	14

SAFETY

Workboat/chase boat	Zodiac RHIB utility/rescue boat; length: 5 m Zodiac inflatable utility boat; length: 14 ft; propulsion: 25 hp Evinrude gasoline outboard motor

SCIENTIFIC SPACES

Oceanographic wet lab	Wet oceanographic lab: 275 sq ft Specimen lab: 100 sq ft
Multipurpose dry lab	Instrumentation lab: 75 sq ft Hydrographic lab: 210 sq ft

SURVEY SYSTEMS

Echo-sounder (single beam)	Shallow water; vertical fish finder; Simrad EK500
Oceanographic sensors (CTDs/XBTs and so on)	XBT system; Shipboard Environmental *Data* Acquisition System (SEAS); flow-through thermosalinograph; CTD system; acoustic Doppler current profiler

DECK MACHINERY

Cranes	Aurora Model: 30TSC3000 telescoping, rotating; length: 30 ft; location: foredeck, centreline; lifting capacity: 3,000 lb at maximum reach Morgan rotating; boom length: 26 to 40 ft; location: aft; lifting

VERIFIED

NOAA Office of Marine and Aviation Operations

Ronald H Brown

GENERAL

	Undertakes oceanographic and atmospheric research worldwide. Home Port: Charleston, South Carolina		2 fully rotating, stern Z-Drives Lips, Type FS 2500-450/1510 BO; rated power (each): 3,000 hp
Official number	R104	**Thrusters**	Bow: azimuthing jet: Elliot White Gill, Model 50 T 35: rated power: 1,180 hp
Classification	American Bureau of Shipping	**Speed (max)**	15 kt
Call sign	WTEC	**Speed (cruising)**	12 kt
Built (yard and date)	Halter Marine, Inc, Moss Point, Mississippi; delivered April 18, 1997	**Endurance**	11,300 n miles at 12 kt, plus 30 days on station/60 days
Length overall	83.5 m (274 ft)	**Electrical power**	3 Caterpillar Model: 3508TA diesels; rated power (each): 715 kW; output voltage: 600 V AC, 60 Hz, 3-phase
Breadth moulded	16.0 m (52.5 ft)		480 V AC, 60 Hz, 3-phase; 120 V AC, 60 Hz, 1-phase
Max draught	5.2 m (17.0 ft)		

PROPULSION

Main engine(s)	3 Caterpillar diesels Model: 3516TA; rated power (each): 1,500 kW; output voltage: 600 V AC, 60 Hz, 3-phase		

BRIDGE NAVIGATION AIDS

Satellite	Global Positioning System (GPS) receivers

Radar	X- and S-band with ARPA display
Gyrocompass	Ring laser
Speed log	Doppler
Echo-sounder	Raytheon RD-500

COMMUNICATIONS

Inmarsat (type)	GMDSS compliant; Standard A radio transceiver with 56 kbyte high-speed data modem; Standard C radio transceiver; Mini-M radio transceiver
MF/HF	Yes
VHF	Yes

DECK MACHINERY

Cranes	2 telescopic boom: Alaska: boom length: 50 ft; lifting capacity: 42,000 lb; location: 02 level, port, amidships, and main deck, starboard, aft Portable foldable boom: HIAB 180 SeaCrane: boom length: 40 ft; lifting capacity: 2,205 lb; location: portable Hydrographic boom: Allied Systems: location: 02 level, starboard, frame 90
A-frame(s)	Movable: clearance over the side: 9 ft: location: stern
Winches	2 electric CTD: Markey DESH-5: maximum pull: 8,100 lb; drum capacity: 10,000 m of 0.322 in conductor cable; location: 02 level, starboard

Traction with dual drum stowage: Markey: drum capacity: 30,000 ft of 0.690 in fibre optic cable, or 30,000 ft of 0.680 in EM cable, or 40,000 ft of 9/16 in 3 × 19 torque-balanced wire rope: cable currently installed: approximately 7,500 m of 0.680 in coaxial EM cable; location: stern, below deck

ACCOMMODATION

Crew	24
Scientists/surveyors	35

SCIENTIFIC SPACES

Oceanographic wet lab	230 sq ft
Multipurpose dry lab	Main lab: 1,730 sq ft Hydro lab: 700 sq ft Electronics/Computer lab: 720 sq ft
Chemistry lab	Biochemical lab: 720 sq ft

SURVEY SYSTEMS

Multibeam/swath system	SEABEAM 2112A multibeam echo-sounding system
Sub-bottom profiler	Deep/shallow bottom profiler Sub-bottom profiler
Oceanographic sensors (CTDs/XBTs and so on)	Acoustic Doppler current profiler; CTD system; XBT system; thermosalinograph; autosalinometer; Shipboard Environmental *Data* Acquisition System (SEAS)

VERIFIED

Ronald H Brown

2000/0093796

NOAA Office of Marine and Aviation Operations

Rude

GENERAL

Performs inshore hydrographic surveys along the northeast coast in support of NOAA's nautical charting mission, specialising in

Official number

the location and accurate positioning of submerged hazards to navigation.
Home Port: Norfolk, Virginia
S 590

Classification	American Bureau of Shipping
Call sign	WTET
Built (yard and date)	Jackobson Shipyard, Oyster Bay, New York; delivered: December 1966
Rebuilt (yard and date)	Brooklyn, New York; commissioned August 28, 1998
Length overall	27.4 m (90 ft)
Breadth moulded	6.7 m (22 ft)
Max draught	4.6 m (15 ft)
Tonnage (grt)	150

PROPULSION

Main engine(s)	2 Cummins geared diesel; rated power (each): 400 hp
Propellers	2 Columbian fixed pitch, Kort nozzle; 3.5 ft diameter; blades: 4
Speed (cruising)	10 kt
Endurance	1,000 n miles/5 days
Fuel capacity	3,900 gallons
Fuel consumption	40 gallons/h
Electrical power	2 Detroit Diesel/Delco; rated power (each): 60 kW; output voltage: 230 V AC, 60 Hz
Fresh water capacity	3,800 gallons

SAFETY

Workboat/chase boat	1 Boston Whaler open utility/ rescue boat; length: 19 ft; propulsion: gasoline outboard

DECK MACHINERY

Cranes	1 Appleton telescoping boom; boom length: 27 ft; lifting capacity: 7,500 lb (2,000 lb boom extended); location: aft
Winches	1 Sea-Mac Marine Products Model: 301EMLW electric side scan; line speed: 130 ft/min (variable); maximum pull: 250 lb; drum capacity: 500 ft

ACCOMMODATION

Crew	11

SURVEY SYSTEMS

Positioning	DGPS Seatex Seapath 200
Echo-sounder (single beam)	Odom Echotrac DF-3200 dual-frequency survey
Multibeam/swath system	Reson SeaBat 9003
Sidescan sonar	EdgeTech 262 side scan sonar

UPDATED

Rude   **2000**/0093795

NOAA Office of Marine and Aviation Operations

Townsend Cromwell

GENERAL

Conducts fishery and living marine resource research in support of the National Marine Fisheries Service (NMFS), Honolulu Laboratory in Honolulu, Hawaii. The ship normally operates in the Pacific in and around the Hawaiian island archipelago. The ship collects fish and crustacean specimens using bottom trawls, longlines, and fish traps. Fish larvae, eggs and plankton are also collected using plankton nets and surface and mid-water larval nets.
Home Port: Honolulu, Hawaii

Official number	R443
Classification	American Bureau of Shipping
Call sign	WTDF
Built (yard and date)	J Ray McDermott Co, Morgan City, LA; delivered November 1963
Length overall	49.7 m (163 ft)
Breadth moulded	10.1 m (33 ft)
Max draught	3.9 m (12.7 ft)
Tonnage (grt)	564

PROPULSION

Main engine(s)	2 White-Superior diesel engines; rated power (each): 400 hp
Thrusters	1 Hundested SFT 4 tunnel thruster; rated power: 200 hp
Propellers	2 × 5.5 ft diameter controllable pitch; Manufacturer: Liaaen
Speed (cruising)	10 kt
Endurance	8,160 n miles/30 days
Fuel capacity	42,000 gallons
Fuel consumption	44 gallons/h
Electrical power	2 Northern Lights diesel ship service generators; rated power (each): 230 kW; output voltage: 450 V AC, 60 Hz, 3-phase 1 Northern Lights emergency generator; rated power: 45 kW; output voltage: 450 V AC, 60 Hz, 3-phase Electrical service: 450/120 V AC, 60 Hz, 3-phase
Fresh water capacity	10,000 gallons

BRIDGE NAVIGATION AIDS

Satellite	Global Positioning System (GPS) receivers
Radar	With ARPA display
Gyrocompass	Yes

COMMUNICATIONS

Inmarsat (type)	Standard A radio transceiver; Standard C radio transceiver
MF/HF	Yes
VHF	Yes
Cellular	Yes
Facsimile	Weather facsimile receiver NAVTEX receiver

SAFETY

Workboat/chase boat	1 SAFE boat, American Eagle utility boat; length: 15 ft 1 Boston Whaler utility boat; length: 17 ft 1 Achilles inflatable utility boat; length: 14 ft

DECK MACHINERY

Cranes	1 Alaska Marine telescoping boom; lifting capacity: 2,000 lb; boom length: 40 ft; location: well deck 1 Morgan Crane Co articulated; lifting capacity: 2,250 lb; boom length: 40 ft; location: boat deck, midship
A-frame(s)	1 J-Frame; SWL 8,000 lb; sheave travel: 8 ft to 6 in inboard of deck edge to 8 ft outboard of deck edge; vertical clearance: 13 ft between cross member and deck; location: well deck, starboard, aft 1 plankton boom; SWL 600 lb; clearance over the side: 8 ft; location: well deck, starboard
Winches	2 Rowe Machine Works hydraulic main deck; line speed: 250 ft/min; maximum pull: 1,200 lb; drum capacity: 15,000 ft of 0.322 in conductor cable

Townsend Cromwell

2000/0093794

1 Pacific Fisherman hydraulic net reel; line speed: 50 ft/min; maximum pull: 2,000 lb; drum capacity: Aberdeen bottom trawl or OSU rope trawl
1 Markey hydraulic CTD winch; line speed: 240 ft/min; maximum pull: 2,750 lb; drum capacity: 30,000 ft of ³/₁₃ in wire rope
1 Marco electric oceanographic
1 hydraulic Power Block pot hauler

ACCOMMODATION

Crew	17
Scientists/surveyors	11

SCIENTIFIC SPACES

Oceanographic wet lab	390 sq ft
Multipurpose dry lab	Electronic lab: 120 sq ft
	Scientific specimen freezers: 200 sq ft

SURVEY SYSTEMS

Sensors	Netsonde
Sub-bottom profiler	Shallow water echo-sounding system
	Chromoscope echo-sounder
Oceanographic sensors (CTDs/XBTs and so on)	Acoustic Doppler current profiler; CTD system; Rosette water sampling system; XBT system; Shipboard Environmental Data Acquisition System (SEAS)

VERIFIED

NOAA Office of Marine and Aviation Operations

Whiting

GENERAL

Designed and outfitted for hydrographic and bathymetric surveys involving nautical charting and ocean mapping. The ship normally operates off the US Atlantic coast, Gulf of Mexico, and the US Caribbean Island territorial waters.
Home Port: Norfolk, Virginia
Sister Ship: R/V *Pierce*

Official number	S 329
Classification	American Bureau of Shipping
Call sign	WTEW
Built (yard and date)	Marietta Manufacturing Company, Pt Pleasant, West Virginia; delivered: July 1963
Length overall	49.7 m (163 ft)
Breadth moulded	10.1 m (33 ft)
Max draught	3.7 m (12.2 ft) with IDSSS dome
Tonnage (grt)	696

PROPULSION

Main engine(s)	2 General Motors geared diesel; rated power (each): 800 hp
Propellers	2 controllable pitch; 6.0 ft diameter; blades: 3
Speed (cruising)	12 kt
Endurance	5,700 n miles/20 days
Fuel capacity	44,347 gallons
Fuel consumption	80 gallons/h
Electrical power	2 Detroit Diesel/Delco generators; rated power (each): 174 kW; output voltage: 450 V AC, 60 Hz, 3-phase
	1 Detroit Diesel/Delco emergency

Whiting   *2000*/0093793

	generator; rated power: 60 kW; output voltage: 450 V AC, 60 Hz, 3-phase
	Electrical service: 450/220 V AC, 60 Hz, 3-phase; 120 V AC, 60 Hz, 1-phase
Fresh water capacity	9,400 gallons

BRIDGE NAVIGATION AIDS

Satellite	DGPS
Radar	X- and S-band with an ARPA display
Gyrocompass	Yes
Speed log	Doppler

COMMUNICATIONS

Inmarsat (type)	Standard A radio transceiver; Standard C radio transceiver
MF/HF	HF Marine band transceivers HF Alarm Watch radio receiver (2,182 kHz)
VHF	Yes
Cellular	Yes
Facsimile	Weather facsimile receiver NAVTEX receiver

SAFETY

Workboat/chase boat	2 Type 1 aluminium survey launches; Manufacturer: The Boatyard (Jensen); length: 29 ft; propulsion: diesel
	1 SeaArk Marine open utility boat; length: 17 ft; propulsion: gasoline outboard

DECK MACHINERY

Cranes	1 C H Wheeler telescoping boom; boom length: 27 ft; lifting capacity: 2,500 lb; location: foredeck
A-frame(s)	1 H articulating boom; boom length: 27 ft; lifting capacity: 2,758 lb; location: after deck
	1 movable electric/hydraulic; location: starboard side amidships; clearance over the side: 6.5 ft; height above deck: 16 ft; dimensions: 8 ft wide at base, 5 ft wide at top; lifting capacity: 6,250 lb maximum load; 5,000 lb working load
Winches	1 Sea Mac electric/hydraulic bathythermograph; maximum pull: 1,000 lb; drum capacity: 10,000 m of ¼ in. wire rope (upper drum); unknown length of $\frac{3}{16}$ in. wire rope (lower drum); maximum line speed: 400 ft/min (upper drum); 35 ft/min (lower drum)

ACCOMMODATION

Crew	35

SURVEY SYSTEMS

Echo-sounder (single beam)	Deep water (12 kHz)
	Shallow water (100 kHz)
	Hydrographic survey sounder (24 and 100 kHz)
Multibeam/swath system	Intermediate Depth Swath Survey System (IDSSS) (36 kHz)
Sidescan sonar	EdgeTech 270
	Klein T-5000 high-speed/high-resolution
Oceanographic sensors (CTDs/XBTs and so on)	Sea-Bird Electronics, Inc SBE 19, SEACAT CTD profiler; XBT system; Shipboard Environmental Data Acquisition System (SEAS); TSS heave and pitch sensor

VERIFIED

Occidental College; Moore Laboratory of Zoology

Vantuna

GENERAL

Background information	Custom-built twin-screw diesel power commercial fishing vessel of heavy wood construction; 'vee' bottom with hard chine built with heavy wooden planking over sawn frames
Call sign	WUV 6093
Rebuilt (yard and date)	Modified in 1969
Length overall	24.50 m
Breadth moulded	6.90 m
Max draught	1.80 m
Tonnage (grt)	94

PROPULSION

Main engine(s)	Twin (D343A-Caterpillars) 920 shp
Speed (cruising)	10 kt
Endurance	7 days/2,000 n miles
Fuel capacity	2,700 gallons
Electrical power	2 × 120/240 VAC, 40 and 20 kW each; 12/32 VDC 200 AH battery bank
Fresh water capacity	600 gallons

BRIDGE NAVIGATION AIDS

Satellite	Magnavox MX 100 GPS; Magellan 5200 D GPS
Radar	Epsco 36 mile; Raytheon Pathfinder 24 mile
Echo-sounder	V820 Raytheon colour depth-sounder; Furuno recording fathometer
Other ship navigation	Trimble 100A Loran-C

COMMUNICATIONS

VHF	2 × transceivers
Cellular	Phone

SAFETY

Workboat/chase boat	12 ft Avon inflatable with 15 hp outboard; 2 × 17 ft Boston Whalers with 90 hp outboard

DECK MACHINERY

A-frame(s)	Stern: max lifting capacity 1,800 lb; 12 ft vertical clearance under block; 9 ft horizontal clearance between the frame; 6 ft horizontal clearance over stern
Winches	Hydrographic: midships upper deck with 5,000 ft of $\frac{5}{32}$ in wire rope; lift capacity mid-drum rating 550 lb; 250 ft/min; main drag winch aft on main deck with

7,500 ft of ½ in IWRC wire rope; lift capacity mid-drum 5,900 lb at 100 ft/min

ACCOMMODATION

Crew	3 – 5
Scientists/surveyors	40 days/10 nights

SCIENTIFIC SPACES

Oceanographic wet lab	2 × Live wells, 800 gallons each; 2 × bait tanks, 15 scoops each

SURVEY SYSTEMS

Sensors	Sonar; net sounder

NEW ENTRY

Oceanographer of the Navy

Bent

GENERAL

	T-AGS 26 Class Oceanographic Survey Ship
Official number	TAGS 26
Built (yard and date)	1965
Length overall	85.50 m (285 ft)
Breadth moulded	14.40 m (48 ft)
Operational draught	6.00 m (20 ft)

PROPULSION

Main engine(s)	Diesel electric, 3,600 shp
Propellers	Single screw, fixed-pitch
Speed (cruising)	13 kt
Endurance	12,000 n miles

BRIDGE NAVIGATION AIDS

Radar	Yes

Gyrocompass	Yes
Speed log	Yes
Echo-sounder	Yes

SAFETY

Workboat/chase boat	No

ACCOMMODATION

Crew	48
Scientists/surveyors	26

SCIENTIFIC SPACES

Total scientific deck space	2,855 sq ft
Multipurpose dry lab	3,560 sq ft

VERIFIED

Oceanographer of the Navy

John McDonnell

GENERAL

	T-AGS 51 Class Oceanographic Survey Ship
Official number	TAGS 51
Built (yard and date)	Halter Marine; Delivered November 1991
Length overall	208 ft
Breadth moulded	45 ft
Operational draught	20 ft

PROPULSION

Main engine(s)	Diesel, 2,550 shp
Speed (cruising)	12 kt
Endurance	12,000 n miles

BRIDGE NAVIGATION AIDS

Radar	Yes
Gyrocompass	Yes
Speed log	Yes
Echo-sounder	Yes

John McDonnell (A Sharma)

2000/0084180

SAFETY

Workboat/chase boat	2 × 34 ft, 16 kt, 16.5 t, 3 ft draft

ACCOMMODATION

Crew	22
Scientists/surveyors	11

SCIENTIFIC SPACES

Total scientific deck space	1,500 sq ft
Multipurpose dry lab	700 sq ft

SURVEY SYSTEMS

Multibeam/swath system	EM 1002

UPDATED

Oceanographer of the Navy

Kane

GENERAL

	'Silas Bent' class T-AGS 26 Class Oceanographic Survey Ship
Official number	TAGS 27
Built (yard and date)	Christy Corp Sturgeon Bay; completed 19 May 1967
Length overall	85.50 m (285 ft)
Breadth moulded	14.40 m (48 ft)
Operational draught	6.00 m (20 ft)

PROPULSION

Main engine(s)	2 × Alco diesel generators; 1 × Westinghouse/GE motor; 3,600 shp (2.69 MW)
Thrusters	Bow, 350 hp (261 kW)
Propellers	Single screw,
Speed (cruising)	13 kt
Endurance	12,000 n miles

BRIDGE NAVIGATION AIDS

Radar	RM 1650/9x; TM 1660/12s
Gyrocompass	Yes
Speed log	Yes
Echo-sounder	Yes

SAFETY

Workboat/chase boat	No

ACCOMMODATION

Crew	31
Scientists/surveyors	28

SCIENTIFIC SPACES

Total scientific deck space	2,855 sq ft
Multipurpose dry lab	3,560 sq ft

UPDATED

Kane

2001/0084179

Oceanographer of the Navy

Littlehales

GENERAL

	T-AGS 51 Class Oceanographic Survey Ship
Official number	TAGS 52
Built (yard and date)	Delivered February 1992
Length overall	208 ft
Breadth moulded	45 ft
Operational draught	20 ft

PROPULSION

Main engine(s)	Diesel, 2,550 shp

Speed (cruising)	12 kt
Endurance	12,000 n miles

BRIDGE NAVIGATION AIDS

Radar	Yes
Gyrocompass	Yes
Speed log	Yes
Echo-sounder	Yes

SAFETY

Workboat/chase boat	No

ACCOMMODATION

Crew	22
Scientists/surveyors	11

SCIENTIFIC SPACES

Total scientific deck space	1,500 sq ft
Multipurpose dry lab	700 sq ft

SURVEY SYSTEMS

Multibeam/swath system	Simrad EM 1002

UPDATED

Office of Wetlands, Oceans, & Watersheds, Environmental Protection Agency

Peter W Anderson

GENERAL

Background information	Constructed 1966 for the US Navy as the fourth of the 'Ashville' class of patrol gunboats PG 86 USS *Antelope*, designed for blockade, surveillance, and related naval support missions. Transferred to EPA in 1978 and converted for EPA use in 1979. Renamed in June 1985. Equipped with over-the-side sampling equipment for monitoring ocean dumping sites and other coastal environments
Former names	USS *Antelope* (PG 86)
Current operational status	Atlantic coast and Gulf of Mexico
Built (yard and date)	Tacoma Boatbuilding Co, Tacoma, Washington; launched 1966, commissioned 1967

Rebuilt (yard and date)	Converted 1979
Length overall	49.50 m
Breadth moulded	7.20 m
Max draught	3.20 m

PROPULSION

Main engine(s)	2 × Cummins VT12-875M diesels, 1,450 shp
Speed (cruising)	13 kt
Endurance	6 days transit, 10 days @ operating speed
Fuel capacity	11,244 gallons
Fuel consumption	64 gallons/h @ 13 kt

ACCOMMODATION

Crew	15 (incl four officers)
Scientists/surveyors	15

NEW ENTRY

Old Dominion University

Linwood Holton

GENERAL

Current operational status	Chesapeake Bay and its tributaries; Atlantic Ocean coastal waters from Chincoteague to False Cape, Virginia
Length overall	19.50 m
Breadth moulded	5.55 m
Max draught	2.10 m
Tonnage (grt)	99

PROPULSION

Main engine(s)	Detroit Diesel 12V-71T
Speed (cruising)	10 kt
Endurance	800 n miles
Electrical power	33 kW diesel-driven generator; 240/120 VAC single-phase 12/24/120 VDC

BRIDGE NAVIGATION AIDS

Satellite	GPS
Radar	Furuno
Gyrocompass	2 × video sounders
Other ship navigation	3 × Loran C

COMMUNICATIONS

VHF	2

DECK MACHINERY

Cranes	Articulating hydraulic with 20 ft reach; 1,000 lb capacity at full flat extension; port: boat davit with 3/16 in stainless wire; 500 lb capacity; starboard: hero platform/boom with 3/16 in stainless wire; 500 lb capacity
Winches	2 × hydro; 350 ft of 3/16 and 5/16 in stainless wire

ACCOMMODATION

Scientists/surveyors	8 (21 on day cruises)

SCIENTIFIC SPACES

Total scientific deck space	Forward: 225 sq ft

NEW ENTRY

Oregon State University

Wecoma

GENERAL

Owner	National Science Foundation
Built (yard and date)	1975

Rebuilt (yard and date)	Mid-life refit 1994
Length overall	56.4 m (184.5 ft)
Breadth moulded	10.1 m (33 ft)
Max draught	5.6 m (18.5 ft)

PROPULSION

Main engine(s)	EMD 16 645 E7 diesel, 3,000 hp
Thrusters	Bow: 350 hp omnidirectional
Propellers	Single cp
Speed (max)	14 kt
Speed (cruising)	12 kt
Endurance	7,200 n miles/30 days
Electrical power	2 × 300 kW, diesel-driven ship's service generators

BRIDGE NAVIGATION AIDS

Satellite	Northstar 9000; "P-Code" receiver – Trimble Tasman
Radar	Furuno X- and S-band digital
Gyrocompass	2 Sperry MK 37
Speed log	EDO 250 kHz
Echo-sounder	Raytheon model 570
Other ship navigation	Transas Marine electronic chart display and information system

COMMUNICATIONS

Inmarsat (type)	A, Mobile Telesystems MTS 2100; M, ABB Nera Saturn M; C, Trimble Galaxy
MF/HF	Harris RF3200; Sailor 1000B transceiver
VHF	2
Cellular	2 Motorola MC 310

DECK MACHINERY

Cranes	Telescoping boom mounted on the centreline aft; boom extension 65 ft, capacity 12,000 lb (max)
A-frame(s)	Stern – working capacity of 15,000 lb, a clearance height of 17 ft and a clearance width of 11 ft. The A-frame is hydraulic and swings from 5 ft inboard to 10 1/2 ft outboard which gives a 5 1/2 ft clearance over the stern. It can be used with either the trawl or deep sea winches.
	Hydro – working capacity of 7,000 lb, a clearance height of 12 ft and a clearance width of 8 ft. The A-frame is hydraulic and swings from 5 ft inboard to 7 ft outboard of the starboard side.
Winches	Markey DESH-5 hydrographic capable of approximately 7,000 lb of line pull at 60 m/min. Two drums are available; one with 10,000 m of 0.322 in diameter, 3

conductor electro-mechanical cable and the other with 9,150 m of 1/4 in diameter 3 × 19 wire rope.

Dynacon deep sea traction capable of 20,000 lb line pull (the capacity is limited by the strength of the A-frame) and line speeds of up to 90 m/min (at light load). Two drums are available; one with about 6,000 m of 9/16 in 3 × 19 wire rope and the other with 0.680 in coaxial cable.

Markey DESH-6 trawl winch capable of a 5,000 lb line pull at 45 m/min and a maximum pull of 7,000 lb.

ACCOMMODATION

Crew	13
Scientists/surveyors	18

SCIENTIFIC SPACES

Oceanographic wet lab	35.5 m^2
Multipurpose dry lab	53.5 m^2

SURVEY SYSTEMS

Positioning	Benthos Model 2214 12 kHz pingers
Echo-sounder (single beam)	EDO 323B 12 kHz; ORE 137D 3.5 kHz
Corer(s)	Piston coring facility, 20 ft core sample/reefer van
Other sampling	MOCNESS multiple plankton net.
Vehicle(s) (ROVs/AUVs and so on)	SEASOAR towed undulating vehicle
Oceanographic sensors (CTDs/XBTs and so on)	Guildline 8 PortaSal salinometer; Turner Designs Field Model 10-AU fluorometer; automated dissolved oxygen titration system; nutrient analysis facility; high-performance Pellicon ultrafiltration system; B&L UV-Viz spectrophotometer; Seabird 911 + CTD system; General Oceanics Niskin samplers; General Oceanics 5 litre or 1.7 litre Niskins; General Oceanics 20L Go-Flo bottles, 30 litre Niskins; digital reversing thermometers; RDI ADCP (300 and 150 kHz); Sippican Mk 12 XBT

UPDATED

Quest Marine Services

Quest

GENERAL

Length overall	12.90 m
Breadth moulded	4.80 m
Max draught	1.35 m

PROPULSION

Endurance	400 n miles
Electrical power	6/71 Detroit Diesel, 100 VAC

BRIDGE NAVIGATION AIDS

Satellite	GPS
Radar	32 mile

Echo-sounder	Video, 50/200 kHz
Other ship navigation	Loran

COMMUNICATIONS

MF/HF	SSB
VHF	Yes
Cellular	Yes

DECK MACHINERY

Cranes	Mast with crow's nest and 1,200 lb capacity boom
A-frame(s)	Articulating stern and trawl gallows, 3,000 lb capacity

Winches	Gearmatic GH7, 485 ft ⅜ in wire, 5,000 lb line pull	SCIENTIFIC SPACES	
		Total scientific deck space	19 × 14 ft

NEW ENTRY

ACCOMMODATION
Crew   6 berths

Raytheon Polar Services Company

Laurence M Gould

GENERAL

Background information	Antarctic research and supply vessel
Owner	Edison Chouest, Galliano, Louisiana
Official number	1057229
Classification	ABS Ice Class A1; USCG Subchapter U (oceanographic research vessel)
Built (yard and date)	North American Shipbuilding, Larose, Louisiana; 1997
Length overall	70.10 m
Breadth moulded	14.02 m
Max draught	5.49 m
Tonnage (grt)	1,599

PROPULSION

Main engine(s)	2 × Caterpillar 3606 diesels, 4,576 hp (3,000 hp ice operations)
Thrusters	Bow: 800 hp
Propellers	2
Endurance	75 days/12,000 n miles
Electrical power	3 × 700 kW 3508 Caterpillar diesels; 1 × 500 kW 3408 Caterpillar emergency diesel

BRIDGE NAVIGATION AIDS

Satellite	Trimble Centurion P-code GPS receiver (primary); Trimble NT200 GPS receiver (secondary)
Radar	2 × Furuno model FAR2835-SW

COMMUNICATIONS

MF/HF	250 W SEA HF radio; bridge 100 W Sailor HF radio; bridge: 2 × Sunair HF radios

DECK MACHINERY

Cranes	Aft knuckle crane
A-frame(s)	Stern: 10 t; starboard: 5 t

Winches   Markey DUSH-4, 0.25 in wire rope × 9,000 m, 0.322, 3 × conductor × 6,000 m, ⁵⁄₁₆ × 6,000 m: 01 deck aft; Markey DUSH-5 CTD, 0.322 EMC × 10,000 m: Baltic Room CTD Staging Area; Markey DUSH-6, 0.5 in wire cable × 4,500 m, 0.68 in coaxial × 4,000 m: aft

ACCOMMODATION

Crew	16
Scientists/surveyors	24

SCIENTIFIC SPACES

Oceanographic wet lab	425 sq ft
Multipurpose dry lab	356 sq ft; hydro lab 526 sq ft

SURVEY SYSTEMS

Echo-sounder (single beam)	Knudsen 12 kHz
Sub-bottom profiler	Knudsen 3.5 kHz
Oceanographic sensors (CTDs/XBTs and so on)	RDI acoustic Doppler current profiler; Biospherical Instruments PUV/GUV ultraviolet radiometers; Sea-Bird CTD 9-11 plus; Sea-Bird underway thermosalinograph system; CI fluorometer; Sea-Tech transmissometer; Sippican Mk12 XBT/ XCTD

SEISMIC SYSTEMS

Compressor numbers and types	2 × 135 CFM

NEW ENTRY

Laurence M Gould

2001/0097434

Raytheon Polar Services Company

Nathaniel B Palmer

GENERAL

Background information	Antarctic research and supply vessel
Owner	Edison Chouest, Galliano, Louisiana
Official number	1057229
Classification	ABS Ice Class A2; USCG Subchapter U
Built (yard and date)	North American Shipbuilding, Larose, Louisiana; 1992
Length overall	94.00 m
Breadth moulded	18.30 m
Max draught	6.75 m
Tonnage (grt)	6,172

PROPULSION

Main engine(s)	4 × 3608 Caterpillar diesels, 6,750 hp (13,500 hp ice operations)
Thrusters	Bow: water jet azimuthing, flush mounted; 1,400 bhp (1,050 kW); Stern: tunnel; 800 hp
Propellers	2
Endurance	75 days/12,000 n miles
Electrical power	4 × 1,050 kW 3512 Caterpillar diesels; 1 × 300 kW 3406 Caterpillar diesel emergency generator

BRIDGE NAVIGATION AIDS

Satellite	GPS

COMMUNICATIONS

MF/HF	Bridge: 100 W Sailor HF radio; Bridge: 2 × Sunair HF radios

DECK MACHINERY

Cranes	Aft: articulated; forward: auxilliary
A-frame(s)	Aft: 20 t; starboard: 20 t
Winches	Markey DUSH-5, 0.322 EMC × 10,000 m; deep sea trawl, $^9/_{16}$ in wire rope × 10,000 m; 0.68 EM wire, coaxial × 5,000 m; waterfall hydrographic winch, $^5/_{16}$ in wire rope × 9,000 m and 0.322 EM, 3 × conductor wire × 9,000 m

ACCOMMODATION

Charterers	7
Crew	26
Scientists/surveyors	32

SCIENTIFIC SPACES

Oceanographic wet lab	420 sq ft
Multipurpose dry lab	2,340 sq ft; hydro lab 480 sq ft

SURVEY SYSTEMS

Multibeam/swath system	Yes
Gravimeter	Yes
Oceanographic sensors (CTDs/XBTs and so on)	SeaBird CTD; 2 × ADCP; fluorometer; thermosalinograph

SEISMIC SYSTEMS

Compressor numbers and types	2 x 1200 CFM

NEW ENTRY

Nathaniel B Palmer

2001/0097435

Rosenstiel School

FG Walton Smith

GENERAL

Background information	Catamaran. Went into service in February 2000
Built (yard and date)	Eastern Shipbuilding Group, Panama City, Florida; 1999
Length overall	28.80 m
Breadth moulded	12.00 m
Operational draught	1.65 m
Tonnage (grt)	97

PROPULSION

Main engine(s)	Twin Cummins QSK 19, 760 hp each
Propellers	Servogear variable pitch
Speed (max)	12 kt
Fuel capacity	10,000 gallons
Electrical power	Twin 80 kW generators 208 VAC, 3 phase, 110/120 VAC
Fresh water capacity	3,000 gallons plus reverse osmosis water maker

DECK MACHINERY

Cranes	2: Aft
A-frame(s)	Aft
Winches	Conductor wire; hydro wire
Moonpool(s) – size(s)/ function(s)	Moonpool

ACCOMMODATION

Crew	4
Scientists/surveyors	16

SCIENTIFIC SPACES

Total scientific deck space	800 sq ft astern
Oceanographic wet lab	800 sq ft total laboratory space

SURVEY SYSTEMS

Positioning	Kongsberg Simrad DP system; TSS POS/ MV 320 position, attitude, heading, and vertical reference sensor.
Echo-sounder (single beam)	12 kHz transducer
Sub-bottom profiler	7 x 3.5 kHz transducer array
Vehicle(s) (ROVs/AUVs and so on)	WS Oceans U-Tow undulating system
Oceanographic sensors (CTDs/XBTs and so on)	ADCP Seawater flowing systems with inlets at the bow; thermosalinograph; partial CO_2 monitor; nutrient monitor; fluorometers; dissolved oxygen monitor; meteorological sensors include wind speed and direction, air temperature, relative humidity, barometric pressure, and solar radiation; Sea Bird CTD system with a fluorometer on a 12 bottle rosette

NEW ENTRY

FG Walton Smith   *2001*/0097683

FG Walton Smith
2001/0097688

Sarbanes Coop Oxford Laboratory

Laidly

GENERAL

Current operational status	Designed for Chesapeake Bay and near-shore (up to 20 n miles) of the mid-Atlantic coast
Length overall	16.50 m
Breadth moulded	4.20 m
Max draught	1.05 m
Tonnage (grt)	25

PROPULSION

Main engine(s)	2 × Detroit Diesel 8V-71 natural diesel @ 325 hp each

Speed (cruising)	14 kt
Endurance	384 n miles
Electrical power	1997 Onan Model MDKAD 15 kW diesel generator; 110/220 VAC
Fresh water capacity	100 gallons

BRIDGE NAVIGATION AIDS

Satellite	DGPS
Radar	Furuno
Gyrocompass	Yes

COMMUNICATIONS		A-frame(s)	3,000 lb working load hydraulic
VHF	2		(6 ¾ in diameter)
Cellular	Yes	Winches	1,000 lb working load McElroy
			double drum hydraulic

SAFETY
Lifeboats	2 × 8-person rigid liferafts
Lifesaving equipment	5 × cold water immersion suits

NEW ENTRY

DECK MACHINERY
Cranes	500 lb working load davit with
	hydraulic winch

Scripps Institute of Oceanography

Melville

GENERAL
Owner	US Navy
Official number	AGOR 14
Built (yard and date)	1969
Rebuilt (yard and date)	1992
Length overall	278 ft 10 in
Breadth moulded	46 ft
Max draught	16.5 ft

PROPULSION
Propellers	Twin 'Z' drive shrouded propellers
Speed (cruising)	12 kt
Endurance	12,000 n miles at 10 kt
Fresh water capacity	15,896 gallons, generates 4,000 gallons/day

BRIDGE NAVIGATION AIDS
Satellite	Trimble Transon P-Code GPS
	Trimble NT 200 DGPS
Radar	Yes
Gyrocompass	Sperry Mk 23
	Sperry Mk 37
Speed log	Edo Doppler
Echo-sounder	International offshore Furuno FE-600A
Other ship navigation	Trimble Loran C

COMMUNICATIONS
MF/HF	Yes
VHF	2

Facsimile	Furuno FAX-214
	Harris/3M 2110

SAFETY
Lifeboats	Port: 28 person lifeboat;
	Starboard: 37 person lifeboat;
	6 × liferafts, 20 persons each
Workboat/chase boat	Boston Whaler, 10 ft

DECK MACHINERY
Cranes	Pettibone Model 7B Allied
A-frame(s)	Stern: capacity 12,500 lb
	Starboard: amidships
	Forward, starboard: J-Frame
Winches	Hydro: Northern line
	2 × CTD: Markey DESH-6
	Trawl: Northern Line

ACCOMMODATION
Crew	23
Scientists/surveyors	38
Hospital	3

SCIENTIFIC SPACES
Total scientific deck space	3,772 sq ft
Multipurpose dry lab	Main lab: 1,342 sq ft
	Analytical lab: 220 sq ft

SURVEY SYSTEMS
Echo-sounder (single beam)	Edo 3. kHz
	Edo 12 kHz
Multibeam/swath system	Sea Beam 2000

Melville

2001/0109103

Magnetometer	Geometrics G-886	Compressor numbers and	Price
Gravimeter	Bell BGM-3	types	
Corer(s)	Yes	Total capacity	1,800 psi; 125 cfm
Other sampling	Isaacs-Kidd midwater trawl; 1 m plankton net; 1 m newston net; 10 ft other trawl		
Oceanographic sensors (CTDs/XBTs and so on)	RDI ADCP 150 kHz/300 kHz Sippican XBT		

UPDATED

Scripps Institute of Oceanography

Robert Gordon Sproul

GENERAL

Owner	University of California
Call sign	WSQ2674
Built (yard and date)	1981
Length overall	37.50 m (125 ft)
Breadth moulded	9.60 m (32 ft)
Max draught	2.85 m (9.5 ft)

PROPULSION

Main engine(s)	2 × Detroit Diesels 12V-149, 675 hp
Thrusters	White-Gill Trainable, 155 hp
Propellers	2 × FPP
Speed (max)	10.5 kt
Speed (cruising)	9 kt
Endurance	14 days; 3,250 n miles; 9 kt
Fuel capacity	18,000 gallons
Fuel consumption	1,300 gallons/day (full speed); 650 gallons/day (average)
Electrical power	2 × 75 kW generators, 440 V AC, 3-phase

BRIDGE NAVIGATION AIDS

Satellite	Trimble Transom P-Code GPS Trimble NT 300 DGPS
Radar	2 × Furuno
Gyrocompass	Yes
Speed log	Datamarine 3200
Echo-sounder	Yes

SAFETY

Lifeboats	12 ft Avon; 13 ft Boston Whaler; 17 ft Avon

DECK MACHINERY

Cranes	Aft deck, portside: Huskey 2,500 lb capacity
A-frame(s)	Stern, SWL 10,000 lb
Winches	Trawl: Markey DEYSK-3; CTD/ Hydro: Northern Line; CTD/ Hydro: Western Gear

ACCOMMODATION

Crew	5
Scientists/surveyors	12

SCIENTIFIC SPACES

Total scientific deck space	Space for 2 × portable labs
Oceanographic wet lab	12 × 8 ft
Multipurpose dry lab	12 × 17 ft

SURVEY SYSTEMS

Echo-sounder (single beam)	Knudsen 320 B/R; 12 kHz
Other sampling	Mid-water trawl Plankton net
Oceanographic sensors (CTDs/XBTs and so on)	RDI 300 kHz narrowband ADCP CTD

UPDATED

Robert Gordon Sproul

2001/0101534

Scripps Institute of Oceanography

Roger Revelle

GENERAL COMMENTS
General purpose oceanographic research vessel

Owner	Office of Naval Research
Official number	AGO2 24
Call sign	KAOU
Built (yard and date)	1996
Length overall	82.11 m (273.7 ft)
Breadth moulded	15.75 m (52.5 ft)
Max draught	5.10 m (17 ft)

PROPULSION

Main engine(s)	Twin 'Z' drive propellers aft, trainable 360°
Thrusters	Bow: White Gill
Speed (cruising)	12.0 kt
Fresh water capacity	12,000 gallons, produces up to 4,000 gallons/day

BRIDGE NAVIGATION AIDS

Satellite	Trimble NT 300 DGPS; Trimble Tansmon P-code GPS; Magnavox model 4102
Radar	Sperry 3 cm; Sperry 10 cm
Gyrocompass	2 × Sperry Mk 37
Speed log	ODEC Doppler; EDO DO2 axis Doppler
Echo sounder	Data Marine Inc, International Offshore System 3000, Digital Depth Sounder, 120 kHz; Furuno FPG-512-H
Other ship navigation	Trimble 10X GPS/LORAN-C; Simrad-Taiyo, TD-L1620 automatic digital direction finder

COMMUNICATIONS

Inmarsat (type)	JRC model JUE-45A
MF/HF	Harris 230M; ICOM M800
VHF	3
Cellular	Uniden model CP-1100
Facsimile	Harris/3M model 2110

SAFETY

Workboat/chase boat	23 ft Hurricane semi-rigid inflatable boat

HELIDECK
Deck machinery

Cranes	Main (North American) on starboard quarter, main deck and on port side, 02 level. 2 × Morgan Marine, normally on foredeck
A-frame(s)	Stern: Fritz-Culver, retractable hydroboom on starboard side by staging bay door.
Winches	Markey DUTW-9-11 traction-drum with dual storage drums. Normally 15,000 m of 9/16 in 3 × 19 trawl wire is on one storage drum and 10,000 m of 0.680 in electromechanical cable on the other. Wires over the side lead to A-frame or main deck crane. Capable of fibre optic cable through A-frame. 2 × Markey DESH 5 hydrographic, one with 10,000 m of ¼ in 3 × 19 hydrographic wire, one with 10,000 m of 0.322 in three-conductor electromechanical CTD cable on Lebus grooving. Wires lead over starboard side via retractable hydroboom.
Transducer well	Yes

Roger Revelle   *2001*/0109102

Accommodation			Taiyo ADF; Nautronix RS916
Crew	22		combined short- and long-
Scientists/surveyors	37		baseline acoustic positioning
Scientific spaces			system
Oceanographic wet lab	Wet Lab: 230 sq ft; science	**Echo sounder (single beam)**	ODEC Bathy 2000; Knudsen
	freezer: 63 sq ft; climate control		320B 12 kHz; Raytheon RD-50
	chamber: 63 sq ft	**Multibeam/swath system**	Simrad EM120
Multipurpose dry lab	1,745 sq ft; electronics/computer	**Sub-bottom profiler**	Knudsen 3.5 kHz
	lab: 610 sq ft; hydro lab: 693 sq ft	**Magnetometer**	Geometrics G-886
Chemistry lab	Analytical/biochemical lab: 330	**Corer(s)**	Yes
	sq ft	**Grab(s)**	Yes
		Oceanographic sensors	Sippican Mark 12 digital XBT; RDI
SURVEY SYSTEMS		**(CTDs/XBTs and so on)**	150 kHz broadband and
Sensors	Robertson dynamic positioning		narrowband ADCPs.
	system; Ashtech ADU GPS		*NEW ENTRY*
	attitude-sensing system; Simrad		

Scripps Institute of Oceanography

New Horizon

GENERAL COMMENTS		**Safety**	
Owner	University Of California	Workboat/chase boat	17 ft Boston Whaler, 50 hp
Call sign	WKWB		Johnson outboard
Built (yard and date)	1978		2 × 14 ft Zodiac inflatables, 25 hp
Rebuilt (yard and date)	Mid-Life Refit: 1995-96		or 9.9 hp Johnson outboard.
Length overall	51.00 m (170 ft)		13 ft Boston Whaler, 25 hp
Breadth moulded	10.80 m (36 ft)		Johnson outboard
Max draught	3.65 m		
Tonnage (grt)	294 grt	**HELIDECK**	
		Deck machinery	
PROPULSION			Main Deck: Nautilus Model 3300-
Main engine(s)	2 × 850 hp Caterpillar Marine	**Cranes**	065, 4,000 lb SWL
	Diesels, model D-398		Main Deck: Hiab crane
Thrusters	Bow: LIPS variable speed,	**A-frame(s)**	Stern A-frame, SWL 16,400 lb
	200 kW		Starboard J-frame
Propellers	2 × CPP	**Winches**	DYNACON traction winch with
Speed (max)	12.3 kt		interchangeable drums with
Speed (cruising)	10.0 kt		10,000 m of 0.680 in
Endurance	9,600 n miles @ 10 kt		electromechanical cable or
Fuel capacity	40,000 gallons		10,000 m of 9/16 in 3 × 19
Fuel consumption	1,000 gallons per day		mechanical wire; capable of
Electrical power	2 × GM 8V-71T 1,800 rpm,		handling 0.680 in fibre optic
	200 kW, 440 V, 3-phase		cable.
Fresh water capacity	8,736 gallons, produces up to		Markey CTD winch with 9,100 m
	960 gallons/day		of 0.322 in conductor wire (CTD)
			with Lebus grooving.
BRIDGE NAVIGATION AIDS			Markey hydrographic winch with
Satellite	Trimble NT 300 DGPS		7,600 m of ¼ in 3 × 19
	Trimble Tansmon P-code GPS		hydrographic wire.
	Magnavox model 4102	**Transducer well**	Yes
Radar	Furuno FAR-1622X, 3 cm		
	Furuno FR-1262S, 10 cm	**ACCOMMODATION**	
	Furuno FAR – 1622X, ARPA	**Crew**	12
Gyrocompass	2 × Sperry Mk 37	**Scientists/surveyors**	19
Speed log	Ametek-Straza Doppler 4015		
Echo sounder	Data Marine Inc, International	**SCIENTIFIC SPACES**	
	Offshore System 3000, Digital	**Oceanographic wet lab**	160 sq ft
	Depth Sounder, 120 kHz	**Multipurpose dry lab**	1,105 sq ft
	Furuno FPG-512-H		
Other ship navigation	Trimble 10X GPS/LORAN-C	**SURVEY SYSTEMS**	
	Simrad-Taiyo, TD-L1620	**Echo sounder (single beam)**	Knudsen 320B digital 3.5/12 kHz
	Automatic Digital Direction Finder	**Corer(s)**	Yes
		Grab(s)	Yes
		Oceanographic sensors	RDI 150 kHz narrowband ADCP
COMMUNICATIONS		**(CTDs/XBTs and so on)**	Sippican Mk 12 digital XBT
Inmarsat (type)	JRC model JUE-45A		
MF/HF	Harris 230M		*NEW ENTRY*
	ICOM M800		
VHF	3		
Cellular	Uniden model CP-1100		
Facsimile	Harris/3M model 2110		

Shoals Marine Laboratory

John M Kingsbury

GENERAL

Background information	Certified as a small passenger vessel on ocean routes up to 100 n miles offshore, off Atlantic coast, with small wet/dry laboratory
Built (yard and date)	Gladding-Hearn Shipbuilding
Length overall	14.10 m
Breadth moulded	4.95 m
Max draught	1.50 m
Tonnage (grt)	34.49

PROPULSION

Main engine(s)	Detroit Diesel, 146 hp
Speed (max)	9 kt

BRIDGE NAVIGATION AIDS

Satellite	DGPS
Other ship navigation	Loran C

DECK MACHINERY

Cranes	1 t SWL
A-frame(s)	Yes
Winches	Hydro, 304 m of 'hydrowire'

ACCOMMODATION

Crew	4 berths

SURVEY SYSTEMS

Sensors	Colour fish finder
Echo-sounder (single beam)	Yes
Other sampling	Plankton nets, for both zoo- and phytoplankton; otter trawl; bottom dredge and drag; water sampling bottle
Oceanographic sensors (CTDs/XBTs and so on)	SeaBird CTD

NEW ENTRY

Smithsonian Tropical Research Institute

Urracá

GENERAL COMMENTS

	Glass fibre vessel, built in 1986 in the UK as an underwater photography and archaeological research vessel. Purchased by the Smithsonian Tropical Research Institute in 1994, she was refitted in 1996, and is now based in the Republic of Panama.
Owner	Smithsonian Institution, Washington, DC
Official number	712739; US Coast Guard No CG044444
Built (yard and date)	UK; 1986
Length overall	28.8 m (96 ft)
Breadth moulded	6.60 m (22 ft)
Operational draught	2.70 m (9 ft)

PROPULSION

Main engine(s)	670 hp
Thrusters	Bow: 40 hp
Propellers	1 × CPP
Speed (max)	12.6 kt
Endurance	5,500 n miles at 7 kt; 3,000 n miles at 9.5 kt; 1,500 n miles at 12 kt
Fuel capacity	5,800 gallons
Electrical power	2 × CATSR 4, 55 kW; Northern Lights, 20 kW

BRIDGE NAVIGATION AIDS

Satellite	Trimble Nav-trac; Maguellan Nav 6000
Radar	Decca BridgeMaster E 180; Furuno FR-604D

Urracá (port view)

2001/0097774

Gyrocompass	C-Plath	
Echo sounder	Simrad EC-210	

COMMUNICATIONS

Inmarsat (type)	Trimble Galaxy C model 7001
MF/HF	Icom IC-M 700 PRO; Skanti model 800
VHF	Sailor C 403; Icom IC-M56; 3 × hand-held Icom IC-M15

SAFETY

Workboat/chase boat	2 × Avon RIBs: 4 m with 25 hp engine and a 5 m with 70 hp

HELIDECK

Deck machinery

Cranes	Tico 7,700 lb articulating boom on boat deck (01) with extension

A-frame(s)	capability for work over the stern. 8.7 ft clear width to 5.4 ft above deck, 13.5 ft clear height under sheave, 14,000 lb SWL, 5,000 lb hydraulic lift capacity.
Winches	Dynacon 30 hp electrohydraulic with electro-active level wind and 1,200 m of ⅜ in trawl cable and capable of 3,000 lb continuous and 7,000 lb intermittent line-pull at 200 ft/min at bare drum.

ACCOMMODATION

Crew	5
Scientists/surveyors	9
Scientific spaces	
Multipurpose dry lab	Total: 100 sq ft

Urracá (stern view) *2001*/0097776

Urracá *2001*/0097773

SURVEY SYSTEMS			
Vehicle(s) (ROVs/AUVs and so on)	DOE Phantom 300 XTL	**Oceanographic sensors (CTDs/XBTs and so on)**	General Oceanics, Model 316 CTD (equipped with DO sensor and a Sea Point fluorometer)

NEW ENTRY

Urracá   **2001**/0097775

Southern California Marine Institute

Sea Watch

GENERAL			
Background information	Built as a twin diesel screw commercial sports fishing vessel of broad beam, vee bottom, transom stern design, and plywood glass fibre construction. Modified for oceanographic research by the Hancock Institute for Marine Studies in 1978	**Echo-sounder**	Furuno FE-881
		Other ship navigation	Trimble 100A Loran-C
		COMMUNICATIONS	
		VHF	2 × transceivers
Call sign	WUV 6093	**Cellular**	Phone
Rebuilt (yard and date)	Modified in 1978		
Length overall	19.50 m	**SAFETY**	
Breadth moulded	7.20 m	**Workboat/chase boat**	12 ft Avon inflatable with 15 hp outboard; 17 ft Boston Whaler with 90 hp outboard
Max draught	1.50 m		
Tonnage (grt)	97		
		DECK MACHINERY	
PROPULSION		**Cranes**	Hydrographic davit on port quarter with 2,500 ft of 5/32 in wire rope; lift capacity 400 lb
Main engine(s)	Twin 465 hp (12-71 Detroits) 920 shp		
		A-frame(s)	Stern: max lifting capacity 2,500 lb; 13 ft vertical clearance under block; 8 ft horizontal clearance between the frame; 7 ft horizontal clearance over the stern
Speed (cruising)	10.5 kt		
Endurance	5 days/500 n miles		
Fuel capacity	1,800 gallons		
Electrical power	120/240 VAC, 60 kW, 12/24 VDC, 200 AH battery bank	**Winches**	Main drag aft on main deck with 4,000 ft of 3/8 in IWRC wire rope; lift capacity of 1,800 lb
		ACCOMMODATION	
BRIDGE NAVIGATION AIDS		**Crew**	3 – 5
Satellite	Magnavox MX 100 GPS; Magnavox MX 200 DGPS	**Scientists/surveyors**	40 days/14 nights
Radar	Furuno 48 mile		

NEW ENTRY

Southern California Marine Institute

Yellowfin

GENERAL	
Background information	Built as a long-line and bait boat and modified for oceanographic research by the Ocean Studies Institute in 1987
Call sign	WCW 2778
Rebuilt (yard and date)	Modified in 1987
Length overall	22.80 m
Breadth moulded	7.20 m
Max draught	2.58 m
Tonnage (grt)	109

PROPULSION	
Main engine(s)	Twin 350 hp (8v92 GM Detroits) 720 shp
Speed (cruising)	10 kt
Endurance	10 days/2,000 n miles
Fuel capacity	4,600 gallons
Electrical power	2 × 120/240 VAC, 50 kW, 12 VDC
Fresh water capacity	600 gallons/day; 360 gallons storage

BRIDGE NAVIGATION AIDS	
Satellite	Trimble GPS
Radar	Raytheon 64 mile plotting; R41 raster scan 32 mile
Echo-sounder	Furuno fathometer, 2,000 m
Other ship navigation	Furuno and Raytheon Loran C

COMMUNICATIONS	
MF/HF	One SSB transceiver
VHF	2 × transceivers
Cellular	Phone

SAFETY	
Workboat/chase boat	12 ft Avon inflatable with 15 hp outboard; 17 ft Boston Whaler with 90 hp outboard

DECK MACHINERY	
Cranes	Articulating starboard mid-ship; max lifting capacity 1,000 lb
A-frame(s)	Stern: max lifting capacity 2,500 lb
Winches	Hydrographic: starboard midship with 1,500 m $^5/_{16}$ in wire rope; lift capacity 500 lb at mid-drum; one additional spool of 330 m of eight-conductor $^3/_8$ in electromechanical cable; main drag aft on main deck with 5,000 m of $^7/_{16}$ in torque-balanced galvanized wire rope; lift capacity of 5,000 lb at mid-drum

ACCOMMODATION	
Crew	3 – 5
Scientists/surveyors	40 days/8 nights

NEW ENTRY

Texas A & M University

Gyre

GENERAL	
Owner	US Navy
Official number	TX2980CJ
Classification	American Bureau of Shipping
Built (yard and date)	1973
Length overall	55.0 m
Breadth moulded	11.0 m
Max draught	3.5 m
Tonnage (grt)	292

PROPULSION	
Main engine(s)	Twin diesel Caterpillars Model 398D, 1,700 bhp at 1,100 rpm
Thrusters	Bow: electrohydraulic
Propellers	2 Liaanen variable pitch
Speed (max)	11.5 kt
Speed (cruising)	9.5 kt
Endurance	8,000/21 days (nominal), 35 days (extended), 60 days (emergency)
Fuel capacity	86,000 gallons
Electrical power	Twin diesel Caterpillars, Model 379B 440 V AC, each 300 kVA, 3-phase, 50 Hz
Fresh water capacity	8,600 gallons

BRIDGE NAVIGATION AIDS	
Satellite	Magnavox 200 SATNAV receiver; DGPS
Radar	Yes
Gyrocompass	Yes
Speed log	EM; Doppler
Other ship navigation	Loran C

COMMUNICATIONS	
Inmarsat (type)	Yes
Facsimile	Yes

SAFETY	
Workboat/chase boat	"Avon" semi-rigid inflatable; Zodiac

DECK MACHINERY	
Cranes	2 articulated: stern – 38 ft reach amidships; starboard – 28 ft reach
A-frame(s)	2 U-frames: stern and starboard quarter
Winches	$^5/_{16}$ in CTD/hydro: 2 amidships, 23,000 ft and 30,000 ft. 1 ½ in coring/trawling aft, 30,000 ft
Moonpool(s) – size(s)/ function(s)	24 in

ACCOMMODATION	
Crew	10
Scientists/surveyors	23

SCIENTIFIC SPACES	
Total scientific deck space	181 m²
Oceanographic wet lab	15 m²
Multipurpose dry lab	81 m²

SURVEY SYSTEMS	
Echo-sounder (single beam)	3.5/12 kHz transceivers
Magnetometer	Yes
Corer(s)	Yes
Grab(s)	Yes
Other sampling	Niskin rosette sampler
Oceanographic sensors (CTDs/XBTs and so on)	RDI ADCP 150 kHz; CTDs: Neil Brown Mk III; Seabird SBE 9; Seabird SEACat Profiler XBT salinometers.

UPDATED

University of Alaska, School of Fisheries and Ocean Sciences

Alpha Helix

GENERAL

Comments	Operated as a year-round platform supporting oceanographic research on the open ocean and in Alaska's shelf and coastal waters. Home port: Seward, Alaska
Owner	National Science Foundation
Classification	ABS
Built (yard and date)	1966
Length overall	41.0 m
Breadth moulded	9.44 m
Max draught	4.20 m
Tonnage (grt)	289

PROPULSION

Main engine(s)	Diesel, 825 bhp at 780 rpm
Speed (max)	10.5 kt
Speed (cruising)	9.5 kt
Endurance	6,500 n miles/30 days
Fuel capacity	104 m³
Electrical power	100 kVA, 440 V, 3-phase, 60 Hz
Fresh water capacity	1 m³/day generated

BRIDGE NAVIGATION AIDS

Satellite	GPS
Radar	Yes
Gyrocompass	Yes
Speed log	Yes
Other ship navigation	Loran

DECK MACHINERY

Cranes	Midships hydraulic with extendable boom: SWL 1 t, clearance above deck 9 m, outboard extension 6 m
A-frame(s)	SWL 1 t, clearance above deck 5 m, outboard extension 2 m
Winches	Hydrographic: conducting cable 8,000 m, SWL 1 t. Deep sea: 2,000 m

ACCOMMODATION

Crew	9
Scientists/surveyors	15

SCIENTIFIC SPACES

Total scientific deck space	119 m²
Oceanographic wet lab	7 m²
Multipurpose dry lab	42 m²

SURVEY SYSTEMS

Sensors	
Echo-sounder (single beam)	12 kHz
Oceanographic sensors (CTDs/XBTs and so on)	ADCP

UPDATED

University of Connecticut

Connecticut

GENERAL

Background information	Home port: Marine Sciences & Technology Center, Groton, Connecticut
Built (yard and date)	Washburn and Doughty Associates, Inc, East Boothbay, Maine; launched in July 1998
Length overall	22.95 m
Breadth moulded	7.80 m
Max draught	2.10 m
Tonnage (grt)	94

PROPULSION

Main engine(s)	Caterpillar D3412 DITA, 825 bhp @ 2,100 rpm, 'C' rated
Thrusters	Bow: Schottel SPJ-22 pump jet, 147 hp @ 2,150 rpm input speed, direct driven by a Caterpillar D3116 DITA, 205 hp @ 2,400 rpm; Stern: Schottel SPJ-22 pump jet, 147 hp @ 2,150 rpm driven hydraulically by a Denison M4 SE-185 pump coupled to either generator
Speed (max)	11 kt
Endurance	7 – 10 days
Fuel consumption	35 gallons/h @ 10.2 kt
Electrical power	Two diesel generator sets, Caterpillar D3304 DIT, each rated 105 kW @ 1,800 rpm, 208 VAC,

Connecticut   *2001*/0097768

Connecticut   *2001*/0097767

---

	three phase. Each genset is configured to hydraulically drive the stern thruster
Fresh water capacity	2,400 gallons

BRIDGE NAVIGATION AIDS

Satellite	Northstar GPS
Radar	2 × Furuno 19442
Echo-sounder	Furuno CV/1000/36 colour

COMMUNICATIONS

Inmarsat (type)	Satellite voice and data transmission @ 4,800 bps
MF/HF	SGC SSB radio
VHF	2 × Icom

SAFETY

Workboat/chase boat	Zodiac: 14 ft length, 25 hp outboard

DECK MACHINERY

Cranes	Alaska Marine MCK-623 with self-contained 40 hp electro-hydraulic power pack and controls, 9,700 lb lift capacity at 15 ft; 5,000 lb lift capacity at 23 ft extension
A-frame(s)	Stern: 23,000 lb capacity, dimensions: 18 ft high × 15 ft wide
Winches	Hawbolt HFS-1235P heavy-duty, drum capacity: 1,200 ft of ⅝ in wire; full drum line pull: 10,000 lb;

oceanographic: InterOcean 707-10 electric; 1,000 lb lift capacity; with 600 m of seven-conductor EM cable; trawl: Two Hawbolt SFD-0620 with drum capacity of 2,100 ft of ⅜ in wire, full drum line pull of 3,600 lb. Mounted on focsle deck and fair lead through A-Frame brackets. Starboard winch aligns with side work deck area to double as second oceanographic.; Sea-Mac electric with 1,500 ft of ¼ in single conductor EM cable with a max lift capacity of 300 lb

Transducer well	ADCP well pipe amidships, 20 in diameter

ACCOMMODATION

Crew	Berths for 12 people
Scientists/surveyors	Max: 40 for day cruises

SCIENTIFIC SPACES

Total scientific deck space	625 sq ft
Oceanographic wet lab	100 sq ft
Multipurpose dry lab	100 sq ft

SURVEY SYSTEMS

Positioning	Trimble attitude GPS (heading, pitch, and roll to 0.1° accuracy updated 10 Hz)

NEW ENTRY

University of Hawaii

Moana Wave

GENERAL

Comments	No longer in operation as an oceanographic research vessel. To be replaced by the *Kilo Mona* in 2002.
Owner	US Navy
Classification	American Bureau of Shipping
Built (yard and date)	Halter Marine Corporation in New Orleans, Louisiana; 1973
Rebuilt (yard and date)	1984
Length overall	65.5 m
Breadth moulded	11.25 m
Max draught	4.20 m
Tonnage (grt)	293

PROPULSION

Main engine(s)	2 Caterpillar 398, each BS 850 hp
Thrusters	Bow: electric 150 hp
Propellers	2 – Liaanen variable pitch
Speed (max)	11 kt
Speed (cruising)	10 kt
Endurance	14,000 n miles/50 days
Fuel capacity	128,500 gallons
Fuel consumption	2,000 gallons/day
Electrical power	Caterpillar 379B (2 each) 400 kW, 440 V, 3-phase; auxiliary generator: 75 kW, 440 V, 3-phase
Fresh water capacity	21,000 gallons

BRIDGE NAVIGATION AIDS

Satellite	Trimble GPS receiver with differential receiver
Radar	Furuno, colour, Model FRC 1411 with GD2000 plotter; Furuno, Model FR 2020 Daylight Bright

Gyrocompass	2 Sperry MK 37 Model C
Speed log	Yes
Echo-sounder	FE 880 Model 400-A

COMMUNICATIONS

Inmarsat (type)	JRC Model JUE-45a, satellite communicator
MF/HF	HF-SSB transceivers: Raytheon Ray 152
VHF	Simrad VHF ADF Model TDI 1520; Raytheon Ray 90; VHF Raytheon, 25 W Ray 88

DECK MACHINERY

Cranes	2 Alaskan Marine knuckle booms; 1 on back deck; 1 on 0-1 deck
A-frame(s)	Stern, fixed, rated at 50 t with sheave 27 ft above deck; starboard side, main deck, movable, rated at 10 t (used for CTD work)
Winches	Markey DUS-9 trawling and coring, single drum with 42,000 ft 9/16 in wire; Markey DESH-5 hydrographic with 10,000 m of 0.322 3 wire and slip rings

ACCOMMODATION

Crew	13
Scientists/surveyors	19

SCIENTIFIC SPACES

Total scientific deck space	244 m²
Oceanographic wet lab	99 m²

Multipurpose dry lab	99 m² Computer lab, electronic lab, science lab, darkroom 1,160 sq ft	**SURVEY SYSTEMS** **Multibeam/swath system**	SeaMarc II

UPDATED

University of Maryland
Chesapeake Biology Laboratory

Aquarius

GENERAL
Built (yard and date)	1964
Length overall	19.50 m
Breadth moulded	4.80 m
Max draught	1.65 m
Tonnage (grt)	53

PROPULSION
Main engine(s)	Twin Detroit Diesel 12V71N main, 900 total hp
Speed (cruising)	18 kt
Endurance	500 n miles
Electrical power	One 20 kW, 120/240 VAC, 60 cycle, single phase Onan generator powered by a Cummins 4B3.9 diesel engine

BRIDGE NAVIGATION AIDS
Satellite	Northstar 941XD DGPS
Radar	Raytheon R81
Echo-sounder	Raytheon V850 colour video

COMMUNICATIONS
MF/HF	Raytheon Ray 150 SSB radio
VHF	Raytheon Ray 78; Icom 1C-59m

SAFETY
Lifeboats	8-person Viking inflatable liferaft

DECK MACHINERY
Cranes	Stern boom, port side boom, capacity 2,000 lb
Winches	Hancock Marine 18 in double drum trawl with warping head, each drum has 750 ft of ⁵⁄₁₆ in 6 × 19 stainless steel wire

ACCOMMODATION
Crew	2
Scientists/surveyors	4 (28 day trip)

SCIENTIFIC SPACES
Total scientific deck space	Aft: 300 sq ft
Multipurpose dry lab	100 sq ft

NEW ENTRY

University of Maryland
Chesapeake Biology Laboratory

Orion

GENERAL
Built (yard and date)	1965
Length overall	15.80 m
Breadth moulded	4.00 m
Max draught	1.40 m
Tonnage (grt)	32

PROPULSION
Main engine(s)	Twin Detroit Diesel 8V71N main, 600 total hp
Speed (cruising)	15 kt
Endurance	180 n miles
Electrical power	One 20 kw, 120/240 VAC, 60 cycle, single phase Onan generator powered by a Cummins 4A2.3 diesel engine

BRIDGE NAVIGATION AIDS
Satellite	Northstar 941XD DGPS
Radar	Furuno FR-7111
Echo-sounder	Furuno FCV-582 colour video

COMMUNICATIONS
VHF	Raytheon Ray 90 radio; Icom 1C-59m radio

SAFETY
Lifeboats	8-person Viking inflatable liferaft

DECK MACHINERY
Cranes	Stern boom, port side boom, capacity 1800 lb; starboard boom, capacity 500 lb
Winches	Hancock Marine 18 in double drum trawl with warping head, each drum has 750 ft of ⁵⁄₁₆ in 6 × 19 stainless steel wire

ACCOMMODATION
Crew	2
Scientists/surveyors	4 (18 day trip)

SCIENTIFIC SPACES
Total scientific deck space	Aft: 200 sq ft
Multipurpose dry lab	55 sq ft

NEW ENTRY

University of New Hampshire

Gulf Challenger

GENERAL

Background information	Aluminium research vessel; home port: Portsmouth, New Hampshire
Classification	USCG Subchapter T, Aluminum
Call sign	WBY 6543
Built (yard and date)	Gladding-Hearn Shipbuilding, Somerset, Massachusetts; launched August 10, 1993
Length overall	15.00 m
Breadth moulded	4.80 m
Max draught	1.50 m

PROPULSION

Main engine(s)	Twin Detroit Diesel 8V-92TA-DDECm 600 bhp each at 2, 100 rpm
Speed (max)	22 kt
Speed (cruising)	18 kt
Endurance	3 days
Fuel capacity	1,100 gallons
Electrical power	Northern Lights 8.5 kVA genset, 2,500 W inverter; 12 and 24 VDC, 110/220 VAC
Fresh water capacity	325 gallons

BRIDGE NAVIGATION AIDS

Satellite	GPS: Raystar 398
Radar	Raytheon R41XX; Raytheon R70
Echo sounder	Raytheon V8010 video; Furuno FE881 recorder
Other ship navigation	Loran: Raynav 580; Raytheon infra-red night vision system

COMMUNICATIONS

MF/HF	SSB
VHF	2
Cellular	Yes

SAFETY

Lifeboats	50-person inflatable rescue platform
Workboat/chase boat	14 ft inflatable with 25 hp outboard

DECK MACHINERY

Cranes	2 × 750 lb capacity davits on foredeck
A-frame(s)	Transom-mounted 6000 lb capacity hydraulic U-frame
Winches	Hydraulic deck with winch head, 1,500 lb capacity; hydro 'Wire': 2,000 ft of ¼ in diameter, plasma braid, 2,000 lb SWL

ACCOMMODATION

Crew	2
Scientists/surveyors	7 (43 on day cruises)

SCIENTIFIC SPACES

Total scientific deck space	240 sq ft
Oceanographic wet lab	6 ft × 8 ft

SURVEY SYSTEMS

Oceanographic sensors (CTDs/XBTs and so on)	RDI 600 kHz ADCP; experimental, downward-looking underwater camera in ADCP well; weather station (wind, air temperature, relative humidity, atmospheric pressure)

NEW ENTRY

University of Rhode Island

Endeavour

GENERAL

Owner	National Science Foundation
Official number	RI-59A
Classification	ABS: A1 AMS Research Vessel
Call sign	WCE5063
Built (yard and date)	Peterson Builders Inc, Sturgeon Bay, Wisconsin; 1976
Rebuilt (yard and date)	Mid-life refit 1993
Length overall	57.5 m
Breadth moulded	9.9 m
Max draught	5.55 m
Tonnage (grt)	298

PROPULSION

Main engine(s)	1 GM/EMD diesel, 16-645-e5, 3,050 shp at 900 rpm (max)
Thrusters	J Samuel White Waterjet, 320 hp, DC variable speed, variable direction
Propellers	Single screw, cp, Kort steering nozzle
Speed (max)	14.5 kt
Speed (cruising)	11.0 kt
Endurance	8,000 n miles at 12 kt/30 days
Fuel capacity	56,100 US gallons
Electrical power	2 Caterpillar 300 kW 460 V AC, 3-phase, 60 Hz; 1 Caterpillar 175 kW 460 V AC, 3-phase, 60 Hz
Fresh water capacity	8,200 US gallons

BRIDGE NAVIGATION AIDS

Satellite	Trimble Tasman P-code GPS receiver; Trimble NavTrack DGPS receiver; Magellan 5000 DGPS receiver
Gyrocompass	Sperry Mk 37
Speed log	EDO Doppler
Other ship navigation	Northstar 800/8000 LORAN

ACCOMMODATION

Crew	12
Scientists/surveyors	18

SURVEY SYSTEMS

Echo-sounder (single beam)	12 kHz bathymetric system, UQN hull transducers, Raytheon PTR-105 transceiver
Sub-bottom profiler	EG&G X-Star
Other sampling	MOCNESS biological net sampling system;

Oceanographic sensors (CTDs/XBTs and so on)	BESS 1 Meter2 Multi-Sampler net system with 155 μ and 330 μ nets with CTD sensors Sea Bird SBE-21 sea surface salinograph; Turner model 10AU Flow Through fluorometer; Niskin bottles (1.7, 5, 10 and 30 litre); Niskin Teflon Go-Flo® 10 litre Teflon® lined sample bottles; G-O Sterile water samplers; salinometers (2 Guildline Autosal 6000A units, 1 AGE Minisal);	spectrophotometer (with sipper cell, 10 cm cell, analogue recorder); Sea Bird 9 11+ CTD system; Sea Bird SBE-25 Sealogger CTD profiler; oxygen sensor; Sea Tech fluorometer 3,000 m max depth; Sea Tech transmissometer 5,000 m max depth; RDI 150 kHz acoustic Doppler current profiler

UPDATED

University of Washington, School of Oceanography

Clifford A Barnes

GENERAL
Comments	Intended for use primarily in the sheltered waters of Western Washington and British Columbia.
Owner	National Science Foundation
Length overall	65 ft 5½ in
Breadth moulded	19 ft 7½ in

PROPULSION
Main engine(s)	Caterpillar D379 400 hp
Speed (max)	10 kt
Speed (cruising)	8.5 to 9 kt
Endurance	1,600 n miles/7 days
Fuel capacity	1,920 gallons
Electrical power	450 V AC, 80 kW, 3-phase; 117 V, 1.5 kW, 1-phase

BRIDGE NAVIGATION AIDS
Satellite	Northstar 800 Loran C/8000 GPS
Radar	Furuno FR 8051
Gyrocompass	Sperry SR 220
Speed log	Paddle wheel type
Echo-sounder	Raytheon V-820

COMMUNICATIONS
MF/HF	ICOM M600 SSB
VHF	ICOM M120 VHF-FM; ICOM M127 VHF-FM
Cellular	Cellular phone

SAFETY
Workboat/chase boat	Avon Searider (RHIB), 4 m, 20 hp outboard

DECK MACHINERY
Cranes	Alaska Marine MCT 3-30 (1,600 lb)
Winches	Hydro: Rowe with 1,000 m of 0.25 in wire rope; CTD: Rowe 0.322 in 3 conductor cable; Portable: Two Rowe general purpose; Kolstrand with 0.322 in 3 conductor cable; Kolstrand with level wind, user-supplied wire

ACCOMMODATION
Crew	2
Scientists/surveyors	6

SURVEY SYSTEMS
Positioning	Northstar 951x DGPS
Echo-sounder (single beam)	Simrad EA-501p
Sidescan sonar	Klein 402

UPDATED

Clifford A Barnes (Kathleen Newell, School of Oceanography, University of Washington)   *2001*/0101613

University of Washington, School of Oceanography

Thomas G Thompson

GENERAL

Comments	Also known as AGOR-23
Owner	Office of Naval Research
Built (yard and date)	Halter Marine; delivered 8 July 1991
Length overall	274 ft
Breadth moulded	52.5 ft
Max draught	19 ft

PROPULSION

Main engine(s)	3 generators – 1,500 kW CAT/ KATO
Thrusters	Twin 360° azimuthing stern rated at 3,000 hp each, 1,100 hp water-jet bow
Speed (max)	14.5 kt
Speed (cruising)	13 kt
Endurance	33 days at 14 kt;
Fuel capacity	248,000 gallons
Electrical power	3 service generators – 715 kW CAT/KATO; emergency generator 250 kW CAT/KATO
Fresh water capacity	13,000 gallons

BRIDGE NAVIGATION AIDS

Satellite	Magnavox 1107, 4 channel, 2 receiver with GPS and transit capabilities
Radar	Raytheon Pathfinder/ST KW 16 in S-band with CAS; Raytheon Pathfinder/ST TM 25KW 16 in X-band
Gyrocompass	Dual Sperry MK 37
Speed log	Ocean Data Equipment Corp dual-axis Doppler
Echo-sounder	2 Raytheon RD-500

COMMUNICATIONS

Inmarsat (type)	JRL with PABX, modem, facsimile, and IBM PS/2
MF/HF	Mackay MSR 8050A (1.6-30 MHz) 125 W PEP; Mackay MSR 8050 (2-23 MHz) with MSR 1020 1 kW linear amplifier
VHF	SAILER SP3210
Cellular	Cellular phone

SAFETY

Lifeboats	19 ft rigid inflatable boat
Workboat/chase boat	26 ft Avon SR-8 rigid inflatable boat; 15 ft Achilles inflatable

DECK MACHINERY

Cranes	Telescoping boom: starboard side on top of staging bay, 2 t static load, 2 t in motion. Vertical clearance of 20 ft, outreach 8 ft, inboard 6 ft. 2 Alaska Marine, Model MCS 1565 NO, one each on main deck aft starboard side, and on 01 level port side; capacities: 42,000 lb at 10 ft radius, 3,400 lb at 65 ft; 12,500 lb winch; boom crutches for 2 trawling positions. Hiab FOCO 180 Sea crane on port quarter, main deck, 27 ft reach. Hiab FOCO 180 Sea crane on starboard side, 43 ft reach
A-frame(s)	Stern, 12 t static load, 6 t in motion, vertical clearance 25 ft; outreach 13 ft, inboard 9 ft, inside width 20 ft at base, 16 ft at top
Winches	2 Markey DESH-5, electric with SCR control, 30,000 ft of 0.25 in 3 × 19 torque-balanced wire or 30,000 ft of 0.322 in E-M cable. Markey DESH-9-11WF double-drum electric mounted below deck, 30,000 ft of 0.25 in 3 × 19 torque-balanced wire and 30,000 ft of 0.68 in E-M cable

ACCOMMODATION

Crew	22
Scientists/surveyors	34 plus 2 technicians

SCIENTIFIC SPACES

Total scientific deck space	3,500 sq ft, including 12 × 100 ft contiguous handling area on starboard side
Oceanographic wet lab	235 sq ft

Thomas G Thompson (Kathleen Newell, School of Oceanography, University of Washington)   *2001*/0101612

Multipurpose dry lab	Main lab: 1,730 sq ft; bio/ analytical clean lab: 359 sq ft; electronic/comp lab: 820 sq ft; hydro lab: 700 sq ft	Other sampling	General Oceanics Rosettes (12 and 14); Niskin bottles (1.5, 2.5, 5, 10 and 30 litre)
		Oceanographic sensors (CTDs/XBTs and so on)	SeaBird SBE-9. Seatech Transmissometer (25 cm); Seatech fluorometer; RD Instruments, acoustic Doppler, 150 kHz
SURVEY SYSTEMS			
Positioning	Robertson Shipmate with inputs from GPS and acoustic positioning system; Honeywell R/S 906 (with SBL and LBL)		
		SEISMIC SYSTEMS	
Echo-sounder (single beam)	Simrad EA-501p	Compressor numbers and types	2 LMF VHGD 4622 W15; 300 scfm capacity, 2,000 psi working pressure
Multibeam/swath system	STN-ATLAS Hydrosweep DS		
Sub-bottom profiler	3.5 kHz sub-bottom system using 12 ODEC TR 109 transducers and 2 × 12 kHz bottom profilers using single ODEC TC-12/34 transducers		*VERIFIED*

Virginia Institute of Marine Science

Bay Eagle

GENERAL		**COMMUNICATIONS**	
Background information	Welded aluminium hull (crewboat type)	VHF	2
		Cellular	Telephone
Current operational status	Chesapeake and Delaware Bays; near-coastal waters of the Atlantic Ocean from Atlantic City, New Jersey to Beaufort, North Carolina	**SAFETY**	
		Workboat/chase boat	10 ft inflatable boat, 6 hp outboard
Length overall	19.50 m		
Breadth moulded	5.55 m	**DECK MACHINERY**	
Max draught	1.5 m	Cranes	Mast with two adjustable booms/ boom-mounted hydraulic winches
Tonnage (grt)	64	Winches	Port: 1,800 lb capacity, 16 ft vertical lift, 350 ft of 5/16 in galvanized wire; starboard: 1,000 lb capacity, 16 ft vertical lift, 200 ft of 1/4 in stainless wire
PROPULSION			
Main engine(s)	Twin Detroit Diesel 12V-71N		
Speed (cruising)	15 kt		
Endurance	400 n miles		
Electrical power	20 kW diesel-driven generator; 208/120 VAC three-phase; 12/32 VDC		
		ACCOMMODATION	
		SCIENTIFIC SPACES	
BRIDGE NAVIGATION AIDS		Total scientific deck space	Aft: 280 sq ft; quarterdeck: 280 sq ft
Satellite	Yes		
Radar	Yes	Oceanographic wet lab	50 sq ft
Echo-sounder	Dual-frequency colour video	Multipurpose dry lab	60 sq ft
Other ship navigation	2 × Loran C		*NEW ENTRY*

Virginia Institute of Marine Science

Langley

GENERAL		Endurance	450 n miles
Background information	Glass fibre trawler	Electrical power	20 kW diesel-driven generator; 240 /110 VAC single-phase; 12 VDC
Current operational status	Chesapeake and Delaware Bays; near-coastal waters of the Atlantic Ocean from Atlantic City, New Jersey to Rudee Inlet, Virginia		
		BRIDGE NAVIGATION AIDS	
Length overall	13.20 m	Satellite	Yes
Breadth moulded	4.35 m	Radar	Yes
Max draught	1.8 m	Echo sounder	2 × colour video sounder
Tonnage (grt)	28	Other ship navigation	2 × Loran C
PROPULSION		**COMMUNICATIONS**	
Main engine(s)	Twin Caterpillar 3208 diesels	VHF	Yes
Speed (cruising)	10 kt	Cellular	Telephone

DECK MACHINERY
Cranes

Winches

Mast with two adjustable booms/
boom-mounted hydraulic winches
Port: 1,000 lb capacity, 14 ft
vertical lift, 350 ft of 3/16 in stainless
wire; starboard: 1,000 lb capacity,
14 ft vertical lift, 350 ft of 3/16 in
stainless wire

SCIENTIFIC SPACES
Total scientific deck space
Multipurpose dry lab

Aft: 100 sq ft
162 sq ft

NEW ENTRY

Woods Hole Oceanographic Institution

Asterias

GENERAL
Length overall   46 ft 2 in
Breadth moulded   15 ft 4 in
Max draught   5 ft 2 in

PROPULSION
Main engine(s)   GM 8V-92N 300 horsepower
                              diesel with Twin Disc 514 M
                              Omega Gear (variable slow
                              speeds)
Speed (cruising)   9.5 kt
Endurance   500 n miles or 50 hours
Electrical power   Diesel generator, 15 kW, 230 V
                              AC or 7.5 kW, 115 V AC; main
                              battery banks provide 32 V DC
                              with limited 12 V DC; 2 kW
                              battery-supplied, 120 V AC
                              available

BRIDGE NAVIGATION AIDS
Satellite   Northstar 941XD DGPS receiver
Radar   Furuno
Gyrocompass   Yes
Speed log   Yes
Echo-sounder   Raytheon R246pW; Datamarine

COMMUNICATIONS
MF/HF   Stephens SEA 209 single
                              sideband radio

VHF   2 ICOM M80; hand-held ICOM
Cellular   Motorola

SAFETY
Workboat/chase boat   Avon 8-person inflatable raft

DECK MACHINERY
Cranes   Boom rigged for 2,000 lb
                              maximum working load, lifting
                              clearance 16 ft over stern and
                              20 ft over starboard side
Winches   Hathaway special hydraulic winch
                              with 3-section drum, line pull
                              2,000 lb at 35 rpm, with 400 ft of
                              3/8 in trawl wire, 2,500 ft of 5/32 in
                              hydro wire or 900 ft of 3/8 in
                              electromechanical cable

ACCOMMODATION
Crew   4 berths

SCIENTIFIC SPACES
Total scientific deck space   144 sq ft
Multipurpose dry lab   72 sq ft

VERIFIED

Asterias   *2000*/0093782

Woods Hole Oceanographic Institution

Atlantis

GENERAL

Owner	US Navy – Office of Naval Research
Call sign	KAQP
Built (yard and date)	1997
Length overall	83.5 m
Breadth moulded	16.0 m
Max draught	5.18 m
Tonnage (grt)	3,200

PROPULSION

Main engine(s)	Diesel-electric, azimuthing stern thrusters
Thrusters	Bow: azimuthing jet 1,180 shp
Speed (max)	15 kt
Speed (cruising)	12 kt
Endurance	17,280 n miles/60 days
Fuel capacity	296,470 gallons
Electrical power	3 × 715 kW 600 V AC

BRIDGE NAVIGATION AIDS

Satellite	Trimble Tasman P-Code GPS; Northstar 941 XD differential GPS; Magnavox 1107 GPS
Radar	2 Sperry Marine RASCAR JA23-5123C
Speed log	ODEC Doppler
Echo-sounder	Raytheon RD-500

COMMUNICATIONS

Inmarsat (type)	"A": Magnavox MX 2400; "B": Nera Saturn B
MF/HF	Mackey MRU 35 MT 1,000 W voice and SITOR; Sperry GMDSS station with Standard C, HF/MF transceiver, SITOR
VHF	2 Sperry digital selective calling radios
Facsimile	Alden weather

SAFETY

Workboat/chase boat	2 Avon 5.4 m hard-bottom inflatable boats with outboard motors

DECK MACHINERY

Cranes	2 Alaska, Model MCS 1565-NO; location: main deck, starboard quarter and 01 deck, midship section, port side; fitted with one fixed boom (main shipper) and two extendible booms (crowds), mounted on a tubular pedestal which raises all moving components well off the deck with an 8 ft vertical clearance; working reach 6 to 70 ft over a full 360° arc; lift capacity 42,000 lb. 2 small portable; working reach 4 to 26 ft over a full 360° arc; lift capacity 2,205 lb.
Winches	Markey DESH-5; electric, AC-SCR/DC, 75 hp; rated line pull: 7,000 lb mid-scope; average

Atlantis (Woods Hole Oceanographic Institute)   **2000**/0093784

working speed: 80 m/min; wire capacity: 10,000 m of 0.322 in E-M cable, 9,150 m of ¼ in wire rope; location: starboard side midships, 02 level.

Markey DUTW-9-11; wire capacity: 10,000 m of 0.690 in fibre optic cable; 10,000 m of 0.680 in EM cable; 15,000 m of ⁹⁄₁₆ in 3 × 19 torque-balanced wire rope

ACCOMMODATION

Crew	23
Scientists/surveyors	24 plus 13 technicians

SCIENTIFIC SPACES

Oceanographic wet lab	Wet lab: 200 sq ft
Multipurpose dry lab	Main lab: 1,600 sq ft; bio/analytical lab: 375 sq ft; hydro lab: 650 sq ft; electronics/computer lab: 750 sq ft

SURVEY SYSTEMS

Positioning	Nautronix RS906 ultrashort/long baseline acoustic navigation system with pingers and tracking transponders
Sensors	
Multibeam/swath system	Seabeam 2112A
Sub-bottom profiler	ODEC dual-frequency (12/33 kHz) bottom/sub-bottom profiler/PTR-105 transceiver; TC 12/34 and TR-109 transducers
Oceanographic sensors (CTDs/XBTs and so on)	RDI VM-150-18 hp 150 kHz Acoustic Doppler Current Profiler (ADCP); XBT: Sippican MK 12 with 386 PC

UPDATED

Atlantis – starboard side view (Woods Hole Oceanographic Institute)   **2000**/0093783

Woods Hole Oceanographic Institution

Knorr

GENERAL

Owner	US Navy – Office of Naval Research
Call sign	KCEJ
Built (yard and date)	1969
Rebuilt (yard and date)	Mid-life overhaul 1989-91
Length overall	85.06 m
Breadth moulded	14.02 m
Max draught	5.03 m
Tonnage (grt)	2,518

PROPULSION

Main engine(s)	Twin Lips diesel-electric, azimuthing stern thrusters
Thrusters	Bow: Lips retractable azimuthing jet 900 shp
Speed (max)	14.5 kt
Speed (cruising)	12 kt
Endurance	12,000 n miles/60 days
Fuel capacity	160,500 gallons

BRIDGE NAVIGATION AIDS

Satellite	2 Magnavox MX200D 5-channel GPS with differential capability; Trimble Tasman P(Y)-P-code GPS
Radar	2 Raytheon ST (3 cm) ARPA; Raytheon ST (10 cm) ARPA; Furuno 2400 (3 cm)
Gyrocompass	2 Sperry MK-37
Speed log	EDO MRQ-4015D-250 kHz dual-axis Doppler
Echo-sounder	Furuno FE-880 50 kHz

COMMUNICATIONS

Inmarsat (type)	2 Magnavox MX-2400 Standard "A"; MTI MDT-6000 Standard "C"
MF/HF	Mackay MRU-35 high-frequency SITOR; Stephens SEA-222; Mackay MRU-21 medium frequency; Mackay MRU-22 high frequency
VHF	Raytheon Ray-55; 2 Standard Eclipse Ten Icom M-11 hand-held; Ross DSC 500
Facsimile	Furuno FAX-208A

SAFETY

Workboat/chase boat	17.9 ft Avon rigid inflatable work boat powered by an 80 hp outboard motor

DECK MACHINERY

Cranes	2 Allied Marine, Model TB 60-70; location: trawl – starboard quarter; utility – 01 deck, midship section and 01 deck, midship section, port side; fitted with one fixed boom (main shipper) and two extendible booms (crowds), mounted on a tubular pedestal which raises all moving components well off the deck with an 8 ft vertical clearance; working reach 6 to 70 ft over a full 360° arc; lift capacity 8,000 to 60,000 lb.

Winches	Hiab portable; working reach 4 to 26 ft over a full 360° arc; lift capacity 5,600 to 10,700 lb 2 hydrographic: Markey DESH-5; electric, AC-SCR/DC, 75 hp; rated line pull: 10,300 lb bare drum, 5,926 lb at 102 m/min at mid-scope, 4,547 lb at 133 m/min at full drum; average working speed: 80 m/min; wire capacity: 10,000 m of 0.322 in E-M cable, 9,200 m of wire rope; location: starboard side midships. Trawl: Northern Line #3155-ETRW; power: electric, AC-SCR/DC, 150 hp; rated line pull: 24,000 lb bare drum, 5,200 lb full drum; average working speed: 100 m/min; wire capacity: 9,200 m of 9/16 in 3 × 19 wire rope

ACCOMMODATION

Crew	22
Scientists/surveyors	32 plus 2 technicians

SCIENTIFIC SPACES

Oceanographic wet lab	Wet lab: 150 sq ft
Multipurpose dry lab	Main lab: 1,310 sq ft; analytical lab: 240 sq ft; upper lab: 450 sq ft; lower lab: 250 sq ft

SURVEY SYSTEMS

Multibeam/swath system	SeaBeam 2112
Sub-bottom profiler	Raytheon LSR-1807M recorder; PTR-105 B transceiver; CESP-III correlator; 10 cycle programmer; EDO 323 B 12 kHz transducer; array of 12 × 3.5 kHz transducers
Oceanographic sensors (CTDs/XBTs and so on)	RDI 150 kHz Acoustic Doppler Current Profiler (ADCP); IMET meteorological sensor system: 2 XBT: Sippican MK 12 with 386 PC

UPDATED

Knorr (Thomas Kleindist, Woods Hole Oceanographic Institute)   **2000**/0093781

Woods Hole Oceanographic Institution

Oceanus

GENERAL

Owner	National Science Foundation	Built (yard and date)	1975
Call sign	WXAQ	Rebuilt (yard and date)	Mid-life overhaul 1994
		Length overall	53.94 m

Breadth moulded	10.05 m
Max draught	5.18 m
Tonnage (grt)	298

PROPULSION

Main engine(s)	1 EMD diesel, 2,875 shp
Thrusters	Bow: White Gill 350 hp trainable
Propellers	Single screw, cp, Kort steering nozzle
Speed (max)	14 kt
Speed (cruising)	11 kt
Endurance	7,000 n miles/30 days
Fuel capacity	48,000 gallons
Electrical power	2 × 300 kW, 480 V AC, 60 Hz, 3-phase

BRIDGE NAVIGATION AIDS

Satellite	Northstar 941X GPS receiver (with DGPS capability); Northstar 800 GPS receiver; Trimble Tasman P(Y)-P-Code GPS receiver
Radar	Raytheon ST (3 cm) ARPA; Raytheon ST (10 cm) ARPA
Gyrocompass	2 Sperry MK-37
Speed log	Sperry Marine SRD-301 Doppler
Echo-sounder	Furuno FE-880 50 kHz

COMMUNICATIONS

Inmarsat (type)	Japan Radio Corp Model JUE-45 MKII Standard "A"; Trimble Galaxy Standard "C"
MF/HF	Mackay MRU-35 high-frequency SITOR; Stephens SEA-222
VHF	Standard Omni; 2 Ross DSC 500
Facsimile	Furuno+ 208A

SAFETY

Workboat/chase boat	15.5 ft Avon inflatable work boat powered by a 40 hp outboard motor

DECK MACHINERY

Cranes	Allied Marine Model TB 60-65 hydraulic, fitted with one fixed boom (main shipper) and two extendible booms (crowds), working reach 10 to 65 ft over a full 360° arc; lift capacity 6,890 to 40,000 lb. Hiab portable; working reach 4 to 26 ft over a full 360° arc; lift capacity 5,600 to 10,700 lb
A-frame(s)	Stern: inside horizontal clearance: 2.7 m (9 ft); maximum vertical clearance: 4.2 m (14 ft); maximum inboard reach: 1.8 m (6 ft); maximum outboard reach: 2.4 m (8 ft); SWL: 26,000 lb

ACCOMMODATION

Crew	12
Scientists/surveyors	14 plus 1 technician

SCIENTIFIC SPACES

Oceanographic wet lab	Wet lab: 240 sq ft
Multipurpose dry lab	Main lab: 800 sq ft; top lab: 350 sq ft

SURVEY SYSTEMS

Sub-bottom profiler	Raytheon LSR-1807M recorder ; PTR-105 B transceiver; 10 cycle programmer; EDO 323 B 12 kHz transducer; array of four 3.5 kHz transducers
Oceanographic sensors (CTDs/XBTs and so on)	RDI 150 or 300 kHz Acoustic Doppler Current Profiler (ADCP); IMET meteorological sensor system:; 2 XBT: Sippican MK 12 with 386 PC

UPDATED

Oceanus (Chris Grimes, Woods Hole Oceanographic Institute)   *2000*/0093780

URUGUAY

Uruguay Navy

Comandante Pedro Campbell

GENERAL

Former names	Former US fleet minesweeper *Chickadee,* MSF 59
Official number	24 (ex-4, ex-MS31, ex-MSF1)
Built (yard and date)	Defoe B & M Works; launched 20 July 1942
Length overall	67.50 m
Breadth moulded	9.80 m
Max draught	3.30 m

PROPULSION

Main engine(s)	Diesel-electric; 4 Alco 539 diesels; 3,532 hp (2.63 MW); 4 generators

Propellers	2 shafts
Speed (max)	18.0 kt
Speed (cruising)	10.0 kt
Endurance	4,300 n miles at 10 kt

ACCOMMODATION

Crew	105

UPDATED

Comandante Pedro Campbell

2000/0084224

VENEZUELA

Coordinating Office of Hydrography & Navigation (OCHINA)

Punta Brava

GENERAL BACKGROUND

A multipurpose ship for oceanography, marine resource evaluation, geophysical and biological research. Developed from the Spanish 'Malaspina' class.

Official number	BO-11
Built (yard and date)	Bazan, Cartagena; commissioned 14 March 1991
Length overall	61.70 m
Breadth moulded	11.90 m
Max draught	3.70 m

PROPULSION

Main engine(s)	2 Bazan-MAN 7L20/27 diesels; 2,500 hp(m) (1.84 MW)
Thrusters	Bow
Propellers	2 shafts
Speed (cruising)	13.0 kt
Endurance	8,000 n miles at 13.0 kt

BRIDGE NAVIGATION AIDS

Radar	ARPA; I-band.

SAFETY

Workboat/chase boat	2 survey launches

ACCOMMODATION

Crew	49
Scientists/surveyors	15

SURVEY SYSTEMS

Multibeam/swath system	Sea Beam 1050D

UPDATED

Punta Brava

2000/0084239

VIETNAM

Research Institute of Marine Products

Bien Dong

GENERAL

Owner	Ministry of Fisheries
Built (yard and date)	1976
Length overall	47.50 m
Breadth moulded	10.30 m
Max draught	4.30 m
Tonnage (grt)	495

PROPULSION

Main engine(s)	1 diesel, 1,500 hp
Speed (max)	14.0 kt

BRIDGE NAVIGATION AIDS

Radar	Yes
Gyrocompass	Yes
Speed log	Yes
Echo-sounder	Yes

UPDATED

SEISMIC EXPLORATION VESSELS

AZERBAIJAN

Caspian Geophysical

Baki

GENERAL		**SEISMIC SYSTEMS**	
Owner	Caspian Geophysical – joint venture between Schlumberger and the State Oil Company of Azerbaijan (SOCAR)	Number of airguns	2 arrays
		Size of airguns	65,876 cm³ each
		Streamer numbers and lengths per number	3 × 480 channels
Built (yard and date)	1994		*VERIFIED*
Length overall	81.85 m		
Breadth moulded	14.80 m		

Caspian Geophysical

Gilavar

GENERAL		**SEISMIC SYSTEMS**	
Former names	*Geco Gamma*	Number of airguns	2 arrays
Owner	Caspian Geophysical – joint venture between Schlumberger and the State Oil Company of Azerbaijan (SOCAR)	Size of airguns	65,826 cm³ each
		Streamer numbers and lengths per number	3 × 400 channels, 1 × 560 channels
Built (yard and date)	1994		*UPDATED*
Length overall	84.90 m		
Breadth moulded	15.60 m		

Gilavar

2001/0110473

Kasporneftegeophyzrazdedka (KMNG)

Geofizik 1

GENERAL		**Rebuilt (yard and date)**	1994
Built (yard and date)	1989	Length overall	55.78 m

VERIFIED

Kasporneftegeophyzrazdedka (KMNG)

Geofizik 2

GENERAL		**Rebuilt (yard and date)**	1994
Built (yard and date)	1989	Length overall	55.78 m

VERIFIED

Kasporneftegeophyzrazdedka (KMNG)

Geofizik 3

GENERAL		**Rebuilt (yard and date)**	1994
Built (yard and date)	1989	Length overall	55.78 m

VERIFIED

CANADA

Continental Holdings Ltd

Calgary

GENERAL		**SEISMIC SYSTEMS**	
Owner	Continental Holdings	Size of airguns	$1 \times 50,000 \text{ cm}^3$
Built (yard and date)	1994	Streamer numbers and	1×480 channels
Length overall	56.00 m	lengths per number	
Breadth moulded	14.00 m		

VERIFIED

Continental Holdings Ltd

Houston

GENERAL		**SEISMIC SYSTEMS**	
Owner	Continental Holdings	Size of airguns	$2 \times 60,000 \text{ cm}^3$
Built (yard and date)	1998	Streamer numbers and	4×720 channels
Length overall	66.00 m	lengths per number	
Breadth moulded	17.00 m		

VERIFIED

Geophysical Service International (GSI)

Admiral

GENERAL		**HELIDECK**	
		Size, aircraft capacity	Yes
Former names	*Geco Alpha, Austral Horizon*		
Current operational status	East coast of Canada	**ACCOMMODATION**	
Owner	Geophysical Service International, Canada	Charterers	Total accommodation for 40
Built (yard and date)	1998	**SEISMIC SYSTEMS**	
Length overall	91.00 m	Energy source (type and manufacturer)	Airguns
Breadth moulded	15.00 m		
Tonnage (grt)	2,777	Number of airguns	2 arrays
		Size of airguns	$64,400 \text{ cm}^3$ each
PROPULSION		Streamer numbers and	4
Speed (cruising)	12 kt	lengths per number	

UPDATED

CHINA, PEOPLE'S REPUBLIC

China Ministry of Geology

Feng DU4

GENERAL		**SEISMIC SYSTEMS**	
Owner	China Ministry of Geology	Number of airguns	1 array

VERIFIED

China Ministry of Geology

Feng DU6

GENERAL		**SEISMIC SYSTEMS**	
Owner	China Ministry of Geology	Number of airguns	1 array

VERIFIED

China Ministry of Geology

Feng DU7

GENERAL		**SEISMIC SYSTEMS**	
Owner	China Ministry of Geology	Number of airguns	1 array

VERIFIED

China Offshore Oil Geophysical Corporation (COOGC)

Bin Hai 501

GENERAL		**SEISMIC SYSTEMS**	
Owner	China Offshore Oil Geophysical Corporation (COOGC)	Energy source (type and manufacturer)	Sleeve
Length overall	78.70 m	Compressor numbers and types	2,250 psi
Breadth moulded	16.00 m	Streamer type	Digital
Operational draught	5.20 m	Streamer numbers and lengths per number	2 at 6,000 m; 4 at 4,500 m; 6 at 3,000 m
Tonnage (grt)	3,787	Acquisition system	RS-6000
PROPULSION		Recording system	Titan 1000
Speed (cruising)	15 kt		
SURVEY SYSTEMS			
Positioning	Wisdom		

NEW ENTRY

China Offshore Oil Geophysical Corporation (COOGC)

Bin Hai 504

GENERAL		**SEISMIC SYSTEMS**	
Owner	China Offshore Oil Geophysical Corporation (COOGC)	Size of airguns	420 cm^3
Built (yard and date)	1984	Streamer numbers and lengths per number	2 × 140 channels
Length overall	74.98 m		
Breadth moulded	14.94 m		

NEW ENTRY

China Offshore Oil Geophysical Corporation (COOGC)

Bin Hai 511

GENERAL		Built (yard and date)	1979
Owner	China Offshore Oil Geophysical Corporation (COOGC)	Length overall	78.03 m
		Breadth moulded	13.41 m

Max draught	4.61 m	Size of airguns	6,000 cu in
Operational draught	3.18 m	Compressor numbers and types	2,000 psi
Tonnage (grt)	1,257		
		Streamer type	Digital
PROPULSION		Streamer numbers and lengths per number	3 × 720 channels
Speed (cruising)	15.8 kt		
		Acquisition system	SGI Power Challenge
SURVEY SYSTEMS		Recording system	Syntrak-480
Positioning	Seisnet		

NEW ENTRY

SEISMIC SYSTEMS	
Energy source (type and manufacturer)	Airguns

China Offshore Oil Geophysical Corporation (COOGC)

Bin Hai 512

GENERAL		**SEISMIC SYSTEMS**	
Owner	China Offshore Oil Geophysical Corporation (COOGC)	Energy source (type and manufacturer)	Sleeve
Built (yard and date)	1979	Size of airguns	
Length overall	78.94 m	Compressor numbers and types	2,000 psi
Breadth moulded	13.41 m		
Max draught	4.61 m	Streamer type	Digital
Operational draught	3.18 m	Streamer numbers and lengths per number	2 × 480 channels; 2 at 4,500 m
		Acquisition system	Micromax
PROPULSION		Recording system	Titan 1000
Speed (cruising)	15.8 kt		

SURVEY SYSTEMS	
Positioning	MCS

NEW ENTRY

China Offshore Oil Geophysical Corporation (COOGC)

Bin Hai 514

GENERAL		**SEISMIC SYSTEMS**	
Owner	China Offshore Oil Geophysical Corporation (COOGC)	Size of airguns	420 cm³
		Streamer numbers and lengths per number	2 × 120 channels
Built (yard and date)	1986		
Length overall	54.86 m		
Breadth moulded	11.58 m		

NEW ENTRY

China Offshore Oil Geophysical Corporation (COOGC)

Bin Hai 518

GENERAL		**SEISMIC SYSTEMS**	
Owner	China Offshore Oil Geophysical Corporation (COOGC)	Size of airguns	2,040 cu in
		Streamer numbers and lengths per number	240 channels
Built (yard and date)	1995		
Length overall	49.59 m		
Breadth moulded	12.59 m		

NEW ENTRY

China Offshore Oil Geophysical Corporation (COOGC)

Nan Hai/502

GENERAL		**SEISMIC SYSTEMS**	
Owner	China Offshore Oil Geophysical Corporation (COOGC)	Size of airguns	3,660 cu in
		Streamer numbers and lengths per number	336 channels
Built (yard and date)	1980		
Length overall	65.84 m		
Breadth moulded	11.28 m		

NEW ENTRY

China Offshore Oil Geophysical Corporation (COOGC)

Orient Pearl

GENERAL

Owner	China Offshore Oil Geophysical Corporation (COOGC)
Built (yard and date)	1994
Length overall	78.64 m
Breadth moulded	16.15 m

SEISMIC SYSTEMS

Size of airguns	2 × 3,660 cu in
Streamer numbers and lengths per number	4 × 480 channels

NEW ENTRY

China Offshore Oil Geophysical Corporation (COOGC)

Party No 2335

GENERAL

Owner	China Offshore Oil Geophysical Corporation (COOGC)
Built (yard and date)	1995
Length overall	57.50 m
Breadth moulded	11.60 m
Max draught	5.60 m
Operational draught	3.80 m
Tonnage (grt)	897.5

PROPULSION

Speed (max)	12.5 kt
Speed (cruising)	9 kt

SURVEY SYSTEMS

Positioning	Gesnav

SEISMIC SYSTEMS

Energy source (type and manufacturer)	Sleeve
Size of airguns	4,075 cu in
Compressor numbers and types	2,000 psi
Streamer type	Digital
Streamer numbers and lengths per number	960 channels
Acquisition system	Grisys
Recording system	Syntrak-480

NEW ENTRY

FRANCE

CGG

CGG Alize

GENERAL

Owner	Sismique, SA
Port of reg/flag	French
Classification	Deepsea, ICE III, AUT, DEP
Built (yard and date)	Chantiers de l'Atlantique, 1999
Length overall	100.00 m
Breadth moulded	29.00 m

Max draught	7.55 m
Tonnage (grt)	11,407 displacement UMS

PROPULSION

Main engine(s)	Diesel-electric. 19,000 kW – 4 Wartsila
Thrusters	Bow 650 kW

CGG Alize　　　　　　　　　　　　　　　　　　　　　　*2001*/0109836

Propellers	Twin fixed-pitch	**Lifesaving equipment**	Liferafts: 4 × 25 persons, 2 × 12 persons, 1 × 6 persons
Speed (cruising)	14.50 kt		
Fuel capacity	HFO: 3,200 m³; DO: 1,100 m³	**HELIDECK**	
Fresh water capacity	230 m³	**Size, aircraft capacity**	CAA-approved for Sikorsky S61N

BRIDGE NAVIGATION AIDS

ACCOMMODATION

Satellite	2 Inmarsat B Saturn class; 1 DGPS: DSNS NR 51 Mk III; 1 GPS: Koden KGP 912	**Charterers**	Total accommodation for 62
Radar	2 × Furuno Raserscan ARPA F.A.R.	**SURVEY SYSTEMS**	
Gyrocompass	Plath GMC Navigat XMK1	**Positioning**	Onboard: GIN 2000; streamer and source: DigiCourse; RGPS on source; Sonardyne SIPS; laser range/bearing; tailbuoys: DSNP
Speed log	Furuno DS50		
Echo-sounder	Skipper GDS 101		
Other ship navigation	Robtrack system: Kongsberg SJS 500 + AP9 Mk III autopilot		

SEISMIC SYSTEMS

		Energy source (type and manufacturer)	Sodera G-guns
COMMUNICATIONS		**Number of airguns**	Up to 12 per sub-array
Inmarsat (type)	2 × B Saturn class	**Size of airguns**	Combination of 1,070 cu in, 1,320 cu in and/or 1,640 cu in sub-array
MF/HF	Sailor		
VHF	Sailor	**Compressor numbers and types**	3 × LMF
Facsimile	Weather fax: 1 FX 220 JMC; Navtex: 1 NT 900 JMC		
		Total capacity	1,600 cu ft/min at 2,000 psi
		Streamer numbers and lengths per number	16, total length 100 km
SAFETY			
Lifeboats	1 × 62 persons	**Recording system**	Syntrak 960-24, 16 × 960 channels + 48 auxiliaries at 2 ms sample rate
Workboat/chase boat	UFAS 'Seisworker' Seabear + Fassmer FRB 675 waterjet 170 hp		

UPDATED

CGG Alize

2001/0109835

CGG

CGG Amadeus

GENERAL		**Operational draught**	6.20 m
Former names	*Aker Amadeus*	**Tonnage (grt)**	Displacement 5,600
Owner	CGG, France		
Port of reg/flag	Oslo/Norwegian/NIS	**PROPULSION**	
Classification	DnV + 1A1, E0, Helideck	**Main engine(s)**	3 × Wartsila 9L32, 4,050 kW
Call sign	LAMF5	**Thrusters**	Bow: Ulstein 423 kW
Built (yard and date)	Aker Finnyards, 1999	**Propellers**	2 × Ulstein Compass, 2,500 kW
Length overall	84.00 m	**Speed (cruising)**	13.50 kt
Breadth moulded	18.50 m	**Endurance**	48 days

Fuel capacity	1,750 m³	**SURVEY SYSTEMS**	
Electrical power	3 × Leroy Somer 4,860 kW generators	Positioning	Concept Systems Spectra INS, Sprint processing. Fugro-Geoteam Starfix-MN8; Fugro-Geoteam, Starfix-Spot
			In sea positioning: DigiCourse, 5011 Compass birds; DigiCourse, DigiRange acoustics; Fugro-Geoteam, RGPS Geo/Gun track III (streamer and source)
BRIDGE NAVIGATION AIDS			
Satellite	Trimble NT200D		
Radar	Norcontrol 1029, ARPA, 10 cm; Norcontrol, 1029, ARPA, 3 cm		
Gyrocompass	C-Plath Navigat X Mk I	Echo-sounder (single beam)	Simrad EA 500, 18/38/200 kHz
Echo-sounder	Skipper GDS 101		
Other ship navigation	Norcontrol, AP2000 Mk III autopilot; heading/position/attitude: Seatex, SeaPath 200, GPS system	**SEISMIC SYSTEMS**	
		Energy source (type and manufacturer)	Sodera G-gun (automatic shut-off)
		Number of airguns	Up to 16 guns/sub-array, 2,000-3,000 psi operating pressure
COMMUNICATIONS		Compressor numbers and types	3 × LMF 1,660 cu ft/min
Inmarsat (type)	'B', Norsat 'C'; data transfer up to 512 kb/s vessel to shore	Total capacity	2,000 psi
Facsimile	JRC JAX-9 weather fax	Streamer manufacturer	Syntron
		Streamer type	Syntrak RDA II O (optical)
SAFETY		Streamer numbers and lengths per number	Up to 8; group length multiples of 6.26 m, up to 960 groups per streamer 2 ms; streamer length up to 8,000 m; Benthos Geopoint hydrophones Syntron, 960/24 MSTS
Lifeboats	Norsafe Mathilde, 50-person lifeboat; 4 × Viking 25-person liferafts		
Workboat/chase boat	Norpower 25; Norsafe Magnum MOB boat		
		Acquisition system	Syntron, 960/24 MSTS
HELIDECK		Recording system	Syntron, MSRS; 32 × IBM Power 3 CPU computers for onboard processing
Size, aircraft capacity	CAA, Super Puma Mk II, 19.50 m; Seatex HMS-100		
DECK MACHINERY			*UPDATED*
Winches	Odim Spectrum with automatic spooling		
ACCOMMODATION			
Charterers	Total accommodation for 50		

CGG

CGG Fohn

GENERAL		Streamer numbers and lengths per number	6 × 7,200 m
Length overall	84.50 m		
Breadth moulded	18.00 m	Recording system	Syntrak 480
SURVEY SYSTEMS			*UPDATED*
Positioning	CGG's GPS-ADV; CGG's integrated nav system GIN 2000		
SEISMIC SYSTEMS			
Energy source (type and manufacturer)	G-gun		

CGG

CGG Harmattan

		Streamer numbers and lengths per number	6 × 7,200 m
GENERAL		Recording system	Syntrak 480
Length overall	96.50 m		
Breadth moulded	18.00 m		*UPDATED*
SURVEY SYSTEMS			
Positioning	CGG's GPS-ADV; CGG's integrated nav system GIN 2000		
SEISMIC SYSTEMS			
Energy source (type and manufacturer)	Sleeve-gun or G-gun		
Number of airguns	Combination of 1,020 cu in and 1,000 cu in sub-arrays		

CGG

CGG Mistral

GENERAL

Length overall	94.00 m
Breadth moulded	15.60 m

Streamer numbers and lengths per number	6 × 7,200 m
Recording system	Syntrak 480

SURVEY SYSTEMS

Positioning	CGG's GPS-ADV; CGG's integrated nav system GIN 2000

UPDATED

SEISMIC SYSTEMS

Energy source (type and manufacturer)	Sleeve-gun or G-gun
Number of airguns	Combination of 1,020 cu in and 1,000 cu in sub-array

CGG Mistral

2001/0109834

CGG

CGG Symphony

GENERAL

Former names	*Atlantic Horizon, Aker Symphony*
Owner	Aker Geo Seismic AS
Port of reg/flag	Nassau/Bahamas

Classification	DnV + 1A1, EO, HELDK SH
Call sign	C6QB9
Built (yard and date)	Cammell Laird, UK, 1998
Length overall	121.00 m

CGG Symphony

2001/0109833

Breadth moulded	23.00 m	**Workboat/chase boat**	UFAS Seabear 750; Norsafe Magnum MOB boat
Operational draught	7.20 m		
Tonnage (grt)	Displacement 10,043	**HELIDECK**	
		Size, aircraft capacity	CAA, Sikorsky S-61, 23 m
PROPULSION			
Main engine(s)	2 × Wärtsilä 9R32 low Nox, 3,690 kW	**DECK MACHINERY**	
		Winches	Odim with automatic spooling
Thrusters	Bow: Ulstein 800 kW; 2 × Ulstein retractable compass, 1,500 kW		
		ACCOMMODATION	
Speed (cruising)	16 kt	**Charterers**	Total accommodation for 60
Endurance	Unlimited, 100 days between offshore refuelling		
		SURVEY SYSTEMS	
Fuel capacity	3,500 m³	**Positioning**	Fugro-Geoteam Starfix-MN8; Fugro-Geoteam Starfix-Spot; Spectra INS; Sprint processing; DigiCourse 5011 compass birds; DigiCourse DigiRange acoustics
BRIDGE NAVIGATION AIDS			
Satellite	Leica MX4000 DGPS		
Radar	Raytheon Pathfinder ST Mk II, X-band ARPA		
	Raytheon Pathfinder ST Mk II, S-band ARPA	**SEISMIC SYSTEMS**	
Gyrocompass	Anschutz STD 20GM; Robertson SKR82	**Energy source (type and manufacturer)**	Sodera G-gun
Echo-sounder	Odom Echotrac DF3200 Mk 2; Skipper, GDS 101	**Number of airguns**	Up to 10 per sub-array
		Size of airguns	2,000 to 3,000 psi
Other ship navigation	Robertson AP9 Mk III autopilot	**Compressor numbers and types**	3 × LMF
		Total capacity	1,600 cu ft/min at 2,000 psi
COMMUNICATIONS		**Streamer manufacturer**	I/O
Inmarsat (type)	Norsat C, B	**Streamer type**	Digital MSX
Facsimile	Furuno 207 d-fax weather	**Streamer numbers and lengths per number**	Up to 10, 8,000 m
		Recording system	I/O System MSX
SAFETY			
Lifeboats	2 × 70 persons TEMPSC lifeboats; 6 × 25 persons liferafts + back deck Jon-Buoy		*UPDATED*

INDIA

Oil & Natural Gas Commission

Sagar Sandhavi

GENERAL		**Number of airguns**	3 arrays
Built (yard and date)	1986	**Size of airguns**	1,000 cm³ each
Length overall	70.20 m		
Breadth moulded	15.00 m		*VERIFIED*
SEISMIC SYSTEMS			
Energy source (type and manufacturer)	Airguns		

ITALY

OGS Italy

OGS Explorer

GENERAL		**SEISMIC SYSTEMS**	
Built (yard and date)	1997	**Energy source (type and manufacturer)**	Sleeve airgun
Length overall	71.90 m		
Breadth moulded	12.80 m		*VERIFIED*

MALAYSIA

TL Geohydrographics

Teknik Glora

GENERAL

Built (yard and date)	1996
Length overall	64.91 m
Breadth moulded	10.10 m

SEISMIC SYSTEMS

Energy source (type and manufacturer)	Airguns

Number of airguns	1 array
Size of airguns	160 cu in
Streamer numbers and lengths per number	1 × 600 m

VERIFIED

TL Geohydrographics

Teknik Kembara

GENERAL

Built (yard and date)	1993
Length overall	56.40 m
Breadth moulded	12.20 m

SEISMIC SYSTEMS

Energy source (type and manufacturer)	Airguns

Number of airguns	2 arrays
Size of airguns	160 cu in
Streamer numbers and lengths per number	1 × 1,500 m

VERIFIED

NORWAY

Fugro-Geoteam AS

Geo Arctic

GENERAL

Former names	*Ak. Namotkin*
Current operational status	Worldwide exploration
Owner	SE Amige
Port of reg/flag	Murmansk/Russian
Official number	8409018
Classification	KM*ULI A2
Call sign	UGXK
Built (yard and date)	1988
Rebuilt (yard and date)	2000
Length overall	81.85 m
Breadth moulded	14.80 m
Max draught	7.50 m
Tonnage (grt)	3,631

PROPULSION

Main engine(s)	Zgoda-Zulcer 6ZL 40/48, 3090 kW
Thrusters	Bow, 220 kW
Propellers	Single
Speed (max)	14.2 kt
Speed (cruising)	12.5 kt
Endurance	60 days
Fuel capacity	900 t
Fuel consumption	Sailing 12.80 t; working 8.40 t; port 2.80 t
Electrical power	3,090 kW
Fresh water capacity	200 t

BRIDGE NAVIGATION AIDS

Satellite	Furuno GP50 MkII
Radar	Kelvin Hughes + Nayada-5

Gyrocompass	Vega
Speed log	Atlas Dolog + IEL-2M
Echo-sounder	NEL-M3B
Other ship navigation	Satellite: PHC ML 3000 LORAN C; gyrocompass: Navigat-II; speed log: Atlas-Dolog-22

COMMUNICATIONS

VHF	Sailor, 0.025 kW
Cellular	Yes
Facsimile	Yes

SAFETY

Lifeboats	1 × R-65, 6 persons
Lifesaving equipment	12 × PSN-10

HELIDECK

Size, aircraft capacity	1 × 200 m²

DECK MACHINERY

Cranes	1 × 4 t, 2 × provisions
Winches	Streamer, 6,000 m; spare streamer 4,500 m, gravity/FF

ACCOMMODATION

Charterers	Total accommodation for 60
Scientists/surveyors	29
Hospital	Yes

SCIENTIFIC SPACES

Total scientific deck space	2 × 200 m²
Multipurpose dry lab	1 × 40 m²; 1 × 20 m²

SURVEY SYSTEMS

Positioning	I/O Total/Nav
Echo-sounder (single beam)	DESO-25
Magnetometer	Yes
Gravimeter	Yes

SEISMIC SYSTEMS

Energy source (type and manufacturer)	G-gun Manufacture, France
Number of airguns	4 × 6
Size of airguns	3,660 cu in

Compressor numbers and types	4 × EK10A-1 (Russia); 1 × LMF (Germany)
Streamer manufacturer	I/O
Streamer type	MSX digital, 6,000 m
Streamer numbers and lengths per number	1 × 9 km
Acquisition system	MSX (USA)
Recording system	I/O MSX 24-bit, 480 channels SEG-D

UPDATED

Geo Arctic

2001/0106423

Fugro-Geoteam AS

Geo Baltic

GENERAL

Current operational status	Mediterranean and West Africa
Owner	K/S North Sea Shipping
Port of reg/flag	Bergen/NIS
Classification	Lloyds +100 A1 ICE1B + LMC VMS
Built (yard and date)	1980
Rebuilt (yard and date)	1998
Length overall	73.00 m

Breadth moulded	14.00 m
Operational draught	4.05 m
Tonnage (gt)	2,450

PROPULSION

Main engine(s)	2 × Caterpillar
Propellers	KaMeWa cp in nozzle
Speed (cruising)	15 kt, 13 kt one engine
Fuel capacity	252 m³

Geo Baltic   0110460

Fuel consumption	Sailing 22 m³, working 7 m³
Electrical power	3 × Hedemora V8/10, each 780 hp, 1,000 rpm, 680 kVA; 380/220 V AC, 50 Hz; total power 2,040 kVA; emergency: Scania V8 DS1, 206 kVA
Fresh water capacity	204 m³

BRIDGE NAVIGATION AIDS

Satellite	Koden GPS
Radar	2 × Decca ARPA 2690 BT, S and X band
Gyrocompass	2 × Anschutz Std 4
Speed log	Doppler

COMMUNICATIONS

MF/HF	Furuno
VHF	Furuno

HELIDECK

Size, aircraft capacity	Landing for 5 t aircraft

DECK MACHINERY

Cranes	Hiab 3 t/m at stern; fixed arm 3 t/m at bow
Winches	Streamer 2 × 6,000 m; gun 4 × 300 m

ACCOMMODATION

Charterers	Total accommodation for 72

SURVEY SYSTEMS

Positioning	Online – Fugro PCSeis; offline – Fugro PCMap
Echo-sounder (single beam)	Elac LAZ 72 E, 12 kHz

SEISMIC SYSTEMS

Energy source (type and manufacturer)	Sodera G-gun
Size of airguns	3,440 cu in
Streamer manufacturer	I/O
Streamer type	MSX digital
Streamer numbers and lengths per number	6,000-9,000 m total
Recording system	I/O MSX 24-bit, 460 channels SEG-D

VERIFIED

Fugro-Geoteam AS

Geolog Dmitriy Nalivkin

GENERAL

Owner	MAGE
Port of reg/flag	Murmansk/Russian
Classification	KM UL (1) A2
Call sign	UAMN
Built (yard and date)	1985
Rebuilt (yard and date)	1990/1991
Length overall	71.70 m
Breadth moulded	12.80 m
Max draught	5.40 m
Operational draught	4.50 m
Tonnage (gt)	1,932

PROPULSION

Main engine(s)	2 × 1,560 bhp, 6-74 (36/4S)
Thrusters	Bow: Zstzam-Werke, BI 1545, 200 hp
Propellers	KaMeWa 86 × F4
Speed (max)	14.5 kt
Speed (cruising)	12.5 kt
Endurance	50 days cruising
Fuel capacity	285 m³
Fuel consumption	11 m³
Electrical power	Deutz 3 × 384 Kva Shaft: 384 kVA all 3 × 380 (220 V AC, 50 Hz)
Fresh water capacity	230 m³

BRIDGE NAVIGATION AIDS

Satellite	Navigator
Radar	Furuno 2010 ARPA interfaced to DGPS Okean-14
Gyrocompass	Sperry Mk37 E 2 × Vega
Speed log	Nel-2

Geolog Dmitry Nalivkin   ***2001***/0106455

COMMUNICATIONS

Inmarsat (type)	EB Saturn 3S
MF/HF	Skanti TRP 8401 D
	Brig
VHF	Skanti
	Reyd-1

DECK MACHINERY

Cranes	2 × Hydroplan 2 and 3 t
Winches	2 × streamer, 3,000 and 1,500 m
	2 × supersede, 2 × 125 m
	1 × lead-in
	1 × gravity

ACCOMMODATION

Charterers	Total accommodation for 60

SURVEY SYSTEMS

Positioning	Online – Fugro PCSeis; offline – Fugro PCMap;

SEISMIC SYSTEMS

Energy source (type and manufacturer)	I/O
Size of airguns	3,440 cu in
Streamer manufacturer	I/O
Streamer type	MSX digital
Streamer numbers and lengths per number	6,000 m total
Recording system	I/O MSX 24-bit, 480 channels SEG-D

streamer: DigiCourse 5011 compass bird; source position: time measurements; tailbuoy: radar reflector, optional Geo-Track DGPS; echo-sounder: Elac LAZ 72E

UPDATED

Fugro-Geoteam AS

Geo Pacific

GENERAL

Owner	Fugro-Geoteam AS
Port of reg/flag	Panama/Panamanian
Classification	KM ULI A2
Built (yard and date)	1987
Rebuilt (yard and date)	1998
Length overall	81.85 m
Breadth moulded	14.80-18.00 m
Max draught	5.70 m
Tonnage (gt)	3,225; net 850

PROPULSION

Main engine(s)	Zgoda-Zulcer 6ZL 40/48, 4,200 hp
Thrusters	Azimuth: Ulstein 1,630 hp; bow: electrical 300 hp
Propellers	Single Zanen 4-blade stainless steel
Speed (max)	14.5 kt
Speed (cruising)	12.5 kt
Endurance	60 days cruising

Geo Pacific

2001/0106422

Fuel capacity	1,200 m³	**ACCOMMODATION**	
Fuel consumption	Sailing 12.80 t, working 16 t, port 2.80 t/24 hr	**Charterers**	Total accommodation for 60
Electrical power	Shaft generator 1 × 122 kW; others: 2 × 500 kW, 1 × 1,500 kW, 3 × 280 (220 V AC, 50 Hz); total: 3,700 kW; emergency: 200 kW	**SURVEY SYSTEMS**	
		Positioning	Online nav: Concept Spectra; offline processing: Concept Sprint; binning: Concept Reflex; streamer: DigiCourse 4011 compass, Sonardyne SIPSII acoustic; source position: laser and RGPS; tailbuoy: RGPS
Fresh water capacity	200 t (11 t/24 h)		
BRIDGE NAVIGATION AIDS			
Satellite	Furuno GP50 MkII		
Radar	Furuno ARPA S and X (3 and 10 cm)	**Echo-sounder (single beam)**	Simrad EA500, 33 and 120 kHz
Gyrocompass	2 × S G Brown	**SEISMIC SYSTEMS**	
Speed log	Atlas Dolog; IEL-2M	**Energy source (type and manufacturer)**	Sodera G-gun
COMMUNICATIONS		**Number of airguns**	2
Inmarsat (type)	Saturn B, Phone + Telenor, Sealink	**Size of airguns**	3,400 cu in each
		Streamer manufacturer	I/O
MF/HF	Raytheon STR 2000-800	**Streamer type**	MSX digital
VHF	Raytheon STR 8400 and Sailor portable	**Streamer numbers and lengths per number**	6 × 3,600 m or 4 × 4,500 m
		Recording system	I/O MSX 24-bit, 4-6 × 288 SEG-D
DECK MACHINERY			
Cranes	8 t, 16 m max, 2.5 m min 2 × provisions, front deck		*UPDATED*
Winches	Streamer 6 × 4,800 m; spare streamer 6,500 m; gravity/FF		

Geco-Prakla

Geco Marlin

GENERAL		**Number of airguns**	2 × 3 subarrays
Built (yard and date)	1993	**Streamer numbers and lengths per number**	1 × 960 channels
Length overall	70.10 m		
Breadth moulded	17.98 m		
			VERIFIED
SEISMIC SYSTEMS			
Energy source (type and manufacturer)	Airguns		

Geco-Prakla

Geco My

GENERAL		**Number of airguns**	2 × 3 subarrays
Built (yard and date)	1990	**Streamer numbers and lengths per number**	1 × 960 channels
Length overall	86.87 m		
Breadth moulded	14.33 m		
			VERIFIED
SEISMIC SYSTEMS			
Energy source (type and manufacturer)	Airguns		

Multiwave Geophysical Company (MGC)

Polar Duke

GENERAL COMMENT			
Owner	Polar Ship Management AS, Norway	**Call sign**	LACS4
		Built (yard and date)	Vaagen Verft AS, Norway, 1983
Port of reg/flag	Bergen/Norwegian	**Rebuilt (yard and date)**	2001
Official number	8200838	**Length overall**	66.80 m
Classification	DnV 1A1-EO-HELDK-Sealer (for max draught 5.30 m) pwdk; DnV ID No: 13520	**Breadth moulded**	13.00 m
		Operational draught	5.80 m
		Tonnage (grt)	1,696; net 509; deadweight 1,050

PROPULSION

Main engine(s) 2 × MAK 6M 453AK, 1,650 kW each

Thrusters Brunvoll 578 hp electric, one fore, one aft

Propellers Hjelset

Fuel capacity Gas oil: 660 m³; kerosene (seismic): 55 m³

Fuel consumption 14 t/day at 13 kt; 8 t/day at 11.5 kt; 10 t/day at 4.5 kt (all seismic gear out, 4 gunlines + 6,000 m single streamer); 4 t/day at stand-by (1 engine running); 14 t/day icebreaking

Fresh water capacity 125 m³

BRIDGE NAVIGATION AIDS

Gyrocompass 1 × Anschutz ST4; 1 × Anschutz Standard 20 Compact

Echo-sounder 1 × Simrad ED 161; 1 × Furuno colour video sounder FCV271

Other ship navigation Anschutz autopilot

COMMUNICATIONS

Inmarsat (type) Yes

SAFETY

Workboat/chase boat 1 × Malo 20

HELIDECK

Size, aircraft capacity Gross weight 5,080 kg, Bell 212 or equivalent

DECK MACHINERY

Cranes 1 × 12 t at 15 m, 22 t at 8 m; 1 × 1.2 t at 7.5 m; 1 × 1.5 t at 7.5 m

Winches 2 × MPD dual umbilical; 1 × MPD streamer

ACCOMMODATION

Charterers 14 cabins, 26 berths

Crew 12 cabins, 13 berths

Hospital 3-berth

SURVEY SYSTEMS

Positioning Compasses: DigiCourse 5011; tailbuoy; RGPS; source; RGPS; INS: Concept Spectra

SEISMIC SYSTEMS

Energy source (type and manufacturer) I/O sleeve

Number of airguns 32

Size of airguns Typically: 4-string source, 3,500 cu in

Compressor numbers and types 3 × Hamworthy

Total capacity 2,400 scfm

Streamer manufacturer Sercel Syntrak

Streamer type 24-bit digital

Streamer numbers and lengths per number 1 × 6 km

Acquisition system Sercel Syntrak 960, 24-bit, 960 channels

Recording system IBM 3590; ProMAX offline QC; OYO plotters

NEW ENTRY

Polar Duke

2001/0110520

Multiwave Geophysical Company

Polar Princess

GENERAL

Current operational status	Gulf of Mexico
Port of reg/flag	Norwegian
Official number	8501074
Classification	Det Norske Veritas 1A1 Ice 1A HLDCK
Call sign	JXBV3
Built (yard and date)	Kleven Løland, Leirvik, Norway, 1985
Rebuilt (yard and date)	Upgraded 2001
Length overall	76.20 m
Breadth moulded	14.00 m
Working deck width	Area 380 m²
Max draught	5.53 m
Tonnage (grt)	2,508; net 752

PROPULSION

Main engine(s)	3,460 hp
Speed (cruising)	14-15 kt
Endurance	60 days
Fuel capacity	817 m³
Fresh water capacity	12,940 m³

BRIDGE NAVIGATION AIDS

Gyrocompass	Anschutz Kiel, Standard 4
Echo-sounder	Atlas Echograph 461
Other ship navigation	Autopilots: Anschutz & Robertson

HELIDECK   Yes

ACCOMMODATION

Charterers	Total accommodation for 47
Crew	14

SURVEY SYSTEMS

Positioning	Spectra; MDL FanBeam laser tracking; RGPS active tailbuoy tracking

SEISMIC SYSTEMS

Energy source (type and manufacturer)	Multiple tuned Bolt 'LL' airgun arrays
Streamer manufacturer	Syntrak
Streamer type	480 digital (flexible to 4 × 7,200 m)
Streamer numbers and lengths per number	Total of 16+ capacity
Recording system	Syntrak 480-24

UPDATED

PGS Exploration AS

Ramform Challenger

GENERAL

Owner	PGS Exploration, Norway
Port of reg/flag	Norwegian, NIS
Classification	DnV + 1A1, ICE-C, Heldk
Built (yard and date)	Langsten, 1996
Length overall	86.20 m
Breadth moulded	39.60 m
Operational draught	7.30 m
Tonnage (grt)	9,000

PROPULSION

Main engine(s)	4 × BRG-6
Thrusters	Azimuth: 1 × Ulstein 2000 kW, 2 × Ulstein 2,550 kW

Ramform Challenger

2000/0088242

Propellers	Triple screw
Speed (cruising)	13 kt
Endurance	150 days
Fuel capacity	4,000 m³

BRIDGE NAVIGATION AIDS

Satellite	2 × Magnavox MX300 GPS
Radar	Nucleus II 6000A
Gyrocompass	2 × Anschutz std 20
Echo-sounder	Skipper GDS – 101
Other ship navigation	Robertson AP9 Mk II Robtrack autopilot

COMMUNICATIONS

Inmarsat (type)	2 × ABB Marisat, Inmarsat B, Norsat B
MF/HF	1 × Skanti TRP 9000 DT; 1 × Skanti TRP 7000
VHF	Jotron TR 6101 (helicopter)
Facsimile	Furuno DFAX-210 weather fax

SAFETY

Lifeboats	2 × 60 persons, Harding
Workboat/chase boat	Norsafe 7.62 m × 10 persons; Norpower 6.71 m × 6 persons

HELIDECK

Size, aircraft capacity	Super Puma/EH-101

ACCOMMODATION

Charterers	Total accommodation for 60
Hospital	Yes

SURVEY SYSTEMS

Positioning	3D Navigation: Spectra (Concept Systems); 3D Binning: Census (QC Tools); streamer and source: DigiCourse 5011 compass birds; RGPS on source; Sonardyne SIPS; laser range/bearing; float: RGPS tailbuoy; S G Brown 1000S gyrocompass
Echo-sounder (single beam)	Simrad EA500 200/38 kHz

SEISMIC SYSTEMS

Energy source (type and manufacturer)	Sodera G-gun
Number of airguns	Six subarrays
Compressor numbers and types	3LMF × 1,500 cu ft/min
Streamer manufacturer	Teledyne
Streamer type	Digital model 40645
Streamer numbers and lengths per number	Steps of 6.25 m group lengths; 750 m max outer streamer separation
Recording system	Syntrak 480 – 24 bit; 480 channels per streamer; 1, 2, 3 or 4 ms sample rates; tape format SEG D 8015, 2.5 byte; 4 × IBM 3590 (NTP) recording drive

VERIFIED

PGS Exploration AS

Ramform Explorer

GENERAL

Owner	PGS Exploration AS, Norway	**Classification**	DnV + 1A1, ICE-C, Heldk
Port of reg/flag	Norwegian, NIS	**Built (yard and date)**	1995
		Length overall	82.00 m

Ramform Explorer

2000/0088243

Breadth moulded	39.60 m		
Operational draught	5.80 m		
Tonnage (grt)	8,380		

PROPULSION
Main engine(s)	4 × BRG-6
Thrusters	Azimuth: 1 × Ulstein 2,000 kW; 2 × Ulstein 2,550 kW
Propellers	Triple screw
Speed (cruising)	12 kt
Endurance	60 days
Fuel capacity	1,800 m³

BRIDGE NAVIGATION AIDS
Satellite	2 × Magnavox MX300 GPS
Radar	Raytheon 3410/12 SU ARPA; Raytheon 3425/9SU ARPA; Kelvin Hughes 5000R
Gyrocompass	2 × Robertson RGC 11
Echo-sounder	Skipper GD 101
Other ship navigation	Robertson AP9 Mk II Robtrack autopilot

COMMUNICATIONS
Inmarsat (type)	2 × ABB Marisat, Saturn B
MF/HF	2 × Skanti 8750 DSC
VHF	Jotron TR 6101 (helicopter)
Facsimile	Furuno DFAX-210 weather

SAFETY
Lifeboats	1 × 60 persons, Harding
Workboat/chase boat	Norsafe 7.62 m × 10 persons; Norpower 6.71 m × 6 persons

HELIDECK
Size, aircraft capacity	Super Puma/Chinook

ACCOMMODATION
Charterers	Total accommodation for 60
Hospital	Yes

SURVEY SYSTEMS
Positioning	3-D Navigation: Spectra (Concept Systems); 3-D Binning: Census (QC Tools); streamer and source: DigiCourse 5011 compass birds; RGPS on source; Sonardyne SIPS; laser range/bearing; float: RGPS, GEO-TRACK or similar, powered through streamer
Echo-sounder (single beam)	Simrad EA500 200/38 kHz

SEISMIC SYSTEMS
Energy source (type and manufacturer)	Sodera G-gun
Number of airguns	10 sub-arrays
Compressor numbers and types	3LMF × 1,500 cu ft/min
Streamer manufacturer	Teledyne
Streamer type	Digital model 40645
Streamer numbers and lengths per number	Up to 12 × 480 channels; length up to 6,000 m; 720 m max outer streamer separation
Recording system	2 × Syntrak 480; 480 channels per streamer; 1, 2, 3 or 4 ms sample rates; tape format SEG D 8015, 2.5 byte; 4 × IBM 3590 (NTP) recording drive

UPDATED

Ramform Explorer

2001/0110465

TGS-NOPEC Geophysical Company ASA

Northern Access

GENERAL

Owner	Baltic Tugs
Port of reg/flag	Limassol, Cyprus
Classification	Vessel for Special Purpose
Call sign	P3FG8
Built (yard and date)	Singapore, 1987
Rebuilt (yard and date)	Landskrona, Sweden, 1998
Length overall	76.00 m
Breadth moulded	14.00 m
Max draught	4.50 m
Tonnage (grt)	3,072; net 922

PROPULSION

Main engine(s)	2 × Leroy Somers motors, 1,300 kW each
Thrusters	Bow: Ulstein 260 kW
Propellers	2 × vp
Speed (cruising)	11.50 kt
Endurance	40 days cruising; 40 days seismic
Fuel capacity	655 m³
Fuel consumption	14 m³/day
Fresh water capacity	270 m³

BRIDGE NAVIGATION AIDS

Satellite	LMX 400 DGPS Navigator (Litton)
Radar	S Band and X Band: Decca Bridgemaster (ARPA)
Gyrocompass	Sperry Mk37 VT
Speed log	Naviknot EM 200 (electromagnetic)
Echo-sounder	Odom Echotrac DF 3200 Mk II (200/24 kHz transducer)
Other ship navigation	Robertson AP9 Mk II autopilot

COMMUNICATIONS

Inmarsat (type)	NERA B
MF/HF	Yes
VHF	5 × hand-held; 1 × Sperry
Cellular	GSM
Facsimile	NAV5 GMDSS Navtex/weatherfax

SAFETY

Lifeboats	1 × 37 persons; 4 × Zodiac BH-7B Quingdao Behai 4 25 persons; 1 × VEB 714-1 20 persons 2 × Jon Buoy mob rafts; 1 × 6 persons jet boat

DECK MACHINERY

Cranes	Brissoneau Lotz, 15 t SWL, 10 m

ACCOMMODATION

Charterers	Total accommodation for 36

SURVEY SYSTEMS

Positioning	Concept Spectra 2D INS; 2 × Trimble GPS; Racal Multifix DGPS; Sperry gyro
Echo-sounder (single beam)	Odom Echotrac DF3200 Mk II 200/24 kHz

SEISMIC SYSTEMS

Energy source (type and manufacturer)	Bolt Longlife 1900 LLX air guns
Number of airguns	40
Compressor numbers and types	3 × Ingersoll Rand LP; 2 × Ariel HP electric driven: 2 × 1,700 cu ft/min
Total capacity	5,000 cu in fired at 2,500 psi
Streamer manufacturer	Hydroscience
Streamer type	24 bit SeaMUX Digital Slim
Streamer numbers and lengths per number	8,100 m length + spare streamer sections; up to 624 channels × 12.50 m
Acquisition system	ProMAX with Sun workstation
Recording system	Hydroscience SeaMUX 2000/24

UPDATED

TGS-NOPEC Geophysical Company ASA

Odin Explorer

GENERAL

Port of reg/flag	Norwegian
Classification	Germanischer Lloyds
Call sign	LAGO4
Built (yard and date)	1967
Rebuilt (yard and date)	1981/1990
Length overall	74.30 m
Breadth moulded	10.80 m
Max draught	6.80 m
Tonnage (grt)	1,345

PROPULSION

Main engine(s)	2 × Deutz 1,320 bhp
Thrusters	Bow: Brunvoll 475 hp
Propellers	Escher-Wyss vp
Speed (cruising)	11.5 kt
Endurance	40+ days

BRIDGE NAVIGATION AIDS

Satellite	2 × Furuno Magnavox MX-200, 6 channel receiver
Radar	10 cm, Atlas 6500 ARPA; 3 cm, Kelvin Hughes 6000 A

Gyrocompass Robertson

Other ship navigation 3 × Sailor RT2048; 1 × Sailor C403

COMMUNICATIONS

Inmarsat (type)	Marisat
VHF	SAIT 5000

SAFETY

Lifeboats	Harding 7.22 m MCM; TEMPSC 35 persons/3 × 25 persons; 1 × 20 persons Viking
Workboat/chase boat	Stringer 741, 200HK Volvo Diesel
Lifesaving equipment	Full compliance with E&P Forum/IAGC/SOLAS regulations

ACCOMMODATION

Charterers	Total accommodation for 33

SURVEY SYSTEMS

Positioning	EIVA Navipac
Echo-sounder (single beam)	Simrad EA300 38 kHz

SEISMIC SYSTEMS

Energy source (type and manufacturer)	HGS sleeve guns I and II	Streamer manufacturer	Syntron
		Streamer type	Digital RDA 480
Number of airguns	4	Streamer numbers and lengths per number	1 × 6,000 m
Size of airguns	2,660 cu in	Acquisition system	ProMAX QC
Compressor numbers and types	4 × LMF	Recording system	Syntrak 480
Total capacity	2 × electric driven, 550 cu ft/min; 2 × diesel driven, 480 cu ft/min		

UPDATED

TGS-NOPEC Geophysical Company ASA

Zephyr 1

GENERAL

Owner	Dalmorneftegeofizika (DMNG); managed by Westland GeoProjects Ltd, UK
Port of reg/flag	Panamanian
Classification	Bureau Veritas KM UL1
Call sign	3FXN4
Built (yard and date)	1987
Length overall	81.85 m
Breadth moulded	14.80 m
Max draught	5.00 m
Tonnage (grt)	2,833

PROPULSION

Main engine(s)	Zgoda-Sulzer 6ZL 40/48, 3,090 kW
Speed (max)	Survey 4-6 kt
Endurance	12,000 n miles

BRIDGE NAVIGATION AIDS

Satellite	1 × JLR 6000
Radar	1 × NAYADA; 1 × Kelvin Hughes ARPA
Gyrocompass	Vega
Echo-sounder	NEL – 5M
Other ship navigation	TS-75 1111M autopilot

COMMUNICATIONS

Inmarsat (type)	Marisat 1 × DRC
MF/HF	SSB: 1 × 400 W; 1 × 1,500 W; 1 × 150 W

ACCOMMODATION

Charterers	Total accommodation for 60

SURVEY SYSTEMS

Positioning	DGPS; Sperry Mk37 gyro
Echo-sounder (single beam)	Atlas Deso 20

SEISMIC SYSTEMS

Energy source (type and manufacturer)	Bolt airguns
Size of airguns	2,800 cu in
Compressor numbers and types	Cherco CSU
Total capacity	1600-05/44 m^3
Streamer manufacturer	Seismic Engineering digital
Streamer type	Shell digital 240/480
Streamer numbers and lengths per number	1 × 6,000 m
Acquisition system	ProMAX
Recording system	Syntrak 480

UPDATED

PERU

Petro-Tech SA

Gulf Supplier

GENERAL

Built (yard and date)	1998
Length overall	58.00 m
Breadth moulded	11.50 m

SEISMIC SYSTEMS

Energy source (type and manufacturer)	Airguns
Number of airguns	2 arrays
Size of airguns	1,020 cm^3 each

UPDATED

RUSSIAN FEDERATION

Dalmorneftegeofizika (DMNG)

Orient Explorer

GENERAL

Owner	Dalmorneftegeofizika (DMNG)	Call sign	3FFX-5
Port of reg/flag	Panama/Panamanian	Built (yard and date)	Poland 1988
Classification	DnV 1A1 ECO HELDK Ice-1A	Rebuilt (yard and date)	Singapore 1995
		Length overall	81.80 m

Breadth moulded	14.80 m	
Operational draught	6.00 m	
Tonnage (grt)	3,478; net 1,044	

PROPULSION

Main engine(s)	Sulzer-Zgoda 6ZL40/48
Speed (cruising)	11 kt
Endurance	50 days
Fuel capacity	750 m³

BRIDGE NAVIGATION AIDS

Radar	Furuno ARPA
Echo-sounder	Krupp Atlas Deso 25

COMMUNICATIONS

Inmarsat (type)	Marisat A, 2 × EB Nera Saturn 3
MF/HF	2 × Furuno FS 5000/FS-156
VHF	3 × Furuno FM 7000/DSC-5V

SAFETY

Lifeboats	Jorgensen + Vik (1 × 60 persons); 3 × 20 + 12 × 10 persons inflatable liferafts; 1 × Norsafe FRC Magnum MOB boat

HELIDECK

Size, aircraft capacity	Rated for Super Puma 332/Bell 212 SI

ACCOMMODATION

Charterers	Total accommodation for 60
Hospital	Yes

SURVEY SYSTEMS

Positioning	Spectra INS; Trimble 4000DL GPS; Sonardyne SIPS; MDL Fanbeam laser; Sprint Concept or IBM RISC6000 processing

SEISMIC SYSTEMS

Energy source (type and manufacturer)	Bolt Long Life
Number of airguns	2 arrays
Size of airguns	2 × 2,920 cu in
Compressor numbers and types	5 × Hamworthy 4TH565W100, 400 cu ft/s at 2,000 psi
Streamer manufacturer	Teledyne/Syntron
Streamer type	digital
Streamer numbers and lengths per number	4 × 480 channels, up to 6,000 m
Recording system	Syntrak 16 bit MSRS

VERIFIED

Seismic exploration vessel Orient Explorer   **2000**/0089993

Sevmorneftegeofizika (SMNG)

Akademic Lazarev

GENERAL

Owner	Sevmorneftegeofizika (SMNG)
Port of reg/flag	Murmansk/Russian
Official number	Russian register, Pc 851 438
Classification	KM* A2, ice class
Call sign	UAJS, MSI 273 450 600 (for DSC)
Built (yard and date)	Varskego Shipyard, Szczecin, Poland, 1987
Length overall	81.85 m
Breadth moulded	14.80 m
Max draught	5.00 m

Tonnage (grt)	2,833; displacement 3,631; dwt 1,313

PROPULSION

Main engine(s)	Zgoda-Sulzer 6ZL 40/48, diesel, 3,090 kW, 505 rpm
Thrusters	Bow: N 1.3, 220 kW
Propellers	1 × vp
Speed (cruising)	12.50 kt
Endurance	11,000 n miles (cruising)/60 days
Fuel capacity	820 t

Fuel consumption	Cruise: 10 t/day; survey: 8 t/day	**ACCOMMODATION**	
Fresh water capacity	210 t	**Charterers**	Total accommodation for 57
BRIDGE NAVIGATION AIDS		**SURVEY SYSTEMS**	
Satellite	Felcom 81A Furuno	**Positioning**	RGP-2D INS; Racal SkyFix;
Radar	Racal Decca BT-501; Furuno 20 in FR 2110		2 × NR-103 DGPS receivers
Gyrocompass	Anschutz, Vega	**Echo-sounder (single beam)**	Simrad EA 500
Speed log	Atlas Dolog 12D		
Echo-sounder	NEL-M3B	**SEISMIC SYSTEMS**	
Other ship navigation	Vega autopilot	**Energy source (type and manufacturer)**	Bolt 1900 LL-X
		Number of airguns	4 × 8 guns each sub-array
COMMUNICATIONS		**Size of airguns**	4,258 cu in total capacity
Inmarsat (type)	Volna-C	**Compressor numbers and types**	4 × EK 30A-1, each 400 cu ft/min;
MF/HF	Skanti TRP 8401 S		2 × LMF 240E – VC2214W14,
VHF	Reyd-1, 24 channels; Skanti VHF-3000		each 850 cu ft/min
Facsimile	Shipmate-RS6100 navtex; GM-6 weather fax	**Total capacity**	2,000 psi working pressure
		Streamer manufacturer	Syntrak
		Streamer type	960-24 digital, 8,000 m
SAFETY		**Streamer numbers and lengths per number**	480 channels
Workboat/chase boat	Magnum-750		
Lifesaving equipment	Rescue boat LR-6	**Recording system**	Syntrak 480-24

DECK MACHINERY

Cranes   4 t

UPDATED

M/V *Akademik Lazarev*

2000/0084679

Sevmorneftegeofizika (SMNG)

Akademik Nemchinov

GENERAL		**Built (yard and date)**	Varskego Shipyard, Szczecin, Poland, 1988
Owner	Sevmorneftegeofizika (SMNG)		
Port of reg/flag	Murmansk/Russian	**Rebuilt (yard and date)**	Tyne Tees Dockyard, Newcastle, UK, 1997
Official number	Russian register, PC 873946		
Classification	KM* YJl1/A2, ice class	**Length overall**	84.00 m
Call sign	UETM	**Breadth moulded**	14.80 m

Max draught	5.40 m
Tonnage (grt)	3,224; dwt 1,328

PROPULSION

Main engine(s)	Zgoda-Sulzer 6ZL 40/48, 3,090 kW, 505 rpm
Thrusters	Bow: Zamech N 1.3 – 220 kW
Propellers	1 × vp (222 rpm)
Speed (cruising)	12 kt
Endurance	10,000 n miles./60 days
Fuel capacity	530 t
Fuel consumption	Cruise 10 t/day; survey: 14 t/day
Fresh water capacity	210 t

BRIDGE NAVIGATION AIDS

Satellite	Norsat C – Ricoh 110
Radar	Kelvin Hughes, 25 kW; HR 3000 ARPA-3 cm; Kelvin Hughes, ARPA-10 cm
Gyrocompass	Vega
Speed log	Dolog 12D
Echo-sounder	NEL-M3B
Other ship navigation	Robertson AP9 Mark 3 autopilot

COMMUNICATIONS

Inmarsat (type)	B
MF/HF	Mousson-2, 250 W
VHF	Reyd-1, 24 channels; Sailor RT 2048; GX 2310 Standard (UK)
Facsimile	Weather fax: INEY-P

SAFETY

Lifesaving equipment	Rescue boat FRB-700

HELIDECK

Size, aircraft capacity	14.80 m (4.30 t)

DECK MACHINERY

Cranes	HSBC-80 (SWL 6.5 t) arm 10-4 m

ACCOMMODATION

Charterers	Total accommodation for 56

SURVEY SYSTEMS

Positioning	Trinav RT integrated nav; MDL laser; DigiCourse acoustic; Plath Navigat II gyrocompass

SEISMIC SYSTEMS

Energy source (type and manufacturer)	Bolt 1500 LL; 1900 LL-X
Number of airguns	6 × 8-gun arrays
Size of airguns	8,000 cu in total capacity
Compressor numbers and types	2 × LMF 51/138 D VCS 2414 W14, each 1,800 cu ft/min
Streamer manufacturer	Nessie-3
Streamer numbers and lengths per number	4 × 4, 500 m
Recording system	TRIACQ

UPDATED

M/V Akademik Nemchinov   *2000*/0084681

Sevmorneftegeofizika (SMNG)

Akademik Shatskiy

GENERAL

Owner	Sevmorneftegeofizika (SMNG)
Port of reg/flag	Murmansk/Russian
Official number	Russian register PC No. 852820
Classification	KM* A2, ice class
Call sign	UAJR

Built (yard and date)	Varskego Shipyard, Szczecin, Poland, 1986
Rebuilt (yard and date)	Lindenau Shipyard, Kiel, Germany, 1991
Length overall	83.15 m
Breadth moulded	14.80 m

Max draught	5.20 m	**HELIDECK**	
Tonnage (grt)	2,779; dwt 1,259	**Size, aircraft capacity**	19 m diameter; 9 t capacity
PROPULSION		**DECK MACHINERY**	
Main engine(s)	Zgoda-Sulzer 6ZL 40/48, 3,110 kW, 506 rpm	**Cranes**	R-4/12.5 (4 t)
Thrusters	Bow: N 1.3, 220 kW	**ACCOMMODATION**	
Propellers	1 vp (225 rpm)	**Charterers**	Total accommodation for 56
Speed (cruising)	12 kt		
Endurance	50 days	**SURVEY SYSTEMS**	
Fuel capacity	510 t	**Positioning**	Trinav QC + Trinav GPS
Fuel consumption	10 t/day cruising; 12 t/day survey		integrated nav; S G Brown gyro
Fresh water capacity	114 t	**Echo-sounder (single beam)**	Simrad EA 500

BRIDGE NAVIGATION AIDS

Satellite	Saturn 3S 90, Saturn BM	**SEISMIC SYSTEMS**	
Radar	Kelvin Hughes HR-3000; Kelvin Hughes Nucleus 2-5000A	**Energy source (type and manufacturer)**	Bolt 1500 LL, Bolt 1900 LL-X; Gunco synchroniser
Gyrocompass	Vega	**Number of airguns**	6 × 8-gun sub-arrays
Speed log	Dolog 12D	**Size of airguns**	6,800 cu in
Echo-sounder	NEL-M3B	**Compressor numbers and types**	2 × LMF 370E – VCS2413W14, each 1,300 cu ft/min
Other ship navigation	Robertson AP9 Mark 3 autopilot	**Total capacity**	2,000 psi working pressure
		Streamer manufacturer	Nessie 3-4
COMMUNICATIONS		**Streamer type**	24 bit digital
MF/HF	Mousson 2, 250 W	**Streamer numbers and lengths per number**	1 × 4,000 m (max 8,000 m) or 2 × 4,000 m
VHF	Reyd-1, 24 channels; Sailor RT 2048; GX 2310 Standard (UK)	**Recording system**	TriAq digital onboard system
Facsimile	Furuno NX 500 navtex		

UPDATED

SAFETY

Lifesaving equipment	Mob-boat: GTC-70 with Volvo Penta TAMD 41A

M/V *Akademik Shatskiy*

2000/0084680

Sevmorneftegeofizika (SMNG)

Iskatel-3

GENERAL		**Breadth moulded**	18.20 m (catamaran)
Owner	Sevmorneftegeofizika (SMNG)	**Operational draught**	2.15 m
Port of reg/flag	Murmansk/Russian	**Tonnage (grt)**	878; net 263; dwt 143
Official number	Russian register, PC862517		
Classification	KM* [1] 1 A2	**PROPULSION**	
Call sign	UFZZ	**Main engine(s)**	2 × 6 AL 20/24 diesels, 420 kW each at 750 rpm
Built (yard and date)	Catamaran, built Vista Shipyard, Gdansk, Poland, 1987	**Propellers**	2 × vp
Length overall	49.29 m	**Speed (cruising)**	10.0 kt

Endurance	25 days cruise; 17 days survey; range at cruising speed: 200 n miles	**DECK MACHINERY**	
		Cranes	1 × deck
Fuel capacity	102 t	**Winches**	2 × streamer, total 6,000 m
Fuel consumption	4.50 t/day cruising; 6.00 t/day surveying		
		ACCOMMODATION	
Electrical power	Auxiliary engines: 4 × 145 kW	**Charterers**	Total accommodation for 35
Fresh water capacity	20 t; fresh water maker 4 t/day		
		SURVEY SYSTEMS	
		Positioning	RGP-2D integrated nav; Vega gyro; IEL 2M e/m log; Sercel NR-103 DGPS
BRIDGE NAVIGATION AIDS			
Satellite	Felcom 81A		
Radar	Furuno FR2110	**Echo-sounder (single beam)**	Deso 25
Gyrocompass	Vega		
Speed log	IEL-2M e/m	**SEISMIC SYSTEMS**	
Echo-sounder	NEL-M3B	**Energy source (type and manufacturer)**	Sleeve gun airguns; Hydra Sys gun controller 200X/32
Other ship navigation	TS-75A 2232 autopilot	**Number of airguns**	Sub-arrays: 4 × 8 guns each, total 32 guns, 11.50 m long
COMMUNICATIONS		**Size of airguns**	Total capacity 2,680 cu in
MF/HF	Mousson-2, 250 W SSB		
VHF	Reyd-1, 24 channels		

Iskatel-3   **2000**/0088245

Iskatel-3   **2000**/0093185

Compressor numbers and types	2 × Sullair 600; 1 × LMF VGd 261 OW14, total 1,200 cu ft/min; 4 × EK 7.50, each 90 cu ft/min	Recording system	Syntrak 480-16 marine digital telemetry system; SEG D demultiplexed, IBM 3490 cartridges; 3 × 3490E cartridge drives; Model GS-624-24 in OYO plotter
Total capacity	Pressure: 2,000 psi		
Streamer manufacturer	Syntrak		
Streamer type	480-16 digital streamer LDA		
Streamer numbers and lengths per number	1 × 6,000 m; group lengths 12.5 m, 25 m		

VERIFIED

Sevmorneftegeofizika (SMNG)

Iskatel-5

GENERAL

Owner	Sevmorneftegeofizika (SMNG)
Port of reg/flag	Murmansk/Russian
Official number	Russian register, PC884080
Classification	KM* [1] 1 A2
Call sign	UAJT
Built (yard and date)	Catamaran, built Vista shipyard, Gdansk, Poland, 1989
Length overall	49.29 m
Breadth moulded	18.20 m (catamaran)
Operational draught	2.15 m
Tonnage (grt)	915; net 274; dwt 166

PROPULSION

Main engine(s)	2 × 6 AL 20/24 diesels 420 kW each at 750 rpm
Propellers	2 × vp
Speed (cruising)	10.0 kt
Endurance	18 days cruise; 13 days survey; range at cruising speed: 200 n miles
Fuel capacity	80 t
Fuel consumption	4.50 t/day cruising; 6.00 t/day surveying
Electrical power	Auxiliary engines: 4 × 145 kW
Fresh water capacity	20 t; fresh water maker 4 t/day

BRIDGE NAVIGATION AIDS

Satellite	Scansat-M 900
Radar	2 × Racal Decca BT 501/6
Gyrocompass	Vega
Speed log	IEL-2M
Echo-sounder	NEL-M3B
Other ship navigation	TS-75A 2232 autopilot

COMMUNICATIONS

MF/HF	Mousson-2, 250 W SSB
VHF	Reyd-1, 24 channels

DECK MACHINERY

Cranes	2 × deck
Winches	Seismic cable WWS-6000

ACCOMMODATION

Charterers	Total accommodation for 30

SEISMIC SYSTEMS

Number of airguns	Sub-arrays: 4 × 10 m long
Compressor numbers and types	4 × EK 7.5 – 3, each 90 cu ft/min; 2 × LMF 120D-VGd 3680 W35, each 400 cu ft/min
Total capacity	Pressure: 2,000 psi

VERIFIED

Iskatel-5

2000/0088246

Sevmorneftegeofizika (SMNG)

Professor Polshkov

GENERAL	
Owner	Sevmorneftegeofizika (SMNG)
Port of reg/flag	Murmansk/Russian
Official number	Russian register PC 820196
Classification	KM* YJI1/A2, ice class
Call sign	UAIS
Built (yard and date)	Turku, Finland, 1984
Length overall	71.60 m
Breadth moulded	12.80 m
Max draught	4.50 m
Tonnage (grt)	1,984; dwt 598
PROPULSION	
Main engine(s)	2 × PH 36/45, diesel, G-74; 1,150 kW/500 rpm
Thrusters	Bow: 150 kW
Propellers	1 × vp
Speed (cruising)	12 kt
Endurance	60 days
Fuel capacity	340 t
Fuel consumption	Cruise: 10 t/day; survey: 8 t/day
Fresh water capacity	200 t
BRIDGE NAVIGATION AIDS	
Radar	Furuno; Racal Decca
Gyrocompass	Vega
Speed log	Dolog 12D
Echo-sounder	NEL-M3B
Other ship navigation	Racal Decca 550 autopilot; Shipmate-RS 6100
COMMUNICATIONS	
Inmarsat (type)	SAT-B

MF/HF	Mousson-2, 250 W
VHF	Reyd-1, 24 channels; Sailor RT 2048; GX 2310 Standard (UK)
DECK MACHINERY	
Cranes	R-4/12.5 (4 t)
ACCOMMODATION	
Charterers	Total accommodation for 60
SURVEY SYSTEMS	
Positioning	Norstar 906-970203 integrated nav; Primary: Multifix; Secondary: Sercel; Anschutz, S G Brown 1000S gyrocompass
Echo-sounder (single beam)	Atlas Deso 20
SEISMIC SYSTEMS	
Energy source (type and manufacturer)	HGS sleeve guns
Number of airguns	4 × 10 guns each
Size of airguns	Total capacity 3,800 cu in
Compressor numbers and types	1 × LMF 510 HD; VCS2413W14, 1,800 cu ft/min; 1 × Hamworthy 4TH190, 170 cu ft/min
Streamer manufacturer	Syntrak
Streamer type	480-16 digital streamer
Streamer numbers and lengths per number	480 channels/6,000 m
Acquisition system	IBM RISC with ProMAX
Recording system	Syntrak 480-16

UPDATED

Professor Polshkov

2001/0106458

Sevmorneftegeofizika (SMNG)

Professor Rjabinkin

GENERAL	
Owner	Sevmorneftegeofizika (SMNG)
Port of reg/flag	Murmansk/Russian
Official number	Russian register, PC870551
Classification	KM* [1] 1 A2
Call sign	UAJU
Built (yard and date)	Rauma-Repola, Finland, 1989
Length overall	49.90 m

Breadth moulded	10.50 m
Operational draught	2.37 m
Tonnage (grt)	952; dwt 163
PROPULSION	
Main engine(s)	4 × Wartsila diesels, SACM Ud25 6LS5, 348 kW each
Thrusters	Bow: 110 kW, KPR 225

Propellers	2 × Aquamaster propulsion units in nozzles, 2 × 460 kW, 360° steerable	
Speed (cruising)	10.0 kt	
Endurance	25 days cruise; 20 days survey; range at cruising speed: 4,000 n miles	
Fuel capacity	117 t	
Fuel consumption	5.00 t/day cruising; 5.00 t/day surveying	
Electrical power	85 kW diesel generator + 25 kW emergency generator	
Fresh water capacity	76 t; fresh water maker 4 t/day	

BRIDGE NAVIGATION AIDS

Satellite	Sailor TT-3064A
Radar	Racal Decca BT-501; Nayada-5
Gyrocompass	Vega, SGB 1000S
Speed log	SAL 860 Doppler
Echo-sounder	NEL-M3B; SAL-860 Doppler
Other ship navigation	Robertson Ap9 Mk II autopilot

COMMUNICATIONS

Inmarsat (type)	'C': Thrane & Thrane TT3020B
MF/HF	Mousson-2, 250 W SSB; Compact SSB RE 2100
VHF	Kelvin Hughes 2048; Reyd-1, 24 channels; River's KAMA
Facsimile	Furuno DFAX-207 weather fax; Shipmate RS 6100 navtex

SAFETY

Workboat/chase boat	7 m boat with Simrad echo-sounder

DECK MACHINERY

Cranes	1 × 2 t deck

Winches	2 × airgun launch; 1 × 6,000 m streamer with 5 cm cable

ACCOMMODATION

Charterers	Total accommodation for 30

SURVEY SYSTEMS

Positioning	RGP-2-D integrated navigation system; SGB 1000S gyro; Sercel NR-103 DGPS
Echo-sounder (single beam)	Elac LAZ 4700, NEL-M3B

SEISMIC SYSTEMS

Energy source (type and manufacturer)	Sleeve gun
Number of airguns	Sub-arrays: 2 × 10 guns each
Size of airguns	Total capacity: 2 × 1,140 cu in
Compressor numbers and types	2 × LMF VHG 5621 W20, each 250 cu ft/min; 1 × LMF 120D –VGd 3608 W35, 400 cu ft/min; 2 × Hamworthy 4TH190, each 170 cu ft/min
Total capacity	Pressure: 2,000 psi
Streamer manufacturer	Hydroscience
Streamer type	Century MUX-2, 24-bit digital, 392 channels
Streamer numbers and lengths per number	4,900 m
Recording system	Alliant Tech System, AESOP, SPARC 20 system controller, 392 ch, 2 ms sample rate; SEG D demultiplexed tape recorder, IBM 3480 cartridges; 2 × STK 4280 cartridge drives A02; Sparc 20 QC; GS-624 OYO plotter

VERIFIED

Professor Rjabinkin

2000/0088247

SINGAPORE

Veritas DGC Asia Pacific Ltd

Pacific Sword

GENERAL

Current operational status	Active in Asia-Pacific Region
Owner	Swire Pacific Offshore Operations Pte, Ltd, Singapore
Port of reg/flag	Singapore
Official number	8024349
Classification	AS + AI(E), AMS, International; Load Line Cert
Call sign	9V5801
Built (yard and date)	Teraoka Zosen, Japan, 1981
Length overall	57.70 m
Breadth moulded	12.20 m
Max draught	3.90 m
Tonnage (grt)	1,307; net 392

PROPULSION

Main engine(s)	2 × Yanmar G250E
Thrusters	1 × Kamome cp
Propellers	2 × 4-blade fp open
Speed (cruising)	11 kt
Endurance	60 days at cruising speed
Fuel capacity	55 m³
Fresh water capacity	163 m³

BRIDGE NAVIGATION AIDS

Satellite	Inmarsat B, Inmarsat M
Radar	2 × Furuno
Gyrocompass	1 × Tokyo Keiki
Echo-sounder	1 × Simrad ED 162

COMMUNICATIONS

MF/HF	Yes
VHF	Yes
Cellular	Yes
Facsimile	Yes

SAFETY

Lifeboats	1 × RTK Model 606 rescue craft
Workboat/chase boat	Yes
Lifesaving equipment	Yes

ACCOMMODATION

Charterers	21
Crew	14

SURVEY SYSTEMS

Positioning	Spectra INS DGPS, gyrocompass, acoustics, laser-ranging
Echo-sounder (single beam)	Odom Echotrak DF3200 Mk II, with 12 kHz and 200 Hz transducers
Gravimeter	Yes
Sound velocity profiler	Yes

SEISMIC SYSTEMS

Energy source (type and manufacturer)	Bolt 1500LL and 1900 LL-XT airguns
Number of airguns	40
Size of airguns	40-460 cu in

Pacific Sword   *2001*/0110521

Compressor numbers and types	1 × LMF 350 HD; 1 × LMF 480D	Streamer numbers and lengths per number	Syntrak 960-24 LDA: 1 × 7,050 m; 2 × 4,500 m
Total capacity	2,950 scfm	Recording system	Syntrak 960-24 MSRS
Streamer manufacturer	Sercel		

UPDATED

UNITED KINGDOM

TGS-NOPEC

M/V Northern Access

GENERAL

Port of reg/flag	Cyprus
Classification	Vessel for Special Purpose
Built (yard and date)	1987
Rebuilt (yard and date)	1998
Length overall	76.00 m
Breadth moulded	14.00 m
Max draught	4.50 m
Tonnage (grt)	3,072

PROPULSION

Main engine(s)	2 × Leroy Somers motors, 1,300 kW each
Thrusters	Bow: Ulstein 260 kW
Speed (cruising)	11.50 kt
Endurance	40 days

BRIDGE NAVIGATION AIDS

Satellite	LMX 400 DGPS Navigator (Litton)
Radar	S Band & × Band: Decca Bridgemaster + ARPA
Gyrocompass	Sperry Mk37 VT
Other ship navigation	Robertson AP9 MkII

COMMUNICATIONS

Inmarsat (type)	NERA B
MF/HF	Yes
VHF	5 hand-held; 1 Sperry

SAFETY

Lifeboats	1 × 37 BH-7B Qingdao Behai/4 × Zodiak–4 – 25 persons; 1 × VEB 714–1 – 20 persons

Workboat/chase boat	2 × Jon Buoy; 1 × 6 persons jet boat

ACCOMMODATION

Charterers	Total accommodation for 36

SURVEY SYSTEMS

Positioning	Concept Spectra 2D
Echo-sounder (single beam)	Odom Echotrac DF3200 Mk II 200/24 kHz

SEISMIC SYSTEMS

Energy source (type and manufacturer)	Bolt Longlife 1900 LLX air guns
Number of airguns	4
Compressor numbers and types	3 × Ingersoll Rand LP; 2 × Ariel HP Electric driven: 2 × 1,700 cu ft/min
Total capacity	5,000 cu in
Streamer manufacturer	Hydroscience
Streamer type	24 bit SeaMUX Digital Slim
Streamer numbers and lengths per number	8,000 m length, up to 624 channels
Acquisition system	ProMAX with Sun workstation
Recording system	Hydroscience SeaMUX 2000/24

VERIFIED

Thales Survey Ltd

Thales Eastern

GENERAL

Port of reg/flag	Belize
Official number	76982437
Classification	DnV + 1A1
Call sign	V3ZU
Built (yard and date)	1975
Rebuilt (yard and date)	1991, 1998 (upgraded to ISM)
Length overall	58.90 m
Breadth moulded	14.50 m
Operational draught	4.40 m
Tonnage (grt)	1,278; net 384

PROPULSION

Main engine(s)	2 × B+W Alpha 10V23L-VO, 1,550 bhp
Thrusters	Bow: 1 × 365 hp, 5 t thrust
Propellers	2 × cp

Speed (max)	11 kt
Speed (cruising)	9 kt; 0-5 kt survey speed
Endurance	30-35 days/6,500+ n miles
Fuel capacity	400 m³
Fuel consumption	Passage: 7 t/day; survey: 4.5 t/day 9 t/day during seismic acquisition using all compressors
Electrical power	Auxiliary engines: 3 × Caterpillar D343; generators: 2 × Stamford 212 kVA/440 V/60 Hz; 2 × Stamford 40 kVA/240 V/50 Hz – clean power; 1 × Stamford 175 kVA
Fresh water capacity	175 m³; water maker 8,000 litres/day max at cruising speed

BRIDGE NAVIGATION AIDS

Radar	1 × Decca ARPA 2490MT; 1 × Decca RM 2090 BT
Gyrocompass	1 × Sperry SR-120
Echo-sounder	Furuno EM-225
Other ship navigation	Robertson AP8 autopilot

COMMUNICATIONS

Inmarsat (type)	'A': JRC JUE 45A Mk II 'B': Nera Saturn B
MF/HF	ICOM M700; Skanti TRP 8000
VHF	Sailor C401
Facsimile	JRC JAX8 weather fax

SAFETY

Lifeboats	1 × rubber/glass fibre MOB boat with 36/40 hp outboard. Liferafts: 4 × 25-persons, 2 × 10-persons
Lifesaving equipment	200% lifejackets Halon firefighting system + streamer De-luge system

DECK MACHINERY

Cranes	1 × Hiab
A-frame(s)	6.50 m hydraulic
Winches	ROV handling

ACCOMMODATION

Charterers	Total accommodation for 40

SURVEY SYSTEMS

Positioning	Racal SkyFix DGPS; MultiFix QC software; Racal GNS, Concept Spectra; SGB 1000S gyro; Nautronix ATS 2 USBL; streamer/gun positioning: Tracs GeoPod; DigiCourse; DigiRange; MDL Fanbeam laser

Echo-sounder (single beam)	Marimatech E Seasound 206C; Atlas Deso 20; Odom Echotrack Mk II; hull-mounted 12/33/38/200/210 kHz transducers
Multibeam/swath system	Elac Bottomchart Mk II, 180 kHz or 50 kHz
Sidescan sonar	GeoAcoustics dual frequency; Coda DA200 and Delph-2 sonar workstations
Sub-bottom profiler	GeoAcoustics or X-Star Chirp; 10 cu in mini-airgun; Sodera S15 watergun; Applied Acoustics surface or sub-tow boomer
Corer(s)	3 m gravity; 3 m vibrocoring
Grab(s)	Yes
Vehicle(s) (ROVs/AUVs and so on)	Racal Sealion Mk II work class ROV, 100 hp; Racal Sea Pup observation class ROV, 25 hp
Oceanographic sensors (CTDs/XBTs and so on)	Applied Microsystems STD-12

SEISMIC SYSTEMS

Number of airguns	Single or dual 4 × 10 cu in, 4 × 20 cu in or 4 × 40 cu in sleeve gun arrays; 2 × 640 cu in LL Bolt and sleeve gun arrays; 2 × Syntron GCU-90 gun controllers; Syntron gun depth transducers
Compressor numbers and types	4 × LMF 400 cu ft/min
Streamer manufacturer	Geco
Streamer type	GX600
Streamer numbers and lengths per number	3,000 m active length
Recording system	ProMAX 2D; Sun Ultra Enterprise 2 with 200 MHz Ultra Sparc; Fujitsu 3490E cartridge drive; OYO-GS624 Versatec plotter; Concept Reflex online/offline binning

UPDATED

Thales Eastern   *2000*/0088251

WesternGeco

Arctic Star

GENERAL

Owner	WesternGeco
Built (yard and date)	1944
Length overall	30.20 m
Breadth moulded	9.10 m

SEISMIC SYSTEMS

Energy source (type and manufacturer)	Sleeve airgun

UPDATED

WesternGeco

Geco Angler

GENERAL

Owner	REM Maritime, Norway
Built (yard and date)	Flekkefjord Slipp AS, Norway, 1998
Length overall	65.84 m
Breadth moulded	14.02 m

SEISMIC SYSTEMS

Energy source (type and manufacturer)	Airguns
Number of airguns	2 × 3 subarrays

UPDATED

Geco Angler

2001/0110470

WesternGeco

Geco Beta

GENERAL

Built (yard and date)	1995
Length overall	91.14 m
Breadth moulded	19.81 m

SEISMIC SYSTEMS

Energy source (type and manufacturer)	Airguns

Number of airguns	2 × 3 subarrays
Streamer numbers and lengths per number	8 × 640 channels

UPDATED

WesternGeco

Geco Bluefin

GENERAL

Current operational status	2-D and 3-D multicomponent (4C) surveys
Owner	Volstad Shipping AS, Aalesund, Norway
Classification	DnV + 1A1 E O – Dynpos AUTR – Heldk
Built (yard and date)	Baatbygg AS, Norway, 1999
Length overall	80.00 m
Breadth moulded	19.00 m
Max draught	9.40 m
Tonnage (grt)	4,735; dw 2,800

PROPULSION

Main engine(s)	1 × 2,685 kW at 600 rpm
Thrusters	Bow: 1 × electric, 1,200 kW; stern: 1 × electric; 1,200 kW; 2 × electric azimuth, each 1,500 kW
Propellers	1 × cp in nozzle
Fuel capacity	1,090 m³
Electrical power	Generators: 4 × 1,530 kW each at 900 rpm; 1 × auxiliary diesel, 455 kVA
Fresh water capacity	120 m³; water-making capacity 20 t/day

BRIDGE NAVIGATION AIDS

Satellite	Yes
Radar	2
Gyrocompass	Yes
Speed log	Yes
Echo sounder	1 × navigational, 55 kHz
Other ship navigation	Autopilot

COMMUNICATIONS

MF/HF	1 × Sea Area 3 GMDSS
VHF	3

SAFETY

Lifeboats	MOB boat
Lifesaving equipment	Full safety equipment to SOLAS regulations; full firefighting equipment

HELIDECK

Size, aircraft capacity	AS 322 Super Puma MkII rated

DECK MACHINERY

Cranes	Electric-hydraulic deck: 1 × knuckle arm, 10 t at 12 m; 1 × knuckle arm, 6 t at 14.5 m; 2 × telescopic arm, 2 t at 12 m
Winches	Proprietary de-tensioning device, to enable Nessie 4C Multiware array to be handled at water depths of more than 1,000 m

ACCOMMODATION

Charterers	Total accommodation for 46

SURVEY SYSTEMS

Positioning	DP system + underwater acoustic
Sensors	Seismic current meter
Echo-sounder (single beam)	Hydrographic: 38 kHz; survey: 200 kHz

SEISMIC SYSTEMS

Streamer manufacturer	54,000 m Nessie 4C Multiware array

NEW ENTRY

Geco Bluefin   **2001**/0110469

WesternGeco

Geco Diamond

GENERAL	
Built (yard and date)	Flekkefjord Slipp AS, Norway, 1993
Length overall	80.77 m
Breadth moulded	14.94 m
SEISMIC SYSTEMS	
Energy source (type and manufacturer)	Airguns

Number of airguns	2 × 3 subarrays
Streamer numbers and lengths per number	10 × 380 channels

UPDATED

WesternGeco

Geco Dolphin

GENERAL	
Current operational status	Ocean bottom cable vessel
Built (yard and date)	1996
Length overall	58.52 m
Breadth moulded	12.19 m

SEISMIC SYSTEMS	
Energy source (type and manufacturer)	Airguns
Streamer numbers and lengths per number	4 × 480 channels

UPDATED

WesternGeco

Geco Eagle

GENERAL	
Owner	WesternGeco
Classification	DnV + 1A1 EO, Ice C, DynPos Aut, Heldk, SF

Built (yard and date)	Mjellem & Karlsen Verft AS, Norway, 1999
Length overall	94.80 m
Breadth moulded	24.00 m

Geco Eagle

2000/0093779

Working deck width	37.00 m (back deck)
Operational draught	7.50 m
Tonnage (grt)	10,800; dw 5,400

PROPULSION

Main engine(s)	2 × Siemens 1RN2803 diesel-electric
Thrusters	Bow: 1 × Brunvoll FN-80-LTC 2000, 1,000 kW; retractable: 1 × Brunvoll FN-80-FRC 2100, 1,500 kW
Propellers	2 × Wichmann, PR100/41COO cp in nozzle
Speed (max)	16 kt
Endurance	90 – 120 days
Fuel capacity	3,400 m³
Electrical power	Generators: 4 × Siemens, each 4,335 kVA; auxiliaries: 4 × Wärtsilä 9L32, MCR 4,050 kW at 720 rpm; emergency generator plant: 1 × Stamford MHC 434F, 305 kVA at 1,800 rpm; power: 1 × Scania, 260 kW at 1,800 rpm
Fresh water capacity	275 m³; fresh water generator: 2 × Alfa-Laval Nirex JWP-26-C80, 15 t/day each

BRIDGE NAVIGATION AIDS

Satellite	1 × Phillips AP Mk10 DGPS
Radar	1 × Norcontrol Databridge
Gyrocompass	1 × Simrad RGC 12

Speed log	1 × Furuno CI-60G + DS-70 Doppler
Echo sounder	1 × Simrad EN250

COMMUNICATIONS

Inmarsat (type)	Sailor C; Nera Saturn BM B
MF/HF	1 × Sailor Compact
VHF	1 × Sailor
Cellular	1 × Skanti helicopter communication

SAFETY

Lifeboats	1 × Miriam 8.85 m for 66 persons; 1 × Norsafe Magnum 750 MOB boat
Workboat/chase boat	Workboats: 1 × Norpower Malo 35; 1 × Maritime Partner, Springer 26

HELIDECK

Size, aircraft capacity	22.2 m; Sikorsky S61 acc to CAP 437

DECK MACHINERY

Cranes	Deck: Aukra Industrier: 1 × 3 t at 14 m; 1 × 12 t at 20 m; 1 × 6 t at 14.5 m; 1 × 2 t at 12 m
Winches	Odim seismic for towing 20 seismic cables

ACCOMMODATION

Charterers	Total accommodation for 66

Geco Eagle

2001/0110466

SURVEY SYSTEMS

Positioning	Simrad HPR and Sonardyne SIPS
	2 streamer
Echo-sounder (single beam)	1 × Simrad EA500

SEISMIC SYSTEMS

Energy source (type and manufacturer)	Airguns
Number of airguns	8 sub-arrays

Streamer type	120 km +, to give survey footprint of 11 km^2 rising to 16 km^2
Streamer numbers and lengths per number	up to 12

UPDATED

Geco Eagle   **2001**/0110472

WesternGeco

Geco Emerald

GENERAL

Owner	WesternGeco
Built (yard and date)	Flekkefjord Slipp AS, Norway, 1992
Length overall	81.69 m
Breadth moulded	14.94 m

SEISMIC SYSTEMS

Energy source (type and manufacturer)	Airguns
Number of airguns	2 × 3 subarrays
Streamer numbers and lengths per number	10 × 380 channels

UPDATED

WesternGeco

Geco Manta

GENERAL

Current operational status	Ocean bottom cable vessel
Built (yard and date)	1996
Length overall	36.27 m
Breadth moulded	7.92 m

SEISMIC SYSTEMS

Streamer numbers and lengths per number	4 × 480 channels

UPDATED

WesternGeco

Geco Resolution

GENERAL
Built (yard and date)   1998
Length overall   75.29 m
Breadth moulded   15.54 m

SEISMIC SYSTEMS
Energy source (type and   Airguns
  manufacturer)

Number of airguns   2 × 3 subarrays
Streamer numbers and   8 × 240 channels
  lengths per number

UPDATED

WesternGeco

Geco Sapphire

GENERAL
Owner   WesternGeco
Built (yard and date)   Flekkefjord Slipp AS, Norway,
    1991
Length overall   75.90 m
Breadth moulded   14.94 m

SEISMIC SYSTEMS
Energy source (type and   Airguns
  manufacturer)

Number of airguns   2 × 3 subarrays
Streamer numbers and   8 × 240 channels
  lengths per number

UPDATED

WesternGeco

Geco Searcher

GENERAL
Built (yard and date)   1995
Length overall   82.91 m
Breadth moulded   19.81 m

SEISMIC SYSTEMS
Energy source (type and   Airguns
  manufacturer)

Number of airguns   2 × 3 subarrays
Streamer numbers and   8 × 640 channels
  lengths per number

UPDATED

WesternGeco

Geco Snapper

GENERAL
Current operational status   Ocean bottom cable vessel
Built (yard and date)   1997
Length overall   63.40 m
Breadth moulded   13.72 m

SEISMIC SYSTEMS
Energy source (type and   Airguns
  manufacturer)
Number of airguns   2 × 3 subarrays

UPDATED

WesternGeco

Geco Tau

GENERAL
Built (yard and date)   1992
Length overall   77.72 m
Breadth moulded   14.02 m

SEISMIC SYSTEMS
Energy source (type and   Airguns
  manufacturer)

Number of airguns   2 × 3 subarrays
Streamer numbers and   4 × 640 channels
  lengths per number

UPDATED

WesternGeco

Geco Topaz

GENERAL

Owner	WesternGeco
Built (yard and date)	Brattvaag Skipsverft AS, Norway, 1993
Length overall	81.08 m
Breadth moulded	14.94 m

SEISMIC SYSTEMS

Energy source (type and manufacturer)	Airguns
Number of airguns	2 × 3 subarrays
Streamer numbers and lengths per number	8 × 380 channels

UPDATED

WesternGeco

Geco Triton

GENERAL

Rebuilt (yard and date)	Converted to seismic vessel, Tyne Tees Dockyard, UK, 1998
Length overall	82.60 m
Breadth moulded	21.03 m

SEISMIC SYSTEMS

Energy source (type and manufacturer)	Airguns
Number of airguns	2 × 3 subarrays
Streamer numbers and lengths per number	10 × 640 channels

UPDATED

WesternGeco

Kenda

GENERAL

Owner	WesternGeco
Built (yard and date)	1997
Length overall	61.90 m
Breadth moulded	12.80 m

SEISMIC SYSTEMS

Energy source (type and manufacturer)	Sleeve airgun
Streamer numbers and lengths per number	1 × 8,000 m

UPDATED

WesternGeco

Mintrop

GENERAL

Built (yard and date)	1993
Length overall	92.35 m
Breadth moulded	15.24 m

SEISMIC SYSTEMS

Energy source (type and manufacturer)	Airguns
Number of airguns	2 × 3 subarrays
Streamer numbers and lengths per number	6 × 320 channels

UPDATED

WesternGeco

Seisranger

GENERAL

Built (yard and date)	1996
Length overall	85.95 m
Breadth moulded	20.73 m

SEISMIC SYSTEMS

Energy source (type and manufacturer)	Airguns
Number of airguns	2 × 3 subarrays
Streamer numbers and lengths per number	8 × 368 channels

UPDATED

WesternGeco

Tucano

GENERAL		SEISMIC SYSTEMS	
Owner	WesternGeco	Energy source (type and manufacturer)	Sleeve airgun
Built (yard and date)	1985		
Length overall	20.90 m		
Breadth moulded	6.10 m		

UPDATED

WesternGeco

Western Aleutian

GENERAL		SEISMIC SYSTEMS	
Owner	WesternGeco	Energy source (type and manufacturer)	Sleeve airgun
Built (yard and date)	1982		
Length overall	42.10 m		
Breadth moulded	9.80 m		

UPDATED

WesternGeco

Western Anchorage

GENERAL		SEISMIC SYSTEMS	
Owner	WesternGeco	Energy source (type and manufacturer)	Sleeve airgun
Built (yard and date)	1977		
Length overall	54.90 m		
Breadth moulded	12.20 m		

UPDATED

WesternGeco

Western Atlas

GENERAL		SEISMIC SYSTEMS	
Owner	WesternGeco	Energy source (type and manufacturer)	Sleeve airgun
Built (yard and date)	1988	Streamer numbers and lengths per number	1 × 32,000 m
Length overall	80.80 m		
Breadth moulded	18.00 m		

UPDATED

WesternGeco

Western Cove

GENERAL		SEISMIC SYSTEMS	
Owner	WesternGeco	Energy source (type and manufacturer)	Sleeve airgun
Built (yard and date)	1994	Streamer numbers and lengths per number	1 × 7,200 m
Length overall	78.60 m		
Breadth moulded	12.80 m		

UPDATED

WesternGeco

Western Horizon

GENERAL		SEISMIC SYSTEMS	
Owner	WesternGeco	Energy source (type and manufacturer)	Sleeve airgun
Built (yard and date)	1982	Streamer numbers and lengths per number	1 × 8,000 m
Length overall	60.00 m		
Breadth moulded	11.90 m		

UPDATED

WesternGeco

Western Inlet

GENERAL		SEISMIC SYSTEMS	
Owner	WesternGeco	Energy source (type and manufacturer)	Sleeve airgun
Built (yard and date)	1981		
Length overall	61.00 m	Streamer numbers and lengths per number	1 × 7,500 m
Breadth moulded	11.90 m		

UPDATED

WesternGeco

Western Legend

GENERAL		SEISMIC SYSTEMS	
Owner	WesternGeco	Energy source (type and manufacturer)	Sleeve airgun
Built (yard and date)	1997		
Length overall	71.30 m	Streamer numbers and lengths per number	1 × 45,000 m
Breadth moulded	16.90 m		

UPDATED

WesternGeco

Western Meteor

		SEISMIC SYSTEMS	
		Energy source (type and manufacturer)	Sleeve airgun
GENERAL			
Owner	WesternGeco		
Built (yard and date)	1995		
Length overall	17.80 m		
Breadth moulded	4.90 m		

UPDATED

WesternGeco

Western Monarch

GENERAL		SEISMIC SYSTEMS	
Owner	WesternGeco	Energy source (type and manufacturer)	Sleeve airgun
Built (yard and date)	1992		
Length overall	92.40 m	Streamer numbers and lengths per number	1 × 48,000 m
Breadth moulded	19.80 m		

UPDATED

WesternGeco

Western Neptune

GENERAL		SEISMIC SYSTEMS	
Owner	WesternGeco	Energy source (type and manufacturer)	Sleeve airgun
Built (yard and date)	1999		
Length overall	92.50 m		
Breadth moulded	23.00 m		

UPDATED

WesternGeco

Western Orient

GENERAL		Length overall	43.90 m
Owner	WesternGeco	Breadth moulded	12.20 m
Built (yard and date)	1981		

UPDATED

WesternGeco

Western Pacific

GENERAL		SEISMIC SYSTEMS	
Owner	WesternGeco	Energy source (type and manufacturer)	Sleeve airgun
Built (yard and date)	1996		
Length overall	54.90 m		
Breadth moulded	11.90 m		

UPDATED

WesternGeco

Western Patriot

GENERAL		SEISMIC SYSTEMS	
Owner	WesternGeco	Energy source (type and manufacturer)	Sleeve airgun
Built (yard and date)	1993	Streamer numbers and lengths per number	1 × 45,000 m
Length overall	78.00 m		
Breadth moulded	17.00 m		

UPDATED

Western Patriot

2001/0110462

WesternGeco

Western Polaris

GENERAL		SEISMIC SYSTEMS	
Owner	WesternGeco	Energy source (type and manufacturer)	Sleeve airgun
Built (yard and date)	1993		
Length overall	41.50 m		
Breadth moulded	9.80 m		

UPDATED

WesternGeco

Western Pride

GENERAL		SEISMIC SYSTEMS	
Owner	WesternGeco	Energy source (type and manufacturer)	Sleeve airgun
Built (yard and date)	1992	Streamer numbers and lengths per number	1 × 45,000 m
Length overall	71.30 m		
Breadth moulded	16.80 m		

UPDATED

WesternGeco

Western Regent

GENERAL		SEISMIC SYSTEMS	
Owner	WesternGeco	Energy source (type and manufacturer)	Sleeve airgun
Built (yard and date)	1992	Streamer numbers and lengths per number	1 × 60,000 m
Length overall	92.40 m		
Breadth moulded	19.80 m		

UPDATED

WesternGeco

Western Shore

GENERAL		SEISMIC SYSTEMS	
Owner	WesternGeco	Energy source (type and manufacturer)	Sleeve airgun
Built (yard and date)	1982		
Length overall	49.10 m		
Breadth moulded	11.60 m		

UPDATED

WesternGeco

Western Spirit

GENERAL		SEISMIC SYSTEMS	
Owner	WesternGeco	Energy source (type and manufacturer)	Sleeve airgun
Built (yard and date)	1993	Streamer numbers and lengths per number	1 × 36,000 m
Length overall	78.00 m		
Breadth moulded	16.90 m		

UPDATED

WesternGeco

Western Trident

GENERAL		SEISMIC SYSTEMS	
Owner	WesternGeco	Energy source (type and manufacturer)	Sleeve airgun
Built (yard and date)	1999	Streamer numbers and lengths per number	1 × 60,000 m
Length overall	92.50 m		
Breadth moulded	23.00 m		

UPDATED

WesternGeco

Western Voyager

GENERAL		SEISMIC SYSTEMS	
Owner	WesternGeco	Energy source (type and manufacturer)	Sleeve airgun
Built (yard and date)	1980	Streamer numbers and lengths per number	1 × 3,000 m
Length overall	25.00 m		
Breadth moulded	7.90 m		

UPDATED

WesternGeco

Western Wave

GENERAL		SEISMIC SYSTEMS	
Owner	WesternGeco	Energy source (type and manufacturer)	Sleeve airgun
Built (yard and date)	1982	Streamer numbers and lengths per number	1 × 5,200 m
Length overall	48.20 m		
Breadth moulded	12.20 m		

UPDATED

Westland GeoProjects Ltd

GeoMariner 1

GENERAL		PROPULSION	
Owner	BGP-NOREX Shipping Ltd	Main engine(s)	2 × Caterpillar D398 – 850 bhp
Port of reg/flag	Valetta/Malta	Thrusters	Bow: 1 × White Gill 321 turbo diesel; Caterpillar 3406 – 375 bhp; stern: 1 × White Gill 241 direct drive; Caterpillar D3304 – 165 bhp
Classification	ABS A1 (E)		
Call sign	9H5771		
Built (yard and date)	Canada, 1978		
Rebuilt (yard and date)	1997		
Length overall	35.10 m	Speed (cruising)	10.5 kt
Breadth moulded	12.80 m	Fuel capacity	172.9 m³
Operational draught	3.70 m (1.50 m min)	Fresh water capacity	50.10 m³
Tonnage (grt)	723; net 216		

GeoMariner 1   **2000**/0099201

BRIDGE NAVIGATION AIDS

Radar	1 × Furuno 1948 MkII; 1 × Decca RM 121C; 1 × Decca RMS 1230
Echo-sounder	Raytheon DE731
Other ship navigation	Cortex Nav5 weather fax

COMMUNICATIONS

Inmarsat (type)	B (+HSD), C
MF/HF	Raytheon GMDSS

SAFETY

Lifeboats	4 × liferafts for 64 persons total
Workboat/chase boat	2 × 4 persons

ACCOMMODATION

Charterers	Total accommodation for 28

SURVEY SYSTEMS

Positioning	Spectra INS: Trimble 4000DS II GPS; Racal Multifix DGPS

SEISMIC SYSTEMS

Energy source (type and manufacturer)	Bolt LLX 1900/2800
Size of airguns	200-1,000 cu in
Compressor numbers and types	Hamworthy 425D
Total capacity	425 cu ft/min
Streamer type	Syntrak RDA – 1, 24 bit
Streamer numbers and lengths per number	1 × 3,000 m
Recording system	Syntrak 480-24 MSTS

UPDATED

UNITED STATES OF AMERICA

Fairfield Industries

Diamond River

GENERAL

Owner	Trico Marine
Port of reg/flag	US
Official number	556352
Classification	ABS
Call sign	WCS 9879
Built (yard and date)	Halter Marine, Moss Point, Mississippi, 1974
Length overall	54.86 m
Breadth moulded	11.58 m
Operational draught	3.96 m
Tonnage (grt)	264; net 179

PROPULSION

Main engine(s)	2 × EMD diesels, 1,000 hp each
Thrusters	Bow: 1 × Detroit 671, 200 hp
Propellers	2 × fp
Endurance	50 days; 9,500 n miles at cruising speed
Fuel capacity	56,000 gallons
Fuel consumption	1,100 gallons/day
Electrical power	3 × 99 kW Detroit 671 diesels
Fresh water capacity	83,000 gallons

BRIDGE NAVIGATION AIDS

Satellite	1 × Garmin 120

Radar	2 × Furuno
Gyrocompass	1 × Sperry; 1 × Sperry gyropilot
Echo-sounder	1 × Furuno FCV-581

COMMUNICATIONS

MF/HF	1 × SEA-222 SSB
VHF	2 × Standard Horizon

SURVEY SYSTEMS

Positioning	Trimble 4000 RS GPS receivers, John E Chance StarFix

SEISMIC SYSTEMS

Energy source (type and manufacturer)	Bolt 1900 'Long Life' airguns; Syntron GCS90 controller; I/O 200 encoder/ synchroniser
Size of airguns	Total volume 2,830 cu in
Compressor numbers and types	2 × LMF compressors
Total capacity	1,300 cu ft/min
Streamer manufacturer	Teledyne
Recording system	Teleseis RTDT telemetry system (520 channels)

UPDATED

Fairfield Industries

Fairfield Expedition

GENERAL

Owner	Fairfield Industries
Port of reg/flag	US
Official number	1050794
Classification	ABS
Call sign	WCX 5383
Built (yard and date)	Geo Shipyard, New Iberia, Louisiana, 1996
Length overall	54.86 m
Breadth moulded	11.58 m
Operational draught	3.96 m

PROPULSION

Main engine(s)	2 × Daytona Mack 550 hp diesels, Twin Disc model 5114 marine transmissions with 3:1 ratio
Thrusters	Bow: 2 × North American Marine TJ600 water-jet drives
Electrical power	2 × Northern Light 16 kW generators

BRIDGE NAVIGATION AIDS

Satellite	1 × Garmin 120

Radar	1 × Furuno F1731
Gyrocompass	1 × Sperry
Echo-sounder	1 × Furuno FCV-581

COMMUNICATIONS

MF/HF	1 × SEA-222 SSB
VHF	2 × Standard Horizon
Cellular	Yes

SURVEY SYSTEMS

| Positioning | Trimble 4000 GPS RS receivers, utilising John E Chance Starfix differential corrections |

UPDATED

Fairfield Industries

Fairfield Explorer

GENERAL

Owner	Fairfield Industries
Port of reg/flag	US
Official number	619902
Classification	ABS ✠ A-1, AMS, ABS International Load Line
Call sign	WCX 8239
Built (yard and date)	Modern Marine, Houma, Louisiana, 1980
Length overall	56.69 m
Breadth moulded	12.19 m
Operational draught	4.57 m
Tonnage (grt)	290; net 197

PROPULSION

Main engine(s)	2 × Wichman 4AXA 1,350 hp 4 cylinder diesels
Thrusters	Bow: Fixed pitch 200 hp with Detroit 671 diesel
Propellers	2 × 3-blades, vp with Kort nozzles
Endurance	76 days; 18,240 n miles at cruising speed
Fuel capacity	149,796 gallons
Fuel consumption	1,950 gallons/day (average)
Electrical power	3 × Delco 150 kW generators, powered by Detroit 871 diesels
Fresh water capacity	72,018 gallons

BRIDGE NAVIGATION AIDS

Radar	2 × Furuno 1930
Gyrocompass	1 × Sperry; 1 × Sperry gyropilot
Echo-sounder	1 × Furuno FCV-668

COMMUNICATIONS

MF/HF	1 × SEA-222 SSB
VHF	2 × Standard Horizon
Facsimile	1 × Shipmate RS 6100 Navtex

SURVEY SYSTEMS

| Positioning | Trimble 4000 RS GPS receivers with John E Chance StarFix differential corrections |

SEISMIC SYSTEMS

Energy source (type and manufacturer)	Bolt 1900 'Long Life' airguns; Syntron GCS90 Controller; I/O 200 encoder/synchroniser
Size of airguns	Total volume 2,830 cu in
Compressor numbers and types	2 × 1,100 cu ft/min Cooper coupled to main engines
Streamer manufacturer	Teledyne
Recording system	Teleseis RTDT telemetry system (520 channels)

VERIFIED

Fairfield Industries

Fairfield Hunter

GENERAL

Owner	Fairfield Industries
Port of reg/flag	US
Official number	1034819
Call sign	WCX 6862
Built (yard and date)	Geo Shipyard, New Iberia, Louisiana, 1995
Length overall	17.68 m
Breadth moulded	4.88 m
Operational draught	0.91 m
Tonnage (grt)	31; net 24

PROPULSION

Main engine(s)	2 × Cummins 6CTA diesels, 30 hp each at 2,500 rpm, Twin Disc model 5061 marine transmissions, 2.45:1 ratio
Propellers	2 × North American Marine TJ11 water-jet drives
Electrical power	Generators: 1 × Cummins 4BT diesel; 1 × 40 kW; 1 × Northern Light 20 kW

BRIDGE NAVIGATION AIDS

| Satellite | 1 × Koden KGP 911 |

Radar	1 × Furuno 1731
Gyrocompass	1 × Sperry
Echo-sounder	1 × Furuno FCV-581

COMMUNICATIONS

MF/HF	1 × Sailor RE 2100 HF SSB
VHF	2 × Standard Horizon; 2 × Icom IC
Cellular	Yes

SURVEY SYSTEMS

| Positioning | Trimble 4000 RS GPS receivers with John E Chance StarFix differential corrections |

SEISMIC SYSTEMS

Energy source (type and manufacturer)	Bolt 2800 'Long Life' airguns; Syntron GCS90 controller; I/O 200 encoder/synchroniser
Size of airguns	Total volume 1,680 cu in
Compressor numbers and types	2 × A300 Price

UPDATED

Fairfield Industries

Fairfield Mirage

GENERAL	
Owner	Fairfield Industries
Port of reg/flag	US
Official number	1060662
Classification	ABS
Call sign	WCX9148
Built (yard and date)	Geo Shipyard, New Iberia, Louisiana, 1996
Length overall	19.81 m
Breadth moulded	5.49 m
Operational draught	0.91 m
Tonnage (grt)	45; net 36

PROPULSION	
Main engine(s)	2 × Daytona Mack 550 hp diesels, with Twin Disc model 5114 marine transmissions, 3:1 ratio
Thrusters	2 × North American Marine TJ600 water-jet drives

Electrical power	2 × Northern Light 16 kW generators

BRIDGE NAVIGATION AIDS	
Radar	1 × Furuno F1731
Gyrocompass	1 × Sperry
Echo-sounder	1 × Furuno FCV-581

COMMUNICATIONS	
VHF	2 × Standard Horizon
Cellular	Yes

SURVEY SYSTEMS	
Positioning	Trimble 4000 RS GPS receivers with John E Chance StarFix differential corrections

UPDATED

Fairfield Industries

Fairfield Quest

GENERAL	
Owner	Fairfield Industries
Built (yard and date)	1996
Length overall	19.81 m
Breadth moulded	5.49 m

SEISMIC SYSTEMS	
Energy source (type and manufacturer)	Airguns
Number of airguns	2 arrays
Size of airguns	2,920 cm³ each

VERIFIED

Fairfield Industries

Fairfield Speculator

GENERAL	
Owner	Fairfield Industries
Port of reg/flag	US
Official number	1046278
Classification	ABS
Call sign	WCX5381
Built (yard and date)	Geo Shipyard, New Iberia, Louisiana, 1996
Length overall	19.20 m
Breadth moulded	5.49 m
Operational draught	0.91 m
Tonnage (grt)	45; net 36

PROPULSION	
Main engine(s)	2 × Cummins 6CTA diesels, each rated at 300 hp at 2,500 rpm, with Twin Disc model 5061 marine transmissions, 3:1 ratio
Thrusters	2 × North American Marine 300-1 water-jet drives
Electrical power	2 × Cummins 4BT diesels with 2 × 40 kW generators

BRIDGE NAVIGATION AIDS	
Radar	1 × Furuno F1731
Gyrocompass	1 × Sperry

COMMUNICATIONS	
VHF	2 × Standard Horizon
Cellular	Yes

SURVEY SYSTEMS	
Positioning	Trimble 4000 RS GPS receivers with John E Chance StarFix differential corrections

SEISMIC SYSTEMS	
Energy source (type and manufacturer)	Bolt 2800 'Long Life' airguns; Syntron GCS90 controller; I/O 200 encoder/synchroniser
Size of airguns	Total volume 1,680 cu in
Compressor numbers and types	2 × A300 Price

UPDATED

Fairfield Industries

Fairfield Vision

Owner	Fairfield Industries	Official number	1058458
Port of reg/flag	US	Classification	ABS

Call sign	WCX7648	**BRIDGE NAVIGATION AIDS**	
Built (yard and date)	Geo Shipyard, New Iberia, Louisiana, 1996	**Radar**	1 × Furuno F1731
		Gyrocompass	1 × Sperry
Length overall	19.20 m	**Echo-sounder**	1 × Furuno FCV-581
Breadth moulded	5.49 m		
Operational draught	0.91 m	**COMMUNICATIONS**	
Tonnage (grt)	45; net 36	**VHF**	2 × Standard Horizon
		Cellular	Yes
PROPULSION			
Main engine(s)	2 × Daytona Mack 550 hp diesels, Twin Disc model 5114 marine transmissions with 3:1 ratio	**SURVEY SYSTEMS**	
		Positioning	Trimble 4000 RS GPS receivers, utilising John E Chance StarFix differential corrections
Thrusters	2 × North American Marine TJ600 water-jet drives		
Electrical power	2 × Northern Light 16 kW generators		*UPDATED*

Fairfield Industries

Geo Tide

GENERAL		**Electrical power**	3 × Delco 150 kW generators, powered by Detroit 871 diesels
Owner	Tidewater Marine	**Fresh water capacity**	72,018 gallons;
Port of reg/flag	US		Village Marine water maker: 4,000 gallons/day
Official number	642135		
Classification	ABS + A1 AMS		
Call sign	WRA 8558	**BRIDGE NAVIGATION AIDS**	
Built (yard and date)	Mississippi Marine Towboat, Morgan City, Louisiana, 1982	**Satellite**	1 × Koden KGP 911
		Radar	2 × Furuno 8600 D
Length overall	43.59 m	**Gyrocompass**	1 × Sperry; 1 × Sperry gyropilot
Breadth moulded	10.97 m	**Echo-sounder**	1 × Kodiak 2650
Operational draught	2.74 m		
Tonnage (grt)	295, net 201	**COMMUNICATIONS**	
		MF/HF	1 × Sailor RE 2100 HF SSB
PROPULSION		**VHF**	2 × Icom IC
Main engine(s)	3 × 3412 Caterpillar at 625 hp each		
		SEISMIC SYSTEMS	
Thrusters	Bow: Schottel 508/4 with Detroit 871, 300 hp	**Recording system**	Teleseis STAR Telemetry System (520 channels); Frontline 3D Binning, Max 3D Verify, Vista Field
Propellers	2 × fixed; 1 × vp		
Endurance	76 days; 18,240 n miles range at cruising speed		
Fuel capacity	149,796 gallons		*VERIFIED*
Fuel consumption	1,950 gallons/day		

Fairfield Industries

Roxanne T

GENERAL		**SEISMIC SYSTEMS**	
Owner	Fairfield Industries	**Energy source (type and manufacturer)**	Airguns
Built (yard and date)	2000		
Length overall	54.86 m	**Number of airguns**	2 arrays
Breadth moulded	11.58 m	**Size of airguns**	2,920 cm³ each
			NEW ENTRY

PGS Exploration

American Explorer

GENERAL		**Number of airguns**	2 arrays
Built (yard and date)	1994	**Size of airguns**	3,090 cm³ each
Length overall	91.50 m	**Streamer numbers and lengths per number**	6 × 240 channels
Breadth moulded	22.00 m		
			VERIFIED
SEISMIC SYSTEMS			
Energy source (type and manufacturer)	Airguns		

PGS Exploration

Atlantic Explorer

GENERAL

Built (yard and date)	1994
Length overall	91.50 m
Breadth moulded	18.00 m

SEISMIC SYSTEMS

Energy source (type and manufacturer)	Airguns

Number of airguns	2 arrays
Size of airguns	3,090 cm^3 each
Streamer numbers and lengths per number	6 × 240 channels

VERIFIED

PGS Exploration

Falcon Explorer

GENERAL

Built (yard and date)	1997
Length overall	81.20 m
Breadth moulded	16.30 m

SEISMIC SYSTEMS

Energy source (type and manufacturer)	Airguns
Number of airguns	2 arrays
Size of airguns	3,090 cm^3 each

VERIFIED

PGS Exploration

Kondor Explorer

GENERAL

Built (yard and date)	1997
Length overall	60.90 m
Breadth moulded	13.00 m

SEISMIC SYSTEMS

Energy source (type and manufacturer)	Airguns
Number of airguns	2 arrays
Size of airguns	3,090 cm^3 each

VERIFIED

PGS Exploration

Nordic Explorer

GENERAL

Built (yard and date)	1993
Length overall	82.00 m
Breadth moulded	16.50 m

SEISMIC SYSTEMS

Energy source (type and manufacturer)	Airguns

Number of airguns	2 arrays
Size of airguns	3,090 cm^3 each
Streamer numbers and lengths per number	6 × 240 channels

VERIFIED

PGS Exploration

Ocean Explorer

GENERAL

Built (yard and date)	1995
Length overall	82.00 m
Breadth moulded	18.00 m

SEISMIC SYSTEMS

Energy source (type and manufacturer)	Airguns

Number of airguns	2 arrays
Size of airguns	3,090 cm^3 each
Streamer numbers and lengths per number	6 × 240 channels

VERIFIED

PGS Exploration

Ramform Valiant

GENERAL		**Number of airguns**	2 arrays
Built (yard and date)	1998	**Size of airguns**	3,090 cm³ each
Length overall	86.60 m	**Streamer numbers and**	20 × 240 channels
Breadth moulded	39.60 m	lengths per number	
			VERIFIED
SEISMIC SYSTEMS			
Energy source (type and	Airguns		
manufacturer)			

PGS Exploration

Ramform Vanguard

GENERAL		**Number of airguns**	2 arrays
Built (yard and date)	1999	**Size of airguns**	3,090 cm³ each
Length overall	86.60 m	**Streamer numbers and**	20 × 240 channels
Breadth moulded	39.60 m	lengths per number	
			VERIFIED
SEISMIC SYSTEMS			
Energy source (type and	Airguns		
manufacturer)			

PGS Exploration

Ramform Victory

GENERAL		**Length overall**	86.60 m
Built (yard and date)	1999	**Breadth moulded**	39.60 m

Ramform Victory   *2001*/0109840

SEISMIC SYSTEMS		**Size of airguns**	3,090 cm³ each
Energy source (type and manufacturer)	Airguns	**Streamer numbers and lengths per number**	20 × 240 channels
Number of airguns	2 arrays		

UPDATED

Ramform Victory   2001/0109839

PGS Exploration

Ramform Viking

| **GENERAL** | | **Length overall** | 86.60 m |
| Built (yard and date) | 1998 | **Breadth moulded** | 39.60 m |

Ramform Viking   2001/0109838

SEISMIC SYSTEMS

Energy source (type and manufacturer)	Airguns	Size of airguns	3,090 cm³ each
		Streamer numbers and lengths per number	20 × 240 channels
Number of airguns	2 arrays		

UPDATED

Ramform Viking   **2001**/0109837

PGS Reservoir Services

Bergen Surveyor

GENERAL		**SEISMIC SYSTEMS**	
Built (yard and date)	1996	Energy source (type and manufacturer)	Airguns
Length overall	66.00 m	Number of airguns	2 arrays
Breadth moulded	14.60 m	Size of airguns	3,690 cm³ each

NEW ENTRY

PGS Reservoir Services

Beulah Chouest

GENERAL		**SEISMIC SYSTEMS**	
Built (yard and date)	1996	Energy source (type and manufacturer)	Airguns
Length overall	59.50 m	Number of airguns	2 arrays
Breadth moulded	12.20 m	Size of airguns	3,690 cm³ each

NEW ENTRY

PGS Reservoir Services

Carlson Tide

GENERAL			
Built (yard and date)	1995	Length overall	59.20 m
		Breadth moulded	12.20 m

NEW ENTRY

PGS Reservoir Services

Dickerson Tide

GENERAL		Length overall	59.20 m
Built (yard and date)	1995	Breadth moulded	12.20 m

NEW ENTRY

PGS Reservoir Services

Elda Chouest

GENERAL		Number of airguns	2 arrays
Built (yard and date)	1992	Size of airguns	3,690 cm³ each
Length overall	65.20 m		
Breadth moulded	12.20 m		

NEW ENTRY

SEISMIC SYSTEMS	
Energy source (type and manufacturer)	Airguns

PGS Reservoir Services

Jonathan Chouest

GENERAL		Length overall	54.90 m
Built (yard and date)	1996	Breadth moulded	10.40 m

NEW ENTRY

PGS Reservoir Services

Owen Tide

GENERAL		Length overall	56.10 m
Built (yard and date)	1995	Breadth moulded	11.60 m

NEW ENTRY

Seismic Explorations International (SEI)

Laurentian

GENERAL		SEISMIC SYSTEMS	
Former names	*Labrador Horizon*	Energy source (type and manufacturer)	Airguns
Owner	British Linen Bank		
Built (yard and date)	1991	Number of airguns	2 arrays
Rebuilt (yard and date)	1998	Size of airguns	64,400 cm³ each
Length overall	81.00 m	Streamer numbers and lengths per number	6 × 360 channels
Breadth moulded	17.00 m		

UPDATED

Thales GeoSolutions Inc

Albuquerque

GENERAL		Number of airguns	1 array
Built (yard and date)	1987	Size of airguns	200 cu in
Length overall	39.00 m	Streamer numbers and lengths per number	1 × 48 channels
Breadth moulded	9.70 m		

SEISMIC SYSTEMS	
Energy source (type and manufacturer)	Airguns

UPDATED

Thales GeoSolutions Inc

Reflection

GENERAL			**Number of airguns**	1 array
Built (yard and date)	1997		**Size of airguns**	200 cu in
Length overall	36.50 m		**Streamer numbers and**	1 × 48 channels
Breadth moulded	9.10 m		**lengths per number**	

SEISMIC SYSTEMS

UPDATED

Energy source (type and manufacturer)   Airguns

University of Hawaii

Ka'imikai-O-Kanaloa

GENERAL				1 × Pitman, 4,536 kg; Hiab,
Former names	*Western Strait*			907.20 kg
Current operational status	Operational		**A-frame(s)**	Moveable, 18,144 kg; CTD boom,
Owner	State of Hawaii			8,505 kg
Port of reg/flag	Honolulu, Hawaii		**Winches**	1 × CTD, Markey DESH 6;
Official number	HA 343 XS			1 × trawl, Northernline
Classification	ABS		**Moonpool(s) – size(s)/**	Straza tower, 1.22 × 1.22 m, used
Call sign	WBN 4310		**function(s)**	for deploying communication
Built (yard and date)	Mangone Shipbuilding, 1979			equipment during manned
Rebuilt (yard and date)	Bender Shipyard, 1991			submersible operations
Length overall	67.97 m			
Breadth moulded	11.58 m		**ACCOMMODATION**	
Working deck width	10.97 m		**Crew**	14
Max draught	4.88 m		**Scientists/surveyors**	19
Operational draught	4.88 m			
Tonnage (grt)	259		**SCIENTIFIC SPACES**	
			Total scientific deck space	96 m²
PROPULSION			**Oceanographic wet lab**	30 m²
Main engine(s)	2 × 16V149 Detroit		**Multipurpose dry lab**	30 m²
Thrusters	Bow: Electric DC Westinghouse		**Chemistry lab**	15 m²
	MTR Amarillo Anate Drive			
Propellers	2 × fixed, 4-blade		**SURVEY SYSTEMS**	
Speed (max)	11 kt		**Multibeam/swath system**	Seabeam
Speed (cruising)	10 kt		**Magnetometer**	Model Geometrics G-886 Proton
Endurance	60 days			Precession
Fuel capacity	175, 355 gallons		**Gravimeter**	Yes
Fuel consumption	2,000 gallons/day		**Corer(s)**	Piston
Electrical power	440 V/220 V/110 V		**Sound velocity profiler**	ADCP
Fresh water capacity	53,044 gallons		**Oceanographic sensors**	Seabird 9/11 + CTD System; 24
			(CTDs/XBTs and so on)	place rosette (24-10-litre bottles);
BRIDGE NAVIGATION AIDS				12 place rosette (mix of 10/12-
Satellite	GPS: Northstar 951XD, Trimble			litre bottles); SeaCat 21
	NAVTRAC XL			thermosalinograph; XBT launcher
Radar	2 × Furuno FCR 1411 Mk 3			
	(X-band)		**SEISMIC SYSTEMS**	
Gyrocompass	1 × Sperry Mk 37 MOD D/E;		**Energy source (type and**	Water gun, type S-80 model 01,
	1 × Sperry Mk 29 MOD 3A		**manufacturer)**	80 cu in; Bolt 1500C air guns
Speed log	Display from GPS		**Number of airguns**	4
Echo-sounder	Raytheon DSF 6000 (12 kHz)		**Size of airguns**	80, 120, 200, 300 cu in chambers
			Streamer manufacturer	Hydroscience Technologies/
COMMUNICATIONS				French AMG; Fast Tow, 6 channel
Inmarsat (type)	Trimble Galaxy (Type C)			streamer
MF/HF	SSB Raytheon Ray 152		**Streamer type**	AMG 37/43 mm (inner/outer dia);
VHF	2 × Raytheon Ray 90			active section 50 m × 2 active
Cellular	Motorola 19055			sections (each 2 groups of 24
Facsimile	Yes			HC202 geomechanical
				hydrophones mounted in 3 × 8
SAFETY				series parallel)
Lifeboats	4 × 20-persons Elliott liferafts		**Acquisition system**	Sun SPARC 10/41 workstation
Workboat/chase boat	1 × 5 m Avon RHI, 1 × 3.96 m			with proprietary data acquisition
	Avon inflatable			and display software
Lifesaving equipment	EPIRB (Type 1)		**Recording system**	SEGY on to both DAT and
				Exabyte tape
DECK MACHINERY				
Cranes	1 × Aurora folding, 18,144 kg;			*VERIFIED*

Veritas

Acadian Searcher

GENERAL		SURVEY SYSTEMS	
Current operational status	USA	Positioning	Spectra INS
Classification	ABS ⊕ A1, AMS, Ice Class 'C'		
Length overall	66.10 m	SEISMIC SYSTEMS	
Breadth moulded	13.40 m	Energy source (type and	Single tuned Bolt 'LL' airgun array
Max draught	4.00 m	manufacturer)	
Tonnage (grt)	193; 131 net	Streamer manufacturer	Syntrak
		Streamer type	480-24 RDA digital (1 × 3,000 – 6,000 m)
PROPULSION		Streamer numbers and	6.25 m, 12.50 m, 18.75 m or
Main engine(s)	5 × 900 kW	lengths per number	25.00 m group lengths
Speed (cruising)	10 kt	Recording system	Syntrak 480-24 MSRS
Endurance	50 days		

ACCOMMODATION			
Charterers	Total accommodation for 43		*VERIFIED*

Veritas

New Venture

GENERAL		SURVEY SYSTEMS	
Classification	ABS	Positioning	Spectra INS; DigiCourse streamer tracking
Built (yard and date)	1985		
Rebuilt (yard and date)	1992		
Length overall	76.20 m	SEISMIC SYSTEMS	
Breadth moulded	17.00 m	Energy source (type and	Tuned Bolt 'Long-Life' airguns, up
Max draught	4.90 m	manufacturer)	to 4 strings/5,600 cu in
Tonnage (grt)	3,338	Streamer manufacturer	Syntrak
		Streamer type	480 digital (to 8,000 m)
PROPULSION		Streamer numbers and	6.26 m, 12.50 m, 18.75 m or
Main engine(s)	6,140 hp	lengths per number	25.00 m group lengths
Speed (cruising)	14 kt	Recording system	Syntrak 480-16
Endurance	40 days		

ACCOMMODATION			
Charterers	Total accommodation for 49		*VERIFIED*

Veritas

Polar Search

		SURVEY SYSTEMS	
		Positioning	Spectra INS; MDL FanBeam laser tracking; RGPS active tailbuoy tracking; DigiCourse System-3 (full network) acoustic ranging
GENERAL			
Former names	*Mobil Search*		
Classification	ABS, A1(E), AMS2ACCUI		
Built (yard and date)	Mitsubishi, Japan, 1982		
Rebuilt (yard and date)	1993; equipment upgrade 1996 (Syntron)	SEISMIC SYSTEMS	
Length overall	98.50 m	Energy source (type and	Multiple tuned Bolt 'LL' airgun
Breadth moulded	15.40 m	manufacturer)	arrays
Max draught	5.30 m	Streamer manufacturer	Syntrak
Tonnage (grt)	4,084	Streamer type	480 digital
		Streamer numbers and	Flexible to 4 × 7,200 m: 6.25 m,
PROPULSION		lengths per number	12.5 m, 18.75 m or 25.00 m group
Main engine(s)	9,600 hp		lengths
Speed (cruising)	15-20 kt	Recording system	Syntrak 480-24
Endurance	56 days		

HELIDECK	yes		
			VERIFIED

ACCOMMODATION			
Charterers	Total accommodation for 58		

Veritas

Professor Kurentsov

GENERAL
Classification | Det Norske Veritas 1A1 Ice 1A
Length overall | 68.86 m
Breadth moulded | 12.40 m
Max draught | 5.75 m
Tonnage (grt) | 1,675

PROPULSION
Main engine(s) | 2,000 hp
Speed (cruising) | 12 kt
Endurance | 40 days

ACCOMMODATION
Charterers | Total accommodation for 55

SURVEY SYSTEMS
Positioning | Spectra INS; DigiCourse streamer tracking

SEISMIC SYSTEMS
Energy source (type and manufacturer) | Tuned Bolt 'Long-Life' dual-string airgun array
Streamer manufacturer | Digicon
Streamer type | DSS-240 digital (to 5,500 m)
Streamer numbers and lengths per number | 12.50 m or 25.00 m group lengths
Recording system | Digicon DSS-240

VERIFIED

Veritas

Seabulk Ross Seal

GENERAL
Classification | ABS Class ✠ A1, AMS
Length overall | 53.64 m
Breadth moulded | 11.59 m
Max draught | 3.28 m
Tonnage (grt) | 299; 203 net

PROPULSION
Main engine(s) | 3,400 hp
Speed (cruising) | 10 kt
Endurance | 33 days

ACCOMMODATION
Charterers | Total accommodation for 31

SURVEY SYSTEMS
Positioning | Spectra INS; RGPS tailbuoy tracking

SEISMIC SYSTEMS
Energy source (type and manufacturer) | Bolt airgun array, single tuned
Streamer manufacturer | Syntrak
Streamer type | 480-16 digital (1 × 6,000 m)
Streamer numbers and lengths per number | 6.25 m, 12.50 m, 18.75 m or 25.00 m group lengths
Recording system | Syntrak 480-16

VERIFIED

Veritas

Veritas Viking

GENERAL
Classification | DNV ✠ A1, SF, EO, HELDK, DK ✠, SBM
Built (yard and date) | Bergen, Norway, 1998
Length overall | 93.35 m
Breadth moulded | 22.00 m

Veritas Viking

2001/0110471

| Max draught | 6.50 m | Speed (cruising) | 15.50 kt |
| Tonnage (grt) | 8,000 | Endurance | 118 days |

| **PROPULSION** | | **ACCOMMODATION** | |
| Main engine(s) | 12,000 hp | Charterers | Total accommodation for 60 |

Veritas Viking

2001/0110468

SURVEY SYSTEMS		Streamer numbers and	Up to 12 km deployment;
Positioning	Spectra INS; MDL FanBeam laser tracking; RGPS active tailbuoy tracking; DigiCourse System-3 acoustic ranging	lengths per number	potential to handle and tow over 16 × 4-bit RDA streamers. 6.25 m, 12.50 m, 18.75 m or 25.00 m group lengths
		Acquisition system	Sprint 3-D (onboard data processing)
SEISMIC SYSTEMS		Recording system	Syntrak 960-24
Energy source (type and manufacturer)	Multiple (up to 3) tuned Bolt 'LL' airgun arrays		
Streamer manufacturer	Syntrak		
Streamer type	960 RDA digital		

UPDATED

Veritas

Veritas Viking II

GENERAL		Length overall	93.35 m
Classification	DNV ✠ SF, EO, HELDK, DK ✠, SBM	Breadth moulded	22.00 m
		Max draught	6.50 m
Built (yard and date)	Bergen, Norway, 1998	Tonnage (grt)	8,000

Veritas Viking II   *2001*/0110463

Veritas Viking II   *2001*/0110467

PROPULSION

Main engine(s)	12,000 hp
Speed (cruising)	15.50 kt
Endurance	118 days

ACCOMMODATION

Charterers	Total accommodation for 60

SURVEY SYSTEMS

Positioning	Spectra INS; MDL FanBeam laser tracking; RGPS active tailbuoy tracking; DigiCourse System-3 acoustic ranging

SEISMIC SYSTEMS

Energy source (type and manufacturer)	Multiple (up to 3) tuned Bolt 'LL' airgun arrays
Streamer manufacturer	Syntrak
Streamer type	960 RDA digital
Streamer numbers and lengths per number	Up to 12 km deployment; potential to handle and tow over 16 × 24-bit RDA streamers. 6.25 m, 12.50 m, 18.75 m or 25.00 m group lengths
Acquisition system	Sprint 3-D (onboard data processing)
Recording system	Syntrak 960-24

UPDATED

UNKNOWN

None at present

Discoverer

GENERAL

Owner	China Offshore Geophysical Corporation
Built (yard and date)	1996
Length overall	72.00 m
Breadth moulded	16.00 m

SEISMIC SYSTEMS

Energy source (type and manufacturer)	Airguns

Number of airguns	2 arrays
Size of airguns	91,440 cm³ each
Streamer numbers and lengths per number	3 × 480 channels

NEW ENTRY

OFFSHORE SITE AND ROUTE SURVEY VESSELS

AUSTRALIA

Svitzer Australia Pty Ltd

Svitzer Meridian

GENERAL
Owner	Svitzer Ltd
Port of reg/flag	Nassau/Bahamian
Official number	732239
Classification	DNV 1A1 E-O
Call sign	C6QR4
Built (yard and date)	1982
Rebuilt (yard and date)	November 1997
Length overall	72.50 m
Breadth moulded	13.80 m
Max draught	6.80 m
Tonnage (grt)	2,255; net 421.33

PROPULSION
Main engine(s)	Normo KVMB-12 2,600 bhp
Thrusters	Bow: 2 × 600 bhp; stern: 1 × 600 bhp
Propellers	Single vp

SAFETY
Lifeboats	Two covered
Lifesaving equipment	One FRC; 200 survival suits

HELIDECK
Size, aircraft capacity	Yes

SURVEY SYSTEMS
Positioning	Racal SkyFix; Simrad HPR300/309T SSBL; TSS HS-50 heave compensator
Echo-sounder (single beam)	2 × Atlas Deso 25
Multibeam/swath system	Atlas MD 50 kHz
Sidescan sonar	GeoAcoustics dual frequency

Sub-bottom profiler	Raytheon 3.5 kHz through hull profiler; shallow towed EG&G sub-tow boomer
Magnetometer	G880
Corer(s)	3 m gravity
Grab(s)	Van Veen
Sound velocity profiler	SVP, SVP+, Valeport

SEISMIC SYSTEMS
Energy source (type and manufacturer)	210 cu in GI and 150 cu in TI sleeve guns
Streamer manufacturer	HTI Digital
Streamer type	HydroScience
Acquisition system	SeisUP QC
Recording system	HydroScience SeaMUX NTRS

UPDATED

Svitzer Meridian   **2001**/0109082

CANADA

Deep Sea Trawlers

Anne S Pierce

GENERAL
Current operational status	Fibre optic cable installation assistance
Owner	Clearwater Fine Foods
Port of reg/flag	Lunenberg, Nova Scotia/Canadian
Official number	802013
Classification	SIC17 Cargo, Home Trade I
Call sign	VY3890
Built (yard and date)	Lunenburg, Nova Scotia, 1981
Rebuilt (yard and date)	Lunenburg, Nova Scotia, 1999
Length overall	35.50 m
Breadth moulded	8.00 m
Working deck width	8.00 m
Max draught	3.71 m
Operational draught	3.20 m
Tonnage (grt)	295

PROPULSION
Main engine(s)	Caterpillar D399
Propellers	4-blade R H, 1,943 mm pitch, 1,892 mm diameter fixed
Speed (max)	11 kt
Speed (cruising)	10 kt
Endurance	30 days
Fuel capacity	85,350 litres
Fuel consumption	2,500 litres/day
Electrical power	1 × Stamford Type MC334C, 112.5 kVA, 240/3/60 V; 1 × Stamford Type MC334C, 94 kVA, 240/3/60 V
Fresh water capacity	Maxim HJ10C producing 600 gallons/day

BRIDGE NAVIGATION AIDS

Satellite	Koden 930 DGPS	**Echo-sounder**	Koden CVS88; Furuno FE502
Radar	Amartizer 720 and 771	**Other ship navigation**	Ocean Vision ECS; Wagner
Gyrocompass	KVH		rudder angle indicator; Loran;
Speed log	DGPS		autopilots

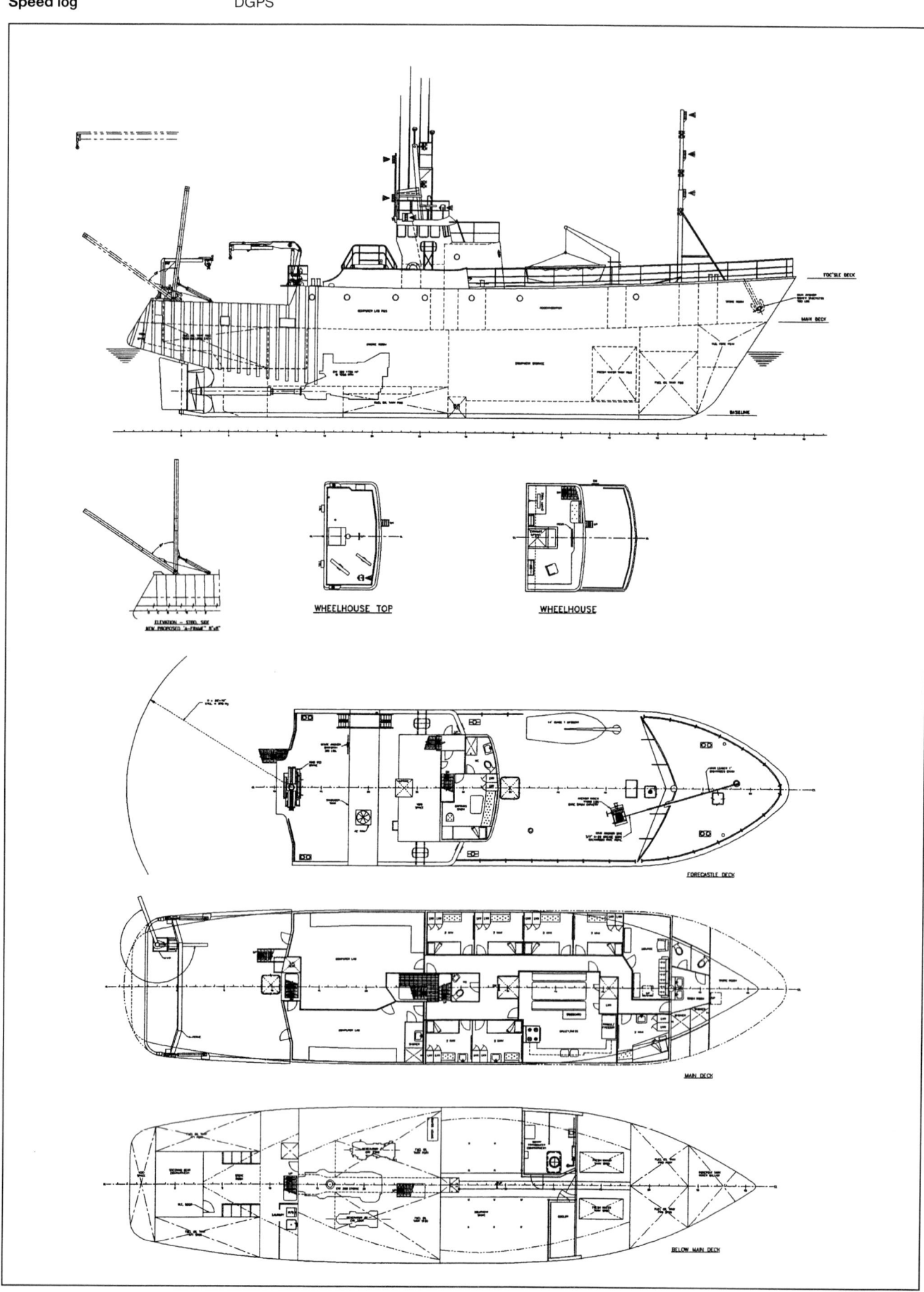

Anne S Pierce

COMMUNICATIONS

Inmarsat (type)	C
MF/HF	1 × Icom M700 SSB
VHF	1 × Sailor RT144; 1 × Icom M56
Cellular	MTT; MSAT

SAFETY

Lifeboats	1 × fibreglass for 8 persons
Lifesaving equipment	Conforms to SIC17 Cargo Vessel Certification requirements

DECK MACHINERY

Cranes	1 × Hiab 950 hydraulic
A-frame(s)	Hydraulically actuated
Winches	Hydraulic capstan
Transducer well	Yes

ACCOMMODATION

Crew	7
Scientists/surveyors	9

SCIENTIFIC SPACES

Total scientific deck space	550 sq ft

SURVEY SYSTEMS

Positioning	DGPS with Winfrog INS; TSS POS M/V
Echo-sounder (single beam)	1 × Koden CVS88; 1 × Furuno FE502
Multibeam/swath system	1 × Simrad EM1002
Sidescan sonar	1 × Klein 2000
Sub-bottom profiler	1 × GeoAcoustics
Magnetometer	1 × Geometrics
Corer(s)	1 × gravity
Grab(s)	1 × Shipek
Sound velocity profiler	1 × MVP200
Oceanographic sensors (CTDs/XBTs and so on)	1 × SV&P; 1 × SV&T

SEISMIC SYSTEMS

Energy source (type and manufacturer)	Airguns
Number of airguns	As required
Size of airguns	As required
Streamer type	48 channels
Recording system	OYO Geospace

NEW ENTRY

FRANCE

Comex S A

Janus

GENERAL

Owner	Comex S A, France
Port of reg/flag	French
Official number	French custom No 057258/615
Classification	Bureau Veritas: I 3/3 (E) ✠ Hull Engine
Built (yard and date)	Comex Marine Construction, 2000
Length overall	28.00 m
Breadth moulded	10.00 m
Working deck width	10.00 m
Max draught	3.50 m
Operational draught	3.00 m
Tonnage (grt)	400 UMS

PROPULSION

Main engine(s)	2 × Baudoin 6M26SR
Thrusters	2 × Schottel SPR 2000 (stern)
Propellers	Bow: 2 × Hydroma hydraulic, 38 kW each
Speed (max)	12 kt
Speed (cruising)	10 kt
Endurance	45,000 n miles, economic speed 10 kt
Fuel capacity	48,800 litres
Fuel consumption	2,500-3,000 litres/day, two generators
Electrical power	2 × 175 kVA, 1 × 44 kVA
Fresh water capacity	11 m³ generated

BRIDGE NAVIGATION AIDS

Satellite	GPS
Radar	Furuno FR 2115 ARPA; Furuno M1832
Gyrocompass	S G Brown Meridian Surveyor
Echo-sounder	Furuno FCU 6000

COMMUNICATIONS

Inmarsat (type)	C & M
MF/HF	Furuno RC 1500-1T GMDSS radio station
Cellular	Yes
Facsimile	Yes

SAFETY

Lifeboats	2 × 20 persons
Workboat/chase boat	Tender for 12 persons
Lifesaving equipment	Lifejackets + life suits

DECK MACHINERY

Cranes	1 × 15 t
A-frame(s)	1 × 7 t
Winches	1 × 5 t; 1 × 500 kg
Transducer well	600 mm diameter

ACCOMMODATION

Charterers	Total accommodation for 16 (14 single beds + two queen-sized beds)

SCIENTIFIC SPACES

Total scientific deck space	Workshops: electronic 7 m², mechanical 5 m²; navigation bridge 25 m²; oceanographic room 12 m²

SURVEY SYSTEMS

Positioning	DGPS Ag132 with Omnistar licence, RTK optional
Multibeam/swath system	Reson 2101-2 (optional)
Sidescan sonar	Klein 2000 m, with ISIS digital recording
Magnetometer	Sinomag

NEW ENTRY

Comex S A

Minibex

GENERAL

Owner	Comex S A, France
Port of reg/flag	Port aux Français/French
Official number	829493
Classification	Bureau Veritas
Call sign	FKSS
Built (yard and date)	Chantiers Navals de Rovere, 1987
Rebuilt (yard and date)	Chantiers Naval de Marseille, 1994
Length overall	29.75 m
Breadth moulded	6.80 m
Working deck width	5.50 m
Operational draught	2.50 m
Tonnage (grt)	166

PROPULSION

Main engine(s)	2 × MAN diesels
Thrusters	2 × Schottel
Speed (max)	10 kt
Speed (cruising)	9 kt
Endurance	2,000 n miles

Fuel capacity	23,500 litres
Fuel consumption	90 litres/h
Electrical power	2 × 70 kVA
Fresh water capacity	3,500 litres (2 × water makers, 200 litres/h)

BRIDGE NAVIGATION AIDS

Satellite	GPS
Radar	Furuno FR1115
Gyrocompass	S G Brown 1000
Speed log	BG & G
Echo-sounder	1 × Furuno FR81

COMMUNICATIONS

Inmarsat (type)	Mini M&C
MF/HF	Furuno GMDSS system

SAFETY

Lifeboats	2
Workboat/chase boat	1
Lifesaving equipment	For 12 persons

Minibex

2001/0106450

DECK MACHINERY

Cranes	1 × 1 t
A-frame(s)	1 × 5.5 t
Winches	1 × 5 t; 1 × 500 kg; 1 × 1.2 t
Moonpool(s)-size(s)/ function(s)	1 m × 1 m

ACCOMMODATION

Charterers	3
Crew	3
Scientists/surveyors	3

SCIENTIFIC SPACES

Total scientific deck space	18 m²
Multipurpose dry lab	6 m²

SURVEY SYSTEMS

Positioning	DGPS: AG132 with Omnistar licence – DSNP NR 203
Echo-sounder (single beam)	Furuno FR82
Sidescan sonar	Klein 2000 with ISIS system
Magnetometer	Sinomag
Vehicle(s) (ROVs/AUVs and so on)	Super Achilles observation ROV, 1,000 m depth capability, recovery and sampling tools; Remora 2000 manned submarine, 600 m depth capability, recovery and sampling tools

UPDATED

Minibex
2000/0093774

GERMANY

OSAE (Offshore Survey & Engineering) GmbH

Geniusbank

GENERAL

Owner	OSAE, Germany
Port of reg/flag	German
Classification	SeeBG
Length overall	14.10 m
Breadth moulded	4.00 m
Operational draught	0.85 m

PROPULSION

Main engine(s)	800 hp Rolls Royce diesel; KaMeWa 450S Waterjet
Electrical power	220 V 18 kW auxiliary diesel generator; 2 × 2 kW constant or regulated power

SURVEY SYSTEMS

Positioning	Trimble 4000 ssi (RTK) DGPS; TSS DMS 2-5 motion sensor; Anschutz Standard 20 survey gyro; EIVA Navipac data acquisition system with C-Map electronic chart overlay
Echo-sounder (single beam)	Atlas Deso 25 hull-mounted 33/ 210 kHz
Multibeam/swath system	Reson SeaBat 8101, hull-mounted; EIVA Navibat multibeam data acquisition system linked to Navipac

---

Sidescan sonar	EG&G 260 TH/272TD, both options, hull-mounted or towed fish
Sub-bottom profiler	GeoAcoustics Pipeliner SBP, hull-mounted
Sound velocity profiler	Robotron
Oceanographic sensors (CTDs/XBTs and so on)	Radio tide gauge receiver

NEW ENTRY

Geniusbank
2001/0110534

OSAE (Offshore Survey & Engineering) GmbH

Kommandor Jack

GENERAL

Former names	Valdivia
Owner	Hays Ships Ltd, UK
Port of reg/flag	Bahamas
Classification	GL + 100 A4, (E), MC
Length overall	73.85 m
Breadth moulded	11.00 m
Working deck width	Area: 180 m²
Operational draught	6.50 m
Tonnage (grt)	1,318; 422 net

PROPULSION

Main engine(s)	MAN G6V 52/74 A, 1,588 kW at 225 rpm
Thrusters	DP system Emri JS integrated with ATS11 acoustic positioning system; bow: 1 × Pleuger, 386 kW, 6 t thrust; aft: 1 × Schottel, 220 kW, 3.5 t thrust
Propellers	1 × Escher Wyss vp
Fuel capacity	210 t
Fuel consumption	7 t/day at 11 kt
Electrical power	Generators: 2 × 275 kVA 50 Hz diesels; 1 × 465 kVA 50 Hz shaft
Fresh water capacity	50 t; generator producing approx 10 t/day

BRIDGE NAVIGATION AIDS

Satellite	DGPS
Radar	2
Gyrocompass	1 with autopilot
Echo-sounder	3

COMMUNICATIONS

Inmarsat (type)	'A'
MF/HF	Raytheon GMDSS

SAFETY

Lifesaving equipment	Conforms to SOLAS requirements

DECK MACHINERY

Cranes	Central: 8 t at 12 m; starboard: AK 600, 2.6 t at 12 m
A-frame(s)	Stern: 15 t SWL; 2 × over-side

Winches	1 × double bathymetric 2000 m/500 m; 1 × survey with 6000 m calde; 1 × 1200 m coring; forward derrick 3 t SWL

ACCOMMODATION

Charterers	Total accommodation for 36

SURVEY SYSTEMS

Positioning	ATS 11
Echo-sounder (single beam)	1 × Simrad EM 1002; 1 × Simrad EA 500
Multibeam/swath system	1 × Simrad EM 120
Sidescan sonar	GeoAcoustics 159
Sub-bottom profiler	1 × Datasonics Chirp 11
Sound velocity profiler	2 × Robotron probes

VERIFIED

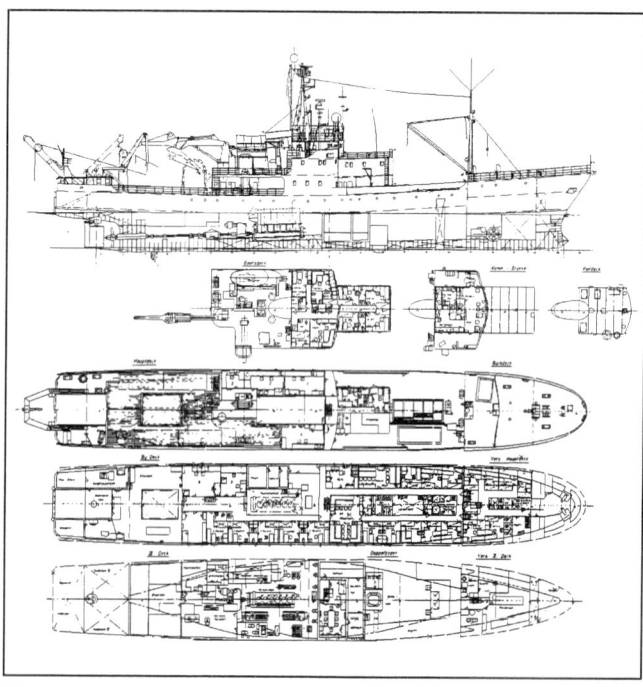

Kommandor Jack

0121298

OSAE (Offshore Survey & Engineering) GmbH

Scout II

GENERAL		**PROPULSION**	
Classification	(Semi-rigid inflatable cabin workboat)	**Main engine(s)**	180 hp BMW diesel/PP90 Jetdrive
Built (yard and date)	1996	**Speed (max)**	27 kt
Length overall	7.40 m		
Breadth moulded	2.50 m		
Operational draught	0.35 m		

NEW ENTRY

Scout II   **2001**/0110548

OSAE (Offshore Survey & Engineering) GmbH

Sounding Symphony

GENERAL		**PROPULSION**	
Port of reg/flag	Rostock	**Main engine(s)**	960 shp (continuous)
Classification	Bureau Veritas 3/3 coastal waters/special duty	**Thrusters**	Bow: 80 shp (electrical/joystick)
		Propellers	Twin
Length overall	27.00 m	**Speed (cruising)**	13.5 kt; survey 2.6 – 4.5 kt
Breadth moulded	6.00 m	**Electrical power**	2 × 60 kVA/380 V generator output
Operational draught	2.00 m		
Tonnage (grt)	101		

Sounding Symphony   **2000**/0089148

BRIDGE NAVIGATION AIDS

Radar	2
Gyrocompass	Magnetic and digital
Echo-sounder	Yes
Other ship navigation	Autopilot

COMMUNICATIONS

Inmarsat (type)	'C'
MF/HF	Yes
VHF	Yes
Facsimile	Yes

DECK MACHINERY

Cranes	1 × Hiab Sea-crane 8.5 m/t, 14 m reach
Winches	Hydraulic on crane; electrical on deck

SURVEY SYSTEMS

Positioning	Sub-surface: Nautronix ATS Trimble & Sercel DGPS; Eiva Navipac
Echo-sounder (single beam)	STN Atlas DESO 25 (210/33/15 kHz, limit 2,000 m); Simrad EA500 (200/38/12 kHz, limit 4,000 m); TSS 335B heave/roll/pitch sensor; TSS 340 Pipetracker
Multibeam/swath system	Atlas Fansweep, 180 kHz
Sidescan sonar	EG&G 260 (400/100 kHz)
Sub-bottom profiler	GeoAcoustic Pipeliner (3.5, 5, 7, 12, 14, 200 kHz)

VERIFIED

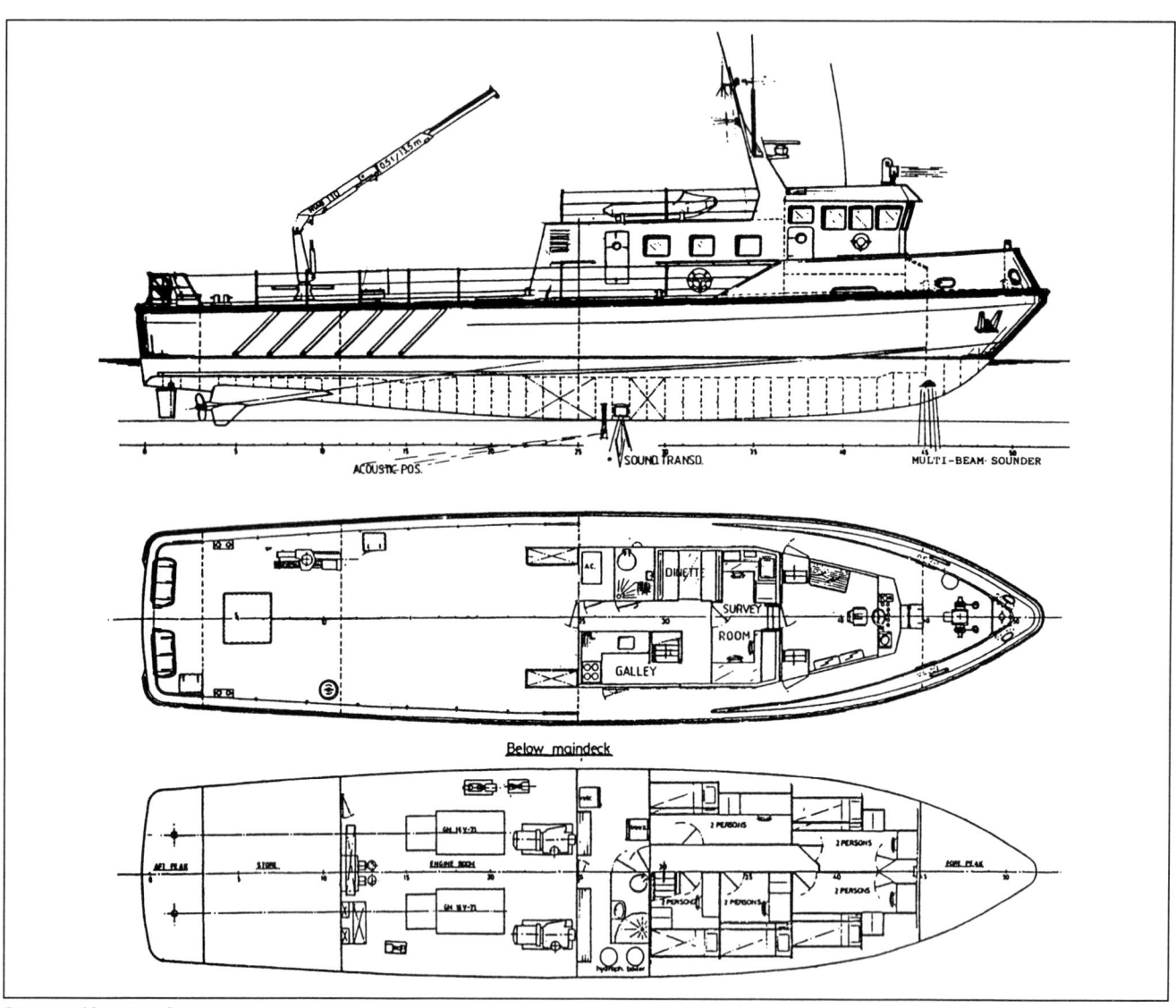

Diagram of Sounding Symphony

2000/0089149

INDIA

Elcome Surveys Pvt Ltd

Flamboyan

GENERAL

Former names	*Teratai; Osam Dragon*
Current operational status	Survey vessel

Owner	Elcome Surveys Pvt Ltd, India
Port of reg/flag	Indian
Official number	2853

Classification	ABS/IRS	**Gyrocompass**	1
Call sign	VWTH	**Speed log**	1
Built (yard and date)	Goriki Shipyard, Japan, 1983	**Echo-sounder**	1
Length overall	39.00 m		
Breadth moulded	3.60 m	**COMMUNICATIONS**	
Working deck width	7.50 m	**MF/HF**	Sailor GMDSS A3 with STD-C
Max draught	3.20 m		telex
Operational draught	3.00 m	**VHF**	Sailor Mini 'M'
Tonnage (grt)	392		
		DECK MACHINERY	
PROPULSION		**Cranes**	1 × Hiab 110 sea crane
Main engine(s)	2 × 800 bhp Otsuka SODHS	**A-frame(s)**	1
	6 × 26		
Thrusters	Bow: one fixed-pitch electric, 1.7 t	**ACCOMMODATION**	
Propellers	2 × fixed pitch	**Charterers**	Total accommodation for 22
Speed (max)	10 kt		
Fuel capacity	172 m³	**SCIENTIFIC SPACES**	
Electrical power	2 × 160/125 kVA 415 V 50 Hz	**Total scientific deck space**	Clear deck space 22.00 × 7.50 m
Fresh water capacity	140 m³		
		SURVEY SYSTEMS	
BRIDGE NAVIGATION AIDS		**Positioning**	Leica DGPS with beacon receiver
Satellite	GPS		
Radar	1		*VERIFIED*

IRELAND

The Commissioners of Irish Lights

Granuaile

GENERAL		**Max draught**	5.00 m
Current operational status	Aids to navigation	**Operational draught**	4.40 m
Owner	Commissioners of Irish Lights	**Tonnage (grt)**	2,625
Port of reg/flag	Irish		
Official number	403374	**PROPULSION**	
Classification	Lloyds 100 A1, LMC, UMS,	**Main engine(s)**	5 × 740 kW, 8-cylinder MAN and
	DP(AM), NRI, PCR		BW 16/24L diesel alternators
Call sign	EIPT	**Thrusters**	Bow: 360° Gill Jet (DP system)
Built (yard and date)	Damen Shipyards, The	**Propellers**	2 × 360° Schottel
	Netherlands, 2000	**Speed (max)**	13.1 kt
Length overall	79.70 m	**Speed (cruising)**	12.63 kt
Breadth moulded	16.10 m	**Endurance**	24 days at cruising speed
Working deck width	15.8 m	**Fuel capacity**	320 m³

Granuaile   *2001*/0110535

Fuel consumption	13.34 m³/day at cruising speed	**VHF**	4 × Kelvin Hughes/Husun;
Electrical power	3,700 kW		3 × Husan hand-held GMDSS;
Fresh water capacity	457 t		6 × Kenwood hand-held;
			2 × Husun hand-held
BRIDGE NAVIGATION AIDS		**Cellular**	2
Satellite	2 × Trimble NT 300D DGPS;	**Facsimile**	1 × cellular
	1 × Trimble NT 200D portable		
	DGPS; 1 × Garmin handheld	**SAFETY**	
	DGPS	**Workboat/chase boat**	2 × 7.5 m Timber motor boats;
Radar	2 × Kelvin Hughes Nucleus		1 × 8 m RIB (32 kt); 1 × semi-rigid
	2/5,000 (S and X band)		rescue boat
Gyrocompass	2 × C Plath	**Lifesaving equipment**	As per Class 7 ship
Speed log	Consilium Marine SAL (SD 2.1)		
	Doppler	**HELIDECK**	
Other ship navigation	1 × Loran C receiver; 1 × Kelvin	**Size, aircraft capacity**	D value 13 m (any helicopter of
	Hughes ECDS electronic chart;		13 m overall length or less), max
	1 × Furuno forward-looking sonar		weight 3.2 t
COMMUNICATIONS		**DECK MACHINERY**	
Inmarsat (type)	Satcom C	**Cranes**	1 × Liebherr 20 t SWL, 20 m max
MF/HF	Kelvin Hughes/Husan		outreach

Granuaile

2001/0110536

Winches	1 × towing (40 t bollard pull); 2 × 5 t tugger; capstans: 2 × 10 t and 2 × 15 t
Moonpool(s) – size(s)/ function(s)	0.5 m diameter

ACCOMMODATION

Charterers	Total accommodation for 27

SURVEY SYSTEMS

Positioning	DGPS and DP system; Trac C and Caris post-processing
Echo-sounder (single beam)	1 × Elac
Multibeam/swath system	1 × Elac
Sound velocity profiler	Yes

UPDATED

Granuaile survey vessel

2000/0093771

Granuaile's cranes at rear of the vessel

2000/0093772

Global Ocean Technologies Ltd

Bligh

GENERAL
Former names   *HMS Hecla*

SURVEY SYSTEMS
Echo-sounder (single beam)   Kongsberg Simrad EM1002
(95 kHz)

Multibeam/swath system   Kongsberg Simrad EM120
12 kHz, 11,000 m depth range
Sub-bottom profiler   Kongsberg Simrad 4 × 4

VERIFIED

Bligh   *2001*/0110525

Hunter Marine Ltd

Kilquade

GENERAL
Former names   *R M A S Denmead*
Owner   Hunter Marine Ltd

Port of reg/flag   Dublin/Irish
Official number   O/N 402951

Kilquade   *2001*/0109097

Classification	Class VIII A with passenger licence
Call sign	E I 4537
Built (yard and date)	Charles Holmes & Co Ltd, Hull, 1970
Length overall	24 m
Breadth moulded	6.49 m
Max draught	2.21 m
Operational draught	2.21 m
Tonnage (grt)	111.99

PROPULSION

Main engine(s)	Lister Blackstone ERS4M
Propellers	3-blade 59 in diameter, graphite iron
Speed (max)	10.5 kt
Speed (cruising)	9.5 kt
Endurance	800 n miles
Fuel capacity	5.25 t
Fuel consumption	12 gallons/hour @ 9.5 kt
Electrical power	Perkins 6.354, 80 bhp @ 1,800 rpm 30 kW DC
Fresh water capacity	3.7 t

BRIDGE NAVIGATION AIDS

Satellite	DGPS, MLR
Radar	Furuno 24 miles range
Echo sounder	A P Precision Type 787

COMMUNICATIONS

VHF	Pye Beaver F M 900

SAFETY

Workboat/chase boat	Zodiac Mk 111
Lifesaving equipment	As necessary by classification/full

SURVEY SYSTEMS

Sensors	
Echo sounder (single beam)	Charterer supply
Multibeam/swath system	Charterer supply
Sidescan sonar	Charterer supply
Sub-bottom profiler	Charterer supply
Magnetometer	Charterer supply

NEW ENTRY

NETHERLANDS

Rederij Waterweg BV

Coastal Explorer

GENERAL

Former names	*Warlock*
Owner	Rederij Waterweg BV, Netherlands
Classification	Bureau Veritas I 3/3 E, special service coastal waters Dutch Shipping Inspectorate coastal waters up to 30 n miles
Call sign	PIML
Built (yard and date)	Netherlands, 1994
Length overall	25.20 m
Breadth moulded	6.96 m
Operational draught	0.75 m
Tonnage (grt)	98; 28 net

PROPULSION

Main engine(s)	2 × GM 6V92, 480 hp
Thrusters	Bow: 55 hp
Propellers	Twin, fixed-pitch
Speed (max)	9.5 kt
Fuel capacity	12,500 litres

Electrical power	Auxiliary engines: 2 × Valmet/ Stamford: 1 at 145 kVA, 1 at 57 kVA
Fresh water capacity	3,000 litres

BRIDGE NAVIGATION AIDS

Radar	Furuno FR 2110
Gyrocompass	Tikomec GM-20/21
Echo-sounder	Furuno FCV-665
Other ship navigation	Robertson AP9 Mk II autopilot; Furuno Navtex NX500

COMMUNICATIONS

VHF	2 × Sailor RT 2048
Cellular	GSM

SAFETY

Workboat/chase boat	Tender vessel *Coastal Mate*: length 8.40 m, 190 hp

DECK MACHINERY

Cranes	Deck: 25 t/m

Coastal Explorer   *2001*/0106424

Coastal Explorer   *2001*/0106425

ACCOMMODATION
Charterers   Total accommodation for 8

SURVEY SYSTEMS
Positioning   Sercel NR 103 DGPS

Echo-sounder (single beam)   Atlas Deso 22 hull-mounted
                                  transducers (33/210 kHz)
Multibeam/swath system   Tritech scanning sonar

VERIFIED

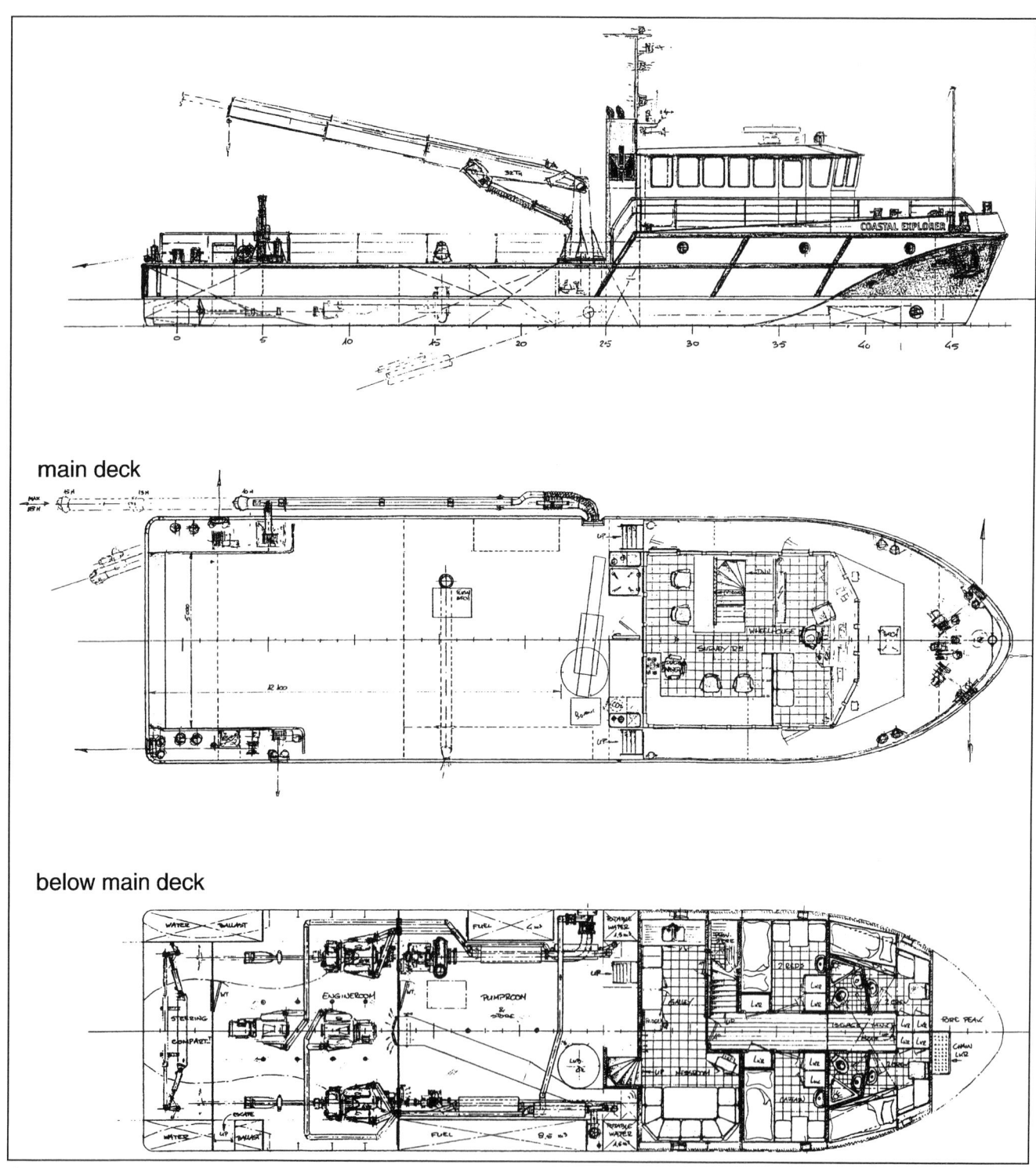

main deck

below main deck

Coastal Explorer   **2001**/0106440

Rederij Waterweg BV

Coastal Force

GENERAL
Owner   Rederij Waterweg BV,
                             Netherlands
Port of reg/flag   Workum, Netherlands

Classification   Bureau Veritas, I 3/3 E tug coastal
                             waters, Dutch Shipping
                             Inspectorate, coastal waters up to
                             30 n miles

Call sign	PCEL		CRK3/Stamford ECM, 31.50 kVA,
Built (yard and date)	Damen Shipyards, Netherlands,		220/380 V
	1997	**Fresh water capacity**	3,000 litres
Length overall	19.50 m		
Breadth moulded	6.20 m	**BRIDGE NAVIGATION AIDS**	
Operational draught	2.50 m	**Satellite**	GP70
Tonnage (grt)	70; 21 net	**Radar**	Furuno FR-8050 DA
		Echo-sounder	Furuno FE-606
PROPULSION		**Other ship navigation**	Robertson AP45 autopilot; Navtex
Main engine(s)	2 × GM 16V92 TA, 1,460 hp		NX500
Speed (max)	11.50 kt		
Fuel capacity	28,000 litres	**COMMUNICATIONS**	
Electrical power	Auxiliary engines: 2 × Lister	**VHF**	2 × Sailor RT 2048

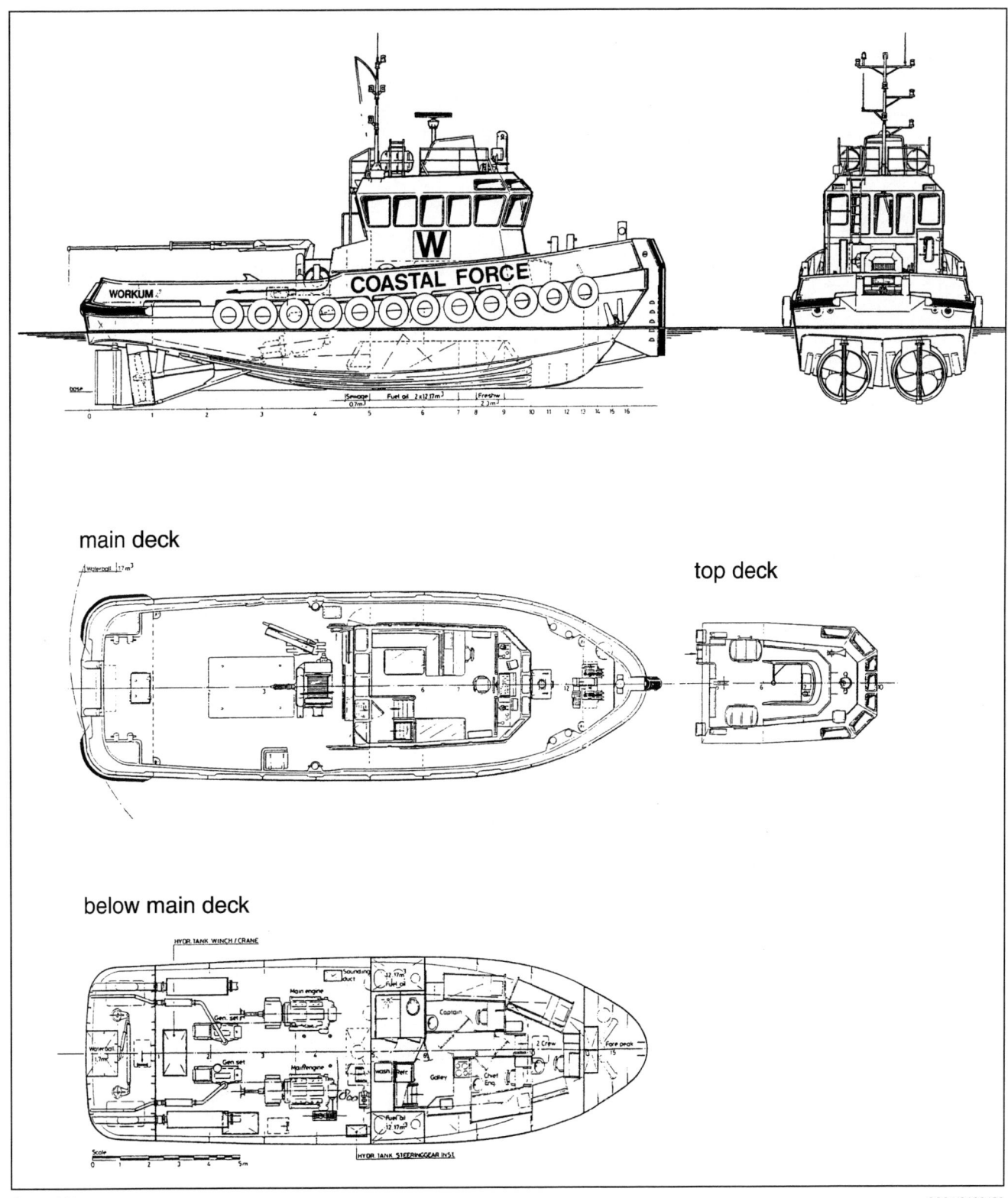

main deck

top deck

below main deck

Coastal Force

2001/0106428

DECK MACHINERY		**ACCOMMODATION**	
Cranes	Effer 6 t/m	**Charterers**	Total accommodation for 4

UPDATED

Coastal Force

2001/0106427

Rederij Waterweg BV

Coastal Liner

GENERAL
Owner   Rederij Waterweg BV,
                             Netherlands

Classification   BV I 3/3 (E) ⊕ Light Ship, High
                             Speed

Coastal Liner

2001/0106429

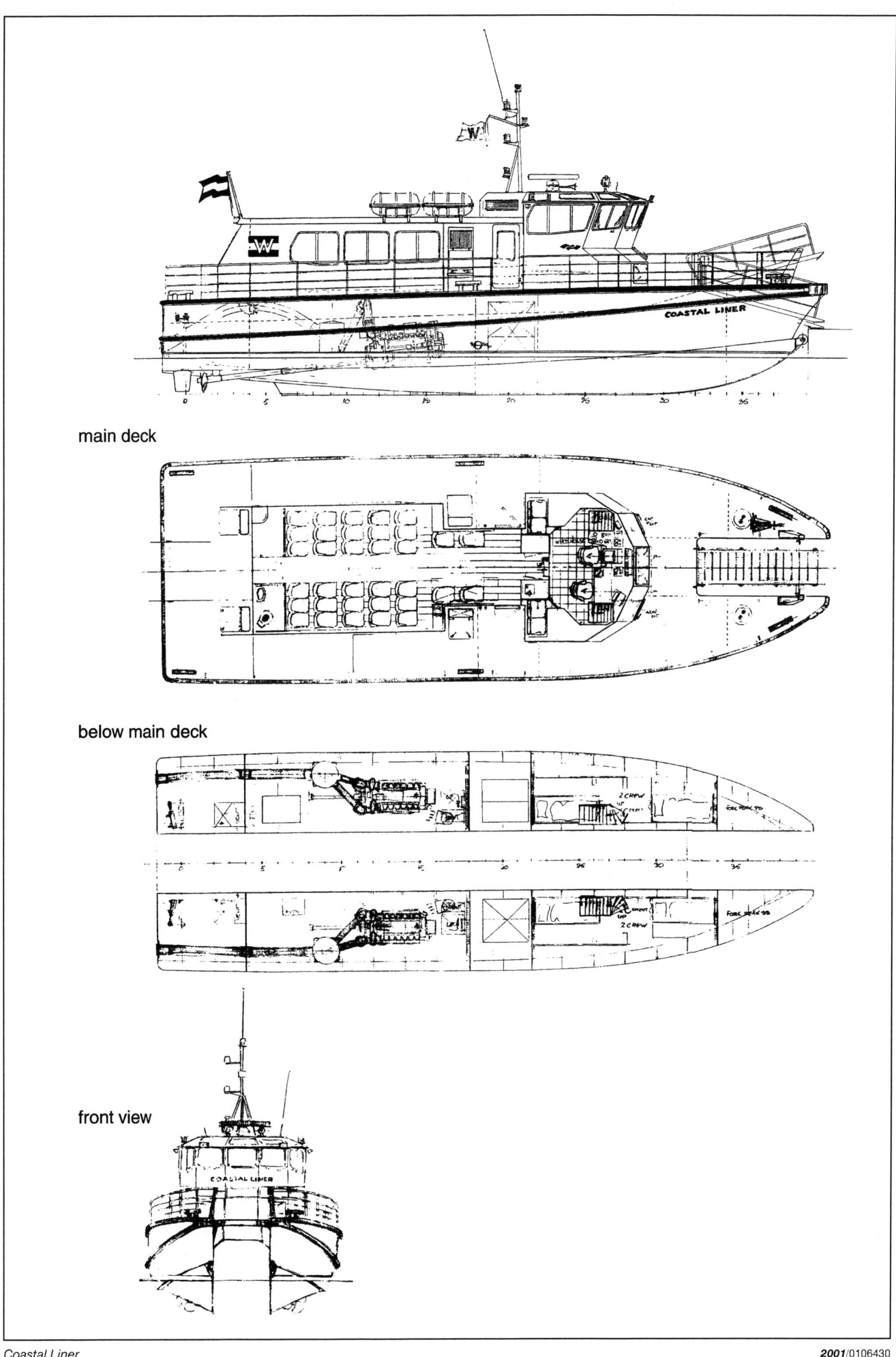

main deck

below main deck

front view

Coastal Liner

2001/0106430

	Passenger Craft Cat A 'Deep Sea' Mach Dutch Shipping Inspectorate, 30 miles (day service 100 miles)	**BRIDGE NAVIGATION AIDS**	
		Satellite	ADMK 10D Philips DGPS
		Radar	Furuno FR 8051
Call sign	PEDC	Echo-sounder	Furuno FE 606; Radio Holland ES 2000
Built (yard and date)	Shipyard Luyt, Den Oever, Netherlands, 2000	Other ship navigation	Robertson AP45 autopilot; Tsunamis plotter
Length overall	21.00 m	**Communications**	
Breadth moulded	6.70 m (catamaran)	VHF	2 × Sailor RT 2048; 1 × Sailor RM 2042 DSC; SSB radio Furuno FS 1562/15; 3 × hand-held GMDSS VHF
Operational draught	1.15 m		
Tonnage (grt)	90; net 27		
		Cellular	GSM mobile phone
PROPULSION			
Main engine(s)	2 × Detroit Diesel MTU 12V2000M70, 2,150 hp	**ACCOMMODATION**	
		Crew	4; 36 passenger seats
Propellers	Twin screw		
Speed (max)	25 kt		
Fuel capacity	6,000 litres		*NEW ENTRY*
Electrical power	Auxiliary engine: Hatz 3L41C/ Stamford, 24 kVA, 50 Hz, 220/380 V		
Fresh water capacity	2 × 120 litres		

Rederij Waterweg BV

Coastal Mate

GENERAL		**PROPULSION**	
Current operational status	Tender and survey vessel for *Coastal Explorer*	**Main engine(s)**	2 × GM 353, 190 hp
		Thrusters	Twin, fixed-pitch
Owner	Rederij Waterweg BV, Netherlands	**Speed (max)**	12 kt
		Fuel capacity	500 litres
Classification	Dutch Shipping Inspectorate		
Built (yard and date)	1995		*NEW ENTRY*
Length overall	8.40 m		
Breadth moulded	3.50 m		
Operational draught	0.80 m		

Coastal Mate

2001/0106426

Rederij Waterweg BV

Coastal Power

GENERAL

Classification	Bureau Veritas, tug coastal waters, Dutch Shipping Inspection, coastal waters up to 30 n miles
Call sign	PDKH
Built (yard and date)	Damen Shipyards, Hardinxveld, Netherlands, 1995
Length overall	16.89 m

Breadth moulded	5.29 m
Operational draught	2.10 m
Tonnage (grt)	41; net 12

PROPULSION

Main engine(s)	2 × Caterpillar 3408 TA/B, 940 hp, 700 kW
Speed (max)	10 kt
Fuel capacity	13.70 m³

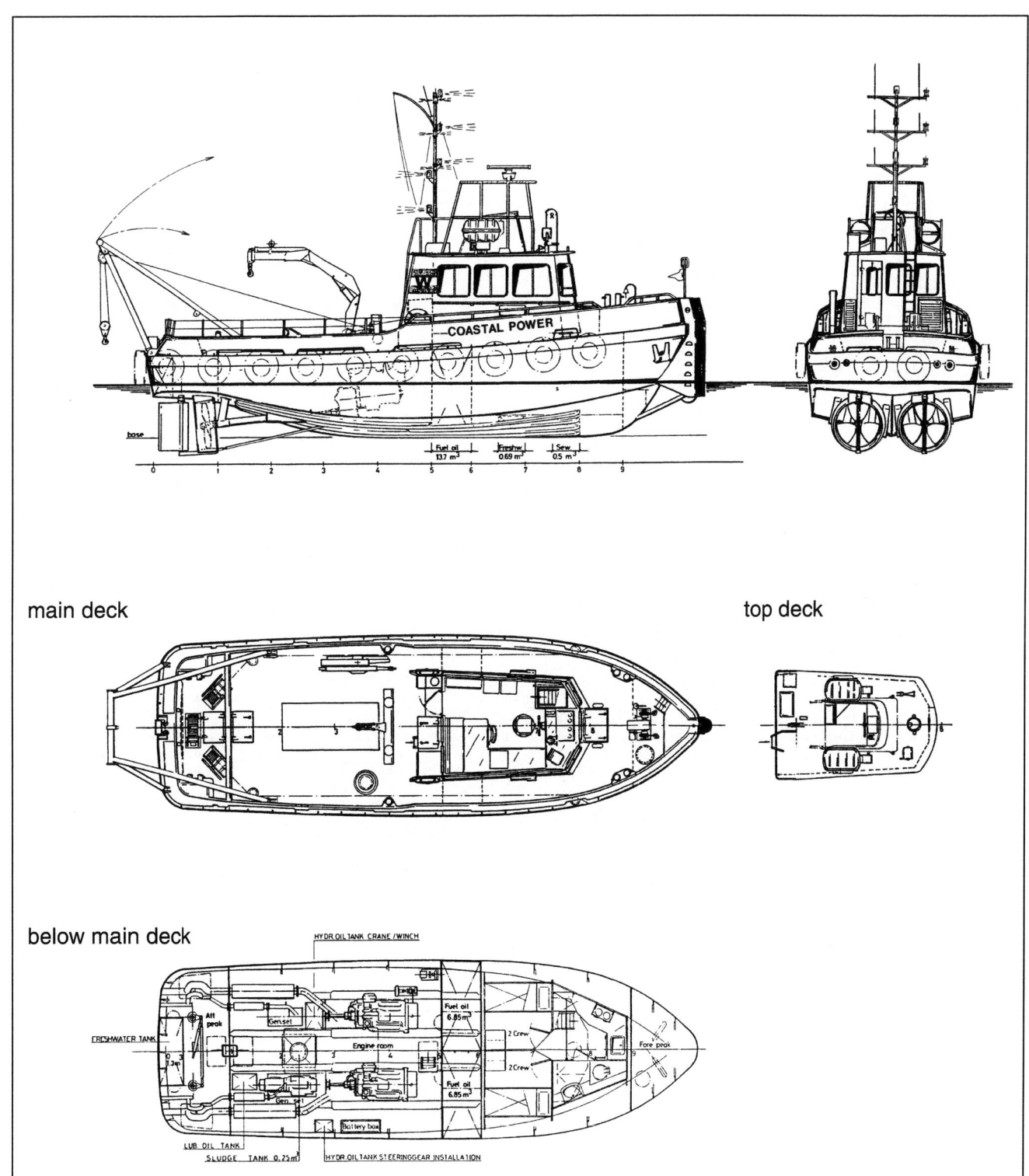

Coastal Power

2001/0106432

Electrical power Auxiliary engine: Onan 31 kVA, 220/380 V; Onan 15 kVA, 220/380 V

BRIDGE NAVIGATION AIDS
Satellite GPS navigator GP70
Radar Furuno FR-8050 DA
Echo-sounder Furuno FCV 667; Radio Holland EZ 2000
Other ship navigation Robertson AP45 autopilot; Navtex NX 500

COMMUNICATIONS
VHF 3 × Sailor RT 2048

DECK MACHINERY
Cranes Effer 6 t/m
A-frame(s) Optional
Winches 7 t hydraulic

ACCOMMODATION
Charterers Total accommodation for 4

SURVEY SYSTEMS
Echo-sounder (single beam) Hull-mounted Atlas Deso 33 kHz and 210 kHz

UPDATED

Coastal Power

2001/0106431

Rederij Waterweg BV

Coastal Service

GENERAL
Owner Rederij Waterweg BV, Netherlands
Port of reg/flag Netherlands
Classification Bureau Veritas, tug coastal waters, Dutch Shipping Inspection, coastal waters up to 15 n miles
Call sign PDMC

Built (yard and date) H de Haas, Maassluis, Netherlands, 1970
Length overall 16.24 m
Breadth moulded 4.50 m
Operational draught 1.60 m
Tonnage (grt) 32.46; 1.91 net

PROPULSION
Main engine(s) GM 12V71N 400 hp/265 kW

Propellers	4-blade	**Echo-sounder**	Furuno FMV-603
Speed (max)	10 kt	**Other ship navigation**	AP navigator
Fuel capacity	10 m³		
Electrical power	Auxiliary engines: Lister TR3, 17.5 kVA, 220/380 V; Samofa 24 V	**COMMUNICATIONS**	
		VHF	1 × Sailor RT 144; 1 × Sailor RT 2048
Fresh water capacity	13 m³		
		DECK MACHINERY	
BRIDGE NAVIGATION AIDS		**Cranes**	Atlas 3006, 6 t/m
Radar	Furuno FR-8050 DA		

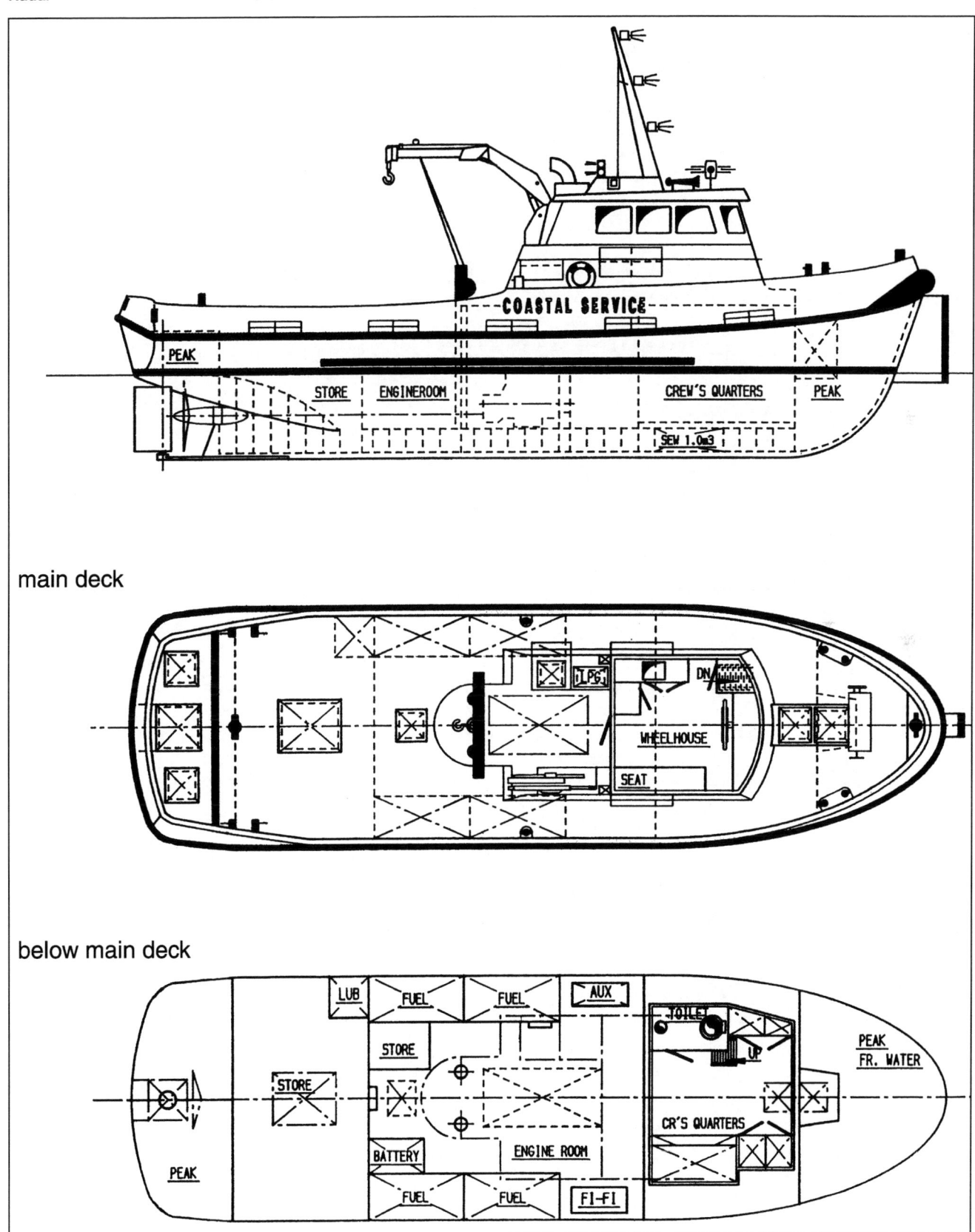

main deck

below main deck

Coastal Service

2001/0106434

ACCOMMODATION

Charterers	Total accommodation for 2

SURVEY SYSTEMS

Echo-sounder (single beam)	Hull-mounted Atlas Deso 33 kHz and 210 kHz

UPDATED

Coastal Service

2001/0106433

Rederij Waterweg BV

Coastal Sprinter

GENERAL

Owner	Rederij Waterweg BV, Netherlands
Classification	Bureau Veritas I 3/3, Seagoing Launch – Mach
Built (yard and date)	1997
Length overall	12.84 m
Breadth moulded	3.42 m
Max draught	0.90 m

PROPULSION

Main engine(s)	Caterpillar 3208 DITA, 435 hp
Propellers	Single, fixed-pitch
Speed (max)	18.5 kt
Fuel capacity	1,000 litres
Electrical power	Auxiliary engine: Mitsubishi S4Q/ Stamford 20 kVA, 220/380 V, 50 Hz
Fresh water capacity	75 litres

BRIDGE NAVIGATION AIDS

Satellite	Furuno GP 500 GPS
Radar	Koden MD-3850
Echo-sounder	Koden CV5-106
Other ship navigation	Robertson AP45 autopilot

COMMUNICATIONS

VHF	2 × Debeg 5506-76; 1 × Sailor RT 144 B

ACCOMMODATION

Charterers	Total accommodation for 1, 8 passenger seats

VERIFIED

Rederij Waterweg BV

Coastal Surveyor 2

GENERAL		Length overall	20.16 m
Former names	*Selsdum*	**Breadth moulded**	6.11 m
Owner	Rederij Waterweg BV,	**Operational draught**	0.75 m
	Netherlands	**Tonnage (grt)**	75; net 22
Classification	Bureau Veritas, I 3/3 E seagoing		
	launch, coastal waters up to 15 n	**PROPULSION**	
	miles Dutch shipping inspectorate	**Main engine(s)**	2 × DAF DK1160, 380 hp
Call sign	PHKJ	**Propellers**	Twin, fixed-pitch
Built (yard and date)	Forward Engineering,	**Speed (max)**	9 kt
	Papendrecht, Netherlands, 1993	**Fuel capacity**	5,000 litres

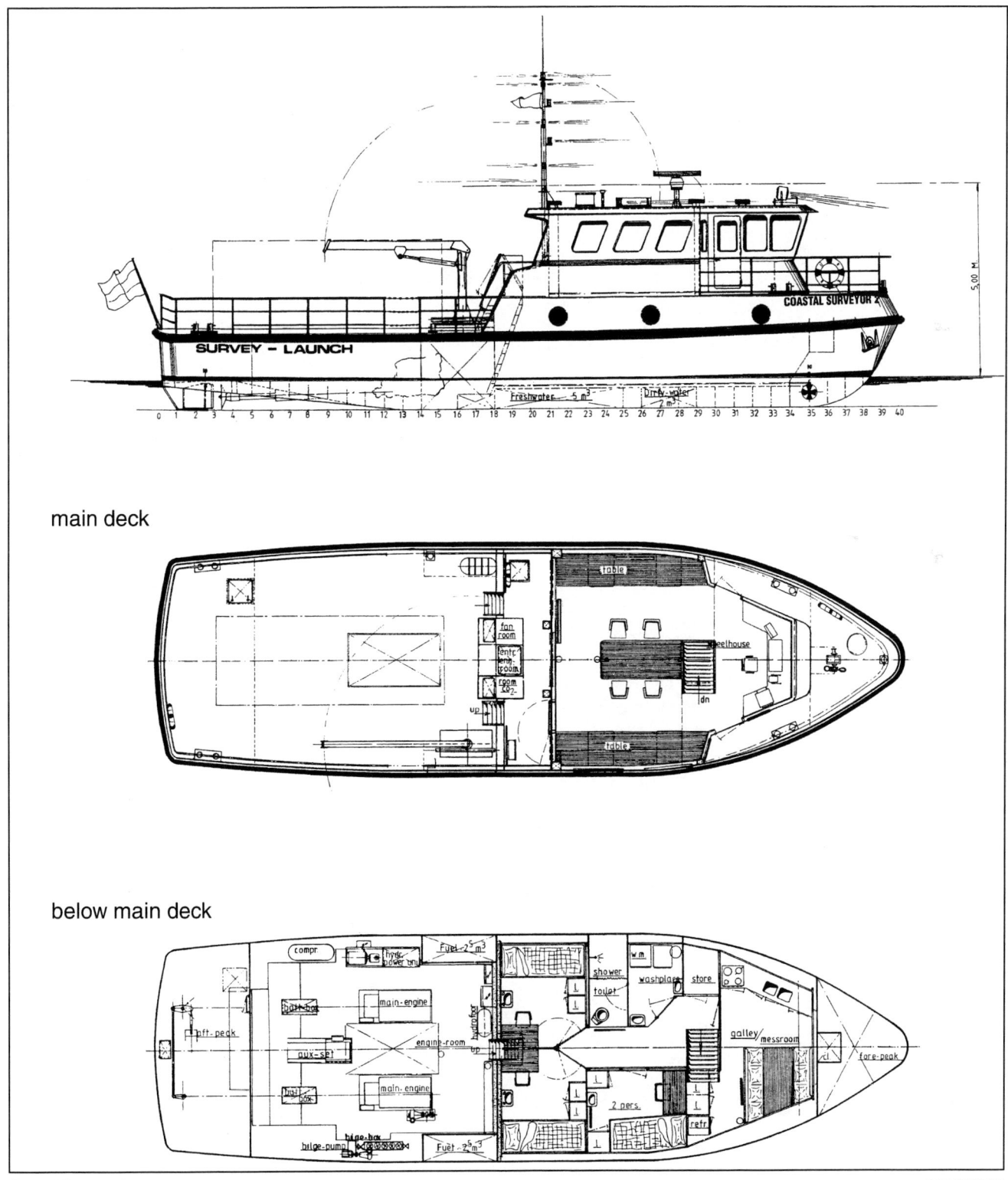

main deck

below main deck

Coastal Surveyor 2   ***2001***/0106436

Electrical power	Auxiliary engines: 1 × DAF-Stamford 65 kVA, 1 × Hatz-Stamford 12.50 kVA	**BRIDGE NAVIGATION AIDS**	
		Satellite	Furuno GP50
		Radar	Furuno FR 7061
Fresh water capacity	5,000 litres	**Echo-sounder**	Dogger 42

Coastal Surveyor 2

2001/0106435

Coastal Surveyor 2

2000/0093865

| Other ship navigation | Robertson AP45 autopilot; Furuno Navtex NX500 | **ACCOMMODATION** **Charterers** | Total accommodation for 6 |

COMMUNICATIONS
VHF   2 × Sailor RT 2048, 1 × Sailor RM 2042

UPDATED

DECK MACHINERY
Cranes   2 t

Rederij Waterweg BV

Coastal Tender

| **GENERAL** | | **Owner** | Rederij Waterweg BV, Netherlands |
| **Former names** | *Bruinvis* | | |

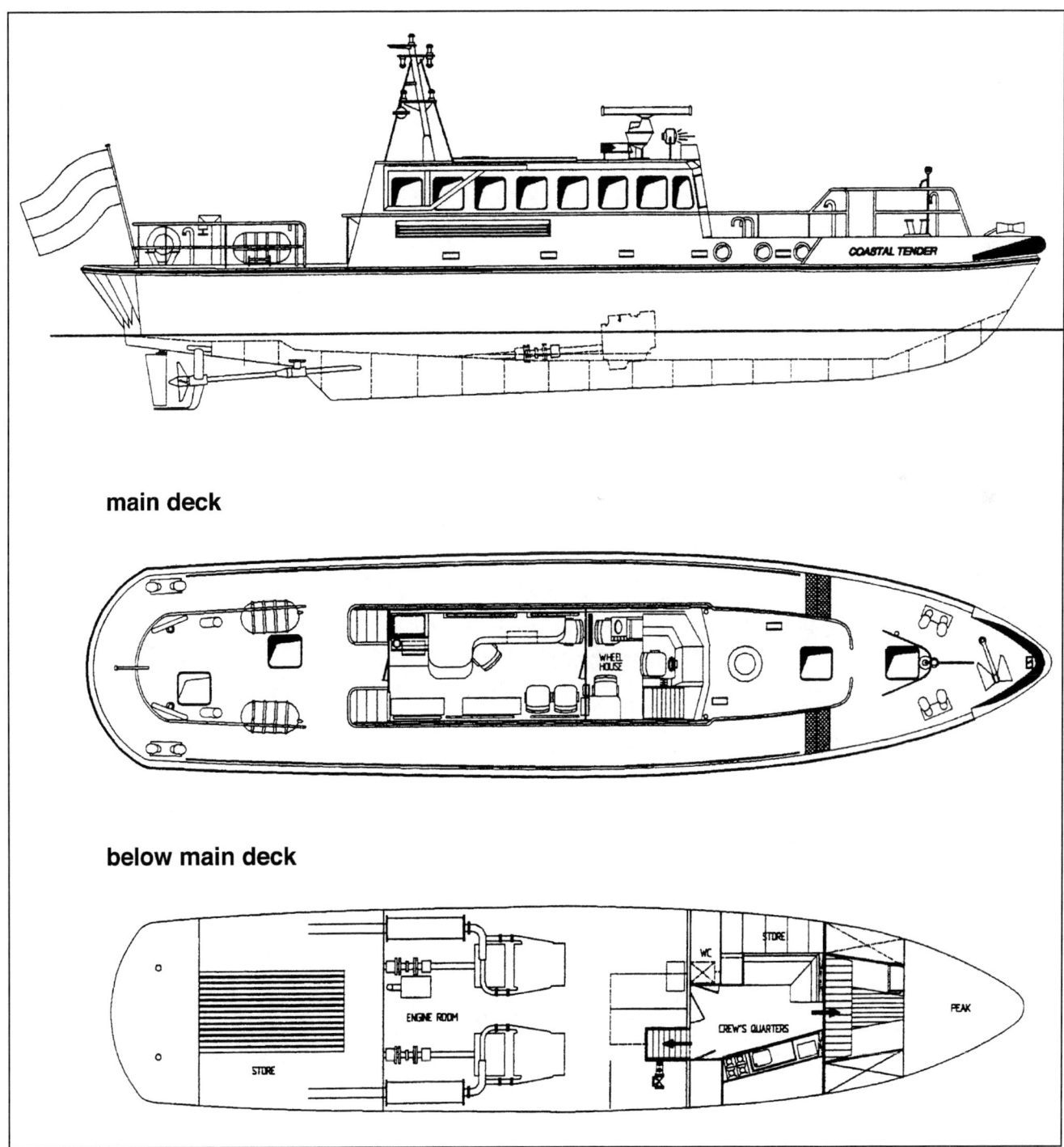

main deck

below main deck

Coastal Tender   *2001*/0106438

Port of reg/flag	Netherlands	**BRIDGE NAVIGATION AIDS**	
Classification	Dutch Shipping Inspectorate, coastal waters up to 30 n miles	Satellite	GPS navigator
		Radar	Bridgemaster CA 180
Call sign	PDHG	Gyrocompass	Yes
Built (yard and date)	Netherlands, 1964	Other ship navigation	Navtex
Rebuilt (yard and date)	1984/1994		
Length overall	21.35 m	**COMMUNICATIONS**	
Breadth moulded	4.65 m	VHF	2 × RT 925
Operational draught	1.30 m		
Tonnage (grt)	37; net 11	**ACCOMMODATION**	
		Crew	4
PROPULSION		Scientists/surveyors	12 passengers
Main engine(s)	2 × GM12V 71N, 375 hp each		*UPDATED*
Propellers	Twin, fixed-pitch		
Speed (max)	13 kt		
Fuel capacity	3,000 litres		
Electrical power	Auxiliary engines: Lister Petter BV3TR3 generator set, 17.20 kVA, 220/380 V		
Fresh water capacity	500 litres		

Coastal Tender   **2001**/0106437

Rederij Waterweg BV

Don Quichot

GENERAL		Breadth moulded	3.39 m
Former names	*Rietgraaf*	Operational draught	1.20 m
Owner	Rederij Waterweg BV, Netherlands	**PROPULSION**	
Port of reg/flag	Workum, Netherlands	Main engine(s)	DAF DT 615 M, 120 hp/92 kW
Call sign	PE 5991	Electrical power	Auxiliary engine: Mercedes 15 kVA, 220/380 V
Built (yard and date)	Damen Shipyards, Netherlands, 1972		
Rebuilt (yard and date)	Re-engined 1988	**BRIDGE NAVIGATION AIDS**	
Length overall	12.65 m	Radar	Decca RR 1216

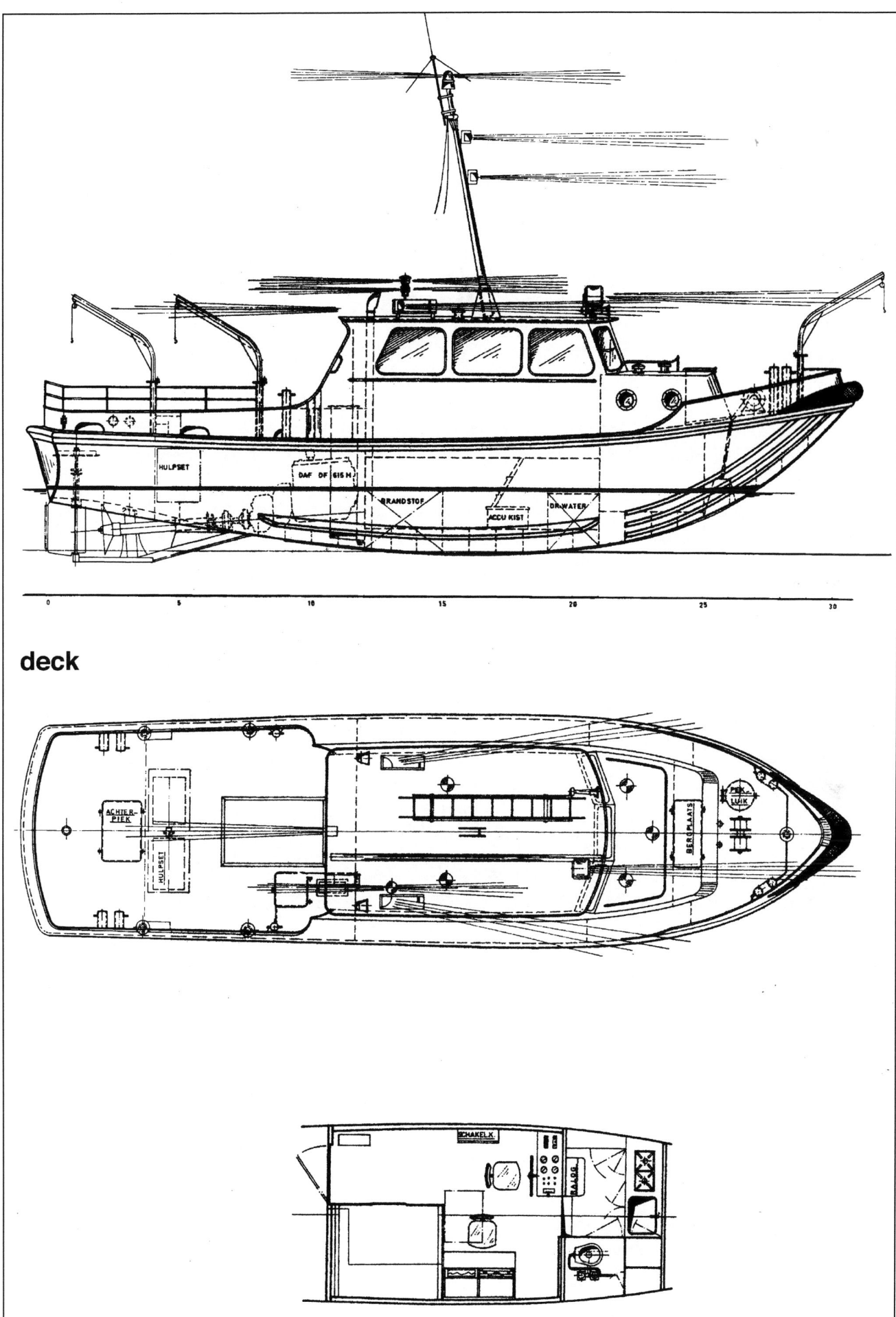

deck

Don Quichot

2001/0106441

COMMUNICATIONS		**SURVEY SYSTEMS**	
VHF	2 × Sailor RT 2048	**Echo-sounder (single beam)**	Atlas Deso 22 hull-mounted transducers (33/210 kHz)

UPDATED

Don Quichot

2001/0106439

Rederij Waterweg BV

Merijn

GENERAL

Former names	*Leda*
Owner	Rederij Waterweg BV, Netherlands
Port of reg/flag	Netherlands
Classification	Bureau Veritas, coastal waters, Dutch Shipping Inspection, coastal waters up to 30 n miles
Call sign	PFXK
Built (yard and date)	Simoneau-Marine, France, 1989
Rebuilt (yard and date)	Re-engined 1997
Length overall	14.50 m
Breadth moulded	6.15 m
Operational draught	1.05 m
Tonnage (grt)	36; net 10

PROPULSION

Main engine(s)	2 × Volvo TAMD 71 A, 360 hp each
Speed (max)	18 kt
Fuel capacity	2,000 m³
Electrical power	Auxiliary engine: Pols 10 kVA, 220 V

BRIDGE NAVIGATION AIDS

Satellite	GP70
Radar	Furuno FR-7040
Echo-sounder	2 × Furuno
Other ship navigation	Robertson AP45 autopilot

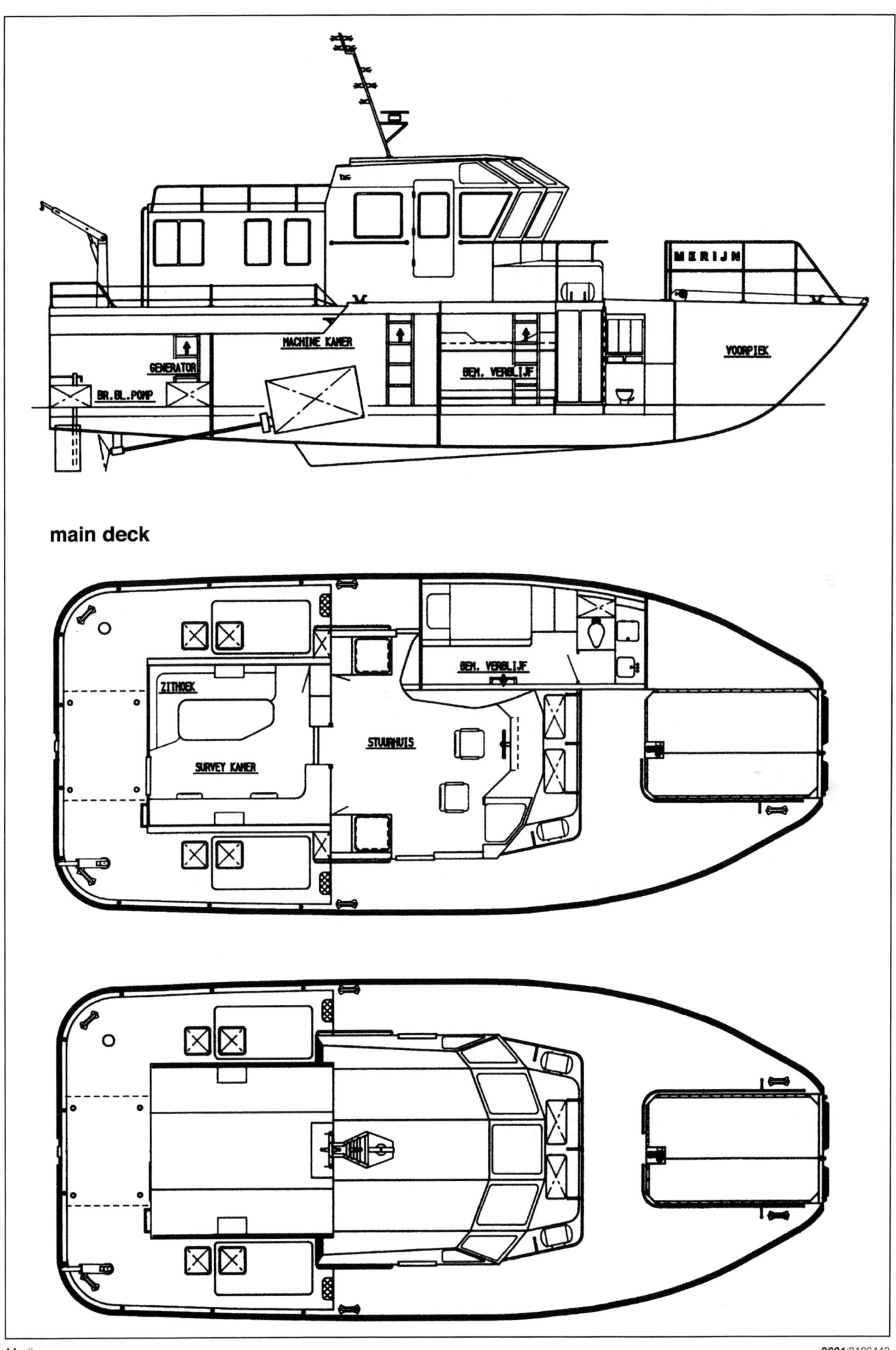

main deck

Merijn

2001/0106443

COMMUNICATIONS
VHF	2
Facsimile	Navtex

ACCOMMODATION
Crew	4
Scientists/surveyors	20 passengers in deckhouse

UPDATED

Merijn

2001/0106442

Rederij Waterweg BV

Nicoline 4

GENERAL

Owner	Rederij Waterweg BV, Netherlands
Port of reg/flag	Workum, Netherlands
Classification	Bureau Veritas, tug coastal waters, Dutch Shipping Inspection, coastal waters up to 30 n miles
Call sign	PFSU
Built (yard and date)	Damen Shipyards, Netherlands, 1998
Length overall	16.89 m
Breadth moulded	5.29 m
Operational draught	2.10 m
Tonnage (grt)	41; net 12

PROPULSION

Main engine(s)	2 × Caterpillar 3408 TA/B, 940 hp/700 kW at 1,800 rpm
Propellers	Twin, 3-blade, fixed-pitch in nozzles
Speed (max)	10 kt
Fuel capacity	13.70 m³
Electrical power	Auxiliary engines: 2 × Lister Stamford 31 kVA, 220/380 V

BRIDGE NAVIGATION AIDS

Satellite	Philips DGPS Mk 10
Radar	Furuno FR-8051 DA
Echo-sounder	Furuno FCV 667; Radio Holland EZ 2000

COMMUNICATIONS

VHF	2 × Sailor RT 2048	**Cellular**	GSM
		Facsimile	Navtex NX 500

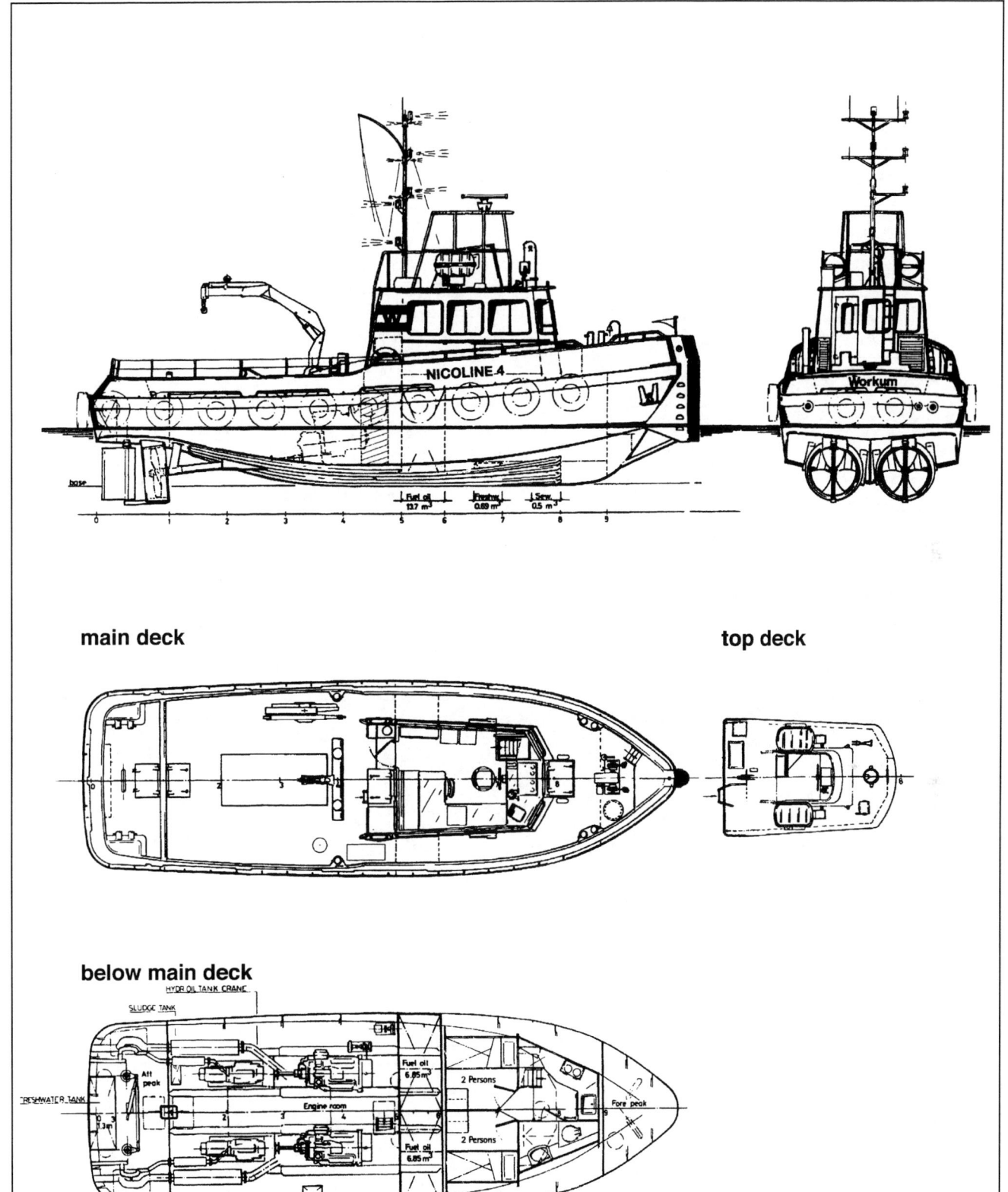

main deck   **top deck**

below main deck

Nicoline 4

2001/0106445

ACCOMMODATION

Crew	2
Scientists/surveyors	2

SURVEY SYSTEMS

Echo-sounder (single beam)   Hull-mounted transducers: Atlas
Deso 2 × 210 kHz, 1 × 33 kHz

UPDATED

Nicoline 4

2001/0106444

Seaworx

Swallow

GENERAL

Owner	Red West Friesland BV, Netherlands
Port of reg/flag	Kingstown/St Vincent
Official number	8339
Classification	Deep Sea
Call sign	J8XM5
Built (yard and date)	Shimoda Dockyard, 1972
Length overall	50.33 m
Breadth moulded	11.58 m
Working deck width	8.50 m
Max draught	3.62 m
Operational draught	± 3.30 m
Tonnage (grt)	615

PROPULSION

Main engine(s)	2 × Caterpillar/820 kW
Thrusters	Bow, 380 hp
Propellers	2
Speed (max)	12 kt

Speed (cruising)	10 kt
Endurance	65 days at max speed
Fuel capacity	480 m³
Electrical power	440-60 Hz
Fresh water capacity	100 m³

BRIDGE NAVIGATION AIDS

Satellite	Furuno GPS, GP 80
Radar	1 × Furuno 2115; 1 × Furuno 7062
Gyrocompass	1 × Hokushin
Echo-sounder	1 × Furuno FCV 582

COMMUNICATIONS

Inmarsat (type)	C, Trimble Galaxy Sentinel
MF/HF	Sailor RE 2100
VHF	2 × Sailor RT 2048; 1 × Sailor RT 4822
Cellular	1 × Carvoc
Facsimile	Philips Magic; Mini M Satellite telephone

SAFETY

Workboat/chase boat	1 × Avon chase boat, 2 × 55 hp Yamaha
Lifesaving equipment	Full equipment for 20 persons

DECK MACHINERY

Cranes	1 × Effer, 10 t SWL
Transducer well	Yes

ACCOMMODATION

Charterers	Total accommodation for 16

NEW ENTRY

Van Stee Survey & Supply B V

Sara Maatje V

GENERAL

Owner	Van Stee Survey & Supply B V
Port of reg/flag	Netherlands

Classification	Germanischer Lloyd (100 A5K) E; NSI certified
Call sign	PHHR

Sara Maatje V

2001/0110540

Sara Maatje V

2001/0110541

Length overall	39.50 m
Breadth moulded	9.70 m
Working deck width	170 m² freeload
Max draught	1.80 m
Operational draught	1.40 m

PROPULSION

Main engine(s)	2 × 400 hp; 1 × 500 hp
Thrusters	Bow: 100 hp
Propellers	Triple screw fp, one in nozzle
Speed (max)	11 kt

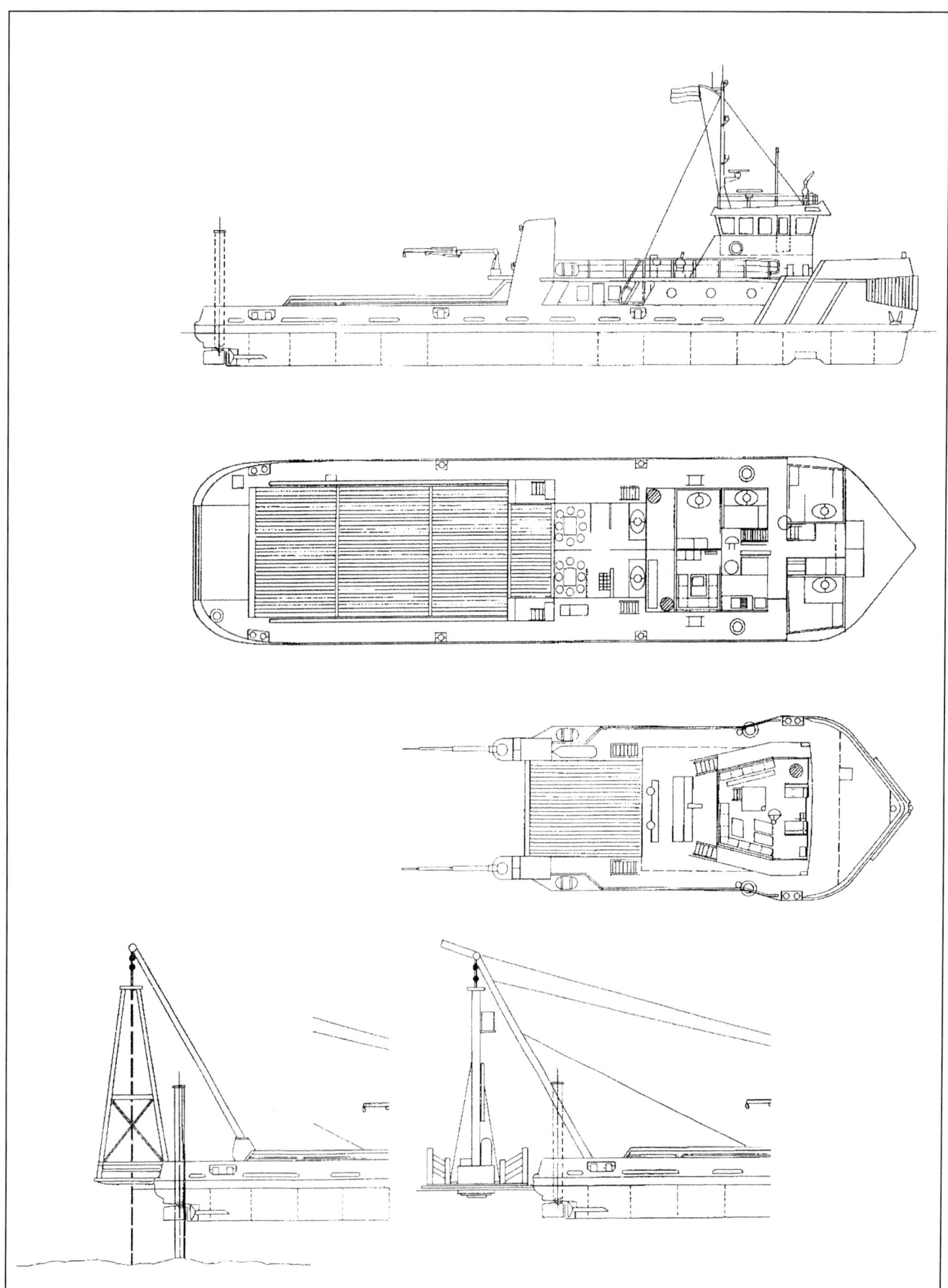

Sara Maatje V

2001/0110542

Fuel capacity	55 m³	**Workboat/chase boat**	1 × 6 persons MOB boat
Electrical power	Auxiliaries: 2 × 80 kVA, 380/220 V, 50 Hz; 24 V + 12 V available	**Lifesaving equipment**	Full requirement of survival suits and life jackets; complies with SOLAS 1974
Fresh water capacity	70 m³		

BRIDGE NAVIGATION AIDS

Satellite	2 × DGPS	**DECK MACHINERY**	
Radar	2 × daylight	**Cranes**	2 × Atlas, 2 t at 9 m
Echo-sounder	1 × digital; 1 × recording, 50 Hz	**A-frame(s)**	Up to 18 t
Other ship navigation	1 × autopilot; 1 × weather fax	**Winches**	Towing and anchor handling, 4 drums at 20 t

COMMUNICATIONS

MF/HF	2 × hand-held GMDSS	**ACCOMMODATION**	
VHF	2 + VHF incl DSC	**Charterers**	Total accommodation for 16

SAFETY

Lifeboats	2 × 12 persons liferafts

NEW ENTRY

Van Stee Survey & Supply BV

Sara Maatje VI

GENERAL

Owner	Van Stee Survey & Supply BV, Netherlands
Port of reg/flag	Netherlands
Classification	Germanischer Lloyd 100 A5K; NSI certified
Call sign	PHUA
Length overall	32.42 m
Breadth moulded	10.00 m
Working deck width	185 m² freeload
Max draught	1.60 m
Operational draught	0.90 m

PROPULSION

Main engine(s)	3 × 350 hp
Thrusters	Bow: 125 hp
Propellers	Triple screw fp in nozzles
Speed (max)	10 kt
Fuel capacity	35 t
Electrical power	Auxiliary generators: 2 × 60 kVA, 380 × 220 V, 50 Hz; 1 × 230 kVA, 380 × 220 V, 50 Hz; 110 V + 24 V + 12 V available
Fresh water capacity	35 t

Sara Maatje VI

2001/0110544

BRIDGE NAVIGATION AIDS

Satellite	1 × DGPS + electronic chart system
Radar	2 × daylight
Echo-sounder	1 × digital; 1 × recording
Other ship navigation	1 × autopilot; 1 × weather fax

COMMUNICATIONS

VHF	3 including DSC

SAFETY

Lifeboats	2 × 12 persons liferafts
Workboat/chase boat	1 × MOB boat, 40 hp outboard
Lifesaving equipment	Full requirement of survival suits and life jackets; complies with SOLAS 1974

DECK MACHINERY

Cranes	Main deck: 1 × Hiab Seacrane 25 t/m; fore deck: 1 × Hiab Seacrane 4 t/m
A-frame(s)	20 t SWL optional
Winches	Towing and anchor handling

ACCOMMODATION

Charterers	Total accommodation for 12

SURVEY SYSTEMS

Echo-sounder (single beam)	2 × hull-mounted 33/210 kHz transducers for Deso 10 or 20

NEW ENTRY

Sara Maatje VI

2001/0110543

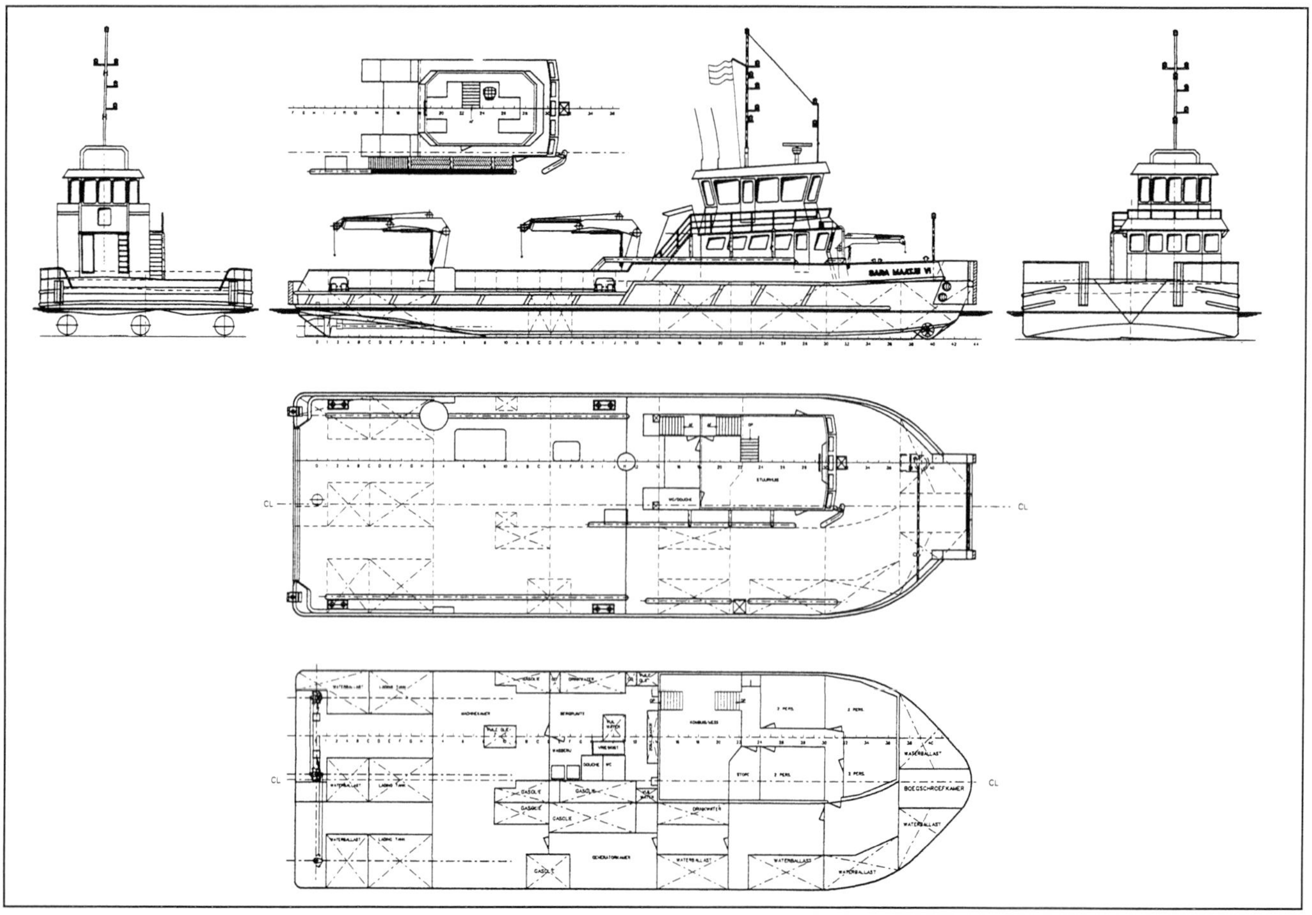

Sara Maatje VI

2001/0110545

NEW ZEALAND

Seaworks Ltd

Seasurveyor

GENERAL

Owner	Seaworks Ltd, New Zealand
Classification	Bureau Veritas
Built (yard and date)	Selco Pte Ltd, Singapore, 1978
Length overall	28.00 m
Breadth moulded	7.70 m
Max draught	2.80 m
Tonnage (grt)	180; net 54

PROPULSION

Main engine(s)	2 × CAT D343 TA diesels, 4-cycle, 6-cylinder
Thrusters	Bow: 70 hp hydraulic
Speed (max)	11 kt
Endurance	3,700 n miles
Fuel capacity	72 t
Fuel consumption	2.2 t/day
Electrical power	Generators: 1 × Cat D3306; 1 × Lister (25 kW); power supply: 125 kW at 440/3/50
Fresh water capacity	22 t

BRIDGE NAVIGATION AIDS

Satellite	Yes
Radar	Yes
Gyrocompass	Yes

Echo sounder	Yes
Other ship navigation	Weather fax; autopilot

COMMUNICATIONS

Inmarsat (type)	Yes
MF/HF	SSB
VHF	Yes

DECK MACHINERY

Cranes	Hiab 1 t Hydraulic Speedloader
A-frame(s)	8 t articulated
Winches	Cargo: 2 t at 10 m/min, for A frame

ACCOMMODATION

Charterers	Total accommodation for 24

SURVEY SYSTEMS

Echo sounder (single beam)	Charterer supply
Multibeam/swath system	Charterer supply
Sidescan sonar	Charterer supply
Sub-bottom profiler	Charterer supply
Magnetometer	Charterer supply
Grab(s)	Charterer supply
Oceanographic sensors (CTDs/XBTs and so on)	Charterer supply

NEW ENTRY

Seaworks Ltd

Seaworker

GENERAL

Owner	Seaworks Ltd, New Zealand
Classification	International Coastal
Built (yard and date)	Nelson, New Zealand, 1991
Length overall	28.70 m
Breadth moulded	10.50 m
Operational draught	2.40 m
Tonnage (grt)	200

PROPULSION

Main engine(s)	2 × Cummins KTA 19M at 500 hp
Thrusters	Dynamically positioned, Simrad 701: main engine: 2 × Aquamaster US 381 360; bow: 2 × HRP 200 360 driven by 2 × Cummins 6 BTA 5 9-M at 150 hp
Propellers	Lips vp
Fuel capacity	4,000 litres
Fuel consumption	DP: 1,500 litres/day; steaming: 1,400 litres/day
Electrical power	Main generator: 90 kVA 3-phase 400 V 50 Hz, 40 kVA 3-phase 400 V 50 Hz ROV generator: 200 kVA 3-phase 400 V 50 Hz or 60 Hz
Fresh water capacity	20,000 litres; 4,000 litres/day water maker

BRIDGE NAVIGATION AIDS

Satellite	Trimble Nav Trac XL GPS

Radar	Furuno FR-8100D 72 miles; Furuno 1731 48 miles
Gyrocompass	2 × TG 5000 SGB 1000

COMMUNICATIONS

Inmarsat (type)	1 × C
MF/HF	Sailor 800 W SSB; NDBP GLOBALE SSB
VHF	2 × multichannel

SAFETY

Lifeboats	Liferafts: 2 × 15 persons, 1 × 25 persons,1 × 6 persons, 1 × 5.40 m Stabicraft rescue craft with 40 hp outboard

DECK MACHINERY

Cranes	1 × Hiab 140 AW 6 t at 2 m
Winches	ROV moonpool launch/retrieval
Moonpool(s) – size(s)/function(s)	2.50 × 4.80 m with sliding hatch

ACCOMMODATION

Charterers	Total accommodation for 28

SURVEY SYSTEMS

Positioning	DGPS
Echo-sounder (single beam)	Charterer supply
Multibeam/swath system	Charterer supply
Sidescan sonar	Charterer supply
Sub-bottom profiler	Charterer supply
Magnetometer	Charterer supply

Corer(s)	Charterer supply	Sound velocity profiler	Charterer supply
Grab(s)	Charterer supply	Oceanographic sensors (CTDs/XBTs and so on)	Charterer supply
Vehicle(s) (ROVs/AUVs and so on)	Charterer supply		

UPDATED

NORWAY

DeepOcean AS

Edda Freya

GENERAL
Port of reg/flag — Haugesund/Norwegian
Classification — DnV + 1A1 DYNPOS AUTR, supply vessel EO Ice C SF BIS Dk(+)HL(2.5) TMON PMS ISM (LFL*)
Built (yard and date) — Ulstein Verft AS, Ulsteinvik, Norway, 1991
Rebuilt (yard and date) — 2000
Length overall — 87.10 m
Breadth moulded — 17.50 m
Working deck width — 14.60 m; length 57.00 m; deck area 817.3 m³
Tonnage (grt) — 3,001; net 944; deadweight 3,493

PROPULSION
Main engine(s) — 2 × Ulstein Bergman BRM-6, 6-cylinder, each 3,300 bhp at 750 rpm
Thrusters — Kongsberg Simrad SD21 DYNPOS AUTR DP system driving 2 × Ulstein 375 TV-C 1,000 bhp (bow), 2 × Ulstein 150 TV-A 800 bhp (stern); interfaces: Simrad HiPap, SeaPath 200, Sercel DGPS with Inmarsat B and spot beam modulators, MDL Fanbeam laser, 2 × wind sensors, 3 × gyrocompasses, 2 × motion reference units
Propellers — 2 × Ulstein 600 AGSC vp, 2,900 mm
Speed (max) — 13.5 kt
Speed (cruising) — Economical/service: 11 kt
Fuel consumption — 22 t/day at max speed; 8 t/day at service
Electrical power — Generators: 2 × shaft, each 2,300 kVA; 2 × Caterpillar/Leroy Somer, each 450 kVA; total power: 440 V/220 V – 60 Hz

BRIDGE NAVIGATION AIDS
Satellite — 1 × Furuno GP80/GR80 DGPS; 1 × ShipMate 5310 GPS
Radar — 1 × JRC/Raytheon TM 3410/12SU ARPA 10 cm; 1 × JRC/Raytheon TM 2525/7XU 3 cm; 1 × JRC/Raytheon SRD 15 monitor; 1 × Telechart 2024 chartplotter
Gyrocompass — 1 × Tokyo Keiki TG5000
Speed log — 1 × JRC-203 Doppler with remote displays
Echo-sounder — 1 × Skipper ED 161 with digital depth indicator
Other ship navigation — 1 × Robertson AP9 Mk II autopilot; 1 × ShipMate RS 6100 navtex; 1 × Taiyo TD-L1520 and 1 × Taiyo TL-L1100 direction-finders

COMMUNICATIONS
Inmarsat (type) — B; ABB Saturn B, Class II phone and fax
MF/HF — 1 × Skanti TRP 8750, 800 W SSB; 1 × Skanti TRP 7200, 200 W SSB
VHF — 2 × Sailor RT 2047; 3 × AXIS 250 GMDSS
Cellular — NMT; GSM

DECK MACHINERY
Cranes — 1 × Norlift GPCO 1250-2020, 20 t SWL at 20 m in Sea State 5
Moonpool(s) – size(s)/function(s) — Mini moonpool for deploying multibeam sounders

ACCOMMODATION
Charterers — Total accommodation for 50
Hospital — 2-berth

SURVEY SYSTEMS
Positioning — 1 × Furuno DGPS; 1 × Simrad HiPap subsea; 1 × Thales Skyfix/Multifix; 1 × MRU-5E motion sensor
Multibeam/swath system — 1 × Reson 8111 100 kHz; 1 × Reson 8125 455 kHz; both on hydraulic driven pole to fit mini moonpool
Sidescan sonar — 1 × GeoAcoustics SS941
Sub-bottom profiler — 1 × Probe 5001

NEW ENTRY

DeepOcean AS

Normand Tonjer

GENERAL
Port of reg/flag — Skudeneshavn/Norwegian
Classification — DnV + 1A1 + EO + Dynpos AUT R + HELDK SH
Built (yard and date) — Georg Eide's Sonner AS, Norway, 1983
Rebuilt (yard and date) — Converted Ulstein Verft, Norway, 2000
Length overall — 80.77 m
Breadth moulded — 18.00 m
Working deck width — 15.50 m × 37.00 m length
Tonnage (grt) — 3,349; net 1,004

PROPULSION

Main engine(s)	2 × MAK diesels, type 8M 435, producing 2 × 3,000 bhp at 600 rpm
Thrusters	Kongsberg Simrad SDP-OS1+OS2 6248 DP system controlling bow and stern; 2 × transverse Ulstein 150 TV, 800 bhp; HiPap acoustics, 3 × DGPS reference; Fanbeam laser
Propellers	2 × Ulstein, type 600 AGSC, vp
Speed (max)	15 kt
Speed (cruising)	14 kt economical
Fuel consumption	22 t/day (max); 17 t/day (economical)
Electrical power	Main generators: 2 × Caterpillar diesels, type 3408 T JWHC, 375 bhp; 2 × Stamford, type MC 534, 317 kVA; 1 × Caterpillar, type 3304 T, 133 bhp; 1 × Stamford, type MC334, 111 kVA; 2 × shaft, type NEBB WAB 800 D12

1,750 kVA; emergency generator: 2 × Caterpillar, type 3408 T, 133 bhp; 2 × Stamford, type MC 334, 111 kVA

BRIDGE NAVIGATION AIDS

Satellite	1 × Furuno GP80 GPS
Radar	1 × Furuno FR 2030s S-band m/ARP2; 1 × Furuno Marine FR-2115 x-band
Gyrocompass	1 × Robertson SKR-82; 2 × Robertson RGC-12; 1 × Anschutz Standard 20
Speed log	1 × JCR JNL 203-b Doppler
Echo-sounder	1 × Furuno FR-881
Other ship navigation	1 × Robertson AP-8 autopilot; 1 × Furuno NX 500 navtex

COMMUNICATIONS

Inmarsat (type)	1 × Sailor C
MF/HF	1 × Sailor compact GMDSS
VHF	1 × RT-143/25 W/55 channels; 1 × Sailor RT-143/25 W/55

Normand Tonjer   **2001**/0110538

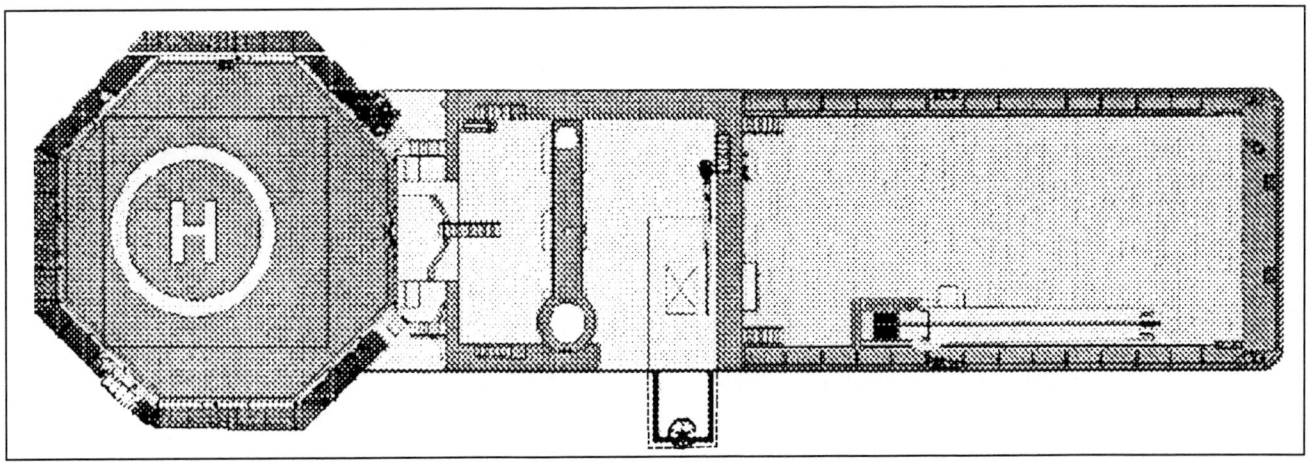

Normand Tonjer   **2001**/0110539

	channels; 5 × Tron/Motorola Mx 1000 handsets; 4 × Motorola GP 900 UHF handsets	**A-frame(s)**	Integrated ROV side launch; heave compensated umbilical winch
Cellular	1 × NMT 900; 1 × GSM		
		ACCOMMODATION	
HELIDECK		**Charterers**	Total accommodation for 58
Size, aircraft capacity	Super Puma rated, 19.5 m	**Hospital**	1-berth
DECK MACHINERY			*NEW ENTRY*
Cranes	1 × seabed 20 t/20 m; optional 50 t/15 m		

Fugro-Geoteam AS

Geo Scanner

GENERAL

Owner	Eidesvik & Co A/S
Port of reg/flag	Haugesund, Norway
Classification	DnV + A-ICE C, EO
Call sign	LDFZ
Built (yard and date)	1962
Rebuilt (yard and date)	1982/84/90/92/97
Length overall	58.40 m
Breadth moulded	10.50 m
Operational draught	4.00 m
Tonnage (grt)	1,001, 300 net

PROPULSION

Main engine(s)	MAK, 1,200 hp
Thrusters	Bow, electric, 450 hp
Propellers	3-blade, vp, Becker rudder
Speed (cruising)	11 kt
Endurance	4 weeks
Fuel capacity	128 m³
Fuel consumption	5 m³/day
Electrical power	4 × generators, total 1,283 kVA; 3 × 380/220 VAC, 50 Hz
Fresh water capacity	114 m³, 3.5 m³/day

BRIDGE NAVIGATION AIDS

Satellite	Magnavox MX 200
Radar	Decca Pilot 450

Gyrocompass	Robertson SKR 82
Speed log	SAGEM LHS
Echo-sounder	Simrad 512

COMMUNICATIONS

Inmarsat (type)	ABB Saturn B
MF/HF	Skanti TRP 5000
VHF	Sailor RT143; Sailor RT2047; DSCRM 2042 (GMDSS); 3 × Navico Axis (GMDSS); Motorola MX1000

DECK MACHINERY

Cranes	Palfinger 30 t/m, 12.5 m; Tico Marine 200, 20 t/m
A-frame(s)	4.50 m, 2.50 t
Winches	Streamer (3,000 m cable); 2 × gun, 100 m umbilical; sidescan (1,500 m cable); DTB (500 m cable); gravity corer (2,000 m cable); far field monitor (200 m cable)
Gate valve	185 mm id

ACCOMMODATION

Charterers	Total accommodation for 28

Geo Scanner

2001/0103613

SURVEY SYSTEMS

Positioning	Fugro PCSeis interfaced to Starfix Georef DGPS with Trimble 4000DL GPS and Seadiff DGPS software; TSS VRU; Acoustic: Simrad HPR 309T; Tailbuoy: radar, optional DGPS
Echo-sounder (single beam)	Simrad EA500 (38/120/200 kHz)
Multibeam/swath system	Simrad EM1000
Sidescan sonar	GeoAcoustics, 59 kHz, 1,000 m depth rating
Sub-bottom profiler	Huntec deep tow boomer; mini air gun: HGS SG1, 10 cu in; hydrophone streamers: Benthos, 50 hydrophones, 7.5 m; Fjord Instruments HA1-C9, 24 hydrophones, 15 m; graphic recorders: 2 × EPC9800; 2 × Dowty 200-138. G-LOG for simultaneous digital processing of sidescan, boomer/sparker, mini-sleeve gun

Corer(s)	Gravity, 3 m
Grab(s)	Thule
Sound velocity profiler	AML SVP-16 (1,000 m)
Oceanographic sensors (CTDs/XBTs and so on)	AML STD-12 (1,000 m) CTD

SEISMIC SYSTEMS

Energy source (type and manufacturer)	HGS sleeve air guns and Sodera G-guns
Streamer manufacturer	Teledyne
Streamer type	Analogue with transformers
Streamer numbers and lengths per number	3,000 m total
Recording system	Sercel 358 DMX, 120 channel at 1 ms sample

UPDATED

Fugro-Geoteam AS

Geo Searcher

GENERAL

Owner	Eidesvik & Co A/S
Port of reg/flag	Haugesund, Norway
Classification	DnV + 1A1-ICE C, EO, HELDK
Call sign	LKTO
Built (yard and date)	1982
Rebuilt (yard and date)	1989/1993
Length overall	69.20 m
Breadth moulded	12.80 m
Operational draught	5.25 m
Tonnage (grt)	1,549

PROPULSION

Main engine(s)	MAK 8MN 452 AK, 1,770 kW
Thrusters	Bow, Ulstein 150TV hydraulic, 600 hp
Propellers	1 × vp, Heinz Hinze flap rudder

Speed (cruising)	12 kt
Endurance	60 days at 85% MCR
Fuel capacity	643 m³
Fuel consumption	5 m³ at 12 kt; 8 m³ at 14 kt
Electrical power	4 generators. Total 987 kVA; 3 × 380/220 VAC, 50 Hz
Fresh water capacity	120 m³, 4 m³/day

BRIDGE NAVIGATION AIDS

Satellite	Furuno NX500
Radar	Decca Bridgemaster; Decca RM 916C; Decca TM 1226
Gyrocompass	Sperry Mk 23
Speed log	Simrad NL, Doppler log

COMMUNICATIONS

Inmarsat (type)	Phone, fax, telex and modem

Geo Searcher   ***2001**/0103619*

MF/HF	Skanti TRP 5000, telex	**Sub-bottom profiler**	EG&G 230 Uniboom; 10 cu in mini sleeve gun; 15 cu in Sodera mini water gun; Benthos and Fjord hydrophhones; 3 × Ultra recorders; 2 × TSS TVG; G-Log simultaneous digital processing of sidescan, boomer/sparker, mini sleeve gun
VHF	2 × Sailor RT 143; Motorola MX1000 hand-held		

DECK MACHINERY

Cranes	Karm 20 t/m (10 m); 2 × provisions handling, each 6 t/m		
Winches	2 × streamer, 1,200 m cable; guns: 2 × 175 m umbilical; Barovane 2 × 250 m; sidescan; boomer: 400 m cable; gravity corer: 1,500 m wire; far field monitor: 800 m cable	**Corer(s)**	Gravity 2 or 3 m, 60 mm dia, 450 kg: UMEL 2 m
		Grab(s)	Shipek
		Sound velocity profiler	AML SVP-16, 1,000 m depth

ACCOMMODATION

SEISMIC SYSTEMS

Charterers	Total accommodation for 42	**Energy source (type and manufacturer)**	HGS sleeve air guns, 140 cu in, 3 × 2 clusters
Hospital	1 berth	**Streamer manufacturer**	Dual, Fjord Instruments
		Streamer type	1,500 m or dual 600 m, with transformers

SURVEY SYSTEMS

Echo-sounder (single beam)	Simrad EA 501P, 38 and 200 kHz	**Recording system**	Sercel 358 DMX, 96-channel at 1 ms sample
Multibeam/swath system	Simrad EM1000		
Sidescan sonar	EG&G 272-TD with 260- TH recorder		*UPDATED*

Fugro-Geoteam AS

Geo Surveyor

GENERAL

Owner	Eidesvik AS	**Speed (cruising)**	11 kt
Port of reg/flag	Haugesund, Norway	**Endurance**	4 weeks
Classification	DnV+1A1-ICE C, EO	**Fuel capacity**	104 m³
Call sign	JXIF	**Fuel consumption**	5 m³/day
Built (yard and date)	1965	**Electrical power**	125 kVA, 3 × 380 (220) VAC
Rebuilt (yard and date)	1981/83, 1990/96		212 kVA, 3 × 380 (220) VAC
Length overall	58.40 m		420 kVA, 3 x 380 (220) VAC
Breadth moulded	10.50 m	**Fresh water capacity**	114 m³; 4 m³/day
Operational draught	3.5 m		
Tonnage (grt)	951; 285 net	**BRIDGE NAVIGATION AIDS**	
		Satellite	Magnavox MX200
PROPULSION		**Radar**	Furuno RDP 062; FRS 48
Main engine(s)	MAK, 1,200 bhp	**Gyrocompass**	Robertson SKR 82
Thrusters	Bow, Brunvoll, electric 450 hp	**Speed log**	Simrad NL
Propellers	1 × vp, Becker rudder	**Echo-sounder**	Simrad 572-11-13

Geo Surveyor

2001/0103618

COMMUNICATIONS

Inmarsat (type)	Phone, fax, telex
MF/HF	Skanti TRP 5000
VHF	2 × Sailor RT 143

DECK MACHINERY

Cranes	Tico 12.5 t/m, 10.3 m, SWL 1.5 t; Bergensen 45 t/m, 9 m, SWL 5 t
A-frame(s)	5.5 m height, SWL 3 t
Winches	Streamer: 600-1,200 m cable; guns: 1 × 150 m umbilical; sidescan: 3,000 m cable; boomer: 400 m cable; corer: 750 m wire, 7.5 t; davit: 4.5 m length, 0.5 t

ACCOMMODATION

Charterers	Total accommodation for 23

SURVEY SYSTEMS

Positioning	Micro PDP 11/83 online with GEONAV; Micro PDP 11/83 + Fugro-Geoteam-developed software for offline processing, analysis and graphic presentation of nav and bathy data; VRU: Seatex MRU-5; Datawell Hippy 120C; acoustic: Simrad HPR 309T; streamer, source and tailbuoy by HPR (optional DGPS for tailbuoy)
Echo-sounder (single beam)	Simrad EA501P, 38 kHz

Multibeam/swath system	Simrad EM1000
Sidescan sonar	EG&G 260 TH recorder with 2 × 272TD towfishes
Sub-bottom profiler	Boomer/sparker: Huntec deeptow, 540 J; mini-sleeve gun: 10 cu in; single-channel streamer, Benthos Mesh 50/24P; graphic recorders, 2 × Ultra 3710, 1 × Dowty 3640 TVG: 2 × TSS; TVF: 2 × Chi; swell filter: 2 × TSS; digital recording: G-Log for simultaneous digital processing of sidescan, boomer/ sparker, mini-sleeve gun
Corer(s)	Freefall 450 kg, 2 × 3 m barrel, 83 mm diameter, 750 m cable
Grab(s)	Shipek
Sound velocity profiler	AML SVP-16, 1,000 m

SEISMIC SYSTEMS

Energy source (type and manufacturer)	HGS sleeve air guns
Number of airguns	4
Size of airguns	40 cu in each
Streamer manufacturer	Teledyne
Streamer numbers and lengths per number	120 channels, 1,200 m
Recording system	Sercel 358 DMX, 96 channel at 1 ms sample

UPDATED

Fugro-Geoteam AS

Jean Charcot

GENERAL

Owner	Jean Charcot Shipping BV
Port of reg/flag	Panama/Panamanian
Classification	DnV 13/3E
Call sign	3EFG8
Built (yard and date)	1965
Rebuilt (yard and date)	1983/1997
Length overall	74.18 m
Breadth moulded	14.10 m
Max draught	5.01 m
Tonnage (grt)	2,141; 642 net

PROPULSION

Main engine(s)	2 × 1,150 hp DC motors driven by 3 × MAN 1,200 hp diesels
Thrusters	1 × 300 hp bow, 1 × 300 hp stern
Propellers	2 × vp
Speed (cruising)	12 kt; service 10.5 kt
Endurance	35 days
Fuel capacity	275 m³
Fuel consumption	12 kt = 11.2 t/day; 10.5 kt = 7.5 t/day; 4.5 kt = 3 t/day

Jean Charcot

2001/0103611

Electrical power	1 × 250 kVA, 380 V, 50 Hz;	A-frame(s)	3.50 m high, 15 t SWL
	1 × 100 kVA 380 V, 50 Hz	Winches	2 × coring
Fresh water capacity	168 m³	Transducer well	For USBL system
		Gate valve	Yes

BRIDGE NAVIGATION AIDS

Satellite	1 × GPS	**ACCOMMODATION**	
Radar	Tokimec 3 cm ARPA; Decca	Charterers	Total accommodation for 39
	10 cm ACS	Hospital	2 berths
Gyrocompass	Arma Brown HK10201		
Speed log	Thomson Doppler	**SURVEY SYSTEMS**	
Echo-sounder	Simrad ED162	Positioning	Fugro Starfix DGPS-MN8;
			2 × Trimble receivers; S G Brown

COMMUNICATIONS

			gyro; acoustic: Nautronix ATS;
Inmarsat (type)	MJ2111		VRU: TSS320 and Hippy 120
MF/HF	Furuno FS1550; Skanti WR6000,	Echo-sounder (single beam)	Simrad EA501
	2182 watchkeeping	Multibeam/swath system	Simrad EM1000 (10-1,000 m);
VHF	2 × Sailor RT2048; 1 cm IC M56		Simrad EM12 (50-11,000 m)
		Sidescan sonar	EG&G 272; 260 recorder
		Sub-bottom profiler	Datasonics chirp
DECK MACHINERY		Sound velocity profiler	SVP16
Cranes	1 × aft, 7.50 t, 17 m; 2 × fore		
	cargo booms, 3 t SWL		*UPDATED*

Fugro-Geoteam AS

Seabulk Fulmar

GENERAL

Owner	Care Offshore, Switzerland	A-frame(s)	3.5 m high, 2 t SWL
Port of reg/flag	Kingstown, St Vincent/St Vincent	Winches	1 × coring
Classification	Lloyds +100A1/+LMC	Transducer well	For USBL system
Call sign	J8FL6	Gate valve	Yes
Built (yard and date)	1968		
Rebuilt (yard and date)	1992	**ACCOMMODATION**	
Length overall	57.78 m	Charterers	Total accommodation for 12
Breadth moulded	11.43 m	Hospital	2 berths
Operational draught	4.12 m		
Tonnage (grt)	986; 295 net	**SURVEY SYSTEMS**	
		Positioning	Starfix MN8, 2 × Trimble rx;

PROPULSION

			online: WINS software, HP 320
Main engine(s)	4 × Lister Blackstone, total 2,400		computers; offline: WINS/Echo
	hp		geosurvey on VAX with HP 7585
Thrusters	1 x 400 hp, 300 kW Ulstein TV-90		AO plotter; acoustic: Nautronics
Propellers	2 × vp		ATS USBL; VRU: TSS 320;
Speed (max)	13.5 kt		tailbuoy: radar, optional DGPS
Speed (cruising)	12 kt	Echo-sounder (single beam)	Simrad EA501 (33 and 200 kHz)
Endurance	4,000 n miles at 11 kt	Sidescan sonar	EG&G 272 and 999 +
Fuel capacity	119 m³/103 t		GeoAcoustics towfishes; EG&G
Fuel consumption	Cruise at 12 kt = 9 t/day; 10 kt =		260 recorder
	6 t/day; survey = 3 t/day	Sub-bottom profiler	Hull-mounted pinger array;
Electrical power	4 × 225 kVA – 440/240/115 V,		Huntec 540 J deeptow boomer
	60 Hz		with sparker option; Bolt 600B
Fresh water capacity	119 m³		mini airgun; Benthos 50/24P
			hydrophone streamer; DELPH 2
BRIDGE NAVIGATION AIDS			digital recorder; Waverley 3710
Satellite	Furuno GP70		graphic recorder; TVG: TSS 307
Radar	Furuno FR 7040 + FR 7100D		amplifiers; TVF: Chi TV3
Gyrocompass	Arma Brown	Corer(s)	UMEL Sargent 3 m, 750 kg
Speed log	Chernikeef	Grab(s)	Shipek
Echo-sounder	2 × general, 1 × high-precision		
		SEISMIC SYSTEMS	
COMMUNICATIONS		Energy source (type and	
		manufacturer)	HGS sleeve
Inmarsat (type)	Marconi Oceanray 2	Size of airguns	160 or 80 cu in
MF/HF	Furuno FS 1550; 2182 Skanti WR	Streamer manufacturer	Prakla
	6000	Streamer type	1,500 m analogue with
VHF	2 × Sailor RT 2048; 1 × 1 cm IC		transformers
	M56	Recording system	TSS System 2, 120 channels at
			1 ms sample. MicroMAX QC and
DECK MACHINERY			processing
Cranes	Hiab Seacrane 200 – 9.10 t at		
	2 m; 1.02 t at 15.6 m; hydraulic,		*VERIFIED*
	1.5 t at 7 m		

Geoconsult AS

Geobay

GENERAL

Port of reg/flag	Norwegian/NIS
Classification	DnV 1A1, E0, HELDK-SH, DYNPOS AUTR
Call sign	LAHX5
Built (yard and date)	1978
Rebuilt (yard and date)	Converted 1999
Length overall	88.20 m
Breadth moulded	15.60 m
Working deck width	Area: 450 m²
Operational draught	6.90 m
Tonnage (grt)	3,590; 1,077 net; 2,455 deadweight

PROPULSION

Main engine(s)	4 × Mitsubishi diesel-electric, 6,000 kW (total), 440 V, 60 Hz
Thrusters	DP system Simrad SDP 21 (dual-redundant); interfaced to DGPS and 2 × Simrad HiPAP; systems; bow: 2 × KaMeWa, CP, 925 kW (tunnel); 1 × Ulstein, CP, 883 kW (azimuth) – electrically driven; stern and main propulsion: 2 × Aquamaster, CRP, 1,400 kW (azimuth) – electrically driven, frequency controlled
Propellers	(see thrusters)
Speed (max)	13 kt
Speed (cruising)	12 kt
Fuel capacity	1,000 m³
Electrical power	Auxiliary engines: 2 × Yanmar, 500 kW (each), 440 V, 60 Hz
Fresh water capacity	550 m³; evaporator 15 t/day

BRIDGE NAVIGATION AIDS

Satellite	1 × Trimble DGPS; 1 × Ashtech GPS/GLONASS
Radar	2 × Consilium Selesmar ARPA
Gyrocompass	2 × Anschutz 20 digital; 1 × Tokyo Keiki MK.ES
Echo-sounder	1 × Furuno
Other ship navigation	1 × Simrad AP 9 Mk III autopilot

COMMUNICATIONS

Inmarsat (type)	'A' Satcom; 1 × Norsat Sealink
MF/HF	GMDSS distress system

SAFETY

Lifeboats	Liferafts: 6 × 25- persons; 1 × Norsafe 580 Merlin, 85 hp, rescue boat

HELIDECK

Size, aircraft capacity	Super Puma rated (19.50 × 19.50 m)

DECK MACHINERY

Cranes	Knuckle-boom (aft), 30 t 650 m lift height (1,500 m optional)
A-frame(s)	6 t for survey and seabed sampling
Winches	Anchor; spring (foredeck); 2 × capstans
Moonpool(s) – size(s)/ function(s)	1 × 4.70 × 5.00 m for ROV

ACCOMMODATION

Charterers	Total accommodation for 50
Hospital	Yes

SCIENTIFIC SPACES

Multipurpose dry lab	Instrument room, offline room × 136 m²

SURVEY SYSTEMS

Echo-sounder (single beam)	1
Multibeam/swath system	1 × surface; 1 × ROV-mounted
Sidescan sonar	1
Sub-bottom profiler	1
Magnetometer	1
Gravimeter	1
Corer(s)	Yes
Grab(s)	Yes
Vehicle(s) (ROVs/AUVs and so on)	Triton XL-37 150 hp

VERIFIED

Geobay

2000/0088231

Geoconsult AS

Geofjord

GENERAL

Port of reg/flag	Norwegian/NIS
Classification	DnV 1A1, E0, HELDK-SH, DYNPOS AUTR, ICE-1A*
Call sign	LADU5
Built (yard and date)	1984
Rebuilt (yard and date)	Converted 1997
Length overall	92.90 m
Breadth moulded	16.00 m
Working deck width	Area: 550 m²
Operational draught	5.10 m
Tonnage (grt)	3,736; 1,121 net; 1,978 deadweight

PROPULSION

Main engine(s)	2 × Sulzer 6 ZL 40/48, 2,650 kW each, 500 rpm
Thrusters	DP system Simrad SDP21 (dual redundant), interfaced to DGPS and Simrad HPR 410 narrow beam, fixed-head and Simrad HiPAP; bow (electrically driven): 1 × KaMeWa, cp, 1,150 kW (tunnel); 1 × Aquamaster, cp, 1,100 kW (azimuth); stern (electrically driven): 2 × KaMeWa, cp, 925 kW (tunnel)
Propellers	(see thrusters)
Speed (max)	11 kt
Speed (cruising)	10 kt (with open moonpool)
Fuel capacity	550 m³
Electrical power	Auxiliary engines: 3 × Sulzer 6 AL 20/24, 750 rpm; generators: Main: 3 × 500 kW, 380 V 50 Hz; shaft: 2 × 2,300 kW, 440 V 60 Hz; emergency: 1 × 100 kW, 380 V 50 Hz
Fresh water capacity	236 m³; evaporator 15 t/day

BRIDGE NAVIGATION AIDS

Satellite	1 × Trimble DGPS
Radar	2 × Furuno
Gyrocompass	2 × Anschutz 20 digital
Echo-sounder	1 × Furuno

COMMUNICATIONS

Inmarsat (type)	1 × Inmarsat 'B' Satcom
MF/HF	GMDSS distress system
Cellular	2 × NMT 450; 1 × NMT 900

SAFETY

Lifeboats	Liferafts: 8 × 25-person; 1 × Norsafe 580 Merlin, 85 hp rescue boat

HELIDECK

Size, aircraft capacity	Super Puma rated (19.50 × 19.50 m)

DECK MACHINERY

Cranes	1 × Hydralift subsea (50 t at 10 m radius, 25 t at 18 m radius, 600 m lift height); 1 × Heila telescopic knuckle-boom (35 t/m)
Winches	1 × anchor; 2 × capstans
Moonpool(s) – size(s)/ function(s)	5.20 × 6.00 m

ACCOMMODATION

Charterers	Total accommodation for 58
Hospital	Yes

SURVEY SYSTEMS

Positioning	Trimble DGPS
Echo-sounder (single beam)	1
Multibeam/swath system	1
Sidescan sonar	1
Sub-bottom profiler	1
Magnetometer	1
Gravimeter	1
Corer(s)	Yes
Grab(s)	Yes
Vehicle(s) (ROVs/AUVs and so on)	ROV

VERIFIED

Geofjord

2000/0088230

Geoconsult AS

Geograph

GENERAL

Port of reg/flag	Norwegian/NIS
Classification	DnV 1A1 ICE C
Call sign	JXPY3
Built (yard and date)	1972
Rebuilt (yard and date)	Converted 1987/1990/1996
Length overall	59.50 m
Breadth moulded	10.20 m
Working deck width	Area: 200 m²
Operational draught	3.80 m
Tonnage (grt)	1,035; 311 net

PROPULSION

Main engine(s)	1 × B & W Alpha Diesel 10 V 23 LU, 1,250 hp/920 kW @ 800 max, 345 rpm service
Thrusters	DP system Simrad SDP 600 interfaced to Simrad HPR 310T and HiPAP; bow: Ulstein, CP, 600 hp (electrically driven); stern: Ulstein, CP, 450 hp (electrically driven)
Speed (max)	11 kt
Speed (cruising)	10 kt
Fuel capacity	107.60 t
Electrical power	Auxiliary engines: 2 × Caterpillar D 398 B diesels; 2 × Cummins NT855 G6 diesels; generators: 2 × Stamford MHC 434F, 345 kW (each), 440 V, 60 Hz, 1,800 rpm; 2 × Kato, 510 kW (each), 440 V, 60 Hz, 1,200 rpm; 2 × Stewart & Stevenson (electrically driven), 40 kW (each), 120/220 V, 60 Hz
Fresh water capacity	132.50 t; evaporator 3-4 t/day

BRIDGE NAVIGATION AIDS

Satellite	1 × Raytheon 398 DGPS
Radar	1 × Furuno FR2130S ARPA; 1 × Racal Decca Colour BT 501
Gyrocompass	1 × Sperry Mk 27; 1 × Anschutz Gyrostar
Echo-sounder	1 × ELAC LA2 50
Other ship navigation	1 × Robertson AP 9 Mk II (incl SDP 600 joystick) autopilot; 1 × Shipmate RS 4000 AP navigator

COMMUNICATIONS

Inmarsat (type)	'B'
MF/HF	GMDSS distress system
Cellular	1 × NMT
Facsimile	1 × Navtex NCR-300A receiver

SAFETY

Lifeboats	Liferafts: 3 × 16-person; 1 × 20-person; 1 × 25-person; rescue boat: 1 × 6-man MOB boat

DECK MACHINERY

Cranes	1 × Effer 34, 34 t/m, 3 t winch; 1 × Effer 20, 20 t/m, 2 t winch
A-frame(s)	Aft: 8 t SWL, height 6 m Midships: 15 t SWL, height 9 m
Winches	Deck: 9 t SWL (two drums); hydrography, 1 t

SCIENTIFIC SPACES

Multipurpose dry lab	Instrument rooms 80 m²

SURVEY SYSTEMS

Positioning	Raytheon DGPS
Echo-sounder (single beam)	1
Multibeam/swath system	1 × Simrad EM 1000
Sidescan sonar	1
Sub-bottom profiler	1
Magnetometer	1
Gravimeter	1
Vehicle(s) (ROVs/AUVs and so on)	ROV

VERIFIED

Geograph

2000/0088229

Polar Ship Management AS

Ernest Shackleton

GENERAL

Former names	*Polar Queen*
Owner	Silverseas Shipping Ltd, Isle of Man, UK
Port of reg/flag	Falkland Islands
Official number	DnV ID No 1860
Classification	DnV at 1A1 EO Icebreaker ICE 05 – HELDK – ICS – DYNPOS – AUTR
Call sign	ZDLS1
Built (yard and date)	Kverner Leven Lervik A/S, Norway, 1995
Length overall	80.00 m
Breadth moulded	17.00 m
Working deck width	17.00 m (length 33.60 m)
Operational draught	6.85 m
Tonnage (grt)	1,910

PROPULSION

Main engine(s)	2 × Bergen Diesel BRG-6, each 2,650 kW at 720 rpm

Thrusters	Kongsberg Simrad DP system driving 1 × 600 kV, 1 × 800 kV, 1 × 800 kV (bow)
Propellers	1 × cp in nozzle
Speed (max)	14 kt
Speed (cruising)	12 kt
Endurance	130 days
Fuel capacity	1,250 m³
Fuel consumption	9.5 t at 12 kt
Electrical power	Auxiliary units: 2 × 600 kW, 450 V, 60 Hz; 120 and 230 V UPS
Fresh water capacity	165 m³ + fresh water maker

BRIDGE NAVIGATION AIDS

Satellite	3
Radar	2
Gyrocompass	2
Echo-sounder	1 × Skipper GDS101; 1 × Simrad EA500

Ernest Shackleton   **2001**/0110531

Ernest Shackleton   **2001**/0110533

Ernest Shackleton   **2001**/0110532

COMMUNICATIONS

Inmarsat (type)	B + C; GMDSS
VHF	3
Cellular	Yes
Facsimile	RDF and helicopter homing; weather fax, Nav Tex; Aero VHF

SAFETY

Lifeboats	1
Workboat/chase boat	1
Lifesaving equipment	Survival suits for all personnel

HELIDECK

Size, aircraft capacity	19.5 m² Super Puma, or equivalent 10 t/d

DECK MACHINERY

Cranes	1 × ROV on upper deck 5 t/10 m; 1 × 10 t at stern
Transducer well	1 × 16 in unit

ACCOMMODATION

Charterers	Total accommodation for 25
Hospital	Yes

SCIENTIFIC SPACES

Oceanographic wet lab	45 m²
Multipurpose dry lab	45 m²

SURVEY SYSTEMS

Positioning	1 × Kongsberg Simrad for DP including Simrad HiPap; 1 × taut wire unit
Echo-sounder (single beam)	12 kHz
Multibeam/swath system	Hull engineered to fit bottom mapping system

NEW ENTRY

Stolt Offshore AS

Seaway Commander

GENERAL

Former names	*Archimedes*
Owner	DSND
Port of reg/flag	Bergen/Norway
Classification	DnV 1A1 + DYNPOS AUTR
Call sign	LJYP
Built (yard and date)	1967
Rebuilt (yard and date)	1982, 1988
Length overall	74.83 m
Breadth moulded	12.34 m
Working deck width	Clear deck area 275 m²
Tonnage (grt)	1,317

PROPULSION

Thrusters	DP system controlling: forward 1 × diesel Brunvoll azimuth cp; 1 × Brunvoll tunnel vp, 605 hp; 1 × Brunvoll tunnel vp, 420 hp; aft: 2 × Brunvoll tunnel vp, 605 hp each
Speed (cruising)	Over 11 kt
Fuel capacity	450 m³
Electrical power	2 × 300 kW at 415 V, 50 Hz; 1 × 300 kW, 50 Hz; 1 × 239 kW, 380 V
Fresh water capacity	150 m³; water making capacity: 6 m³/day

COMMUNICATIONS

Inmarsat (type)	Telenor V-Sat; Norsat B

SAFETY

Lifeboats	1
Workboat/chase boat	1 × MOB boat
Lifesaving equipment	8 × liferafts for 20 persons each; survival suits and lifejackets for 50 persons

HELIDECK

Size, aircraft capacity	Yes

DECK MACHINERY

Cranes	1 × Hydralift with winches for 35 t at 7.5 m radius, 25 t at 8.5 m radius, 5 t at 18 m radius; 1 × Hydralift, 1.5 t at 7 m radius; 1 × Hydralift, 1 t at 11 m and 2 t at 5 m radius
A-frame(s)	1 × 5 t T-frame
Winches	1 × Brattvagg, 2 t on aft deck; 2 × anchor on stern deck; 1 × anchor on foredeck
Transducer well	1 for HPR 309T, 1 for HiPap acoustic tracking systems

Seaway Commander   *2001*/0110549

ACCOMMODATION

Charterers	36
Crew	9
Hospital	2-berth

SCIENTIFIC SPACES

Multipurpose dry lab	275 m²; 1 × 30 m² survey room integrated with ROV control room; 1 × 50 m² processing room

SURVEY SYSTEMS

Positioning	2 × lightweight taut wires; Simrad 309T; Simrad HiPap acoustic tracking systems
Echo-sounder (single beam)	1 × Kongsberg Simrad ADP 503 Mk 2
Multibeam/swath system	1 × Kongsberg Simrad EM 300; 1 × EM 3000

NEW ENTRY

Stolt Offshore AS

Seaway Invincible

GENERAL

Former names	*Seaboard Invincible*	Breadth moulded	12.00 m
Port of reg/flag	Port Villa/Vanatu	Working deck width	11.00 m
Official number	339814	Max draught	9.20 m
Classification	Bureau Veritas 1/3/3E BV No 82N214	Operational draught	5.40 m
		Tonnage (grt)	1,311
Call sign	YJRF5		
Built (yard and date)	1971	**PROPULSION**	
Rebuilt (yard and date)	1980s	Main engine(s)	Ruston 9ATCM, 2,160 bhp at 520 rpm
Length overall	71.30 m		

Thrusters	Cegelec/GEC GEM80 Mk2-302 DP system controlling 1 × forward azimuth Aquamaster VL631, 549 kW; 1 × aft tunnel Brunvoll 655BD, 254 kW	**DECK MACHINERY** **Cranes**	1 × Hydralift fixed boom, 10 t at 5 m or 2 t at 10 m, includes hydraulic winch
Propellers	1 × KaMeWa cp	**A-frame(s)**	Space available on stern
Speed (max)	12.0 kt	**Winches**	2 × deck-mounted wire, approx 1 t
Speed (cruising)	10.5 kt		
Endurance	30 days	**Gate valve**	1 for Kongsberg Simrad 309T acoustic tracking system
Fuel capacity	293 t		
Fuel consumption	2-3 m³ at survey speed; 2-5 m³ on DP (per day)	**Moonpool(s) – size(s)/ function(s)**	1 × 1.2 m diameter (port) for HiPap; 1 × 300 mm diameter (starboard) for LBL transducer
Electrical power	Vessel supplies 2 × 300 kW 220 V DC; charterers supplies, 2 × 313 kVA off 440 V 60 Hz phase; 2 × 20 kVA, 220 V 50 Hz single phase		

Electrical power (cont.)

Fresh water capacity 185 t; water maker 10 m³/day

ACCOMMODATION
Charterers Total accommodation for 29
Crew Max 13
Hospital 1-berth

BRIDGE NAVIGATION AIDS
Radar 1 × JRC JMA-627-6; 1 × Kelvin Hughes 5000R
Gyrocompass 2 × Sperry ST-130
Speed log 1 × JRC JLN-203 Doppler
Echo-sounder JRC JFE-570SD

SCIENTIFIC SPACES
Total scientific deck space 240 m²
Multipurpose dry lab 70 m²

COMMUNICATIONS
MF/HF 1 × Skanti TRP 6000; 1 × Skanti TRP 8250
VHF 2 × Sait SD72; 1 × Kelvin Hughes Husun 65; 1 × Sailor RT 144C
Cellular GSM Europe
Facsimile Yes

SURVEY SYSTEMS
Positioning Cegelec/GEC GEM80 Mk2-302 DP system; DGPS, Kongsberg Simrad HPR 309-T; 1 × VRU; 2 × wind sensors
Echo-sounder (single beam) Optional
Multibeam/swath system Optional
Sidescan sonar Optional
Sub-bottom profiler Optional
Magnetometer Optional
Gravimeter Optional
Corer(s) Optional
Grab(s) Optional
Other sampling Optional
Sound velocity profiler Optional

SAFETY
Lifeboats 6 × liferafts for 135 persons
Workboat/chase boat 1 × small MOB unit
Lifesaving equipment 42 immersion suits, 50 lifejackets

NEW ENTRY

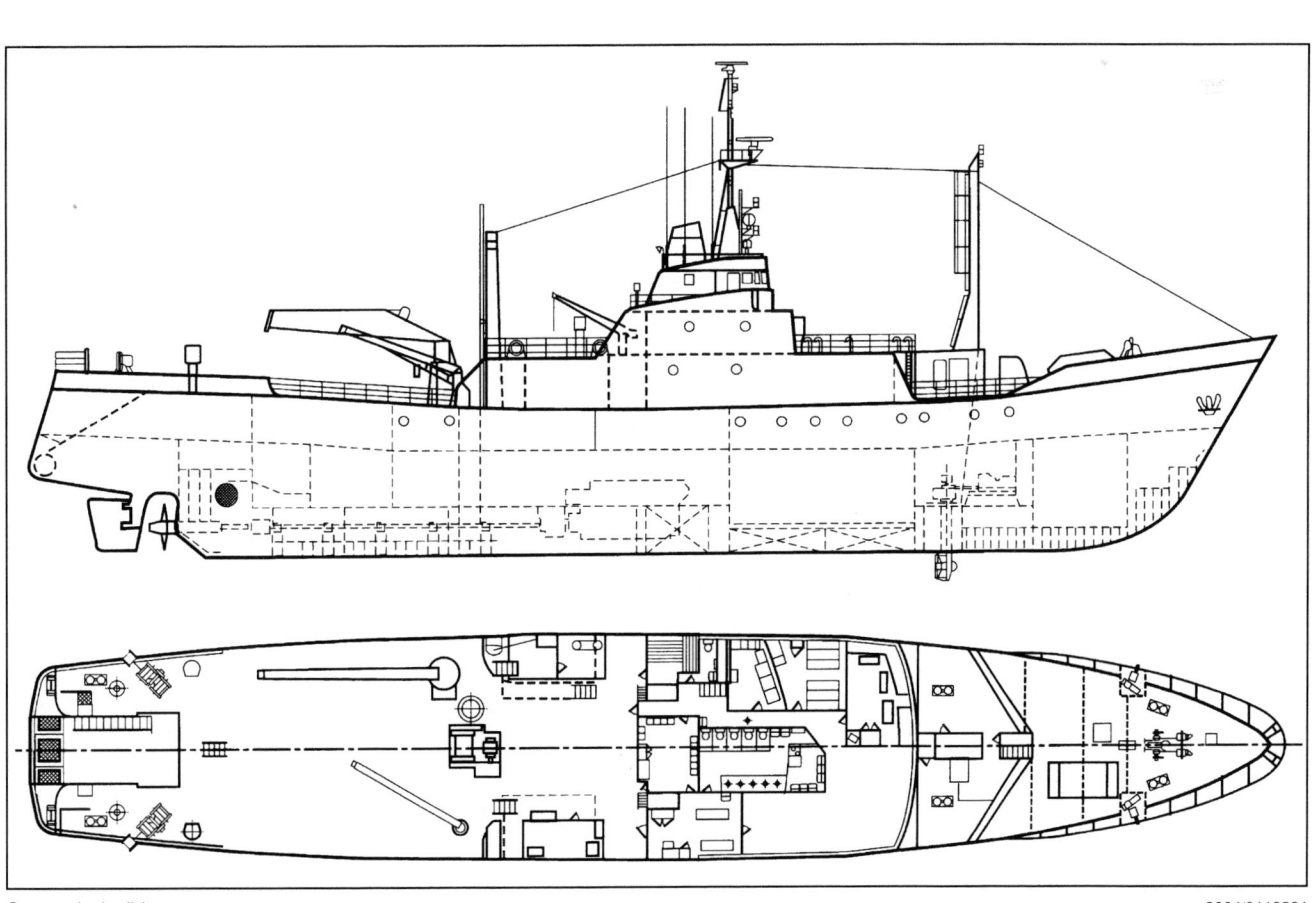

Seaway Invincible   **2001**/0110564

RUSSIAN FEDERATION

Arctic Marine Engineering Geological Expeditions (AMIGE)

Kern

GENERAL

Owner	Arctic Marine Engineering Geological Expeditions (AMIGE)
Port of reg/flag	Murmansk, Russian
Official number	8837942
Classification	KM*L2A1
Call sign	UFVD
Built (yard and date)	1991
Rebuilt (yard and date)	2000
Length overall	55.76 m
Breadth moulded	9.30 m
Max draught	5.16 m
Tonnage (grt)	1,157

PROPULSION

Main engine(s)	1 × 736 kW, Russia, GHBD48A-2U
Propellers	Single
Speed (max)	11.5 kt
Speed (cruising)	10.5 kt
Endurance	30 days
Fuel capacity	137 t
Fuel consumption	3 t
Electrical power	736 kW
Fresh water capacity	109 t

BRIDGE NAVIGATION AIDS

Satellite	GPS
Radar	Nayada-5
Gyrocompass	Kurs-4
Speed log	Pel-4
Echo-sounder	NEL-M3B

COMMUNICATIONS

VHF	Sailor, 0.025 kW
Cellular	Yes
Facsimile	Yes

SAFETY

Lifeboats	2 × 000222, 26 persons
Workboat/chase boat	Zodiac
Lifesaving equipment	12 x PSN-10

DECK MACHINERY

Cranes	Yes
A-frame(s)	Yes
Winches	Four

ACCOMMODATION

Crew	24
Scientists/surveyors	14
Hospital	Yes

SCIENTIFIC SPACES

Total scientific deck space	1 × 50 m²
Multipurpose dry lab	1 × 25 m²; 1 × 4 m²

SURVEY SYSTEMS

Corer(s)	Yes
Grab(s)	Yes

SEISMIC SYSTEMS

Energy source (type and manufacturer)	Shallow geophysical seismic complex: EdgeTech Subscan; GeoAcoustics sparker
Acquisition system	EdgeTech
Recording system	EdgeTech

UPDATED

Arctic Marine Engineering Geological Expeditions (AMIGE)

Kimberlit

GENERAL

Owner	Arctic Marine Engineering Geological Expeditions (AMIGE)
Port of reg/flag	Murmansk, Russian
Official number	8725008
Classification	KM*L21
Call sign	UAIN
Built (yard and date)	1985
Rebuilt (yard and date)	2000
Length overall	53.66 m
Breadth moulded	10.49 m
Max draught	5.55 m
Tonnage (grt)	1,217

PROPULSION

Main engine(s)	1 × 970 kW, Russia, 8NVD 48A-2U
Propellers	Single
Speed (max)	12.4 kt
Speed (cruising)	11.6 kt
Endurance	25 days
Fuel capacity	150 t
Fuel consumption	3 t
Electrical power	970 kW
Fresh water capacity	108 t

BRIDGE NAVIGATION AIDS

Satellite	GPS
Radar	MIUS, Nayada-5
Gyrocompass	Amur
Speed log	Pel-4
Echo-sounder	NEL-M3B

COMMUNICATIONS

VHF	Sailor, 0.025 kW
Cellular	Yes
Facsimile	Yes

SAFETY

Lifeboats	1 × PR1446, 26 persons
Lifesaving equipment	12 × PSN-10

DECK MACHINERY

Cranes	Two
Winches	Three
Moonpool(s) – size(s)/function(s)	10.5 × 1 m; drill function

ACCOMMODATION

Crew	20
Scientists/surveyors	10
Hospital	Yes

SCIENTIFIC SPACES

Total scientific deck space	1 × 60 m²
Oceanographic wet lab	1 × 8 m²
Multipurpose dry lab	1 × 20 m²

SURVEY SYSTEMS

Corer(s)	Yes
Grab(s)	Yes

SEISMIC SYSTEMS

Energy source (type and manufacturer)	Shallow geophysical seismic complex: EdgeTech Subscan; GeoAcoustics sparker
Acquisition system	EdgeTech
Recording system	EdgeTech

UPDATED

SINGAPORE

Fugro Geodetic Pte Ltd

Setouchi Surveyor

GENERAL

Port of reg/flag	Panama
Classification	ABS + A1 AMS
Call sign	HP 9549
Built (yard and date)	1979
Rebuilt (yard and date)	Upgraded Pan United Shipyard, Singapore, 2000
Length overall	64.80 m
Breadth moulded	11.30 m
Working deck width	Open deck space 385 m²
Operational draught	4.80 m
Tonnage (gt)	1,290; net 387

PROPULSION

Main engine(s)	2 × 3508B Caterpillar diesels
Thrusters	Simrad SDP 11 DP to ABS DPI with auto track and follow-target modes; Simrad SJS01 stand-alone joystick control
Propellers	Two stern-mounted HRP511 omni-directional fp thrusters with 5-bladed propeller
Speed (max)	12 kt
Speed (cruising)	10 kt
Fuel capacity	384 m³
Fuel consumption	Cruising 7 m³/day; survey (4 kt) 4.50 m³/day
Electrical power	1,300 kVA from 3 × 530 hp Daihatsu diesel generators
Fresh water capacity	240 m³; 8 t/day from fresh water generators (3 t/day in DP)

BRIDGE NAVIGATION AIDS

Satellite	1 × Koden
Radar	1 × Tokimex, 1 × Tokyo Keiki

Gyrocompass	1 × Hokushin
Speed log	1 × Hokushin Denki
Echo-sounder	2 × Furuno

COMMUNICATIONS

Inmarsat (type)	1 × Nera B; 1 × Raytheon C
VHF	Raytheon

DECK MACHINERY

Cranes	8 t at 3 m, 3 t at 17 m
A-frame(s)	29 t at 3 m extension
Winches	5 t SWL
Moonpool(s) – size(s)/function(s)	3 × 3 m

ACCOMMODATION

Charterers	Total accommodation for 36
Hospital	Two-berth

SURVEY SYSTEMS

Positioning	Starfix MN8 DGPS; for DP referencing: wind sensor, 2 × VRUs, 2 × gyros, Sonardyne USBL
Echo-sounder (single beam)	Yes
Multibeam/swath system	Yes
Sidescan sonar	Yes
Sub-bottom profiler	Yes
Magnetometer	Yes
Corer(s)	Yes
Grab(s)	Yes

UPDATED

Fugro Geodetic Pte Ltd

Singaora

GENERAL

Port of reg/flag	Singapore
Classification	ABS + A1 + AMS + E
Call sign	9V3216
Built (yard and date)	1984
Length overall	43.30 m
Breadth moulded	10.00 m
Working deck width	90 m² open deck space

Operational draught	3.76 m
Tonnage (grt)	488; 146 net

PROPULSION

Main engine(s)	2 × 2,420 bhp Fuji diesels
Thrusters	1 × bow
Propellers	2 × fixed pitch
Speed (max)	10 kt

Speed (cruising)	8 kt	**Gyrocompass**	1 × Hokushin
Endurance	30 days	**Echo-sounder**	1 × Furuno
Fuel consumption	Cruising 4.2 t/day; survey (5 kt)		
	3 t/day	**COMMUNICATIONS**	
Electrical power	500 kVA from 2 × Yanmar diesel	**MF/HF**	1 × Furuno
	generators	**VHF**	1 × Skanti
Fresh water capacity	138 t		
		DECK MACHINERY	
BRIDGE NAVIGATION AIDS		**Cranes**	4 t at 5 m, 2.5 t at 12 m
Satellite	1 × Furuno	**Winches**	5 t SWL
Radar	2 × Furuno		

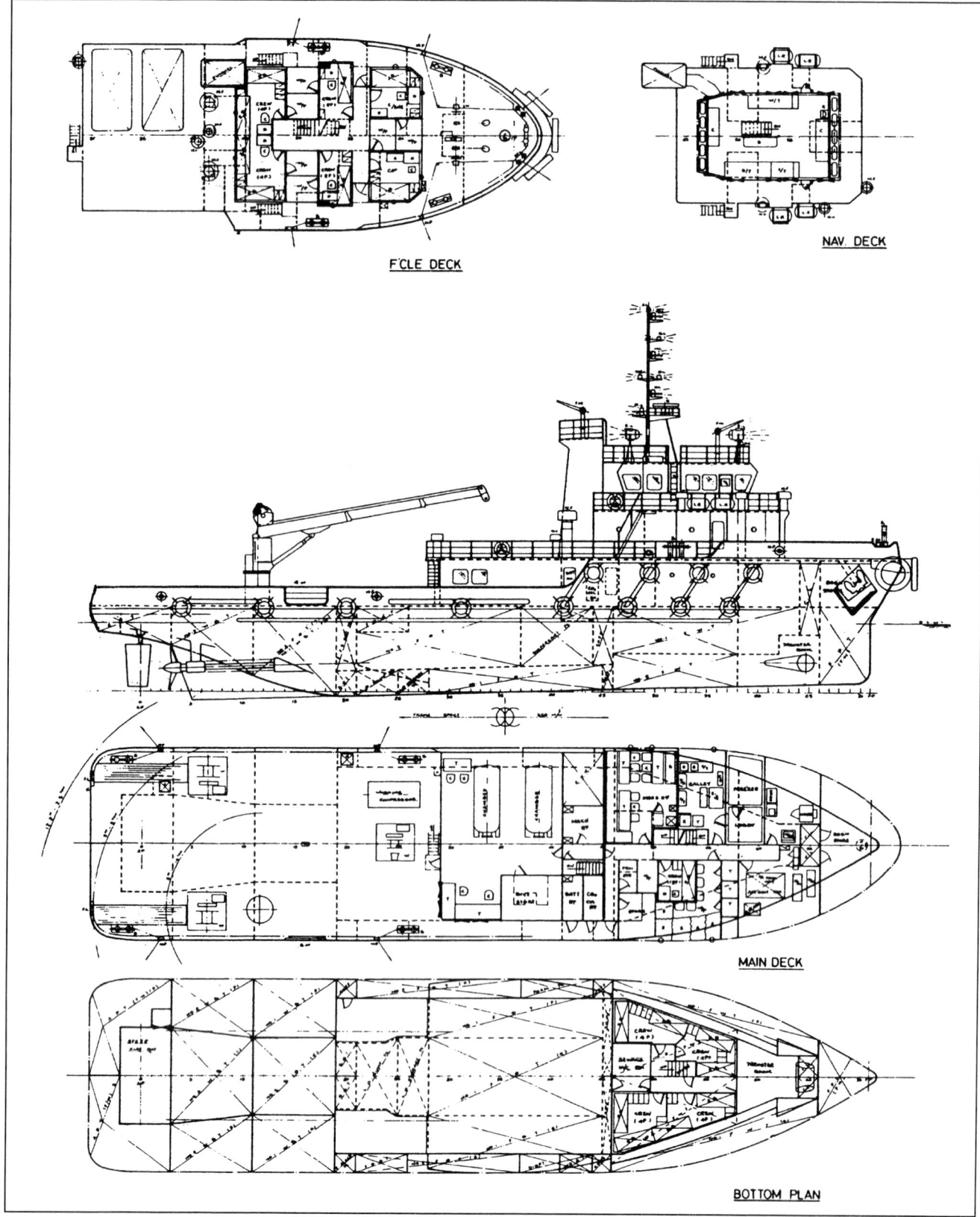

Singaora GA

ACCOMMODATION		Corer(s)	3 m/600 m cable
Charterers	Total accommodation for 32	**Grab(s)**	Shipek

SURVEY SYSTEMS

		SEISMIC SYSTEMS	
Positioning	Starfix MN8 DGPS; SG Brown survey gyro	**Energy source (type and manufacturer)**	HGS 4 × 4 sleeve gun array
Echo-sounder (single beam)	Simrad EA500	**Streamer manufacturer**	Syntron
Multibeam/swath system	Simrad EM1000	**Streamer numbers and lengths per number**	120 channels, 1,500 m
Sidescan sonar	EdgeTech SMS260		
Sub-bottom profiler	Pinger: ORE 143, 4 × 4 hull mounted; boomer: GeoAcoustics surface tow	**Recording system**	Digital: TTS 2
Magnetometer	Geometrics G876		

UPDATED

Maritime and Port Authority of Singapore (MPA)

Mata Ikan (Eye of the Fish)

GENERAL		SURVEY SYSTEMS	
Owner	Maritime and Port Authority, Singapore	**Positioning**	DGPS
		Multibeam/swath system	Yes
Port of reg/flag	Singapore	**Sidescan sonar**	Yes
Built (yard and date)	1966	**Sub-bottom profiler**	Yes
Rebuilt (yard and date)	2000	**Magnetometer**	Yes
Length overall	30.00 m	**Corer(s)**	Yes
Tonnage (grt)	150	**Grab(s)**	Yes

BRIDGE NAVIGATION AIDS	
Satellite	DGPS and ECDIS

UPDATED

Stolt Offshore

Seaway Pioneer

GENERAL			
Former names	*Northern Surveyor*	**Electrical power**	3 × Stamford 220 V 50 Hz, total 375 kW; 2 × Delco 440 V 60 Hz, total 300 kW
Owner	Stolt USA		
Port of reg/flag	Panama/Panamanian		
Classification	DnV meeting all SOLAS and USCG	**Fresh water capacity**	17,377 gallons; water making for one week
Built (yard and date)	1976		
Length overall	63.63 m	BRIDGE NAVIGATION AIDS	
Breadth moulded	9.69 m	**Satellite**	2 × Trimble 4000SE, interfaced to Racal Skyfix
Working deck width	7.00 m		
Operational draught	4.24 m	**Radar**	Decca RM926; Furuno FRS48
Tonnage (grt)	1,007	**Gyrocompass**	1 × Anschutz Kiel; S G Brown

PROPULSION		SAFETY	
Main engine(s)	1 × MAK type 8M 451 AK 1300 IHK	**Lifeboats**	Lifeboat/rescueboat for 20 persons; lifeboat for 24 persons; 4 × liferafts for 45 persons
Thrusters	Kongsberg Simrad DP controlling bow and aft each: 1 × Brunvoll diesel OM 404A Liaaen T63		
		HELIDECK	
		Size, aircraft capacity	
Speed (cruising)	10 kt		
Endurance	23 days	DECK MACHINERY	
Fuel capacity	47,953 gallons	**Cranes**	1 × Hydralift MCV-3-8, 3 t at 3 m radius; 1 × Effer 34TM 3S
Fuel consumption	1,200 gallons/day		

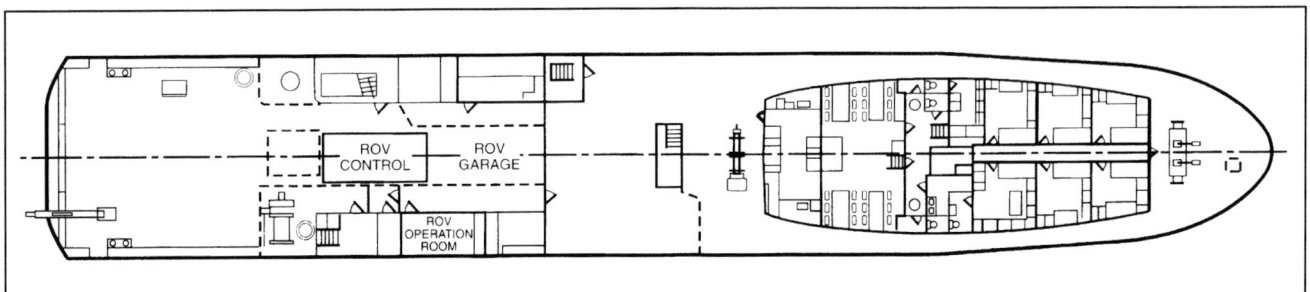

Seaway Pioneer   *2001*/0110554

A-frame(s)	Capacity up to 5 t	**Magnetometer**	Elsec Littlemore 7708
Winches	Sonar, drop corer, fast corer to 2,000 m	**Corer(s)**	Capacity to 2,000 m
Transducer well	For Simrad HPR transducer and echo-sounder	**Sound velocity profiler**	Yes

ACCOMMODATION

Charterers Total accommodation for 37

SCIENTIFIC SPACES

Multipurpose dry lab Yes

SURVEY SYSTEMS

Positioning Kongsberg ADP 311 MK2 DP system (H58 Class I DP system + H31 em); 1 × Simrad HPR 310T

Echo-sounder (single beam) Atlas Deso 15
Sidescan sonar GeoAcoustics + EG&G
Sub-bottom profiler GeoAcoustics Uniboom 300 Joules

SEISMIC SYSTEMS

Number of airguns 2 arrays
Size of airguns 150 cu in
Compressor numbers and types 1 × electrical, type 5436
Total capacity 77 cu ft/min
Streamer manufacturer Litton
Streamer numbers and lengths per number 1 × 600 m, 48 channel
Acquisition system OYO Das 1, installed if required
Recording system OYO Das 1, installed if required

NEW ENTRY

Seaway Pioneer

SOUTH AFRICA

De Beers Marine

Zealous

GENERAL

Owner De Beers Marine, South Africa

DECK MACHINERY

Winches NPD

SURVEY SYSTEMS

Vehicle(s) (ROVs/AUVs and so on)   1 × Maridan M600 AUV with Reson 8125 imaging sonar, Klein 2000 digital sidescan and

GeoAcoustics Geo-chirp sub-bottom profiler

NEW ENTRY

Zealous   **2001**/0110558

UNITED ARAB EMIRATES

Oceonics (Asia-Pacific) Ltd

Al Massah

GENERAL
Owner	Oceonics (Asia-Pacific) Ltd
Length overall	8.50 m
Operational draught	0.70 m

PROPULSION
Main engine(s)	2 × Yamaha 75 hp outboards
Fuel capacity	80 gallons

COMMUNICATIONS
VHF	Ship-to-shore
Cellular	Yes

ACCOMMODATION
Charterers	Total accommodation for 5

SURVEY SYSTEMS
Positioning	Starfix MN8, Seastar, Omnistar, PVNav, PCBarge, PCMap

UPDATED

Al Massah   **2001**/0103616

UNITED KINGDOM

Andrews Survey

Tsunami

GENERAL COMMENT

Owner	Andrews Survey
Classification	Customised RIB; MCA category 3 certified
Length overall	6.80 m
Breadth moulded	2.00 m
Max draught	0.75 m
Operational draught	0.75 m

PROPULSION

Main engine(s)	2 × 100 hp Yamaha outboard
Propellers	2
Speed (max)	40 kt
Speed (cruising)	28 kt
Endurance	320 n miles
Fuel capacity	280 litres (petrol)
Electrical power	220/12 V/24 V

BRIDGE NAVIGATION AIDS

Satellite	2 × GPS
Radar	Yes
Gyrocompass	KVH
Echo sounder	2 × Garmin/Odom

COMMUNICATIONS

VHF	2
Cellular	Yes
Facsimile	PC only

SAFETY

Lifeboats	1 × 4 persons liferaft

DECK MACHINERY

Transducer well	2

ACCOMMODATION

Crew	2
Scientists/surveyors	1

SCIENTIFIC SPACES

Total scientific deck space	2 m²

SURVEY SYSTEMS

Positioning	2 × DGPS
Echo sounder (single beam)	Dual frequency
Multibeam/swath system	Yes
Sidescan sonar	Yes
Sub-bottom profiler	Yes
Magnetometer	Yes
Sound velocity profiler	Yes

NEW ENTRY

Tsunami   **2001**/0109101

Atlantic Marine Sales & Charter Co

Bremen

GENERAL

Former names	*Mintrop*
Owner	Maritime Atlantic Ltd
Port of reg/flag	Kingstown/St Vincent and the Grenadines
Official number	8781
Classification	100 A5 + MC/AUT
Call sign	J8B2309
Built (yard and date)	Schipbau-Unterweser AG Bremerhaven, Germany, 1972
Rebuilt (yard and date)	1993
Length overall	92.00 m
Breadth moulded	15.00 m
Working deck width	11.00 m
Max draught	7.40 m
Operational draught	6.80 m
Tonnage (grt)	4,112

PROPULSION

Main engine(s)	2 × MAK 6M55 1AK
Thrusters	1 × Ulstein 150TV-A, 680 hp
Propellers	Single
Speed (max)	14 kt
Speed (cruising)	12.5 kt
Endurance	Transit: 44 days: economical 54 days
Fuel capacity	1,000 m³
Fuel consumption	Cruising: 12.3 m³; economical: 11.5 m³; port: 2 m³
Electrical power	1 × AEG 680 kVA; 2 × AvK 290 kVA; 2 × AEG 1,000 kVA
Fresh water capacity	59.10 t; 20 t/day from water maker

BRIDGE NAVIGATION AIDS

Satellite	1 × Transas ECD (world chart folio)
Radar	1 × Atlas 900 ARPA, 10 cm; 1 × Atlas 900 ARPA, 3 cm
Gyrocompass	1 × Anschutz Standard IV
Speed log	1 × JRC JLN-203 Doppler
Echo-sounder	1 × Elac LAZ 72

COMMUNICATIONS

Inmarsat (type)	C; telex; Skanti B; Skanti B high-speed data Iridium satellite handset
MF/HF	Areas A1 + A2 + A3: 1 × Skanti TRP 8251 D; 1 × Skanti DSC 9000; 2 × Sailor DSC
VHF	3 × Sailor RT2048; 1 × Sailor RT2047; 3 × portable Sailor SP3110 GMDSS
Facsimile	1 × Rocoh 1700L

SAFETY

Lifeboats	1 × Hatecke for 45 persons
Workboat/chase boat	1 × 6.50 m
Lifesaving equipment	45 × survival suits and lifejackets; 1 × 25 persons liferaft; 3 × 20 persons liferafts

HELIDECK

Size, aircraft capacity	18.95 m × 8.60 t (Bell 214/Super Puma); CAA and NMD approved

Bremen

DECK MACHINERY		**SURVEY SYSTEMS**	
Cranes	1 × HMC 229 k 1.4 t SWL	Positioning	Charterer supply
Winches	4 × 15 t streamer,	Sensors	Charterer supply
	6,000 m × 74 mm; 2 × 8 t	Echo-sounder (single beam)	Charterer supply
	streamer, 3,000 m × 74 mm	Multibeam/swath system	Charterer supply
		Sidescan sonar	Charterer supply
ACCOMMODATION		Sub-bottom profiler	Charterer supply
Charterers	Total accommodation for 40	Magnetometer	Charterer supply
Crew	14	Other sampling	Charterer supply
Scientists/surveyors	19	Sound velocity profiler	Charterer supply
Hospital	Yes	Oceanographic sensors	Charterer supply
		(CTDs/XBTs and so on)	
SCIENTIFIC SPACES			
Multipurpose dry lab	3 × lab spaces = 180 m²		*NEW ENTRY*

Atlantic Marine Sales & Charter Co

Pacific Horizon

GENERAL		**BRIDGE NAVIGATION AIDS**	
Owner	Maritime Atlantic Ltd, UK	Satellite	ECDIS computer with DGPS
Port of reg/flag	Kingstown, St. Vincent and the		tracking + data output for surveys;
	Grenadines		2 × DGPS units
Official number	8305/N	Radar	1 × Furuno 2110 with ARPA;
Classification	Lloyds + 100A1 LMC DTp Class		1 × Furuno 1505 with ARPA
	VII	Gyrocompass	1 × Anschutz; 1 × SG Brown
Call sign	J8X13	Speed log	1 × Walker
Built (yard and date)	A G Weser Werk Seebeck,	Echo-sounder	1 × Elac
	Germany, 1973	Other ship navigation	Anschutz and Cetrek autopilots
Rebuilt (yard and date)	Globe Engineering, Hull, UK,		
	1981; upgraded 1988 + Small &	**COMMUNICATIONS**	
	Co, Lowestoft, UK, 1999,	Inmarsat (type)	C; high-speed data via Sat B; mini
	including DP system		C; B Iridium multichannel
Length overall	79.80 m	MF/HF	1 × Furuno 1550
Breadth moulded	12.60 m	VHF	1 × Sailor; 2 × Robertson
Max draught	5.47 m	Cellular	GSM mobile
Operational draught		Facsimile	GSM; Inmarsat
Tonnage (grt)	1,598; net 551		
		SAFETY	
PROPULSION		Workboat/chase boat	1 × Humber 5.5 m RIB
Main engine(s)	3 × Deutz BV8M diesels, total	Lifesaving equipment	1 × DOTI 4 m MOB boat; life
	2,700 bhp driving 3 × AEG		jackets
	600 kW 500 V DC generators		
Thrusters	Bow: 1 × Schottel 340 shp	**DECK MACHINERY**	
Propellers	2	Cranes	2 × Atlas midships; 1 × Hiab aft
Speed (max)	12 kt	A-frame(s)	2 × 2 t; 1 × 15 t
Endurance	12,000 n miles	Transducer well	3
Fuel capacity	325 t	Gate valve	3
Fuel consumption	Survey speed: 4 m³/day; cruising		
	speed: 6 m³/day		
Electrical power	1 × Deutz BV6M 536, 460 kW 380		
	V 50 Hz AC, 1 × Motorgen		
	460 kW 380 V 50 Hz AC, 1 × CAT		
	380 kW 380 V 50 Hz AC, 1 × 110		
	kVA Perkins		
Fresh water capacity	110 t; +10 t/day from evaporators		

Pacific Horizon   *2000*/0088241

Pacific Horizon   *2001*/0110561

ACCOMMODATION

Charterers	Total accommodation for 42
Hospital	1-berth

SCIENTIFIC SPACES

Total scientific deck space	450 m²
Multipurpose dry lab	100 m²

SURVEY SYSTEMS

Positioning	Charterer supply
Echo-sounder (single beam)	1 × Elac
Multibeam/swath system	Charterer supply
Sidescan sonar	Charterer supply

Sub-bottom profiler	Charterer supply
Magnetometer	Charterer supply
Gravimeter	Charterer supply
Sound velocity profiler	Charterer supply
Oceanographic sensors (CTDs/XBTs and so on)	Charterer supply

SEISMIC SYSTEMS

Compressor numbers and types	Yes

UPDATED

Atlantic Marine Sales & Charter Co

Scotian Shore

GENERAL

Former names	*Western Crest, Fred J Agnich*
Current operational status	Working West African waters
Owner	Maritime Atlantic Ltd
Port of reg/flag	Kingstown, St Vincent and the Grenadines
Official number	7029
Classification	INSB
Call sign	J8RE7
Built (yard and date)	Ferguson Industries, Pictou, Nova Scotia, 1973
Rebuilt (yard and date)	1981
Length overall	51.98 m
Breadth moulded	11.89 m
Working deck width	11.00 m
Max draught	5.10 m
Tonnage (grt)	939; net 282

PROPULSION

Main engine(s)	2 × Lister Blackstone 4 SA 2942 2,000 bhp
Thrusters	Bow: Brunvoll 320 hp tunnel
Propellers	Twin screw in Kort nozzles
Speed (max)	12 kt
Speed (cruising)	8 kt
Endurance	60 days
Fuel capacity	410 m³
Fuel consumption	Steaming: 5 t/day
Electrical power	2 × Caterpillar 240 kW/415 V/60 Hz; 1 × Caterpillar 112 kW/415 V/60 Hz
Fresh water capacity	185 t

BRIDGE NAVIGATION AIDS

Satellite	2 × Furuno GPS navigator + DGPS

Survey and support vessel for charter Scotian Shore

2000/0089138

Radar	1 × Furuno FR 1505; 1 × Furuno 2110 with ARPA
Gyrocompass	1 × Sperry survey standard (step)
Echo-sounder	2
Other ship navigation	1 × Sperry autopilot + heading for ARPA output; Transas worldwide folio charting system and ECDIS computer, with DGPS tracking and data output for route surveys

COMMUNICATIONS

Inmarsat (type)	'M' with internal exchange; Iridium; e-mail high-speed data link
MF/HF	1 × Furuno 1550 transceiver with DSC; full GMDSS A1 + A2 + A3
VHF	2 × Sailor
Cellular	GSM mobile
Facsimile	GSM; Inmarsat

SAFETY

Workboat/chase boat	1 × Avon 5.4 m RIB rescue boat; 1 × 80 hp motor
Lifesaving equipment	Lifejackets and survival suits

DECK MACHINERY

Cranes	1 × Atlas Hiab midships; 1 × Hiab aft
A-frame(s)	1 × 50 t SWL

Winches	1 × double drum 42 t direct pull tow; capacity 2,000 m of 44 mm; 2 × 15 t tugger
Transducer well	Yes
Gate valve	Yes

ACCOMMODATION

Charterers	2
Crew	15
Scientists/surveyors	10

SCIENTIFIC SPACES

Total scientific deck space	160 m²
Oceanographic wet lab	20 m²
Multipurpose dry lab	40 m²

SURVEY SYSTEMS

Positioning	Charterer supply
Echo-sounder (single beam)	Charterer supply
Multibeam/swath system	Charterer supply
Sidescan sonar	Charterer supply
Sub-bottom profiler	Charterer supply
Magnetometer	Charterer supply
Gravimeter	Charterer supply
Other sampling	Charterer supply
Sound velocity profiler	Charterer supply
Oceanographic sensors (CTDs/XBTs and so on)	Charterer supply

UPDATED

Blue Water Recoveries Ltd

Challenger I

GENERAL

Former names	*Columbus Iselin*
Current operational status	Cable route survey
Owner	Valurex International
Port of reg/flag	Bahamas
Official number	731049
Classification	ABS + A1E + AMS
Call sign	C6QB3
Built (yard and date)	Bellinger Shipyards, Jacksonville, Florida, 1972
Rebuilt (yard and date)	Atlantic Drydock, Jacksonville, Florida, 1995; Bender Shipbuilding & Repair, Mobile, Alabama, 1998

Length overall	51.30 m
Breadth moulded	10.97 m
Max draught	3.30 m
Operational draught	3.20 m
Tonnage (grt)	648

PROPULSION

Main engine(s)	2 × Caterpillar D398 (1,500 hp total)
Thrusters	Bow: hydraulic 175 hp
Propellers	Twin screw – 3 blade cp
Speed (max)	12 kt
Speed (cruising)	10 kt
Endurance	30 days/10,000 n miles

Challenger 1

2001/0103612

Fuel capacity	150 t	**ACCOMMODATION**	
Fuel consumption	3 t/day at 10 kt	Charterers	17 berths
Electrical power	2 × Kato 200 kW; 1 × 200 kW deck generator	Crew	15 berths
Fresh water capacity	24 t (2 × water-making units 15 t/day)	**SCIENTIFIC SPACES**	

SCIENTIFIC SPACES

Total scientific deck space	220 m² on two decks
Multipurpose dry lab	46 m²

BRIDGE NAVIGATION AIDS

Satellite	Magnavox MX300 GPS
Radar	2 × Furuno FR2020
Gyrocompass	1 × Sperry Marine MK37
Speed log	1 × Sperry Marine SRD-331
Echo-sounder	1 × ELAC Nautik LAZ 5000 (50/200 kHz)

SURVEY SYSTEMS

Positioning	Racal SkyFix DGPS with Trimble 4000 receivers; Multifix + GNSII Navigation software; Trackpoint II plus USBL with 3 transponders; TSS HRP10 motion sensor; 1 × Sperry Marine SR-180 survey gyrocompass
Echo-sounder (single beam)	Marimatech E-Sea Sound 206C (33/200 kHz)
Multibeam/swath system	Provision for pole mounting
Sidescan sonar	Klein 2000 with 100/500 kHz towfishes; Coda DA100 processing including twin MO drives and Coda TrackPlot overview; EPC GSP-1086 printer
Sub-bottom profiler	Klein 3.5 kHz
Magnetometer	Dual Geometrics G-880 cesium; Geosoft Oasis Montaj post-processing
Vehicle(s) (ROVs/AUVs and so on)	Sub-Atlantic Cherokee ROV (1,000 m rated) with 4-function manipulator, Tritech SeaKing scanning sonar + Insite colour and monochrome video cameras

COMMUNICATIONS

Inmarsat (type)	Furuno Felcom 81B B phone/fax; Sailor Mini M phone
MF/HF	2 × SEA 322 (150 W)
VHF	Sperry Marine RT2047/D; 2 × Standard Horizon Explorer II (25 W)
Cellular	Yes
Facsimile	JRC NCR-300A Navtex; Furuno Fax 207 weather fax

UPDATED

SAFETY

Workboat/chase boat	Zodiac 4.57 m
Lifesaving equipment	4 liferafts: 2 × 25 persons, 2 × 16 persons

DECK MACHINERY

Cranes	1 × Slattery 95 knuckle-boom; 3 t at 3.05 m radius; 0.5 t at 15.24 m radius; 1 × Appleton articulated boom; 10 t SWL at 1.13 m radius; 1.5 t SWL at 15.24 m radius
A-frame(s)	Stern: 1 × 6.5 t SWL hydraulic, min 3.66 m wide by 6.25 m high; starboard: 1 × 1.5 t SWL hydraulic side launching
Winches	1 × 5 t SWL pneumatic tugger; 3 × Dynacon hydraulic towing
Gate valve	4 in

British Waterways

Elf

GENERAL

Current operational status	Operational UK inland waterways
Owner	British Waterways
Classification	Survey launch

Built (yard and date)	Porta-Bote International, California, USA, 2001
Length overall	3.20 m
Breadth moulded	1.20 m

Elf folds up for car transportation   **2001**/0110528

Working deck width	1.10 m	**SAFETY**	
Max draught	0.30 m	Lifesaving equipment	Wide range
Operational draught	0.20 m		
Tonnage (grt)	0.2	**DECK MACHINERY**	
		Transducer well	Yes
PROPULSION			
Main engine(s)	5 hp outboard	**ACCOMMODATION**	
Speed (max)	5 kt	Crew	1
Speed (cruising)	4 kt	Scientists/surveyors	1
Endurance	15 n miles		
Electrical power	12 V invertors	**SCIENTIFIC SPACES**	
		Total scientific deck space	2 m²
BRIDGE NAVIGATION AIDS			
Satellite	Yes	**SURVEY SYSTEMS**	
Radar	Yes	Positioning	Trimble DGPS
Gyrocompass	Yes	Echo-sounder (single beam)	Yes
Speed log	Yes	Multibeam/swath system	Yes
Echo-sounder	Yes	Corer(s)	Yes

COMMUNICATIONS	
VHF	Yes
Cellular	Yes

NEW ENTRY

British Waterways

Hydra III

GENERAL		**COMMUNICATIONS**	
Current operational status	Operational UK inland waterways	VHF	Yes
Owner	British Waterways	Cellular	Yes
Classification	Survey launch		
Built (yard and date)	Birmingham, 1995	**SAFETY**	
Length overall	6.00 m	Lifesaving equipment	Wide range
Breadth moulded	2.00 m		
Working deck width	1.90 m	**DECK MACHINERY**	
Max draught	0.30 m	Transducer well	Yes
Operational draught	0.30 m		
Tonnage (grt)	1.5	**ACCOMMODATION**	
		Crew	2
PROPULSION		Scientists/surveyors	1
Main engine(s)	25 hp outboard		
Speed (max)	15 kt	**SCIENTIFIC SPACES**	
Speed (cruising)	6 kt	Total scientific deck space	4 m²
Endurance	150 n miles		
Electrical power	12 V invertors	**SURVEY SYSTEMS**	
		Positioning	Trimble DGPS
BRIDGE NAVIGATION AIDS		Echo-sounder (single beam)	Yes
Satellite	Yes	Multibeam/swath system	Yes
Radar	Yes		
Gyrocompass	Yes		
Speed log	Yes		
Echo-sounder	Yes		

NEW ENTRY

Coastline Surveys Ltd

Coastline Surveyor

GENERAL		**COMMUNICATIONS**	
Owner	Coastline Surveys Ltd, UK	VHF	2
Length overall	7.30 m		
Breadth moulded	2.60 m	**ACCOMMODATION**	
Operational draught	0.5 m	Charterers	Enclosed cabin for helmsman + surveyor
PROPULSION			
Main engine(s)	165 hp Ford Mermaid with Vospower water-jet	**SURVEY SYSTEMS**	
		Positioning	2 × DGPS; ECDIS plotter; Trimble Hydropro
Speed (max)	18 kt		
Speed (cruising)	3-6 kt surveying	Sensors	
Electrical power	3.5 kW stable sine wave	Echo-sounder (single beam)	Dual frequency

Sidescan sonar	Dual frequency and real-time mosaic	**Magnetometer**	Yes
Sub-bottom profiler	Yes	**Grab(s)**	Day or Van Veen

VERIFIED

Coastline Surveyor

2000/0093767

Coastline Surveys Ltd

Flat Holm

GENERAL

Owner	Coastline Surveys Ltd, UK
Classification	ABS A1 E Towing Service, Full International Loadline, 12 passengers + 4 crew
Length overall	23.30 m
Breadth moulded	7.50 m
Max draught	2.50 m loaded
Operational draught	2.00 m

PROPULSION

Main engine(s)	2 × Cummins NTA 855M continuous at 350 hp each, 425 hp max, 2 × Twin Disc MG514 gearboxes
Propellers	2 × Kort nozzles
Speed (max)	10 kt
Endurance	4,000 n miles
Fuel capacity	44 m³
Electrical power	Auxiliaries: 2 × Volvo Penta D70 CHC 85 kVA; 415 VAC (3 ph) 240 VAC (1 ph), 24 VDC, 12 VDC
Fresh water capacity	9 m³

BRIDGE NAVIGATION AIDS

Satellite	2 × DGPS
Radar	2 × 48 n miles

COMMUNICATIONS

MF/HF	1
VHF	2
Cellular	1

DECK MACHINERY

Cranes	HyTek SeaCrane 14 t/m
A-frame(s)	7.50 t
Winches	SAMIA Hydrobloc S35 3.5 t SWL; bollard pull 10 t

ACCOMMODATION

Charterers	Total accommodation for 14

SCIENTIFIC SPACES

Multipurpose dry lab	9 m²

SURVEY SYSTEMS

Positioning	Dual DGPS with Trimble Hydropro software; ECDIS plotter	**Grab(s)**	0.5 m³; Hamon; Day; Van Veen
Echo-sounder (single beam)	1, with in-hull transducer	**Other sampling**	6 m 2,000 kg rake for seabed ploughing; crane-mounted dredge pump
Multibeam/swath system	1	**Oceanographic sensors**	Bow-mounted RDI 1,200 kHz
Sidescan sonar	1 × dual frequency	**(CTDs/XBTs and so on)**	ADCP
Sub-bottom profiler	1		
Magnetometer	1		
Corer(s)	1		

UPDATED

Flat Holm   **2000**/0085816

Delta Marine

Elizabeth-G

GENERAL

Former names	*Bergen Kreds*	**Propellers**	2
Owner	Bob Spanswick	**Speed (max)**	11 kt
Port of reg/flag	Lerwick/UK	**Speed (cruising)**	10 kt
Official number	901037	**Endurance**	3,000 n miles
Classification	SCVC Ureg No SOO3MV0220136 150 miles from safe haven	**Fuel capacity**	24,000 litres
		Fuel consumption	50-70 litres/h
Call sign	MXSF8	**Electrical power**	2 × 30 kVA GM2-71
Built (yard and date)	Leirvik Sueis, Skudenshaven, Norway, 1963	**Fresh water capacity**	6,500 litres
Length overall	22.85 m		
Breadth moulded	6.00 m	**BRIDGE NAVIGATION AIDS**	
Working deck width	5.00 m	**Satellite**	2 × GPS
Max draught	3.00 m	**Radar**	2
Operational draught	2.90 m	**Echo-sounder**	Furuno
Tonnage (grt)	84.45		
		COMMUNICATIONS	
PROPULSION		**MF/HF**	1 × Furuno SSB
Main engine(s)	2 × Detroit 12V71 365 bhp; Twin Disc 4.5:1 gearbox	**VHF**	2 × Sailor
		Cellular	1 × Panasonic
		Facsimile	Navtex

SAFETY
Lifeboats   1 × Zodiac
Lifesaving equipment   15-persons liferaft

DECK MACHINERY
Cranes   1 × 1 t
Winches   1 × 3.50 t capstan

ACCOMMODATION
Crew   3
Scientists/surveyors   5

SCIENTIFIC SPACES
Total scientific deck space   10 m²

SURVEY SYSTEMS
Echo-sounder (single beam)   Hull housing fitted
Multibeam/swath system   Hull housing fitted

VERIFIED

Elizabeth-G   *2000*/0088252

DSND Subsea Ltd

Commander

GENERAL
Owner   DSND
Port of reg/flag   Norway
Classification   DnV 1A1 + Dynpos AUTR
Call sign   LJYP
Built (yard and date)   1967
Rebuilt (yard and date)   Converted 1982, 1988
Length overall   74.83 m
Breadth moulded   12.34 m
Working deck width   Area: 275 m²
Max draught   5.70 m
Operational draught   4.00 m

PROPULSION
Main engine(s)   2 × CAT 3516 BTA
Thrusters   Kongsberg Simrad DP system;
                             bow: 1 × 600 bhp diesel electric,
                             retractable azimuth, vp in steering
                             nozzle; 1 × 802 bhp tunnel
                             thruster, electric vp; 1 × 490 bhp
                             tunnel thruster, electric, vp; aft:
                             2 × 802 hp tunnel thrusters,
                             electric, vp
Speed (max)   15 kt

Electrical power   22 × Stamford LSH81402
                             generators; auxiliaries: 1 × 380 V,
                             283 kVA, 50 Hz; 1 × 440 V 570
                             kVA for azimuth thruster; 4 × AC
                             motors 3,400 bhp

BRIDGE NAVIGATION AIDS
Satellite   1 × Shipmate R55100;
                             1 × GP-500 APNAV GPS
Radar   1 × JRC 3510S, 10 cm;
                             1 × Furuno FP-2020, 3 cm + half
                             ARPA
Gyrocompass   1 × Sperry 120; 1 × Sperry MK 37
                             Mod E
Speed log   1 × Ben GA 120
Echo-sounder   1 × Furuno FE 881
Other ship navigation   1 × Robertson AP9 MK2 autopilot

COMMUNICATIONS
Inmarsat (type)   1 × Mascot 3000
MF/HF   1 × SSB Radiotelefon Mod
                             FST-500; 2 × main receivers,
                             emergency receiver
VHF   2 × Sailor

Cellular	1 × Dancall with fax	Liferafts: 1 × Autoflug, 20
Facsimile	1 × Skanti Navtex 2 weather fax	persons; 2 × RFD, 16 persons;
		1 × RFD, 12 persons;
SAFETY		1 × Viking, 12 persons;
Lifeboats	1 × Harding lifeboat, 7.92 m, 50	1 × Dunlop, 12 persons
	persons	

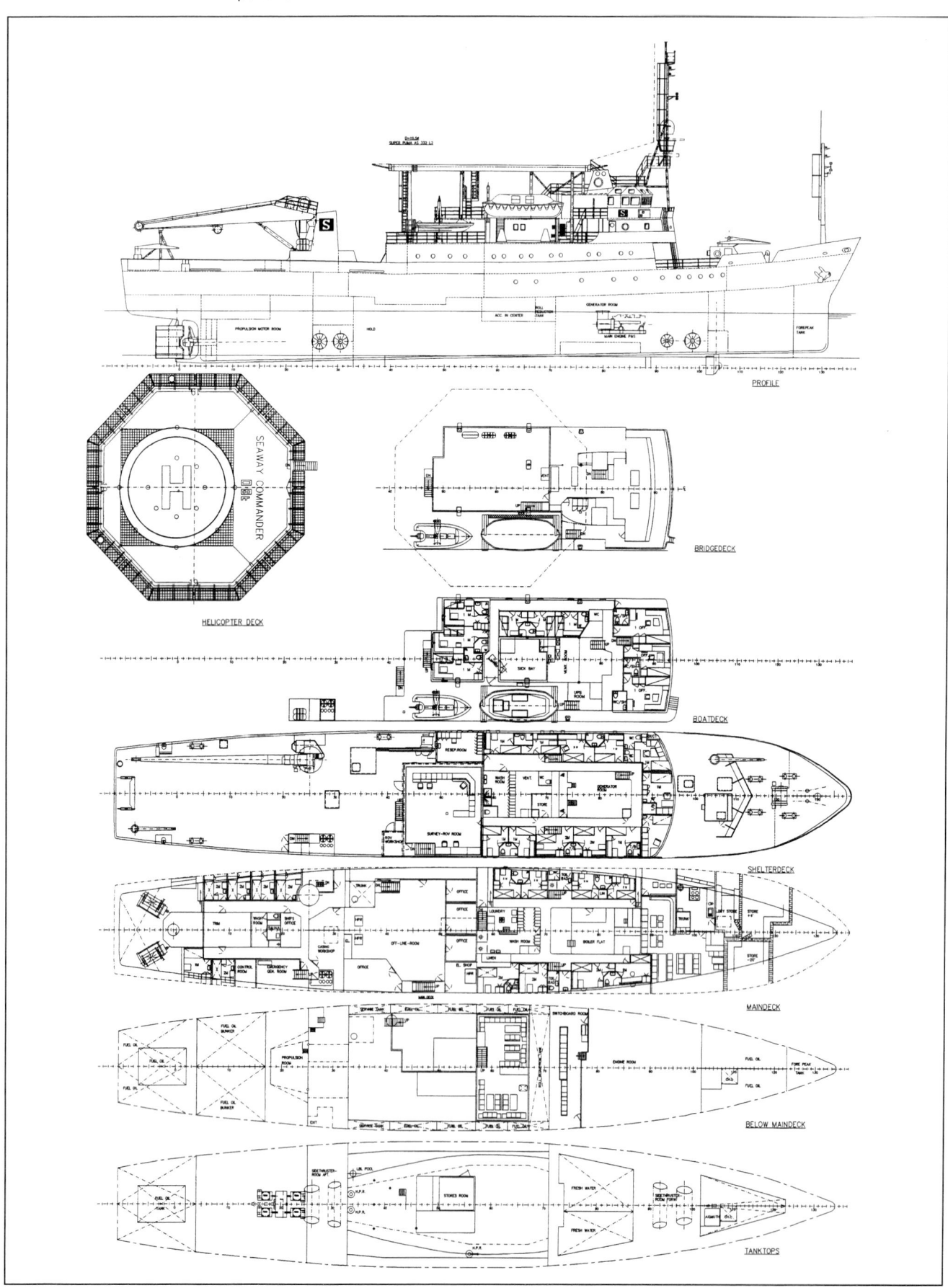

Dimensions of the Commander vessel

2000/0088232

Workboat/chase boat	MOB boat: 1 × Jørgensen & Vik, 6 persons		25 t at 8.50 m, 5 t at 18 m; 1 × Hydralift electrohydraulic, 1.5 t
HELIDECK		**Winches**	Anchor: 1 × LP Hyd Brattvaag
Size, aircraft capacity	Super Puma or similar		B9-50; mooring: 2 × 26 t, 1,800 m steel cables each
DECK MACHINERY			
Cranes	1 × Hydralift electrohydraulic telescopic, 1 t at 11 m, 2 t at 5 m; 1 × Hydralift electrohydraulic with 3 winch systems, 35 t at 7.50 m,	**SURVEY SYSTEMS** Positioning	1 × Furuno 50 KM3 DGPS

VERIFIED

Commander

2000/0088244

DSND Subsea Ltd

DSND Surveyor

GENERAL

Owner	DSND
Port of reg/flag	Norway NIS
Classification	DnV 1A1 EØ ICE DYNPOS AUTR
Built (yard and date)	1986
Rebuilt (yard and date)	Converted 1991
Length overall	65.70 m
Breadth moulded	11.00 m
Working deck width	Area: 300 m²; deck load max 60 t, 2.3 t/m²
Operational draught	6.10 m
Tonnage (grt)	414 net; 1,716 deadweight

PROPULSION

Main engine(s)	1 × Bergen diesel, KRMB-9 2480 eHK 1825
Thrusters	Kongsberg Simrad SPD 21 DP system with HiPAP USBL, Tautwire system, 2 × DGPS, 1 × VRU, 1 × MRU 5 attitude sensor, Seapath 200 heading and attitude sensor; bow: 1 × 882 kW

	Ulstein retractable azimuth VROS; 1 × 368 kW Ulstein tunnel 90 TV-A; 1 × 600 kW Brunvoll tunnel FU 632 TC 1550; stern: 1 × 368 kW Ulstein Tunnel 90 TV-A; 1 × 552 kW Ulstein tunnel 150 TV-A
Propellers	1 × Ulstein nozzle, bollard pull approx 35 t
Speed (max)	11.50 kt; bollard pull 35 t at 4.50 kt
Fuel consumption	Max: 10 t/day; transit: 6.50 t economic; on DP: ± 6.5 t/day
Electrical power	Generators: 1 × shaft, Siemens 1,060 kVA 440 V 60 Hz; 3 × Stamford MHC 920 kVA 440 V 60 Hz; 1 × Stamford MHC 320 kVA emergency generator 440 V 60 Hz; auxiliary: 3 × Detroit Diesels 16 V – 92 Ta Mod 8163-7416; 1 × Volvo TAMD 122A

BRIDGE NAVIGATION AIDS

Radar	1 × Raytheon R84, 1 × Raytheon R81
Gyrocompass	3

COMMUNICATIONS

Cellular	Yes
Facsimile	Furuno GP 500 weather fax

SAFETY

Lifeboats	Liferafts: 2 × RFD, 15-man; 2 × Viking, 16-persons; 2 × Viking, 12-persons

DECK MACHINERY

Cranes	1 × Hiab 450, 4.30 t/9.90 m; 1 × Hydralift 6 t 12 m ROV crane
A-frame(s)	1 × 15 t, 10 m high

ACCOMMODATION

Charterers	Total accommodation for 43

VERIFIED

DSND Surveyor

2000/0088233

DSND Subsea Ltd

Kommandor 2000

GENERAL

Owner	DSND
Port of reg/flag	Nassau/Bahamas
Classification	Lloyds + 100A1, LMC UMS DP (AA) offshore support vessel NMD Class 2
Built (yard and date)	North Sea Shipyard, Ringkobing, Denmark, 1996
Length overall	78.50 m
Breadth moulded	13.50 m
Working deck width	Enclosed hangar area: 275 m²; aft open deck: 225 m²; deck loading: 3 t/m²
Operational draught	4.10 m
Tonnage (grt)	2,449; 734 net; 1,100 deadweight

PROPULSION

Main engine(s)	2 × Deutz BA12M 816U diesel electric each 707 hp (520 kW) at 1,800 rpm coupled to 593 kVA Ares-type A3560M alternator; 2 × Cummins KTA 38G3 each 1,340 hp (1,000 kW) coupled to Stamford 840 kW alternator
Thrusters	DP system Simrad ADP 702 interfaced to dual DGPS, Simrad HPR 410, Sonardyne LUSBL, taut wire; bow: 2 × Hundested, each driven by 500 kW electric motor (nominal 7,000 kg each); Aquamaster 500 kW retractable azimuthing, type 601/3500 with MCD clutch; 2 × electrical synchronous motors, 1,300 kW 1,800 rpm, 2 × azimuth thrusters; Aquamaster type US1701/3250 (see thrusters)
Propellers	
Speed (max)	14 kt; bollard pull 35 t at 4.5 kt
Fuel consumption	9 t/day at 13 kt; on DP: 6-9 t/day
Electrical power	4 × Cummins-type KTA 50-G1, each 1,007 kW at 1,800 rpm with 1,280 kVA alternator; auxiliary: 1 × Cummins type NTA855-G3 358 kW at 1,800 rpm with 425 kVA alternator; 1 × Cummins type NT855-G4 280 kW at 1,800 rpm with 190 kVA alternator

BRIDGE NAVIGATION AIDS

Satellite	1 × MBX-2 DGPS
Radar	2 × Furuno FR-2110, 1 with ARPA
Gyrocompass	2 × Robertson RGCII gyrocompasses; 1 × Sperry SR220
Echo-sounder	1 × Furuno FE-680
Other ship navigation	Emri SEM200 autopilot

COMMUNICATIONS

Inmarsat (type)	'C'
MF/HF	Skanti TRP 7200 GMDSS communication station with radio/ telex

VHF   2 with DSC

SAFETY

Lifeboats   Liferafts: 2 fully enclosed 60-persons Watercraft

HELIDECK

Size, aircraft capacity   Folding, forward of bridge, rated for Super Puma

DECK MACHINERY

Cranes   Acta 50 t electrohydraulic, mounted port side; main deck SWL 5 t at 10 m; foundation for 350 t

A-frame(s)   30 t SWL with internal width 7.00 m and 5.50 m clear height; can extend 6 m beyond stern of vessel at 30 t

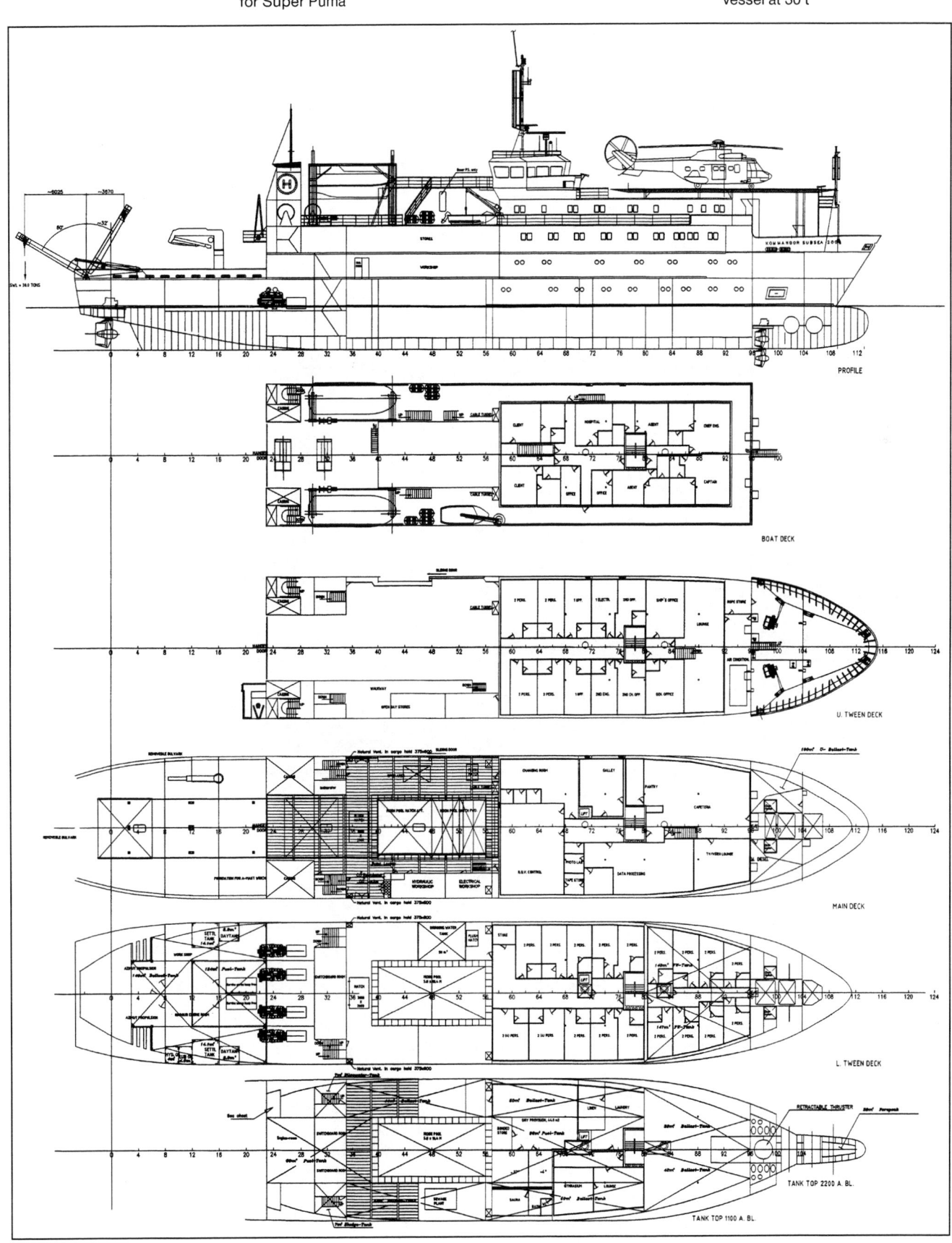

Dimensions of the Kommandor 2000

2000/0088228

Moonpool(s) – size(s)/ function(s)	10 × 5 m – can be configured as 2 × 5 × 5 m or 7.5 × 5 m; totally enclosed	**Vehicle(s) (ROVs/AUVs and so on)**	Stealth workclass ROV (3,000 m); eyeball ROV

VERIFIED

ACCOMMODATION
Charterers	Total accommodation for 60
Hospital	Yes

SURVEY SYSTEMS
Positioning	Simrad ADP 702; DGPS (dual system); Simrad HPR 410; Sonardyne LUSBL, taut wire

Kommandor 2000

2000/0088227

DSND Subsea Ltd

Markab

GENERAL
Port of reg/flag	Netherlands
Classification	BV 1 3/3 E, IMCA Class 1 (NMD Class 1)
Call sign	PHTZ
Rebuilt (yard and date)	Converted 1995
Length overall	70.20 m
Breadth moulded	13.00 m
Working deck width	Area: 400 m²
Max draught	6.00 m
Operational draught	4.30 m

PROPULSION
Main engine(s)	2 × B & W Alpha diesels, each 1,100 kW
Thrusters	DP system Kongsberg Simrad SDO

interfaced to 2 × DGPS, HPR 410 and HiPAP; bow: 1 × tunnel Brunvoll, 5 t CPP; 1 × tunnel Ulstein, 6 t CCP; stern: 1 × tunnel Ulstein, 6 t CCP

Propellers	2 × cp
Speed (max)	10.5 kt
Fuel capacity	340 m³
Electrical power	Auxiliary engines: 2 × 250 kVA Mercedes, 60 Hz/440 VAC (ship's use); 2 × 250 kVA Detroit Diesels (client's use); 1 × 1,000 kVA Deutz generator set for side thrusters
Fresh water capacity	410 m³

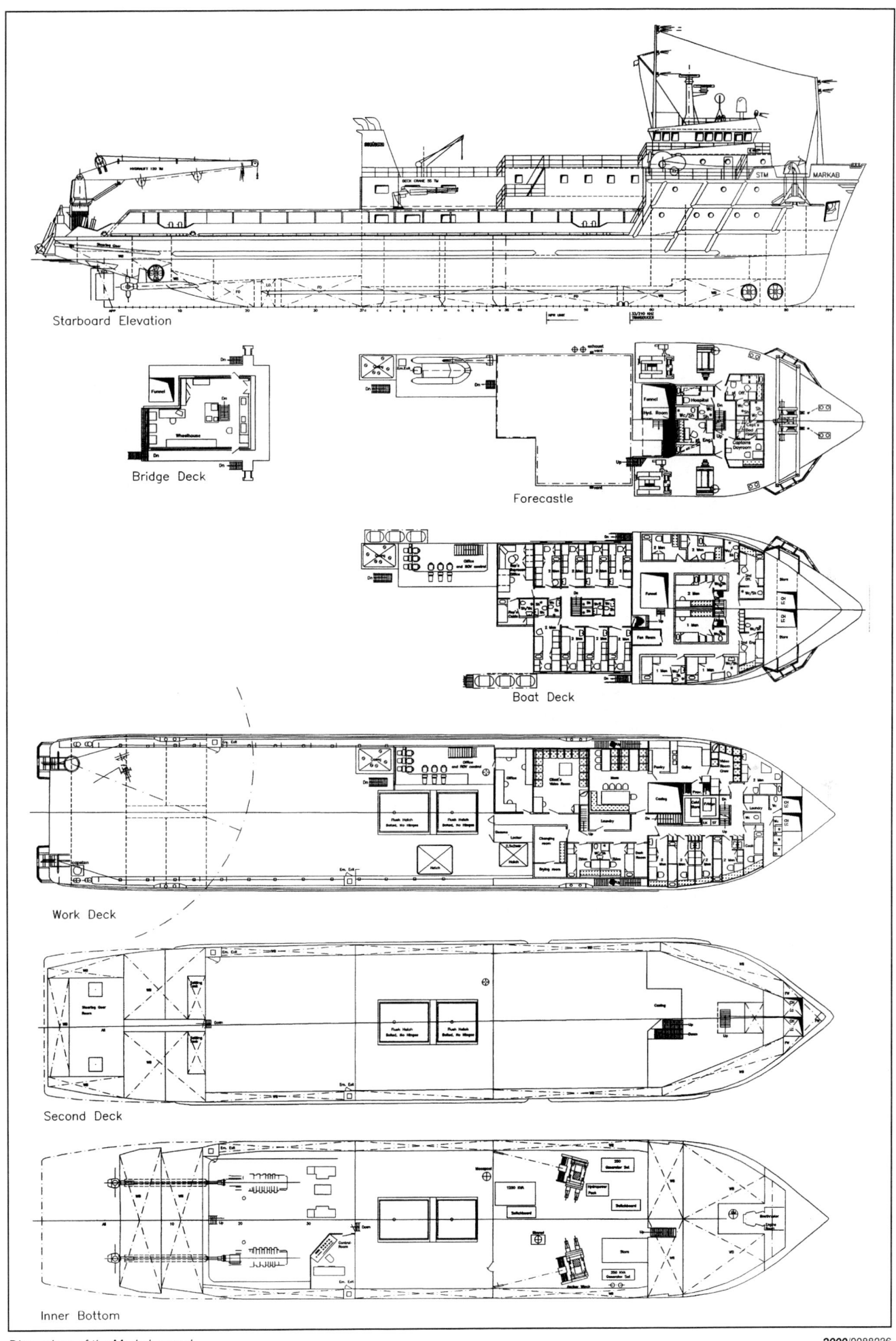

Starboard Elevation

Bridge Deck

Forecastle

Boat Deck

Work Deck

Second Deck

Inner Bottom

Dimensions of the Markab vessel

BRIDGE NAVIGATION AIDS
Satellite   2 × DGPS
Radar   1 × Furuno FP-2010
Gyrocompass   Anschutz
Echo-sounder   Simrad EX 38D
Other ship navigation   Robertson autopilot

COMMUNICATIONS
Inmarsat (type)   'A'
MF/HF   1 × Sailor GMDSS

DECK MACHINERY
Cranes   1 × hydraulic 8 t SWL – 15 m
                           (120 t/m); 1 × ROV knuckle-
                           boom; 58 t/m near moonpools;
                           1 × man riding for MOB boat

Winches   Forward: 2 × Brattvaag SL 30; aft:
                           2 × Luyt; 1 × general purpose
                           tugger; 5 t with capstan PS aft;
                           1 × capstan 10 t SB aft;
                           1 × windlass with 2 × 1.5 t anchor
                           and 2 capstans
Moonpool(s) – size(s)/   2: 1 = 3.50 × 3.50 m;
   function(s)   1 = 4.00 × 3.50 m

ACCOMMODATION
Charterers   Total accommodation for 31

VERIFIED

Markab   **2000**/0088235

DSND Subsea Ltd

Mirfak

GENERAL
Port of reg/flag   Netherlands
Classification   Bureau Veritas, ocean-going
Call sign   PFZU
Built (yard and date)   1966
Rebuilt (yard and date)   Converted 1986, 1991
Length overall   59.80 m
Breadth moulded   11.70 m
Working deck width   Total area: 170 m²;
                           behind streamer winch: 47 m²
Operational draught   3.60 m

PROPULSION
Main engine(s)   2 × 1,350 hp Industrial Diesels
Thrusters   Bow: Tornado 2/1 200 hp electric
                           driven
Propellers   2 × vp
Speed (max)   11 kt
Electrical power   Generators: 2 × fully stabilised
                           220 VAC, 25 kVA; 1 × 380 VAC
                           50 Hz, 250 kVA

BRIDGE NAVIGATION AIDS

Satellite	Furuno FSN 80
Radar	Furuno FR 1211
Gyrocompass	Arma Brown
Echo-sounder	Kelvin Hughes
Other ship navigation	MK 33 autopilot

COMMUNICATIONS

Inmarsat (type)	'A'

MF/HF	Sailor T1130/R1119 500 W
VHF	Sailor

DECK MACHINERY

Cranes	Deck midships: Hiab, 1 t starboard side; deck aft: 16 t/m at stern port side
A-frame(s)	6 t SWL at stern, height 8 m
Winches	Coring: aft upperdeck, 2 t SWL

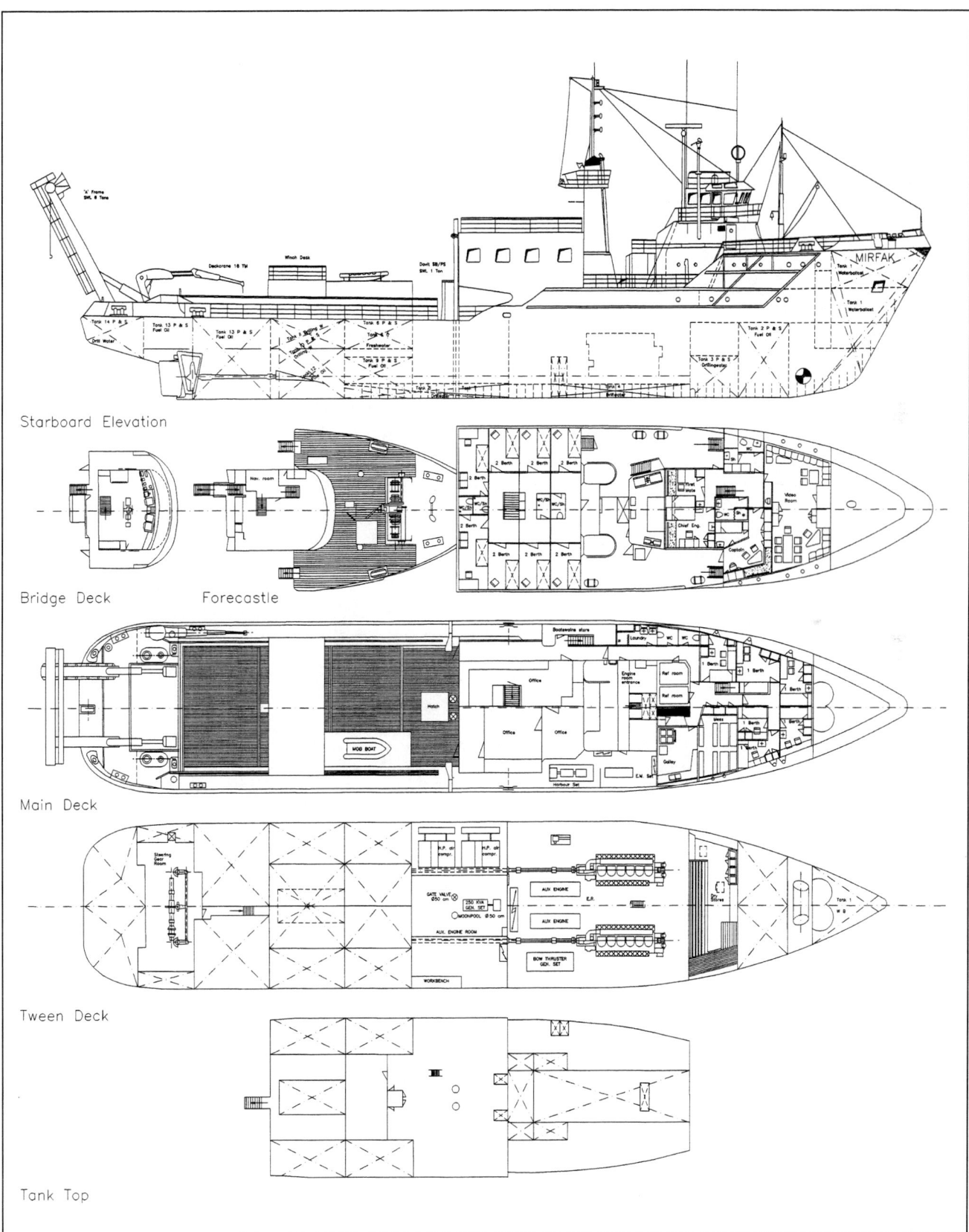

Starboard Elevation

Bridge Deck   Forecastle

Main Deck

Tween Deck

Tank Top

Dimensions of the Mirfak vessel

2000/0088238

ACCOMMODATION

Charterers	Total accommodation for 25

SURVEY SYSTEMS

Positioning	DGPS
Echo-sounder (single beam)	Atlas Deso 25, heave compensated, Hippy 120 B with hull-mounted 33/210 kHz transducers
Sidescan sonar	Dowty 3010 Widescan II 100/325 kHz; ORE 160 100 kHz
Sub-bottom profiler	Seapro Mk II dual-frequency 3.5 to 14 kHz, heave compensated; EG&G 1 kJ multi-electrode sparker; Huntec deeptow sparker; Huntec deeptow boomer; TSS signal processing suite; Dowty 3710 thermal recorders
Corer(s)	2 m Piston
Grab(s)	Shipek, Van Veen samplers; vibrocorer (3 m) and CPT

SEISMIC SYSTEMS

Energy source (type and manufacturer)	Sleeve gun
Size of airguns	160 cu in (4 × 40)
Compressor numbers and types	2 × Price 275 cu ft/min; 1 × LMF 400 cu ft/min
Streamer manufacturer	Teledyne
Streamer type	Programmable quick coupling cable to 96 channels, 1,200 m active
Streamer numbers and lengths per number	1
Recording system	TTS-2 programmable to 120 channels; MicroMax near field and far field monitoring

VERIFIED

Mirfak   **2000**/0088237

Echoscan Ltd

Scan Scarab

GENERAL

Port of reg/flag	United Kingdom
Classification	Lloyds + 100 A1 + LMC (97)
Built (yard and date)	D C Holmes, Beverley, UK, 1971
Length overall	35.21 m
Breadth moulded	8.99 m
Operational draught	3.00 m (loaded)
Tonnage (grt)	283

PROPULSION

Main engine(s)	1 × Lister Blackstone ERS8, 660 bhp at 750 rpm
Propellers	Single
Speed (max)	10 kt
Fuel capacity	26.70 t
Fuel consumption	1.5 t/day at 8 kt

Electrical power	Generators: 1 × Foden 100 kVA; 1 × Perkins 30 kVA
Fresh water capacity	20.11 t

BRIDGE NAVIGATION AIDS

Radar	2 × Racal Decca 501
Gyrocompass	1 × S G Brown, interfaced with radar and autopilot
Echo-sounder	1 × Furuno dual-frequency 50/250 Hz

COMMUNICATIONS

MF/HF	1 × Furuno 1562 150 W GMDSS SSB radio
VHF	1 × Sailor RT2048; 2 × waterproof hand-held

Cellular	Vodafone with fax
Facsimile	Navtex
SAFETY	
Workboat/chase boat	1 × 150 hp Rigid Raider with GPS + Widescan
DECK MACHINERY	
Cranes	1 × 3 t Hiab; 1 × 20 t twin wire derrick
Winches	DD winch 500 × 24 mm crane wire; S & P 5 t deck + S & P 3 t aft anchor
ACCOMMODATION	
Charterers	Total accommodation for 16
SURVEY SYSTEMS	
Magnetometer	1 × Aquascan MC5

NEW ENTRY *Scan Scarab* *2001*/0110546

Echoscan Ltd

Scan Warrior

GENERAL

Owner	Echoscan Ltd, UK
Port of reg/flag	Rochester, Beverley/UK
Classification	Lloyds + 100 A1 + LMC
Built (yard and date)	1966
Rebuilt (yard and date)	Converted 1990; modified 1992
Length overall	52.27 m
Breadth moulded	11.43 m
Working deck width	Lower: 12 × 10 m; upper: 15 × 10 m
Max draught	4.10 m
Tonnage (grt)	797

PROPULSION

Main engine(s)	2 × Lister Blackstone, 800 bhp
Thrusters	Bow: 160 hp tunnel, 600 hp Aquamaster diesel
Propellers	2 × fp
Speed (max)	12 kt
Fuel capacity	200 t
Fuel consumption	1.4 t/day
Electrical power	Generators: 2 × 125 kVA, 220 V DC/220 V 50 Hz; Deutz 180 kVA 3-phase, 50/60 Hz; 1 × 60 kVA
Fresh water capacity	200 t

BRIDGE NAVIGATION AIDS

Satellite	Philips DGPS and C-Map computer navigation system
Radar	1 × Furuno FR2010 ARPA; 1 × Furuno FR1510 DA; 1 × Furuno FR1940
Gyrocompass	1 × Sperry SR120
Echo-sounder	1 × Furuno FCV665
Other ship navigation	1 × Ceitek 747 autopilot; Navtex Nav 5 GMDSS

COMMUNICATIONS

MF/HF	1 × Kelvin Hughes Huscan 2100
VHF	3 × Kelvin Hughes RT2048
SAFETY	
Lifeboats	9 t Miranda RIB
DECK MACHINERY	
Cranes	1 × Hiab hydraulic
A-frame(s)	40 t with double drum winch
ACCOMMODATION	
Charterers	Total accommodation for 40
SURVEY SYSTEMS	
Echo-sounder (single beam)	Hull-mounted transducer for Atlas dual-frequency 33/210 kHz

NEW ENTRY

Scan Warrior *2001*/0110547

Emu Environmental Ltd

Emu Surveyor

GENERAL

Current operational status	Nearshore site surveying
Owner	Emu Environmental Ltd, UK
Classification	MCA coding Category 2
Built (yard and date)	
Length overall	12.50 m
Operational draught	2.00 m

PROPULSION

Main engine(s)	2 × John Deere 300 hp turbocharged diesels
Speed (max)	20 kt
Endurance	Up to 60 n miles

Electrical power   12 V + 24 V supplies; 240 V supply from 6 kVA generator and 1.4 kVA UPS

ACCOMMODATION

Charterers	Can carry 12 passengers

SURVEY SYSTEMS

Positioning	Leica MX412 DGPS
Echo-sounder (single beam)	Knudsen dual frequency; Seatex MRU heave compensator
Sidescan sonar	EdgeTech
Sub-bottom profiler	EdgeTech

NEW ENTRY

Emu Surveyor

2001/0121297

Emu Environmental Ltd

Mariner

GENERAL

Owner	Emu Environmental Ltd, UK
Length overall	11.00 m

PROPULSION

Main engine(s)	Gardner diesel
Speed (max)	11 kt

DECK MACHINERY

A-frame(s)	1.5 t

SURVEY SYSTEMS

Positioning	DGPS
Echo-sounder (single beam)	Yes
Sidescan sonar	EdgeTech with Triton digital processor

Sub-bottom profiler	EdgeTech	Oceanographic sensors	RDI ADCPs
Corer(s)	Yes	(CTDs/XBTs and so on)	
Grab(s)	Yes		*VERIFIED*

Mariner   ***2000**/0093769*

Fugro Survey Ltd

Geo Prospector

GENERAL

		Length overall	72.64 m
Owner	Fugro-Geoteam Ltd	**Breadth moulded**	11.80 m
Port of reg/flag	Haugesund, Norway	**Operational draught**	5.50 m
Classification	DnV + 1A1 EO	**Tonnage (grt)**	1,417; 425 net
Call sign	LADE 5		
Built (yard and date)	1970	**PROPULSION**	
Rebuilt (yard and date)	1997	**Main engine(s)**	2 × Deutz RBV8M 546 (1,760 bhp/1,313 kW) through Lohmann & Stolterfoht gearbox

Geo Prospector   ***2001**/0103615*

Thrusters	Bow: electric 177 kW (237 hp)
Propellers	Escher-Wyss vp
Speed (max)	16.50 kt
Speed (cruising)	16 kt
Endurance	15,000 n miles
Fuel consumption	13 t/day at 16.50 kt
	9 t/day at 14.00 kt
	6 t/day at 9.00 kt
Electrical power	4 × Deutz diesels BF6M 716, each
	246 hp (184 kW) driving 215 kVA
	400/230 V 50 Hz alternator
Fresh water capacity	4-5 t/day consumption

BRIDGE NAVIGATION AIDS

Satellite	Furuno GP80 GPS
Radar	Kelvin Hughes Nucleus 25,000 A;
	full ARPA; Furuno FR 1510 DA
Gyrocompass	Anschutz + Robertson 82
Speed log	Anthea

COMMUNICATIONS

Inmarsat (type)	Furuno B and C
MF/HF	2 × Furuno DSC-6;
	MMSI-2598114000 (MID)
VHF	Debeg 7606 (2182); 2 × Furuno
	FM-8500; Sailor C403 remotes

DECK MACHINERY

Cranes	2 × Hiab 200 sea cranes
A-frame(s)	'T' type
Winches	1 × SSS/far field coring winch
	(3.50 m corer)
Transducer well	Simrad 410, 6 m
Gate valve	Standard

ACCOMMODATION

Charterers	Total accommodation for 43
Hospital	1 berth

SURVEY SYSTEMS

Positioning	Fugro Starfix MN8 and Starfix
	Spot DGPS; 2 × Trimble 4000
	RDS; online nav: Fugro PCSeis;
	offline: Fugro GMENU/GMAP;
	VRU: Seatex MRU8; acoustic
	positioning: Simrad HPR 410T
Echo-sounder (single beam)	Simrad EA 500, 38/27/200 kHz
Multibeam/swath system	Multibeam sounder: Simrad
	EM300
Sidescan sonar	GeoAcoustics 159
Sub-bottom profiler	GeoAcoustics 4 × 4 hull-mounted;
	TI 10 cu in sleeve gun; Benthos
	single channel hydrophone
	streamer; TTS 2 digital recorder;
	Waverley 3710 graphic recorder;
	TSS 360 TVG, TVF and swell filter
Corer(s)	Malakoff 3-5 m drop corer
	(2,000 m cable)
Grab(s)	Shipek

SEISMIC SYSTEMS

Energy source (type and manufacturer)	6 × sleeve gun array (140 cu in)
Streamer manufacturer	Fjord Instruments
Streamer numbers and lengths per number	1,500 m total, 96 channel
Recording system	TTS2, 120 channel; MicroMAX QC

UPDATED

Fugro Survey Ltd

Svetlomor 2

GENERAL

Current operational status	2D exploration, Caspian Sea
Classification	MRS KM A2 supply vessel
Call sign	4 JGF
Built (yard and date)	1987
Rebuilt (yard and date)	1996
Length overall	61.00 m
Breadth moulded	14.00 m
Max draught	4.50 m
Tonnage (gt)	1,695; net 509

PROPULSION

Speed (max)	12 kt (service)
Endurance	4,500 n miles
Fuel capacity	300 m³
Electrical power	3 × 238 kW generators

BRIDGE NAVIGATION AIDS

Satellite	Yes
Radar	3 cm/10 cm
Speed log	Doppler

DECK MACHINERY

Cranes	1
A-frame(s)	Yes

ACCOMMODATION

Charterers	Total accommodation for 34

SURVEY SYSTEMS

Positioning	Starfix MN8; PC Seis
Echo-sounder (single beam)	Simrad EA501
Sidescan sonar	EG&G 260TH/272TD
Sub-bottom profiler	EG&G
Other sampling	Drop corer + grab

SEISMIC SYSTEMS

Energy source (type and manufacturer)	4 × 40 cu in sleeve gun cluster; 10 cu in mini-sleeve gun
Streamer numbers and lengths per number	56 channel
Recording system	TTS 128

UPDATED

Fugro-UDI Ltd

Fugro Surveyor

GENERAL

Owner	Fugro-UDI Ltd, UK
Classification	MCA Class 2, catamaran; road transportable (towed by a modified Land Rover), with specially designed self-sufficient launch system
Built (yard and date)	Cheetah Marine, Isle of Wight, UK, 2001
Length overall	7 m
Operational draught	40 cm

PROPULSION

Main engine(s)	2 × Honda 50 hp
Speed (max)	15 kt
Electrical power	6 kVA generator, 3 kVA UPS to operate for 30 min on full load

ACCOMMODATION

Charterers	1
Crew	3

SURVEY SYSTEMS

Positioning	Starfix DGPS, Starfix.NAV
Sensors	Dual KVH 1000 compass
Echo sounder (single beam)	Knudsen dual-frequency

Multibeam/swath system	Yes
Sidescan sonar	Yes
Sub-bottom profiler	Yes
Magnetometer	Yes
Vehicle(s) (ROVs/AUVs and so on)	"Eyeball" ROV

NEW ENTRY

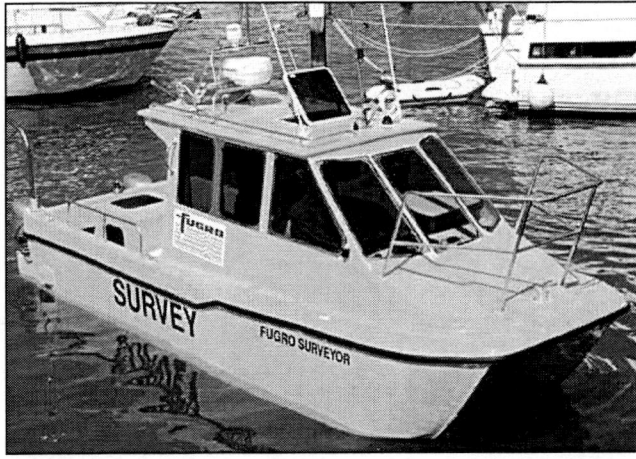

Fugro Surveyor   *2001*/0109079

Fugro-UDI Ltd

Northern Prince

GENERAL

Owner	Fugro-UDI Ltd, UK
Port of reg/flag	Hull, UK/British
Classification	Lloyds + 100A1
Call sign	GPHH
Built (yard and date)	1972
Rebuilt (yard and date)	1986/1993
Length overall	70.20 m
Breadth moulded	12.65 m
Working deck width	Main deck 337 m² capacity; fore deck 170 m² area
Operational draught	5.74 m
Tonnage (grt)	1,421; 560 net

PROPULSION

Main engine(s)	Mirrlees KMR 6-cyl
Thrusters	Duplex GEM 802; Simrad HPR410T, plus taut wire; azimuth: forward 850 hp, 360°, aft 700 hp, 360°; lateral: forward 600 hp, vp, aft 450 hp, vp
Propellers	AM Liaaen
Speed (max)	16 kt
Speed (cruising)	14 kt
Endurance	60+ days
Fuel capacity	400 t
Fuel consumption	Cruising 8-10 t/day; survey/dp: 3.5 t/day
Electrical power	Main alternator produces 440 V 3-phase; DC: 220 kW alternator; 220 kW generator; 2 × auxiliary 475 kW alternators; 2 × ROV alternators; shaft-driven constant voltage generator
Fresh water capacity	100 t

BRIDGE NAVIGATION AIDS

Satellite	Magnavox MX 4102
Radar	2 × Furuno
Gyrocompass	2 × Sperry SR 220
Speed log	EMY1/C Decca Walker
Echo-sounder	Atlas

COMMUNICATIONS

Inmarsat (type)	Marisat
MF/HF	Sailor 800 W; Skanti SSB 250 W
VHF	Dual

Northern Prince   *2001*/0121299

DECK MACHINERY

Cranes	15 t SWL survey; 31 t/m SWL ROV
A-frame(s)	20 t SWL
Winches	Traction, 15 t SWL, 10,000 m of 20 mm wire; 2 × corer handling davits
Moonpool(s) – size(s)/ function(s)	1 m diameter

ACCOMMODATION

Charterers	Total accommodation for 44
Hospital	Yes

SCIENTIFIC SPACES

Total scientific deck space	Survey 50 m²; deck (survey) 25 m²; deck (ROV) 23 m²; ROV workshop 12 m²
Multipurpose dry lab	Tween deck 100 m³ independent lab space

VERIFIED

Fugro-UDI Ltd

Skandi Carla

GENERAL

Owner	District Offshore ASA, Norway
Classification	DnV + 1A1-EO-SF, dk (+), hl (2, 8), dynpos AUTR/NMD2, HELDK
Built (yard and date)	Building Aukra Industrier AS, Norway, delivering 2001
Length overall	83.85 m
Breadth moulded	19.70 m
Working deck width	Back deck area: 600 m²

PROPULSION

Main engine(s)	4 × 2,500 kW, total 10,000 kW
Thrusters	Forward: 2 × tunnel 1,000 kW, 1 × azimuth; aft: 2 × azimuth
Fuel capacity	1,300 m³

HELIDECK

Size, aircraft capacity	19.5 × 19.5 m, Super Puma rated

Artist's impression of Skandi Carla

2000/0093768

DECK MACHINERY

Cranes	50 t, heave-compensated — lift capacity: 50 t at 10 m radius, 30 t at 16 m radius, 10 t at 33 m radius, 15 t at 2,000 m depth
Moonpool(s) – size(s)/ function(s)	5.50 × 5.40 m

ACCOMMODATION

Charterers	Total accommodation for 80

UPDATED

Skandi Carla   **2001**/0110566

Fugro-UDI Ltd

Skandi Inspector

GENERAL

Classification	NMD Class II DP
Built (yard and date)	1998
Length overall	81.00 m
Breadth moulded	18.00 m
Working deck width	Open deck space 540 m²
Max draught	5.00 m
Tonnage (grt)	2,560

PROPULSION

Main engine(s)	2 × MAK diesels, 2,407 bhp
Thrusters	Simrad DP; 5 × 750 hp vp
Propellers	2 × vp
Electrical power	2 × 1,000 kVA generators

HELIDECK

Size, aircraft capacity	Super Puma capability

DECK MACHINERY

Cranes	1 × 50 t to 600 m; 20 t to 2,000 m
Winches	10 t; heave-compensated traction (ROV)
Moonpool(s) – size(s)/ function(s)	1: 5.00 × 5.80 m for ROVs. 2: 5.00 × 5.20 m

ACCOMMODATION

Charterers	Total accommodation for 64
Hospital	Yes

SURVEY SYSTEMS

Positioning	Starfix MN8 DGPS; taut wire: Simrad HiPAP and 418 HPR

UPDATED

Gardline Surveys Ltd

Elinor TH

GENERAL

Former names	*Lady Fiona, British Enterprise Two, Ocean Enterprise*
Current operational status	Hydrographic survey
Owner	Imsco
Port of reg/flag	Hamilton/Bermudian
Official number	384827

Classification	LRS+100A1+LMC
Call sign	Z FW N
Built (yard and date)	Brooke Marine, Lowestoft, UK, 1966
Rebuilt (yard and date)	Rickmerswerft, Bremerhaven, Germany, 1975; refitted Richards Dry Dock, 1999

Length overall	51.82 m
Breadth moulded	11.28 m
Max draught	4.12 m
Tonnage (grt)	959

PROPULSION

Main engine(s)	Lister Blackstone ESS L8 MGR 2 x 800 bhp
Thrusters	Bow: azimuth 650 bhp
Propellers	2 × fp
Speed (max)	13 kt
Speed (cruising)	10 kt
Endurance	30 days +
Fuel capacity	295 m³
Fuel consumption	4.5 t/day at 10.5 kt; 1.5 t/day at 5 kt
Electrical power	30 kVA 240 V (50 Hz)
Fresh water capacity	289 m³

BRIDGE NAVIGATION AIDS

Satellite	JRC 3800 series
Radar	2 × Decca RM 1070/916
Gyrocompass	Anschutz 110-203
Echo sounder	Simrad ES 2 BN

COMMUNICATIONS

Inmarsat (type)	2 × Mini M telephone C
MF/HF	Icom M 710
VHF	Sailor 144 B/C Icom RS 8400
Cellular	Yes
Facsimile	SAT A

SAFETY

Lifeboats	4 × 25-person liferafts; Lifeguard IR455 rescue boat
Lifesaving equipment	Firefighting (3 × B A set and firefighting outfits) CO_2 system in engine room; full safety equipment to SOLAS regulations

DECK MACHINERY

Cranes	Hydraulic Hiab 360 SEA, 516 t at 6.8 m, 2.71 t at 11.9 m, 8 t at min radius

A-frame(s)	4 t SWL/5 m
Winches	3 t
Moonpool(s) – size(s)/ function(s)	2

ACCOMMODATION

Crew	10
Scientists/surveyors	21
Scientific spaces	
Total scientific deck space	450 m²
Oceanographic wet lab	108 m²
Multipurpose dry lab	65 m²

SURVEY SYSTEMS

Positioning	surface: DGPS SkyFix, QC, QPS or VGPS; sub-surface: Nautronix ATS II
Echo sounder (single beam)	Simrad EA 502/Deso 15
Sidescan sonar	GeoAcoustics dual frequency (100/500 kHz)
Sub-bottom profiler	EG&G 240 sub tow boomer; EG&G 230 surface tow boomer; deep tow sparker; SIG sparker; TSS signal processing suite/ thermal recorders; Elics Delph recorder and Coda processing optional
Magnetometer	Geometrics 880 caesium
Corer(s)	3 m UMEL Sargent gravity; 3 m Kullenberg piston; 5 m vibrocorer, optional; 5 m acoustic CPT, optional
Grab(s)	Van Veen
Sound velocity profiler	SVP + velocimeter

NEW ENTRY

Elinor TH

2001/0110474

Gardline Surveys Ltd

Ocean Seeker

GENERAL

Former names	*Granuille II*
Current operational status	Hydrographic survey
Owner	Gardline Shipping Ltd, UK
Port of reg/flag	Dublin/Irish
Official number	401142
Classification	Lloyds + 100A1 UMS
Call sign	EICQ
Built (yard and date)	1970
Rebuilt (yard and date)	2000
Length overall	80.68 m
Breadth moulded	12.80 m
Working deck width	12.00 m
Max draught	3.95 m
Tonnage (grt)	1,943

PROPULSION

Main engine(s)	2 × W H Allen 8-cylinder, coupled to 2 × 215Lohmann and Stolterfoht reduction/reverse gearboxes; 3 × Rushton 300 kW
Thrusters	Bow: Stone Vickers, 300 kW
Propellers	twin fp
Speed (max)	12 kt
Speed (cruising)	10 kt
Endurance	35 days
Fuel capacity	284.80 t
Fuel consumption	2.50 t/day

Electrical power	400 V 60 Hz 3 Phase and 240 V 26 A
Fresh water capacity	190.80 t

BRIDGE NAVIGATION AIDS

Satellite	Trimble GPS – NT300D
Radar	Racal Bridgemaster
Gyrocompass	S G Brown

COMMUNICATIONS

Inmarsat (type)	Mini M telephone
MF/HF	Sailor MF 400 W SSB
VHF	Sailor C4014
Cellular	Yes
Facsimile	SAT A

SAFETY

Lifeboats	2 × 53 persons
Lifesaving equipment	50 immersion suits; 1 × Jotron EPIRB; SARTS Lokata 3; 4 × 20-person liferafts; scale A fire alarm signal

HELIDECK

Size, aircraft capacity	18.3 m²

DECK MACHINERY

Cranes	1 × Liebherr 5 t
Gate valve	14 in diameter

Ocean Seeker   **2001**/0110475

ACCOMMODATION

Charterers	Total accommodation for 50
Crew	13
Scientists/surveyors	36
Hospital	Yes

SCIENTIFIC SPACES

Multipurpose dry lab	65.40 m²

SURVEY SYSTEMS

Positioning	Surface: DGPS SkyFix, QC: QPS or VGPS; sub-surface: Nautronix ATSII
Echo sounder (single beam)	Simrad EA 502
Multibeam/swath system	EM120/1002 (scheduled installation mid-2001)
Sidescan sonar	GeoAcoustics dual frequency (100/500 kHz)

Sub-bottom profiler	EG&G 240 sub tow boomer; EG&G 230 surface tow boomer; deep tow sparker; SIG sparker; TSS signal processing suite/ thermal recorders; Elics Delph recorder and Coda processing optional
Magnetometer	Geometrics 880 caesium
Corer(s)	3 m UMEL Sargent gravity; 3 m Kullenberg piston; 5 m vibrocorer + 5 m acoustic CPT, optional
Grab(s)	Van Veen
Sound velocity profiler	SVP+ velocimeter

NEW ENTRY

Gardline Surveys Ltd

Ocean Voyager

GENERAL

Owner	Gardline Shipping Ltd, UK
Port of reg/flag	Port aux Francais, French (Kergue'len)
Official number	SP 76 7833
Classification	Bureau Veritas
Call sign	FKJM
Built (yard and date)	Bel Air Shipyard, Vancouver, Canada, 1974
Rebuilt (yard and date)	Reconfigured 1994
Length overall	60.20 m
Breadth moulded	13.72 m
Max draught	5.28 m

Operational draught	4.33 m
Tonnage (grt)	1,586; 651 net

PROPULSION

Main engine(s)	2 × Polar 4-stroke 2 × 2,600 hp
Thrusters	DP system Kongsberg Simrad SDP 01; bow: 280 and 500 hp; stern: 600 hp azimuth
Propellers	2 × vp
Speed (max)	12 kt
Speed (cruising)	10 kt
Endurance	40 days; 30 days surveying
Fuel capacity	438 t

Ocean Voyager

2000/0088239

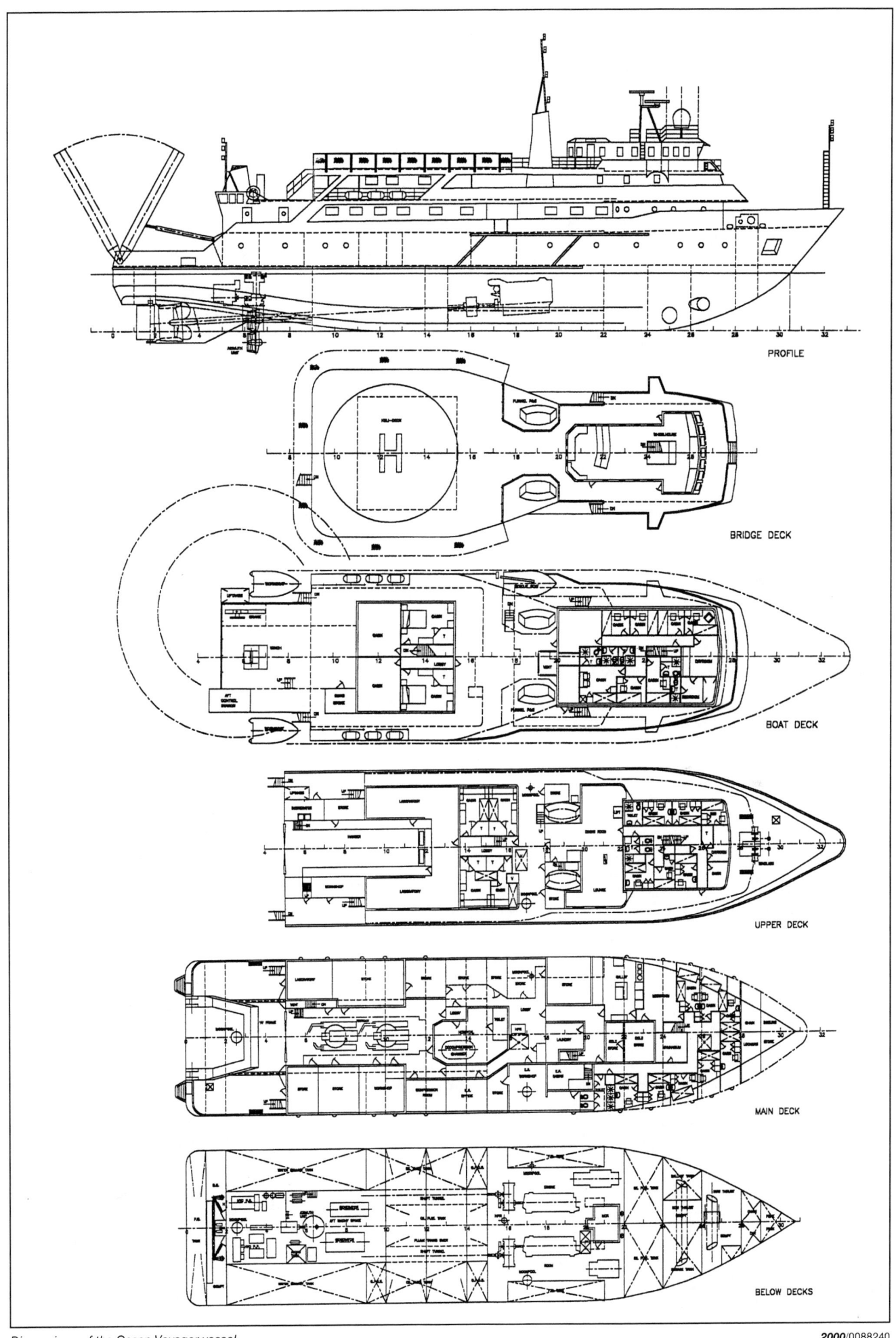

PROFILE

BRIDGE DECK

BOAT DECK

UPPER DECK

MAIN DECK

BELOW DECKS

Dimensions of the Ocean Voyager vessel

2000/0088240

Fuel consumption	12 t/day at maximum speed, 5 t/day surveying
Electrical power	HP 620 kVA (3 generating set 440 V 60 Hz); 380 VAC, 220 VAC, 110 VAC 60 Hz; additional 519 kVA generator
Fresh water capacity	166.60 t (production: 20 t/day)

BRIDGE NAVIGATION AIDS

Satellite	Trimble NT 100GPS
Radar	Furuno FCR 1411; Racal Decca Bridgemaster 180/250
Gyrocompass	Sperry SR 120
Echo-sounder	Skipper GDS 101; 2 × Simrad EQ50
Other ship navigation	Sperry/Navitron autopilot

COMMUNICATIONS

Inmarsat (type)	A: Saturn 3S90; C: Nera GMDSS
MF/HF	RE2100 SSB
VHF	Skanti 3000; Sailor RT 2048
Cellular	Yes
Facsimile	Furuno 207 weather fax

SAFETY

Lifeboats	Rigid MOB and inflatable + liferafts
Lifesaving equipment	Decompression chamber (permanent)

HELIDECK

Size, aircraft capacity	Suitable for 13 m, type AS 350B

DECK MACHINERY

Cranes	2
A-frame(s)	1 × 20 t
Winches	1 × 15 t

Moonpool(s) – size(s)/function(s)	2 × 0.90 m

ACCOMMODATION

Charterers	Total accommodation for 46

SCIENTIFIC SPACES

Multipurpose dry lab	100 m² survey room

SURVEY SYSTEMS

Positioning	Surface: DGPS; sub-surface: Simrad HPR 309 (T)
Echo-sounder (single beam)	Simrad EA502 (38/200 kHz)
Multibeam/swath system	Elac bottomchart
Sidescan sonar	GeoAcoustics 160 DF; Dowty 3710 (× 3) graphic recorders
Sub-bottom profiler	Boomer: EG&G 240 sub-tow; Pinger: hull-mounted nine element; Sparker: Gardline deep tow
Corer(s)	UMEL Sargent Gravity; vibrocorer
Grab(s)	Van Veen

SEISMIC SYSTEMS

Energy source (type and manufacturer)	TI sleeve airgun cluster
Number of airguns	4
Size of airguns	40 cu in each
Streamer manufacturer	Geco
Streamer numbers and lengths per number	1 at 1,200 m, 96 channels
Recording system	Geometrics Strata View, 120 channel, MicroMAX QC

VERIFIED

Gardline Surveys Ltd

Sea Explorer

Former names	*Marjata II*	Owner	Gardline Shipping Ltd, UK
Current operational status	Hydrographic and geophysical survey vessel	Port of reg/flag	Nassau/Bahamas
		Official number	726167

M.V. Sea Explorer

2000/0089140

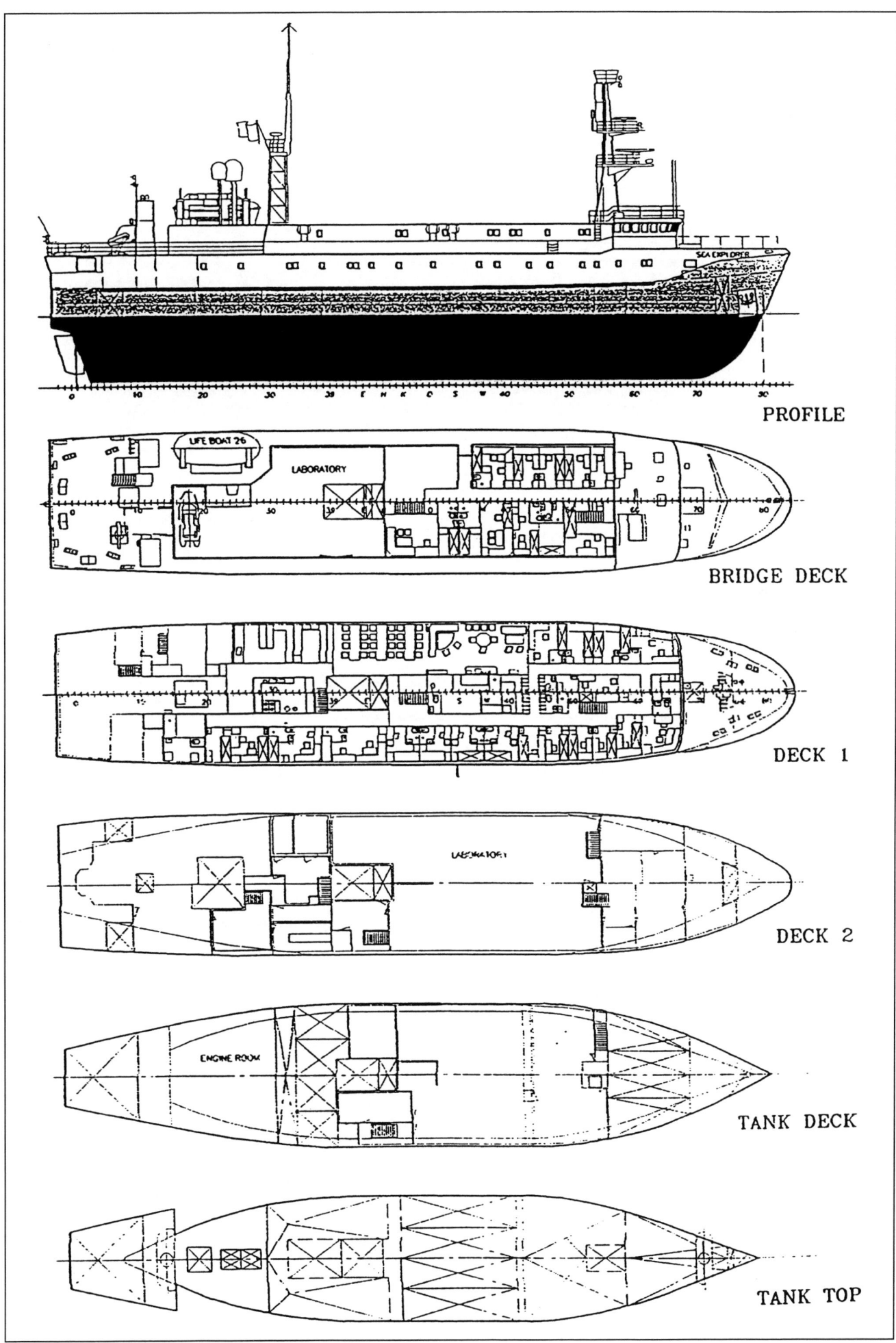

PROFILE

BRIDGE DECK

DECK 1

DECK 2

TANK DECK

TANK TOP

Diagram of M.V. Sea Explorer

Classification	DnV + 1A1 MV EO ICE C
Call sign	C6NG6
Built (yard and date)	1976
Rebuilt (yard and date)	1983 (reconfigured)
Length overall	58.85 m
Breadth moulded	11.00 m
Operational draught	5.07 m
Tonnage (grt)	1,385; 415 net

PROPULSION

Main engine(s)	2 × MAK 6M451Ak, 2,000 bhp total (1,612 kW)
Thrusters	Simrad Albatross DP with Simrad HPR tracking transducers; bow + stern: 1 × 800 bhp Brunvoll
Propellers	2 × cp
Speed (cruising)	10 kt
Endurance	30 days
Fuel capacity	240 t
Fuel consumption	Max speed: 6.8 t; digital surveying: 2.8 t with compressors
Electrical power	3 × Cummins VTA 1710 G/28G2 generators; total 1,350 kW
Fresh water capacity	170 t

BRIDGE NAVIGATION AIDS

Satellite	GPS
Radar	Krupp Atlas 7600 ARPA
Gyrocompass	1 × S G Brown; 1 × Anschutz
Speed log	1 × Marinavox Doppler sonar
Echo-sounder	Deso 20
Other ship navigation	Robertson AP9 autopilot

COMMUNICATIONS

Inmarsat (type)	2 × 'A'
MF/HF	2 × Skanti
VHF	Skanti multichannel
Facsimile	Radiocom Arden Marinefax V weather fax

SAFETY

Lifeboats	1 × Harding MCM totally enclosed 26-person; Liferafts: 3 × Viking 16-person; 2 × Viking 12-person; 1 × Benfort 12-person
Lifesaving equipment	Rescue boat: FRC – Atlantic 21 – 15-person; firefighting: Fixed Halon system in machinery spaces/compressor room/ incinerator

DECK MACHINERY

Cranes	1 × 6 t
A-frame(s)	1 × 5 t (over moonpool)

Winches	Streamer: hydraulic 3,000 m capacity
Moonpool(s) – size(s)/ function(s)	1 × 3 m²

ACCOMMODATION

Charterers	Total accommodation for 34
Hospital	Yes

SCIENTIFIC SPACES

Multipurpose dry lab	500 m²

SURVEY SYSTEMS

Positioning	Surface: Veripos HF/I DGPS; QPS DGPS QC; sub-surface: Nautronix ATSII; TSS DMS305 heave compensator
Echo-sounder (single beam)	Atlas Deso 15 (33/210 kHz)
Multibeam/swath system	Simrad EM 1000
Sidescan sonar	GeoAcoustics 160 dual-frequency with Dowty 3710 thermal recorder + DAT recorder
Sub-bottom profiler	Deep tow sparker; 16 element hull-mounted pinger; sub-tow boomer; 10 cu in mini airgun; TSS signal processing suite

MAGNETOMETER

	Geometrics 880 caesium (optional)
Corer(s)	3 m UMEL Sargent gravity; optional vibrocorer, optional acoustic CPT (5 m)
Grab(s)	Van Veen
Sound velocity profiler	SVP16; SVP+; Valeport 600

SEISMIC SYSTEMS

Energy source (type and manufacturer)	TI sleeve airgun cluster
Number of airguns	4
Size of airguns	40 cu in each
Compressor numbers and types	3 × Hamworthy 4TH87
Streamer manufacturer	Geco
Streamer numbers and lengths per number	1 × 1,200 m, 96 channels, 12.5 m group length interval; Digicourse 5010 birds
Recording system	Strataview R, 120 channel; 3490 tape drive; MicroMAX QC

VERIFIED

Gardline Surveys Ltd

Sea Profiler

GENERAL

Former names	*Profiler, Geotek Beta, R S Shackleton*
Current operational status	Hydrographic and geophysical survey vessel
Owner	Gardline Shipping Ltd, UK
Port of reg/flag	Panama/Panamanian
Official number	21720-LI
Classification	Lloyds 100 A1
Call sign	HP 6791
Built (yard and date)	1954
Rebuilt (yard and date)	1971, reconfigured 1992

Length overall	65.78 m
Breadth moulded	11.08 m
Operational draught	4.66 m
Tonnage (grt)	1,082; 324 net

PROPULSION

Main engine(s)	MAN G6V40/60 999 bhp
Thrusters	Bow: Samuel White 32 in 260° Gilljet
Propellers	KaMeWa cp
Speed (cruising)	10 kt
Endurance	28 days

Fuel capacity	150 t		
Fuel consumption	2.4 t/day at maximum speed; 1.9 t/day digital survey with compressors; 1.7 t/day analogue survey		
Electrical power	2 × MAN W5V100HP engines driving 220 V/65 kW DC generators; 2 × Volvo Penta TMD102 158 kW engines driving English Electric 175 kVA/440 V/50 Hz alternators; 1 × Ruston 6YEC 156 kW engine driving English Electric 175 kVA/440 V/50 Hz alternator		
Fresh water capacity	100 t		

BRIDGE NAVIGATION AIDS

Satellite	Trimble 4000SL
Radar	Decca Bridgemaster 180; Decca RM914C
Gyrocompass	Sperry 120
Speed log	Readout from survey navigation
Echo-sounder	Simrad EX 330
Other ship navigation	Decca Arkas 550 autopilot

COMMUNICATIONS

Inmarsat (type)	Standard 'A'; Marconi Oceanray II
MF/HF	Skanti 6000; Skanti 5000
VHF	Sailor RT 144B; Sailor RT 144C; 3 × portable
Cellular	Yes
Facsimile	Yes

SAFETY

Lifeboats	Lifeguard IR455 25 hp rescue boat; liferafts: 2 × Dunlop 15- person; 1 × Dunlop 20-person; 1 × RFD 25-person
Lifesaving equipment	Firefighting: engine room CO_2 system; full safety equipment to Solas, Panama regulations

DECK MACHINERY

Cranes	6,000 kg; 3 × telescopic booms 20,000 kg aft
A-frame(s)	3,000 kg
Winches	Streamer winch: 1,200 m of 70 mm diameter streamer
Gate valve	2 × 16 in (USBL, Swathe)

M.V Sea Profiler

ACCOMMODATION

Charterers	Total accommodation for 30
Crew	12
Scientists/surveyors	15
Hospital	Yes

SCIENTIFIC SPACES

Multipurpose dry lab	88 m²

SURVEY SYSTEMS

Positioning	Surface: DGPS – SkyFix; QC: QPS or VGPS; sub-surface: Nautronix ATS II; Sonardyne LUSBL TTS 320B heave compensator Seatex Seapath 200 attitude position and heading system
Echo-sounder (single beam)	Simrad EA502 (38/200 kHz)
Multibeam/swath system	Simrad EM1000; Elac bottomchart
Sidescan sonar	GeoAcoustics dual-frequency (100/500 kHz)
Sub-bottom profiler	9-element hull-mounted pinger array; EG&G 240 sub-tow boomer; EG&G 230 surface-tow boomer; deep-tow sparker; TSS signal processing suite/thermal recorders; Elics Delph recorder and Coda processing optional

Magnetometer	Geometrics 880 caesium
Corer(s)	2-3 m UMEL Sargent gravity; 3 m Kullenberg piston; 5 m vibrocorer optional; 5 m acoustic CPT optional
Grab(s)	Grab Vanveen
Sound velocity profiler	Sound velocity profiler SCP4 velocimeter or similar

SEISMIC SYSTEMS

Energy source (type and manufacturer)	TI sleeve airgun cluster
Number of airguns	4
Size of airguns	40 cu in each
Compressor numbers and types	Price W2
Total capacity	180 cu ft/min at 2,000 psi
Streamer manufacturer	Geco
Streamer numbers and lengths per number	1 × 600 m, 48 channels, 12.5 m groups; or 1 × 1,200 m, 96 channels, 12.5 m groups
Recording system	Strataview R 120 channel; MicroMAX or ProMAX QC

VERIFIED

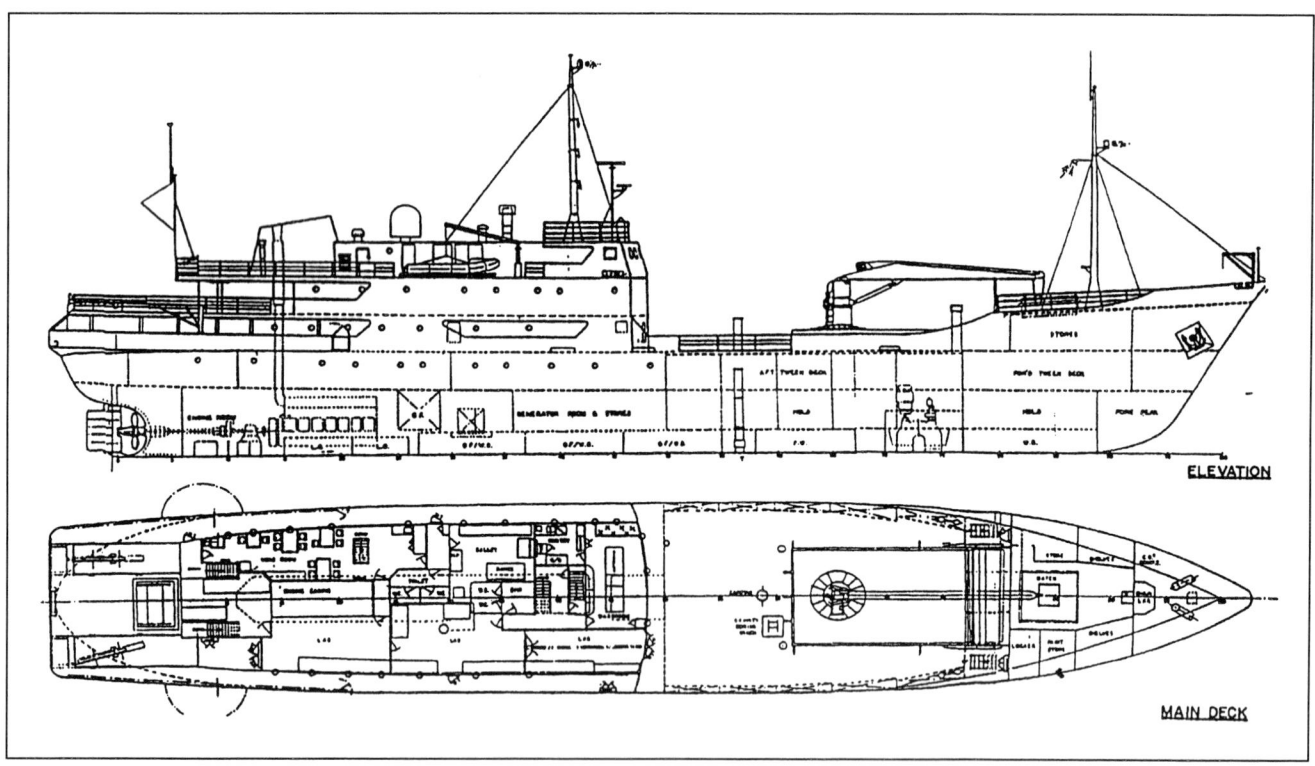

Diagram of M.V. Sea Profiler

2000/0089143

Gardline Surveys Ltd

Sea Surveyor

GENERAL

Former names	RMAS *Magnet*
Current operational status	Hydrographic and Geophysical survey
Owner	Gardline Shipping Ltd, UK
Port of reg/flag	Nassau/Bahamas
Official number	732193
Classification	Lloyds – 100 A1 LMC

Call sign	C6QL6
Built (yard and date)	1979
Rebuilt (yard and date)	1998
Length overall	64.40 m
Breadth moulded	11.40 m
Operational draught	3.50 m
Tonnage (grt)	1,275; 382 net

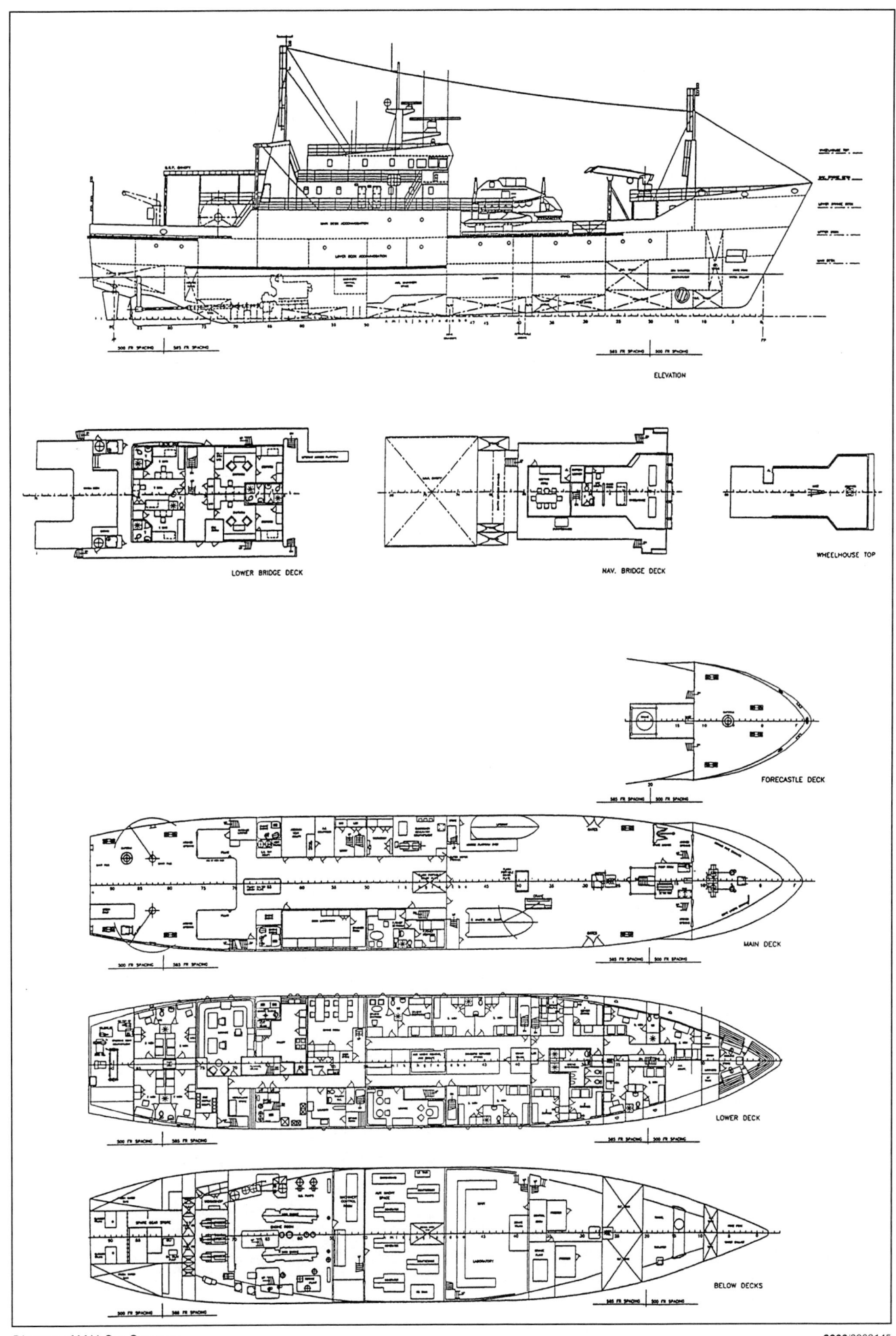

Diagram of M.V. Sea Surveyor

***2000**/0089145*

PROPULSION

Main engine(s)	2 × Mirrleees Blackstone ESL6, each 825 bhp @ 900 rpm, driving 2.5:1 reversible reduction gearboxes
Thrusters	Bow: 1 × Jastram Buzof, tunnel, 175 hp, fixed pitch, diameter 840 mm; stern: 1 × Jastram Buzof, tunnel, 175 hp, fixed pitch, diameter 840 mm
Propellers	Twin Ajax Bamford fixed pitch 4 blades, diameter 1,650 mm
Speed (cruising)	12 kt
Endurance	35-40 days
Fuel capacity	200 m³
Fuel consumption	4.5 t/day
Fresh water capacity	80 t; 5 t/day from 2 × water makers

BRIDGE NAVIGATION AIDS

Satellite	Trimble
Radar	Simrad SDP01 Simplex; Furuno; Kelvin Hughes HR 3000 ARPA
Gyrocompass	Arma Brown Mk 12
Speed log	Chernikeef 100/14
Echo-sounder	Kelvin Hughes M545
Other ship navigation	Robertson AP9 Mk 3 autopilot

COMMUNICATIONS

Inmarsat (type)	Saturn 3S; A, M, C (primary and secondary)
MF/HF	2 × Sailor SSB
VHF	Vingtor Pamex 16/2M

SAFETY

Lifeboats	5 × 20 persons; 1 × 30 persons Waterman; TEMPSC rescue boat
Lifesaving equipment	Fire fighting: E/R CO_2 fixed flooding; streamer deck fixed foam

DECK MACHINERY

Cranes	1 main deck – 150 t/m; 1 articulated, 2.25 t @ 7 m
Gate valve	1, diameter 16 in
Moonpool(s) – size(s)/ function(s)	1 m × 1.1 m (access from main deck)

ACCOMMODATION

Charterers	Total accommodation for 38
Crew	12

SURVEY SYSTEMS

Positioning	Trimble DGPS; acoustic: Nautronics ATSII; TSS DMS05/ Seapath 200 heave/motion compensation
Echo-sounder (single beam)	Simrad EA502 (30/200 kHz); Simrad Combi 50/200 B
Multibeam/swath system	Simrad EM12S (13 kHz) (full ocean depth); Simrad EM950 (95 kHz); Simrad Neptune/Smedvig C-Floor processing
Sidescan sonar	GeoAcoustics 160 DF dual frequency with optional Coda/ Elixs DelphMap processing
Sub-bottom profiler	Deeptow sparker; 16-element hull-mounted pinger; sub-tow boomer; mini airgun; Dowty 3710 recorders; TSS signal processing suite; DAT recorder
Magnetometer	Geometrics 880 caesium
Corer(s)	2 m UMEL Sargent gravity; optional 3/6 m vibrocorer; optional acoustic 5 m CPT
Grab(s)	Van Veen
Sound velocity profiler	SVP16/SD200

SEISMIC SYSTEMS

Energy source (type and manufacturer)	TI sleeve gun cluster
Number of airguns	4 or 2 × 4 and 320 cu in Bolt gun array
Size of airguns	40 cu in per gun
Compressor numbers and types	2 × Hamworthy 425E electric, each 390 cu ft/min @ 3,000 psi; 1 × Hamworthy 4 TH87145 cu ft/min electric 2,000 psi
Total capacity	390 cu ft/min at 3,000 psi
Streamer manufacturer	Geco
Streamer numbers and lengths per number	1 × 3,000 m, 240 channels, 12.5 m groups
Acquisition system	Strataview R
Recording system	MicroMAX or ProMAX QC

UPDATED

M.V. Sea Surveyor

2000/0089144

Gardline Surveys Ltd

Sea Trident

GENERAL

Former names	*Western Trident, Kirsten Bravo*
Current operational status	Hydrographic and Geophysical survey vessel
Owner	Gardline Shipping Ltd, UK
Port of reg/flag	Panama/Panamanian
Official number	14133-84-C
Classification	DnV + 1A1 ICE IC
Call sign	HO 2883
Built (yard and date)	1974
Rebuilt (yard and date)	1984 (reconfigured)
Length overall	57.90 m
Breadth moulded	10.20 m
Operational draught	3.80 m
Tonnage (grt)	964, 289 net

PROPULSION

Main engine(s)	B&W Alpha 10 V 23L-VO 1,450 bhp @ 800/345 rpm
Thrusters	Bow: White 360° Gilljet 160 kW
Propellers	cp
Speed (cruising)	10 kt max; 8 kt economical
Endurance	28 days
Fuel capacity	115 t
Fuel consumption	3.2 t/day (max speed); 1.7 t/day (digital survey with compressors)

Electrical power	Generators: 2 × Volvo Penta TD121CHC 192 kW engines, driving 2 × Newage NHC 434C 210 kVA/415 V/60 Hz alternators; 1 × Volvo Penta TD100GG 180 kW engine driving 1 × Newage MHC434C 210 kVA/415 V/60 Hz alternator; 1 × Scania DS8 120kW engine driving 1 × Roheico BRF280 120 kVA/415 V/60 Hz alternator; 2 × ECC 15 kVA/220 V/50 Hz clean power alternators; 1 × Onan 12.5 RDJC 15 kW engine driving Onan RDJC 12.5 kVA/220 V/50 Hz clean power alternator
Fresh water capacity	136 t; reverse osmosis 4 t/day

BRIDGE NAVIGATION AIDS

Satellite	1 × Magnavox MX1107; 1 × Raytheon Raystar 390
Radar	1 × Koden 3210S; 1 × Furuno 1721
Gyrocompass	1 × Sperry SR-130; 1 × Sperry SR-120

M.V. Sea Trident   **2000**/0089146

Echo-sounder	1 × Elac LAZ 50 AW; 1 × Elac LVG 4D/W
Other ship navigation	Robertson Tritech AP9 Mk II autopilot

COMMUNICATIONS

Inmarsat (type)	'A' and 'M', including e mail facility; 1 × Magnavox MX2400 with Panafax UF-150
MF/HF	1 × Marconi Oceanlink 400; Icom IC-M700
VHF	IC-M120; IC-M100; 4 × IC-M12 (portable)
Facsimile	Raytheon Rayfax 500 weather fax

SAFETY

Lifeboats	Achilles SK140 with 30 hp outboard rescue boat; 3 × Dunlop 30-person and 1 × Viking 10-person liferafts
Lifesaving equipment	Firefighting: Halon system fitted to engine room and recording room; compressor room fixed CO_2 system; full safety and fireighting equipment to Solas 8.3 Panama regulations

DECK MACHINERY

Cranes	1 × National Crane 4,000 kg; 1 × Hiab 5,300 kg; 1 × Hiab 3,000 kg
Winches	Streamer winch, capacity 3,500 m of 65 mm diameter streamer
Moonpool(s) – size(s)/ function(s)	1 × 600 mm, 1 × 1.00 m

ACCOMMODATION

Charterers	Total accommodation for 37
Crew	12
Scientists/surveyors	8 nominal

SCIENTIFIC SPACES

Multipurpose dry lab	10 m × 9 m

SURVEY SYSTEMS

Positioning	Surface: DGPS (SkyFix/StarFix); sub-surface: Nautronix ATS; TTS 320B heave compensator
Echo-sounder (single beam)	1 × Atlas Deso 20 (33/210 kHz) with deep water transducer (33 kHz)
Multibeam/swath system	1 × Elac BottomChart Compact BCC Mk II 50 kHz

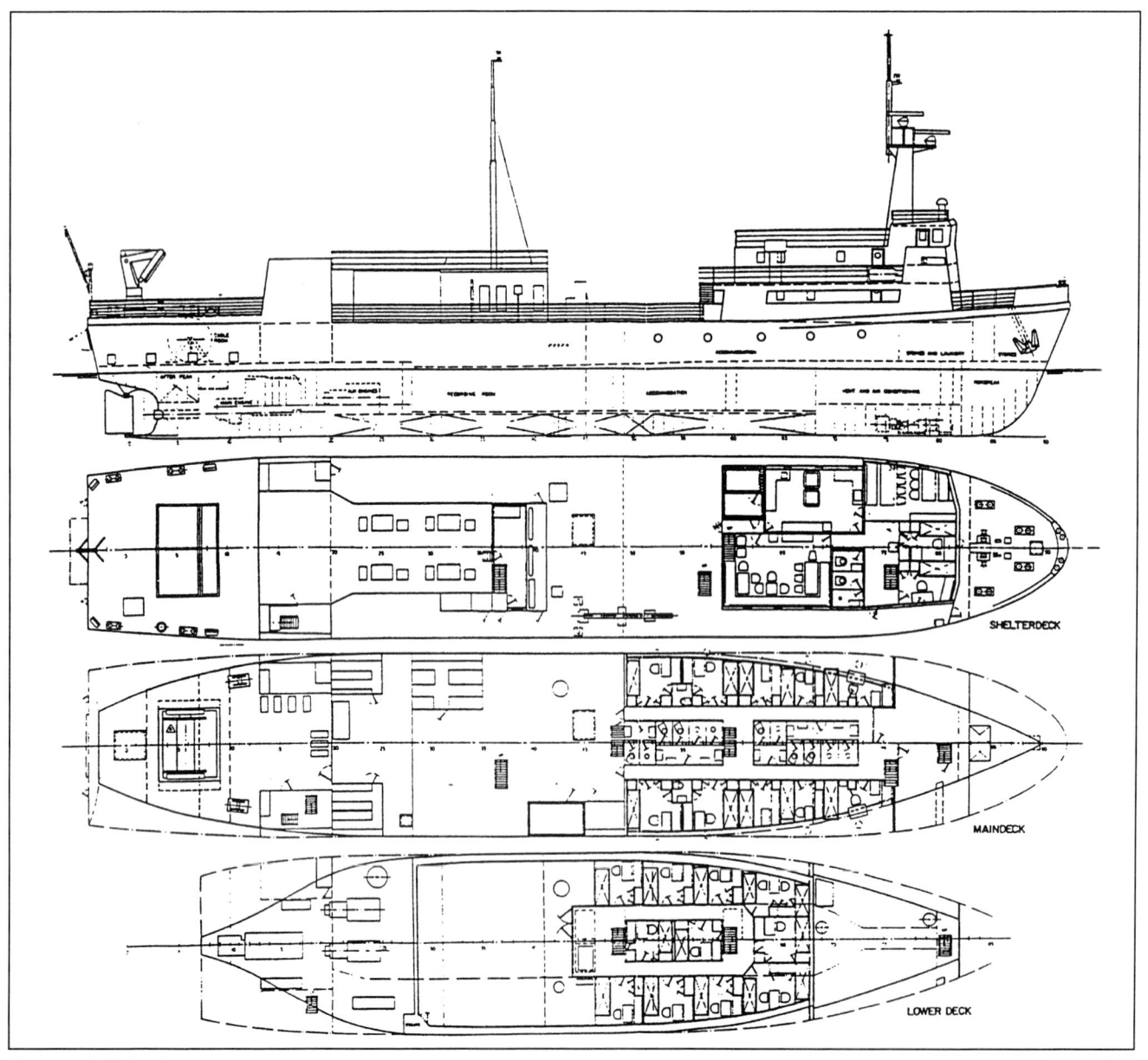

Diagram of M.V. Sea Trident

2000/0089147

Sidescan sonar	1 × GeoAcoustics, DF nominal 100 kHz/500 kHz, 1,500 m depth capacity (ISIS mosaic system optional)	Oceanographic sensors (CTDs/XBTs and so on)	1 × Hugron Seamon TD tide gauge; 1 × Aanderaa RCM7
Sub-bottom profiler	1 × 9-element hull-mounted pinger array; 1 × mini airgun; 1 × EG&G sub-tow boomer; 1 × SIG multi-electrode sparker; 1 × deep tow sparker; 1 × Probe 5000 deep tow profiler; 1 × TSS signal processing suite; 1 × DAT recorder; Elics Delph processing (optional); 1 × Dowty 3710 recorder	**SEISMIC SYSTEMS**	
		Energy source (type and manufacturer)	TI sleeve airgun cluster
		Number of airguns	4
		Size of airguns	40 cu in
		Compressor numbers and types	2 × Price W2
		Streamer manufacturer	Geco
		Streamer type	HSSQ
		Streamer numbers and lengths per number	1. Programmable up to 1,500 m/ 120 channels
Magnetometer	Geometrics 880 caesium	Recording system	1 × TTS 2, 120 channels; 1 × MicroMAX QC
Corer(s)	1 × 2-3 m UMEL Sargent gravity; 1 × 3 m Kullenburg piston; 5 m vibrocore and 5 m CPT		
Grab(s)	Van Veen		*UPDATED*
Sound velocity profiler	Profiler SVP+ velocimeter or similar		

GeoLab Technical Services Ltd

Fres

GENERAL		**COMMUNICATIONS**	
Former names	*Marion Dufresne*	Inmarsat (type)	Yes
Owner	GeoLab Group	VHF	1 × Skanti; 1 × Furuno GMDSS
Classification	BV + I3/3 Special Service – AUT+	Facsimile	1 × Met; 1 × Navtex
Built (yard and date)	1973		
Length overall	112.00 m	**HELIDECK**	
Breadth moulded	18.50 m	Size, aircraft capacity	16 × 12 m
Operational draught	6.30 m		
Tonnage (grt)	6,640; net 3,044	**DECK MACHINERY**	
		Cranes	2 × 5 t; 1 × 40 t boom (forward); 1 × 10 t SWL (stern)
PROPULSION			
Main engine(s)	2 × SEMT Pielstick 8PC 2 400, 8-cylinder, 3,500 bhp each	A-frame(s)	1 × 10 t SWL (stern)
Thrusters	Bow: KaMeWa 700 hp, approx 7 t; stern: KaMeWa 700 hp, approx 7 t	Winches	1 × oceanographic with 7,000 m cable
Propellers	Single	**ACCOMMODATION**	
Speed (max)	15 kt	Charterers	Total accommodation for 146
Speed (cruising)	12 kt (economical)	Hospital	Yes
Endurance	20,000 n miles at 15 kt; 22,400 n miles at 12 kt		
		SCIENTIFIC SPACES	
Fuel capacity	Fuel oil: 1,020 t; diesel oil: 366 t	Total scientific deck space	300 m² clear deck deployment at stern
Electrical power	Auxiliaries: 3 × Dresser Dujardin 6 BC 5 12 D 560 kW; generators: 440 V at 50 Hz; 2 × Jeumont Schneider A100G12 750 kW shaft 1 × Alsthom/JS A48 emergency	Oceanographic wet lab	2
		SURVEY SYSTEMS	
Fresh water capacity	755 t	Positioning	1 × Thales Skyfix DGPS; 1 × Seapath 200 precise heading
BRIDGE NAVIGATION AIDS		Echo-sounder (single beam)	1 × Simrad EA 500
Satellite	1 × Ben Galatee	Multibeam/swath system	1 × Simrad EM 120; 1 × Simrad EM 1002 with Neptune data acquisition system
Radar	1 × Sperry 340S (ARPA); 1 × Sperry	Sub-bottom profiler	Hull-mounted 4 × 4
Gyrocompass	1 × Sperry SR220	Magnetometer	Geometrix 880 caesium
Echo-sounder	1 × Skipper ED163; 1 × Skipper 603	Sound velocity profiler	Valeport
Other ship navigation	1 × Sperry autopilot		*NEW ENTRY*

Hays Ships Ltd

Kommandor Amalie

GENERAL

Owner	Hays Ships Ltd, UK
Port of reg/flag	Douglas, Isle of Man/British
Classification	Bureau Veritas I 3/3E for world wide trading
Call sign	MGDD 7
Built (yard and date)	Rickmers Werft, Germany, 1962
Rebuilt (yard and date)	Norway, 1983; further converted 1989/90
Length overall	67.25 m
Breadth moulded	9.60 m
Operational draught	5.40 m
Tonnage (grt)	1,053; net 315

PROPULSION

Main engine(s)	Deutz Diesel type SBV8M-358, 1,655 bhp (1,225 kW) at 250 rpm
Thrusters	Bow: 1 × Brunvoll 250 bhp tunnel, hydraulically driven; stern: 2 × Brunvoll 400 bhp tunnel, electrically driven
Propellers	Liaaen cp
Speed (max)	13.5 kt
Speed (cruising)	10 kt
Fuel capacity	182 m³
Fuel consumption	6.5 t/day at max speed; 4.0 t/day at economical
Electrical power	Auxiliaries: Deutz BAM 816 driving 570 kW alternator (440 V 60 Hz 3 ph); Dorman 6LE driving 100 kW alternator (380 V 50 Hz, 3 ph); Caterpillar D333C driving 80 kW alternator; Caterpillar D334 driving 165 kW alternator
Fresh water capacity	155 m³

BRIDGE NAVIGATION AIDS

Satellite	1 × Furuno GPS 70; 1 × Furuno GPS 50
Radar	1 × Furuno FR 1500 DA; 1 × Furuno RDP – 115A
Gyrocompass	1 × Anschutz ST-4; 1 × Robertson
Echo-sounder	1 × Simrad 603
Other ship navigation	1 × Anschutz autopilot

COMMUNICATIONS

Inmarsat (type)	M and C
MF/HF	Furuno Area A3 GMDSS
VHF	2 × Furuno FM8500 with DSC

SAFETY

Lifeboats	2 × Avon 6.4 m Searider rescue craft; 1 × Harding motorised 32 persons rescue boat
Lifesaving equipment	Conforms to international regulations, full equipment for 40 persons

DECK MACHINERY

Cranes	Hiab 360 sea crane (hyd/elec), aft of ROV hangar starboard side: 3.06 t at 7.6 m (max 12 m)
Gate valve	2 × 12 in, installed in forward hold for survey echo-sounder/HPR transducers; 1 × 12 in, installed for charterer's use

ACCOMMODATION

Charterers	Total accommodation for 38

SCIENTIFIC SPACES

Total scientific deck space	Online survey/ROV control room on shelterdeck; offline survey room on tweendecks

NEW ENTRY

Kommandor Amalie

2001/0110537

Hydrocharter Associates

Hydrotech

GENERAL

Owner	Hydrocharter Associates, UK
Classification	Lloyd's, Department of Transport SSR 44788; Code of Practice Category One (Class VIBIIA Loadline)

Call sign	MNLL2
Length overall	17.00 m
Breadth moulded	4.50 m
Max draught	2.30 m
Operational draught	1.80 m

Hydrotech   **2000**/0093773

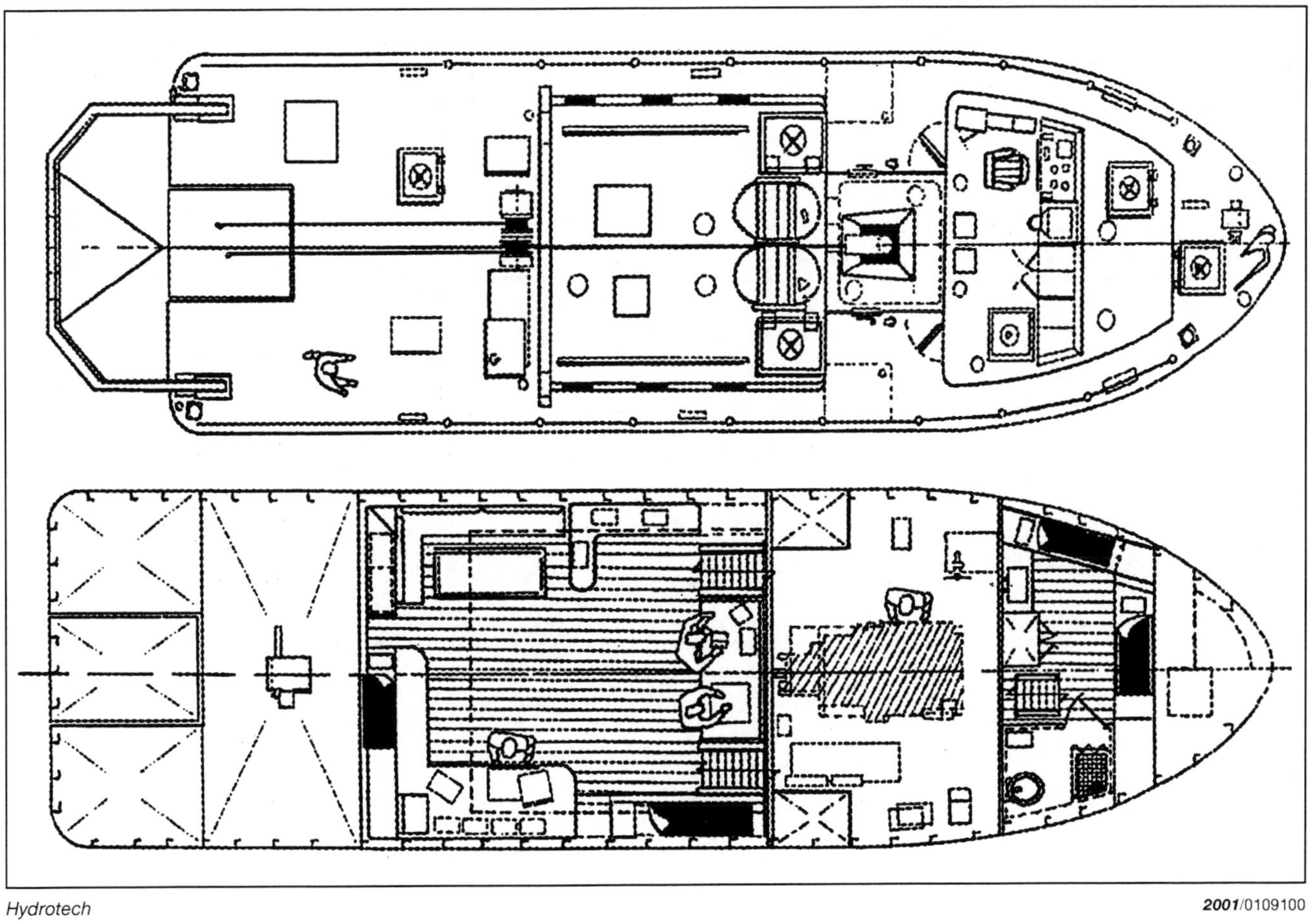

Hydrotech   **2001**/0109100

PROPULSION

Main engine(s)	Dorman Diesel Type 8JTM; 270 bhp at 1,800 rpm
Thrusters	Bow: Vetus (electric driven), rated Sea State 5
Propellers	Brunton fp via MRF 350 reverse reduction gearbox, ratio 2.55:1
Speed (cruising)	12 kt (free run)
Fuel capacity	2.40 t
Electrical power	Alternators: 2 × CAV AC90, 90 A battery charging; 3 × independent battery banks, 265 A/hour each; generator: diesel powered producing 4.5 kVA at 220/240 V
Fresh water capacity	1.5 t

BRIDGE NAVIGATION AIDS

Satellite	Magellan 5000 DGPS
Radar	Koden M3000
Echo-sounder	Sounders-Seasport Mk V Colour Set; Echo Pilot FLS2 Professional

COMMUNICATIONS

MF/HF	Sailor multi-frequency
VHF	Icom

DECK MACHINERY

Cranes	Hydraulic Hiab, 0.50 t – 1 t capacity, extension arm and winch
A-frame(s)	4 t adjustable, with dedicated outrigger sonar boom
Winches	3 drum hydraulic
Moonpool(s) – size(s)/ function(s)	Recess for + facility for deck extension

ACCOMMODATION

Charterers	Total accommodation for five

SURVEY SYSTEMS

Multibeam/swath system	Charterer supply
Sidescan sonar	Charterer supply
Sub-bottom profiler	Charterer supply
Magnetometer	Charterer supply

UPDATED

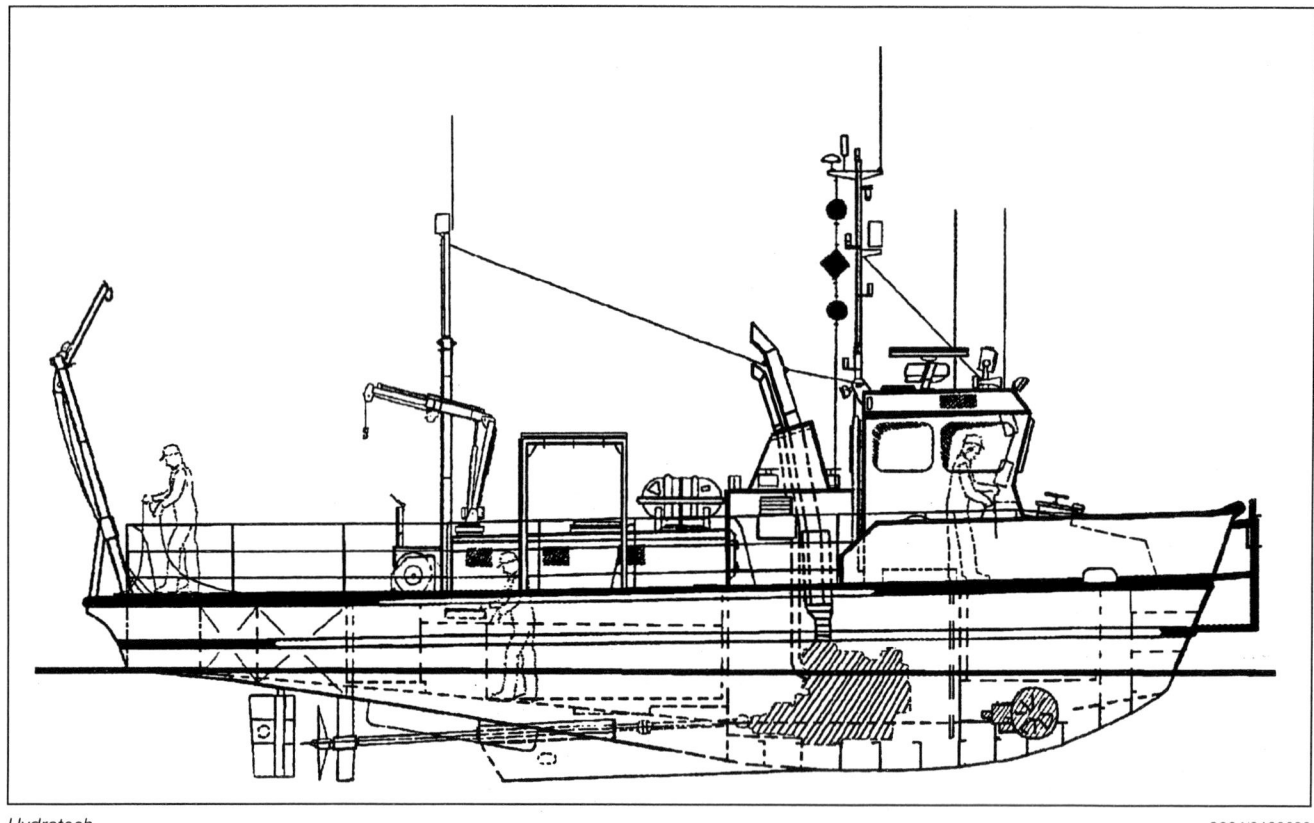

Hydrotech

2001/0109099

Hydrosurveys (Salveson Fox Ltd)

Sandkat

GENERAL

Owner	Hydrosurveys (Salveson Fox Ltd)
Port of reg/flag	Southampton, UK
Official number	903354
Call sign	ZQCAZ
Built (yard and date)	Cheetah Marine, Isle of Wight, UK
Length overall	8 m (twin hull GRP)
Breadth moulded	2.50 m
Working deck width	2.40 m
Max draught	0.60 m

Operational draught	0.30 m
Tonnage (grt)	2.14

PROPULSION

Main engine(s)	2 × 90 hp Honda 4-stroke OBM
Speed (max)	30 kt
Speed (cruising)	15 kt
Endurance	150 n miles
Fuel capacity	230 litres
Fuel consumption	0.70 – 1 mile/litre

Electrical power	12/24 VDC, 250 VAC
Fresh water capacity	50 litres

BRIDGE NAVIGATION AIDS

Satellite	MLR FX412 DGPS
Radar	Furuno M1832 4 kW
Echo-sounder	Koden CVS 106D
Other ship navigation	Raytheon 620 chart plotter

COMMUNICATIONS

VHF	Navico Axis DSC 1400; ICOM 1500E
Facsimile	Furuno Navtex NX300

SAFETY

Lifeboats	6-persons Solas B Zodiac
Workboat/chase boat	2.50 m Avon Rover workboat

DECK MACHINERY

Cranes	Overside hoist 400 kg
A-frame(s)	Stern tow frame
Winches	Spencer Carter 400 kg

SURVEY SYSTEMS

Positioning	Trimble DSM 212H DGPS; Ashtech Z. Surveyor RTK GPS for real-time tide/wave height

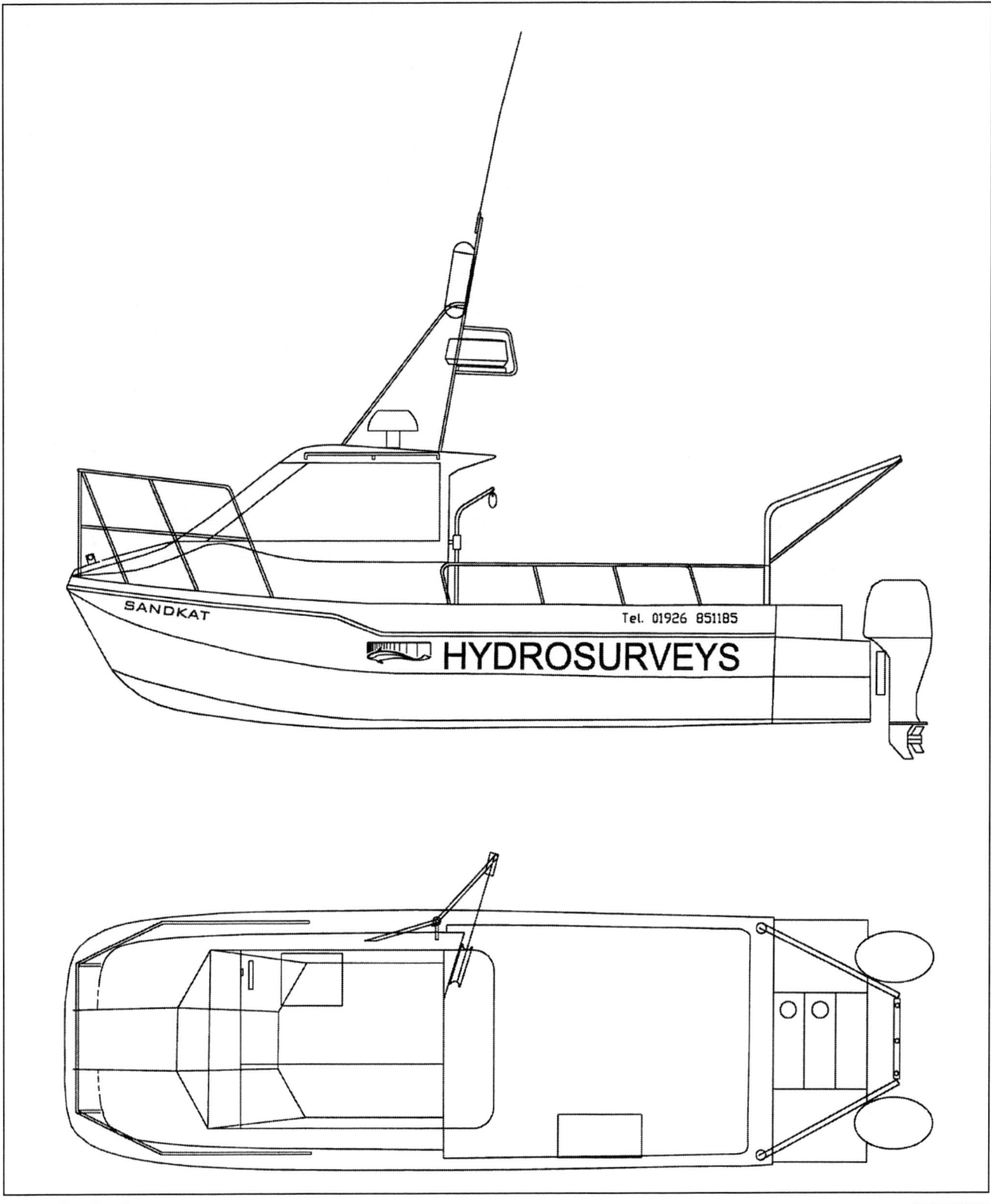

Outline of the Sandkat

2000/0093775

Echo-sounder (single beam)	Odom Hydrotrack	**Other sampling**	Survey beam trawl 2 m
Multibeam/swath system	Optional	**Oceanographic sensors**	Multiparameter YS1 6000 +
Sidescan sonar	Optional CM800	**(CTDs/XBTs and so on)**	YSI6920
Sub-bottom profiler	Optional		*VERIFIED*
Corer(s)	2 m gravity		
Grab(s)	Day 0.1 m²; Van Veen 0.45 m²		

Sandkat   **2000**/0093766

Osiris Hydrographic & Geophysical Projects Ltd

Osprey

GENERAL		**BRIDGE NAVIGATION AIDS**	
Owner	Osiris Hydrographic &	**Radar**	Furuno 16 mile radar
	Geophysical Projects Ltd, UK	**Other ship navigation**	Digital fluxgate compass
Length overall	7.97 m		
Breadth moulded	2.80 m	**COMMUNICATIONS**	
Max draught	0.80 m	**VHF**	2
PROPULSION		**SAFETY**	
Main engine(s)	200 hp turbo diesel	**Lifeboats**	1 × 6 persons liferaft
Propellers	Duoprop stern drives		
Speed (max)	30 kt	**SURVEY SYSTEMS**	
Speed (cruising)	26 kt	**Positioning**	Furuno DGPS
Endurance	250 n miles	**Echo-sounder (single beam)**	Widebeam
Fuel capacity	300 litres		*VERIFIED*

Osiris Hydrographic & Geophysical Projects Ltd

Seker

GENERAL		**Built (yard and date)**	Finland – Botnia Targa 35 type
Owner	Osiris Hydrographic &		boat
	Geophysical Projects Ltd, UK	**Length overall**	11.50 m

Breadth moulded	3.50 m
Operational draught	1.00 m
Tonnage (grt)	7 t displacement

PROPULSION

Main engine(s)	2 × 260 hp Volvo Penta KAD44P 24 valve diesels
Propellers	Duoprop stern drives
Speed (max)	36 kt
Speed (cruising)	28 kt
Endurance	Over 300 n miles at cruising speed
Fuel capacity	980 litres

BRIDGE NAVIGATION AIDS

Radar	Simrad 772

COMMUNICATIONS

VHF	2 × VHF radios with DSC

SAFETY

Lifeboats	6 persons liferaft with SOLAS B pack

ACCOMMODATION

Charterers	Total accommodation for 6

SURVEY SYSTEMS

Positioning	Trimble DGPS; HYDROpro software
Echo-sounder (single beam)	Dual frequency with in-hull transducers
Sidescan sonar	1 + Coda DA-200 acquisition
Sub-bottom profiler	Yes
Magnetometer	Caesium
Grab(s)	Yes
Vehicle(s) (ROVs/AUVs and so on)	Mini ROV with high-resolution colour camera

UPDATED

Seker   *2000*/0093778

Port of London Authority

Chartwell

GENERAL

Current operational status	Thames Estuary survey vessel
Owner	Port of London Authority
Port of reg/flag	London/British
Official number	717172
Classification	Lloyd's LRBC Dot Class VIII A
Call sign	MHGV6
Built (yard and date)	McTay, Birkenhead, 1989
Length overall	26.00 m
Breadth moulded	5.80 m
Max draught	1.80 m
Operational draught	1.80 m
Tonnage (grt)	105

PROPULSION

Main engine(s)	Paxman X2, 1,440 hp + Volvo driving 380 hp jet

Thrusters	Twin screw + water jet
Speed (max)	22 kt
Speed (cruising)	18 kt
Fuel capacity	10,900 litres
Electrical power	2 × 62.5 kVA generators
Fresh water capacity	500 litres

Bridge navigation aids

Satellite	Trimble NT100 GPS
Radar	Furuno FR1510DA
Gyrocompass	Fluxgate compass
Echo-sounder	Koden CVS 108

COMMUNICATIONS

VHF	Sailor VHF RT 2048
Cellular	Vodafone

SAFETY
Lifeboats	2 × 10 persons liferafts
Workboat/chase boat	5.50 m RIB with Mercury 25 outboard

DECK MACHINERY
Cranes	Hydraulic, 1 t max SWL
Winches	Aft: hydraulic capstan; forward: electric windlass

SURVEY SYSTEMS
Positioning	DGPS
Echo-sounder (single beam)	Yes
Sidescan sonar	Yes
Sub-bottom profiler	Yes

NEW ENTRY

Thales Geosolutions Group Ltd

Askelad

GENERAL
Port of reg/flag	St Vincent and the Grenadines
Classification	Bureau Veritas, 13/3E Cargo Ship, Deepsea, MACH
Built (yard and date)	Norway, 1979
Rebuilt (yard and date)	As survey vessel, Norway, 1996
Length overall	34.00 m
Breadth moulded	8.00 m
Max draught	4.00 m

PROPULSION
Main engine(s)	Cummins 700 hp
Thrusters	2 × dual hydraulic bow
Propellers	Heimdal variable pitch
Endurance	Three weeks
Fuel capacity	70 m³
Fresh water capacity	50 m³

BRIDGE NAVIGATION AIDS
Radar	2 × Furuno
Gyrocompass	Yes

SAFETY
Lifeboats	2 × 20-person liferafts
Lifesaving equipment	Zodiac fast rescue boat with 25 hp outboard

DECK MACHINERY
Cranes	1 ton Hiab crane
A-frame(s)	Yes
Winches	3 ton cargo; 5 ton hydraulic; 1 ton Hiab

ACCOMMODATION
Charterers	Total accommodation for 18

SURVEY SYSTEMS
Positioning	Furuno GPS

VERIFIED

Thales Geosolutions Group Ltd

Whitethorn

GENERAL
Port of reg/flag	St Vincent and the Grenadines
Classification	Lloyds + 100A1, DOT Class 8
Built (yard and date)	1963
Length overall	79.50 m
Breadth moulded	11.80 m
Operational draught	5.10 m
Tonnage (grt)	1,587; 476 net

PROPULSION
Main engine(s)	British Polar MN 19S 2290 bhp at 310 rpm
Thrusters	Bow: 4.50 t, 360° Azimuthing White-Gill driven by an independent Dorman 8QVT diesel
Propellers	1 × fixed
Fuel capacity	186 m³
Electrical power	3 × 20 V DC, 73 kW Laurence Scott generators; 3 × 415 V AC, 3 phase, 50 Hz, 250 kVA Stamford alternators; 1 × 415 V AC, 3 phase, 50 Hz, 125 kVA alternator
Fresh water capacity	114 m³

BRIDGE NAVIGATION AIDS
Satellite	Furuno GPGP50
Radar	Sperry 104; Decca BT 501
Gyrocompass	Sperry SR 120
Echo-sounder	Atlas Deso 10

COMMUNICATIONS
Inmarsat (type)	JRC JAX 830 'A' receiver, Sailor 'C', Thrane Mini 'M'
MF/HF	1 × SSB
VHF	3

DECK MACHINERY
Cranes	1 × 3 t crane; 2 × 1.5 t cranes; 19 m derrick, 40 t; 7 m CPT derrick
Winches	Drawworks: 82 kW, 8 t pull hydraulic Rooster box: 1.5 t SWL, 400 m of 9.5 mm wire Four-point mooring: 4 × electro-hydraulic 15.5 t Robertson, 1,150 m of 32 mm wire each

ACCOMMODATION
Charterers	Total accommodation for 39

SURVEY SYSTEMS
Other sampling   Full flush rotary drilling system
with 5 in API drillpipe; seabed
template and cone penetrometer

– continuous 3 m stroke at
2 cm/sec

VERIFIED

Whitehorn   ***2000***/0089150

Sea Boston Ltd

Terschelling

GENERAL		**Built (yard and date)**	NV Zaanlandschem, Netherlands,
Port of reg/flag	Gibraltar		1963
Classification	Lloyds ICE Class II	**Length overall**	40.50 m
Call sign	Z DCT 7	**Breadth moulded**	7.90 m

Terschelling   ***2000***/0089151

Max draught	3.00 m		**DECK MACHINERY**	
Operational draught	2.676 m		**A-frame(s)**	2: port and stern
Tonnage (grt)	229.41; net 66.15			
			ACCOMMODATION	
PROPULSION			**Charterers**	Total accommodation for 18
Speed (max)	11 kt			
Speed (cruising)	9 kt		**SURVEY SYSTEMS**	
			Positioning	DGPS
BRIDGE NAVIGATION AIDS			**Echo-sounder (single beam)**	Charterer supply
Satellite	DGPS		**Multibeam/swath system**	Charterer supply
Radar	Decca 402 Colour		**Sidescan sonar**	Klein
Echo-sounder	Atlas		**Sub-bottom profiler**	Charterer supply
			Magnetometer	Yes
COMMUNICATIONS			**Corer(s)**	Charterer supply
Inmarsat (type)	'M'		**Grab(s)**	Charterer supply
MF/HF	Sailor SSB Radio 400 W		**Vehicle(s) (ROVs/AUVs and**	Seacat and Hyball ROVs
VHF	2 × Sailor		**so on)**	

UPDATED

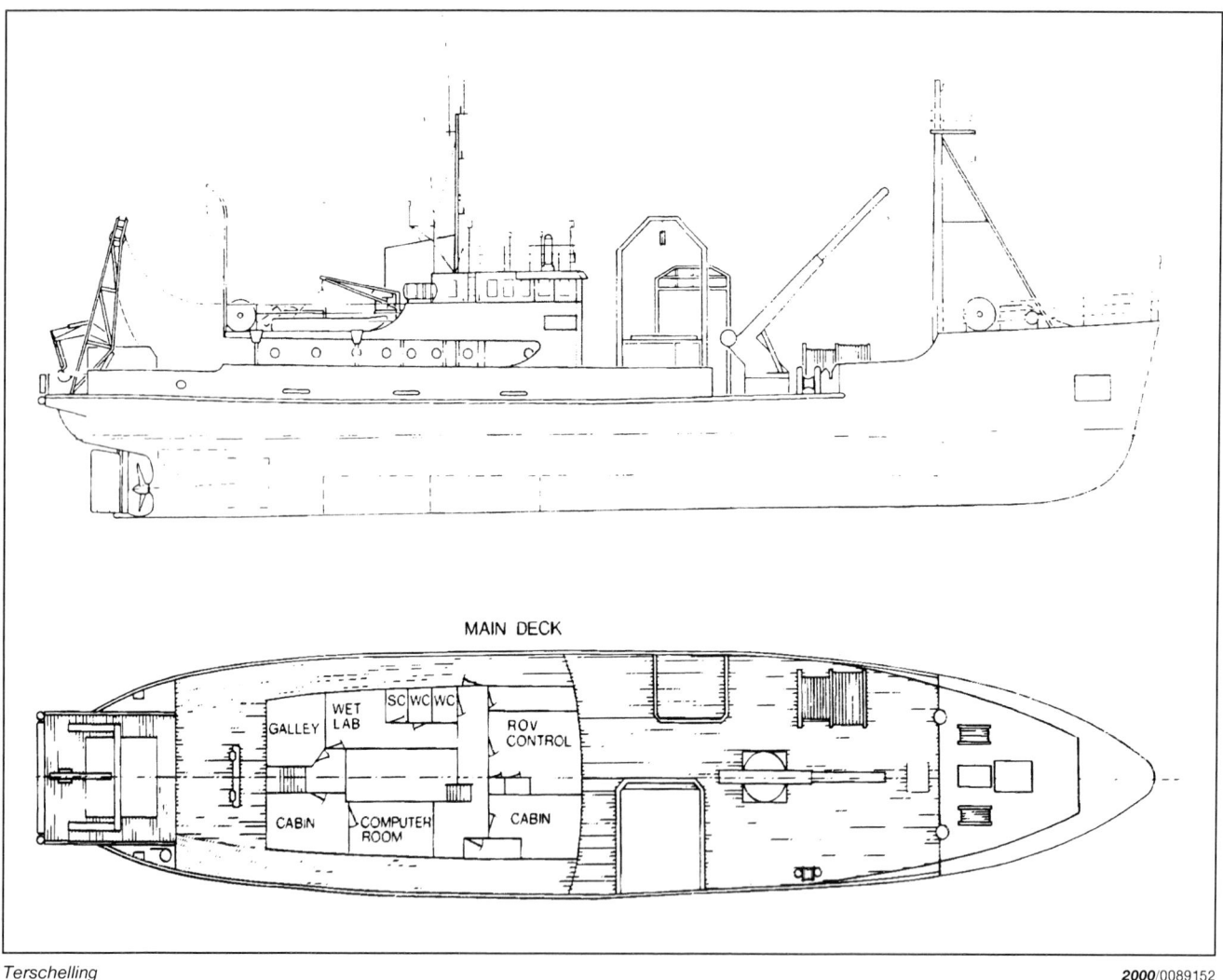

MAIN DECK

Terschelling   **2000**/0089152

Sea-Trax

Scimitar

GENERAL				
			Length overall	10.00 m (twin hull)
Current operational status	UK coastal waters		**Breadth moulded**	5.00 m
Owner	D I and J L Burden		**Working deck width**	5.00 m
Port of reg/flag	Bristol, UK		**Max draught**	1.30 m
Official number	SSR 43510		**Operational draught**	1.20 m
Classification	MCA Workboat Cat 2			
Call sign	MNZM 8		**PROPULSION**	
Built (yard and date)	Canvey Island, UK, 1991		**Main engine(s)**	2 × Yanmar, 170 hp
			Propellers	2

Speed (max)	18 kt
Speed (cruising)	15 kt
Endurance	225 n miles at cruising speed
Fuel capacity	900 litres
Fuel consumption	45 litres/hour cruising,
	15 litres/hour surveying
Electrical power	3.60 kVA
Fresh water capacity	100 litres

BRIDGE NAVIGATION AIDS

Satellite	Garmin GPS; Furuno DGPS
Radar	Kelvin Hughes 16 mile
Speed log	B & G
Echo-sounder	Raytheon V720, Koden
Other ship navigation	Navmaster ARCS charts

COMMUNICATIONS

VHF	Huson 75; Icom 70; Sailor 2047
Cellular	Yes

SAFETY

Lifeboats	6 and 8 person liferafts
Workboat/chase boat	Avon inflatable

DECK MACHINERY

Cranes	Atlas hydraulic crane fitted with winch drum
Winches	450 kg, 75 m 6 mm s/s wire; 1,000 kg deck capstan
Transducer well	Survey mounts fitted, adaptable for most systems

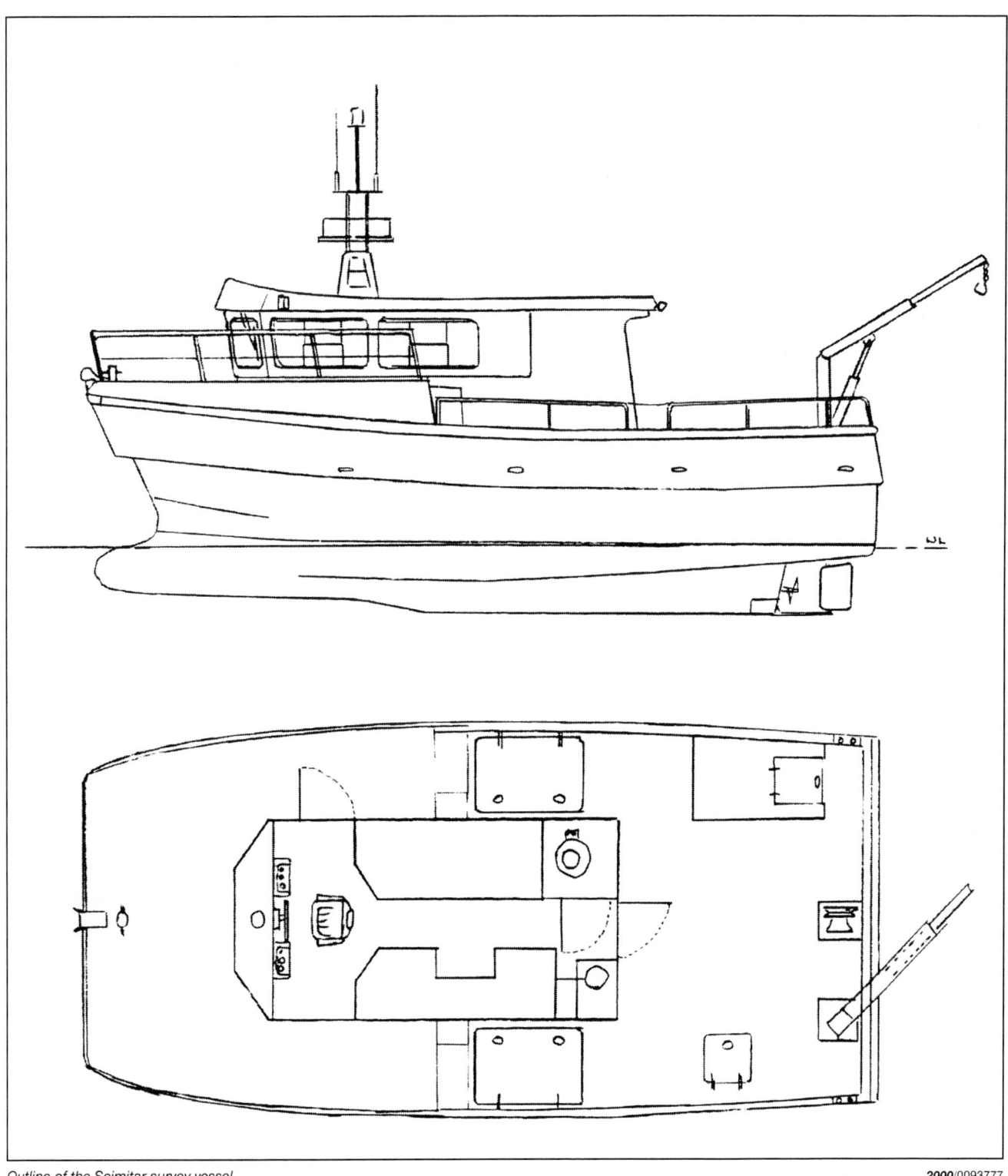

Outline of the Scimitar survey vessel

2000/0093777

ACCOMMODATION

Charterers	Capacity to carry 12 (accommodation for 1 person in cabin)
Crew	2

SURVEY SYSTEMS

Positioning	Trimble DGPS
Echo-sounder (single beam)	Charterer supply
Multibeam/swath system	Charterer supply
Sidescan sonar	Charterer supply
Sub-bottom profiler	Charterer supply
Magnetometer	Charterer supply
Oceanographic sensors (CTDs/XBTs and so on)	Charterer supply

UPDATED

Scimitar
2000/0093776

Shoreline Surveys Ltd

Wozee

GENERAL

Owner	Emile M J Foote
Port of reg/flag	None, trailed vessel
Official number	M99WB0050061
Classification	Survey dory
Call sign	MQZA7
Length overall	5.50 m
Breadth moulded	2.00 m
Working deck width	1.75 m
Max draught	0.30 m
Operational draught	0.60 m
Tonnage (grt)	1.3

PROPULSION

Main engine(s)	75 hp Mariner outboard
Propellers	1
Speed (max)	30 kt
Speed (cruising)	22 kt
Endurance	Varies on fuel loading – canned containers
Fuel consumption	30 litres/12 hours surveying
Electrical power	12 V

BRIDGE NAVIGATION AIDS

Gyrocompass	2
Speed log	DGPS
Echo-sounder	Raytheon DE 719 Mk II

COMMUNICATIONS

VHF	1 × fixed, 1 × portable
Cellular	2
Facsimile	Via laptop

SAFETY

Lifesaving equipment	Complies with MECAL Class 3

DECK MACHINERY

A-frame(s)	If required
Winches	If required
Transducer well	Mounting over bow

SURVEY SYSTEMS

Positioning	Del Norte 1008, 12-channel DGPS
Echo-sounder (single beam)	Raytheon DE 719 Mk II
Multibeam/swath system	If required
Sidescan sonar	If required
Sub-bottom profiler	If required
Magnetometer	If required
Gravimeter	If required
Corer(s)	If required
Grab(s)	If required
Other sampling	If required
Sound velocity profiler	If required
Oceanographic sensors (CTDs/XBTs and so on)	If required

UPDATED

Wozee
2001/0109090

Svitzer Ltd

L'Espoir

GENERAL

Owner	Bon Espoir Survey, Den Helder
Port of reg/flag	Den Helder/The Netherlands
Official number	8018
Classification	Bureau Veritas (Special Survey Deep Sea)
Call sign	PFPY
Built (yard and date)	1971
Rebuilt (yard and date)	1996
Length overall	67.43 m
Breadth moulded	10.60 m
Max draught	4.50 m
Tonnage (grt)	1,168; net 350

PROPULSION

Main engine(s)	1 × B&W Alpha (1,590 bhp)
Thrusters	Bow: 1 × Gill Jet 360° (480 hp)
Propellers	Single vp
Speed (cruising)	13 kt
Fuel capacity	253 m³
Fresh water capacity	70 m³

SAFETY

Lifeboats	4 × liferafts (total 64 persons)

Workboat/chase boat	Frassmer MOB boat
Lifesaving equipment	29 survival suits

DECK MACHINERY

Cranes	Hiab 1,650 kg at 8.6 m
A-frame(s)	Hydraulic 15 t SWL 8.5 m

SURVEY SYSTEMS

Positioning	2 independent DGPS systems; ORE Trackpoint II; TSS 320 heave compensator
Echo-sounder (single beam)	2 × Atlas Deso 20
Multibeam/swath system	Atlas DS (6,000 m)
Sidescan sonar	GeoAcoustics 160D
Sub-bottom profiler	ORE through-the-hull pinger
Magnetometer	Geometrics G880
Corer(s)	3 m gravity
Grab(s)	Van Veen
Sound velocity profiler	SVP, SVP+, Valeport
Oceanographic sensors (CTDs/XBTs and so on)	Sippican XBT

UPDATED

Svitzer Ltd

Svitzer Magellan

GENERAL

Owner	Svitzer Ltd	Call sign	GKGR
Port of reg/flag	Lowestoft/UK	Built (yard and date)	1974
Official number	373192	Rebuilt (yard and date)	1994
Classification	Lloyds 100 A1	Length overall	58.00 m
		Breadth moulded	12.50 m

Svitzer Magellan   **2001**/0109083

Max draught	4.50 m	Sub-bottom profiler	Deep tow sparker; EG&G boomer; hull-mounted pinger G880
Tonnage (grt)	1,683	Magnetometer	
		Corer(s)	3 m gravity
PROPULSION		Grab(s)	Van Veen
Main engine(s)	2 × Normo LDM-5 (750 bhp each)	Sound velocity profiler	SVP, SVP+, Valeport
Thrusters	1 × Brunvoll bow (330 hp)		
Propellers	2 × vp	**SEISMIC SYSTEMS**	
		Energy source (type and manufacturer)	TI sleeve guns; Sodera G & GI guns
BRIDGE NAVIGATION AIDS		Number of airguns	Up to 4
Gyrocompass	Anschutz	Size of airguns	20-21 cu in
		Streamer manufacturer	Litton
SAFETY		Streamer type	Up to 120 channels programmable
Lifeboats	One totally enclosed		
Lifesaving equipment	6 × Viking 24-person liferafts; 36 survival suits	Streamer numbers and lengths per number	300-1,500
		Acquisition system	MicroMAX or SeisUP QC
SURVEY SYSTEMS		Recording system	Sercel 358 DMX with 3490 tape decks
Positioning	Two independent DGPS systems; Simrad HPR309(T)		
Echo-sounder (single beam)	1 × Atlas Deso 25; 1 × Atlas Deso 20		
Multibeam/swath system	Atlas MD2		*UPDATED*
Sidescan sonar	GeoAcoustics 160D		

Svitzer Ltd

Svitzer Mercator

GENERAL		**SAFETY**	
Owner	Svitzer Ltd, UK	Lifeboats	One totally enclosed
Port of reg/flag	Nassau/Bahamian	Lifesaving equipment	One fast rescue craft; five life rafts (total 50 persons)
Official number	727532		
Classification	Lloyds 100 A1 LMC		
Call sign	C6NV9	**SURVEY SYSTEMS**	
Built (yard and date)	1967	Positioning	Two independent DGPS; Simrad Hipap SSBL
Rebuilt (yard and date)	1996		
Length overall	72.90 m	Echo-sounder (single beam)	1 × Atlas Deso 25; 1 × Atlas Deso 20
Breadth moulded	11.60 m		
Max draught	5.30 m	Multibeam/swath system	Atlas Fansweep, MD 28
Tonnage (grt)	1,538; net 463	Sidescan sonar	GeoAcoustics 160D
		Sub-bottom profiler	NSRF deep tow sparker; EG&G boomer; hull-mounted pinger G880
PROPULSION			
Main engine(s)	1 × Mirrlees Monarch (2,308 bhp)	Magnetometer	
Thrusters	Bow: 1 × Brunvoll (900 hp); stern: 1 × Brunvoll (900 hp)	Corer(s)	3 m gravity
		Grab(s)	Van Veen
Propellers	Single vp		

Svitzer Mercator   *2001*/0109084

Vehicle(s) (ROVs/AUVs and so on)	ROTV	Compressor numbers and types	LMF Price
Sound velocity profiler	SVP, SVP+, Valeport	Streamer manufacturer	Fjord
Oceanographic sensors (CTDs/XBTs and so on)	Sippican XBT	Streamer type	Up to 120 channels programmable
		Streamer numbers and lengths per number	6.25 and 12.5 m groups
SEISMIC SYSTEMS		Acquisition system	MicroMAX or SeisUP QC
Energy source (type and manufacturer)	Sodera G & GI guns	Recording system	Sercel 358 DMX with 3490E tape decks
Number of airguns	3		
Size of airguns	210 cu in		*UPDATED*

Svitzer Ltd

Tridens I

GENERAL

Owner	Chase Seismic Survey, Den Helder	**SAFETY**	
		Lifeboats	4 × liferafts (total 64 persons)
Port of reg/flag	Den Helder/The Netherlands		
Official number	6270	**SURVEY SYSTEMS**	
Classification	Bureau Veritas (Special Survey Deep Sea)	Positioning	Two independent DGPS systems; Simrad HPR410(T) SSBL; TSS 320
Call sign	PIAO	Echo-sounder (single beam)	1 × Atlas Deso 25; 1 × Atlas Deso 20
Built (yard and date)	1968		
Rebuilt (yard and date)	1997	Multibeam/swath system	Atlas Fansweep 20
Length overall	60.85 m	Sidescan sonar	GeoAcoustics 160D; Klein 595
Breadth moulded	9.80 m	Sub-bottom profiler	EG&G surface & sub-tow boomer
Max draught	4.40 m	Magnetometer	G880
Tonnage (grt)	934; net 280	Vehicle(s) (ROVs/AUVs and so on)	ROTV

PROPULSION

Main engine(s)	2 × Bolnes (1 × 1,200 bhp/1 × 600 bhp)		*UPDATED*
Thrusters	Bow: 1 × Brunvoll (175 hp)		
Propellers	Single vp		

Thales GeoSolutions Group Ltd

Petr Kottsov

GENERAL

Port of reg/flag	St. Petersburg	**COMMUNICATIONS**	
Classification	Worldwide, KM*UL 1 A2 USSR Register of Shipping	Inmarsat (type)	B (voice and fax)
		MF/HF	Yes
Built (yard and date)	Hollming Shipyard, Finland, 1991	VHF	Yes
Rebuilt (yard and date)	Upgraded 1998		
Length overall	65.30 m	**SAFETY**	
Breadth moulded	12.70 m	Workboat/chase boat	1 × 7 m survey launch; 1 × 4 m MOB, 36 hp
Operational draught	3.60 m		
Tonnage (grt)	1,698; dwt 557	**DECK MACHINERY**	
		Cranes	Aft, 3 t SWL at 10 m; port and starboard deployment frames: 10 kN, SWL at 1.8 m outreach; 4 t SWL at 16 m

PROPULSION

Main engine(s)	2 × 1,300 kW Wärtsilä Vasa SR22 HF-D diesels		
Thrusters	Bow: 2 t		
Speed (max)	12.5 kt	**ACCOMMODATION**	
Fuel capacity	260 t (HOF), 42 t (GO)	Charterers	Total accommodation for 25
Electrical power	Auxiliaries: 2 × 240 kW Deutz MWM TBD2 34VO8.2; 300 kW shaft generator	**SURVEY SYSTEMS**	
Fresh water capacity	6 t/day water maker	Positioning	SkyFix DGPS; Nautronix ATS acoustic positioning; Racal GNS online navigation

BRIDGE NAVIGATION AIDS

Satellite	SkyFix DGPS; Trimble GPS	Echo-sounder (single beam)	Simrad EA 500
Radar	Decca 2690 3 cm/10 cm	Multibeam/swath system	Simrad EM12 S 120; Elac Bottomchart Mk II
Gyrocompass	2 × SG 1000	Sidescan sonar	GeoAcoustics with Coda DA-200

Sub-bottom profiler	GeoAcoustics Chirp (integrated with sidescan)	**Other sampling**	CPT
Magnetometer	Geometrics G876S	**Oceanographic sensors**	AML STD 12 deepwater
Corer(s)	Gravity piston; vibrocorer	**(CTDs/XBTs and so on)**	velocimeter; Sippican XBT and
Grab(s)	Yes		XSV

UPDATED

Petr Kottsov   **2000**/0088248

Thales GeoSolutions Group Ltd

Thales Venturer

GENERAL

Former names	*Seisventurer*
Port of reg/flag	NOR (Norwegian National Register)
Official number	DNV 14842; IMO 851673
Classification	DNV + IAI EO HELDK ICE-IB + MV
Call sign	JXBU
Built (yard and date)	Drammen Slip and Mek Verksted, Drammen, Norway, 1986
Rebuilt (yard and date)	Upgraded, Th Hellesoy Skipsbyggeri Lofallstrand, Norway, 1992
Length overall	89.55 m
Breadth moulded	14.40 m
Tonnage (grt)	3,935

PROPULSION

Main engine(s)	3 × 2,255 hp Rolls Royce type KRG 9, 4,965 kW, total 6,750 hp
Thrusters	Bow: 1 x 500 kW Brunvoll, vp, 670 hp, type SPX-VP/QOV 400 DB 6
Propellers	Twin Liaaen vp
Speed (max)	14.5 kt

Endurance	Max 60 days seismic production before refuelling; fully equipped for offshore refuelling over bow
Fuel capacity	620 m³
Fuel consumption	15 m³/day at 14 kt (cruising at full speed); 8-10 m³/day during seismic production
Electrical power	Generators: 3 × 1,963 kVA, 380 V, type WA-B 630 F8; 1 × 300 kW Cummins (emergency)
Fresh water capacity	120 m³; 2 × ECS Reverse Osmosis, 20 m³/day

BRIDGE NAVIGATION AIDS

Satellite	Furuno GP-80 DGPS; Shipmate RS 5310
Radar	10 cm Furuno FAR 2835-S ARPA, 30 kW with PM 50 performance monitor; 3 cm Furuno FAR 2825 ARPA, 25 kW with PM 30 performance monitor; interswitch RJ-7 for 10 cm and 3 cm radar gyro-interface GC-8 for both

Gyrocompass	Robertson SKR-82
Echo sounder	Skipper GDS 101, 50 kHz, range 1,000 m
Other ship navigation	Robertson AP 9 MK11 autopilot

COMMUNICATIONS

Inmarsat (type)	A: JRC JUE 35A; C: Sailor H 2095 B
MF/HF	Skanti 8750 D, 750 W SSB
VHF	2 × Kelvin Hughes 2047/2048; 1 × Sailor RT 2047
Cellular	Yes
Facsimile	Yes

SAFETY

Lifeboats	Viking 6.70 m, fully enclosed for 24 persons with SA-BB 22 hp diesel; Jorgensen & Vik, 6.5 m, davit-deployed combined MOB/lifeboat with SA-BB70 hp diesel, for 20 persons; Viking/RFD liferafts, 4 × 16 persons + 2 × 20 persons
Lifesaving equipment	Halon fire-fighting in engine and compressor room

HELIDECK

Size, aircraft capacity	Up to Sikorsky S61N (9,300 kg)

DECK MACHINERY

Cranes	Forward: 1 × Hydralift SNVL 2 t at 10 m radius; aft: 1 × Hydralift SNVL 2 t at 11 m radius; hydraulic single-arm davit for seismic workboat, max weight 5,400 kg

ACCOMMODATION

Charterers	Total accommodation for 44
Hospital	3 beds

SEISMIC SYSTEMS

Compressor numbers and types	6 × Hamworthy model 425E, single speed, 402/392 cu ft/min at 2,000/3,000 psi; 2 × Hamworthy model 425E, 2-speed, 402/392 cu ft/min at 2,000/3,000 psi

NEW ENTRY

Thales Venturer   *2001*/0109080

Thales Geosolutions Group Ltd

Baruna Jaya III

GENERAL

Port of reg/flag	Jakarta/Indonesia
Classification	BV+1 3/310A1
Built (yard and date)	Chantiers Atlantique, France, 1989
Rebuilt (yard and date)	US$3 million refit at Pan United Shipyard, Singapore, 2000
Length overall	60.40 m
Breadth moulded	11.60 m
Operational draught	4.20 m
Tonnage (grt)	1,300 displacement

PROPULSION

Main engine(s)	2 × 1,100 hp Niigata SEMT-Pielstick; Model PA5-225
Thrusters	Bow: 200 hp

Speed (max)	14 kt
Speed (cruising)	12 kt
Endurance	7,500 n miles at 12 kt
Electrical power	Auxiliaries: 1 × 200 kVA
Fresh water capacity	Water maker 5.50 t/day

COMMUNICATIONS

MF/HF	Yes with high-speed datalink

SAFETY

Workboat/chase boat	Survey launch

DECK MACHINERY

Cranes	1 × 6 t at 7 m
A-frame(s)	1 × 10 t

ACCOMMODATION

Charterers	Total accommodation for 40
Crew	16
Scientists/surveyors	24

SURVEY SYSTEMS

Positioning	SkyFix DGPS; FOG (2); Thomson Marconi Sonar Posidonia 6000 underwater acoustic; Racal WinFrog online navigation; acquisition, processing and charting by CARIS HIPS, Racal Chart-X; Simrad Merlin
Echo-sounder (single beam)	Dual-frequency Simrad EA500
Multibeam/swath system	Simrad EM12D 150 × 176, full ocean depth
Sidescan sonar	Elac BottomChart Mk II medium; Shallow water swath bathymetry GeoAcoustics GeoChirp II with Triton sidescan and profiler
Sub-bottom profiler	GeoAcoustics Chirp II (integrated with sidescan); GeoPulse 16-element hull-mounted array
Magnetometer	Geometrics G880 (Cesium)
Corer(s)	Gravity piston and grab sampler; Vibrocorer (optional); CPT (optional)
Oceanographic sensors (CTDs/XBTs and so on)	Sippican XBT and XSV probes

UPDATED

Baruna Jaya III

Thales Geosolutions Group Ltd

Mansal 18

GENERAL

Current operational status	Multipurpose ROV and survey support vessel
Port of reg/flag	Qatar
Classification	DnV 100 A1 DYNPOS AUTR EO HLDK
Built (yard and date)	Ulstein Hatlo A/S, Norway, 1975
Rebuilt (yard and date)	Upgraded La Spezia to DSV and submersible support, 1980; upgraded Malta to DP Class II and ROV support vessel, 1997
Length overall	80.77 m
Breadth moulded	18.00 m
Working deck width	Free deck area: 800 m²
Max draught	7.10 m moulded
Operational draught	5.10 m
Tonnage (grt)	3,665; 2,539 dwt

PROPULSION

Main engine(s)	2 × MaK 6M453 AK
Thrusters	DP system Kongsberg SDP interfaced to 2 × DGPS, 1 × Simrad HPR 309, tracking and standard transducers, 1 × fanbeam, 2 × VRS, 3 × gyros, 2 × wind sensors; bow: 2 × Ulstein 90, 380 kW (510 hp); 1 × Brunvoll FU80, 1,000 kW (1,340 hp); aft: 1 × Brunvoll FU63, LTC 155 660 kW; (885 hp); 1 × Ulstein TV150, 600 kW (806 hp)
Propellers	2 × Ulstein 4-bladed, CPP 1,429 kW (2,000 hp)
Speed (max)	10 kt
Speed (cruising)	9 kt (economical)
Endurance	16,000 n miles
Fuel capacity	840 m³
Fuel consumption	10 t/day passage; 8-12 t/day Class 2 DP; 4-6 t/day Class 1 DP

Electrical power	3 × 720 kW Deutz diesels; 1 × 525 kW Deutz diesel; 1 × 358 kW at 440 V emergency diesel; 2 × 800 kW shaft alternators	**HELIDECK** **Size, aircraft capacity**	15.00 × 15.00 m for Augusta Bell 206 L1, Dauphin N and N2, Bakow 105, S76
Fresh water capacity	326 m³	**DECK MACHINERY** **Cranes**	Linkbelt fmc-tc 238; 50 t SWL at 6.10 m; 11 t SWL at 27.00 m
BRIDGE NAVIGATION AIDS **Radar**	Furuno ARPA FAR2815; Furuno FR2020	**A-frame(s)** **Winches**	Caley Hydraulics – 30 t SWL 4 × Hatlapa 250 kN, 1,700 m wire length each
Gyrocompass	3 × Robertson RGC 11		
Echo-sounder	Simrad EN	**ACCOMMODATION**	
Other ship navigation	Robertson AP9 autopilot	**Charterers**	Total accommodation for 69
COMMUNICATIONS **Inmarsat (type)**	Satcom B and C	**SURVEY SYSTEMS** **Vehicle(s) (ROVs/AUVs and so on)**	2 × Racal Sealion Mk II, 100 hp workclass ROV, 2,000 m depth rating
MF/HF	GMDSS		
Facsimile	Furuno weather fax		
SAFETY **Lifeboats**	2 × davit-launched liferafts; 2 × hand-launched		
Lifesaving equipment	1 × 6-person rescue boat; survival suits		

UPDATED

Mansal 18   **2001**/0103614

Thales Geosolutions Group Ltd

Mansal 19

GENERAL **Current operational status**	Multipurpose ROV and survey support vessel	**Port of reg/flag**	Qatar
		Classification	DnV – 100 A1 DYNPOS AUTR EO
		Built (yard and date)	Aker, Norway, 1967

Rebuilt (yard and date)	Conversion, Malta Drydocks to DP Class II and ROV support, 1998/99	**Speed (max)**	12 kt
		Speed (cruising)	10 kt (economical)
Length overall	80.32 m	**Endurance**	8,000 n miles operating range
Breadth moulded	13.33 m	**Fuel capacity**	460 m³
Working deck width	Free deck area: 400 m², deck loading: 2 t/m²	**Fuel consumption**	9 t/day passage; 6-8 t/day DP
		Electrical power	2 × Caterpillar 3412 diesels
Operational draught	5.50 m		500 kW (780 bhp); 2 × 500 kW
Tonnage (grt)	3,665; 1,099 net; 1,050 dwt		alternators, 2 × 575 kW and;
			2 × 640 kW shaft alternators,
			1 × 140 kW; emergency generator
PROPULSION		**Fresh water capacity**	180 m³
Main engine(s)	2 × Wartsila 814TK diesels, 803 kW (1,080 bhp); 2 × Wartsila 614TK diesels, 603 kW (810 bhp)		
		BRIDGE NAVIGATION AIDS	
Thrusters	DP system Kongsberg SDP 21 interfaced to 2 × DGPS, 1 × Simrad HiPAP, 1 × fanbeam; 2 × VRU, 2 × gyros, 2 × wind sensors; bow: 1 × KaMeWa 446 kW (600 bhp); 1 × Brunvoll 372 kW (500 bhp); stern tunnel: 1 × KaMeWa 446 kW (600 bhp); stern azimuth: 1 × Brunvoll 372 kW (500 bhp)	**Satellite**	1 × Garmin 120XL
		Radar	2 × Furuno
		Gyrocompass	1 × Sperry Mk 37; 2 × Anschutz Standard 20 digital
		Echo-sounder	1 × Skipper 161
		Other ship navigation	Decca 450 autopilot
		COMMUNICATIONS	
		Inmarsat (type)	'C' and 'M'
		MF/HF	GMDSS full Furuno system
		Facsimile	Furuno weather fax
Propellers	Liaanen vp 1,488 kW (2,000 bhp)		

Mansal 19

2000/0088250

SAFETY		**SURVEY SYSTEMS**	
Lifeboats	2 × davit-launched liferafts;	Positioning	2 × DGPS
	2 × hand-launched liferafts	Multibeam/swath system	Yes, with Coda DA 200
Lifesaving equipment	1 × 6-person rescue boat		processing
		Sidescan sonar	Yes
DECK MACHINERY		Sub-bottom profiler	Yes
Cranes	2 × Aurora telescopic, 12 t SWL at	Vehicle(s) (ROVs/AUVs and	2 × Racal workclass
	6.00 m and 6 t SWL at 12.00 m,	so on)	
	wire length 450 m each		
Winches	Forward: 2 × Van Rietschoten &		*UPDATED*
	Houwens		

ACCOMMODATION	
Charterers	Total accommodation for 67

Titan Environmental Surveys Ltd

Titan Explorer

GENERAL		**BRIDGE NAVIGATION AIDS**	
Owner	Titan Environmental Surveys Ltd,	Satellite	DGPS
	UK		
Classification	Catamaran	**DECK MACHINERY**	
Built (yard and date)	Cheetah Marine, Isle of Wight, UK	A-frame(s)	Yes
Length overall	8.40 m		
Operational draught	0.38 m	**SURVEY SYSTEMS**	
		Positioning	3 × DGPS
PROPULSION			
Main engine(s)	Twin 130 hp Honda, 4-stroke	Echo sounder (single beam)	Yes
	petrol outboards	Sidescan sonar	EdgeTech dual frequency
Endurance	60 n miles offshore	Sub-bottom profiler	EdgeTech Chirp
Electrical power	Lombardini 6 kVA generator,	Oceanographic sensors	RDI ADCP
	3 kVA UPS to operate for 30 min	(CTDs/XBTs and so on)	
	on full load		*NEW ENTRY*

UK Dredging

UKD Surveyor

GENERAL		Owner	Associated British Ports plc, UK
Former names	*Humber Surveyor*	Port of reg/flag	Swansea, UK
Current operational status	Operating in Bristol Channel	Official number	1248

UKD Surveyor   *2001*/0109087

Classification	MCA Category 2	Gyrocompass	Ritchie – electronic
Call sign	MZCJ	Speed log	All logging via PC – PDS1000 software
Built (yard and date)	Watercraft (Shoreham) Ltd, UK, 1968	Echo-sounder	Atlas Deso 15

Length overall — 18.00 m
Breadth moulded — 5.50 m
Working deck width — 6.00 m
Max draught — 1.80 m
Operational draught — 1.80 m
Tonnage (grt) — 50

COMMUNICATIONS
VHF — Husun 60 Kelvin Hughes and Sailor A1, VHF-DSC
Cellular — Motorola International 2700

PROPULSION
Main engine(s) — 2 × Lister JWS6A, 185 hp (335.70 kW)
Propellers — Two
Speed (max) — 11 kt
Speed (cruising) — 8 kt
Endurance — 36 hours
Fuel capacity — 600 gallons
Fuel consumption — 8 gallons each engine @ max speed
Electrical power — 6 kVA generator 240/ 24/ 12 V power
Fresh water capacity — 200 gallons

SAFETY
Lifeboats — 1 × 12-persons 'A' pack throwover liferaft
Lifesaving equipment — Jacob's Cradle

DECK MACHINERY
Winches — Anchor winch hand operated

ACCOMMODATION
Charterers — Total accommodation for 4

SURVEY SYSTEMS
Positioning — Sercel NR 103 DGPS; Trimble DSM 212L DGPS
Echo-sounder (single beam) — Atlas Deso 15 (210/33 kHz)
Grab(s) — Small sampling grab
Sound velocity profiler — Bar check

BRIDGE NAVIGATION AIDS
Satellite — Sercel DGPS
Radar — Racal Decca

UPDATED

UKD Surveyor   **2001**/0109085

UKD Surveyor   **2001**/0109086

WesternGeco

Geco Scorpio

GENERAL
Owner — Remøy Shipping, Fosnavaag, Norway
Classification — DnV + 1A1, E0, SF
Built (yard and date) — Søviknes Verft AS, Norway, 2000
Length overall — 55.80 m
Breadth moulded — 13.00 m
Operational draught — 11.60 m
Tonnage (grt) — 1,429: dw at 5.8 m: 1,500

PROPULSION
Main engine(s) — Ulstein Bergen KRMB-8, 2 × 1,785 kW

Thrusters — Bow/azimuth: Ulstein, TNC 83/ 56-220, 880 kW
Propellers — 2
Speed (max) — 15 kt
Fuel capacity — 1,390 m³
Electrical power — Generators: shaft: 1 × Newage, 600 kW, 450 V/60 Hz; auxiliaries: 1 × Volvo Penta TAMD 162 A, 360 kW
Fresh water capacity — 72 m³; Gefico fresh water maker

BRIDGE NAVIGATION AIDS
Satellite — 1 × Furuno GPS-GP80

Radar	1 × Furuno FAR 2135S;	**SAFETY**	
	1 × Furuno FAR 2115X	**Lifeboats**	MOB boat
Gyrocompass	1 × Anschutz standard 20		
Speed log	1 × Skipper EML 224	**DECK MACHINERY**	
Echo-sounder	1 × Furuno FCV 700	**Cranes**	1 × ABAS 5 t SWL at 12 m
Other ship navigation	1 × Anschutz Pilotstar D autopilot	**Winches**	Brødrene Rogne
COMMUNICATIONS		**ACCOMMODATION**	
Inmarsat (type)	1 × Skanti D/Mini M	**CHARTERERS**	Total accommodation for 26
MF/HF	1 × Skanti A3 GMDSS		
VHF	1 × Skanti		

NEW ENTRY

UNITED STATES OF AMERICA

Alpine Ocean Seismic Survey Inc

Atlantic Twin

GENERAL		**DECK MACHINERY**	
Length overall	27.43 m	**Cranes**	800-1,200 lb capacity, 11.80 m reach
Breadth moulded	8.53 m (catamaran)	**A-frame(s)**	1 × side; 1 × stern
Working deck width	Total 102.19 m² back deck space	**Winches**	Dual drum
Max draught	2.31 m		
		ACCOMMODATION	
PROPULSION		**Charterers**	Total accommodation for 14
Main engine(s)	2 × Detroit diesels		
Fuel capacity	8,000 gallons	**SCIENTIFIC SPACES**	
Electrical power	2 × 30 kW generators	**Oceanographic wet lab**	Total lab space 16.72 m²
Fresh water capacity	1,000 gallons		
		SURVEY SYSTEMS	
BRIDGE NAVIGATION AIDS		**Sidescan sonar**	Charterer supply
Satellite	Trimble DGPS	**Sub-bottom profiler**	Charterer supply
Radar	Furuno 16-mile	**Magnetometer**	Charterer supply
Echo-sounder	Raytheon		
Other ship navigation	Wood-Freeman model 500 autopilot		*NEW ENTRY*
COMMUNICATIONS			
VHF	2		

Beaufort Oceanics

Weatherbird

GENERAL		**Fuel consumption**	15 gallons/hour
Former names	*Whitefoot*	**Electrical power**	220 V, 40 kW
Owner	Marine Towing and Salvage Inc, USA	**Fresh water capacity**	1,200 gallons; 500 gallons/day; R/O
Port of reg/flag	Beaufort, NC/USA		
Classification	Small passenger vessel	**BRIDGE NAVIGATION AIDS**	
Built (yard and date)	Halter Marine, New Orleans, USA, 1970	**Satellite**	3 × Northstar DGPS, Furuno
		Radar	2 × Furuno
Rebuilt (yard and date)	1983, 1997	**Gyrocompass**	Anschutz
Length overall	19.50 m	**Speed log**	Yes
Breadth moulded	6.70 m	**Echo sounder**	Furuno
Working deck width	6.70 m		
Max draught	2.13 m	**COMMUNICATIONS**	
Operational draught	1.98 m	**Inmarsat (type)**	KVH
Tonnage (grt)	61	**MF/HF**	Furuno M-700
		VHF	3 × Icom
PROPULSION		**Cellular**	Motorola
Main engine(s)	2 × 8-71 Detroit Diesel	**Facsimile**	Available
Propellers	48 × 40		
Speed (max)	9 kt	**SAFETY**	
Speed (cruising)	8.5 kt	**Lifeboats**	2 × Solas liferafts
Endurance	16 days	**Workboat/chase boat**	Avon 3.3 m, 15 hp; Honda outboard
Fuel capacity	6,000 gallons		

DECK MACHINERY

Cranes	Appleton knuckle, 6 t
A-frame(s)	Stern, 7 t capacity
Winches	Trawl, CTD; 2 × capstans; anchor
Transducer well	12 and 6 in

ACCOMMODATION

Charterers	Total accommodation for 6
Crew	3 – 4
Scientists/surveyors	6

SCIENTIFIC SPACES

Total scientific deck space	70 m²
Oceanographic wet lab	6 m²

Multipurpose dry lab	6 m²
Chemistry lab	6 m²
Echo sounder (single beam)	Furuno
Sidescan sonar	Available
Sub-bottom profiler	Available
Magnetometer	Available
Corer(s)	Available
Grab(s)	Available

NEW ENTRY

Donjon Marine Co Inc

Atlantic Surveyor

GENERAL

Owner	Donjon Marine Co Inc, USA
Port of reg/flag	New York, USA
Official number	1092744
Call sign	WCZ7162
Built (yard and date)	Peterson Builders, 1968
Length overall	28.68 m
Breadth moulded	6.43 m
Tonnage (grt)	145; net 99

PROPULSION

Main engine(s)	4 × GM 12 V-711, 600 hp with 4:1 reduction
Propellers	2
Speed (max)	19 kt

Speed (cruising)	16 kt
Fuel capacity	6,000 gallons
Electrical power	Generators: 2 × 30 kW driven by GM 2 V-71, 110/440 V
Fresh water capacity	2,264 gallons

SAFETY

Lifesaving equipment	Full complement firefighting equipment; 2 × 1.5 in electric pump

ACCOMMODATION

Charterers	Total accommodation for 16

NEW ENTRY

Fugro GeoServices Inc

Geodetic Surveyor

GENERAL

Owner	Survey Boats Inc, USA
Port of reg/flag	Morgan City, LA/USA
Official number	637873
Classification	Utility

Call sign	WBB8832
Built (yard and date)	Universal Iron Works, US, 1986
Rebuilt (yard and date)	1985
Length overall	37.90 m
Breadth moulded	9.14 m

Geodetic Surveyor

Max draught	3.00 m	**DECK MACHINERY**	
Operational draught	3.00 m	Cranes	Alaska 8-30 K for deep-tow deployment
Tonnage (grt)	97	A-frame(s)	Hydraulic 5,000 lb SWL
		Winches	5 × utility for sonar, 10,000 ft coring, mag, VSP, deep tow 30,000 ft wire on Dynacon

PROPULSION

Main engine(s)	2 × V-16-92-N
Propellers	62 in × 54 in
Speed (max)	10 kt
Speed (cruising)	10 kt
Endurance	17.5 days
Fuel capacity	21,300 gallons
Fuel consumption	50-68 gallons/h
Electrical power	2 × 6-71 N-75 kW
Fresh water capacity	17,000 gallons

ACCOMMODATION

Crew	4
Scientists/surveyors	12

SCIENTIFIC SPACES

Multipurpose dry lab	Dry/electronics 192 sq ft; electronics 266 sq ft

BRIDGE NAVIGATION AIDS

Satellite	DGPS
Radar	2 × Furuno GP 50 Mark 3
Gyrocompass	Sperry and POS/MV
Echo-sounder	Raytheon R246M – International Offshore 3000
Other ship navigation	Robertson AP-9 autopilot

SURVEY SYSTEMS

Positioning	Fugro Starfix
Echo-sounder (single beam)	Simrad EA500; EchoTrac DF 3200
Multibeam/swath system	Reson 8101 or Deep Tow 2
Sidescan sonar	EDO Deeptow; EG&G 272-TD
Sub-bottom profiler	Geopulse 3.5 kHz pinger; EG&G 16KJ-9-tip sparker; heave compensator: TSS320; boomer: Datasonics Chirp

COMMUNICATIONS

Inmarsat (type)	M-Sat Westinghouse 1000 Super Hygain
MF/HF	SSB Sea 330 Necode
VHF	2
Cellular	Yes
Facsimile	Satellite and cellular

Magnetometer	SeaSpy
Corer(s)	3 in bore to 20 ft length
Grab(s)	Available on request
Other sampling	VSP
Vehicle(s) (ROVs/AUVs and so on)	Deep Tow 2
Oceanographic sensors (CTDs/XBTs and so on)	Seabird CTD

SAFETY

Lifeboats	2 × 25 person liferafts
Workboat/chase boat	USCG-approved rescue boat
Lifesaving equipment	Epirb 406, 2 fire suits, 2 Scott Pack breathing gear, Lith-X extinguisher

UPDATED

Fugro GeoServices Inc

L'Arpenteur

GENERAL		**Breadth moulded**	9.14 m
Owner	Survey Boats Inc, USA	**Working deck width**	Open deck space: 1,990 sq ft
Port of reg/flag	New Orleans	**Operational draught**	3.20 m
Official number	646846	**Tonnage (gt)**	99
Classification	Utility		
Call sign	WBB8827	**PROPULSION**	
Built (yard and date)	Universal Iron Works, USA, 1982	Main engine(s)	2 × GM V-16-92-N, 1,300 hp
Length overall	37.18 m	Propellers	62 in × 54 in

L'Arpenteur

2001/0106447

Speed (max)	10 kt
Speed (cruising)	10 kt
Endurance	4,200 n miles/17.50 days
Fuel capacity	21,300 gallons
Fuel consumption	50-68 US gallons/h
Electrical power	2 × GM 6-71-N, 208 V, 75 kW
Fresh water capacity	40,000 gallons

BRIDGE NAVIGATION AIDS

Satellite	DGPS
Radar	2 × Furuno FR-8100D
Gyrocompass	Sperry
Speed log	Pressley 8500
Echo-sounder	Simrad 802, Data Marine 3000, ORE 4600

COMMUNICATIONS

Inmarsat (type)	M-Sat
MF/HF	SEA 330
VHF	ICOM IC-M80; Motorola Modar, Motorola L51JJB1400BM
Cellular	Yes
Facsimile	Satellite and cellular

SAFETY

Lifeboats	2 × 25 persons liferafts
Workboat/chase boat	USCG approved rescue boat
Lifesaving equipment	Epirb 406, 2 fire suits, 2 Scott Pack breathing gear, Lith-X extinguisher

DECK MACHINERY

A-frame(s)	1 × 6 ft 6 in internal opening, 7,000 lb/ft line tension, 5,000 lb/ft dead lift
Winches	5 t utility for sonar, 5,000 ft coring, magnetometer, velocity profiling, streamer

ACCOMMODATION

Crew	4
Scientists/surveyors	12

SCIENTIFIC SPACES

Multipurpose dry lab	Dry/electronics 192 sq ft; electronics 266 sq ft

SURVEY SYSTEMS

Positioning	Fugro Starfix
Echo-sounder (single beam)	Simrad EA500; EchoTrac DG 3200
Multibeam/swath system	Reson 8101 available
Sidescan sonar	EG&G 272-TD
Sub-bottom profiler	Geopulse 3.5 kHz pinger; TSS heave compensator; boomer available
Magnetometer	SeaSpy
Corer(s)	3 in bore, 20 ft length
Grab(s)	Available on request
Sound velocity profiler	SVP-16

SEISMIC SYSTEMS

Energy source (type and manufacturer)	GI gun
Size of airguns	90-120 cu in
Compressor numbers and types	2 × Price W-5
Total capacity	340 cu ft/min
Streamer manufacturer	Litton
Streamer type	48 channels
Streamer numbers and lengths per number	1 at 600 m, 12.5 m groups
Recording system	OYO 48-trace DAS-1; Seiscam

UPDATED

Fugro GeoServices Inc

Seis Surveyor

GENERAL

Owner	Survey Boats Inc, USA	Call sign	WBB8821
Port of reg/flag	New Orleans	Built (yard and date)	1976
Official number	575398	Rebuilt (yard and date)	1985
Classification	Subchapter C; ABS L/L	Length overall	45.70 m
		Breadth moulded	11.60 m

Seis Surveyor

2001/0106448

Max draught	3.80 m	**Winches**	5 t utility for sonar, 5,000 ft coring, magnetometer, velocity profiling, streamer
Operational draught	3.80 m		
Tonnage (gt)	199; net 133		

PROPULSION

Main engine(s)	2 × Caterpillar D-398, 1,700 hp total	**ACCOMMODATION**	
		Crew	5
Thrusters	Schottel 300 hp		
Propellers	72 in × 64 in	**SCIENTIFIC SPACES**	
Speed (max)	10 kt	**Multipurpose dry lab**	Dry/electronics 130 sq ft; electronics 484 sq ft
Speed (cruising)	10 kt		
Endurance	6,000 n miles, 26 days	**SURVEY SYSTEMS**	
Fuel capacity	59,000 gallons	**Positioning**	I/O Total Nav; I/O Total Net; DGPS; Decca radar
Fuel consumption	80 gallons/h		
Electrical power	3 × CAT, 225 kW, 480 V, 300 A	**Echo-sounder (single beam)**	Simrad EA500; EchoTrac DF3200
Fresh water capacity	80,000 gallons	**Multibeam/swath system**	Reson 8101 available
		Sidescan sonar	EG&G 272-TD
BRIDGE NAVIGATION AIDS		**Sub-bottom profiler**	Pinger: Geopulse 3.5 kHz; heave compensator: TSS; boomer available
Satellite	Magnavox MX 4400		
Radar	2 × Furuno FR8100D		
Gyrocompass	Sperry	**Magnetometer**	SeaSpy
Echo-sounder	Int'l Offshore Data 3000; Furuno 881II; ORE transceiver 140	**Corer(s)**	3 in bore × 20 ft length
		Grab(s)	Available
		Sound velocity profiler	SeaBird
COMMUNICATIONS			
Inmarsat (type)	M-Sat	**SEISMIC SYSTEMS**	
MF/HF	SSB: Seacom	**Energy source (type and manufacturer)**	GI Gun 90-120 cu in
VHF	2 × Sailor; Motorola		
Cellular	Yes	**Compressor numbers and types**	2 × Price W-5
Facsimile	Satellite and cellular		
		Total capacity	340 cu ft/min
SAFETY		**Streamer manufacturer**	Litton
Lifeboats	2 × 25 person liferafts	**Streamer type**	48-channel, 12.5 m groups
Workboat/chase boat	Avon RIB rescue boat	**Streamer numbers and lengths per number**	1 × 600 m, 1 × 1,200 m, 2 × 600 m, 4 × 200 m, 6 × 100 m
Lifesaving equipment	Epirb 406, 2 fire suits, 2 Scott Pack breathing gear, Lith-X extinguisher	**Recording system**	OYO 96 Trace DAS-1

UPDATED

DECK MACHINERY

A-frame(s)	7,500 lb hydraulic

Fugro GeoServices Inc

Universal Surveyor

GENERAL		**Breadth moulded**	9.14 m
Owner	Survey Boats Inc, USA	**Working deck width**	Open deck space: 1,200 sq ft
Port of reg/flag	New Orleans	**Max draught**	3.10 m
Official number	627510	**Operational draught**	3.10 m
Classification	Utility	**Tonnage (gt)**	94
Call sign	WBB8829		
Built (yard and date)	1980	**PROPULSION**	
Length overall	37.18 m	**Main engine(s)**	2 × GM V-16-92-N, total 1,300 hp

Universal Surveyor

2001/0106449

Propellers	62 in × 54 in
Speed (max)	10 kt
Speed (cruising)	10 kt
Endurance	4,200 n miles, 17.5 days
Fuel capacity	21,300 gallons
Fuel consumption	50-68 gallons/h in transit
Electrical power	2 × GM generators – 60 kW
Fresh water capacity	40,000 gallons

BRIDGE NAVIGATION AIDS

Satellite	GPS
Radar	2 × Furuno FR-8100D
Gyrocompass	Sperry
Echo-sounder	Raytheon R2460S

COMMUNICATIONS

Inmarsat (type)	M-Sat
MF/HF	SSB SEA 330
VHF	Motorola Triton/ICOM IC-M80
Cellular	Yes
Facsimile	Satellite and cellular

SAFETY

Lifeboats	1 × 20 person liferaft, 1 × 25 person liferaft
Workboat/chase boat	USCG-approved rescue boat
Lifesaving equipment	Epirb 406, 2 fire suits, 2 Scott Pack breathing gear, Lith-X extinguisher

DECK MACHINERY

A-frame(s)	7,000 lb/ft dead lift, height 20 ft, 12 ft internal opening
Winches	Branden 30,000 lb/ft, 400 ft cable; 5,500 lb/ft, 1,000 ft cable

ACCOMMODATION

Crew	4
Scientists/surveyors	10

SCIENTIFIC SPACES

Multipurpose dry lab	Electronics 250 sq ft

SURVEY SYSTEMS

Positioning	Fugro Starfix
Echo-sounder (single beam)	Simrad EA500; EchoTrac DF3200
Multibeam/swath system	Reson 8101 available
Sidescan sonar	DataSonics 1500 Chirp
Sub-bottom profiler	Pinger: Geopulse 3.5 kHz; heave compensator: TSS
Magnetometer	SeaSpy
Gravimeter	3 in × 20 ft length
Corer(s)	Available
Sound velocity profiler	SVP-16

SEISMIC SYSTEMS

Energy source (type and manufacturer)	GI Gun 90-120 cu in
Number of airguns	Varies
Size of airguns	90-120 cu in
Compressor numbers and types	2 × Price W5
Total capacity	340 cu ft/min
Streamer manufacturer	Geco
Streamer type	96 channels
Streamer numbers and lengths per number	1 × 600 m
Recording system	OYO 48-trace DAS-1; Seiscam

UPDATED

Fugro-McClelland Marine

Fugro Explorer

GENERAL

Former names	*Western Magellan*
Owner	Fugro-McClelland Marine, Houston, Texas, USA
Built (yard and date)	Kwong Soon Engineering, Singapore, 1999
Rebuilt (yard and date)	Being converted 2001
Length overall	67.36 m

Breadth moulded	16.00
Operational draught	6.00 m

PROPULSION

Main engine(s)	2 × Wärtsilä G626 diesels, 4,988 bhp
Propellers	cp

NEW ENTRY

Marex Oceanographic Services

Atlantic Explorer

GENERAL
Length overall	53.00 m
Breadth moulded	12.07 m
Working deck width	Main/aft: 10.66 m × 15.84 m; load capacity: 111,000 lb

PROPULSION
Main engine(s)	1 × B&W Alpha 8-cylinder diesel
Thrusters	Nautronix ASK 4000 JS dynamic positioning system driving 1 × 360° Thrustmaster retractable (bow) and 2 × 360° Thrustmaster (stern) via three Caterpillar 540 hp diesels and Gulf Coast Air and Hydraulics power units
Speed (max)	10 kt
Endurance	7,000 n miles
Fuel capacity	61,000 gallons
Electrical power	2 × Caterpillar Model 3406 diesels driving 2 × 165 kW generators
Fresh water capacity	40 t; 1,500 gallons/day water maker

BRIDGE NAVIGATION AIDS
Satellite	GPS: 1 × Trimble Nav NT 200; 1 × Furuno Nav GP 80
Radar	2 × Furuno: 1 × 1510 Mark II; 1 × FR1510D
Gyrocompass	1 × Anschutz Kiel
Echo-sounder	1 × Datamarine International Offshore
Other ship navigation	1 × Navtex NCR 300A weather fax; 1 × Bergen Nautic 8 in magnetic compass; 1 × Anschutz Kiel Compilot 8 autopilot

COMMUNICATIONS
MF/HF	1 × Skandi TRP 8258S; 1 × Sea model 330
VHF	1 × JRC JHS-31; 1 × Sea 7156 with Seacall; 1 × Standard Horizon Eclipse
Cellular	1 × Sea Sat 3

SAFETY
Lifesaving equipment	For 40 persons

DECK MACHINERY
Cranes	1 × 12 t North American telescoping

ACCOMMODATION
Charterers	Total accommodation for 37

NEW ENTRY

Marex Oceanographic Services

Beacon

GENERAL
Owner	Marex Oceanographic Services, USA
Port of reg/flag	US
Built (yard and date)	Halter Marine, New Orleans
Length overall	30.48 m
Breadth moulded	7.31 m
Working deck width	Open deck space: 1,200 sq ft
Max draught	2.43 m
Tonnage (grt)	172

PROPULSION
Main engine(s)	2 × 1271 Detroit Diesels
Speed (max)	10 kt
Fuel capacity	24,000 gallons diesel
Electrical power	Generators: 2 × 66 kW Caterpillar
Fresh water capacity	7,400 gallons

BRIDGE NAVIGATION AIDS
Satellite	1 × Magnavox DGPS
Radar	1 × Decca RM 926C
Gyrocompass	1 × Anschutz Standard 20 compact
Echo-sounder	1 × Furuno Video
Other ship navigation	1 × Anschutz Pilotstar D autopilot

COMMUNICATIONS
VHF	Yes
Cellular	Yes

SAFETY
Workboat/chase boat	1 × Zodiac with 14 hp Johnson outboard; 1 × Boston Whaler with 30 hp Johnson outboard

DECK MACHINERY
Cranes	1 × 5 t
A-frame(s)	1 × 25 t on hydraulic rams
Winches	5,000 ft coring; 4 × hydraulic capstans

ACCOMMODATION
Charterers	Total accommodation for 19

SCIENTIFIC SPACES
Multipurpose dry lab	Electronics, 250 sq ft

SURVEY SYSTEMS
Positioning	DGPS
Echo-sounder (single beam)	Charterer supply
Multibeam/swath system	Charterer supply
Sidescan sonar	Charterer supply
Sub-bottom profiler	Charterer supply
Magnetometer	Charterer supply
Sound velocity profiler	Charterer supply

NEW ENTRY

Marex Oceanographic Services

Heck

GENERAL

Former names	(Former NOAA survey vessel)
Owner	Marex Oceanographic Services, USA
Rebuilt (yard and date)	1998
Length overall	27.43 m
Breadth moulded	6.70 m
Max draught	2.43 m

PROPULSION

Electrical power	Generators: 125 and 140 kW
Fresh water capacity	Water maker

BRIDGE NAVIGATION AIDS

Other ship navigation	1 × Anschutz autopilot

COMMUNICATIONS

MF/HF	1 × ICOM 710 SSB

ACCOMMODATION

Charterers	Total accommodation for 14

SURVEY SYSTEMS

Positioning	1 × Furuno DGPS
Multibeam/swath system	Stabilising keel accepts Reson 8101 transducer

NEW ENTRY

Marex Oceanographic Services

Plus Ultra

GENERAL

Former names	*HMS Fox*
Owner	Marex Oceanographic Services
Port of reg/flag	Hull, UK
Official number	712708
Classification	Lloyds + 10CA1 + LMC DTp Class VII
Call sign	GKCD
Built (yard and date)	Brooke Marine, Lowestoft, UK, 1968
Rebuilt (yard and date)	1989
Length overall	57.70 m
Breadth moulded	11.40 m
Operational draught	3.825 m
Tonnage (grt)	1,022; net 306; displacement 1,134

PROPULSION

Speed (max)	16 kt
Speed (cruising)	12 kt service
Endurance	3 months; range: 4,500 n miles at service speed
Fuel capacity	139 t
Fresh water capacity	52 t + reserve: osmosis plant capacity 5 t/day

ACCOMMODATION

Charterers	Total accommodation for 30
Crew	12

NEW ENTRY

Monterey Canyon Research Vessels, Inc

Retriever

GENERAL

Current operational status	San Francisco Bay; Sacrament-San Joaquin Delta; moveable overland by truck
Owner	Monterey Canyon Research Vessels, Inc, USA
Port of reg/flag	San Francisco/USA
Official number	1076750
Classification	Motor vessel
Call sign	WAI 6560
Built (yard and date)	Port Orchard, Washington, USA, 1985
Length overall	15.24 m
Breadth moulded	4.62 m
Working deck width	3.96 m
Max draught	1.22 m
Operational draught	1.21 m
Tonnage (grt)	35

PROPULSION

Main engine(s)	Isuzu 150 hp twin inboard/outboards
Propellers	Twin, counter-rotating 19 in × 14 in
Speed (max)	9 kt
Speed (cruising)	7 kt

Endurance	Day operations only
Fuel capacity	300 gallons
Fuel consumption	5 gallons/hour
Electrical power	3.5 kW 110/220 V AC, 20 kW planned
Fresh water capacity	60 gallons

BRIDGE NAVIGATION AIDS

Satellite	Northstar 951 DGPS/plotter
Radar	24-mile
Speed log	DGPS
Echo sounder	Lorance

COMMUNICATIONS

VHF	King
Cellular	3 W, external antenna and DC source

SAFETY

Lifeboats	22 persons rigid float
Workboat/chase boat	4.87 m/25 hp
Lifesaving equipment	35 lifejackets, flares and so on

DECK MACHINERY

A-frame(s)	Over-the-bow: 7.00 m high, 3.35 m wide, 1,818 kg max

---

Winches	Hydraulic (soy-based), 200 m wire, 4 t capstan
Transducer well	Transducers all fixed through hulls
Gate valve	2 in
Moonpool(s) – size(s)/ function(s)	In preparation, estimated 24 in

ACCOMMODATION

Crew	1
Scientists/surveyors	6

SCIENTIFIC SPACES

Total scientific deck space	40 m²
Multipurpose dry lab	3 m²

SURVEY SYSTEMS

Positioning	Charterer supply

Sensors

Echo sounder (single beam)	Charterer supply
Multibeam/swath system	Charterer supply
Sidescan sonar	Charterer supply
Sub-bottom profiler	Charterer supply
Magnetometer	Charterer supply
Corer(s)	0.25 m² box
Other sampling	Charterer supply
Sound velocity profiler	Charterer supply
Oceanographic sensors (CTDs/XBTs and so on)	Charterer supply

NEW ENTRY

Monterey Canyon Research Vessels, Inc

Shana Rae

GENERAL

Current operational status	Coastal waters central and southern California, into B C, Canada and Baja California, Mexico
Owner	Monterey Canyon Research Vessels, Inc, USA
Port of reg/flag	Juneau, Alaska
Official number	618458
Classification	Motor vessel
Call sign	WAI 6560
Built (yard and date)	Delta Marine Industries, Seattle, USA, 1980
Length overall	15.85 m
Breadth moulded	5.03 m

Working deck width	4.72 m
Max draught	2.13 m
Operational draught	2.13 m
Tonnage (grt)	46

PROPULSION

Main engine(s)	Caterpillar 3406 TA
Propellers	45 in x 40 in, right hand
Speed (max)	10 kt
Speed (cruising)	8 kt
Endurance	8 (24-hour) days
Fuel capacity	1,500 gallons
Fuel consumption	7-8 gallons/hour
Electrical power	20 kW 120/240 V AC and 6 kW 120/240 V AC
Fresh water capacity	450 gallons

Shana Rae

2001/0109098

BRIDGE NAVIGATION AIDS

Satellite	Northstar 951 DGPS receiver/ plotter
Radar	48-mile Anritsu; 48-mile Furuno
Speed log	DGPS
Echo sounder	Simrad
Other ship navigation	Furuno LC-90 Loran; Furuno GP-1250 GPS plotter

COMMUNICATIONS

MF/HF	Icom SSB
VHF	Icom and LRS
Cellular	3 W, external antenna and DC source
Facsimile	Furuno DFAX

SAFETY

Lifeboats	Elliot 8 persons with full offshore pack; 22 persons rigid float
Workboat/chase boat	4.87 m, 25 hp, storable on deck
Lifesaving equipment	8 survival suits, 40+ lifejackets, 2 × EPIRBS, flares and so on

DECK MACHINERY

A-frame(s)	Hydraulic stern-mounted, 3.2 m wide, 3.04 m high, 2,273.00 kg max
Winches	4,000 m; two overhead boom-mounted deck winches, 1,364.00 kg

Transducer well	Transducers all fixed through hulls
Gate valve	3 in

ACCOMMODATION

Crew	2
Scientists/surveyors	5

SCIENTIFIC SPACES

Total scientific deck space	24 m²
Oceanographic wet lab	10 m²
Multipurpose dry lab	10 m²

SURVEY SYSTEMS

Positioning	Charterer supply
Sensors	Charterer supply
Echo sounder (single beam)	Charterer supply
Multibeam/swath system	Charterer supply
Sidescan sonar	Charterer supply
Sub-bottom profiler	Charterer supply
Magnetometer	Charterer supply
Corer(s)	0.25 m² box
Other sampling	Charterer supply
Sound velocity profiler	Charterer supply
Oceanographic sensors (CTDs/XBTs and so on)	Charterer supply

NEW ENTRY

Ocean Services

Davidson

GENERAL

Owner	Ocean Services, Seattle, USA (subsidiary of Pacific Genesis Applications Group)
Length overall	55.00 m

SURVEY SYSTEMS

Multibeam/swath system	1 × Reson SeaBat 8150-F, dual frequency

NEW ENTRY

Davidson

2001/0110526

Raytheon Systems Co

Sensor

GENERAL

Owner	Raytheon Systems Co, USA
Port of reg/flag	USA
Length overall	41.45 m
Breadth moulded	10.97 m
Working deck width	Area: 250 m²
Max draught	2.43 m
Tonnage (grt)	193; net 134

PROPULSION

Main engine(s)	2 × Enterprise DMM 363, 500 hp each
Thrusters	Bow: 1 × Omnithruster HTC 600 at 200 hp
Speed (max)	10 kt
Fuel capacity	34,000 gallons
Fresh water capacity	1,000 gallons; 600 gallons/day from water maker

BRIDGE NAVIGATION AIDS

Radar	1 × Furuno 1941, 48 n miles; 1 × Furuno Mk 24, 24 n miles
Gyrocompass	1 × Sperry 130
Other ship navigation	1 × Sperry ADG 2000VT autopilot

COMMUNICATIONS

MF/HF	Yes
VHF	Yes
Cellular	Yes

DECK MACHINERY

Cranes	1 × Olympic 2410-45, 9,000 lb at 13.71 m and 40,000 lb at 3.04 m; auxiliary: 1 × Continental US 6-2
A-frame(s)	1 × 30,000 lb SWL: 7.01 m wide at trunions; 7.01 m vertical lift; 3.81 m reach aft of stern; 5.33 m reach forward of stern
Winches	Anchor: 1 × WT202, 182.88 m depth at 5:1; deck: 1 × Landtec with 20,000 lb full drum; A-frame: 1 Pullmaster M50
Moonpool(s) – size(s)/ function(s)	13 in diameter

ACCOMMODATION

Charterers	Total accommodation for nine
Crew	5

SURVEY SYSTEMS

Positioning	GPS: 1 × Trimble Nav Trac; 1 × Trimble 4000 DS; 1 × Trimble Nav Beacon XL
Sidescan sonar	1 × SeaMARC®
Vehicle(s) (ROVs/AUVs and so on)	1 × RCV® 225/ROV 425; 1 × 4.87 m aluminium skiff with 50 hp outboard

NEW ENTRY

Sensor   **2001**/0110556

Stolt Offshore Inc

Seaway Legend

GENERAL

Former names	*Laney Chouest*
Owner	S & H Diving LLC, USA
Port of reg/flag	USA
Official number	680844
Classification	+A1 towing services, Ice Class C, AMS Class; ABS
Call sign	WCY 8548
Built (yard and date)	1985
Rebuilt (yard and date)	1988
Length overall	71.63 m
Breadth moulded	18.93 m
Working deck width	16.70 m
Max draught	4.70 m
Operational draught	4.09 m
Tonnage (grt)	2,022

PROPULSION

Main engine(s)	3 × EMD model 16-645-E7B, total 9,210 hp
Thrusters	DP controlling 3 × Azimuth Gill Jet units (2 aft, 1 forward); 1 × Brunvoll tunnel unit forward; total 3,525 hp
Propellers	Fp, right/steering in Kort nozzle
Speed (max)	14.5 kt
Speed (cruising)	10 kt
Endurance	50 – 75 days
Fuel capacity	192,840 gallons

Fuel consumption	Cruising: 1,500 gallons/hour; on DP: 62.5-85 gallons/hour
Electrical power	Generators: 4 × 300 kW 60 Hz, 2 × 500 kW
Fresh water capacity	12,062 gallons; water maker 3,000 gallons/day

BRIDGE NAVIGATION AIDS

Satellite	1 × Furuno DGPS
Radar	2 × Furuno 72NM; 1 × JRC-2254
Gyrocompass	2 × Anschutz Standard 20; 1 × Sperry SR-130
Speed log	EM
Echo-sounder	International Offshore/Data Marine depth sounder

COMMUNICATIONS

Inmarsat (type)	C-Band
MF/HF	Seacall GMDSS; Bridge office SEA-222
VHF	4 × Sailor
Cellular	1 × Petrom
Facsimile	1 × Furuno/D-FAX/FAX-208 A/N

SAFETY

Lifeboats	7 × 10 persons liferafts
Workboat/chase boat	Yes
Lifesaving equipment	Yes

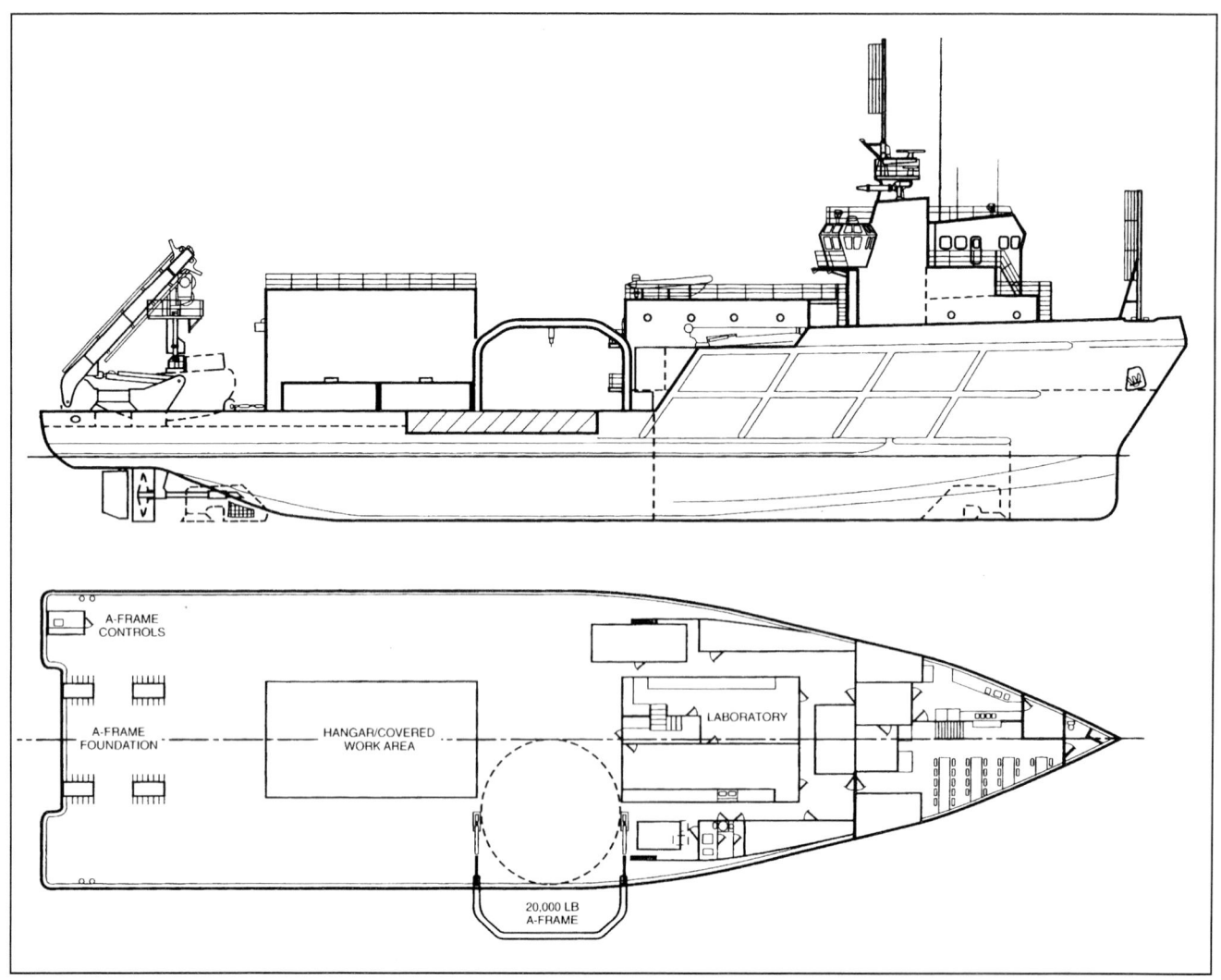

Seaway Legend   **2001**/0110552

DECK MACHINERY
Cranes	Aurora 30 t boom
A-frame(s)	Caley Hydraulics 18 SWL
Transducer well	1 for Sonardyne transponders; 1 for HiPap
Gate valve	2 for USBL acoustics

ACCOMMODATION
Charterers	Total accommodation for 54
Hospital	Yes

SURVEY SYSTEMS
Positioning	Nautronix ASK 4002 Class 2 Duplex system; 2 × Trimble NT200D DGPS receivers; 1 × Sonardyne acoustic tracking system; 1 × HiPap acoustic tracking system
Echo-sounder (single beam)	Simrad EA 500

NEW ENTRY

Seaway Legend

2001/0110551

Stolt Offshore Inc

Seaway Rover

GENERAL
Former names	*Ceanic Rover, Tidewater Illustrious, Seaboard Illustrious*
Owner	Ceanic Worldwide Ltd
Port of reg/flag	Panama/Panamanian
Official number	26841-00
Classification	Bureau Veritas
Call sign	HP 9705
Built (yard and date)	UK, 1966
Rebuilt (yard and date)	Bollinger, Texas City, USA, 1998
Length overall	71.32 m
Breadth moulded	12.03 m
Working deck width	Area 3,440 sq ft
Max draught	5.42 m
Operational draught	4.57 m
Tonnage (grt)	1,433

PROPULSION
Main engine(s)	Ruston 9ATCM, 2,160 bhp at 480 rpm
Thrusters	Nautronix ASK 4001 DP system controlling forward: 1 × Aquamaster retractable, 8.50 t thrust; aft 1 × Brunvoll tunnel, 5 t thrust
Propellers	1 × cp

Speed (max)	12.5 kt
Speed (cruising)	11.5 kt
Endurance	40 days
Fuel capacity	56,000 gallons (213 m³)
Fuel consumption	1,400 gallons/day (cruising); 1,100 gallons/day DP; 900 gallons/day (DP – mains idle)
Electrical power	AC units: 2 × Detroit Diesels, 320 kVA each; DC units: 2 × Paxman, 300 kW each; 1 × emergency generator 53 kW (220 V)
Fresh water capacity	124 t; water maker 80 gallons/hour

BRIDGE NAVIGATION AIDS
Satellite	2 × DGPS for DP (Racal and Decca)
Radar	2 × Decca (bridge navigator)
Gyrocompass	2
Speed log	2 × GPS
Echo-sounder	1 × Skipper ED 161

COMMUNICATIONS
Inmarsat (type)	C-band
MF/HF	1 × Sailor SSB 2160

VHF	2 × Sailor; 1 × Apelco	**Charterers**	Total accommodation for 35
Cellular	1 × Petrocom	**Crew**	12
Facsimile	1 × Panasonic UF-B15	**Hospital**	Yes

SAFETY

Lifeboats 1 × MOB boat (Narval SV 400H) for six persons; 4 × Viking liferafts for 80 persons

Lifesaving equipment 70 Duncan III lifevest units

DECK MACHINERY

Cranes Port: 1 × 10 t at 5 m or 2 t at 10 m; starboard: 1 × 2 t at 5 m

Winches 1 × deck unit

Transducer well Yes

Gate valve 1 × FWD hold

Moonpool(s) – size(s)/ function(s) 1 off port side, beside deck winch aft

ACCOMMODATION

SCIENTIFIC SPACES

Oceanographic wet lab Multipurpose, can be converted

Multipurpose dry lab 40 m^2

Chemistry lab Multipurpose, can be converted

SURVEY SYSTEMS

Positioning 1 × Nautronix ASK 4001 'simplex' DP system; 2 × gyro units; 1 × VRU; 2 × wind sensors; 1 × hydro-acoustic system; 2 × DGPS references; 1 × survey interface; 1 × Delpec UPS

NEW ENTRY

Seaway Rover **2001**/0110555

VESSEL OPERATORS —
OPERATORS OF GOVERNMENT HYDROGRAPHIC
AND OCEANOGRAPHIC RESEARCH VESSELS

ALGERIA

Hydrographic Services of Naval Forces
PO Box 81
Alger Bourse
Algeria

ARGENTINA

Consejo Nacional de Investigaciones Científicas y Técnicas (CONICET)
Avenida Rivadavia 1917
CP C1033AAJ Cdad de Buenos Aires
Argentina
Tel: (+54 11) 49 53 72 30/39
Web: http://www.conicet.gov.ar/

National Institute for Fisheries Research & Development
Paseo Victoria Ocampo 1
7600 Mar del Plata
Argentina
Tel: (+54 223) 486 25 86
Fax: (+54 223) 486 18 30
e-mail: postmaster@inidep.edu.
Web: http://www.inidep.edu

Naval Hydrographic Service
Avenida Montes de Oca 2124
Buenos Aires
Tel: (+54 11) 43 01 00 61
Fax: (+54 11) 43 01 38 83
e-mail: shn@rina.hidro.gov.ar
Web: http://www.hidro.gov.ar

AUSTRALIA

Australian Hydrographic Service
Royal Australian Navy
Locked Bag 8801
South Coast Mail Centre
New South Wales 2521
Australia
Tel: (+61 2) 42 21 85 00
Fax: (+61 2) 42 21 85 99
e-mail: marketing.hydro@navy.gov.au
Web: http://www.hydro.navy.gov.au

Australian Institute of Marine Science
PMB 3 Townsville MC
Townsville
Queensland 4810
Australia
Tel: (+61 7) 47 53 44 42
Fax: (+61 7) 47 21 38 60
Web: http://www.aims.gov.au

Australian Maritime College
PO Box 21
Beaconsfield
Tasmania 7270
Australia
Tel: (+61 3) 63 35 44 04
Fax: (+61 3) 63 83 47 66
e-mail: D.Ranmuthugala@fme.amc.edu.au
Web: http://www.amc.edu.au/fme

CSIRO Marine Research
GPO Box 1538
Hobart
Tasmania 7001
Australia
Tel: (+61 3) 62 32 52 22
Fax: (+61 3) 62 32 50 00
e-mail: reception@marine.csiro.au
Web: http://www.marine.csiro.au

BELGIUM

Antwerpse Zeehavendienst
Loodsgebouw
Tavernierkaai 3
B-2000 Antwerpen
Belgium
Tel: (+32 3) 222 08 11
Fax: (+32 3) 231 20 62

Coastal Hydrographic Service
Ministerie van de Vlaamse Gemeenschap
Emiel Jacqmainlan 156, bus 5
B-1000 Brussels
Belgium
Tel: (+32 59) 55 42 11
Fax: (+32 59) 51 00 41
e-mail: arnold.fremont@lin.vlaanderen.be

Management Unit of the North Sea Mathematical Models (MUMM)
3-23 Linieregimenstsplein
B-8400 Ostende
Belgium
Tel: (+32 59) 70 01 31
Fax: (+32 59) 70 49 35
e-mail: info@mumm.ac.be
Web: http://www.mumm.ac.be

BERMUDA

Bermuda Biological Station for Research Inc
17 Biological Lane
Ferry Reach
St George's GE 01
Bermuda
Tel: (+1 441) 297 18 80 ext 208
Fax: (+1 441) 297 18 39
Cell Phone: (+1 441) 235 27 20
e-mail: lblack@bbsr.edu
Web: http://www.bbsr.edu

BRAZIL

Directorate of Hydrography and Navigation
Ministry of the Navy
Rua Bãrao de Jaceguay S/N°
Ponta da Armação
2428-900 Niteroi – RJ
Brazil
Tel: (+55 21) 620 00 73
Fax: (+55 21) 620 00 73

University of São Paulo, Oceanographic Institute
191 Cidade Universitária
São Paulo CEP 05508-900
Brazil
Tel: (+55 11) 818 65 01
Fax: (+55 11) 210 30 92
e-mail: io@edu.usp.br
Web: http://www.io.usp.br

BULGARIA

Institute of Oceanology
PO Box 152
BG-9000 Varna
Bulgaria
Tel: (+359 52) 77 20 38
Fax: (+359 52) 77 42 56
e-mail: office@iobas.io-bas.bg

Navy Hydrographic Service
Bulgarian Navy
PO Box No 50
BG-9000 Varna
Bulgaria
Tel: (+359 52) 60 85 62
Fax: (+359 52) 60 32 59

CANADA

Canadian Hydrographic Service
Department of Fisheries and Oceans
615 Booth Street
Ottawa
Ontario K1A 0E6
Canada
Tel: (+1 613) 995 44 13
Fax: (+1 613) 996 90 53
Web: http://www.chs-shc.dfo-mpo.gc.ca/

CHILE

Chilean Antarctic Institute (INACH)
Luis Thayer Ojeda 814
Casilla 16521 Correo 9
Providencia, Santiago
Tel: (+56 2) 231 81 77
Fax: (+56 2) 232 04 40
e-mail: inach@inach.cl
Web: http://www.inach.cl

Hydrographic and Oceanographic Service (SHOA)
Chilean Navy
Casilla 324
Valparaiso
Chile
Tel: (+56 32) 28 26 97
Fax: (+56 32) 28 35 37
Web: http://www.shoa.cl

Instituto de Formento Pesquero – (IFOP)
Almirante Blanco 1067
Piso 4
Casilla 1287 8 V
Valparaiso
Chile
Tel: (+56 32) 23 41 43
Fax: (+56 32) 21 31 78

CHINA, PEOPLE'S REPUBLIC

China Ministry of Geology
Beijing
People's Republic of China

Dalian Fisheries Research Institute
267 Fujiazhuang
Dalian
Liaoning Province 116013
Tel: (+86 411) 27 27 60

East China Sea Branch SOA
630 Dongtang Road
Pudong, Shanghai 200137
People's Republic of China
Tel: (+86 21) 548 04 75
Fax: (+86 21) 548 04 75

Hydrographic Office
2/F Hydro Building
Government Dockyard
Stonecutters Island
Kowloon
Hong Kong
Tel: (+852) 25 04 02 69
Fax: (+852) 25 04 45 27
e-mail: hydro@mardep.gov.hk
Web: http://www.info.gov.hk/mardep/

Institute of Oceanology of the Chinese Academy of Sciences (IOCAS)
7 Nanhai Road
Qingdao
Shandong Province 266071
People's Republic of China
Tel: (+86 532) 27 08 82
Fax: (+86 532) 27 08 82

Maritime Safety Administration
Ministry of Communications
11 Jianguomennei Avenue
Beijing
People's Republic of China
Tel: (86 10) 529 28 01
Fax: (86 10) 529 22 45

North China Sea Branch (SOA)
22 Fusun Road
Qingdao
Shangdong Province 266033
People's Republic of China
Tel: (+86 532) 33 55 12
Fax: (+86 532) 33 55 13

Oceanic Research Centre, Ocean University of Qingdao
5 Yushan Road
Qingdao 266003
People's Republic of China
Tel: (+86 532) 203 27 93/28 12
Fax: (+86 532) 203 28 03
e-mail: shpcentre@public.qd.sd.cn

South China Sea Branch SOA
Xingang Zhounglu
Guangdong Province 510300
People's Republic of China
Tel: (+86 20) 45 12 46
Fax: (+86 20) 445 29 59

South China Sea Institute of Oceanology
164 Xingang Xilu
Guangzhou
Guangdong Province 510301
Tel: (+86 20) 45 13 35
Fax: (+86 20) 45 16 72

Yellow Sea Fisheries Research Institute (YSFRI)
19 Laiyang Road
Qingdao
Shandong Province 266003
People's Republic of China
Tel: (+86 532) 28 66 50
Fax: (+86 532) 27 07 02

COLOMBIA

Armada Nacional Bas Naval
Arc Bolivar
AA 982 Colombia
Cartagena 982
Colombia

Comunidad Cientifico Nacional Colombiana
Base Naval Apartado aereo 1744
Cartagena 982
Colombia

General Directorate for Shipping (DIMAR)
Colombian Navy
Direccion General Maritima
Calle 41 No 46-20 Oficina 304
Santafe de Bogota
Colombia
Tel: (+57 1) 222 02 47
Fax: (+57 1) 222 26 36
e-mail: ofasi@armada.mil.co
Web: http://www.dimar.mil.co

DENMARK

Danish Institute for Fisheries Research
PO Box 121
DK-9850 Hirtshals
Denmark
Tel: (+45) 98 94 44 48
Fax: (+45) 98 94 50 48
e-mail: dana@dfu.min.dk
Web: http://www.dfu.min.dk

National Environmental Research Institute (NERI)
Frederiksborgvej 399
DK-4000 Roskilde
Denmark
Tel: (+45) 46 30 12 00
Fax:(+45) 46 30 11 14
e-mail: dmu@dmu.dk
Web: http://www.dmu.dk

ECUADOR

Oceanographic Institute of the Navy (INOCAR)
Proantec
PO Box 5940
Guayaquil
Ecuador
e-mail: inocar@inocar.mil.ec
Web: http://www.inocar.mil.ec

ESTONIA

Estonian Marine Institute
University of Tartu
Viljandi Mnt 18B
EE-11216 Tallinn
Estonia
Tel: (+372 2) 628 15 69
Fax: (+372 2) 628 15 63
Web: http://www.sea.ee

Estonian National Maritime Board
Lighthouse and Hydrographic Department
48 Lasnamae Street
EE-00114 Tallinn
Estonia
Tel: (+372 2) 633 91 60
Fax: (+372 2) 633 91 66
e-mail: eva@enmb.ee
Web: http://www.enmb.ee

Institute of Ecology and Marine Research
Paldiski Road 1
EE-10637 Tallinn
Estonia
Tel: (+372 2) 142 45 16 34
Fax: (+372 2) 142 45 37 48

FINLAND

Finnish Institute of Marine Research
PO Box 33
FIN-00931 Helsinki
Finland
Tel: (+358 9) 61 39 41
Fax: (+358 9) 61 39 44 94
e-mail: info@fimr.fi
Web: http://www2.fimr.fi

Finnish Maritime Administration
Hydrography and Waterways Department
Box 171
FIN-00181 Helsinki
Finland
Tel: (+358) 204 48 40
Fax: (+358) 204 48 45 55
Web: http://www.fma.fi

Saimaa Research
University of Joensuu
Box 111
FIN-80101 Joensuu
Finland
Tel: (+358 13) 25 11 11
Fax: (+358 13) 251 34 49
e-mail: saimaa@joensuu.fi

South Savo Regional Environment Centre
Jääkärinkatu 14
FIN-50100 Mikkeli
Finland
Tel: (+358 15) 74 41
Fax: (+358 15) 744 45 09

FRANCE

Institut de Recherche pour le Développement (IRD)
213 rue La Fayette
F-75480 Paris Cedex 10
France
Tel: (+33 1) 48 03 77 77
Fax: (+33 1) 48 03 08 29
Web: http://www.ird.fr

Institut Français de Recherche pour l'exploitation de la mer (IFREMER)
Technopolis 40
155 rue Jean-Jacques Rousseau
F-92138 Issy-les-Moulineaux
France
Tel: (+33 1) 46 48 21 00
Fax: (+33 1) 46 48 22 48
Web: http://www.ifremer.fr/

Institut Français pour la Recherche et la Technologie Polaires (IFRTP)
Technopôle de Brest-Iroise
BP 75
F-29280 Plouzané
France
Tel: (+33 2) 98 05 65 00
Fax: (+33 2) 98 05 65 55
Web: http://www.ifremer.fr/ifrtp/

Naval Hydrographic and Oceanographic Service (SHOM)
3 avenue Octave Gerard – Paris 7ème
BP 5
F-00307 Armées
France
Tel: (+33 1) 44 38 41 16
Fax: (+33 1) 40 65 99 98
Web: http://www.shom.fr

GERMANY

Alfred Wegener Institute Foundation for Polar and Marine Research (AWI)
Postbox 12 0161
D-27515 Bremerhaven
Tel: (+49 471) 483 10
Fax: (+49 471) 48 31 11 49
Web: http://www.awi-bremerhaven.de

BMS Baltic Marine Service GmbH
Marieneher Strasse 11
D-18069 Rostock
Germany
Tel: (+49 381) 811 25 85
Fax: (+49 381) 489 80 17
Web: http://www.rf-bremen.com/bms

Bundesamtes fur Seeschiffahrt und Hydrographie (BSH)
Bernhard-Nocht-Strasse 78
Postfach 30 12 20
D-20305 Hamburg
Germany
Tel: (+49 40) 31 90-0
Fax: (+49 40) 31 90 50 00
Web: http://www.bsh.de

Federal Agency for Agriculture and Food (BLE)
Palmaille 9
D-22767 Hamburg
Germany
Tel: (+49 40) 38 90 50
Fax: (+49 40) 38 90 51 28

GKSS Research Centre
Max-Planck-Strasse
D-21502 Geesthacht
Germany
Tel: (+49 4152) 87-0
e-mail: presse@gkss.de
Web: http://www.gkss.de

Institute for Baltic Sea Research Warnemünde (IOW)
Seestrasse 15
D-18112 Rostock
Tel: (+49 381) 519 70
Fax: (+49 381) 51 97 48 17
Web: http://www.io-warnemuende.de/

Institut für Meereskunde
University of Kiel
Düsternbrooker Weg 20
D-24105 Kiel
Germany
Tel: (+49 431) 597 39 02
Fax: (+49 431) 56 58 76
e-mail: gkortum@ifm.uni-kiel.de
ifm@ifm.uni-kiel.de

K & K Nordseeforschungsschiff – Bereederung GmbH
Kopernikusweg 25
D-26389 Wilhelmshaven
Tel: (+49 4421) 99 81 47
Fax: (+49 4421) 99 81 48

RF Reedereigemeinschaft Forschungsschiffahrt GmbH
Haferwende 3
D-28357 Bremen
Germany
Tel: (+49 421) 20 76 60
Fax: (+49 421) 207 66 70
e-mail: rf@rf-gmbh.de
Web: http://www.rf-bremen.com

University of Hamburg, Centre for Marine and Climate Research (ZMK)
Bundesstrasse 55
D-20146 Hamburg
Germany
Tel: (+49 40) 428 38 45 23/5
Fax: (+49 40) 428 38 52 35
Web: http://www.uni-hamburg.de/Wiss/SE/ZMK/

GREECE

Hellenic Navy Hydrographic Service
TGN 1040
Athens
Greece
Tel: (+30 1) 644 29 66
Fax: (+30 1) 652 02 24
e-mail: info@hnhs.gr
Web: http://www.hnhs.gr

Institute of Marine Biology of Crete (IMBC)
PO Box 2214
GR-71003 Iraklio
Crete
Greece
Tel: (+30 81) 34 68 60
Fax: (+30 81) 24 18 82
e-mail: imbc@imbc.gr
Web: http://www.imbc.gr

National Centre for Marine Research
Agios Kosmos
Hellinikon
GR-16604 Athens
Greece
Tel: (+30 1) 982 02 14
Fax: (+30 1) 983 30 95
Web: http://www.ncmr.gr

ICELAND

Icelandic Hydrographic Service
Landhelgisgæslan
Seljavegi 32
IS-101 Reykjavík
Iceland
Tel: (+354) 511 22 22
Fax: (+354) 511 22 44
e-mail: lhg@lhg.is
Web: http://www.igh.is

Marine Research Institute
Skulagata 4
PO Box 1390
IS-121 Reykjavik
Iceland
Tel: (+354) 552 02 40,
Fax: (+354) 562 37 90
e-mail: librarian@hafro.is
Web: http://www.hafro.is

INDIA

Department of Ocean Development
Block No 9 & 12 CGO Complex
Lodhi Road
New Delhi 110003
Fax: (+91 11) 436 03 36
e-mail: ocean@dod.delhi.nic.in
Web: http://www.oceandev.gov.in

Fishery Survey of India
Botawala Chambers
PM Road
Mumbai 400 001
India
Tel: (+91 22) 261 71 44/5
Fax: (+91 22) 261 71 01

National Institute of Oceanography
Dona Paula,
Goa 403 004
India
Fax: (+91 832) 22 33 40
e-mail: ocean@darya.nio.org
Web: http://www.nio.org/

National Institute of Ocean Technology
Indian Institute of Technology Madras
Velacherry-Tambaram Main Road
Narayanapuram
Chennai, Tamil Nadu
India 601 302
Tel: (+91 44) 246 00 63
Fax: (+91 44) 246 06 45
e-mail: niot@niot.ernet.in
Web: http://www.niot.ernet.in

Naval Hydrographic Office
Post Office Box 75
Dehra Dun 248001 (UP)
India
Tel: (+91 135) 65 48 73
Fax: (+91 135) 65 83 73
e-mail: nho@nde.vsni.net.in

Shipping Corporation of India
Shipping House
245 Madam Cama Road
Mumbai – 400 021
Tel: (+91 22) 202 66 66
Fax: (+91 22) 202 69 05
Web: http://www.shipindia.com

INDONESIA

Hydro-Oceanographic Service (KADISHIDROS)
Jalan Pantai Kuta V No 1
Jakarta 14430
Indonesia
Tel: (+62) 21 68 48 09
Fax: (+62) 68 48 19; 68 48 09
Web: http://www.dephan.go.id/homeal/hidros.html

INTERNATIONAL

NATO SACLANT Undersea Research Centre
Viale San Bartolomeo 400
I-19138 La Spezia
Italy
Tel: (+39 0187) 52 71
Fax: (+39 0187) 52 77 00
Web: http://www.saclantc.nato.int

IRELAND

Marine Institute
80 Harcourt Street
Dublin 2
Ireland
Tel: (+353 1) 476 65 00
Fax: (+353 1) 478 49 88
e-mail: institute.mail@marine.ie
Web: http://www.marine.ie

ISRAEL

Red Sea Surveyor Ltd
PO Box 1854
IL-88104 Eilat
Israel
Tel: (+972 7) 633 66 78
Fax: (+972 7) 633 66 79
e-mail: Seasurv@eilatcity.co.il
Web: http://www.sea-surveyor.co.il

ITALY

Hydrographic Institute of the Navy
Passo dell'Osservatorio 4,
I-16134 Genova
Italy
Tel: (+39 010) 102 44 31
Fax: (+39 010) 10 26 14 00
Web: http://www.marina.difesa.it/idro

Institute of Marine Biology
Castello 1364/a
I-30122 Venice
Italy
Tel: (+39 041) 240 47 11
Fax: (+39 041) 520 41 26
e-mail: biomar@ibm.ve.cnr.it
Web: http://www.ibm.ve.cnr.it

Istituto Nazionale di Oceanografia e di Geofisica Sperimentale (OGS)
Borgo Grotta Gigante 42/C
I-34016 Sgonico
Trieste
Italy
Tel: (+39 040) 214 01
Fax: (+39 040) 32 73 07
e-mail: Mailbox@ogs.trieste.it
Web: http://www.ogs.trieste.it

So Pro Mar SPA
Via Della Pesca N 11
I-00054 Fiumicino (Rome)
Italy
Tel: (+39 06) 650 71 19
Fax: (+39 06) 650 77 49

JAPAN

Fisheries Agency
1-2-1 Kasumigaseki
Chiyoda-ku
Tokyo 100-8907
Tel: (+81 3) 35 02 81 11
Fax: (+81 3) 35 02 82 20

Hydrographic Department
Japan Marine Safety Agency
5-3-1 Tsukiji
Chuo-ku
Tokyo 104-0045
Japan
Tel: (+81 3) 35 41 36 85
Fax: (+81 3) 35 42 71 74
e-mail: ico@cue.jhd.go.jp
Web: http://www.jhd.go.jp

Japan Marine Science and Technology Center (JAMSTEC)
Natsushima-cho 2-15
Yokosuka-shi
Kanagawa Prefecture 237-0061
Japan
e-mail: support@jamstec.go.jp
Web: http://www.jamstec.go.jp

Tokai University
School of Maritime Science and Technology
3-20-1 Orido
Shimizu
Shizuoka 424-8610
Japan
Tel: (+81 543) 34 04 11
Fax: (+81 543) 34 99 82

KOREA, SOUTH

Korea Institute of Geology, Mining & Materials
30, Kajung Dong
Yusug-gu
Taejon 305-350
Korea, South
Tel: (+82 42) 868 31 14
Fax: (+82 42) 861 97 20
e-mail: wmaster@kigam.re.kr
Web: http://www.kigam.re.kr

Korea Ocean Research & Development Institute
Ansan
PO Box
South Korea
Tel: (+82 31) 400 60 00
Fax: (+82 31) 408 58 20
e-mail: hjkang@kordi.re.kr
Web: http://www.kordi.re.kr

National Fisheries Research & Development Institute
408-1 Sirang-ri
Gijang-eup, Gijang-gun
Busan 619-902,
Korea, South
Tel: (+82 51) 720 21 14
Fax: (+82 51) 720 20 54
Web: http://www.nfrda.re.kr

National Oceanographic Research Institute
1-17 7ga Hang-dong
Jung-gu
Incheon
Korea, South
Tel: (+82 32) 885 38 27
Fax: (+82 32) 885 38 29
Web: http://www.nori.go.kr

Office of Hydrographic Affairs
1-17 7-ga Hang-dong
Chung-gu
Inchon 400-037
South Korea
Tel: (+82 32) 885 38 21
Fax: (+82 32) 885 38 29

LIBYA

Marine Biological Research Centre
PO Box 30830
Tajura
Tripoli
Libya
Tel: (+218 21) 369 00 03
Fax: (+218 21) 369 00 02

LITHUANIA

Ministry of Environmental Protection
Centre of Marine Research
Taikos pr 26
5802 Klaipeda
Lithuania
Tel: (+370 6) 41 04 50
Fax: (+370 6) 41 04 60
e-mail: CMR@klaipeda.omnitel.net
Web: http://www1.omnitel.net/juriniai_tyrimai

MALAYSIA

Hydrographic Directorate
Royal Malaysian Navy
Ministry of Defence
Jalan Padang Tembak
50634 Kuala Lumpur
Malaysia
Tel: (+60 3) 960 30 00
Fax: (+60 3) 298 79 72
Web: http://maf.mod.gov.my

University College Terengganu
21030 Kuala Terengganu
Tel: (+60) 96 69 64 11
Fax: (+60) 96 69 64 41
Web: http://www.uct.edu.my/

MEXICO

General Directorate of Naval Oceanography
Eje 2 Oriente Tramo H Escuela Naval Militar No 861
Edificio "B" 1/er Nivel
Col Los Cipreses Delegacion Coyoacan
CP 04830 Mexico DF
Tel: (+52 684) 81 88 12 02
Fax: (+52 684) 81 88 12 05

Institute of Marine and Limnological Sciences
Circuito Exterior s/n
Ciudad Universitaria
CP 04510
Mexico City
Apartado postal 70-305
Tel: (+52 5) 56 22 57 70
Fax: (+52 5) 56 16 27 45
Web: http://www.icmyl.unam.mx/

MOROCCO

Hydrographic and Oceanographic Service of the Royal Navy (SHOMAR)
Etat Major de la Marine Royal
BP 1077 Rabat
Morocco
Tel: (+212 7) 70 47 90
Fax: (+212 7) 76 76 96

MOZAMBIQUE

National Institute of Hydrography and Navigation (INAHINA)
Av Karl Marx 153
Porta 901
Maputo
Mozambique
Tel: (+258 1) 43 01 86/8
Fax: (+258 1) 43 01 85
e-mail: Sitoe@inahina.uem.mz

MYANMAR

Naval Hydrographic Office
Myanmar Navy
55/61 Strand Road
Yangon
Myanmar
Tel: (+95 1) 774 37

NETHERLANDS

Hydrographic Service
PO Box 90704
2509 LS The Hague
Netherlands
Tel: (+31 70) 316 28 00
Fax: (+31 70) 316 28 43
e-mail: info@hydro.nl
Web: http://www.hydro.nl

Netherlands Institute for Fisheries Research (RIVO)
Postbox 68
NL-1970 AB
Ijmuiden
Netherlands
Tel: (+31 255) 56 46 46
Fax: (+31 255) 56 46 44
e-mail: postmaster@rivo.wag-ur.nl
Web: http://www.rivo.wag-ur.nl

Netherlands Institute for Sea Research (NIOZ)
PO Box 59
NL-1790 AB Den Burg
Texel
Tel: (+31 222) 36 93 00
Fax: (+31 222) 31 96 74
Web: http://www.nioz.nl

Netherlands Institute of Ecology (NIOO)
Centre for Estuarine and Coastal Ecology
PO Box 140
NL-4400 AC Yerseke
Netherlands
Tel: (+31 294) 23 93 03
Fax: (+31 294) 23 20 78
e-mail: Rienks@nioo.knaw.nl
Web: http://www.nioo.knaw.nl/

Rijkswaterstaat North Sea Directorate
Koopmanstraat 1
PO Box 5807
NL-2280 HV Rijswijk
Netherlands
Tel: (+31 70) 336 66 00
Fax: (+31 70) 390 06 91
Web: http://www.waterland.net/dnz/

NEW ZEALAND

Ministry of Agriculture & Fisheries
PO Box 297
Wellington
New Zealand
Tel: (+64 4) 386 10 29

National Institute of Water and Atmospheric Research (NIWA) Vessel Management Ltd
269 Khyber Pass Road
Newmarket
Auckland
Tel: (+64 4) 386 05 50
Fax: (+64 4) 386 05 55
Web: http://www.niwa.cri.nz

Royal New Zealand Navy
Hydrographic Business Unit
19 Byron Street
Takapuna
Auckland
New Zealand
Tel: (+64 9) 486 79 00
Fax: (+64 9) 486 35 60
Web: http://www.navyhydro.co.nz

NIGERIA

Nigerian Naval Hydrographic Office
No 5 Point Road
Apapa
Lagos
Nigeria
Tel: (+234 1) 87 63 25
Fax: (+234 1) 87 57 15

NORWAY

Dept of Fisheries and Marine Biology
University of Bergen
Thormøhlensgt 55
N-5020 Bergen
Norway
Tel: (+47) 55 58 44 00
Fax: (+47) 55 58 44 50
Web: http://www.ifm.uib.no/

Institute of Marine Research
Postboks 1870
Nordnes
N-5817 Bergen
Norway
Tel: (+47) 55 23 85 00
Fax: (+47) 55 23 85 31
e-mail: havforskningsinstituttet@imr.no
Web: http://www.imr.no

Norwegian Hydrographic Service
Lervigveien 36
Boks 60
N-4001 Stavanger
Norway
Tel: (+47) 51 56 34 11
Fax: (+47) 51 56 37 40
e-mail: official@uredd.sjo.statkart.no
Web: http://www.statkart.no

University of Tromsø
School of Fisheries
N-9037 Tromsø
Tel: (+47 77) 64 60 00
Web: http://www.nfh.uit.no/

PAKISTAN

Hydrographic Department
Naval Headquarters
Islamabad
Pakistan
Tel: (+92 51) 82 00 32 56
Fax: (+92 51) 82 88 97

PANAMA

Smithsonian Tropical Research Institute
Unit 0948
APO AA 34002-0948
Tel: (+1 507) 212 87 18
Fax: (+1 507) 212 87 91

PERU

Hydrographic and Navigation Directorate of the Navy
Av Gamarra No 500
Chucuito
Callao
Peru
Tel: (+51 1) 429 60 19
Fax: (+51 1) 465 29 95
e-mail: dihidronav@dhn.mil.pe
Web: http://www.hidronav.marina.mil.pe

Marine Institute of Peru (IMARPE)
Lima
Web: http://www.imarpe.gob.pe

PHILIPPINES

Bureau of Fisheries and Aquatic Resources (BFAR)
Fishery Resources Research Division
Arcadia Building
860 Quezon Avenue
Quezon City
Philippines

National Mapping and Resource Information Authority (NAMRIA)
Lawton Avenue
Fort Andres Bonifacio 1201
Makati City
Philippines
Tel: (+63 2) 810 54 68
e-mail: oss@namria.gov.ph
Web: http://www.psdn.org.ph/namria/

POLAND

Hydrographic Office of the Polish Navy
PL-81-912
Gdynia 12
Tel: (+48 58) 626 36 80
Fax: (+48 58) 626 62 03

Institute of Oceanology
Polish Academy of Sciences
Powstancow Warszawy 55
PL-81-712 Sopot
PO Box 68
Tel: (+48 58) 551 72 81
Fax: (+48 58) 551 21 30
e-mail: office@iopan.gda.pl
Web: http://www.iopan.gda.pl/

Sea Fisheries Institute
ul. Kołłątaja 1
PL-81-332
Gdynia
Tel: (+48 58) 620 17 28
Fax: (+48 58) 620 28 31
e-mail: pikom@miryb.mir.gdynia.pl
Web: http://www.mir.gdynia.pl/

Szef Biura Hydrograficznego Marynarki Wojennej
PL-81-812 Gdynia 12
Poland
Tel: (+48 58) 20 74 72

PORTUGAL

Hydrographic Institute
Rua das Trinas 49
P-1296 Lisbon Codex
Portugal
Tel: (+351 21) 391 40 00
Fax: (+351 21) 391 41 98
e-mail: mail@hidrografico.pt
Web: http://www.hidrografico.pt/

Instituto de Investigacção das Pescas e do Mar (IPIMAR)
Web: http://www.ipimar.pt

ROMANIA

Maritime Hydrographic Directorate
Code 8700
Constanta
Romania
Tel: (+40 41) 65 10 40

National Institute for Marine Research & Development "Grigore Antipa"
Mamaia 300
RO-8700 Constanta 3
Romania
Tel: (+40 41) 54 32 88
Fax: (+40 41) 83 12 74
e-mail: abologa@alpha.rmri.ro

RUSSIAN FEDERATION

Department of Navigation and Oceanography
8, 11 Liniya, B-34
St Petersburg 199034
Russia
Tel: (+7 812) 213 81 09
Fax: (+7 812) 213 75 48

Polar Marine Geosurvey Expedition (PMGE)
Pobedy Street 24
Lomonosov
189510
St Petersburg
Tel: (+7 812) 422 12 82
Fax: (+7 812) 423 19 00
e-mail: info@pmge.ru
Web: http://www.pmge.ru

Sea Technology Institute
St Petersburg
199397 Russia
Moika Embankment, 5
Tel: (+7 812) 312 77 75
Fax: (+7 812) 315 18 30
e-mail: sti@linco.spb.su
Web: http://users.nevalink.ru/linco

Yuzhmogeologiya
20 Krymskaya Street
Gelendzhik 353470
Russia
Tel: (+7 86141) 243 31
Fax: (+7 86141) 243 34
e-mail: Info@ymg.sea.ru

SAUDI ARABIA

Military Survey Department
Hydrographic Section
PO Box 8652
Riyadh 11492
Saudi Arabia
Fax: (+966 1) 454 41 92

SOUTH AFRICA

Hydrographic Office
South African Navy
Private Bag X1
Tokai
7966 Cape Town
Tel: (+27 21) 787 24 08
Fax: (+27 21) 787 22 28
e-mail: hydrosan@iafrica.com

Marine and Coastal Management
Dept of Environmental Affairs and Tourism
PO Box X2
Roggebaai 8012
South Africa
Tel: (+27 21) 402 31 06
Fax (+27 21) 21 74 06
e-mail: jcsmith@sfri.wcape.gov.za
Web: http://www.environment.gov.za/mcm

SPAIN

Canary Island Institute of Marine Sciences (ICCM)
Apartado 56
E-35200 Telde
Las Palmas
Canary Islands
Spain
Tel: (+34 28) 13 29 04
Fax: (+34 28) 13 29 08
Web: http://www.iccm.rcanaria.es

Institute of Marine Sciences (CMIMA)
Passeig Maritim de la Barceloneta, 37-49
E-08003 Barcelona
Spain
Tel: (+34 93) 230 95 00
Fax: (+34 93) 230 95 55
e-mail: ugbo-inf@icm.csic.es
Web: http://www.icm.csic.es

Instituto Español de Oceanografía (IEO)
Avenida de Brasil 31
E-28020 Madrid
Spain
Tel: (+34 91) 597 44 43
Fax: (+34 91) 597 47 70
e-mail: ieo@md.ieo.es
Web: http://www.ieo.es

Navy Hydrographic Institute
Tolosa Latour N 1
E-11007 Cadiz
Spain
Tel: (+34 956) 59 94 14
Fax: (+34 956) 27 53 58

SWEDEN

Institute of Marine Research
National Board of Fisheries
PO Box 423
SE-401 26 Gothenburg
Sweden
Tel: (+46 31) 743 03 00
Fax: (+46 31) 743 04 44
Web: http://www.fiskeriverket.se

Kristineberg Marine Research Station (KMRS)
SE-450 34 Fiskebackskill
Sweden
Tel: (+46 523) 185 00
Fax: (+46 523) 185 02
e-mail: Kmf@kmf.gu.se
Web: http://www.kmf.gu.se

Swedish Maritime Administration
Hydrographic Office
SE-601 78 Norrköping
Sweden
Tel: (+46 11) 19 11 19
Fax: (+46 11) 13 39 03
e-mail: sjokarte@sjofartsverket.se
Web: http://www.sjofartsverket.se/

THAILAND

Department of Fisheries
Kasetklang
Chatuchak
Bangkok 10900
Thailand
Tel: (+66 2) 562 06 00 15
Fax: (+66 2) 940 62 03
e-mail: webmaster@fisheries.go.th
Web: http://www.fisheries.go.th

Hydrographic Department
Royal Thai Navy
Aroon-amarin Road
Bangkok 10600
Thailand
Tel: (+66 2) 466 66 87
Fax: (+66 2) 472 12 86
Web: http://www.navy.mi.th/hydro

Southeast Asian Fisheries Development Centre (SEAFDEC)
PO Box 97 Phrasamutchedi
Samutprakan 10290
Thailand
Tel: (+66 2) 425 80 40/5
Fax: (+66 2) 425 85 61
e-mail: sutee@seafdec.org
Web: http://www.seafdec.org

TUNISIA

Hydrographic and Oceanographic Service
Department of Defence
Base Navale Principale de Bizerte
7011 La Pêcherie
Bizerte
Tunisia

TURKEY

Department of Navigation, Hydrography and Oceanography
Dairesi Baskanligi
TR-81647 Çubuklu
Istanbul
Turkey
Tel: (+90 216) 322 25 80
Fax: (+90 216) 331 05 25
e-mail: info@shodb.gov.tr
Web: http://www.shodb.gov.tr/

General Directorate of Mineral Research & Exploration (MTA)
TR-06520 Ankara
Turkey
Tel: (+90 312) 287 34 30
Fax: (+90 312) 287 91 88
Web: http://www.mta.gov.tr/

Middle East Technical University (METU)
Institute of Marine Sciences (IMS)
PO Box 28
TR-33731 Erdemli-Icel
Turkey
Tel: (+90 324) 521 3434
Fax: (+90 324) 521 23 27
e-mail: sukru@ims.metu.edu.tr
Web: http://www.ims.metu.edu.tr

Turkish Navy
Dept of Navigation, Hydrography and Oceanography
TR-81647 Çubuklu
Istanbul
Turkey
Tel: (+90 216) 322 25 80
Fax: (+90 216) 331 05 25
e-mail: director@shodb.mil.tr
Web: http://www.shodb.mil.tr

University of Istanbul, Institute of Marine Sciences & Management
Muskule Sokak
TR-34470 Instanbul
Turkey
e-mail: cemga@istanbul.edu.tr
Web: http://www.istanbul.edu.tr

UKRAINE

Marine Hydrophysical Institute
2 Kapitanskaya Str
Crimea 335000
Ukraine
Web: http://www.mhi.iuf.net

State Hydrographic Service of Ukraine
Ministry of Transport
28 Predslavinska Street
Kiev 252006
Tel: (+38 44) 252 94 23
Fax: (+38 44) 252 82 00

Underwater Scientific Research Center
1/46 Kostomarovskaja Str
Sevastopol
Crimea 335000
Ukraine

UNITED KINGDOM

British Antarctic Survey
High Cross
Madingley Road
Cambridge
CB3 0ET
United Kingdom
Tel: (+44 1223) 22 14 00
Fax: (+44 1223) 36 26 16
e-mail: information@bas.ac.uk
Web: http://www.antarctica.ac.uk

Centre for Environment, Fisheries & Aquaculture Science (CEFAS)
Lowestoft Laboratory
Pakefield Road
Lowestoft
Suffolk NR33 0HT
United Kingdom
Tel: (+44 1502) 56 22 44
Fax: (+44 1502) 51 38 65
Web: http://www.cefas.co.uk

Department of Agriculture for Northern Ireland
Agricultural and Environmental Science Division
Aquatic Systems Group
Newforge Lane
Belfast BT9 5PX
UK
Tel: (+44 28) 90 25 55 13
Fax: (+44 28) 90 38 22 44
e-mail: willie.mccurdy@dardni.gov.uk
Web: http://www.dardni.gov.uk

Dove Marine Laboratory
University of Newcastle
Tel: (+44 191) 252 48 50
Fax: (+44 191) 252 10 54
e-mail: c.l.j.frid@ncl.ac.uk
Web: http://www.ncl.ac.uk/mscmweb

Dunstaffnage Marine Laboratory
PO Box 3
Oban
Argyll
PA34 4AD
UK
Tel: (+44 1631) 55 90 00
Fax: (+44 1631) 55 90 01
e-mail: mail@dml.ac.uk
Web: http://www.sams.ac.uk

Marine Laboratory Aberdeen
Fisheries Research Services
PO Box 101
Victoria Road
Aberdeen
AB11 9DB
UK
Tel: (+44 1224) 87 65 44
Fax: (+44 1224) 29 55 11
e-mail: registry@marlab.ac.uk
Web: http://www.marlab.ac.uk/

Marr Vessel Management
Marr Building
St Andrews Dock
Hull
East Yorkshire HU3 4PN
UK
Tel: (+44 1482) 32 78 73
Fax: (+44 1482) 32 06 09
e-mail: nmvmops@j-marr.co.uk
Web: http://www.j-marr.co.uk

Plymouth Marine Laboratory
Prospect Place
West Hoe
Plymouth
PL1 3DH
United Kingdom
Tel: (+44 1752) 63 31 00
Fax: (+44 1752) 63 31 01
Web: http://www.pml.ac.uk

Port Erin Marine Laboratory
Port Erin
Isle of Man
IM9 6JA
United Kingdom
Tel: (+44 1624) 83 10 00
Fax: (+44 1624) 83 10 01
e-mail: peml@liv.ac.uk
Web: http://www.liv.ac.uk/peml

QinetiQ
Air Systems
Farnborough
Hampshire
GU 14 0LX
United Kingdom
Tel: (+44 1252) 39 39 16
Fax: (+44 1252) 39 33 10

RN Surveying Service
Shackleton Building
MO56
Morice Yard
HM Naval Base
Devonport
Plymouth PL1 4SL
UK

School of Ocean and Earth Science
University of Southampton
Southampton Oceanography Centre
European Way
Southampton
SO14 3ZH
United Kingdom
Tel: (+44 23 80) 59 61 72
Fax: (+44 23 80) 59 68 55

School of Ocean Sciences
University of Wales, Bangor
Menai Bridge
Anglesey
LL59 5EY
United Kingdom
Tel: (+44 1248) 38 28 46
Fax: (+44 1248) 71 63 67
Web: http://www.sos.bangor.ac.uk

Southampton Oceanography Centre
European Way
Empress Dock
Southampton
Hampshire
SO14 3ZH
United Kingdom
Tel: (+44 23 85) 59 62 91
Fax: (+44 23 85) 59 62 95
e-mail: paul.stone@soc.soton.ac.uk
Web: www.soc.soton.ac.uk/RVS/rvsmarine/

University Marine Biological Station
Millport
Isle of Cumbrae
KA28 0EG
United Kingdom
Tel: (+44 1475) 53 05 81/2
Fax: (+44 1475) 53 06 01
Web: http://www.gla.ac.uk/centres/marinestation/

VT Ocean Sciences
223 Southampton Road
Portsmouth
PO6 4QA
UK
Tel: (+44 2392) 35 40 00
Fax: (+44 2392) 35 40 01
e-mail: Princemadog@vtis.com
Web: http://www.rvprincemadog.com

UNITED STATES OF AMERICA

California Department of Fish and Game
San Pedro/Long Beach
United States of America
Tel: (+1 562) 590 51 17
Cape Fear Community College
Wilmington
North Carolina 28401-3393
United States of America
Tel: (+1 910) 251 69 41
Fax: (+1 910) 763 22 79
e-mail: sbeuth@capefear.cc.nc.us

Center for Environmental Science
University of Maryland
Chesapeake Biology Laboratory
PO Box 38
Solomons
Maryland
20688-0038
United States of America
Tel: (+1 410) 326 73 58
Fax: (+1 410) 326 73 42
e-mail: rfo@cbl.umces.edu

Center for Great Lakes and Aquatic Science
University of Michigan
2200 Bonisteel Blvd
Ann Arbor
Michigan 48109
United States of America
Tel: (+1 313) 763 53 93
Fax: (+1 313) 647 27 48
e-mail: Lgoad@umich.edu
Web: http://www.umich.edu

Center for Marine Science Research
University of North Carolina at Wilmington
7205 Wrightsville Avenue
Wilmington
North Carolina 28403
United States of America
Tel: (+1 910) 256 37 21
Fax: (+1 910) 256 88 56
e-mail: bocconcellia@uncwil.edu
Web: http://www.uncwil.edu/cmsr

College of Marine Studies, University of Delaware
700 Pilottown Road
Lewes
Delaware 19958
United States of America
Tel: (+1 302) 645 43 41
Fax: (+1 302) 645 40 06
e-mail: hawkins@udel.edu
Web: http://www.ocean.udel.edu

College of Oceanic and Atmospheric Sciences
Oregon State University
104 Ocean Administration Building
Corvallis
Oregon 97331-5503
United States of America
Tel: (+1 541) 737 35 04
Fax: (+1 541) 737 20 64
e-mail: jonesf@ucs.orst.edu
Web: http://www.oce.orst.edu

College of William and Mary
Virginia Institute of Marine Science
Gloucester Point
Virginia 23062
Tel: (+1 804) 642 70 54
Fax: (+1 804) 642 71 95
e-mail: pongon@vims.edu

Duke University Marine Laboratory
135 Duke Marine Lab Road
Beaufort
North Carolina 28516-9721
United States of America
Tel: (+1 252) 504 75 80
Fax: (+1 252) 504 75 61
e-mail: quentin@duke.edu
Web: http://www.env.duke.edu

Florida Atlantic University
SeaTech Facility
101 N Beach Road
Dania Beach
Florida 33004
Tel: (+1 954) 924 70 00
Fax: (+1 954) 924 70 07
e-mail: rfranks@oe.fau.edu
Web: http://www.oe.fau.edu

Florida Institute of Oceanography
830 First Street South
St Petersburg
Florida 33701
United States of America
Tel: (+1 727) 553 11 00
Fax: (+1 727) 553 11 09
Web: http://www.marine.usf.edu

Great Lakes National Program Office
Environmental Protection Agency
77 W Jackson Blvd
Chicago
Illinois 60604-3590
United States of America
Tel: (+1 312) 353 13 73
Fax: (+1 312) 353 20 18
Web: http://www.epa.gov

Great Lakes Water Institute
University of Wisconsin-Milwaukee
600 East Greenfield Avenue
Milwaukee
Wisconsin 53204
United States of America
Tel: (+1 414) 382 17 00
Fax: (+1 414) 382 17 05
e-mail: jorchard@uwm.edu
Web: http://www.uwm.edu

Gulf Coast Research Laboratory
USM Institute of Marine Sciences
PO Box 7000
Ocean Springs
Mississippi 39566-7000
United States of America
Tel: (+1 228) 872 42 56
e-mail: dale.fremin@usm.edu
Web: http://www.usm.edu

Harbor Branch Oceanographic Institution
5600 US 1 North
Ft Pierce
Florida 34946
United States of America
Tel: (+1 561) 465 24 00 ext 262/271
Fax: (+1 561) 465 21 16
e-mail: taskew@hboi.edu
Web: http://www.hboi.edu

Institute of Marine/Coastal Sciences
Rutgers University
College Farm/Dudley Road
PO Box 231
New Brunswick
New Jersey 08903
United States of America
Tel: (+1 908) 932 65 55
Fax: (+1 908) 932 8578
e-mail: grassle@imcs.rutgers.edu
Web: http://www.imcs.rutgers.edu

Jackson Estuarine Laboratory
University of New Hampshire
85 Adams Point Road
Durham
New Hampshire 03820-3406
United States of America
Tel: (+1 603) 862 21 75
Fax: (+1 603) 862 11 01
e-mail: hmt1@christa.unh.edu
Web: http://marine.unh.edu

Lamont-Doherty Earth Observatory
PO Box 1000/RT 9W
Palisades
New York 10964
United States of America
Tel: (+1 845) 365 88 45
Fax: (+1 845) 359 68 17
e-mail: marscico@ldeo.columbia.edu
Web: http://www.ldeo.columbia.edu

Large Lakes Observatory
University of Minnesota
10 University Drive
Duluth
Minnesota 55812
United States of America
Tel: (+1 218) 726 81 28
e-mail: tcj@d.umn.edu
Web: http://www.d.umn.edu/llo

Louisiana Universities Marine Consortium (LUMCON)
8124 Hwy 56
Chauvin
Louisiana 70344
United States of America
Tel: (+1 504) 851 28 00
Fax: (+1 504) 851 28 74
e-mail: information@lumcon.edu
Web: http://www.lumcon.edu

Marine Science Institute
The University of Texas at Austin
750 Channel View Drive
Port Aransas
Texas 78373-5015
United States of America
Tel: (+1 361) 749 67 11
Fax: (+1 361) 749 67 77
Web: http://wwwutmsi.zo.utexas.edu

Marine Sciences Research Center
State University of New York
Stony Brook
New York 11794-5000
United States of America
Tel: (+1 631) 632 87 00
Fax: (+1 631) 632 88 20
Web: http://www.msrc.sunysb.edu

Maryland Dept Natural Resources
Tawes State Office Building
MANTA C-2
580 Taylor Avenue
Annapolis
Maryland 21401
United States of America
Tel: (+1 410) 326 31 42
Fax: (+1 410) 326 39 61
e-mail: rvkerhin@chesapeake.net

Monterey Bay Aquarium Research Institute (MBARI)
7700 Sandholdt Road
Moss Landing
California 95039-9644
United States of America
Tel: (+1 831) 775 17 00
Fax: (+1 831) 775 16 20
Web: http://www.mbari.org/

Moss Landing Marine Labs
Marine Operations
7700 Sandholdt Road
Building D
Moss Landing
California 95039
United States of America
Tel: (+1 831) 633 35 34
Fax: (+1 831) 633 45 80
e-mail: rmuller@mlml.calstate.edu
Web: http://www.mlml.calstate.edu/marinops/marinops.htm

Naval Oceanographic Office (NAVOCEANO)
1002 Balch Boulevard
Stennis Space Center
Mississippi 39522-5001
United States of America
Web: http://www.navo.navy.mil

Occidental College
Moore Laboratory of Zoology
1600 Campus Road
Los Angeles
California 90041
United States of America
Tel: (+1 213) 259 26 75
Fax: (+1 213) 259 28 87

Office of Marine and Aviation Operations
National Oceanic and Atmospheric Administration
SSMC3, Room 12837
1315 East-West Highway
Silver Spring
Maryland 20910
United States of America
Tel: (+1 301) 713 10 45
Fax: (+1 301) 713 15 41
e-mail: director.omao@noaa.gov

Office of Wetlands, Oceans and Watersheds
Oceans and Coastal Protection Division 4504F
Environmental Protection Agency
1200 Pennsylvania Avenue NW
Washington DC 20460
United States of America
Tel: (+1 202) 260 19 52
Fax: (+1 202) 260 99 20
Web: http://www.epa.gov/OWOW/coastal

Old Dominion University
Dept of Ocean, Earth and Atmospheric Sciences
Norfolk
Virginia 23529-0276
United States of America
Tel: (+1 757) 683 51 62
Fax: (+1 757) 683 53 03
e-mail: rnbray@odu.edu
Web: http://www.odu.edu

Quest Marine Services
PO Box 42
Yarmouthport
Massachusetts 02675
United States of America
Tel: (+1 508) 362 65 01
e-mail: info@questmarineservices.com
Web: http://www.questmarineservices.com

Raytheon Systems Company
Vessel Operations
5355-B 30th Avenue NW
Seattle 98107-4144
United States of America
Tel: (+1 206) 789 14 09
Fax: (+1 206) 789 24 17
e-mail: carl_gower@res.raytheon.com
http://www.polar.org/marine

Rosenstiel School of Marine and Atmospheric Science
University of Miami
4600 Rickenbacker Causeway
Miami
Florida 33149
United States of America
Tel: (+1 305) 361 48 80
Fax: (+1 305) 365 08 40
e-mail: mardep@rsmas.miami.edu
Web: http://www.rsmas.miami.edu/support/mardep

Sarbanes Coop. Oxford Lab.
904 South Morris Street
Oxford
Maryland 21654
United States of America
Tel: (+1 410) 226 51 93
Fax: (+1 410) 226 01 20
e-mail: sjordan@dnr.state.md.us

School of Oceanography
University of Washington
15th Avenue NE and NE Boat Street
Box 357940 Seattle
Washington 98195-7940
United States of America
Tel: (+1 206) 543 50 62
Fax: (+1 206) 543 60 73
e-mail: dschwartz@ocean.washington.edu
Web: http://www.ocean.washington.edu

Scripps Institution of Oceanography
8602 La Jolla Shores Drive
La Jolla,
California 92037
United States of America
Tel: (+1 858) 534 88 84
Fax: (+1 858) 535 18 17
e-mail: shipsked@ucsd.edu
Web: http://www.sio.ucsd.edu

Shoals Marine Laboratory
Cornell University
G-14 Stimson Hall
Ithaca
New York
United States of America
Tel: (+1 603) 964 90 11
Fax: (+1 603) 964 47 39
e-mail: shoals-lab@cornell.edu

Southern California Marine Institute
820 South Seaside Avenue
Terminal Island
California 90731
United States of America
Tel: (+1 310) 519 31 72
Fax: (+1 310) 519 10 54
e-mail: scmi@csulb.edu
Web: http://www-bcf.usc.edu/~scmi

Texas A & M University
Marine Operations (Research Foundation)
PO Box 1675
Galveston
Texas 77553-1675
United States of America
Tel: (+1 409) 740 44 69
Fax: (+1 409) 740 44 56
e-mail: gyreops@tamug.tamu.edu
Web: http://www-ocean.tamu.edu

University of Alaska, Fairbanks
Seward Marine Center
PO Box 730
Seward,
Alaska 99664
United States of America
Tel: (+1 907) 224 52 61
Fax: (+1 907) 224 33 92
e-mail: fnts@aurora.alaska.edu
Web: http://www.ims.alaska.edu

University of California at Los Angeles (UCLA)
Marina Del Rey
Marine Science Center
California
United States of America
Tel: (+1 310) 206 82 47
Fax: (+1 218) 726 69 79

University of Connecticut
Marine Sciences and Technology Center
1084 Shennecosset Road
Groton
Connecticut 06340
United States of America
Tel: (+1 860) 405 91 72
Fax: (+1 860) 405 91 53
Web: http://www.mstc.uconn.edu

University of Hawaii Marine Center
No 1 Sand Island Road
Honolulu,
Hawaii 96819
United States of America
Tel: (+1 808) 847 26 61
Fax: (+1 808) 848 54 51
e-mail: snug@soest.hawaii.edu
Web: http://www.soest.hawaii.edu

University of Maryland
Center for Environmental Science
Research Fleet Operations
Chesapeake Biological Lab
PO Box 38
Solomons
Maryland 20688-0038
United States of America
Tel: (+1 410) 326 73 58
Fax: (+1 410) 326 73 42
e-mail: rfo@cbl.umces.edu

Woods Hole Oceanographic Institution
Woods Hole
Massachusetts 02543-1050
United States of America
e-mail: marineops@whoi.edu
Web: http://www.whoi.edu/

URUGUAY

Oceanographic, Hydrographic and Meteorological Service of the Navy
Capurro 980
Casilla de Correos 1381
Montevideo
Uruguay
Tel: (+598 2) 39 38 61
Fax: (+598 2) 39 92 20

VENEZUELA

Hydrography and Navigation Directorate
Comandancia General de la Armada
Observatorio "Cagigal"
Apartado Postal No 6745 – Carmelitas
Caracas
Venezuela
Tel: (+58 2) 483 16 13
Fax: (+58 2) 481 27 61

VIETNAM

Research Institute of Marine Products (RIMP)
170 Le Lai Street
Ngo Quyen District
Hai Phong
Vietnam
Tel: (+84 31) 83 66 64
Fax: (+84 31) 83 68 12

Vietnam Maritime Bureau
Vietnam Maritime Safety Agency
31 Da Nang Street
Ngo Quyen District
Hai Phong City
Vietnam

VESSEL OPERATORS — OPERATORS OF SEISMIC EXPLORATION AND OFFSHORE SITE AND ROUTE SURVEY VESSELS

Alpine Ocean Seismic Survey, Inc
70 Oak Street
Norwood
New Jersey 07648
USA
Tel: (+1 201) 768 80 00
Fax: (+1 201) 768 57 50
e-mail: alpine@alpineocean.com
Web: http://www.alpineocean.com

Andrews Survey
Salmon Road
Great Yarmouth
Norfolk NR30 3QS
UK
Tel: (+44 1493) 33 21 11
Fax: (+44 1493) 33 22 65
e-mail: email@andrews.co.uk

Arctic Marine Engineering Geological Expeditions (AMIGE)
3 Sverdlov Street
183034 Murmansk
Russian Federation
Tel: (+7 8152) 33 26 44
Fax: (+7 8152) 33 27 00
Tel/fax via Norwegian telecom: (+47) 78 91 03 67
e-mail: office@amige.murmansk.ru

Atlantic Marine Sales & Charter Co
Maritime House
Basin Road North
Hove
East Sussex
BN41 1WR
UK
Tel: (+44 1273) 24 88 00
Fax: (+44 1273) 24 87 00
e-mail: paul@atlantic-marine.co.uk
Web: http://www.atlantic-marine.co.uk

Beaufort Oceanics
PO Box 941
Beaufort
North Carolina 28516
USA
Tel: (+1 252) 728 30 33
Fax: (+1 252) 728 28 89
e-mail: Martow@mail.clis.com
Web: http://www.martow.com

Blue Water Recoveries Ltd
Knockhundred House
Knockhundred Row
Midhurst
West Sussex
GU29 9DQ
UK
Tel: (+44 1730) 81 15 00
Fax: (+44 1730) 81 15 01
e-mail: david@bluewater.uk.com
Web: http://www.bluewater.uk.com

British Waterways
Willow Grange
Church Road
Watford WD17 3QA
UK
Tel: (+44 1923) 20 12 92
Fax: (+44 1923) 20 13 00
e-mail: pressoffice@britishwaterways.co.uk
Web: http://www.british-waterways.org

Caspian Geophysical
T Aliyarbekov St 9
370005 Baku
Azerbaijan
Tel: (+994 12) 98 25 60
Fax: (+994 12) 98 27 32
e-mail: office@caspgeo.baku.az
Web: http://www.azer.com

China Ministry of Geology
Beijing
People's Republic of China

China Offshore Oil Geophysical Corporation (COOGC)
Box 502
Tanggu
Tianjin
People's Republic of China
Web: http://www.coogc.com

Coastline Surveys Ltd
Marine Operations Base
Units 17 & 18
Frampton on Severn Industrial Park
Bridge Road
Frampton on Severn
Gloucestershire
GL10 7HE
UK
Tel: (+44 1452) 74 09 41
Fax: (+44 1452) 74 08 11
e-mail: info@coastlinesurveys.co.uk
Web: http://www.coastlinesurveys.co.uk

Comex SA
36 boulevard des Océans
BP 143
F-13275 Marseille Cedex 9
Tel: (+33 4) 91 29 75 00
Fax: (+33 4) 91 29 75 07
e-mail: Comexsa@comex.fr
Web: http://www.comex.fr

Commissioners of Irish Lights
16 Lower Pembroke Street
Dublin 2
Ireland
Tel: (+353 1) 662 45 25
Fax: (+353 1) 661 80 94
e-mail: marine@cil.ie
Web: http://www.cil.ie

Compagnie Générale de Géophysique (CGG)
1 rue Leon Migaux
F-91341 Massy Cedex
France
Tel: (+33 1) 64 47 30 00
Fax: (+33 1) 64 47 39 70
Web: http://www.cgg.com

Continental Holdings Ltd
3030 3rd Avenue
Suite 210
Calgary
Alberta T2A 6T7
Canada

Dalmorneftegeofizika (DMNG)
426 Prospect Mira
Yuzhno-Sakhalinsk 693004
Russian Federation
Tel: (+7 424) 242 76 18
Fax: (+7 50441) 620 90
e-mail: A.Livshits@dmng.ru
Web: http://www.dmng.ru

De Beers Marine
101 Hertzog Boulevard
Cape Town
South Africa
Tel: (+21 21) 410 42 31
Fax: (+21 21) 410 42 57
e-mail: bayly@debeers.co.za

DeepOcean AS
Postboks 2144
N-5504 Haugesund
Norway
Tel/Fax: (+47) 52 70 04 00
e-mail: post@deepocean.no
Web: http://www.deepocean.no

Deep Sea Trawlers
c/o Seaforth Engineering
780 Windmill Road
Suite 302
Dartmouth
Nova Scotia
Canada
Tel: (+1 902) 468 35 79
Fax: (+1 902) 468 68 65
e-mail: info@seamapgeosurveys.com

Delta Marine
5 Gladstone Terrace
Lerwick
Shetland
ZE1 0EG
UK
Tel: (+44 1595) 69 47 99
Fax: (+44 1595) 69 31 32
e-mail: delta.marine@zetnet.co.uk
Web: http://www.delta-marine.co.uk

Donjon Marine Co, Inc
1250 Liberty Avenue
Hillside
New Jersey 07205
USA
Tel: (+1 908) 964 88 12
Fax: (+1 908) 964 74 26
e-mail: divemasters@ameri-com.com
Web: http://www.donjon.com

DSND AS
Radhusgaten 23
PO Box 752 Sentrum
N-0106 Oslo
Norway
Tel: (+47) 22 41 21 50
Fax: (+47) 22 41 06 50
Web: http://www.dsnd.co.uk

DSND Subsea Ltd
Peregrine Road
Westhill Business Park
Aberdeen
AB32 6JL
UK
Tel: (+44 1224) 34 43 00
Fax: (+44 1224) 34 46 00
Web: http://www.dsnd.co.uk

Echoscan Ltd
62 Bagley Lane
Farsley
Leeds LS28 7YY
UK
Tel: (+44 113) 236 33 33
Fax: (+44 113) 236 02 26/236 28 28
e-mail: sales@echoscan.co.uk
Web: http://www.echoscan.co.uk

Elcome Surveys Private Ltd
Elcome House D222/30
TTC INDL Area MIDC
Nerul
New Bombay 400 706
India
Tel: (+91 22) 762 91 26
Fax: (+91 22) 762 91 40
e-mail: elcomsur@bom3.vsnl.net.in

Emu Environmental Ltd
Hayling Island Marine Laboratory
Ferry Road
Hayling Island
Hampshire
PO11 0DG
UK
Tel: (+44 23) 92 63 68 00
Fax: (+44 23) 92 63 72 15
e-mail: mail@emunv.co.uk
Web: http://www.emunv.co.uk

Fairfield Industries
Data Acquisition Division
Suite 600
Sugar Lane
Texas 77478
USA
Tel: (+1 281) 275 75 00
Fax: (+1 281) 275 75 50
e-mail: data.acquisition@fairfield.com
Web: http://www.fairfield.com

Fugro-Geodetic Pte Ltd
Loyang Offshore Supply Base
Loyang Crescent
PO Box 5040
Singapore 508988
Tel: (+65) 543 02 00
Fax: (+65) 543 05 00
e-mail: fgpl@fugro.com.sg
Web: http://www.fugro.nl

Fugro GeoServices Inc
200 Dulles Drive
Lafayette
Louisiana 70506
USA
Tel: (+1 337) 237 26 36
Fax: (+1 337) 268 32 21
e-mail: thampton@fugro.com
Web: http://www.fugro-usa.com

Fugro GeoServices, Inc
6100 Hillcroft
Houston
Texas 77081
USA
Tel: (+1 713) 773 85 00
Fax: (+1 713) 773 85 01
e-mail: thamilton@fugro.com
Web: http://www.fugro-usa.com

Fugro-Geoteam AS
PO Box 490
Hoffsveien 1C
Skøyen
N-0213 Oslo
Norway
Tel: (+47) 22 13 46 00
Fax: (+47) 22 13 46 46
e-mail: geoteam@fugro.geoteam.no
Web: http://www.fugro.geoteam.no

Fugro-McClelland Marine Geosciences, Inc
6100 Hillcroft
Houston
Texas 77081
USA
Tel: (+1 713) 369 56 00
Fax: (+1 713) 369 55 20
e-mail: srainey@fugro.com
Web: www.fugro-usa.com

Fugro Survey Ltd
Regent House
Regent Quay
Aberdeen
AB11 5BE
UK
Tel: (+44 1224) 21 18 60
Fax: (+44 1224) 21 18 61
e-mail: info@fugrosurvey.co.uk
Web: http://www.fugro.nl

Fugro Survey (Middle East) Ltd
PO Box 43088
Abu Dhabi
UAE
Tel: (+971 2) 554 78 10
Fax: (+971 2) 554 78 11/12
e-mail: fugrosur@emirates.net.ae
Web: http://www.fugrome.com

Fugro-UDI AS
PO Box 63
Fabrikkveien 23
N-4033 Forus
Norway
Tel: (+47) 51 95 19 90
Fax: (+47) 51 95 19 91
e-mail: geoteam@fugro.geoteam.no
Web: http://www.fugro.nl

Fugro-UDI Ltd
Denmore Road
Bridge of Don
Aberdeen
AB23 8JW
UK
Tel: (+44 1224) 25 75 00
Fax: (+44 1224) 25 75 01
e-mail: info@fugro-udi.co.uk
Web: http://www.fugro.nl

Fugro-UDI Ltd
14 Brinell Way
Harfreys Industrial Estate
Great Yarmouth
Norfolk NR31 0LU
UK
Tel: (+44 1493) 45 42 03
e-mail: I.Janor@fugro-udi.co.uk
Web: http://www.fugro.nl

Gardline Surveys (Far East) Ltd
371 Beach Road
Keypoint #02-25
Singapore 199597
Tel: (+65) 292 25 33
Fax: (+65) 293 76 94

Gardline Surveys Ltd
Endeavour House
Admiralty Road
Great Yarmouth
Norfolk NR30 3NG
UK
Tel: (+44 1493) 85 07 23
Fax: (+44 1493) 85 21 06/85 23 25
e-mail: dawn.perrin@gardline.co.uk
Web: http://www.gardline.co.uk

Gardline Surveys (Malaysia) Sdn. Bhd.
C10-3 Jalan Ampang Utama 1/1
Off Jalan Ampang
6800 Selangor
Malaysia
Tel: (+60 3) 457 30 17/39 17
Fax: (+60 3) 457 37 16

Geoconsult AS
Nedre Åstveit 12
N-5106 Øvre Ervik
Bergen
Norway
Tel: (+47) 55 53 89 00
Fax: (+47) 55 53 89 01
e-mail: info@geoconsult.no
Web: http://www.geoconsult.no

GeoLab Technical Services Ltd
Ferry House
South Denes Road
Great Yarmouth
Norfolk NR30 2PJ
UK
Tel: (+44 1493) 85 59 92
Fax: (+44 1493) 85 59 93
e-mail: info@geolab.co.uk
Web: http://www.geolab.co.uk

Geophysical Service Intl
Canada

Global Ocean Technologies (GOTECH)
Main Terminal Building
Waterford Regional Airport
Killowen
Co Waterford
Ireland
Tel: (+353 51) 85 84 46
Fax: (+353 51) 30 12 66
e-mail: gotech@eircom.net

Government of Islamic Republic of Pakistan
Web: http://www.pak.gov.pk

Hays Ships Ltd
Ogscastle
Carnwath
MK11 8NE
UK
Tel: (+44 1555) 84 09 33
Fax: (+44 1555) 84 09 45
e-mail: hays@haysships.force9.co.uk

Hunter Marine Ltd
5 Bellevue Lawn
Delgany
Co Wicklow
Ireland
Tel/Fax: (+353 404) 615 66
Mobile: 087 2590195

Hydrocharter Associates
73 Havant Road
Emsworth
Hampshire
PO10 7LE
UK
Tel: (+44 1243) 37 04 64
Fax: (+44 1243) 43 20 27
e-mail: Hydrocharter@cwcom.net

Hydrosurveys
Holmes Court
Bridge Street
Kenilworth
Warwickshire
CV8 1BP
UK
Tel: (+44 1926) 85 11 85
Fax: (+44 1926) 85 16 31
e-mail: info@hydrosurveys.co.uk
Web: http://www.hydrosurveys.co.uk

KMNG – Kasporneftegeophyzrazdedka
Moscovskiye Prospect 83
370033 Baku
Azerbaijan

Marex Oceanographic Services
5100 Poplar Avenue
Memphis
Tennessee 38137
USA
Tel: (+1 901) 681 01 00
Fax: (+1 901) 684 14 05
e-mail: marex@marexmarine.com
Web: http://www.marexmarine.com

Maritime Port Authority of Singapore
460 Alexandra Road
PSA Building
#18-00
Singapore 119963
Tel: (+65) 375 16 00
Web: http://www.mpa.gov.sg

Monterey Canyon Research Vessels, Inc
114 Mason Street
Santa Cruz
California 95060
USA
Tel: (+1 831) 423 48 64
Fax: (+1 831) 423 17 19
Web: http://www.shanarae.com

Multiwave Geophysical Company (MGC) AS
Damsgardsveien 131
N-5162 Laksevag
Bergen
Norway
Tel: (+47) 55 94 77 50
Fax: (+47) 55 94 77 51
e-mail: marketing@mgc.no
Web: http://www.mgc.no

Ocean Services
Seattle
Washington
USA
e-mail: marinegroup@effectnet.com

Offshore Survey & Engineering (OSAE) GmbH
Fahrenheitstrasse 7
D-28359 Bremen
Germany
Tel: (+49 421) 223 91 50
Fax: (+49 421) 223 91 51
e-mail: info@osae.de
Web: http://www.osae.de

OGS Italy
Borgo Grotta Gigante 42c
PO Box 2011
I-34016 Sgonico-Trieste
Italy
Tel: (+39 040) 214 01
Fax: (+39 040) 32 73 07
Web: http://www.ogs.trieste.it/

Oil & Natural Gas Commission
605 Kailash Building
6th Floor
New Delhi 110701
India

Osiris Hydrographic & Geophysical Projects Ltd
Heritage House
91 Eastham Village Road
Eastham
Wirral
Cheshire CH62 0AW
UK
Tel: (+44 151) 328 11 20
Fax: (+44 151) 328 11 39
e-mail: osirisuk@aol.com
Web: http://www.osirisprojects.co.uk

Petro-Tech Peruana SA
Av Los Incas 460 (El Olivar)
San Isidro
Lima 27
Peru
Tel: (+51 1) 440 95 50
Fax: (+51 1) 441 94 30

PGS Exploration AS
Strandveien 4
N-1366 Lysaker
Norway
Tel: (+47) 67 52 64 00
Fax: (+47) 67 52 64 64
Web: http://www.pgs.com

PGS Exploration (US) Inc
16010 Barker's Point Lane
Suite 300
Houston
Texas 77079
USA
Tel: (+1 281) 589 88 18
Fax: (+1 281) 589 94 65
Web: http://www.pgs.com

PGS Reservoir Consultants, Inc
1001 S Dairy Ashford
Suite 300
Houston
Texas 77077
USA
Tel: (+1 281) 848 76 00
Fax: (+1 281) 848 76 76
Web: http://www.pgs.com

Polar Ship Management AS
PO Box 1114, Sentrum
N-5809 Bergen
Norway
Tel: (+47) 55 59 96 00
Fax: (+47) 55 59 96 05
e-mail: info@polarship.no

Port of London Authority
Hydrographic Service
Royal Pier Road
Gravesend
Kent DA12 2BG
UK
Tel: (+44 1474) 56 23 14
Fax: (+44 1474) 56 22 06
e-mail: hydrographic@pola.co.uk

Raytheon Systems Company
5355-B 28th Ave NW
Seattle
Washington 98107-4144
USA
Tel: (+1 206) 789 24 17/789 14 08
Fax: (+1 206) 789
e-mail: carl_gowler@mukilteo.hac.com
(Naval and Maritime Systems – Mukilteo Operations)
Web: http://www.raytheon.com

Rederij Waterweg BV
Het Nieuwe Diep 43A
NL-1781 AE Den Helder
Netherlands
Tel: (+31 223) 61 56 66
Fax: (+31 223) 61 43 60
e-mail: mail@waterweg.nl
Web: http://www.waterweg.nl

Sea Boston Ltd
Bayly's Road
Oreston
Plymstock
Plymouth
Devon PL9 7NQ
Tel: (+44 1752) 40 72 65
Fax: (+44 1752) 48 23 28

Sea-Trax
10 Penwarden Way
Bosham
West Sussex
PO18 8LG
UK
Tel: (+44 1243) 57 37 31 or (0860) 86 81 56
Fax: (+44 1243) 57 37 31
e-mail: david@sea-trax.fsnet.co.uk

Seaworks Ltd
Level 3
Seaworks House
39 Waterloo Quay
PO Box 39
Wellington
New Zealand
Tel: (+64 9) 499 68 91
Fax: (+64 9) 499 68 93
e-mail: contact@seaworks.co.nz
Web: http://www.seaworks.co.nz

Seaworx BV
Nijverheidskade 2
NL-1780 AM Den Helder
Netherlands
Tel: (+31 223) 66 84 00
Fax: (+31 223) 66 84 44
e-mail: sx@seaworx.nl
Web: http://www.seaworx.nl

Seismic Explorations Intl
USA

Sevmorneftegeofizika (SMNG)
17 Karl Marx Street
Murmansk 183025
Russian Federation
Tel: (+7 8152) 55 63 97
Fax: (+7 8152) 55 60 49
e-mail: smng@smng-geophysics.com
Web: http://www.smng-geophysics.com

Shoreline Surveys
PO Box 4179
Lulworth Cove
Wareham
Dorset
BH20 5YF
UK
Tel: (+44 1929) 40 01 01
Fax: (+44 1929) 40 01 04
e-mail: general@shorelinesurveys.freeserve.co.uk
Web: http://www.shorelinesurveys.freeserve.co.uk

Stolt Offshore AS
Verven 4
Postboks 740
N-4004 Stavanger
Norway
Tel: (+47) 51 84 50 00
Fax: (+47) 51 83 59 00
e-mail: nor-info@stoltoffshore.com
Web: http://www.stoltoffshore.com

Stolt Offshore Inc
900 Town & Country Lane
Suite 400
Houston
Texas 77024
USA
Tel: (+1 713) 430 11 00
Fax: (+1 713) 461 00 39
e-mail: gom-info@stoltoffshore.com
Web: http://www.stoltoffshore.com

Stolt Offshore Ltd
Bucksburn House
Howes Road
Aberdeen AB16 7QU
UK
Tel: (+44 1224) 71 82 00
Fax: (+44 1224) 71 51 29
e-mail: info@stoltoffshore.com
Web: http://www.stoltoffshore.com

Stolt Offshore Pte. Ltd
25 Loyang Crescent
Loyang Offshore Supply Base
Sops Way, Mailbox 5136
Singapore 508988
Tel: (+65) 545 60 66
Fax: (+65) 545 66 18
e-mail: apac-info@stoltoffshore.com
Web: http://www.stoltoffshore.com

Svitzer Australia Pty Ltd
1/7 Hardy Street
South Perth
Western Australia 6151
Australia
Tel: (+61 8) 93 67 82 22
Fax: (+61 8) 93 67 83 22
Web: http://www.svitzer.co.uk

Svitzer Ltd
Morton Peto Road
Great Yarmouth
Norfolk
NR31 0LT
UK
Tel: (+44 1493) 44 03 20
e-mail: sales@svitzer.co.uk
Web: http://www.svitzer.co.uk

TGS-NOPEC Geophysical Company
2500 City West Boulevard
Suite 2000
Houston
Texas 77042
Tel: (+1 713) 860 21 00
Fax: (+1 713) 334 33 08
e-mail: tgs@tgsgeo.com
Web: http://www.tgsgeo.com

TGS-NOPEC International ASA
Baarsrudveien 2
N-3478 Naersnes
Norway
Tel: (+47) 31 29 20 24
Fax: (+47) 31 29 20 10
e-mail: kjellaub@tgsnopec.no

TGS-NOPEC (UK) Ltd
Graylaw House
21/21A Goldington Road
Bedford
MK40 3JY
UK
Tel: (+44 1234) 27 24 07
Fax: (+44 1234) 27 24 08
e-mail: nopecgeo@dial.pipex.com
Web: http://www.tgsnopec.no

Thales GeoSolutions Group Ltd (Head Office)
Compass House
Davis Road
Chessington
Surrey KT9 1TB
UK
Tel: (+44 870) 601 00 00
Fax: (+44 208) 391 16 02/16 72
Web: http://www.thales-geosolutions.com

Thales GeoSolutions Group Ltd
Unit 4
White Lodge Business Park
Hall Road
Norwich NR4 6DG
UK
Tel: (+44 1603) 28 18 00
Fax: (+44 1603) 28 18 01

Thales GeoSolutions Inc
36499 Perkins Road
Prairieville
Louisiana 70769
USA
Tel: (+1 800) 999 61 05
Fax: (+1 225) 673 58 77
Web: http://www.thales-geoSolutions.com

Thales GeoSolutions Ltd
Greenwell Road
East Tullos Industrial Estate
Aberdeen AB12 3TA
UK
Tel: (+44 1224) 24 97 00
Fax: (+44 1224) 42 94 46

Titan Environmental Surveys Ltd
Pen-y-bont STW
Ogmore-by-Sea
nr Bridgend
Mid Glamorgan
CF32 0QP
Tel: (+44 1656) 88 12 22
Fax: (+44 1656) 88 12 34
e-mail: george.a.smith@titansurveys.co.uk

TL Geohydrographics (Teknik Lengkap)
Tingkat 15
Menara 2 Faber Towers
Jalan Desa Bahagia
Taman Desa
Off Jalan Klana Lama
58100 Kuala Lumpur
Malaysia

UK Dredging
Port Office
Atlantic Way
Barry
South Wales
CF63 3US
UK
Tel: (+44 1446) 70 08 07
Fax: (+44 1446) 70 01 00
e-mail: ukd@abports.co.uk
Web: http://www.abports.co.uk/dredging/

University of Hawaii at Manoa
School of Ocean and Earth Science and Technology
1680 East-West Road
PO Box 802
Honolulu
Hawaii 96822
Tel: (+1 808) 956 61 82
Fax: (+1 808) 956 91 52
e-mail: soest@soest.hawaii.edu
Web: http://www.soest.hawaii.edu

Van Stee Survey and Supply BV
Nieuwe Vissershaven 5
NL-8861 NX Harlingen
Netherlands
Tel: (+31 517) 41 54 42
Fax: (+31 517) 41 75 76
e-mail: vanstee@vanstee.com
Web: http://www.vanstee.com

Veritas (Corporate Headquarters)
3701 Kirby Drive
Suite 112
Houston
Texas 77098
USA
Tel: (+1 713) 512 83 00
Web: http://www.veritasdgc.com

Veritas DGC Asia Pacific
Union Industrial Building
37 Jalan Pemimpin
Suite #06-01
Singapore 577177
Tel: (+65) 258 12 21
Fax: (+65) 258 09 89
Web: http://www.veritasdgc.com

Veritas DGC Inc
Veritas Geophysical Services
3701 Kirby Drive
Suite #1144
Houston
Texas 77098
USA
Tel: (+1 713) 512 83 00
Fax: (+1 713) 512 87 01
e-mail: contact@veritasdgc.com
Web: http://www.veritasdgc.com

WesternGeco (Corporate Offices)
Schlumberger House
Buckingham Gate
Gatwick Airport
West Sussex RH6 0NZ
UK
Tel: (+44 1293) 55 66 55
Fax: (+44 1293) 55 69 40
e-mail: seismic@slb.com
Web: http://www.westerngeco.com

Westland GeoProjects Ltd
Belle Vue Lane
Bude
Cornwall
EX23 8BR
UK
Tel: (+44 1288) 35 60 90
Fax: (+44 1288) 35 24 60
e-mail: info@wgeo.co.uk
Web: http://www.wgeo.co.uk

INDEXES

SHIP INDEX BY OPERATOR

SHIP INDEX BY NAME